THE SPORTING IMAGE

READINGS IN AMERICAN SPORT HISTORY

Paul J. Zingg
Editor & Contributor

UNIVERSITY
PRESS OF
AMERICA

Lanham • New York • London

Copyright © **1988** by

University Press of America,® **Inc.**

4720 Boston Way
Lanham, MD 20706

3 Henrietta Street
London WC2E 8LU England

All rights reserved

Printed in the United States of America

British Cataloging in Publication Information Available

Library of Congress Cataloging-in-Publication Data

The Sporting image : readings in American sport history / Paul J. Zingg,
editor & contributor.
p. cm.
Includes bibliographies.
1. Sports—United States—History. 2. Sports—Social aspects—United States—History.
I. Zingg, Paul J., 1947–
GV583.S6844   1988   796'.0973—dc19   87–32622 CIP
ISBN 0–8191–6817–3 (alk. paper)
ISBN 0–8191–6818–1 (pbk. : alk. paper)

All University Press of America books are produced on acid-free
paper which exceeds the minimum standards set by the National
Historical Publications and Records Commission.

ACKNOWLEDGMENTS

I wish to express thanks to the authors whose works are represented in this volume and their publishers for granting reprint privileges, to the University of Pennsylvania Research Foundation, the Saint Mary's College Committee for Faculty and Curriculum Development, and especially George Weiss for the funding toward this project, and Laurie Babka, Ann Madell, Elizabeth Abigail Reed and David Silk for their assistance.

Copyright notices

David Riesman and Reuel Denny, "Football in America: A Study in Culture Diffusion," *American Quarterly*, 3 (Winter, 1951), 309-25. Reprinted by permission of the authors, *American Quarterly*, and the American Studies Association. Copyright 1951, American Studies Association.

Richard Harmond, "Progress and Flight: An Interpretation of the American Cycle Craze of the 1890's," *Journal of Social History*, V (Winter, 1971), 235-257. Reprinted by permission of the Journal of Social History.

Steven A. Riess, "Race and Ethnicity in American Baseball: 1900-1919," *Journal of Ethnic Studies*, IV (Winter, 1977), 39-55. Reprinted by permission of the Journal of Ethnic Studies.

Randy Roberts, "Jack Dempsey: An American Hero of the 1920's," *Journal of Popular Culture*, vol. 8:2 (1974), 411/57-426/72. Reprinted with permission of The Popular Press, Bowling Green State University.

Marshall Smelser, "The Babe on Balance," *American Scholar*, LXIV (Spring, 1975), 299-304. Reprinted by permission of Anna Smelser.

Dominic J. Capeci, Jr. and Martha Wilkerson, "Multifarious Hero: Joe Louis, American Society and Race Relations During World Crisis, 1935-1945," *Journal of Sport History*, X (Winter, 1983), pp. 5-25. Reprinted by permission of the North American Society for Sport History.

Donald Spivey and Thomas A. Jones, "Intercollegiate Athletic Servitude: A Case Study of the Black Illini Student-Athletes, 1931-1967." Reprinted from *Social Science Quarterly*, vol. 55, No. 4, March 1975, by permission of the University of Texas Press.

William H. Beazley and Joseph P. Hobbs, "'Nice Girls Don't Sweat': Women in American Sport," *Journal of Popular Culture*, vol. 16:4 (1982), 42-53. Reprinted by permission of The Popular Press, Bowling Green State University.

CONTENTS

Acknowledgments v

Introduction ix

Puritans and Sport:
The Irretrievable Tide of Change
NANCY L. STRUNA 1

Horses and Gentlemen: The Cultural Significance
of Gambling Among the Gentry of Virginia
TIMOTHY H. BREEN 23

The Rise of Sport
FREDERIC L. PAXSON 45

The Promise of Sport in Antebellum America
PETER LEVINE 69

American Sportswomen in the 19th Century
MARGERY A. BULGER 85

The First Modern Sport in America:
Harness Racing in New York City, 1825-1870
MELVIN L. ADELMAN 107

The Quest for Subcommunities and the
Rise of American Sport
BENJAMIN G. RADER 139

America's First Intercollegiate Sport:
The Regattas from 1852 to 1875
GUY M. LEWIS 155

The Technological Revolution and the
Rise of Sport, 1850-1900
JOHN R. BETTS 171

Baseball in St. Louis, 1867-1875:
An Historical Case Study of Civic Pride
GREGG LEE CARTER 195

Football in America: A Study in Culture Diffusion
DAVID RIESMAN & REUEL DENNY 209

Progress and Flight: An Interpretation of the
American Cycle Craze of the 1890's
RICHARD HARMOND 227

Race and Ethnicity in American Baseball: 1900-1919
STEVEN A. RIESS 247

Jack Dempsey: An American Hero of the 1920's
RANDY ROBERTS 267

The Babe on Balance
MARSHALL M. SMELSER 287

Multifarious Hero: Joe Louis, American Society
and Race Relations During World Crisis, 1935-1945
DOMINIC J. CAPECI, JR. & MARTHA WILKERSON ... 297

Intercollegiate Athletic Servitude: A Case Study
of the Black Illini Student-Athletes, 1931-1967
DONALD SPIVEY & THOMAS E. JONES 323

'Nice Girls Don't Sweat':
Women in American Sport
WILLIAM H. BEAZLEY & JOSEPH P. HOBBS 337

Myth and Metaphor: Baseball in the History
and Literature of American Sport
PAUL J. ZINGG 353

INTRODUCTION

Over thirty years ago, Jacques Barzun offered some straight-forward advice to anyone who wanted to know "the heart and mind of America"--learn baseball![1] In 1954, however, few serious scholars followed his advice.[2] The study of baseball and, for that matter, other forms of American sport were stuck in the intellectual badlands. Although competitive sports engaged Native Americans and colonial settlers on a routine basis centuries ago and preoccupy millions of participants and followers in our present day (half the American population watches bowl games over the New Year's holidays[3]), their study enjoyed little credibility as a respectable academic subject. Ignored by scholars who stuck to traditional modes of inquiry in their disciplines and impaired by efforts which reflected *naivete* and simplicity, sport history studies generally provided few contributions to understanding American culture and society.

To a great extent, the criticism and disdain received by those purporting to write sport history were deserved. Embarrassingly hagiographic, tediously statistical, and remarkably superficial, the sport books they produced lacked methodological substance and analytical depth. Although the authors demonstrated a fascination for myths and symbols, an interest that potentially gave them a viable intellectual framework, they usually devoted their energy to creating myths, not understanding them. The world of sport history drifted somewhere between press agency and adolescent fantasy.

This situation has begun to change, slowly, cautiously, but, nonetheless, perceptively. The change has been facilitated by several new and provocative forces that have profoundly affected the present shape of American historiography and the teaching of American history. Foremost among these has been the shaping of new intellectual attitudes. The political ferment of the 1960s contributed to a breakdown of the conservative consensus that had dominated most aspects of American historical scholarship for the previous few decades. The years of the New Frontier and the Great Society revealed deep divisions within American society and culture. The events of that tumultous period underscored the shallowness, elitism and inadequacy that frequently characterized interpretations of the American experience. They opened the door for fresh and respected inquiries into the fields of social history and popular culture. The study of sport fit well within the new imperative to explore the American scene and its many institutions and subcommunities in a considerably broader context.

The growth of "American studies" as a distinct discipline has significantly aided the developing maturity and respectability of sport scholarship. The discipline has expanded and diversified well beyond its

formative emphases on recurring patterns and themes in American literature and intellectual history. In the process, it is still unbounded by the
dictates of any prevailing orthodoxy, which has not yet emerged, and
scholars in the field are unrestrained in exploring new areas and applying
imaginative perspectives to familiar topics. In addition, there are significant intellectual and biographical ties between American studies and
sport history. Among the most important recent contributions to the
study of sport are the works of scholars who emerged from such strong
American Studies programs as the University of Minnesota and Yale.[4].

Aside from an intellectual recognition of the importance of sport
in helping elucidate various themes central to American history and life,
other factors have been at work in accounting for the surge of interest in
the topic in recent years. Historians have begun to draw more heavily and
confidently on the works of scholars in such related disciplines as anthropology, sociology, folklore, psychology and philosophy in order to reveal the patterns of American thought and behavior. Academic demo-
graphics have also played a role in bringing sport history to light.
Concern about declining enrollments prompted many humanities and
social sciences departments to develop courses of topical interest, including sport. Prepared--or pushed--to offer these new courses, scholars
encountereed a dearth of appropriate materials that could be used. Many
simply turned away, convinced that this empty hole in historical scholarship reflected the apparent insignificance of the topic. Those who turned
their attentions and energies to developing new materials in order to enhance the integrity and value of their courses found in the process that
they were uncovering a great deal of history that was not only interesting
but important.

Many of the leaders of the sport history movement have emerged
from a source that has not enjoyed a particularly favorable academic reputation within traditional circles. This is the discipline of physical education. Encompassing sport in all of its dimensions, including history,
physical education has played a major role in focusing attention on sport
history scholarship. Physical educators, or, more precisely, sport historians working in physical education, took the initiative in organizing
scholarly gatherings and symposia that addressed sport history themes,
publishing a professional scholarly journal devoted to sport history, and
forming national and international professional associations that centered on interests and efforts related to the study of the history of sport.
Indeed, the courses on sport history that have recently appeared in the
offerings of other academic departments trace their roots to "phys ed."
Although scholars are often reluctant to mention physical education in
the same breath as their own disciplines, they cannot ignore the contributions the field has made to the design and development of sport history

and to sensitizing the American public to the psychological, sociological, and philosophical aspects of the sports experience.

Another mark of the maturing of sport history has been the appearance of scholarly surveys of the topic.[5] Although they vary greatly in style, quality and value, these surveys underscore the variety and volume of materials produced in sport history in recent years and they provide a useful, if uneven, synthesis of them. For the most part, these surveys have followed a chronological orientation. This is, of course, an appropriate organizational framework, but the surveys can profit from more imaginative and integrative conceptualizations if they are to be more than a sum of the existing literature.[6]

The selections in this volume, with few notable exceptions, are the products of the new efforts in American sport history. All of the selections are drawn from scholarly journals. This has been intentional for several reasons. First, the journals are a primary vehicle for testing new hypotheses and sharing new scholarship. Second, the degree to which studies on sport history have found their way into these sources is a commentary on the respectability that the studies themselves have achieved, the importance that has been attached to their subject matter, and the range of their appeal. The nineteen selections in this collection represent the contributions of twenty-three scholars in twelve different journals. Third, the bibliographies following each article often underscore the seminal value of the piece in citing works that developed from it. The additional references also help identify the larger context in which each article fits and the extent of complementary materials.

This book essentially follows a chronological structure in order to emphasize the historical growth and development of sport in America. Tracing sport from its colonial origins, through its rise in the nineteenth century, to its established place in modern American life, the essays provide a panoramic view of the sporting phenomenon in this country and the image and role of sport in the American historical consciousness. From a historical perspective, these articles reveal the development and refinement of new themes, methodologies and frameworks for the study of sport. They confirm the vitality of sport studies in their own right and the usefulness of sport as a paradigm for understanding the larger culture of which it is a part. They also indicate where some of the most important and innovative work has been done and where opportunities and needs for further study continue to be.

Nearly one hundred and fifty years ago, English historian Joseph Strutt observed that "in order to form a just estimation of the character of any individual people, it is absolutely necessary to investigate the sports and pastimes most generally prevalent among them."[7] Barzun understood this advice clearly when he issued his challenge to study baseball. As this volume demonstrates, they are no longer alone in recognizing the centrality of sport's symbols, rituals and attractions to a society's belief-systems, values and behaviors. Like the American character, though, sport has many faces. Rejecting for the most part elitist formulas of inquiry, the works in this collection suggest that there is much value in scholarship not far from the maddening crowd, but among it.

• • •

Notes

1. Barzun, *God's Country and Mine* (New York: Harper and Row, 1965), 159.

2. See, for example, Jennie Holliman, *American Sports, 1786-1835* (Durham, NC: Seeman Press, 1931); Foster Rhea Dulles, *American Learns to Play: A History of Popular Recreation, 1607-1940*, (New York: Appleton-Century, 1940); John R. Krout, *Annals of American Sport*, The Pageant of America Series, Ralph Gabriel, ed., Vol. 15 (New Haven: Yale University Press, 1929); Herbert Manchester, *Four Centuries of Sport in American Life* (Chicago: University of Chicago Press, 1939); Frederick W. Cozens and Florence S. Stumpf, *Sports in American Life* (Chicago: University of Chicago Press, 1953); and Stewart Culin, *Games of the North American Indians* (Washington: Bureau of American Ethnology, 1907).

3. *Miller Lite Report on American Attitudes Toward Sports*, 1983 (New York: Research and Forecasts, 1983).

4. Among the products of the Minnesota program are Leverett Smith, *The American Dream and the National Game*, (Bowling Green, OH: Bowling Green University Press, 1975) and Mark Harris, whose baseball novels are among the most important sport fiction ever written. The pioneering scholars in American studies at Minnesota included Henry Nash Smith and Leo Marx, who both taught there, and John William Ward and Alan Trachtenberg, who earned their degrees there. Trachtenberg is now at Yale, whose American Studies program has produced some dissertations on sport.

5. John R. Betts, *America's Sporting Heritage, 1850-1950* (Reading, MA: Addison-Wesley, 1974); John Lucas and Ronald Smith, *Saga of American Sport* (Philadelphia: Lea and Febiger, 1978); Benjamin G. Rader, *American Sports: From the Age of Folk Games to the Age of Spectators* (Englewood Cliffs, NJ: Prentice-Hall, 1983); William J. Baker and John M. Caroll, editors, *Sports in Modern America* (St. Louis: River City Publishers, 1981); and Betty Spears and Richard Swanson, *A History of Sport and Physical Activity in the United States* (Dubuque, Iowa: Brown, 1978). Baker, *Sports in the Western World* (Totowa, NJ: Rowan and Littlefield, 1982), includes a significant examination of sport in America. More personal overviews include: James Michener, *Sports in America* (New York: Random House, 1976) and Michael Novak, *The Joy of Sports: End Zones, Bases, Baskets, Balls and the Consecration of the American Spirit* (NY: Basic, 1976).

6. See, for example, Allen Guttman, *From Ritual to Record: The Nature of Modern Sports* (New York: Columbia University Press, 1978) and the neo-Marxist interpretation of Paul Hoch, *Rip Off the Big Game: The Exploitation of Sports by the Power Elite* (New York: Anchor, 1972).

7. Strutt, *Sports and Pastimes of the People of England* (London, 1838), xvii.

PURITANS AND SPORT:
THE IRRETRIEVABLE TIDE OF CHANGE

Nancy L. Struna

Accounts of sporting activity in seventeenth century New England have usually had a Menckenian cast to them. Seeing Puritanism as a major restraint on colonists recreating, much less enjoying themselves in the process, historians routinely portrayed the Puritan world as unusually drab and dour, populated with prigs and *moral athletes*, opposed to the play impulses of saint and stranger alike. As our understanding of the Puritan existence improved, we have come to realize that the founders of Massachusetts Bay and their descendants valued sobriety and industry but neither eschewed the pleasures of the body nor endorsed an ascetic ideal that fostered a retreat from the "real" world.

Tracing the role of sport through three generations of New England Puritans, Nancy Struna sees the transformation and diversification of that society reflected in its habits of physical recreation. From quasi-athletic games of individual chance and skill to more sophisticated contests involving set rules, teams and spectators, sport served as an agent of refreshment, relaxation, and socialization from the earliest days of the settlement. Surviving the occasional efforts of the ministry over the next century to reestablish the orthodoxy of the founding fathers, sport emerged as an integral part of military training and an outlet for the initiative and competitiveness of an increasingly secular and worldly society.

The concept of change is central to Struna's essay. Although Puritans agonized over the potential development of recreation as an end in itself, they recognized that such activity could contribute to an individual's well-being, making him better able to serve God. This concession opened the door to more tolerant attitudes toward leisure time. Colonial New England slowly moved away from an age of intolerance and the effects of this change, evident in all social institutions, were reflected in a more widespread acceptance of sporting activity and the gradual development of sporting codes and practices.

Year after year the historical, or hysterical, battle has raged over the New England Puritans and their sport. Did they, or did they not sport? Did they forbid others within society to sport? Upon what bases did they accept or reject sport? To answer such questions, historians have frequently relied upon evidence provided by certain individuals who lived at distinct times within the colonial period. Newspapers, legal sources, and sermons, as well, have rendered valuable, if limited, information.

Too often, however, these historians have insufficiently considered the perspective of the sources. They have ignored or underrated the importance of chronology and the role in which his society had cast that individual. Thus, historians may have ascertained the scope of participation of selected individuals within Puritan society, and they may have isolated the attitudes toward sport of discrete portions of the population. They have not, however, produced a comprehensive analysis of sport reflecting the dynamic totality of Puritan society. In fact, the failure to acknowledge the perspective of the evidence has frequently obscured the changes evident in the course of Puritan society, particularly in light of the vast research of the last two decades detailing the transformation of that society in America.

A developmental examination of sport within the first century of Puritan society in Massachusetts Bay can perhaps more adequately provide the necessary societal perspective. In Massachusetts Bay, the initial Puritan enterprise in the new world, three generations appeared in the course of the first one hundred years, 1630-1730. During this century a transformation occurred within the value system as structured and interpreted by those Puritans. Initiated as a Puritan attempt to preserve the visible church, the colonial enterprise coalesced as a mercantile outpost of the British empire.[1]

As a behavioral form defined in terms of the seventeenth century,[2] sport becomes a vehicle for the observation of changes in societal attitudes and institutions. Thus, the habits of participation and attitudes in Massachusetts Bay achieve greater clarity as these emerge within the context of that dynamic society, and as they represent similarities and differences among three generations.

THE PLAN FOR SOCIETY, 1630-1730

The initial generation of Puritans who settled in Massachusetts Bay resolved to establish a society dedicated to the preservation of the visible church and bound by a philosophy which clearly defined man's role and niche in the world. As descendents of Adam, the Puritans recognized themselves as corrupt men who had been given a second chance to achieve salvation. To escape the experiences of the disorderly, ungodly world, the Puritans established a "city upon a hill" in Massachusetts Bay.[3]   John Winthrop, the first governor of the Massachusetts Bay Company in the new world, identified for his colonists the values which God had ordained for all his creations.   Hierarchy, inequality, mutuality, variety, and order were all observable in nature.[4] Conformity to the rest of God's works demanded the implanting of these values in society.   Only through self-consciousness of one's emotions and attitudes toward behavior could a Puritan hope to entertain a godly mind.[5]

A few years before the journey to New England, John Downame advised his congregation of the lifetime service required by God and, though possibly inadvertently, of the place that sport might hold in the Puritan value system:

> Wee must constantly and continually, in everything, and at everytime, performe service unto God in all our actions and throughout our whole course and conversation ...in the meanest duties of the basest calling, yea even in our eating and drinking, lawful sports and recreations, when as wee doe them in faith.[6]

Sport might thus be as mutually beneficial to man as eating and drinking, especially if pursued in lawful forms and attentive to order.

In a later publication Downame emphasized the necessity of "due recreation." He acknowledged the fatigue and dissatisfaction bred by dull constance in one's calling and encouraged moderate participation in "...allowable Sports as best fit with mens severall dispositions for their comfort and refreshing."[7] Downame suggested, as well, that sport was a dichotomous concept, implying both conformance and non-conformance to the Puritan value system.

About the same time in Massachusetts Bay, Winthrop struggled with the occurrence of sport in his life:

> When I had some tyme abstained from suche worldly delights as my heart most desired, I grewe melancholick and uncomfortable, for I had been more careful to refraine from an outward conversation in the world, than to keepe the love of the world out of my heart, or to uphold my conversation in heaven...I grewe unto a great dullnesse and discontent: which being at last perceived, I examined my heart, and findinge it needful to recreate my minde with some outward recreation, I yeielded unto it, and by a moderate exercise herein was much refreshed...[8]

Abstention had created disorder in Winthrop's life; melancholy and discomfort had detracted from his attention to God. Yet to ensnare his "heart so farre in worldly delights" forced him to cool "the graces of the spirit by them."[9]

Moderation, Downame had called the key to order in one's life. Winthrop discovered a similar sense of sobriety when "outward recreation" was necessary. The mind dominated God's gift to man, but activities of the body might refresh an overworked mind. The maintenance of order necessitated mutual operations between mind and body. Moderation in sport, in its recreative sense, provided a balancing factor ordained by God.

Unfortunately for the reputation of sport, not all of the Puritan immigrants shared Winthrop's conceptions of values. Even as the earliest settlers embarked from English shores, the Reverend John White of Dorchester noted a diversity present among the voyagers:

As it were absurd to conceive they have all one minde, so were it ridiculous to imagine they have all one scope. Necessitie may presse some; Noveltie draw on others, hopes of gaine in time to come may prevaile with a third sort; but the most and most sincere and godly part have advancement of the Gospel for their maine scope I am confident...[10]

Members of the Company realized that men were corrupt and that few, if any, could adhere to the strict behavioral code every moment of his life. To this end the Puritans employed the civil government, wherein elected magistrates covenanted with freeholding church members to govern according to "God's laws and man's."[11] The people had the liberty to do what was good, just and honest, as exemplified by right thinking men.

As the epitome of right thinking men and guardians of the churches, the magistrates had to ensure the sanctity of the Sabbath. The Court of Assistants in 1630 ordered that John Baker "...shalbe whipped for shooteing att fowle on the Sabbath day."[12] The implication is that the Court punished Baker for his inattention to the Sabbath, rather than for his fowling. Within five years all persons absent from church meetings faced fines or imprisonment.[13] The records indicate that church absentees engaged in sport less frequently than they drank, labored unnecessarily, or traveled. Sport apparently maintained its position in the delicate hierarchy on the Sabbath.

Magistrates similarly restricted sport, or more precisely the occasion for sport, when this detracted from the economic success of the colony and social order. Perhaps the underlying theme of the first generation was the promotion of the public good. Thomas Hooker warned against the designs and devices of individuals whose selfish activities would precipitate "the distraction and desolation of the whole" and "prejudice the publike good."[14] In a society without institutions to care for the poor, the criminals, and other societal malcontents, the magistrates had to prevent such unstabilizing germs, rather than wait to treat the products.

Initially the magistrates assumed that the family, the cornerstone of society since Biblical times, would establish and maintain social order. To the master reverted the responsibilities of maintaining a financially successful calling and ensuring proper behavior.

When heads of families failed in their duties, the General Court enacted legislation providing for the disposition of the poor, and for constables to "search after all manner of gaming, singing and dancing" and "disordered meetings" in private residences.[15] Magistrates regulated occasions for vast expense of money and time and those conducive to disorderly conduct. They apparently perceived that gaming with cards, dice, or tables threatened the financial security of both individuals and colony, and they placed the burden of responsibility predominantly upon the family head.[16]

In many respects the inns and common houses of entertainment disrupted the orderly arrangement of society. Though necessary for the housing of travelers, these houses encountered rigid surveillance of visitor tenure, volume and price of liquors and tobacco, and activities permitted on the premises. The General Court scrutinized the taverns primarily because:

> ...it hath appeared unto this court, upon many sad complaints, that much drunkenness, wast of the good creatures of God, mispence of precious time and other disorders have frequently fallen out in the inns...whereby God is much dishonored, the pfession of religion repoched, & the welfare of this comonwealth greatly impaired, & the true vse of such houses (being the necessary releefe of travellers) subverted ...[17]

Owners who disregarded these laws lost their licenses, while offenders faced fines and corporal punishment.

Since people could not legally enjoy gaming in their own residences, apparently some traveled to the inns for that opportunity. Not until 1647 did the General Court outlaw shovelboard, and shortly after bowling and gaming in general, "...whereby much pcious time is spent unfruitfully, & much wast of wine & beare occasioned thereby ..."[18] The delay in banning these games, as well as the emphasis on unprofitability and drunkenness, suggest that the magistrates did not intend to denounce the nature of the game, but rather to attack overspending and inebriation.

Aside from the desire, in varying degrees, for economic stability and order in society, sport reflected other values and habits of Puritan life. In 1639 the first military company organized and depended upon physical exercise, marksmanship and athletic contests, and mock battles as the core of the training day.[19] Competitive matches emerged as tests of skill.

Military leaders sometimes restricted other occasions for sport. Near Salem in 1636, three men vacated their posts to go fowling. Instead of being happily diverted by birds, they fell prey to lurking Indians. Only one man returned to face the wrath of the lieutenant whose orders had been countered.[20]

Sport provided a means by which some men could support both the hierarchical composition of society and the public welfare. On the *Arbella* Winthrop had announced that "...in all times some must be rich, some poor; some high and eminent in power and dignity; others mean and in subjection."[21] In the first decade alone two men seemingly tried to replicate the English game preserve. In 1632 John Perkins reserved two areas in which he could "...take Fowle wth netts."[22] From the town of Salem in 1639, Emmanuell Downing received five hundred acres for the "...takeing wild foule by way of duck coy." The General Court, "...being desiros to encourage the & others, in such designs as tend to publike good...", forbade all others to shoot within a half mile of the pond.[23]

The experience of Downing and Perkins suggest that sport provided some occasions for society to focus upon the individual, especially when the needs of the individual and the community coincided. By 1641 the rights of freemen appeared printed as the Body of Liberties. One of the articles insured householders of their rights to fish and fowl for sport or livelihood within the limits of their towns.[24] Six years later concerns for horses as property and the rights of their owners instigated a law against "...a very evill practice of some disordred psons ... who do use to take othr mens horses ... & ride them at their pleasure ..."[25] This did not ban horseracing, and was only intended to protect the rights of horse-owners.

Thus, in the first two decades of Puritan life in Massachusetts Bay, the occurrence of sport was very real, reflecting both values and diversity within that society. Frequently the occasions for sport detracted from societal values, at least as conceived of by magistrates. Magistrates sought to limit these occasions and, in effect, may have restricted participation. Yet, when Samuel Maverick described Boston, he noted that its streets were lined with "... good shopps well furnished with all kinds of merchandize ..." and " full of Girles and Boys sporting up and down, with a continued concourse of people."[26]

IMPOSED HOMOGENEITY, 1650-1690

Maverick's approving comments on the progress of society do not in any way predict the crisis which befell the Puritans after mid century. As members of the second generation came of age, fewer of them joined the congregations. In their failure either to experience or relate conversion experiences and thus become baptized members, they threatened the original mission of the colony to preserve the church. Ministers and magistrates reacting to the decline in membership, which reached a record low in the 1650's and continued through the 1680's, transformed their mission into one of preserving an entire people.[27] They isolated groups within society and attacked heterogeneous attitudes. In a miscalculated effort to resurrect the supposedly homogeneous society of the first generation, they succeeded only in arousing hostility, some guilt, and greater diversity.

Ministers believed that the key to the survival of the pure church lay within the grasp of the children. If the children failed in their demonstrations of conversion, God would vent his wrath upon the entire plantation. Magistrates, by virtue of their guardianship of the churches, ordered all family masters and town officials to prevent:

> ...soundry abuses and misdemeanors, comitted by soundry persons of the Lords day, not only by children playing in the streetes and other places, but by youths, majds, and other persons, both straungers and others, uncivily walking the streets and feilds, travailing from toune to toune, going on shipboard, frequenting comon howses and other places to drincke, sport and otherwise mispend that pretjous tyme ...[28]

Youths over the age of fourteen and strangers, "the reputed great provokers of the high displeasure of Almightly God," apparently seized upon sport and other socializing activities as alternatives to Sabbath solitude.

The General Court decried the youths who took the "...liberty to walke & sporte themselves in the streets or feilds ...", disturbed the religious preparations of others, and "...too frequently repaire to publique houses of entertainment & there sitt drincking..."[29] Apparently the Court sought to enforce a rigid homogeneity within a society which had already become diverse. In an effort to preserve the efficacy of the congregations, the Court legislated against religious disturbances and excessive drinking. Many people did not carefully discriminate places or times for their participation, at a time when the colony's leaders had chosen to preserve the plantation from the fire and brimstone of God.

One must realize, however, that within society a common acceptable focus on sport must have existed. Without a sporting vernacular and some recognized values, there would have been no basis for the apparent divisions which arose. John Cotton and Increase Mather concurred that one's perspective determined the efficacy of the activity.[30] In nearly the same breath in which he denounced gaming, the second generation Mather admitted that "For a Christian to use Recreation is very lawful, and in some cases a great duty..."[31]

Ministers generally applied to sport the dictates of service to God. Some Puritans observed that sport provided desirable opportunities for socialization, for military preparedness, or for recreation and catharsis. Whether in London or Boston, Samuel Sewall swam, fished, and recognized bowling greens.[32] In 1679 John Richardson exhorted the militia men to attain greater skill:

> Victory is the Mark that skill aims at; Skill of hand, Strength of
> body, & Courage of mind do make a compleat Champion.[33]

Harvard College officials even allotted a minimum two and one-half hours for sport among their students after 1655.[34]

A man relaxed and refreshed through sport could function more efficiently in his calling. If this calling fulfilled the needs of the community, the benefit to all was obvious. Puritans continued to respond to the communal ideal so obvious during the first twenty years in Massachusetts Bay. However, the degree of commitment to that response varied. Whereas once Winthrop had to judge only for himself and record in his own diary how much sport he might enjoy, now Cotton defined and printed for others similar limitations.[35] Ministers at training days seemingly cajolled, or at least challenged, recruits to strive for skill and to distinguish the play of boys from that of men.[36] Yet, no longer did they act and speak simply to vindicate their own actions. They could not stamp out the heterogeneous attitudes toward sport. Even the Reverend Peter Thatcher of Milton purchased "'a pack of ninepins and bowle'."[38] Soldiers on active duty during King Philip's War in 1675 lost their arms while gaming.[39]

Those who attempted to dictate the acceptable values of sport probably did not fear that men would sport, but rather certain occasions for sport and the aftermath of some of these. The laws and sermons of the second generation anticipated God's wrath, for the most part, because of the largely misunderstood decline in church membership. By instilling order, a sense of conforming order ascertained by more and more artificial officers and institutions, these leaders hoped to return their people to the path of God. The gradual increase in population, Indian threats to a more distant frontier, and vacillating periods of economic expansion and contraction presented new problems to second generation leaders.

In an attempt to enforce uniformity, Harvard College had actually reacted in a positive sense by permitting sport on campus and not allowing students to venture off campus.[40] Magistrates, however, did not so readily solve the problems of filling the churches and preserving the communities. Taverns continually irritated those who tried to order society. Leaders among the second generation became ever more concerned about the opportunities these taverns provided. Shuffleboard and bowling had already become forbidden, at least partly because of the gaming element. In 1651 the General Court forbade dancing at weddings in taverns because "...there are many abuses and disorders by dancing in ordinaryes..."[41]

It is quite possible that dancing itself was not the target of the Court. John Cotton and, later, Increase Mather, accepted dance, although Cotton favored its mixed form, while Mather, unmixed.[42] The abuses and disorders may, in fact, have arisen not from dancing but from the assemblage of a crowd, the containment of which posed grave problems for the few constables and selectmen. Dancing and drinking, when enjoyed together, enabled people to perpetrate actions which threatened the lives around them and elicited God's wrath.

The Essex County Court arrested Thomas Wheeler in 1653 for "...profane and foolish dancing; singing and wanton speeches, probably being drunk..."[43] Wheeler's crime actually lay in his "speakinge sinfull and reprochfull speeches" against Reverend Cobbett of Lynn. His imbibing had probably supplied the impetus for "profane dancing." The court records are replete with cases involving drunkenness, fornication, and lewd behaviors, not with dancing.

On other occasions as well, sport constituted a threat to the safety of the colonists and to the order of society in general. In Boston the selectmen and the council reacted to the dangers of foot-ball:

Forasmuch as sundry complaints are made that several persons have received hurt by boys and young men playing at football in the streets, these are therefore to enjoin that non be found at that game in any of the streets, lanes, or enclosures of this town, under penalty of twenty shillings for every such offense.[44]

By 1662 cases of "violent rideing in the streets" of Boston occurred so frequently that the General Court railed against the effect of "...indaingering the bodies and lives of many persons ..."[45] Apparently, by 1672, the danger had not abated. Coupled with the economic disasters attendant upon horse racing for money, the Court of Assistants cited the

"Hazard of their limbs and lives" as reasons for refusing to permit this sport within four miles of any town.[46]

Men carrying cocks offered an exciting pastime for some Bostonians. Samuel Sewall described one such incident:

> Jos. Maylem carries a Cock at his back, with a Bell in 's hand, in the Main Street; several follow him blindfold, under pretence of striking him or 's cock, with great cartships strike passengers, and make great disturbance.[47]

Judge Sewall ordered the constables to " ... take effectual care to suppress and dissipate all unlawful Assemblies or tumultuous gatherings ..." arising from "...Shailing or throwing at Cocks and such like Disorders, tending to the disturbance of their Magesties liege People, and breach of the peace."[48] Governor Bradford himself signed the order. Though the magistrates uttered not a word against cock scaling itself, they condemned the dangers to the community inherent in the situation.

Perhaps the concept of gaming most adequately represents the diversity in attitude present within Puritan culture. During the first twenty years of settlement, gaming emerged as an illegal activity, primarily as a result of economic necessity. After 1650 gaming seemingly attracted more numerous proponents and opponents.

Concurrent with the unfavorable decline in church membership, John Cotton pictured the enmity of religion to card games. Since the distribution of cards lay in the hands of God, he argued "... to appeal to him and his providence for dispensing these ludicra, seemeth...a taking of God's name in vain."[49] Nearly thirty years later, Increase Mather deplored the lottery even more adamantly:

> Now a Lot is a serious thing not to be trifled with; the Scripture saith not only (as some would have it) of Extraordinary Lots, but of a Lot in general, that the whole Disposing (or Judgment) thereof is of the Lord ... He that makes use of a Lot, wholly commits his affair to a Superior Cause than either nature or art, therefore unto God. But this ought not to be done in a Sportful Lusory way.[50]

Mather's son Cotton, while deploring the further fallen state of young people, even more viciously attacked the "Scandalous Games of Lottery."[51]

The minister's outcries must have fallen on many deaf ears. In 1662 the Pynchon Court heard testimony from John Henryson who, along with five others, played cards because "...I was willing to have recreation for my wife to drive away melancholy." He admitted that "...he was willing to do anything when his wife was Ill to make her merry."[52] Paul Parker, a two time gamester, was finally convicted for "...being a very ill example to the youth ..."[53]

By 1670 the General Court noted the great increase in gaming and issued yet another law on the basis that:

> Whereas the great sin of gaming increaseth wth in this juris-
> diction to the great dishonour of God, corrupting of youth &
> expending of much pretjous time & estate ...[54]

Into the preamble of this law, the Court bound all the major con-cerns of the colony's leaders: sin, wayward or less than ideal youth, and economy, both of time and money.

It is quite possible that gaming was more popular and widespread than the General Court would have liked to have believed. Both civil and military personnel continued to play cards. Masters, innkeepers, and servants alike played cards and used dice.[55] Nor did the Court succeed in halting the importation and sale of devices for gaming. In a single court session in Suffolk County, five ships inventoried packs of cards sold for three shillings apiece.[56]

Two primary factors appeared to negate, or at least limit, the effectiveness of the laws and the desired conformity to first generation values. The first of these was the declining ability of the family to instill discipline and thus preserve social order. To offset this decline, magistrates had to instill more artificial institutions and officers to carry out what were once family responsibilities. By 1655 the General Court had established houses of correction.[57] It empowered constables and selectmen to "...take notice of comon coasters, unprofitable fowlers, and other idle psons...", as well as to restrain the "Unreverent carriage and behavior of divers young psons."[58] Within the next twenty years tithingmen replaced the heads of families as executors of Sabbath discipline and, shortly thereafter, could interfere in all family disorders.[59] The poor, the unbridled, and the indolent faced rehabilitation within the militia, jails, homes of esteemed families, and minor alms houses.[60]

The second emanated from inconsistencies within the calling doctrine and stewardship of wealth concept. Some Puritans envisioned financial gain to be derived from sporting ventures.

Yet the speculation involved in gaming or providing dancing lessons was not recognized by the authorities as a legitimate and fruitful economic venture. As long as men with economic success sat in judgment of the colony, they ruled against the elements of chance in sport, its ap-parent unprofitability, and disorder. At least two dancing masters left

Boston in a state of financial insolvency, while a tavern owner was prevented from renting a room to a man "to shew tricks in."[61]

The second generation society, at least the Puritan leaders among
them, did not preserve a Christian utopia in Massachusetts Bay, nor did
they succeed in impressing a homogeneous character upon the ruled. By
singling out distinct groups, the ministers marked an actual fragmentation
in society. Laws involving sport illustrate the merging of concerns for sin,
economy and order.

For many members of society, sport retained much of its original
essence. Sport provided diversion, recreation, competitive skill training,
and healthful exercise. Henryson even rationalized that an illegal sporting activity might indeed provide the same essential benefits. Others began to envision economic opportunities.

THE FRACTURING OF SOCIETY, 1690-1730

As the second generation merged with the third, this fragmenting
process continued. A new English administration and interference with
Massachusetts introduced several variables into the predominantly
Puritan culture of Massachusetts. More direct colonial contact with
England and greater proximity to British society at home and abroad
helped to diversify colonial society.[62] As a result of both external and
internal factors, Massachusetts society generated a greater degree of attitudinal and role change than it ever had previously. Sport was both affected and reflected in this transformation. Opportunities for the recreational and economic functions of sport increased, while positive and
negative attitudes solidified. Newspaper advertisements of sporting
events appeared and laws regulating sport as a behavior declined in frequency.

After 1690 external factors enhanced the religious fluctuations
within Massachusetts. In the aftermath of the Glorious Revolution, the
English parliament had passed the Act of Toleration. To the Anglican
population and other sects in Massachusetts, coupled with a franchise
based on financial qualifications, this meant greater freedom from
Puritan religious restraint. Ministers reacted intensely to their loss of
dominion and to the failures of their own congregation members to
exhibit conversion experiences. The treatment of sport by the ministers
illustrates their confused and frequently reactionary opinions and
attitudes.

At militia trainings, always a natural forum with an isolated
audience, ministers frequently used metaphors of sport to praise, inspire,
and harangue the men. The Christian soldier, who vigilantly protected
his god and his society, warranted great praise. "Indeed men of Martial
Spirits and Skill ought to be Encouraged. These Trainings and Exercises

are very commendable...", emphasized Peter Thatcher.[63] Benjamin Wadsworth cited biblical injunctions and maneuvers for artillery men and grenadiers. More importantly, however, Boone differentiated between classes in society. He warned the private soldier to avoid drunkenness and gaming,[64] but to gentlemen and commanders he spoke in terms of "healthful Exercise", so becoming to their stations in life.[65]

Joseph Belcher reminded his listeners of the spiritual purpose of one's calling. He urged his comrades to battle effectively, to win the prize, and to obtain victory, and he portrayed the Apostle Paul as the epitome of the ultimate victor in heaven. Possibly Belcher believed that the utilization of talent and training for success in one's particular calling had finally superseded the societal goal of unity and the attainment of heaven. "You are not called to quit your pleasures, only change the objects of them," Belcher advised the militia.[66]

The militia sermons and attitudes toward training days represent a mingling of concerns. At times the ministers appeared as a conservative force trying to revitalize the essence of community with God as the focus. Sport was useful to them as a medium for instilling discipline, cooperation, and the will to struggle. Almost simultaneously however, they recognized other, more personal interpretations of the same elements which could and did exist. The ministers helped to consummate a class society by speaking to gentlemen in a different tone than to others. They advocated rational thought and efficiency of body, mind, and spirit.[67]

The minister's treatment of the family and children is similarly reflective of the struggle to accommodate the style of a fluctuating society to the values of their fathers and grandfathers. For some, such as Cotton Mather and Benjamin Wadsworth, sport provided a medium through which they could regulate and educate their children. Mather even translated sporting phrases into Latin for his son Sam to study.[68]

The society did recognize that childhood represented a stage in maturity distinct from that of youth or adulthood. Benjamin Wadsworth urged parents to distinguish between the play of children and that of youth.[69] Henry Gibbs, by 1727, noted that too many parents cared more for the worldly circumstances of their children than for their spiritual fulfillment, just as the former did for themselves.[70]

In 1709 Increase Mather authored a simmering "Advice to a Young Man" distinguishing between lawful, moderate sporting and the indulgence in "sinful sports and pastimes".[71] William Cooper published an entire sermon dedicated to "How and Why Young People Should Cleanse Their Way," while Thomas Foxcroft admonished impenitent youth to "...abandon evil Company, Forsake the foolish, and live."[72] Daniel Lewes vigorously condemned the "waste" among the young and ministered to youth as an impersonal state of being, an "it."[73]

The impersonality and harsh tones present within Lewes' sermon seemed to indicate a more complete ministerial isolation from society. Rather than to comply with the values of a changing society, many of these ministers chose to follow the paths established by predecessors. They could not meet the needs of the society by developing constructive sermons, so they splintered the flock into distinct groups and criticized those. Azariah Mather attacked travelers and sailors who, he believed, refused to observe the sanctity of the Sabbath when absent from Massachusetts.[74] Cotton Mather, as well, viewed returning seamen as being detrimental to the moral code which the ministers advocated.[75]

As had been the practice of their fathers and grandfathers, the ministers after 1690 turned to magistrates for legitimate support of their position on behavior. The General Court retained its duty to protect the churches throughout the seventeenth century and well into the eighteenth. "An Act for the better Observation and Keeping the Lords-Day," published a minimum of four times between 1692 and 1727, prohibited people from engaging in any unnecessary aspects of their ordinary callings, to travel, or to "...use any Game, Sport, Play or Recreation."[76]

The frequency with which this law appeared, the appearance of penalties for second offenders in 1716 and the additions of proscribed activities suggest, among other ideas, that the laws were disobeyed, ignored, or unknown. These factors may help explain the continuous appearance of lotteries, sport, and drinking at taverns.

By 1719 the General Court concluded that the popularity of private lotteries, "Mischievous and Unlawful Games," had increased among those who could least afford these diversions. The Court illegalized all private lotteries because:

> ...the Children and Servants of Several Gentlemen, Merchants, and Traders and other unwary People have been drawn into a vain and foolish Expence of Money, which tends to the utter Ruin and Impoverishment of many Families, and is to the Raproach of this Government, and against the Common Good, Trade, Welfare and Peace of the Province.[77]

While public lotteries may have promoted the public welfare, private lotteries did no. Yet, continue they did. Three months after the law's passage, Samuel Sewall entered in his diary confirmation of four newspaper advertisements for private lotteries.[78]

Inns and taverns continued to be closely scrutinized by the General Court. To limit incentives for people to misspend or misuse time and money, the magistrates prohibited "...Dice, Cards, Tables, Bowles, Shuffleboard, Billiards, Coyts, Cales, Logats, or any implements used in Gaming."[79] Unfortunately for the gamesters, who now bore the brunt of fines and punishment, many could not afford the luxury of gaming, while the state could not bear the expense of paupers. Magistrates legislated against the root causes of poverty and indolence and assured the colonists that if they did not make the proper choices, the choices would be made for them.

This idea of proper choices permeated society and became a very personal consideration when one's safety became endangered. Citizens of Boston, in reacting to the bodily harm inflicted by young boys sporting in the streets, restricted opportunities for throwing foot-balls, squibs, snowballs, and long bullets. Throwing the long bullet, made of iron, lead, brass, wood, or stone, resulted in "...divers Inconveniences and may be of the Pernicious Consequence..."[80]

The disapproval of foot-ball seems to relate directly to the site of its occurrence. Away from the confines of town streets and yards, players presumably did not endanger spectators or passersby. John Dunton, an English traveler, described the circumstances of such a game in Rowley:

> ...there was that day a great game of Foot-ball to be play'd with their feet, which I thought was very odd; but it was upon a broad Sandy Shoar, free from stones, which made it more easy. Neither were they so apt to end up one anothers heels and quar-rel, as I have seen 'em in England.[81]

The players maintained a sense of fair, competitive play and apparently had chosen to disallow any raucous behavior.

Apparently public recalcitrance to other sport forms diminished as some patrons of horse racing, bear baiting, and billiards removed these from the streets and taverns.[82] Particularly after 1715, newspapers advertised rules, weights, wagers, and prizes, often to "gentlemen and others." The designs of racing competition became increasingly com-plex, as exemplified by this notice in the *Boston Gazette* in 1725:

> This is to give notice to all gentlemen and others that there is to be Thirty Pounds in Money run for ... by Six Horses, Mares or Geldings, Two miles ... to carry 9 stone Weight, the Standard to be 14 hands high ... Each one that Runs to have their Number from 1 to 6, to be drawn, and to run by 2 ..., the 3 first Horses to run a second Heat ...[83]

The colonists who wrote and read this and other notices appar-ently knew how to organize sporting events and understood a concept of competition. Horses of fairly equal stature frequently ran for symbols of wealth and esteem, not merely for money purses. The price signified the achievement of status for a single winner, an individual who relied upon his own talents to his own benefit rather than always for that of the community.

Some members of the third generation seized the opportunities provided by sport among the people to achieve financial gain in legitimate business ventures. Merchants in Salem and Boston stocked children's playthings, at times supplied by privateers.[84] Dancing masters taught for fees in Boston, where the popularity of dancing and balls among British officials probably helped to sway public opinion in their favor.[85] Cabinet makers fashioned card tables for sale to wealthy colonists, as indicated in estate inventories.[86] A farmer sold his orchard in 1712 to the Harvard College Corporation, which designated the land as "... a place of recreation and exercise for the scholars."[87]

A 1714 advertisement in the *Boston Newsletter* of a bowling green includes several intriguing comments about the society of that day. Daniel Stevens, the owner of the British Coffee House, invited men according to their position in society, "... all Gentlemen, Merchants, and others, that have a mind to Recreate themselves, shall be accommodated ..."[88] By accommodating these men Stevens apparently sought to provide a service, in the form of recreation, to three distinct and recognized social groupings. Further, as the owner of the British Coffee House, Stevens was not bound by laws regulating sporting activities in inns or taverns. Either the laws did not apply to coffee houses, or they were simply ineffective.

The Stevens' case is only one of many that reveals how far in practice the third generation had strayed from the ideal values established by the first. Economic success and social position, rather than the authority of od, reckoned the hierarchical organization of society. Individual initiative and a worldly competitive spirit replaced the older sense of mutuality, as the welfare of the individual superseded that of the community in many instances. Rational thought, particularly in matters of economic stability and personal safety, not revelation, helped to transform the concept of order. Men relied upon themselves rather than God for the plan of society.

Even the ministers could not stem the tide of change. Verbal vengeance became their weapon against practices which they did not completely understand or for which they assumed primarily negative consequences. To them the contraction of family responsibilities in maintaining order meant only that the family unit was disintegrating and negating its function in society. Few, if any, ministers realized that this transformation within the family might actually produce a more stable one, with members bound by love rather than fear.

Both Puritans and non-Puritans within the first century in Massachusetts Bay did sport and, undoubtedly, with increasing frequency as the century progressed. Several primary factors have arisen to at least partially explain this phenomenon. Perhaps the most obvious is that the Puritans were human and, as such, they demanded refreshment, relaxation, socialization, and competition, all of which sport provided. Secondly, is the fact that from the onset of the colony the immigrants never formed a uniform society, either in purpose or in action. Consequently, the interpretations of values and social mores varied widely among those possessing authority and those without such. Time and money served both God and men; however, the use of such by men did not always conform to religious dictates or civil enactments. What was idleness to some apparently represented the economic use of time to others.

Throughout this century the initially Puritan-oriented society diversified even further. Non-Puritan immigrants speeded changes within towns and countryside. Massachusetts gradually turned to the world, especially to that of mercantile Britain. The occasions for sport now fit the needs of the world of Daniel Stevens rather than that of John Winthrop.

Thus, the enigmatic status of sport in Puritan society emerges slightly less puzzling when viewed in the perspective of the first century society in Massachusetts Bay. Diverse sporting habits and attitudes existed because of the demands placed on sport and the roles devised for sport by the Puritans themselves. As a behavioral form, sport mirrored developments within Massachusetts Bay and, in turn, was affected by the transformation and diversification of that society. Individuals sported and groups sported, but only in the context of the entire society do their activities and attitudes begin to fit as pieces of an interlocking puzzle.

• • •

Notes

1. Particular treatments of the change in Puritan society to which one should refer include: Paul Conklin, *Puritans and Pragmatists* (New York: Dodd, Mead and Company, 1968); Stephen Foster, *Their Solitary Way: The Puritan Social Ethic in the First Century of Settlement in New England* (New Haven: Yale University Press, 1971); David Hawke, *The Colonial Experience* (New York: The Bobbs-Merrill Company, 1966); Kenneth Lockridge, *A New England Town: The First One Hundred Years* (New York: W.W. Norton and Company, 1970); Robert Middlekauff, *The Mathers: Three Generations of Puritan Intellectuals, 1597-1728* (New York: Oxford University Press, 1971); Darrett B. Rutman, *Winthrop's Boston: Portrait of a Puritan Town* (New York: W.W. Norton and Company, 1972); Gary Warden, *Boston, 1689-1776* (Boston: Little, Brown, and Company, 1970); and Larzar Ziff, *Puritanism in America* (New York: Viking Press, 1973).

2. Sir John Murray, *Oxford English Dictionary*, reprint of *New English Dictionary* (Oxford: Clarendon Press, 1933), X, 665-667. Broadly stated in seventeenth century terms, sport connotes: (1) a pleasant pastime; entertainment or amusement; recreation, diversion; (2) to amuse, entertain, or recreate oneself, especially by active exercise in the open air; to take part in some game or play; to frolic or gambol; (3) to deal with in a light or trifling way. Further limitations on term appear within the literature of the Puritans.

3. John Winthrop, "Modell of Christian Charity," in *Winthrop Papers* (6 vols. Boston: Massachusetts Historical Society, 1929-1947), II, 295.

4. Ibid., 282-283.

5. Robert Middlekauff, op.cit., 6.

6. John Downame, "Guide to Godlynesse" (London, 1622), 164.

7. John Downame, "The Christian Warfare," (London, 1634), 969-990. Puritans used the term calling in three senses, in each of which God always called to man. Most broadly, God called man to commit himself in any given right action. Secondly, God called man to be saved; thus the "general" or "effectual" calling. Finally, God summoned man to a worldly occupation, the "particular" calling for one's own subsistence and that of the public good. Edmund Morgan, *The Puritan Family* (New York: Harper and Row, Publishers, 1966), 69-70.

8. John Winthrop, op.cit., I, 201-202.

9. Ibid.

10. John White, "The Planters Plea: or the Grounds of Plantations Examined and Usuall Objections Answered" (London, 1630), n.p.

11. John Winthrop, "Remarks on Liberty," in Russell Nye and Norman Grabo, eds., *American Thought and Writing* (Boston: Houghton Mifflin Company, 1965), I, 59-61.

12. *Records of the Governor and the Company of the Massachusetts Bay*, edited by Nathaniel B. Shurtleff (Boston: William White Press, 5 vols., 153), I, November 30, 1631, 82. Hereafter cited as *Massachusetts Records*. For the purposes of the paper the colonial practice of double dating the months of January-March has been deleted, and those months are included as the first and third of each new year.

13. *Massachusetts Records*, I, March 4, 1635, 140.

14. Thomas Hooker, "A Survey of the SUmme of Church Discipline" (London, 1648), 188.

15. *Massachusetts Records*, II, 70, 180.

16. *Massachusetts Records*, I, March 22, 1631; November 5, 1639, 280.

17. *Massachusetts Records*, I, November 30, 1637, 213.

18. *Massachusetts Records*, II, May 26, 1647, 195; III, June 19, 1650, 201.

19. *Massachusetts Records*, I, March 13, 1639, 250; John Winthrop, *Journal*, edited by James K. Hosmer (New York: Charles Scribner's Sons, 2 vols., 1908), II, September 15, 1640, 42; Norma Schwendener, *A History of Physical Education in the United States* (New York: A.S. Barnes and Company, 1942), 6.

20. John Winthrop, *Journal*, op.cit., I, October 8, 1636, 192.

21. John Winthrop, *Papers*, op.cit., II, 282.

22. *Massachusetts Records*, I, April 3, 1632, 94.

23. *Massachusetts Records*, I, September 6, 1638, 236; Sidney Perley, *The History of Salem, Massachusetts* (Salem: by the author, 1926), II, 25-27.

24. "Body of Liberties of 1641," number 16, in Edwin Powers, *Crime and Punishment in Early Massachusetts, 1620-1692* (Boston, Beacon Press, 1966), 535.

25. *Massachusetts Records*, II, May 26, 1647, 195; "Body of Liberties," number 92, op.cit., 544.

26. Samuel Maverick, "A Briefe Description of New England and the Severall Townes therein," *Massachusetts Historical Society Proceedings*, Second Series, I (1885), 238.

27. Stephen Foster, op.cit., 177, Boston's First Church entered 265 in 1630, 31 in 1650s; 39 in 1680s; Charleston entered 98 in 1630s, 26 in 1650s, and 39 in 1680s; Roxbury entered 112 in 1630s, 21 in 1650s, and 49 in 1680s. Other congregations substantiated similar declines at a time when the population increased fourfold. Further discussions of these facts and the effect on the quantity of the freeman electorate may be found in: Edmund S. Morgan, *Visible Saints: The History of a Puritan Idea* (New York: New York University Press, 1963), 88,104-105; Richard C. Simmons, "Freemanship in Early Massachusetts: Some Suggestions and a Case Study," *William and Mary Quarterly*, 19 (1962), 422-428; Simmons, "Godliness, Property, and the Franchise in Puritan Massachusetts: an Interpretation," *Journal of American History*, 55, (1968-1969), 495-511; Robert E. Wall, Jr., "The Massachusetts Bay Colony Franchise in 1647," *William and Mary Quarterly*, 27 (1970), 136-344.

29. *Massachusetts Records*, IV part 1, October 19, 1657, 347.

30. John Cotton, "A Practical Commentary, or An Exposition with Observations, Reasons and Uses upon the First Epistle Generall of John" (London, 1656), 125-128; Increase Mather, "A Testimony Against Several Prophane and Superstitious Customs" (Boston, 1688), 37.

31. Ibid.

32. Samuel Sewall, The Diary of Samuel Sewall, 1674-1729, *Massachusetts Historical Society Collections Fifth Series, 1878-1882* (New York, Arno Press, 3 vols., 1972),I, July 8, 1689, 264; July 12, 1687, 182.

33. John Richardson, "The Necessity of a Well-Experienced Soldiery" (Cambridge, 1679), 10.

34. *Harvard College Records* (Boston: Publications of the Colonial Society of Massachusetts, 3 vols., 1935), III, 330-333.

35. John Cotton, op.cit., 125-126.

36. John Richardson, op.cit., 10, Samuell Nowell, "Abraham in Arms" (Boston, 1678), 19.

37. Increase Mather, op.cit., 37.

38. Alice M. Earle, *Customs and Fashions in Old New England* (New York: Charles Scribner's Sons, 1893), 237-238.

39. *Massachusetts Records*, V, October 13, 1675, 50.

40. *Harvard College Records*, op.cit., 330-331.

41. *Massachusetts Records*, II, May 7, 1651, 224.

42. John Cotton, "Letter to R. Levett," quoted in E.D. Hansom, editor, *The Heart of the Puritan* (New York: The Macmillan Company, 1917), 177; *Samuel Foster Damon, The History of Square-Dancing* (Worchester, Massachusetts: The Davis Press, Inc., 1952), 64.

43. *Essex Quarterly Court Records* (Boston: Essex Institute, 8 vols., 1911-1921), I, 286-287.

44. "Second Report of the Boston Records Commissioners," *In The Memorial History of Boston, 1630-1880*, edited by Justin Windsor (Boston: James R. Osgood, 1880), 229.

45. *Massachusetts Records*, IV part II, October 8, 1662.

46. *Massachusetts Court of Assistants Records, 1630-1692* (Boston: published by the County of Suffolk, 3 vols, 1901), II, April 9, 1672.

47. Samuel Sewall, *Diary*, I, February 15, 1687, 167; February 16, 1686, 122.

48. Ibid., March 4, 1690, 312-313.

49. John Cotton, op.cit., 177.

50. Increase Mather, op.cit., 30.

51. Cotton Mather, *The Diary of Cotton Mather*, edited by Worthington C. Ford (New York: Frederick Ungar Publishing Company, 2 vols., 1911), I, July 30, 1690, 202.

52. *Colonial Justice in Western Massachusetts, 1639-1702: Pynchon Court Records*, edited by Joseph H. Smith (Cambridge University Press, 1961), March 20, 1662, 257. Hereafter cited as *Pynchon Court Records*.

53. *Court of Assistants*, III, March 1, 1669, 201; *Massachusetts Records*, IV part II, May 31, 1670, 453.

54. *Massachusetts Records*, IV part II, May 11, 1670, 449.

55. *Pynchon Court Records*, March 20, 1678, 289; *Records of the Suffolk County Court, 1671-1680* (Boston: Published by the Colonial Society of Massachusetts, 2 vols., 1933), I, October 2, 1672, 184; April 29, 673, 259, 263; II, January 27, 1680, 1162. Hereafter cited as *Suffolk Court Records*.

56. *Suffolk Court Records*, I, January 30, 1672, 58.

57. *Massachusetts Records*, IV part 1, May 23, 1655, 222.

58. *Massachusetts Records*, IV part 1, Pay 17, 1658, 325; IV part I, October 19, 1654, 200.

59. Larzar Ziff, op.cit., 193.

60. *Massachusetts Records*, I, June 6, 1639, 264; II, November 4, 1646, 179-180; V, June 1, 1677, 144.

61. Sewall, *Diary*, I, November 12, 1685, 103-104; December 17, 1685, 112; July 28, 1686, 145; December 4, 1687, 196; *Court of Assistants*, I, 1681, 197.

62. Gary B. Warden, op.cit., 36; Stephen Foster, op.cit., 92-93; David Hawke, op.cit., 242-244.

63. Peter Thatcher, "The Saint's Victory" (Boston, 1696), 37.

64. Benjamin Wadsworth, "Good Soldiers A Great Blessing" (Boston, 1700), 8,21.

65. Nicholas Boone, "Military Discipline: The Compleat Solder" (Boston, 1701), 55,57.

66. Joseph Belcher, "A Victory Over Those Habits of Sin Which War Against the Soul" (Boston, 1698), 4-8.

67. Ebenezer Pemberton, "The Souldier Defended and Directed" (Boston, 1701), 15, 17-18.

68. Cotton Mather, *Diary*, II, 1712, 144; II, Jan. 29, 1716, 340.

69. Benjamin Wadsworth, "The Well-Ordered Family" (Boston, 1712), 47.

70. Henry Gibbs, "Godly Children Their Parents Joy" (Boston, 1727), 26,28.

71. Increase Mather, "Advice to a Young Man" (Boston, 1709), 28; "Meditations on the Lords Day" (Boston, 1711), n.p.

72. William Cooper, "How and Why Young People Should Cleanse Their Way" (Boston, 1716), 11; Thomas Foxcroft, "The Secure and Impenitent Youth: Exhortations and Directions to Young People" (Boston, 1721), 20.

73. Daniel Lewes, "The Sins of Youth Remembered" (Boston, 1725), 5.

74. Azariah Mather, "The Sabbath-Day's Rest Asserted" (Boston, 1709), 37-39, 67.

75. Cotton Mather, "The Sailour's Companion" (Boston, 1709), 37-39.

76. *Acts and Laws of the Massachusetts General Court, 1684-1730*, June 8, 1692, 17; 1714, 15; 1716, 279-280; November 22, 1727, 380-381. Hereafter cited as *Acts and Laws*.

77. *Acts and Laws*, May 27, 1719, 319.

78. Samuel Sewall, "Letter to William Dummer," August 12, 1719, in "Letter-book," *Massachusetts Historical Society Collections Sixth Series*, II, 102-103.

79. *Acts and Laws*, June 8, 1692, 16-17; May 25, 1698, 275-276.

80. *Orders and By-Laws of the Inhabitants of Boston, 1701*, 11; 1719-1724, 27.

81. Albert Bushness Hart, *Common Wealth History of Massachusetts* (New York: The States History Company, 5 vols., 1927), II, 280.

82. *Boston News-Letter*, August 22-29, 1715; May 22-29, 1721; *Boston Gazette*, May 2, 1721, May 23-30, 1726; *New England Courant*, April 30, 1722.

83. *Boston Gazette*, April 19-26, 1725.

84. Sidney Perley, op.cit., III, 127; Alice M. Earle, *Child Life in Colonial Days* (New York: The Macmillan Company, 1899), 361.

85. *Boston News-Letter*, March 1, 1713; Thomas J. Wertenbaker, *The Puritan Oligarchy* (New York: Charles Scribners Sons, 1947), 176-177; Sewall, *Diary*, III, November 29, 1716, 111, January 7, 1718, 158; September 8, 1718, 193.

86. George Dow, *Everyday Life in the Massachusetts Bay Colony* (Boston: Published by the Society for the Preservation of New England Antiquities, 1935), 112, 115.

87. *Harvard College Records*, op.cit., I, 401.

88. *Boston News-Letter*, April 26-May 3, 1714.

•　•　•

Suggestions for Further Reading:

Durant, John and Otto Bettmann, *Pictoral History of American Sports: Colonial Times to the Present* (Cranbury, NJ: A.S. Barnes, 1965).

Good, Douglas L., "Colonials at Play: Leisure in Newport, 1723," *Rhode Island History*, XXXIII, 1 (February, 1974), 8-17.

Henderson, Robert W., *Early American Sport*, 3rd ed. (Rutherford, NJ: Fairleigh Dickinson University Press, 1976).

Jable, J. Thomas, "Aspects of Moral Reform in Early Nineteenth-Century Pennsylvania," *Pennsylvania Magazine of History and Biography*, CII (July, 1978), 344-363.

————. "Pennsylvania's Early Blue Laws: A Quaker Experiment in the Suppression of Sport and Amusement, 1682-1740," *Journal of Sport History*, I (November, 1974), 107-121.

Ledbetter, Bonnie S., "Sports and Games of the American Revolution," *Journal of Sport History*, VI (Winter, 1979), 29-40.

Meyer, Heinz, "Puritanism and Physical Training: Ideological and Political Accents in the Christian Interpretation of Sport," *International Review of Sport Sociology*, VIII (1973), 37-51.

Mook, H. Telfer, "Training Day in New England," *New England Quarterly*, XI (December, 1938), 687-697.

Painter, Ruth E., "Tavern Amusements in Eighteenth Century America" in Leon Stein, Ed., *The Leisure Class in America* (New York: Arno, 1975).

Struna, Nancy, "Sport and Colonial Education: A Cultural Perspective," *Research Quarterly for Exercise and Sport*, LII, 1 (March, 1981), 117-133.

_____. "Sport and Societal Values: Massachusetts Bay," *Quest,*
        XXVII (Winder, 1977), 38-46.

Wagner, Peter, "Puritan Attitudes Towards Physical Recreation in 17th
        Century New England," *Journal of Sport History,* III (Summer,
        1976), 139-151.

Weiss, Harry B. and Grace M. Weiss, *Early Sports and Pastimes in New
        Jersey* (Trenton, NJ: Past Times, 1960.

HORSES AND GENTLEMEN:
THE CULTURAL SIGNIFICANCE OF GAMBLING
AMONG THE GENTRY OF VIRGINIA

Timothy H. Breen

In this essay, Timothy Breen explores the utility of a sports paradigm in examining various socio-cultural elements of the American colonial experience. Arguing that "a specific, patterned form of behavior, such as gambling, does not become popular in a society or among the members of a subgroup of that society unless the activity reflects or expresses values indigenous to that culture," Breen recognizes both the role of sport in seventeenth century Virginia and the value in drawing on the perspectives and methodologies of other disciplines in understanding the historical significance of sport.

Noting the factors that contributed to an environment supportive of competitive gaming, Breen focuses on the gentry values that gambling put on public display. These values contributed to a sense of identity and cohesion among the gentry group. Gambling, particularly quarter-horse racing, reinforced the values and preserved class distinctions.

In acknowledging the work of Clifford Geertz, Erving Goffman, and others, Breen affirms the place of cultural anthropology, sociology, and psychology in historical inquiry. His essay emphasizes the interaction among several fields of study in exploring basic patterns of thought and behavior through a society's cultural artifacts. Breen clearly demonstrates that the study of sport fits well within the post-consensus need to examine the American scene and its individual sub-communities more broadly.

In the fall of 1686 Durand of Dauphine, a French Huguenot, visited the capital of colonial Virginia. Durand regularly recorded in a journal what he saw and heard, providing one of the new firsthand accounts of late seventeenth century Virginia society that has survived to the present day. When he arrived in Jamestown the House of Burgesses was in session. "I saw there fine looking men." he noted, "sitting in judgment booted and with belted sword." But to Durand's surprise, several of these Virginia gentlemen "started gambling" soon after dinner, and it was not until midnight that one of the players noticed the Frenchman patiently waiting for the contest to end. The Virginian—obviously a veteran of long nights at the gaming table—advised Durand to go to bed. "'For,' said he, 'it is quite possible that we shall be here all night," and in truth I found them still playing the next morning."[1]

The event Durand witnessed was not unusual. In late seventeenth and early eighteenth-century Virginia, gentlemen spent a good deal of time gambling. During this period, in fact, competitive gaming involved high stakes became a distinguishing characteristic of gentry culture. Whenever the great planters congregated, someone inevitably produced a deck of cards, a pair of dice, or a backgammon board; the quarter-horse racing was a regular event throughout the colony. Indeed, these men hazarded money and tobacco on almost any proposition in which there was an element of chance. Robert Beverley, a member of one of Virginia's most prominent families, made a wager "with the gentlemen of the country" that if he could produce seven hundred gallons of wine on his own plantation, they would pay him the handsome sum of one thousand guineas. Another leading planter offered six-to-one odds that Alexander Spotswood could not procure a commission as the colony's governor. And in 1671 one disgruntled gentleman asked a court of law to award him his winnings concerning "a Servant maid."[2] The case of this suspect-sounding wager—unfortunately not described in greater detail—dragged on until the colony's highest court ordered the loser to pay the victor a thousand pounds of tobacco.

The great planters' passion for gambling, especially on quarter-horse racing, coincided with a period of far-reaching social change in Virginia.[3] Before the mid-1680s constant political unrest, servant risings both real and threatened, plant-cutting riots, and even a full-scale civil war had plagued the colony.[4] But by the end of the century Virginia had achieved internal peace.[5] Several elements contributed to the growth of social tranquility. First, by 1700 the ruling gentry were united as they had never been before. The great planters of the seventeenth century had been for the most part aggressive English immigrants. They fought among themselves for political and social dominance, and during Bacon's Rebellion in 1676 various factions within the gentry attempted to settle their differences on the battlefield. By the end of the century, how-ever, a sizable percentage of the Virginia gentry, perhaps a majority, had been born in the colony. The members of this native-born elite—one historian calls them a "creole elite"—cooperated more frequently in political affairs than had their immigrant fathers. They found it necessary to unite in resistance against a series of interfering royal governors such as Thomas Lord Culpeper, Francis Nicholson, and Alexander Spotswood. After Bacon's Rebellion the leading planters—the kind of men whom Durand watched gamble the night away—successfully consolidated their control over Virginia's civil, military, and ecclesiastical institutions. They monopolized the most important offices; they patented the best lands.[6]

A second and even more far-reaching element in the creation of this remarkable solidarity among the gentry was the shifting racial composition of the plantation labor force. Before the 1680s the planters had relied on large numbers of white indentured servants to cultivate Virginia's sole export crop, tobacco. These impoverished, often desperate servants disputed their masters' authority and on several occasions resisted colonial rulers with force of arms. In part because of their dissatisfaction with the indenture system, and in part because changes in the international slave trade made it easier and cheaper for Virginians to purchase black laborers, the major planters increasingly turned to the Africans. The blacks' cultural disorientation made them less difficult to control than the white servants. Large-scale collective violence such as Bacon's Rebellion and the 1682 plant cutting riots consequently declined markedly. By the beginning of the eighteenth century Virginia had been transformed into a relatively peaceful, biracial society in which a few planters exercised almost unchallenged hegemony over both their slaves and their poorer white neighbors.[7]

The growth of gambling among the great planters during a period of significant social change raises important questions not only about gentry values but also about the social structure of late seventeenth century Virginia. Why did gambling, involving high stakes, become so popular among the gentlemen at precisely this time? Did it reflect gentry values or have symbolic connotations for the people living in this society? Did this activity serve a social function, contributing in some manner to the maintenance of group cohesion? Why did quarter-horse racing, in particular, become a gentry sport? And finally, did public displays such as this somehow reinforce the great planters' social and political dominance?

In part, of course, gentlemen laid wagers on women and horses simply because they enjoyed the excitement of competition. Gambling was a recreation, like a good meal among friends or a leisurely hunt in the woods—a pleasant pastime when hard-working planters got together. Another equally acceptable explanation for the gentry's fondness for gambling might be the transplanting of English social mores. Certainly, the upper classes in the mother country loved betting for high stakes, and it is possible that the all night card games and the frequent horse races were staged attempts by a provincial gentry to transform itself into a genuine landed aristocracy.[8] While both views possess merit, neither is entirely satisfactory. The great planters of Virginia presumably could have favored less risky forms of competition. Moreover, even though several planters deliberately emulated English social styles, the widespread popularity of gambling among the gentry indicates that this type of behavior may have had deeper, more complex cultural roots than either of these explanations would suggest.[9]

In many societies competitive gaming is a device by which the participants transform abstract cultural values into observable social behavior. In his now-classic analysis of the Balinese cockfight Clifford Geertz describes contests for extremely high stakes as intense social dramas. These battles not only involve the honor of important villagers and their kin groups but also reflect in symbolic form the entire Balinese social structure. Far from being a simple pastime, betting on cocks turns out to be an expression of the way the Balinese perceive social reality. The rules of the fight, the patterns of wagering, the reactions of winners and losers—all these elements help us to understand more profoundly the totality of Balinese culture.[10]

The Virginia case is analogous to the Balinese. When the great planter staked his money and tobacco on a favorite horse or spurred a sprinter to victory, he displayed some of the central elements of gentry culture—its competitiveness, individualism, and materialism. In fact, competitive gaming was for many gentlemen a means of translating a particular set of values into action, a mechanism for expressing a loose but deeply felt bundle of ideas and assumptions about the nature of society. The quarter-horse races of Virginia were intense contests involving personal honor, elaborate rules, heavy betting, and wide community interest; and just as the cockfight opens up hidden dimensions of Balinese culture, gentry gambling offers an opportunity to improve our understanding of the complex interplay between cultural values and social behavior in Virginia.

Gambling reflected core elements of late seventeenth and early eighteenth-century gentry values. From diaries, letters, and travel accounts we discover that despite their occasional cooperation in political affairs, Virginia gentlemen placed extreme emphasis upon personal independence. This concern may in part have been the product of the colony's peculiar settlement patterns. The great planters required immense tracts of fresh land for their tobacco. Often thousands of acres in size, their plantations were scattered over a broad area from the Potomac River to the James. The dispersed planters lived in their "Great Houses" with their families and slaves, and though they saw friends from time to time, they led for the most part isolated, routine lives.[11] An English visitor in 1686 noted with obvious disapproval that "their Plantations run over vast Tracts of Ground ... whereby the Country is thinly inhabited; the Living solitary and unsociable." Some planters were uncomfortably aware of the problems created by physical isolation.[12] William Fitzhugh, for example, admitted to a correspondent in the mother country, "Society that is good and ingenious is very scarce, and seldom to be come at except in books."[13]

Yet despite such apparent cultural privation, Fitzhugh and his contemporaries refused to alter their lifestyles in any way that might compromise their freedom of action. They assumed it their right to give commands, and in the ordering of daily plantation affairs they rarely tolerated outside interference.[14] Some of these planters even saw themselves as lawgivers out of the Old Testament. In 1726 William Byrd II explained that "like one of the Patriarchs, I have my Flocks and my herds, my Bond-men and Bond-women, and every Soart of Trade amongst my own Servants, so that I live in a kind of Independence on every one but Providence."[15] Perhaps Byrd exxagerated for literary effect, but forty years earlier Durand had observed, "There are no lords in Virginia, but each is sovereign on his own plantation."[16] Whatever the origins of this independent spirit, it bred excessive individualism in a wide range of social activities. While these powerful gentlemen sometimes worked together to achieve specific political and economic ends, they bristled at the least hint of constraint.[17] Andrew Burnaby later noted that "The public or political character of the Virginians corresponds with their private one: they are haughty and jealous of their liberties, impatient of restraint, and can scarcely bear the thought of being controuled by any superior power."[18]

The gentry expressed this uncompromising individualism in aggressive competitiveness, engaging in a constant struggle against real and imagined rivals to obtain more lands, additional patronage, and high tobacco prices. Indeed, competition was a major factor shaping the character of face-to-face relationships among the colony's gentlemen, and when the stakes were high the planters were not particular about the methods they employed to gain victory.[19] In large part, the goal of the competition within the gentry group was to improve social position by increasing wealth.

Some gentlemen believed that personal honor was at stake as well. Robert "King" Carter, by all accounts the most successful planter of his generation, expressed his anxiety about losing out to another Virginian in a competitive market situation. "In discourse with Colonel Byrd, Mr. Armistead, and a great many others," he explained, "I understand you an English merchant had sold their tobaccos in round parcels and at good rates. I cannot allow myself to come behind any of these gentlemen in the planter's trade."[20] Carter's pain arose not so much from the lower price he had received as from the public knowledge that he had been bested by respected peers. He believed he had lost face. This kind of intense competition was sparked, especially among the less affluent members of the gentry, by a dread of slipping into the ranks of what one eighteenth century Virginia historian called the "common Planters."[21] Gov. Francis

Nicholson, an acerbic English placemen, declared that the "ordinary sort of planters" knew full well "from whence these mighty dons derive their originals."[22] The governor touched a nerve; the efforts of "these mighty dons" to outdo one another were almost certainly motivated by a desire to disguise their "originals," to demonstrate anew through competitive encounters that they could legitimately claim gentility.

Another facet of Virginia gentry culture was materialism. This certainly does not mean that the great planters lacked spiritual concerns. Religion played a vital role in the lives of men like Robert Carter and William Byrd II. Nevertheless, piety was largely a private matter. In public these men determined social standing not by a man's religiosity or philosophic knowledge but by his visible estate—his lands, slaves, buildings, even by the quality of his garments. When John Bartram, one of America's first botanists, set off in 1737 to visit two of Virginia's most influential planters, a London friend advised him to purchase a new set of clothes, "for though I should not esteem thee less, to come to me in what dress thou will, —yet these Virginians are a very gentle, well-dressed people—and look, perhaps, more at a man's outside than his inside."[23] This perception of gentry values was accurate. Fitzhugh's desire to maintain outward appearances drove him to collect a stock of monogrammed silver plate and to import at great expense a well-crafted, though not very practical, English carriage.[24] One even finds hints that the difficulty of preserving the image of material success weighted heavily upon some planters. When he described local Indian customs in 1705, Robert Beverley noted that native Americans lived an easy, happy existence "without toiling and perplexing their mind for Riches, which other people often trouble themselves to provide for uncertain and ungrateful Heirs."[25]

The gentry were acutely sensitive to the element of chance in human affairs, and this sensitivity influenced their attitudes toward other men and society. Virginians knew from bitter experience that despite the best-laid plans, nothing in their lives was certain. Slaves suddenly sickened and died. English patrons forgot to help their American friends. Tobacco prices fell without warning. Cargo ships sank. Storms and droughts ruined the crops. The list was endless. Fitzhugh warned an English correspondent to think twice before allowing a son to become a Virginia planter, for even "if the best husbandry and the greatest forecast and skill were used, yet ill luck at Sea, a fall of a Market, or twenty other accidents may ruin and overthrow the best Industry.[26] Other planters, even those who had risen to the top of colonial society, longed for greater security. "I could wish," declared William Byrd I in 1685, "wee had Some more certain Commodity than tobacco to rely on but see no hopes of it."[27] However desirable such certainty may have appeared, the planters always put their labor and money into tobacco, hoping for a run of luck. One simply learned to live with chance. In 1710, William Byrd II confided in his secret diary, "I dreamed last night ... that I won a tun full of money and might win more if I had ventured."[28]

Gaming relationships reflected these strands of gentry culture. In fact, gambling in Virginia was a ritual activity. It was a form of repetitive, patterned behavior that not only corresponded closely to the gentry's values and assumptions but also symbolized the realities of everyday planter life. This congruence between actions and belief, between form and experience, helps to account for the popularity of betting contests. The wager, whether over cards or horses, brought together in a single, focused act the great planter's competitiveness, independence, and materialism, as well as the element of chance.[29] It represented a social agreement in which each individual was free to determine how he would play, and the gentleman who accepted a challenged risked losing his material possessions as well as his personal honor.[30]

The favorite household or tavern contests during this period included cards, backgammon, billiards, nine-pins, and dice. The great planters preferred card games that demanded skill as well as luck. Put, piquet, and whist provided the necessary challenge, and Virginia gentlemen—Durand's hosts, for example—regularly played these games for small sums of money and tobacco.[31] These activities brought men together, stimulated conversation, and furnished a harmless outlet for aggressive drives. They did not, however, become for the gentry a form of intense, symbolic play such as the cockfight in Bali.[32] William Byrd II once cheated his wife in a game of piquet, something he would never have dared to do among his peers at Williamsburg. By and large, he showed little emotional involvement in these types of household gambling. The exception here proves the rule. After an unusually large loss at the gaming tables of Williamsburg, Byrd drew a pointed finger in the margin of his secret diary and swore a "solemn resolution never at once to lose more than 50 shillings and to spend less time in gaming, and I beg the God Almighty to give me grace to keep so good a resolution ..." Byrd's reformation was short-lived, for within a few days he dispassionately noted losing another four pounds at piquet.[33]

Horse racing generated far greater interest among the gentry than did the household games.[34] Indeed, for the great planters and the many others who came to watch, these contests were preeminently a social drama. To appreciate the importance of racing in seventeenth century Virginia, we must understand the cultural significance of horses. By the turn of the century possession of one of these animals had become a social necessity. Without a horse, a planter felt despised, an object of ridicule. Owning even a slow-footed saddle horse made the common planter more of a man in his own eyes as well as in those of his neighbors; he was reluctant to venture forth on foot for fear of making an adverse impression. As the Rev. Hugh Jones explained in 1724, "almost every or-

dinary Person keeps a Horse; and I have known some spend the Morning
in ranging several Miles in the Woods to find and catch their Horses only
to ride two or three Miles to Church, to the Court-House, or to a Horse-
Race, where they generally appoint to meet upon Business."[35] Such behavior seems a waste of time and energy only to one who does not
comprehend the symbolic importance which the Virginians attached to
their horses. A horse was an extension of its owner; indeed, a man was
only as good as his horse. Because of the horse's cultural significance, the
gentry attempted to set its horsemanship apart from that of the common
planters. Gentlemen took better care of their animals, and, according to
John Clayton, who visited Virginia in 1688, they developed a distinctive
riding style. "They ride pretty sharply," Clayton reported; "a Planter's
Pace is a Proverb, which is a good sharp hand-Gallop."[36] A fast-rising
cloud of dust far down a Virginia road probably alerted the common
planter that he was about to encounter a social superior.

The contest that generated the greatest interest among the gentry
was the quarter-horse race, an all-out sprint by two horses over a quarter-
mile dirt track.[37] The great planters dominated these events. In the
records of the county courts—our most important source of information
about specific races—we find the names of some of the colony's most
prominent planter families—Randolph, Eppes, Jefferson, Swan, Kenner,
Hardiman, Parker, Cocke, Batte, Harwick (Hardidge), Youle (Yowell),
and Washington. Members of the House of Burgesses, including its
powerful speaker, William Randolph, were frequently mentioned in the
contests that came before the courts.[38] On at least one occasion the Rev.
James Blair, Virginia's most eminent clergyman and a founder of the
College of William and Mary, gave testimony in a suit arising from a race
run between Capt. William Sloane and Robert Napier.[39] The tenacity with
which the gentry pursued these cases, almost continuations of the race itself, suggests that victory was no less sweet when it was gained in court.

Many elements contributed to the exclusion of lower social
groups from these contests. Because of the sheer size of the wagers, poor
freemen and common planters could not have participated regularly.
Certainly, the members of the Accomack County Court were embarrassed
to discover that one Thomas Davis, "a very poore Man," had lost 500
pounds of tobacco or a cow and calf in a horse race with an adolescent
named Mr. John Andrews. Recognizing that Davis bore "a great charge of
wife and Children," the justices withheld final judgment until the governor
had an opportunity to rule on the legality of the wager. The Accomack
court noted somewhat gratuitously that if the governor declared the action
unlawful, it would fine Davis five days' work on a public bridge.[40] In such
cases country justices ordinarily made no comment upon a plaintiff's or
defendant's financial condition, assuming, no doubt, that most people
involved in racing were capable of meeting their gaming obligations.

The gentry actively enforced its exclusive control over quarter-horse racing. When James Bullocke, a York County tailor, challenged Mr. Mathew Slader to a race in 1674, the county court informed Bullocke that it was "contrary to Law for a Labourer to make a race being a Sport for Gentlemen" and fined the presumptuous tailor two hundred pounds of tobacco and cask.[41] Additional evidence of exclusiveness is found in early eighteenth century Hanover County. In one of the earliest issues of the colony's first newspaper, the *Virginia Gazette*, an advertisement appeared announcing that "some merry-dispos'd gentlemen" in Hanover planned to celebrate St. Andrew's day with a race for quarter-milers. The Hanover gentlemen explained in a later, fuller description that "all Persons resorting there are desir'd to behave themselves with Decency and Sobriety, the Subscribers being resolv'd to discountenance all Immorality with the utmost Rigour." The purpose of these contests was to furnish the county's "considerable Number of Gentlemen, Merchants, and credible Planters" an opportunity for "cultivating Friendship."[42] Less affluent persons apparently were welcome to watch the proceedings provided they acted like gentlemen.

In most match races the planter rode his own horse, and the exclusiveness of these contests meant that racing created intensely competitive confrontations. There were two ways to set up a challenge. The first was a regularly scheduled affair usually held on Saturday afternoon. By 1700 there were at least a dozen tracks, important enough to be known by name, scattered through the counties of the Northern Neck and the James River valley. The records are filled with references to contests held at such places as Smith's Field, Coan Race Course, Devil's Field, Yeocomico, and Varina.[43] No doubt, many races also occurred on nameless country roads or convenient pastures. On the appointed day the planter simply appeared at the race track and waited for a likely challenge. We know from a dispute heard before the Westmoreland County Court in 1693 that John Gardner boldly "Challeng'd all the horses then upon the ground to run with any of them for a thousand pounds of Tobo and twenty shillings in money."[44] A second type of contest was a more spontaneous challenge. When gentlemen congregated over a jug of hard cider or peach brandy, the talk frequently turned to horses. The owners presumably bragged about the superior speed of their animals, and if one planter called another's bluff, the men cried out "done, and done," marched to the nearest field, and there discovered whose horse was in fact the swifter.[45]

Regardless of the outcome, quarter horse races in Virginia were exciting spectacles. The crowds of onlookers seem often to have been fairly large, as common planters, even servants, flocked to the tracks to watch the gentry challenge one another for what must have seemed immense amounts of money and tobacco. One witness before a

Westmoreland County Court reported in 1674 that Mr. Stone and Mr. Youle had run a challenge for $10 sterling "in sight of many people."[46] Attendance at race days was sizable enough to support a brisk trade in cider and brandy. In 1714 the Richmond County Court fined several men for peddling liquors "by Retaile in the Race Ground."[47] Judging from the popularity of horses throughout planter society, it seems probable that the people who attended these events dreamed of one day riding a local champion such as Prince or Smoaker.

The magnitude of the gentry betting indicates that racing must have deeply involved the planter's self-esteem. Wagering took place on two levels. The contestants themselves made a wager on the outcome, a main bet usually described in a written statement. In addition, side wagers were sometimes negotiated between spectators or between a contestant and a spectator.[48] Of the two, the main bet was far the more significant. From accounts of disputed races reaching the county curts we know that gentlemen frequently risked very large sums. The most extravagant contest of the period was a race run between John Baker and John Haynie in Northumberland County in 1693, in which the two men wagered 4000 pounds of tobacco and 40 shillings sterling on the speed of their sprinter, Prince and Smoaker.[49] Some races involved only twenty or thirty shillings, but a substantial number were run for several pounds sterling and hundreds of pounds of tobacco. While few, if any, of the seventeenth century gentlemen were what we would call gambling addicts, their betting habits seem irrational even by the more prudential standards of their own day: in conducting normal business transactions, for example, they would never have placed so much money in jeopardy.

To appreciate the large size of these bets we must interpret them within the context of Virginia's economy. Between 1660 and 1720 a planter could anticipate receiving about ten shillings per hundredweight of tobacco. Since the average grower seldom harvested more than 1500 pounds of tobacco a year per man, he probably never enjoyed an annual income from tobacco in excess of eight pounds sterling.[50] For most Virginians the conversion of tobacco into sterling occurred only in the neat columns of account books. They themselves seldom had coins in their pockets. Specie was extremely scarce, and planters ordinarily paid their taxes and conducted business transactions with tobacco notes—written promises to deliver to the bearer a designated amount of tobacco.[51] The great preponderance of seventeenth century planters were quite poor, and even the great planters estimated their income in hundreds, not thousands, of pounds sterling[52] Fitzhugh, one of the wealthier men of his generation, described his financial situation in detail. "Thus I have given you some particulars," he wrote in 1686, "which I thus deduce, the yearly Crops of corn and Tobo, together with the surplusage of meat more than will serve the family use, will amount annually to 60000 lb. Tobo wch. at 10 shillings per Ct. is 300 $ annum."[53] These facts reveal that the Baker-Haynie bet—to take a notable example—amounted to approximately £22 sterling, more than 7 percent of Fitzhugh's annual cash return. It is therefore not surprising that the common planters seldom took part in quarter-horse racing: this wager alone amounted to approximately three times the income they could expect to receive in a good year. Even a modest wager of a pound of two sterling represented a substantial risk.

Gentlemen sealed these gaming relationships with a formal agreement, either a written statement laying out the terms of the contest or a declaration before a disinterested third party of the nature of the wager. In either case the participants carefully stipulated what rules would be in effect. Sometimes the written agreements were quite elaborate. In 1698, for example, Richard Ward and John Steward, Jr., "Covenanted and agreed" to race at a quarter-mile track in Henrico County known as Ware. Ward's mount was to enjoy a ten-yard handicap, and if it crossed the finish line within five lengths of Steward's horse, Ward would win five pounds sterling; if Steward's obviously superior animal won by a greater distance, Ward promised to pay six pounds sterling.[54] In another contest William Eppes and Stephen Cocke asked William Randolph to witness an agreement for a ten-shilling race: "each horse was to keep his path, they not being to crosse unlesse Stephen Cocke could gett the other Riders Path at the start at two or three Jumps."[55]

Virginia's county courts treated race covenants as binding legal contracts.[56] If a gentleman failed to fulfill the agreement, the other party had legitimate grounds to sue, and the county justices' first consideration during a trial was whether the planters had properly recorded their agreement.[57] The Henrico court summarily dismissed one gambling suit because "noe Money was stacked down nor Contract in writing made [one of wch] in such cases is by the law required."[58] Because any race might generate legal proceedings, it was necessary to have a number of people present at the track not only to assist in the running of the contest but also to act as witnesses if anything went wrong. The two riders normally appointed an official starter, several judges, and someone to hold the stakes.

Almost all of the agreements included a promise to ride a fair race. Thus two men in 1698 insisted upon "fair Rideing"; another pair pledged "they would run fair horseman's play."[59] By such agreements the planters waived their customary right to jostle, whip, or knee an opponent, or to attempt to unseat him.[60] During the last decades of the seventeenth century the gentry apparently attempted to substitute riding skill and strategy for physical violence. The demand for "fair Rieding" also suggests that the earliest races in Virginia were wild, no-holds-barred affairs that afforded contestants ample opportunity to vent their aggressions.

The intense desire to win sometimes undermined a gentleman's written promise to run a fair race. When the stakes were large, emotions ran high. One man complained in a York Country court that an opponent had interfered with his horse in the middle of the race, "by meanes of whereof the said Plaintiff lost the said Race."[61] Joseph Humphrey told a Northumberland County court that he would surely have come in first in a challenge for 1500 pounds of tobacco had not Capt. Rodham Kenner (a future member of the House of Burgesses) "held the defendt horses bridle in running his race."[62] Other riders testified that they had been "Josselled" while the race was in progress. An unusual case of interference grew out of a 1694 race which Rodham Kenner rode against John Hartly for one pound sterling and 575 pounds of tobacco. In a Westmoreland County court Hartley explained that after a fair start and without using "whipp or Spurr" he found himself "a great distance" in front of Kenner. But as Hartley neared the finish line, Kenner's brother, Richard, suddenly jumped onto the track and "did hollow and shout and wave his hat over his head in the plts [plaintiff's] horse's face." The animal panicked, ran outside the posts marking the finish line, and lost the race. After a lengthy trial a Westmoreland jury decided that Richard Kenner "did no foule play in his hollowing and waveing his hatt."[63] What exactly occurred during this race remains a mystery, but since no one denied that Richard acted very strangely, it seems likely that the Kenner brothers were persuasive as well as powerful.

Planters who lost large wagers because an opponent jostled or "hollowed" them off the track were understandably angry. Yet instead of challenging the other party to a duel or allowing gaming relationships to degenerate into blood feuds, the disappointed horsemen invariably took their complaints to the courts.[64] Such behavior indicates not only that the gentlemen trusted the colony's formal legal system—after all, members of their group controlled it—but also that they were willing to place institutional limitations on their own competitiveness. Gentlemen who felt they had been cheated or abused at the track immediately collected witnesses and brought suit before the nearest county court. The legal machinery available to the aggrieved gambler was complex; and no matter how unhappy he may have been with the final verdict, he could rarely claim that the system had denied due process.

The plaintiff brought charges before a group of justices of the peace sitting as a county court; if these men found sufficient grounds for a suit, the parties—in the language of seventeenth century Virginia—could "put themselves upon the country."[65] In other words, they could ask that a jury of twelve substantial freeholders hear the evidence and decide whether the race had in fact been fairly run. If the sums involved were high enough, either party could appeal a local decision to the colony's general court, a body consisting of the governor and his council. Several men who hotly insisted that they had been wronged followed this path. For example, Joseph Humphrey, loser in a race for 1500 pounds of tobacco, stamped out of a Northumberland County court, demanding a stop to "farther proceedings in the Common Law till a hearing in the Chancery."[66] Since most of the General Court records for the seventeenth century were destroyed during the Civil War, it is impossible to follow these cases beyond the county level. It is apparent from the existing documents, however, that all the men involved in these race controversies took their responsibilities seriously, and there is no indication that the gentry regarded the resolution of a gambling dispute as less important than proving a will or punishing a criminal.[67] It seems unlikely that the colony's courts would have adopted such an indulgent attitude toward racing had these contests not in some way served a significant social function for the gentry.

Competitive activities such as quarter-horse racing served social as well as symbolic functions. As we have seen, gambling reflected core elements of the culture of late seventeenth century Virginia. Indeed, if it had not done so, horse racing would not have become so popular among the colony's gentlemen. These contests also helped the gentry to maintain group cohesion during a period of rapid social change. After 1680 the great planters do not appear to have become significantly less competitive, less individualistic, or less materialistic than their predecessors had been.[68] But while the values persisted, the forms in which they were expressed changed. During the last decades of the century unprecedented external pressures, both political and economic, coupled with a major shift in the composition of the colony's labor force, caused the Virginia gentry to communicate these values in ways that would not lead to deadly physical violence or spark an eruption of blood feuding. The members of the native-born elite, anxious to preserve their autonomy over local affairs, sought to avoid the kinds of divisions within their ranks that had contributed to the outbreak of Bacon's Rebellion. They found it increasingly necessary to cooperate against meddling royal governors. Moreover, such earlier unrest among the colony's plantation workers as Bacon's Rebellion and the plant-cutting riots had impressed upon the great planters the need to present a common fact to their dependent laborers, especially to the growing number of black slaves who seemed more and more menacing as the years passed.

Gaming relationships were one of several ways by which the planters, no doubt unconsciously, preserved class cohesion.[69] By wagering on cards and horses they openly expressed their extreme competitiveness, winning temporary emblematic victories over their rivals without thereby threatening the social tranquility of Virginia. These non-lethal competitive devices, similar in form to what social anthropologists have termed "joking relationships," were a kind of functional alliance developed by the participants themselves to reduce dangerous, but often inevitable, social tensions.[70]

Without rigid social stratification racing would have lost much of its significance for the gentry. Participation in these contests publicly identified a person as a member of an elite group. Greater planters raced against their social peers. They certainly had no interest in competing with social inferiors, for in this kind of relationship victory carried no positive meaning: the winner gained neither honor nor respect. By the same token, defeat by someone like James Bullocke, the tailor from York, was painful, and to avoid such incidents gentlemen rarely allowed poorer whites to enter their gaming relationships—particularly the heavy betting on quarter horses. The common planters certainly gambled among themselves. Even the slaves may have laid wagers. But when the gentry competed for high stakes, they kept their inferiors at a distance, as spectators but never players.

The exclusiveness of horse racing strengthened the gentry's cultural dominance. By promoting these public displays these planters legitimized the cultural values which racing symbolized—materialism, individualism, and competitiveness. These colorful, exclusive contests helped persuade subordinate white groups that gentry culture was desirable, something worth emulating; and it is not surprising that people who conceded the superiority of this culture readily accepted the gentry's right to rule. The wild sprint down a dirt track served the interests of Virginia's gentlemen better than they imagined.

• • •

Notes

1. [Durand of Dauphiné], *A Huguenot Exile in Virginia: or Voyages of a Frenchman Exiled for his Religion with a Description of Virginia and Maryland,* ed. Gilbert Chinard (New York, 1934 [orig. publ. The hague, 1687]), 148.

2. Rev. James Fontaine, *Memoirs of a Huguenot Family* ..., ed. Ann Maury (Baltimore, 1967 [orig. publ. 1853]), 265-266; John Mercer, cited in Jane Carson, *Colonial Virginians at Play* (Williamsburg, 1965), 49, n.l.; H.R. McIlwaine, ed., *Minutes of the Council and General Court of Colonial Virginia, 1622-1632, 1670-1676* ... (Richmond, 1924), 252, 281, 285.

3. Throughout this essay I use the terms gentry, gentlemen, and great planters as synonyms. In each Virginia county a few gentry families dominated civil, ecclesiastical, and military affairs. While the members of these families were substantially wealthier than the great majority of white planters, they were not a class in a narrow economic sense. Their cultural style as well as their financial

position set them apart. The great planters and their families probably accounted for less than 2% of the colony's white population, Louis B. Wright, *The First Gentlemen of Virginia: Intellectual Qualities of the Early Colonial Ruling Class* (San Marino, CA,1940), 57, estimates their number at "fewer than a hundred families." While entrance into the gentry was not closed to newcomers, upward mobility into that group became increasingly difficult after the 1690s. See Philip A. Bruce, *Social Life of Virginia in the Seventeenth Century* (New York, 1907), 39-100; Aubrey C. Land, "Economic Base and Social Structure: The Northern Chesapeake in the Eighteenth Century," *Journal of Economic History*, XXV (1965), 639-654; Bernard Bailyn, "Politics and Social Structure in Virginia," in James Morton Smith, ed., *Seventeenth-Century America: Essays in Colonial History* (Chapel Hill, NC, 1959), 90-115; and Jack P. Greene, "Foundations of Political Power in the Virginia House of Burgesses, 1720-1776," *William and Mary Quarterly*, 3d Ser., XVI (1959), 485-506.

4. These disturbances are described in T.H. Breen, "A Changing Labor Force and Race Relations in Virginia 1660-1710," *Journal of Social History*, VII (1973), 3-25. The fullest account of Bacon's Rebellion remains Wilcomb E. Washburn, *The Governor and the Rebel: A History of Bacon's Rebellion in Virginia* (Chapel Hill, NC: 1957).

5. Several historians have remarked on the unusual political stability of 18th century Virginia. See, for example, Jack P. Greene, "Changing Interpretations of Early American Politics," in Ray Allen Billington, ed., *The Reinterpretation of Early American History: Essays in Honor of John Edwin Pomfret* (San Marino, CA, 1966), 167-168, and Gordon S. Wood, "Rhetoric and Reality in the American Revolution," *WMQ*, 3d Ser., XXIII (1966), 27-30.

6. The phrase "Creole elite" comes from Carole Shammas, "English-Born and Creole Elites in Turn-of-the-Century Virginia," in Thad W. Tate and David L. Ammerman, eds., *Essays on the Seventeenth-Century Chesapeake* (Chapel Hill, NC: forthcoming). See also David W. Jordan, "Political Stability and the Emergence of a Native Elite in Maryland, 1660-1715," ibid. The process of forming a native-born elite is also discussed in Bailyn, "Politics and Social Structure," in Smith, ed., *Seventeenth-Century America*, 90-115; John C. Rainbolt, "The Alteration in the Relationship between Leadership and Constituents in Virginia, 1660 to 1720," *WMQ*, 3d Ser., XXVII (1970), 411-434; and Martin H. Quitt, "Virginia House of Burgesses 1660-1706: The Social, Educational, and Economic Bases of Political Power" (Ph.D. diss., Washington University, 1970).

7. Breen, "Changing Labor Force," *Jour. Soc. Hist.*, VII (1973), 2-25; Edmund S. Morgan, *American Slavery—American Freedom: The Ordeal of Colonial Virginia* (New York, 1975), 295-362; Rainbolt, "Leadership and Constituents," *WMQ*, 3rd Ser., XXVII (1970), 428-429. On the social attitudes of the small planters see David Alan Williams, "Political Alignments in Colonial Virginia, 1698-1750" (Ph.D. diss., Northwestern University, 1959), chap. 1.

8. A sudden growth of gambling for high stakes in pre-Civil War England is discussed in Lawrence Stone, *The Crisis of the Aristocracy, 1558-1641* (Oxford, 1965). For the later period see Robert W. Malcomson, *Popular Recreations in English Society, 1700-1850* (Cambridge, 1973); G.E. Mingay, *English Landed Society in the Eighteenth Century* (London, 1963), 151-153, 249-250; and E.D. Cuming, "Sports and Games," in A.S. Turberville, ed., *Johnson's England: An Account of the Life and Manners of his Age*, I (London, 1933), 362-383.

9. It is important to stress here that the Virginia gentry did not simply copy English customs. As I argue in this essay, a specific, patterned form of behavior, such as gambling, does not become popular in a society or among the members of a subgroup of that society unless the activity reflects or expresses

values indigenous to that culture. In 17th-century Massachusetts Bay, for example, heavy betting did not develop. A small amount of gambling seems to have occured among the poor, especially among servants, but I can find no incidence of gambling among the colony's social, political, or religious leaders. See Nathanial B. Shurtleff, ed., *Records of the Governor and Company of the Massachusetts Bay* ... (Boston, 1853-1854), II, 180, III, 201, IV, pt. 1, 366; *Records of the Suffolk County Court, 1671-1680* (Colonial Society of Massachusetts, Publications [Boston, 1933]), XXIX, 131-259, 263, XXX, 1162, and Joseph H. Smith, ed., *Colonial Justice in Western Massachusetts, 1639-1702. The Pynchon Court Record* (Cambridge, MA: 1961), 109.

10. Two of Clifford Geertz's essays here helped shape my ideas about Virginia society: "Thick Description: Toward an Interpretive Theory of Culture," and "Deep Play: Notes on the Balinese Cockfight" in Geertz, *The Interpretation of Cultures* (New York, 1973), 3-30, 412-453. Also see Erving Goffman's "Fun in Games" in Goffman, *Encounters: Two Studies in the Sociology of Interaction* (Indianapolis, 1961), 17-81; Raymond Firth, "A Dart Match in Tikopia: A Study in the Sociology of Primitive Sport," *Oceania*, I (1930), 64-96; and H.A. Powell, "Cricket in Kiriwana," *Listener*, XLVIII (1952), 384-385.

11. Philip A. Bruce, *Economic History of Virginia in the Seventeenth Century* ..., II (New York, 1935 [orig. publ. 1895]), 151.

12. "A Letter from Mr. John Clayton Rector of Crofton at Wakefield in Yorkshire, to the Royal Society, May 12, 1688," in Peter Force, ed., *Tracts and Other Papers Relating Principally to the Origin, Settlement, and Progress of the Colonies in North America* ..., III (Washington, D.C., 1844), no. 12, 21.

13. Richard Beale Davis, ed., *William Fitzhugh and His Chesapeake World, 1676-1701: The Fitzhugh Letters and Other Documents* (Chapel Hill, NC, 1963), 15.

14. On the independence of the Virginia gentry see Gerald W. Mullin, *Flight and Rebellion: Slave Resistance in Eighteenth-Century Virginia* (New York, 1972), chap. I.

15. William Byrd II to Charles, Earl of Orrery, July 5, 1726, in "Virginia Council Journals, 1726-1753," *Virginia Magazine of History and Biography*, XXXII (1924), 27.

16. [Durand], *A Huguenot Exile*, ed. Chinard, 110.

17. I discuss this theme in greater detail in a paper entitled "Looking Out for Number One: Cultural Values and Social Behavior in Early Seventeenth-Century Virginia" (paper delivered at the Thirty-Second Conference in Early American History, Nove, 1974).

18. Rev. Andrew Burnaby, *Travels through The Middle Settlements in North America, In the Years 1759 and 1760; With Observations Upon the State of the Colonies*, in John Pinkerton, ed., *A General Collection of the Best and Most Interesting Voyages and Travels in All Ports of the World* ..., XIII (London, 1812), 715.

19. According to John Rainbolt, the gentry's "Striving for land, wealth, and position was intense and, at times, ruthless" ("Leadership and Constituents," *WMQ*, 3d Ser., XXVII [1970], 414). See Carole Shammas, "English-Born and Creole Elites," in Tate and Ammerman, eds., *Seventeenth-Century Chesapeake*; Morgan, *American Slavery—American Freedom*, 288-289; and Rhys Isaac, "Evangelical Revolt: The Nature of the Baptists' Challenge to the Traditional Order in Virginia, 1765-1775," *WMQ*, 3d Ser., XXXI, (1974), 345-353.

20. Louis B. Wright, ed., *Letters of Robert Carter, 1720-1727: The Commercial Interests of a Virginia Gentleman* (San Marino, CA, 1940), 93-94.

21. Hugh Jones, *The Present State of Virginia Giving a Particular and Short Account of the Indian, English, and Negroe Inhabitants of that Colony ...* (New York, 1865 [orig. publ. 1724]), 48.

22. Quoted in Thomas Jefferson Wertenbaker, *The Old South: The Founding of American Civilization* (New York, 1942), 19.

23. Peter Collinson to John Bartram, Feb. 17, 1737, *WMQ*, 2d Ser., VI (1926), 304.

24. Davis, ed., *Fitzhugh Letters*, 229, 241-242, 244, 246, 249-250, 257-259. For another example of the concern about outward appearances see the will of Robert Cole (1674), in *WMQ*, 3d Ser., XXXI (1974), 139.

25. Robert Beverley, *The History and Present State of Virginia*, ed., Louis B. Wright (Chapel Hill, NC, 1947), 226.

26. William Fitzhugh to Oliver Luke, August 15, 1690, in Davis, ed., *Fitzhugh Letters*, 280.

27. William Byrd I to Perry and Lane, July 8, 1686, in "Letters of William Byrd I," *VMHB*, XXV (1917), 132.

28. Louis B. Wright and Marion Tinling, eds., *The Secret Diary of William Byrd of Westover, 1709-1712* (Richmond, VA, 1941), 223-224.

29. Gaming was so popular among the gentry, so much an expression of their culture, that it became a common metaphor in their discussion of colonial politics. For example, an unsigned essay entitled "The History of Bacon's and Ingram's Rebellion, 1676" described the relationship between Nathaniel Bacon and Gov. William Berkeley as a card game. Charles M. Andrews, ed., *Narratives of the Insurrections, 1675-1690* (New York, 1915), 57. In another account of Bacon's Rebellion, written in 1705, Thomas Mathew noted that several members of the House of Burgesses were "not docill enough to Gallop the future Races, that Court seem'd dispos'd to Lead'em." Ibid., 32. In May 1697 William Fitzhugh explained to Capt. Roger Jones: "your self will see what a hard Game we have to play the contrary party that it our Opposers, having the best Cards and the trumps to boot especially the Honor. Yet would my Lord Fairfax there [in England], take his turn in Shuffling and Dealing the Cards and his Lordship with the rest see that we were not cheated in our game, I question not but we should gain the Sett, tho' the gaim is so far plaid" (Davis, ed., *Fitzhugh Letters*, 352).

30. Rhys Isaac provides a provocative analysis of the relationship between games and gentry culture on the eve of the Revolution in "Evangelical Revolt," *WMQ*, 3d Ser., XXXI (1974), 348-353. See also Mark Anthony de Wolfe Howe, ed.," Journal of Josiah Quincy, Junior, 1773," *Massachusetts Historical Society, Proceedings*, XLIX (1915-1916), 467, and William Stith, *The Sinfulness and Pernicious Nature of Gaming. A Sermon Preached before the General Assembly of Virginia: At Williamsburg, March 1st, 1752* (Williamsburg, 1752), 5-26.

31. The best discussion of these household games is Carson, *Virginians at Play*, 49-89. See also Charles Cotton, *The Compleat Gamester or Instructions How to Play at Billiards, Trucks, Bowls, and Chess ...* (1674), in Cyril H. Hartmann, ed., *Games and Gamesters of the Restoration: The Compleat Gamester by Charles Cotton, 1674, and Lives of the Gamesters*, by Theophilus Lucas, 1714 (London, 1930).

32. After 1750, however, the gentry's attitude toward household or tavern games seems to have changed. The betting became so heavy that several eminent planters lost fortunes at the gaming tables. A visitor at Williamsburg in 1765 wrote of these men that "they are all professed gamesters. Especially Colonel Burd [William Byrd III], who is never happy but when he has the box and Dices in hand. [T]his Gentleman from a man of the greatest property of any in America has reduced himself to that Degree by gameing, that few or nobody will Credit him for Ever so small a sum of money. [h]e was obliged to sel 400 fine Negroes a few

Days before my arival." "Journal of a French Traveller in the Colonies, 1765, I," *American Historical Review,* XXVI (1920-1921), 742. Byrd was not alone. Robert Wormely Carter and Robert Burwell were excessive gamblers, and as the aging Landon Carter (Robert "King" Carter's son) observed the wagering of the gentry on the eve of the Revolution, he sadly mused, "they play away and play it all away." Jack P. Greene, ed., *The Diary of Colonel Landon Carter of Sabine Hall, 1752-1778,* II (Charlottesville, Va., 1965), 830. On this generations addiction to gambling see Emory G. Evans, "The Rise and Decline of the Virginia Aristocracy in the Eighteenth Century: The Nelsons," in Darrett B. Rutman, ed., *The Old Dominion: Essays for Thomas Perkins Abernethy* (Charlottesville, VA, 1964), 68-70.

33. Wright and Tinling, eds., *Secret Diary,* 75, 442, 449.

34. Only one mention of cockfighting before 1730 has come to my attention, and that one refers to contests among the "common planters." Jones, *Present State of Virginia,* 48. See Carson, *Virginians at Play,* 151-152.

35. Jones, *Present State of Virginia,* 48. This observation was repeated in other accounts of Virginia society throughout the 18th century. William Byrd wrote "my Dear Countryman have so great a Passion for riding, that they will often walk two miles to catch a Horse, in Order to ride One." William K. Boyd, ed., *William Byrd's Histories of the Dividing Line Betwixt Virginia and North Carolina* (Raleigh, N.C., 1929), 258. See also Carson, *Virginians at Play,* 102-105.

36. "A Letter From Clayton," in Force, ed., *Tracts and Other Papers,* no. 12, 35.

37. On the development of racing in Virginia, especially the transition from a quartermile straight track to the oval course, see W.G. Stanard, "Racing in Colonial Virginia," *VMHB,* II (1894-1895), 293-305, and Fairfax Harrison, "The Equine F.F.V.'s: A Study of the Evidence for the English Horses Imported into Virginia before the Revolution," ibid., XXXV (1927), 329-370. I suspect that quarter-horse racing was a sport indigenous to Virginia.

38. Besides Randolph, there were John Stone, William Hardidge, Thomas Yowell, John Hardiman, Daniel Sullivant, Thomas Chamberlain, Rodham Kenner, Richard Kenner, William Soane, and Alexander Swan.

39. Aug. 1690, Henrico County, Order Book, 1678-1693, 340. All references to manuscript county records are to the photostat copies at the Virginia State Library, Richmond.

40. Jan. 16, 1666, Accomack Co., Orders, 1666-1670, 9.

41. Sept. 10, 1674, York Co., Deeds, Orders, Wills, 1672-1694, 85.

42. *Virginia Gazette,* Nov. 19-26, 1736, Sept. 30-Oct. 7, 1737.

43. Bruce, Social LIfe, 195-209; Carson, *Virginians at Play,* 108-110.

44. Apr. 7, 1693, Westmoreland Co., Order Book, 1690-1698, 92; "Racing in Virginia in 1700-05," *VMHB,* X (1902-1903), 320.

45. Aug. 1683, Henrico Co. Records [Deeds and Wills], 1677-1692, 254.

46. Oct. 16, 1674, Westmoreland Co., Deeds, Patents, Etc., 1665-1677, 211; Bruce, *Social Life,* 197-198; Carson, *Virginians at Play,* 109.

47. Beverley Fleet, ed., Richmond County Records, 1704-1724, *Virginia Colonial Abstracts,* XVII (Richmond, VA, 1943), 95-96.

48. Carson, *Virginians at Play,* 105. See Aug. 29, 1694, Westmoreland Co., Order Book, 1690-1698, 146.

49. Aug. 22, 1695, Northumberland Co., Order Book, 1678-1698, Pt. 2, 707-708.

50. Morgan, *American Slavery—American Freedom,* 142, 108, 204.

51. Bruce, *Economic History,* II, 495-512.

52. Aubrey Land's analysis of the probate records in a tobacco-producing area in nearby Maryland between 1690 and 1699 reveals that 74.6% of the estates there were worth less than 100 sterling. According to Land, the differences

between the social structures of Maryland and Virginia at this time were not "very great." Land, "Economic Base and Social Structure," *Jour. Econ. Hist.*, XXV (1965), 641-644.

53. William Fitzhugh to Dr. Ralph Smith, April 22, 1686, in Davis, ed., *Fitzhugh Letters*, 176.

54. The full covenant is reproduced in Stanard, "Racing in Colonial Virginia," *VMHB*, II (1894-1895), 296-298.

55. Ibid., 296.

56. Virginia law prohibited fraudulent gaming, certain kinds of side bets, and gambling by persons who had "no visible estate, profession, or calling, to maintain, themselves." William Waller Hening, ed., *The Statues at Large; Being a Collection of all the Laws of Virginia ...*, IV (Richmond, 1820), 214-218; George Webb, *Office and Authority of a Justice of Peace ...* (Williamsburg, VA, 1736), 165-167. Wagers made between two gainfully employed colonists were legal agreements and enforceable as contracts. The courts of Virginia, both common law and chancery, apparently followed what they believed to be standard English procedure. Whether they were correct is difficult to ascertain. Sir William Holdsworth explains that acts passed by Parliament during the reigns of Charles II and Anne allowed individuals to sue for gaming debts, but he provides no evidence that English courts regularly settled disputed contests such as horse races. Holdsworth, *A History of English Law* (London, 1966), VI, 404, XI, 539-542.

57. Not until the 1750s did Virginians begin to discuss gambling as a social vice. See Stith, *The Sinfulness ... of Gaming*; R.A. Brock, ed., *The Official Records of Robert Dinwiddie*, I (Richmond, VA, 1883), 30-31; Samuel Davies, *Virginia's Danger and Remedy. Two Discourses Occasioned by The Severe Drought ...* (Williamsburg, 1756).

58. Oct. 1690, Henrico Co, Order Book, 1678-1693, 351. See also Aug. 28, 1674, Northampton Co., Order Book No. 9, 1664-1674, 269, and Nov. 4 1674, ibid., No. 10, 1674-1679.

59. Stanard, "Racing in Colonial Virginia," *VMHB*, II (1894-1895), 267; Henrico Co., Records [Deeds and Wills], 1677-1692, 466.

60. Carson, *Virginians at Play*, 109-110.

61. "Some Extracts from the Records of York Co., Virginia," *WMQ*, 1st Ser., IX (1900-1901), 178-179.

62. Jan 1694, Northumberland Co., Order Book, 1678-1698, Pt.2, 643.

63. Aug. 29, 1694, Westmoreland Co., Order Book, 1690-1698, 146-146a. Also see Oct. 1689, Henrico Co., Order Book, 1678-1693, 313, and Stanard, "Racing in Virginia," *VMHB*, II (1894-1895), 296.

64. A gentleman could have challenged an opponent to a duel. Seventeenth- and early 18th-century Virginians recognized a code of honor of which dueling was a part, but they did everything possible to avoid such potentially lethal combats. I have found only four cases before 1730 in which dueling was even discussed. County courts fined two of the challengers before they could do any harm. ("A Virginian Challenge in the Seventeenth Century," *VMHB*, II [1894-1895], 96-97; *Lower Norfolk County Antiquarian*, IV, [1904], 106) And two comic-opera challenges that only generated blustery rhetoric are described in William Stevens Perry, ed., *Historical Collections Relating to the American Colonial Church*, I (Hartford, CT, 1870), 25-28, and Bond, ed., *Byrd's Histories of the Dividing Line*, 173-175. On the court system see Philip A. Bruce, *Institutional History of Virginia in the Seventeenth Century ... I*, (Gloucester, 1910), 484-632, 647-689.

65. Aug. 29, 1694, Westmoreland Co., Order Book, 1690-1698, 146a.

66. Jan 1694, Northumberland Co., Order Book, 1678-1698, Pt. 2, 643.

67. Sometimes the courts had an extremely difficult time deciding exactly what had occurred at a race. A man testified in 1675 that he had served as the official judge for a contest, and that while he knew which horse had finished first, he was "not able to say much less to Sweare that the Horse did Carry his Rider upon his back over the path." Sept. 16, 1675, Surry County, Deeds, Wills and Orders, 1671-1684, 133. For another complex case see Mar. 5, 1685, Rappahannock Co., Orders [no. 1], 1683-1686, 103, 120, 153.

68. For evidence of the persistence of these values among the gentry in the Revolutionary period see Isaac, "Evangelical Revolt," *WMQ*, 3d Ser., XXXI (1674), 348-353.

69. The planter's aggressive hospitality may have served a similar function. Hospitality in Virginia should be analyzed to discover its relationship to gentry culture. Robert Beverley makes some suggestive comments about this custom in his *History and Present State of Virginia*, 312-313. An interesting comparison to the Virginia practice is provided in Michael W. Young, *Fighting with Food: Leadership, Values and Social Control in a Massim Society* (Cambridge, 1971).

70. A.R. Radcliffe-Brown, *Structure and Function in Primitive Society: Essays and Addresses* (New York, 1964), chaps. 4,5.

• • •

Suggestions for Further Reading:

Barnett, C. Robert, "Recreational Patterns of the Colonial Virginia Aristocrat," *Journal of the West Virginia Historical Association*, II (Spring, 1978), 1-11.

Bennett, Bruce, "Sports in the South up to 1865," *Quest*, XXVII (Winter, 1977), 4-17.

Carson, Jane, *Colonial Virginians at Play* (Charlottesville: University of Virginia Press, 1965).

Davis, Thomas R., "Some Notes on Historians' Treatment of Colonial American Sports," *Canadian Journal of the History of Sport and Physical Education*, I (December, 1970), 37-40.

Issac, Rhys, "Evangelical Revolt: The Nature of the Baptist's Challenge to the Traditional Order in Virginia, 1765-1775," *William and Mary Quarterly*, XXXI (July, 1974), 345-368.

Lee, Patricia Ann, "Play and the English Gentleman in the Early Seventeenth Century," *The Historian*, XXXI (May, 1969), 364-380.

Morgan, Edmund S., *Virginians at Home: Family Life in the Eighteenth Century* (New York: Holt, Rinehart and Winston, 1952).

Nye, Russell B., *The Cultural Life of the New Nation,* 1776-1830 (New York: Harper and Row, 1960).

Thompson, E.P., "Patrician Society, Plebian Culture," *Journal of Social History*, VII (Summer, 1974), 382-405.

Wertenbaker, Thomas J., *The First Americans, 1607-1690* (New York: Macmillan, 1929).

Wright, Louis B., *The First Gentlemen of Virginia: Intellectual Qualities of the Early Colonial Ruling Class* (San Marino, CA: Huntington Library, 1940).

THE RISE OF SPORT

Frederic L. Paxson

The real and symbolic influence of the frontier on American life, particularly as stated by Frederick Jackson Turner in his landmark interpretation of 1893, provides the context for this essay. Arguing that the hearty participant in sport had succeeded the rugged individualist of the frontier, Frederic Paxson proposed that "the search for sport revealed a partial substitute for pioneer life." Although tracing sporting activity in the United States from the spectator focus of the early 1800s to the participatory culture of a century later, Paxson emphasized less the causes of the rise of sport than its consequences. As the frontier provided a significant explanation for American development and character, Paxson celebrated sport as an instrument to preserve through play the moral integrity and social equilibrium of the nation.

Just as the frontier experience is an essential context for interpreting American history, Paxson's analysis represents an important starting point for understanding sport history and historiography in this country. Paxson's essay is significant not only for relating the study of sport to a central theme in American history, but also for declaring the value of sport as an institution in its own right that should command scholarly attention.

Paxson's essay coincided with a growing interest in social history that influenced many American scholars in the early twentieth century. The enlarged scope of their inquiry included some work on sport. Stewart Culin's massive ethnographic study, *Games of the North American Indians* (1907), for example, may still be the most useful of its kind. The works of Herbert Manchester, *Four Centuries of Sport in America, 1490-1890* (1931), Jennie Holliman, *American Sports, 1786-1835* (1931), Robert B. Weaver, *Amusements and Sports in American Life* (1939), and A.B. Frost, *Sports and Games in the Open* (1899), however, added information but little insight, to the topic. With few exceptions, John A. Krout, *Annals of American Sport* (New Haven: Yale University Press, 1929), the most notable, only a handful followed Paxson's lead until mid-century.

As scholars then began to explore more thoroughly and perceptively such issues as the impact of technology on the rise of sport, the community bonding and identity which athletic competition and participation represented, and the influences of urbanization, profes-

45

sionalism and commercialism on sport, Paxson's study achieved new
respect and recognition. For in one way or another, he had touched on
all of these issues, raised questions on many others, and opened wider
the lens of historical inquiry.

No people has passed through greater changes in a single lifetime
than did Americans in the generation which saw the closing of the old
frontier. Social groups that had been nearly homogeneous were broken
up, and out of them were selected and combed specialized industrial
colonies to be moved to town and driven before the machinery of economic change. The fathers of this generation had been a sober lot, unable often to bend without a break, living a life of rigid and puritanical
decorum, interspersed perhaps with disease and drunkenness but unen-
livened, for most of them, by spontaneous play. When Barnum started
upon his long career as showman in 1835 he introduced Joice Heth, "nurse
of General George Washington" and now "arrived at the astonishing age of
161 years;" but he was careful to add that she had been "a member of the
Baptist church for upwards of one hundred years" and took pleasure in the
conversation of the clergy.[1] Amusement was under suspicion of wicked-
ness unless disguised as instruction; and sport was hard to find.

"I idled away the morning on Mr. Daniel Greenleaf's wharf," wrote
Charles Francis Adams in his diary in 1843, after playing with his boys for
a few hours; "perhaps this consumption of time is scarcely justifiable; but
why not take some of life for simple enjoyments, provided that they interfere with no known duty?"[2] A few years later the genial Autocrat scolded
at a portion of his fellow-countrymen: "I am satisfied that such a set of
black-coated, stiff-jointed, soft-muscled, paste-complexioned youth as
we can boast in our Atlantic cities never before sprang from loins of
Anglo-Saxon lineage ... We have a few good boatmen, no good horsemen that I hear of, nothing remarkable, I believe, in cricketing, and as for
any great athletic feat performed by a gentleman in these latitudes, society
would drop a man who should run around the Common in five minutes."[3]
Farther south, or father west, if an Adams had criticized himself or a
Holmes his neighbor, the showing might, in spots, have been less dole-
ful; but neither in east nor west did America esteem the human body.[4]
"The taste for athletic sports in America is not over fifteen years old,"
wrote a shrewd observer in 1869.[5] In 1886 some of our journals could still
find "news" in Dr. Peabody's baccalaureate upon the text, "The temple of
God is holy, which temple ye are."[6] But before the boys who heard this
sermon reached middle life their world had changed.

On the first of March, 1909, there gathered in the White House
without rebuke--almost without comment--a group selected not for pur-

poses of state but for play alone[7] An ambassador was there, a scout, a scientist, a soldier, and even a president of the United States, who addressed his guests as "men with whom at tennis, or hunting, or riding, or walking, or boxing, I have played; with whom I have been on the round-up, or in the mountains, or in the ranch country." Proctor's stealthy cougar, in bronze,[8] that the "tennis cabinet"[9] left behind them for their host, was a fair type of the new work and the newer play; of the art of Frederick Remington and the tales of Owen Wister, of a generation that had appraised the spiritual values of its play and that had settled itself into a new environment. Today a president dismisses an ambassador and goes off to golf, with all approving,

> And, while studying closely his putts, to explore the obscurity shrouding the roots of the war."[10]

So late as Arthur's day a vacation trip to the Rockies was a luxury, if not an indiscretion.

The various stages in that disappearance of the frontier that brought one American cycle to an end have been portrayed by various scholars, and Mr. Turner's part in that portrayal is, perhaps, the most distinguished feat in American historical scholarship in the last half century. The free lands were used up. The cow country rose and fell. The social safety valve was screwed down. But the explosion did not come. The reason for continued bearable existence under the increasing pressure generated in industrial society cannot yet be seen from all its sides; but one side is already clear: a new safety valve was built upon the new society. The rumblings and premonitory tremblings were not followed by disaster. The strikes of 1877 seemed to many to presage a revolution, and the anarchistic riots of 1886 appeared to be the first blow. But American society learned to give instead of crack. Perhaps its sense of humor helped to save. *Puck* began in 1877 its career as weekly emollient, cartoonists multiplied in every editorial shop, and *Life* in 1883 found it possible to combine knight-errantry and humor. Mark Twain was at his crest of popularity; not yet a sage, but always sane. Saved by its temper from immediate explosion, American society went to work to provide new outlets.

Between the first race for the America's cup in 1851 and the first American aeroplane show of February last, the safety valve of sport was designed, built, and applied. Between the organization of the oldest of the major leagues--the National league of baseball clubs--in 1876, and the earliest golf tournament in the United States, in 1894, the progress and development were rapid. Between the first meet of the League of American wheelmen in 1880, and the first national tournament of the United States lawn tennis association in 1881, on one hand, and the interdict launched in 1888 by the amateur athletic union against amateurs who

dared participate in unauthorized games or meets, the growing pains of a
society which was entering almost monthly upon a new pastime were min-
gled with the soreness of its muscles as it undertook, on ever broader
scale, baseball, cricket, bicycling, tennis, and roller skating; polo, racing, coaching, field sports, and canoeing; gymnastics, curling, boxing,
hunting, and archery. To enumerate them all would take the space of a
sporting cyclopedia; to describe them all would emphasize the fact that in
nearly every one wholesale participation and adoption came between the
years of the centennial in Philadelphia and the world's fair in Chicago.[11]
Together they constitute the rise of sport.

Spectators' sports found lodgment in American society earlier
than did those in which participation is the price of enjoyment. Racing
and boxing can be traced through the first years of the republic with a train
of admirers behind each champion. In his old age Diomed, who had won
the initial Derby at Epsom Downs, in 1780, came to America[12] to breed a
great family of racing horses on a Virginia stock farm; other victors followed him to reinvigorate the strain, and from time to time Americans
aroused one side of national pride as they endeavored to grasp the Derby
stakes. Iroquois did this at last in 1881, for Pierre Lorillard,[13] his owner;
and in 1907 Richard Croker's Kentucky bred Orby[14] did it again. Racing
that could produce such finest flowers developed an American establishment that grew almost beyond control.

The opening of the American jockey club[15] at Jerome Park, on the
old Bathgate farm at Fordham in 1866, was an epoch for the American
turf.[16] Through the next decade it seemed as though the horse were
coming to own America. Trotting for the humbler at the country fairs,
and running races over the great courses near the cities, drew mighty
audiences. But the spectators who had made possible this high
exploitation killed it in the end. The gamblers and the cheap sports
brought racing into disrepute, and before the Coney Island jockey club[17]
held its inaugural meeting in 1879 the game was outlawed by conservative
society. Yet its evil profits kept it alive during the eighties--through six
hundred and one races run in the vicinity of New York in ninety-five days
in 1888[18]--until at last the legislature and the constitution[19] were invoked
against it. But Maud S. and her successors,[20] and Nancy Hanks before her
pneumatic-tired sulky,[21] made a place in the American imagination that
called for something else to fill it when the race course had run through its
day.

Trotting and racing had gathered their crowds and stirred the
blood, but they produced no sentimental symbol equal to the America's
cup, with which, wrote Caspar Whitney, "there is no trophy in all the
world of sport to compare ... in point of age or distinction."[22] The
American clipper ship knew no superior in the forties of the last century,[23]
and one of its fleet took away the queen's cup from Cowes and the royal
yacht squadron[24] in the year of the London exposition, 1851.[25] This feat

quickened a nation's feelings on either side of the Atlantic, though no challenger came to America to take it back for nineteen years. Then, with the *Cambria* in 1870 a series of adventurers began to seek the trophy guarded by the New York yacht club, its custodian.[26] On the eve of the great war, Sir Thomas Lipton was arranging for the fourth time to try to take the prize. Dunraven had preceded him; and him the *Thistle* (1887), and the *Galatea* (1886), and the *Genesta* (1885), and the *Atlanta* (1881), and the *Countess of Dufferin* (1876), and the *Livonia* (1871), in a gallant succession of vain attempts. Four times in the eighties and thrice each in the seventies and nineties did the autumn races off New York renew the interest, with an ever-widening circle acquainted with the skipper, learned on the points of sail and beam, and ready to debate measurement, centerboard, or keel. And in the intervals between the races they could turn to wrangle over the prospects for Richard Fox's diamond belt.

This diamond belt was designed to adorn the heavyweight champion of the world, and was the donation of Richard K. Fox, editor of the the *Police Gazette*. It followed a precedent that had, in another sport, uncovered the financial possibilities behind the promotion of great spectacles. All through the seventies there had been occasional matches between professional long-distance pedestrians; but these had grown into disrepute through the quarrels of promoters and the trials of referees, who fell foul of the question, What is a walk? In a single issue, in 1879, the *New York Sun* noted that Miss Lulu Loomer, clad in black silk tunic and sky blue hose, was walking 3000 quarter miles in 3000 quarter hours in a public hall; that Van Ness and Belden were at work on a six-days' race in the Fifth regiment armory; and that in Cooper hall, Jersey City, a similar test was underway.[27]

Sir John Astley had already tried to reduce pedestrian chaos to matters of record by offering, in 1878, a purse of £100 more to the winner of a six-days' test, go-as-you-please. In the Agricultural hall at Islington this was the first walked off and won by one O'Leary, a Chicago Irishman, already well-known, who now established a six-day record of five hundred and twenty miles.[28] The trophy was contested again in October, 1878, and three times in the following year. An English walker named Rowell captured it in March, 1879; Edward Payson Weston, an American, took it from him in the following June, and defended it in Madison Square Garden for six days in the following September.[29] Weston had raised the record to five hundred and fifty miles, but Rowell won back the belt this time in a field of thirteen contestants. No new record was made, but for the whole week crowds gathered round the course to smoke and bet and encourage the various entries, and similar contests continued to draw their throngs for many years. Only recently Weston, hearty still on his seventy-first birthday,[30] walked from New York to San Francisco in one hundred days, though the Astley belt has left the sporting recollection.

The Fox diamond belt indicates a revival of the manly art after two decades of well-deserved oblivion. The last great fight that Americans of the centennial decade could remember was fought in a meadow at Farnboro, near London, for thirty-six rounds, on April 17, 1860. Here Heenan, the American, and Sayers, the English champion, fought to a draw in a turf ring, with twenty-one London "pugs" as ringkeepers, who let the ring break in before the American could knock out his opponent.[31]

The recollection of the Heenan-Sayers fight endured through years when pugilists failed to hit each other, until a new slugger with a genius for advertising appeared within the ring. This was John L. Sullivan, born in Boston in 1858, who emerged as a driving fighter about 1881. In February, 1882, he won from Paddy Ryan the title of champion of America,[32] and for the next ten years was as popular a sporting character as the world possessed. The leather football that Mike Donovan,[33] boxing instructor of the New York athletic club, had adapted to new use as a punching bag spread its vogue once it had trained this champion.[34] Audiences repeatedly crowded Madison Square Garden when Sullivan was announced to box, and the paragraphers treasured his words uttered in his cups or sober. "The worship of brute force," wailed Leslie's newspaper, had filled the boxing schools of New York. "Let prize fighters be once more regarded as outlaws, and not as public 'entertainers,'"[35] it urged; but when Sullivan went to England in 1887, he and Buffalo Bill and the Prince of Wales competed on easy terms for space.

The reluctance of fighters to fight was well dispelled by 1887. In this year Jake Kilrain fought Jem Smith for one hundred and six rounds in France, but only to a draw which left the ownership of the new diamond belt in doubt, since this was offered for a finish fight.[36] Sullivan, who had been boxing to huge audiences in the English music halls, and who had been received by the Prince of Wales,[37]—much, it is said, to the mortification of the queen, then celebrating her jubilee,—trained now at Windsor, and in March, 1888, fought Charley Mitchell to a thirty-six round draw near Chantilly. It was a single-handed bout, for the American broke his right arm in the fifth round, and could only defend himself with his left for the rest of the fight.[38] "There is hardly a more disreputable ruffian now breathing than this same Sullivan," commented the *New York Tribune*, "but with all his brutality, his coarseness, and his vices, he certainly is not afraid of meeting any living man with bare fists."[39] Early in 1889 he and Kilrain agreed to fight for $20,000, the title, and the belt; and this time there was no draw, for Sullivan battered his way to a knockout at Richburg, Mississippi, on July 8.[40] They talked of running him for congress on the democratic ticket now; but he went on a boxing tour to Australia instead, and came back to lose his title to a new winner, James J. Corbett, in 1892.

How Corbett's science won the title and maintained it until Robert Fitzsimmons ended his reign; how Fitzsimmons was finally worsted by Jim

Jeffries; and he by Johnson, and he in turn by Willard would bring the boxing story down to date. But none of his successors had equalled Sullivan in his popular appeal, and it was his gold-mounted rabbit's foot, for luck that Colonel Roosevelt carried through his African trip in 1909.[41] Sport had a new appeal to the city crowds of the eighties, and the promoters catered to it. The periodic crisis of the races and the fights were interspersed by the meetings of the national game, baseball.

The major leagues and the shoal of minor leagues that today control the formal side of baseball, with permanent million dollar parks,[42] with a president of the United States to throw the first ball of a season, with over seven million paid admissions to the major leagues alone within a single year,[43] represent an institution that is far removed from the game of ball as it was played by a few private clubs after the Mexican war, and from the earliest of its organizations, the national association of baseball players, of 1858.[44] It seems to have been the civil war that brought potential nines together and nationalized the game. Men who might have joined the militia regiments for exercise or recreation before the war played baseball around the cities, after it. The Cincinnati Red Stockings, a strictly professional team, discovered the financial possibilities of the game in 1869. A national association of professional baseball players emerged in 1871, but its base of organization was faulty, and no financially successful scheme appeared for five years more.[45]

In February, 1876, William A. Hulbert of Chicago, and A.G. Spalding, a prominent professional of Boston, having signed up a strong team for the approaching season made a workable machine for the furtherance of their profits and the game. At the Grand Central hotel, in New York, they organized the National league of baseball clubs, the parent league of today, with eight member teams: Boston, Hartford, Chicago, St. Louis, Louisville, Cincinnati, the Mutuals (New York), and the Athletics (Philadelphia).[46] The transition from an association of players to a league or partnership of managers, gave a firm basis to the sport. It was, indeed, only a spectators' sport. With only changes in detail the scheme continues workable. A second league branched off in 1882 as the American association; a Federal league and various brotherhoods or fraternities have followed it. But baseball as a producer's business in the larger cities has not been shaken. Spalding's Chicago team won the pennant year after year. The pitched ball changed from a toss to a throw, an arsenal of mitts, shields, and masks evolved, and in 1888-1889 Spalding's baseball tour around the world introduced the full-grown national game to other countries.[47] The umpire became a recognized butt for the comic papers. And at last the sedate editor of the *Atlantic Monthly Almanac*, confident that all his readers can understand the lingo, adorns the opening baseball date of 1917 with the alleged oriental maxim, "There are no fans in Hell."

Baseball succeeded as an organized spectator's sport, but it did also what neither racing nor boxing could do in turning the city lot into a playground and the small boy into an enthusiastic player. The cigarette pictures of leading players that small boys of the eighties collected by scores indicate at once their interest and their naughty habits. Like cricket in England, baseball became a game for everyone.

Cricket, indeed, had been played around Boston and New York and chiefly Philadelphia, since the English factory hands had brought it to Kensington and Germantown in the middle forties. The late Dr. S. Weir Mitchell remembered to have played a full-fledged game in 1845;[48] and ever after this there was at least one Newhall to play in Philadelphia,[49] and a growing list of cricket clubs. From time to time an inter-city game enlivened the mild sport; then a visit from Canadian players; then an imported English team that with eleven ordinary veterans could retire an American team of twenty-two without batting out its second innings. But in September, 1885,[50] though cricket was "still an exotic in the United States," a team of eleven Philadelphians beat eleven Britishers for the first time at their own game. The interest of the spectator was being translated into proficiency in sport.

Indoors and out-of-doors city growth and changing habits lured more men to exercise. The notion of participation for the fun there was in it, or for the physical advantage entailed, was more widely spread before the civil war than the existing records would indicate; but it was scant enough. The Young Men's Christian Association, an importation of the early fifties, had begun to group its charges and to see the various sides of the new problem they raised. Their city buildings, undertaken in the later sixties, included room for gymnasiums[51] as well as chapels and class-rooms; and their directors taught gymnastics, upon a basis resembling that of the German immigrants, exhibited through their turner societies a dozen years before.

Father Friedrich Ludwig Jahn and his gymnastic educational revival had done much for German nationalism and democracy before the revolutionary movements of 1848 brought it under suspicion and drove many of its leaders into more or less involuntary exile. Into America the Germans came with common resentments and with familiarity with this bond that might hold them together and cheer their hearts as they struggled against nativistic critics in a strange land.[52] Singing, playing, exercising, drinking beer their together on Sunday evenings, they had immediately started turner societies and had formed a turnerbund with more than one hundred and fifty member societies before the civil war.[53] Many of these societies marched to the front with ranks almost untouched by failure to enlist, and more than one German regiment paid for shelter and hospitality with all it had to give. In the winter of 1864-1865 the league reorganized as the Nordamerikanischer Turnerbund,[54] and since that day its athletic festivals and congresses have at once broadened the influence of comradeship and kept the German-Americans in contact with their common past. A team of Milwaukee turners invaded the fatherland in 1880 and carried off the trophies of a general meet at Frankfort-on-Main;[55] while the twenty-third festival at St. Louis[56] opened the next year with 20,000 people on the fair ground.

The growing wealth of cities,the appearance of a class of men with leisure, and the consequences of sedentary life could not have failed to develop organized provision for play nor to induce young men to start athletic clubs in increasing numbers. The greatest of the clubs was organized in 1868 in New York, and rented a field for athletic games that soon gave fame to Mott Haven, on the Harlem river. This was the New York athletic club,[57] whose growth and expansion would alone illustrate and typify nearly the whole of modern sport. For almost twenty years it flourished on the stern diet of athletics, and only athletics. Its boat house, its track, and its field became the center of general support, while at its various annual games young athletes accumulated records that ought to have gladdened the heart of Dr. Holmes.

In 1876, after the New York athletic club had held its own seventh annual spring meet, it devised a novelty and held the first open amateur handicap field meeting in America.[58] Already the Intercollegiate athletic association had been organized to regulate the play of college boys, and had conducted its first games at Saratoga.[59] But the New York open games represented a new principle possible only because sport was becoming universal, and necessary because definitions and standards were so unsettled as to imperil sport itself. Out of these open games there grew, under the patronage of the New York athletic club, the National association of amateur athletics of America, an organization without a plant of its own, and aspiring to govern sport. In 1888, after a dispute in this association,[60] from which the New York athletic club had withdrawn its countenance, and which the Intercollegiate athletic association was ready to desert,[61] the greatest of the Philadelphia clubs, the Athletic club of the Schuylkill navy, took steps to create the Amateur athletic union.[62] The new union held a first meet at Detroit in September, 1888,[63] and was a success from the beginning. In its first summer, August 25, 1888, it faced the country courageously,—insolently, some thought,—and resolved that any amateur participating in unauthorized games should thereby disqualify himself as entry in games controlled by the Amateur athletic union.[64] This union and other governing bodies are still defining the amateur and adjusting the terms of his competitions; but this interdict of the athletic protestant,—or infidel,—is a high mark in the rising tide.

Long before the Amateur athletic union had been conceived, its parent outgrew its primitive athletic plant and, stimulated by its own needs and the rivalry of eager imitators, had come into town with a great athletic club house. In 1885, with William R. Travers as president and Herman Oelrichs as financial backer, the New York athletic club opened its own

building at Sixth avenue and Fifty-fifth street; three years later it opened a
country home on Travers Island; and in 1896 it moved up Sixth avenue to
a larger city palace on Fifty-ninth street.[65] Meanwhile its development
had been paralleled in Philadelphia by the Athletic club of the Schuylkill
navy, whose rowing had grown into general athletics and produced the
Arch street club house in 1889.[66] In Boston the athletic club boasted
among its members Henry L. Higginson and John Boyle O'Reilly, and
opened modern quarters in 1888.[67] In Chicago the building on Michigan
avenue was regarded as the last word in athletic architecture when it
opened in 1893.[68] In smaller towns and among poorer athletes, where
marble palaces were out of the question, where the Young Men's Christian
Association or the turnverein or the local school or college might be the
agency, the athletic club was extending its stimulation deep into the social
body.

The increasing organization of sport tells one side of the story;
the invention of new activities the other. The mechanical genius of one
Plimpton, about 1863,[69] made roller skating possible and bred a mania
that first infected Australia, then Europe, then America, and that raged,
an intermittent epidemic, for a generation. Tools of the game were
cheap; skill was not hard to acquire; but the rinks in which to skate controlled the sport. The Brooklyn rink, long to be famous as a political
meeting place, was opened in 1877. On the future site of the Auditorium
hotel, Chicago had one in 1880; and A.G. Spalding opened another in
the same city in 1884.[70] There was a great Olympia rink in New York, on
Fifty third street, in 1885. At this time, according to one estimate, there
was $20,000,000 of skating rink property in America,[71] and the capacity
of these was supplemented many fold by the new concrete sidewalks and
the asphalt pavements that invited the small boy to "hitch behind" and
risk his neck. A six-day skating race in New York in 1885 produced a
record 1,090 miles.[72] Women and girls adopted the pastime, while their
elders "viewed with alarm" the demoralization of the growing generation.
Boxwood, the material for skate wheels, in the preferable three-inch
growth, rose from thirty-eight to one hundred and twenty dollars per ton
under the demand of manufacturers, and far-off Persia and Turkey, where
this wood grew, benefited by the craze.[73]

Nearly twenty years before skating thus literally carried its devotees off their feet, another epidemic had "swept over our land," "the
swiftest and most infectious" yet, croquet.[74] To the rules and definitions
of this game the *Nation* devoted a long article in 1866. In England three
years later, writes Alfred Austin, it was "in the heyday of its popularity."[75]
Like roller skating, its paraphernalia was simple and readily set up anywhere, and as a courting game few have surpassed it. It produced in time
its experts who, in 1879, gathered in Chicago at "the first national convention of croquet players ever held in this country,"[76] to debate "loose"
against "tight" methods and to formulate its laws. Such a useless gather-

ing, regretted the *Chicago Times*, was a "severe commentary upon our civilization;" but whether because of the prize tournament mallet offered by A.G. Spalding or because the game had merit of its own, croquet declined to disappear. At Norwich, Connecticut, the National croquet association built its tournament grounds, and here year after year a handful of persistent players reduced the game to one of nice skill, similar to nothing less than billiards.[77] And everywhere croquet, like roller skates, became part of the education of the child.

The wooden-wheeled, iron-tired "bone-shaker" bicycle of the civil war decade brought zest to life at yet another spot. Charles de Drais[78] had experimented with his "draisena" early in the century, and Pierre Lallement[79] had built and ridden a bicycle in Paris in 1863. Thereafter where roads and nerve permitted the old high bicycle gained its advocates and, with velocipede and tricycle, tempted even an occasional girl to learn to ride. A clipping from a scrap book of 1869 celebrates the early sporting girl:

> But I am of the Yankee sort,
> A gutta-percha lady sport,
> Fair and tough, and fast and strong
> And hold to my paces all day long ...
> Stir the dust and take the shoot,
> Pantalettes and gaiter-boot.
> Houp la! houp-la!—needn't try
> To find a lovelier wretch than I.

As the seventies advanced the bicycle became a tool of delicate grace, with a fifty-one inch wheel weighing thirty pounds,[80] although the general public still found interest in articles telling how to pronounce the word.[81] Colonel A.A. Pope, of Hartford, imported several of the English machines in 1878 and then began to build his own Columbia bicycles;[82] and here and there enthusiasts began to organize clubs to ride together, and even held their race meets by 1879. Riding academies multiplied,[83] often using armories or skating rinks, and park commissioners were exasperated by appeals to permit citizens astride their wheels to use the public drives. Horses started upon the long course of nervous education that the motor car has finished. And on May 31, 1880, there met at Newport delegates from twenty-nine bicycle clubs who there organized the League of American wheelmen and held their first parade.[84]

Bicycling is unique among the sports in the extent to which participation was on an individual basis and in the degree to which individuals joined in the national organization. The annual meets of the League of American wheelmen were of increasing interest for twenty years, both as sporting events with fast and furious racing, and as social gatherings to which members and their families went as for a sporting vacation.

Wheeling, a monthly magazine, appeared as organ of the sport in 1882, and still continues, with enlarged scope, as *Outing*. Thomas Stevens crossed the continent a-wheel in 1884,[85] and soon after made his memorable trip recorded in *Around the world on a bicycle*.[86] There were supposed to be thirty thousand bicycles in the United States in 1885[87] and twelve thousand members of the league by 1889; and this while the old high wheel was the one most generally used.

The safety bicycle—chain driven, with wheels of equal size—appeared in the catalogs of 1887, and with the pneumatic rubber tire [88] that was soon devised, opened new worlds to be conquered. By 1898 the league had over one hundred thousand paying members[89] and women had taken their great step toward equal treatment by free participation with the men. After 1900 the league collapsed, but it had widened the effective radius of life, quickened sluggish blood for both sexes and all ages, and reawakened a love for out-of-doors that city dwellers had begun to lose.

Contemporary with wheeling was lawn tennis, fit for both sexes, anywhere and at all ages, and invented at about the same time. In 1881 the United States lawn tennis association[90] was organized and held its first national tournament at Newport, under conditions resembling those which surround the Wimbledon grounds of the All England lawn tennis club, then five years old. The game was first played in America not earlier than 1875,[91] but its conquest was sweeping and complete. On private lawns, in newly-organized clubs, on the commons by the country school house, even on the unused side of at least one burying ground, the nets were stretched and the game begun. By 1890 the women had a national championship tournament of their own[92] and in another decade an American girl invaded England and there held her own against all comers. International matches were an annual feature of the game, and city, state, sectional, and national championships covered the country with their nets. Three hundred tournaments authorized[93] for 1916 by the United States lawn tennis association give a measure for the most perfect of the participating sports.

The love of outdoor sports, spreading each year into new regions and new classes worked on whatever materials it could find. Florida became a playground, opening its west coast to the rich in winter when the Plant system completed its line to Tampa in 1885.[94] Theodore Roosevelt, of an active family whose name is to be found in the initial lists of nearly every sport that I have seen, bought his range on the Little Missouri in the early eighties.[95] Here he rode the roundup and hunted outlaws, and less dangerous wild game, consciously building a frame to carry burdens. Here he saw the cow country in its final phase, and hence he went to write *The winning of the west*. In December, 1887, at a private dinner, he and his outdoor friends organized the Boone and Crockett club[96] for the study and conservation of big game, naming it for the great pathfinders for whom game was no luxury and hunting not a sport. The saving of the Yellowstone park[97] was one of the early public services of this club, the founding of the New York zoological society was another. The love of open country for hunting, camping, hiking, and the respect for common interests that all this entailed were not accidental products of our decade. They came directly from the swelling national interest.

Not every American could take time to hunt big game, or watch it, or to commune with remote nature, but the opportunity for something out of doors was demanded and provided. The rise of the country club is a feature of the later eighties. The institutions that were competent to grew into the country club where the environment was right for evolution were already provided. Here and there an older club could be made over. The old Staten Island cricket and baseball club built a new home with full outdoor equipment in 1886.[98] The Essex county hunt opened the Essex county country club in 1888.[99] The New York athletic club, always partially out-of-doors, finished its complete home and playground on Travers Island in the same year. A Boston country club, with grounds near Brookline, emerged from a racing group in 1887. But the country club that served as text for the most discussion was opened in 1996 on Pierre Lorillard's ancestral estate on Ramapo mountain under the control of the Tuxedo club.[100] At Tuxedo was a resident suburban colony club, where members could build their own cottages and use a club house more elaborate than the old casino at Newport, and with "an aggressively English air" that suggested the country life of a society that wealthy Americans liked to imitate. It was socially exclusive and highly expensive, and novel enough to furnish paragraphs for many years. It represented one of the three clear types toward which the country clubs tended to standardize for thirty years.

"Fifteen years ago," wrote Robert Dunn in 1905, "country clubs seemed fads, were confined to the East, and associated with the somewhat un-American and unrelaxed atmosphere of what one hears called 'society,'"[101] but they served a need too broad to be circumscribed. Some were the country toys of city men, who hurried out of town when work was done, who often slept at the club house, and who were as nearly unconscious of the local world around the grounds as possible. Such was Travers Island for the New York athletic club. Others became the foci for suburban colonies. Like Tuxedo, and in simpler imitations of it, their members chose to live and rear their children within walking and driving distance of the playground; and the ladies' club house and the junior annex became as important as the club itself. Still others were acclimated in the country towns, used without pretense, recruited with little or no parade of society or exclusion, and became as true an organ of local life as the high school or the board of commerce. The community of 20,000 without a country club became an anomaly requiring explanation.

The roots of country clubs sprang from the older games, and were strengthened by tennis and bicycling that widened their opportunity and their availability. But most of all they multiplied from the impetus given by a new game that must be played over the open country if at all, the royal game of golf.

The beginnings of the game of golf, with the leather ball[102] stuffed with feathers, are doubtless based "upon the desire of the Anglo-Saxon to arm himself with a stick and drive a small round body with it,"[103] but they are lost in the antiquity that conceals, perhaps, the common parent of all games of ball. Old prints and casual references carry the game back for several centuries in England and Scotland,[104] but Americans are not known to have played it in the United States before the later eighties. A writer in *Harper's Weekly*, in 1891[105] prophesied that it was likely to take foothold here, but had few facts of playing to produce. The nine hole course at Southampton, in the Shinnecock Hills, was open to play in 1892,[106] while Mr. H.C. Chatfield-Taylor remembers to have played a game over a primitive private course at Lake Forest in the same year.[107] The attractions of the game distributed it from the cities out into the country, and middle age came into its own. The playing season of 1895 was memorable for the new courses over lumpy greens, and for the shoal of old clubs that added golf and new clubs that organized to play it. In Newport the casino acquired a healthy rival in the country club. Already, in 1894, five of the pioneer clubs had organized the United States Golf Association,[108] whose annual meetings and expanding membership brought the rules and players under firm control.[109] And the environs of the cities became embroidered with the turfs and costumes of the new adoption.

It would be easy to overstate the significance and influence of single factors in the change that has altered the old American life beyond recovery or reconstruction, but not the change itself. "The great development and wide diffusion and practice of athletic exercises among our people during the last quarter of a century (this diffusion taking place precisely among those classes where the need of it was greatest)," observed Colonel Roosevelt in 1893, "has been a very distinct advantage to our national type."[110] In proportion as inducement appeared for city folk to go afield mechanical devices speeded up their going. One decade saw the opening of the Brooklyn Bridge, and the beginnings of the perennial fight for rapid transit; the next saw the electric trolley quicken the circulation on city streets and gladden the hearts of promoters of suburban real estate additions; the third is memorable for the extended use of motor cars.

Today there are a few of us who own no Ford, but all are rapidly forgetting the time two decades back when only experimental cars existed, when the debate between steam and gasoline was real, and when the horseless carriage was a carriage, not a car. In January, 1900, New York held its first American automobile show, following the several years' precedent of the bicycle shows. And since that time the physical habits of society have undergone a revolution. Part of this change is chronicled and photographed in *Country Life in America*, appearing first in 1901; more of it is still a part of our unrecorded recollection. The body of man has been freed from the restrictions of space and time; his soul has occupied new realms of nature and of play. No earlier president[111] than Colonel Roosevelt would have denounced a tribe of "nature fakers,"[112] and no earlier generation would have cared or even understood.[113] Only the invention of a portable camera made it practicable for ordinary persons to see life as it really is.[114]

Such are the partial facts to illustrate the major currents in the rise of sport. They might be enlarged to include the college games, and football with its ups and downs. They might embrace the timely subject of marksmanship, and relate the facts about the Creedmoor range and the local and international matches of the National Rifle Association, which opened there in 1873.[115] They might tell of the coaching revival that paraded down Fifth Avenue for the first time in 1876;[116] or of Bennett's introduction of polo[117] in the same year. They might mention the National Archery Association that tried to revive the Anglo-Saxon affection for the long bow, and that opened its series of national tournaments in Chicago, at the White Stockings Park, before "quite a large and certainly a very select audience" in 1879.[118] They might recall the gathering of campers who had learned the charms of the Indian canoe, and formed the American canoe association at Lake George in 1880,[119] and continued for years, in camping meets, to profit by and popularize all water sports.

They might from a different angle record the interests of collectors and owners that turned the successive buildings at Madison Square Garden into the custody of sporting shows and gave to St. Gaudens' gold Diana on the tower a real significance as goddess of the newer chase. In 1895 a series of annual sportsmen's expositions was begun, to amuse the crowds and display the dealers' wares.[120] Already other shows had prepared the way for this. Greatest of all was the horse show, that began in 1883 to aid in defining classes and improving breeds of horses, and that took at least a decade to teach exhibitors and judges genuine types.[121] There had been a dog show—first of a long series—by the Westminster Kennel Club in 1877,[122] on whose benches the uninspiring pug gave way to the terriers and collies[123] of later preference, and in whose chambers exhibitors debated the merits of "bat" and "rose-bud" ears.[124] A poultry show appeared in these same precincts in 1887,[125] with a toy dog show in an annex;[126] and a cat show in the spring of 1895 was "an epoch in the history of the cat in America."[127]

There can be no question as to there having been this rise of sport. It obtrudes from the sources of the eighties, and had created in the daily press the clean-cut sporting page before 1890, giving sharp contrast to the papers of the seventies where sport was only general news, and thin at that. In nearly every game we play today there is evidence that between 1876 and 1893 playing expanded on a widening scale, and organization made its government quasi-national. A new generation appeared taking all this for granted, and living the rounded life unconscious of a change.

It was the open frontier that kept America young during its first century of national existence. Year after year the continuous pressure from the newer states, noisy, ill-informed, but irrepressible, had driven Congress and the nation along the path of liberalism. The free ballot, the public school, the state university had kept America the land of opportunity; and however men despaired in their public utterances, their inner souls were conscious of this spark of youth and life. When the frontier closed in the eighties the habit of an open life was too strong to be changed offhand. The search for sport revealed a partial substitute for pioneer life. City congestion stimulated the need at this immediate moment, but without the cities the transition must any way have occurred. Baseball was already adopted in the small towns; the country club has produced its most numerous and typical examples away from the large cities and even in the remoter west whence the frontier has barely disappeared.

But the causes of the rise of sport, whether in the needs of city life, or in the automatic adaptation of a society whose old safety-valve, free land, was closing down, or in the aptitudes of a community inured to frontier conditions and new deprived of them, are of slighter consequence than its results upon America. No one can probe national character, personal conduct, public opinion of today without bringing out their difference from that which formerly prevailed. The hysteria of the period of the Spanish War and of Cleveland's Venezuela episode has sobered into better deliberation and balance, far enough from the ideal, but notably of higher tone. The moral indifference to methods of achievement, bred somewhat in our own great war and dominant when men smiled at the cipher despatches or the star route frauds; or printed in their advertising pages the lying romances of quack doctors and patent medicines, is giving way to a real concern for honest methods; and those who would not of themselves reform are being squeezed by sheer force of public disapproval into a reluctant degree of compliance with the rules. Personal behavior, too has changed. A cleaner living and a lessened indulgence in strong drink come with the sharpened intellect and the acuter soul. We know that we shall live to see a dry America, and one of equal rights for all. And who shall say that when our women took up tennis and the bicycle they did not as well make the great stride towards real emancipation; or that the quickened pulse, the healthy glow, the honest self-respect of honest sport have not served in part to steady and inspire a new Americanism for a new Century?

• • •

Notes

1. *New York Transcript,* August 8, 1835, advertisement, p. 3. The attempts to expose this hoax are in the *New York Herald,* September 8, 13, 1836, and are commented on in various editions of the Barnum autobiography. Phineas T. Barnum, *Life of P.T. Barnum* (New York,1885); *Struggles and Triumphs* (1873), 73.

2. *Charles Francis Adams, 1835-1915, an Autobiography, with a Memorial Address Delivered November 17, 1915, by Henry Cabot Lodge* (Boston and New York, 1916), 12.

3. Oliver W. Holmes in *Atlantic Monthly,* May 1858, p. 881.

4. In *Sports and Pastimes, a Magazine of Amusements for All Seasons* (Boston, Adams and Company), croquet, ring toss, angling, embroidery, and card and question games are described in July, 1871; and in April, 1875, dialogues, cricket, pet rabbits, magnetism, and "Silent Sam, the conjuror."

5. *The Nation,* September 2, 1869, p. 188, made this assertion while commenting upon the Harvard-Oxford boat race which had just been rowed.

6. *New York Tribune,* June 21, 1886, p. 2.

7. Ibid., March 2, 1909, p. 2.

8. *Theodore Roosevelt, an Autobiography* (New York, 1913), 48.

9. There is a photograph of the famous White House tennis court, in use, in *Harper's Weekly,* March 6, 1909, p. 13; and another of the White House offices built on the same site by President Taft in ibid., November 27, 1909, p. 30.

10. *Punch,* January 31, 1917, p. 75.

11. Gladys Miller, *Certain Aspects of Organized Recreations in the United States, 1876-1889* (Master's thesis, University of Wisconsin, 1916.

12. Edward Spencer, "The classic English Derby," in *Outing,* June, 1902, p. 292.

13. *Frank Leslie's Illustrated Newspaper,* June 18, 1881, p. 263; July 9, pp. 319, 321.

14. Photographs of Orby, Richard Crocker his owner, and "the foremost racing event of the world," in *Outing,* September, 1907, pp. 727-732.

15. Francis Trevelyan, "The American Turf. The Race Courses of the East," in *Outing,* May, 1892, p. 129.

16. *New York Herald,* September 26, 1866, p. 7, devotes three columns to the opening of the club, comparing its equipment with that of Ascot, Epsom, and Longchamps.

17. *Coney Island Jockey Club,* 1879 (pamphlet), gives an account of this new venture. Coney Island had now become famous as a New York resort, having been "discovered" about 1874 by William A. Engeman. *New York World,* January 12, 1884. The Ocean Parkway drive from Brooklyn was completed in 1876.

18. *Frank Leslie's Illustrated Newspaper,* October 27, 1888, p. 167.

19. Betting rings were abolished by the New York constitution of 1894.

20. E.T. Riddick, "Robert Bonner's stock farm," in *Harper's Weekly,* July 23, 1892, p. 709.

21. There is a cut of this sulky in *Outing,* October, 1892, appendix 19.

22. *Outing,* November, 1907, p. 237.

23. A.J. Kenealy, "The New York Yacht Club, a Sea-dog's Yarn of Fifty Years," in *Outing*, August, 1894, p. 388.

24. *New York Daily Tribune*, September 8, 1851; *New York Evening Post*, September 9, 1851.

25. A.J. Kenealy, "The Racers for the America's Cup," in *Outing*, August, 1893, p. 381.

26. R.F. Coffin, "History of American Yachting," in *Outing*, August, 1886, p. 509. The New York yacht club was now established at Clifton, S.I., and was conducting regular regattas and fleet cruises in American waters. Ibid., p. 402.

27. *New York Sun*, February 10, 1879.

28. *New York Herald*, March 18, 24, 1878, September 22, 1879.

29. *Chicago Inter-Ocean*, September, 22, 1879.

30. *Harper's Weekly*, March 27, 1909, p. 31.

31. *New York Herald*, April 29, 1860, describes this fight.

32. The younger Bennett, consistently interested in racing, polo, yachting, and other sports, made the *New York Herald* the best source for sporting news in this period. Sketches of Sullivan are given in the issues for January 30 and February 8, 1882, and July 9, 1889.

33. Mike Donovan, "How to Punch the Ball," in *Outing*, April, 1902, p. 54.

34. A New York correspondent, after a visit to Sullivan's training quarters, described the superiority of the "leather football" over the sand pillow formerly used. *New York Herald*, January 29, 1882, p. 13.

35. *Frank Leslie's Illustrated Newspaper*, March 31, 1883, p. 86; November 29, 1884, p. 227.

36. *New York Herald*, December 20, 1887; *New York Tribune*, December 20, 1887.

37. *New York Sun*, December 10, 1887; *New York Tribune*, December 20, 1887; *New York Herald*, January 5, 1888. John Boyle O'Reilly asserted that "skill in pugilism has always been coincident with political freedom." *New York Tribune*, December 20, 1887.

38. "John L. Sullivan ... has faced his last opponent in the ring, and it is doubtful if he will ever again do the knocking out act." *New York Herald*, March 12, 1888, p. 4.

39. December 30, 1887, p. 4.

40. *Milwaukee Sentinel*, January 8, 1889; *Idaho Avalanche*, July 13, 1889; *Chicago Inter-Ocean*, July 9, 1889.

41. *Theodore Roosevelt, An Autobiography*, 46.

42. Shibe Park, home of the Athletics, and the grounds of the Pirates at Pittsburgh, both opened in 1909, are good specimens of the modern equipment. *Harper's Weekly*, May 1, 2, 1909.

43. Arthur B. Reve, "What America Spends for Sport," in *Outing*, December, 1910, p. 300.

44. H.C.Palmer, J.A. Fynes, F. Richter, and W.I. Harris, *Athletic Sports in America, England and Australia* (1889), 26.

45. Albert G. Spalding, *America's National Game; Historic Facts Concerning the Beginning, Evolution, Development and Popularity of Baseball, with Personal Reminiscences of its Vicissitudes, Victories, and its Votaries* (New York, 1911), 64.

46. The text of the call for this meeting, and an account of its transactions are in the *Chicago Tribune*, February 7, 1876.

47. "The Return of the Ball Players," in *Harper's Weekly*, April 6, 1889, p. 226.

48. *Harper's Weekly*, September 22, 1894, p. 908.

49. The numerous Newhall brothers, famous in cricket annals, are described in ibid., June 22, 1889, p. 495.

50. *Chicago Tribune,* September 18-21, 1885.

51. *Physical Education in the Young Men's Christian Associations of North America* (1914), p. 5. An International training school for directors was organized in Springfield, Massachusetts, in 1885, while a series of annual conferences of the association of general secretaries was continuous from 1871. *Louisville Commercial,* May 6, 11, 1893.

52. Marion D. Learned, *The German-American Turner Lyric* (Baltimore, 1897), 40.

53. *Harper's Weekly,* September 20, 1890, p. 734.

54. Heinrich Metzner, *Geschichte des [Nordamericanischen] Turner-Bunds* (Indianapolis, 1874), 85; *New York Tribune,* September 12, 16, 1864; *New York Herald,* April 6, 1865.

55. *Chicago Tribune, Milwaukee Sentinel,* September 11, 1880.

56. *Frank Leslie's Illustrated Newspaper,* June 25, 1881, pp. 281, 283, gives sketches of the festival; *Chicago Inter-Ocean,* June 6, 1881.

57. *Memorial History of New York,* edited by J.G. Wilson, 4: 258; S.C. Foster, "The New York Athletic Club," in *Outing,* September, 1884, p. 403.

58. On July 29, 1876. *New York Herald,* July 16, 30, 1876.

59. Intercollegiate rowing, since the Harvard-Oxford race, had become a mild "mania." *Frank Leslie's Illustrated Newspaper,* July 15, 1876, p. 302. On the day after the annual Saratoga regatta, July 20, 1876, the Intercollegiate athletic association held its meet. *New York Herald,* Jun 17, July 21, 1876.

60. The Manhattan athletic club organized as a rival to the New York athletic club in 1878, was special patron of the National association of Amateur athletics of America in its later years, and occupied an imposing house at Madison Avenue and Forty-fifth Street between 1890 and 1893. New York Sun, February 19, 1893.

61. The resolutions embodying this desertion are in *Outing,* April, 1889, appendix, 1; June, 1889, appendix, 32.

62. The details of the breach are in *Outing,* November 1888, p. 168, January, 1889, p. 363.

63. *New York Herald,* September 20, 1888.

64. The meeting that passed this resolution was held in the house of the New York Athletic Club. *Outing,* October, 1888, p. 81.

65. M.W. Ford, "The New York Athletic Club," in *Outing,* December, 1898, p. 247.

66. *New York Times,* September 23, 1889.

67. *New York Herald,* December 30, 1888.

68. *Chicago Inter-Ocean,* July 16, 1893.

69. *Annual Cyclopaedia and Register of Important Events of the Year 1884* (New York), 737.

70. *Spalding's Manual of Roller Skating* (1884), 78; *Chicago Times,* May 18, 1864, p. 7.

71. *Frank Leslie's Illustrated Newspaper,* April 18, 1885, p. 149.

72. *New York Herald,* March 8, 1885.

73. *Scientific American,* March 28, 1885, p. 200.

74. *The Nation,* August 9, 1866, p. 113.

75. Alfred Austin, *Autobiography of Alfred Austin,* Poet Laureate, 1835-1910 (London, 1911), 2:1.

76. *Chicago Times,* September 24, 1879, pp. 4,8.

77. E.S. Martin in *The Nation,* September 3, 1898, p. 862.

78. *Wheelman,* March, 1883, p. 460.

79. Charles E. Pratt, "Pierre Lallement and His Bicycle," in *Outing* and the *Wheelman*, October, 1883, p. 4.

80. *Scientific American*, July 17, 1875, p. 39.

81. *Cincinnati Commercial*, November 22, 1879.

82. A.A. Pope, "The wheel," in *Wheelman*, October, 1882, p. 69; an early Columbia advertisement, with cut, is in the *Christian Union*, February 12, 1879, p. 168.

83. *New York Sun*, January 2, 1880, p. 1, describes the opening of a new academy in the American Institute building.

84. New York Tribune, May 31, 1880; Frank Leslie's *Illustrated Newspaper*, June 19, 1880, p. 261.

85. His itinerary, via Humboldt Valley, Laramie City, and the old Platte traile is in *Outing*, May, 1887, p. 187.

86. Before appearing in book form, his journal ran as serial in *Outing*, October, 1885-June, 188.

87. *Chicago Tribune*, November 7, 1885, "Wheeling as a sport."

88. W.T. Farwell, "The Story of the Tire," in *Outing*, January, 1913, p. 472.

89. *Outing*, April, 1900, p. 95.

90. *Wright and Ditson's Lawn Tennis Guide*, 1897, p. 18; *New York World*, May 22, 1881, p. 2.

91. James Dwight, "Lawn Tennis in New England," in *Outing*, May, 1891, p. 157.

92. Miss Ellen C. Roosevelt won the first national championship on the Philadelphia cricket club grounds at Wissahickon. According to Alice Barber Stephens, as well as the illustrator for styles, girls played tennis in 1891 in long skirts, long sleeves, high collars, and trimmed hats. *Harper's Bazaar*, June 6, 1891, p. 443., July 18, 1891, pp. 557, 559.

93. *Chicago Tribune*, January 28, 1917, pt. 2, p.1.

94. With a connecting link in a steel steamer to run to Havana. *Chicago Tribune*, July 28, 1885; G.H. Smythe, *Henry Bradley Plant* (1898), 75.

95. *Theodore Roosevelt, An Autobiography*, 94.

96. George Bird Grinnell, *Brief History of the Boone and Crockett Club, with Officers, Constitution, and List of Members for the Year 1910* (New York [1911?]), 3.

97. Ibid., 10.

98. C.E.Clay, "Staten Island Cricket and Baseball Club," in *Outing*, November, 1887, p. 110; *New York Times*, July 5, 1886; *New York Herald*, July 6, 1886.

99. At Hutton Park on Orange Mountain. *New York Tribune*, December 5, 1887, January 3, 1888; *New York Sun*, December 23, 1887; *New York Herald*, May 6, 13, 1888, gives a description of country clubs near New York.

100. B.L.R. Dana, "An Original Social Experiment—Tuxedo," in *Cosmopolitan*, October, 1899, p. 547; J.N. Smith, "The Tuxedo Club," in *Munsey's*, November, 1891, p. 161; *Harper's Weekly*, December 18, 1886; *New York World*, June 2, 1886.

101. "The Country Club," in *Outing*, November, 1905, p. 165.

102. "The Golf Ball," in *Harper's Weekly*, April 8, 18, 89, p. 351.

103. *The Nation*, August 26, 1869, p. 168.

104. *Country Life in America*, May, 102, p. 35; Andrew Lang discusses the history of the game in H.G. Hutchinson, *Golf* (Badminton Library, 1902), 1.

105. E.N. Lamont, "The royal game of golf," September 12, 1891, p. 695.

106. *Harper's Weekly*, August 27, 1892, p. 832; cf. *Outing*, September, 1894, appendix, 173, October, 1894, appendix, 22, August 1898, p. 498.

107. H.C. Chatfield-Taylor, "The Development of Golf in the West," in *Outing*, August, 1900, p. 531.

108. The earliest American tournament was begun at St. Andrews, October 11, 1894. *New York Times*, October 12, 1894; *Outing*, August, 1895, appendix, 11, February, 1897, p. 502.

109. For the case of Francis Ouimet against the United States Golf Association, see *Chicago Examiner*, January 14, 1917.

110. Theodore Roosevelt, "Value of an athletic training," in *Harper's Weekly*, December 23, 1893, p. 1236.

111. Thomas Jefferson, indeed, while minister in France, had a costly private argument with M. de Buffon over the characteristics of the moose. Jefferson to Rutledge, September 9, 1788, *Writings of Thomas Jefferson* (Monticello edition—Washington, 1904), 7:137.

112. Edward B. Clark, "Roosevelt on the Nature Fakirs," in *Everybody's Magazine*, June 1907, p. 770. The immediate reply of W.J. Long is in *Boston Evening Transcript*, May 23, 24, 1907; he returned indirectly to the attack in "The Bull Moose as a Political Totem," in *Independent*, July 11, 1912, p. 85. When Colonel Roosevelt walked through New Forest on June 9, 1910 with Sir Edward Grey, they identified forty-one forest birds and heard the note of twenty-three. Theodore Roosevelt, *An Autobiography*, 334.

113. The struggles of Audubon to find subscribers for his *Birds of America*, and his final report to a British publisher, give a measure for early American interest in natural science. Washington Irving to Martin Van Buren, October 19, 1836, in *The Life of John James Audubon, the Naturalist*, edited by his widow (New York, 1869), 394.

114. The followers of Daguerre made slow progress until, about 1878, the dry plate was perfected. *Outing*, December, 1889, p. 220. Immediately experimenters began to work towards series-photography and moving pictures. *San Francisco Chronicle* and in *Cincinnati Commercial*, August 21, 1879. Nine years later the Eastman Company brought out its roll-film cameras and began to advertise "You press the button, we do the rest." *Harper's Weekly*, July 20, 1889, p. 583; *Harper's Bazaar*, May 23, 1891, p. 407; *Encyclopaedia Britannica* (eleventh edition), 21: 503. A photographers' association of America completed its organization and held its first national convention in Chicago in 1880. *Chicago Tribune*, August 24-27, 1880. Portraits of living game were shown at the fourth annual sportsmen's show. *Harper's Weekly*, January 22, 1898, p. 101. And a little later, A.R. Dugmore could describe "A revolution in nature pictures," in *World's Work*, November 1900, p. 83.

115. "The American Wimbledon," *New York Tribune*, June 23, 1873. General George W. Wingate, captain of the first international team, participated in the formation of a gigantic public schools athletic league in 1903. *Outing*, September, 1901, p. 616, May, 1908, p. 166. Luther H. Gulick, famous in Y.M.C.A. activities, and associate of General Wingate, became president in 1906 of the new Playground Association of America, with Colonel Roosevelt and Jacob A. Riis as honorary officials. *Playground*, April, 1907, p. 7.

116. Colonel De Lancay Lane expected to start his daily coach to Pelham Bridge on May 1, 1876. *New York Herald*, March 18, 1876.

117. His Westchester polo club built a house at Jerome Park, and played inside the track. "Polo in America," in *Wildwood's Magazine*, November, 1888, p. 10; *Frank Leslie's Illustrated Newspaper*, June 24, 1876, p. 261; *New York Herald*, May 12, June 2, 1876.

118. *Chicago Tribune*, August 14, 1879; Maurice Thompson, "Bow-shooting," in *Scribner's Magazine*, July 1877, p. 273.

119. *New York Herald*, August 5, 1880. Judge Nicholas Longworth, of Cincinnati, first vice-commodore, offered a tournament cup to the Western Canoe Association a few years later. *Western Canoe Association, Seventh Annual Yearbook* (1891), 22.

120. George Bird Grinnell, editor of *Forest and Stream*, and an active member of the Boone and Crockett Club, was connected with the management of the first exposition, May 13-18, 1895. *New York Times*, December 16, 1894, p. 20. Subsequent expositions became, to a great extent, dealers' sporting goods exhibits. *Harper's Weekly*, January 29, 1898, p. 100; March 18, 1899, p. 276.

121. *Topeka Commonwealth*, October 23, 1883; *New York Sun*, October 23, 1883. Alexander J. Cassatt, later president of the Pennsylvania Railroad, but now gentleman-farmer at Haverford, exhibited one of the first hackneys seen in America, "general purpose" type whose period lies between the rise of the modern macadam road and the advent of the automobile. *Harper's Weekly*, April 9, 1892, p. 348; *World's Work*, July 1901, p. 973; *Country Life in America*, December, 1901, p. 41.

122. The first dog show opened Tuesday, May 8, 1877, at the Hippodrome with some 1,300 dogs on exhibition. *New York Times*, May 8, 1877; *Frank Leslie's Illustrated Newspaper*, May 26, 1877, p. 203. In later years Madison Square Garden was utilized.

123. J.P. Morgan collies, American-bred at his Cragston kennels, won the honors of 1894. *Harper's Weekly*, March 3, 1894, p. 215.

124. The introduction of the French bull-dog about 1897 raised the debate over the shape to which the ears should conform. *Harper's Weekly*, February 26, 1898, p. 214.

125. *New York Tribune*, December 15, 22, 1887.

126. The American Toy Dog Club was organized to conduct this show. *New York Tribune*, November 17, 1887, p. 5; *New York Herald*, May 26, 1888, p. 3.

127. *Harper's Bazaar*, May 11, 1895, p. 380; *New York World*, May 12, 1895.

• • •

Suggestions for Further Reading:

Adelman, Melvin L., "Neglected Sports in American History: The Rise of Billiards in New York City, 1850-1871," *Canadian Journal of History of Sport*, XII (December, 1981), 1-4, 24-28.

Betts, John R., *America's Sporting Heritage*, 1850-1950 (Reading, MA: Addison-Wesley, 1974).

_____, "Mind and Body in Early American Thought," *Journal of American History*, LIV (March, 1968), 787-805.

Cole, Arthur, C., "Our Sporting Grandfathers—The Cult of Athletics at Its Source," *Atlantic Monthly*, CL (July, 1932), 88-96.

Dizikes, John, *Sportsmen and Gamesmen* (Boston: Houghton-Mifflin, 1981)

Dulles, Foster Rhea, *America Learns to Play: A History of Popular Recreation, 1607-1940* (New York: Appleton-Century, 1940).

Eyler, Marvin H. "Origins of Contemporary Sports," *Research Quarterly*, XXXII, 3 (December, 1961), 480-489.

Geldbach, Erich, "The Beginnings of German Gymnastics in America," *Journal of Sport History*, III (Winter, 1976), 236-272.

Henderson, Robert W., *Ball, Bat and Bishop: The Origin of Ball Games* (New York: Rockport Press, 1947).

Krout, John A. "Some Reflections on the Rise of American Sport," *Proceedings of the Association of History Teachers of the Middle States and Maryland*, XXVI (1928), 84-93.

Noverr, Douglas A. and Lawrence E. Ziewacz, *The Games They Played: Sports in American History, 1865-1980* (Chicago: Nelson-Hall, 1983).

Swanson, Richard A., "The Acceptance and Influence of Play in American Protestantism," *Quest*, XI (December, 1978), 58-70.

Weaver, Robert B., *Amusements and Sports in American Life* (Chicago: University of Chicago Press, 1939).

Zeigler, Earle F., Ed., *A History of Sport and Physical Education to 1900: Selected Topics* (Champaign, IL: Stipes Publishing Co., 1973).

THE PROMISE OF SPORT
IN ANTEBELLUM AMERICA

Peter Levine

In the following essay, Peter Levine ties the development of sport and physical education in antebellum America to the efforts of some middle class reformers to influence societal values. Focusing on the literature produced by child guidance advisors, health reformers, and the authors of books on sports and amusements, he finds the themes of individual self-improvement and national vitality closely linked. Through these works, the metaphoric quality of sport for the moral health and physical well-being of a nation and its citizens has its beginnings.

Levine acknowledges the work of John Betts, Jennie Holliman, Frederic Paxson and others in identifying the development of a sporting consciousness in America during the Jacksonian era. He does not agree completely, however, with the standard notion that "concern for the development of sound minds and sound bodies emerged out of perfectionist religious and secular thought reflective of egalitarian economic and social circumstances." Emphasizing the period's conservative tendencies, and, in the process, reflecting recent historical analyses of the antebellum socio-economic structure, he sees the advocates of sport essentially addressing an urban, middle class audience—like themselves—and urging this population to pursue physical recreation and games in order to strengthen such traditional values and virtues as order, stability and respect for authority. Levine points out that encouragement along these lines was not exclusively rooted in a nostalgia for past ideals. One also needed to be fit in order to grapple successfully with the fast pace and arduous demands of a rapidly modernizing society.

In the self-conscious efforts of his reformers, Levine identifies a group which fits within the mainstream of romantic reform in antebellum America. Although they did not overtly seek to control subordinate groups, they strove to insure their own place in a society where the old claims on status were changing significantly. There is no Marxian intrigue here, but there is an affirmation of capitalist values and aspirations.

In a recent essay entitled "The Corruption of Sport," Christopher Lasch argues that "the degradation of sport ... consists ... in its subjection to some ulterior purpose, such as a profit-making, patriotism, moral training, or the pursuit of health. Sport may give rise to these things in abundance," he continues, "but ideally it produces them, only as by-products having no essential connection with the game."[1] Whether or not this appraisal correctly identifies problems inherent in contemporary American society, ironically, genuine attempts to promote such associations contributed to an increased interest in sport and physical education in antebellum America. Specifically, the serious attention that Americans gave to sport between 1820 and 1860 coincided with and was encouraged by an articulate attempt to link sport positively with the development of proper citizens possessed with the character traits necessary to preserve and continue American greatness.

This statement comes as no surprise to anyone familiar with the work of John Betts, Jennie Holliman, Guy Lewis and other scholars interested in the history of sport in America. Although they might disagree about the relative contributions of phrenologists, physicians, physical educators and naturalists in giving sport special purpose, their work convincingly locates this tendency in the Jacksonian period and correctly identifies the participants in that process.[2]

Without exception, however, explanations of this significant development rely on uncritical acceptance of outdated and often suspect historical interpretations that prevent a full exploration of the relationships between American sport and American society. Emphasizing the notions of "Progressive" historians including Frederick Jackson Turner, Frederic Paxson and Arthur Schlesinger, Jr., those who have informed us about sport and physical recreation in the Jacksonian period have placed that experience solely in the context of an optimistic, egalitarian society, confident in its ability to achieve individual and societal perfection through social reform. In this framework, concern for the development of sound minds and sound bodies emerged out of perfectionist religious and secular thought reflective of egalitarian economic and social circumstances. It was in the "Age of the Common man," where "democracy seemed to burst the bonds of the past," where "class distinctions were challenged," and where "the desire for human perfection was possibly the most characteristic trait of Americans," that social reformers urged participation in sport as part of an optimistic effort to achieve human perfectibility.[3]

My intention is not to suggest that this complex of ideas is entirely in error nor that reliance on them to explain the emergence of new attitudes about sport and recreation is totally unconvincing. Although recent historical analysis of 19th century American social structure, politics and culture increasingly denies the validity of this celebrant view of an open, optimistic, egalitarian society, nevertheless there is some merit in understanding the movement toward a belief in the positive social purposes of sport in the context of a perfectionist, reform spirit.[4]

There is, however, another side of the story that deserves attention. Articulate attempts to promote positive attitudes about sport and physical recreation also came from individuals who were ambivalent about their society. For them, the possibility of social disorder inherent in their perception of a constantly changing world tempered optimistic appraisals of the future. Particularly for an urbanizing middle class audience with increasing leisure time, this appraisal encouraged new meaning for sport as a way of controlling certain tendencies that, to them, threatened to undermine the virtues and the values of the American republic.

Although there is little agreement about the precise moment when the United States became a modern nation or about the ways in which different groups of people experienced that process, unquestionably, developments usually associated with the transformation of America from a traditional to a modern society occurred in the first half of the 19th century.[5] Expansive economic growth accompanied by technological innovation, dramatic population rise, increased urbanization and geographic mobility were among features of this experience recognized by contemporaries. So too was the feeling that preoccupation with the accumulation of wealth, to the exclusion of other considerations, was producing a new American capable of realizing the ideals of the Founding Fathers.[6]

For many observers, these developments engendered both incredible optimism about American potential and deep pessimism about the possibility of realizing it.[7] Repeated longings for the simplicity of the Old Republic reflected more than simple nostalgia for some ideal past. Explicit in them were expressions of anxiety and fear about the potential for American catastrophe inherent in the drive toward modernity. As David Rothman makes clear in his path-breaking book, *The Discovery of the Asylum*, what concerned many Americans was the need to understand how best to promote the stability implicit in the republican ideal in a new society constantly undergoing rapid social change. In Rothman's words, "Americans in the Jacksonian period could not believe that geographic and social mobility would promote or allow order and stability ... They knew that the old system was passing, but not what ought to replace it. What in their day was to prevent society from bursting apart? For where would the elements of cohesion come."[8]

This desire for stability, often underscored by apocalyptic visions of impending doom, was heightened by the feeling that traditional mechanisms of maintaining order were no longer capable of fulfilling that function. As other historians have shown, the American experiment in republicanism seemed to be under constant siege, with no assurance as to what the outcome might be.[9]

For a whole range of reformers, then, the issue was to shape the values and interests of citizens actively participating in the supposed opportunities of American life in ways that prevented individual and social disintegration while at the same time encouraging personality characteristics relevant to the demands of a new order. Efforts to promote participation in sport and physical recreation between 1820 and 1860 are clearly related to these feelings and to the sense of anxiety and urgency that spawned them. They also reflect an awareness of the fragmentation of time into work and non-work and a concern of how to use a new leisure time in productive ways. A brief look at the literature of three groups involved in this enterprise—child guidance advisors, health reformers, and the authors of books on sport and amusement—underlines these connections.

The enormous popularity enjoyed by domestic tracts on childrearing and on moral guidance for young adults between 1820 and 1860 suggests a shared concern among many Americans about their own future and that of the nation's. Aimed at a predominantly urban, middle class audience, the message of William Alcott's *The Young Man's Guide*, already in its tenth edition by 1846, T.S. Arthur's *Advice to Young Men*, Catherine Beecher's *The Evils Suffered by American Women*, Lydia Child's *The Mother's Book* and other similar works are clear.[10] Order and stability, the keystones of republican society, were under constant attack. Unless family authority was strengthened and children taught proper values and respect, disaster was imminent. In Catherine Beecher's words, "... unless our children are trained to intelligence and virtue, the nation is ruined."[11] It was "American Mothers," as Lydia Child noted, "on whose intelligence and discretion the safety and prosperity of our Republic ... depend."[12]

The role of sport and physical recreation occupied a minor theme in this guidance literature devoted to specific instructions on how to raise productive citizens in a modernizing society. Invariably, however, interspersed among discussions of child government, diet, clothing, moral training and obedience, was advice about the effects of sport on character development that helped impart new meaning to such society.

The most prominent argument present in this nurture literature for physical recreation and sport rested on commonly held assumptions about human development. Drawing on the beliefs of physiologists and phrenologists, Alcott, Child and others emphasized the relationship of a sound mind and a sound body in encouraging readers of both sexes toward participation. Informal out-of-door activities in particular, including playing ball, quoits, ninepines, jumping, running, sliding, skating, calisthenics, croquet and horseback riding were most often recommended for making "the body ... a traveling companion for the journey of life."[13] Arguing that if Americans could remedy the abuses of their bodies they would be "at the head of the human race," Catherine Beecher even urged every community to establish a "Temple of Health," where people could exercise together and learn about proper diet and medical care.[14] Beecher hoped that parents would accompany their children to these temples and join in their games "for nothing so binds the young to those who control them, as aid and sympathy in amusing sports."[15]

Although girls as well as boys were targets of these appeals, discussions of female participation reflected mid-19th century attitudes about distinctions between the sexes. They also anticipated arguments against women's involvement in sport on the same level or for the same purposes as men so prevalent in the 20th century.

Physical recreation for girls would certainly promote health but only if done in ways that preserved supposed female virtues while taking into account assumed differences in the physical capabilities of the sexes. Lydia Child, for instance, in describing calisthenics for girls distinguished these exercises as "a gentler sort of gymnastics, suited to girls ..."[16] And William Alcott, in his *Letters to a Sister* advised women to engage in exercises that were compatible to their "nervous and sanguine" temperament.[17]

Whatever the activity, participation in it required attention to its possible ill-effects on the female character. While it is proper for girls to skate and slide, Child, in *The Mother's Book*, cautioned that such activity should not take place in mixed, public company. "Such sports, when girls unite in them," she noted, "should be confined to the inmates of the house, and away from all possibility of contact with the rude and the vicious. Under these circumstances, a girl's manners cannot be injured by such wholesome recreations."[18]

Appreciation of youthful recreation also received encouragement from modern attitudes about social organization. Viewing life as "warfare," T.S. Arthur warned his readers of the need for "patience, fortitude, energy, and intense thought, in overcoming the difficulties that must be encountered before the day of trial was over." Appealing specifically to an audience of prospective businessmen, he continued that "recreations and innocent amusements" gave young men some diversion from the "strife of life conflict" and allowed them to become "refreshed and invigorated for new combats." In an increasingly fragmented world where "in business ... one sought his own interest," where "there was no general deference to the interests of others," and where "men grew daily more and more selfish," recreation not only renewed their energy but brought them "into associations different from business associations, by which they will be able to see new phases of character, and judge more kindly of their fellows."[19]

Both the optimism and the anxiety about mid-19th century American society explicit in these statements about the purpose of sport and physical recreation reflect a situation experienced by other social reformer of that era. Recognizing that traditional mechanisms for maintaining order and morality had lost meaning in an increasingly segmented society in which rapid material advancement defined success and progress, reformers reached out for new ways to influence individual human character and to encourage social stability. In choosing sport as one means of improving character, however, child guidance writers cautioned against participation in certain activities. Ironically, the way in which they expressed themselves on this point reveals that in their attempts to reestablish traditional eighteenth century notions of stability they also encouraged values more consonant with a society bent on modernity.[20]

Instructions to avoid participation in horseracing, cockfighting and boxing, for instance, appear in the pronouncements of Henry Ward Beecher, William Alcott and others.[21] These activities, inseparable in their minds from intemperance and gambling, led only to the corruption of proper values necessary for American society to survive. "Will races make you more moral?—more industrious?—more careful?—economical?—trustworthy?" Beecher intoned as he reminded his listeners to avoid gamblers, jockeys and other types "who live off society without returning any useful equivalent for their support."[22]

In even stronger terms Alcott urged his readers to avoid gaming and all sports associated with it. "Take not the first step," he admonished, "the moment you do, all may be lost ... If the United States are to be ruined, gaming in some of its forms will be a very efficient agent in accomplishing the work.[23] The reasons for this analysis were obvious. Gambling corrupted manners, discouraged industry and most importantly wasted time. In words reminiscent of a sociologist describing time thrift as a component of the modern personality, Alcott concludes his remarks by noting:

> Every many who enjoys the privileges of civilized society, owes
> it to that society to earn as much as he can; or in other words, to
> improve every minute of his time. He who loses an hour, or a
> minute, is the price of that hour, debtor to the community.
> Moreover, it is a debt which he can never repay.[24]

Even more emphatic than child guidance writers in insisting on a new role for sport were mid-nineteenth century health reformers. Although premised on optimistic notions of the individual's capacity to conquer ill health, their advice also reflected anxiety over the course of American development. In this context, sport and physical recreation became activities essential to individual self-improvement and to national survival.[25]

Writing some twenty-five years apart, Charles Caldwell, a physician and former student of Benjamin Rush, and S.R. Calthrop, a phrenologist, both active in the health reform movement, emphasized the importance of physical health for the proper development of human nature so crucial to individual and social happiness. Referring to man's physical system as machinery, for instance, Caldwell, in a published lecture entitled "Thoughts on Physical Education," first delivered in 1833, compared it to a steam engine and underscored the need to produce "a better piece of machinery" within which the mind and spirit could properly "perform."[26]

This strikingly modern analogy failed to obscure the clear ambivalence both men felt about their own society and their concern over its ability to fulfill its destiny. Although they were hopeful about the possibilities for human perfectibility, their vigorous arguments in defense of sport as part of a broad scheme of physical education emerged as well out of sense of despair for the future and out of nostalgia for a more familiar past.

Constant references to an idealized version of the young American republic fill Calthrop's "Lectures on Physical Development," first published in 1858. His model of the ideal man "who has developed all components of human nature" is none other than George Washington himself. Without his great physical strength nurtured by "all kinds of athletic exercises" Washington might have been "a good man ... but the Father of his Country, never!"[27] Unless Americans gave attention to their physical health, not only would such leaders fail to develop, but the legacy of the Founding Fathers would be wasted. Quoting "an address to America, dictated by an ancient sage," Calthrop told his audience of the dire social consequences neglect of physical fitness would bring:

> Oh! latest born of time, the wise man said,
> A mighty destiny surrounds thy head;
> Great is thy mission, but the puny son
> Lacks strength to finish what the sires begun!
> Sooner or later must the slighted air
> And exercise take vengeance on the fair.
> Ah! one by one I see them fade and fall,
> Both old and young, fair, dark, short or tall,
> Till one stupendous ruin wraps them all.[28]

Caldwell's interest in physical fitness evolved more out of despair about his own world than out of a longing for a vision of the past. A society "tainted with moral corruption," replete with excessive religious and political agitation, and fixed on a restless pursuit of wealth made the future seem "gloomy and potentous."[29] Only a mass commitment to physical education that would make the nation "a nursery of abler statesmen and more virtuous patriots" could secure its future.[30]

Out of these concerns and as part of comprehensive blueprints designed to improve the health of every bodily organ and part, Calthrop,

Caldwell and other health reformers encouraged active involvement for both sexes of all ages in sport and physical recreation.[31] Again, sexual distinctions required different activities for males and females in order to serve anticipated adult roles. Although emphatic about the necessity for girls to participate in physical recreation, Caldwell carefully limited activity to walking, hill-climbing and horseback riding done in moderation. As he put it:

> I do not mean that they ought to run foot-races, wrestle, spar, fence, or vault over six-bar gates ... Such masculine feats would suit neither their taste, delicacy, nor intended pursuits ... No: I mean that they should as a duty to themselves, their contemporaries, and posterity, indulge in graceful and becoming exercise ... to a sufficient extent to invigorate their frames, heighten their beauty, and strengthen their intellects.[32]

As for males, both Caldwell and Calthrop opted for more vigorous activity in order to instruct young men in "personal firmness and self-reliance" essential for life's struggles.[33] Aside from the individual outdoor activities frequently mentioned in the child nurture literature, "the systematic pursuit of health and strength by all manner of manly sports and games" also received encouragement.[34] Echoing contemporary interest in what some historians have labelled muscular christianity, Calthrop, discussing his experiences as headmaster of a boys school, mused: "I cannot tell how much physical weakness, how much moral evil we have batted and bowled, and shinnied away from our door; but I do know that we have batted and bowled away indolence and listlessness, and doing nothing, which I believe is the Devil's greatest engine."[35]

Specific encouragement to emulate the habits of "the sporting world" accompanied criticism of the propensity of Americans to focus their energies solely on the "love of wealth." Commenting on the high rate of insanity in the United States, Caldwell attributed it to excessive "mental excitement" brought on by several factors including "the desire and pursuit of wealth." Greater attention to physical education presumably would temper this obsession and reduce insanity.[36]

In similar fashion, Calthrop noted that the "sporting world" justifiably deserved its reputation as undignified and disreputable. Nevertheless, it contained important lessons for citizens who defined their success only in material terms. " ... Crickett and boating, battledore and archery, shinney and skating, fishing, hunting, shooting, and baseball," Calthrop advised, were "Nature's" way of instructing society that people were "not intended to be made working machines." " ... They have capacities ... for doing some pleasant thing for the mere sake of doing it," he continued, "without any regard to gain or profit ..."[37]

Health reformers, like child nurture writers, then, in demanding a significant role for physical recreation in their society, displayed a curious mixture of a commitment to the requirements of a modernizing society and to the virtues of a simpler past that emerged out of their ambivalent attitudes about 19th century American society. The work of both groups complemented and encouraged a new interest in sport that was not lost on their contemporaries. The popularity of a spate of books specifically about sport and the message they carried illustrates this point.

Books on sport, both English and American in origin, were extremely popular in antebellum America. American editions of Horatio Smith's *Festivals, Games and Amusements, Ancient and Modern,* Pierce Egan's *Sporting Anecdotes,* and William Clarke's *The Boy's Own Book*—all originally published in England—complemented native contributions such as Robin Carver's *The Book of Sport* and Frank Forrester's numerous volumes on field sports in providing detailed information about sports and justification for participating in them.[38]

Carver's work, for example, published in Boston in 1834, devoted nine of its fifteen chapters to descriptions of specific sports and games including separate sections on ball games, sports of agility, gymnastics and swimming. Instructional advice as well as rules and regulations governing activities ranging from baseball to Puss in the Corner made this book an invaluable guide for sportsminded youth. Similar information appeared in Clarke's book, first published in the United States in 1829 and in a number of other places including an openly plagiarized version of a portion of Clarke's "beautiful London work" published in New Haven in 1839 under the title *The Boy's Book of Sports.* For those interested in advice about field sports any number of the titles appearing under the pen name of Forester would have served the purpose.[39]

Obviously aimed at the same middle class urban audience that was the target of child nurture writers, these manuals on sport made similar distinctions about the kinds of activities suitable for boys and girls. Descriptions in verse of children's games appearing in *Juvenile Pastimes* in 1830, for instance, limited hop scotch—a fine game for strengthening limbs—to boys while noting that shuttlecock would "afford good exercise" for girls who spend much of their time in "the still pursuits of the needle or book."[40] And in *Children's Amusements,* published in 1820, descriptions of ball-playing, archery, swimming, football, fives and other sports, along with predictable advice about the need to protect girls from sports that were too rough and physical , also included instruction on amusement designed to prepare them for adulthood. Entitled, "Dressing the Doll," this section noted that such activity was "innocent and pleasing employment for little girls: children are imitative creatures; what the daughters see their mothers, and the sons their fathers do, they will imitate. How necessary then the examples set, be good."[41]

Accompanying this practical instruction were arguments defending sport similar to those employed by health reformers and child guidance writers. The positive relationship between a sound body and a sound mind, and the ability of sport to discourage laziness and indolence while renewing the cutting mental edge necessary to compete in "the headlong race ... for wealth ... preeminence ... and power were common themes in these manuals.[42]

Occasionally the message emerged in the form of brief morality plays interspersed among descriptions of specific sports. Robin Carver's story of Arthur and James, for instance, made clear to his young audience the importance of physical activity to worldly success. As young boys these brothers both were studious and did well in school. Arthur, however, was "averse to exercise in the open air," while James "was the foremost in all sports during play hours." Upon entering college Arthur immediately became ill and was forced to leave. For the rest of his life he "remained an invalid ... regretting deeply his early habits of bodily sloth and inactivity." James, however, "unimpeded by illness or want of strength," successfully concluded his tale by mentioning that he had often heard James declare "that wealth and reputation are nothing compared to the blessing of 'a sound mind and body.'"[43]

Although anxiety about the nation's future and a longing for an ideal past were not major preoccupations of these writers there are even occasional references to such issues. Frank Forester, for instance, defended participation in field sports as "the best, the manliest, and the most desirable ... of national amusements" for preventing "over civilization ... effeminacy and sloth ... in an age" characterized by " ... fanaticism, cant, and hypocracy."[44] And Robin Carver, referring to "the young inmates of the city," who were denied the opportunities of rural life to develop their muscles, urged the building of gymnasiums as "artificial means ... necessary to give them that exercise of which their mode of life deprives them."[45]

On May 17, 1845, the *New York Weekly Herald* reported on the famous intersectional horserace between Fashion and Peytona attended by thousands of people at the Union Racecourse on Long Island, New York.

At a very early hour Tuesday morning, New York showed by evident and significant sights, that this was no common day. It is well known that her industrious citizens are no longer sleepers when business calls to resume the daily task. But say what we will, there is a difference between work and play, toil and enjoyment, care and sport. Yesterday was a day dedicated to the latter ...[46]

It would be incorrect to argue that the situation of most Americans, living in a predominantly agrarian society, reflected the modern attitudes about work and leisure implied by the *Herald's* reporter.[47] Recognition, however, that for a growing urban population, daily life often involved a well-defined separation of activities, represents another sign that the United States underwent dramatic social change during the first half of the 19th century. For certain reformers and sports enthusiasts, fears of social disorder and catastrophe generated by this experience and a conception of reform as a means of social control, encouraged new meaning for sport in these years.

It was not the intention of these individuals to promote sport and physical recreation in order to control the values of some inferior group or class. Although it is possible to argue that such was the case between 1880 and 1920, prior to the Civil War, expressions about the value of sport as a means of developing proper character and as a relief from the pressures of the real world primarily involved the efforts of middle class reformers to shape the values of their own kind.[48] Reflecting ambivalence about their own society, they insisted that involvement in sport might serve several, not always compatible roles. Participation would promote values and character traits necessary for success in a new and changing nation. It would also provide relief from the vigors of the pursuit of material wealth—allowing the individual to reenter the battle with new energy. Finally, it would encourage a traditional sense of order and stability in what appeared to be an increasingly unstable world.

• • •

Notes

1. Christopher Lasch, "The Corruption of Sports," *New York Review of Books*, Vol. XXIV, No. 7, 26.

2. John R. Betts, "American Medical Thought on Exercise as the Road to Health, 1820-1860," *Bulletin of the History of Medicine*," 45 (1971), pp. 138-145; "Mind and Body in Early American Thought," *Journal of American History*, LIV (March, 1968), 787-805; Jennie Holliman, *American Sports, 1783-1835* (Durham, NC, 1931), p. 192. Guy Lewis, "The Muscular Christianity Movement," *Journal of Health, Physical Education and Recreation*, xxxvii (May, 1966), 27-8, 42; John A. Lucas, "A Prelude to the Rise of Sport in Ante-Bellum America, 1850-1860," *Quest* XI (Dec., 1968), 50-57; Roberta Park, "The Attitudes of Leading New England Transcendentalists Toward Healthful Exercise, Active Recreations and Proper Care of the Body: 1830-1860," *Journal of Sport History*, (Spring, 1977), 34-50; and Gerald Redmond, "The First 'Tom Brown's Schooldays' (1804) and Others: Origins and Evolution of 'Muscular Christianity in Children's Literature, 1762-1857," Paper delivered at NASSH Meeting, May 17-21, 1977.

3. Park, pp. 34-5; Lucas, p. 53; Betts, "American Medical Thought," pp. 40-41; Betts, "Mind and Body," pp. 801-5; and Lewis, p. 27 are the sources for this composite quotation and summary of ideas. This dominant interpretive framework, on occasion, also calls on some version of Turner's frontier thesis. For examples, see Betta, "Mind and Body in Early American Thought," p. 805 and Frederic Paxson, "The Rise of Sport," *Mississippi Valley Historical Review,* IV (Sept., 1917), 143-168.

4. There is no need here to list current research that bears on this point. A comprehensive view of the literature can be found in Edward Pessen, *Jacksonian America: Society, Personality, and Politics* (Homewood, 1978).

5. The most recent statement of this viewpoint appears in Richard D. Brown, *Modernization, The Transformation of American Life, 1600-1865,* (New York, 1976). For a perceptive critique of Brown see James A. Henretta, "'Modernization': Toward a False Synthesis," *Reviews in American History,* Vol. 5 (Dec., 1977), 445-452.

6. For a brief summary of contemporary response see Douglas T. Miller, *The Birth of Modern America, 1820-1850* (New York, 1970), pp. 20-22. Numerous citations concerning the effects of the pursuit of wealth on the American character appear later in this essay.

7. This theme is familiar to students of 19th century American history. For example, see Leo Marx, *The Machine in the Garden* (New York, 1967), Marvin Meyers, *The Jacksonian Persuasion, Politics and Belief* (New York, 1957), Miller, *The Birth of Modern America,* and David Rothman, *The Discovery of the Asylum, Social Order and Disorder in the New Republic* (Boston, 1971)

8. Rothman.

9. Explicit discussion of this idea in relation to the family can be found in Anne L. Kuhn, *The Mother's Role in Childhood Education: New England Concepts, 1830-1860* (New Haven, 1947); Rothman, pp. 216-221; Robert Sunley, "Early Nineteenth Century American Literature on Child Rearing." in Margaret Mead and Martha Wolfenstein, eds., *Childhood in Contemporary Cultures* (Chicago, 1955), and Bernard Wishy, *The Child and the Republic* (Phila., 1968). Also see John R. Howe, Jr., "Republican Thought and the Political Violence of the 1790s," *American Quarterly,* 19 (Summer 1967), 147-65 and Linda Kerber, *Federalists in Dissent: Imagery and Ideology in Jeffersonian America* (Ithaca, 1970).

10. The child guidance literature examined for this paper included William Alcott, *Familiar Letters to Young Men on Various Subjects Deigned as a Companion to the Young Man's Guide* (1850); _____ , *Letters to a Sister or Women's Mission* (1850); _____, *The Young Man's Guide* (1836); _____, *The Young Wife or Duties of Woman in the Marriage Relation* (1837); T.S. Arthur, *Advice to Young Men* (1850); Catherine Beecher, *Letters to the People on Health and Happiness* (1855); *The Evils Suffered by American Women and American Children: The Cause and the Remedy* (1846); Beecher, Henry Ward, *Seven Lectures to Young Men on Various Important Subjects* (1844); L. Maria Child, *The Girl's Own Book of Amusements* (1833); _____, *The Mother's Book* (1844); Samuel G. Goodrich, *Sketches From a Student's Window* (1844); Almira Phelps, *The Female Student, or Lectures to Young Ladies on Female Education* (1836); and L.H. Sigourney, *The Child's Book* (1846). Related periodicals such as the *Child's Friend* and *Family Magazine, The Child's Newspaper, The Mother's Assistant and Young Lady's Friend,* and *Godey's Magazine* were also looked at. John C. Crandall, "Patriotism and Humanitarian Reform in Children's Literature, 1825-1860." *American Quarterly,* XXI (Spring 1969), 3-22 notes the appeal to a middle class audience. The literature examined for this paper makes obvious references as well. For example, see Alcott, *The Young Man's Guide,* advertisement in the first edition, that appears at the beginning of the 1836 edition.

11. Beecher, *The Evils Suffered by American Women*, p. 5.

12. Child, *The Mother's Book*, p. 2.

13. Alcott, *The Young Man's Guide*, p. 191. Child, *The Mother's Book*, pp. 58-9; and Phelps, pp. 64-65, 68.

14. Beecher, *Letters to the People on Health and Happiness*, pp. 164, 168-9.

15. Ibid., p. 170.

16. Child, *The Girl's Own Book of Amusements*, p. 165.

17. Alcott, *Letters to a Sister*, p. 52.

18. Child, *The Mother's Book*, p. 59. Also see Alcott, *The Young Wife*, pp. 252-53 and Phelps, pp. 61-68.

19. Arthur, pp. 72-77.

20. This argument is based on Rothman's analysis of reformers involved in the movement to create prisons and asylums to care for criminal and handicapped people in the Jacksonian period. See Rothman, pp. 105-109 for his statement of the argument. For another application see Regina M. Morantz, "Making Women Modern: Middle Class Women and Health Reform in 19th Century America," *Journal of Social History*, vol. 10 (Summer, 1977), 490-507.

21. Alcott, *The Young Man's Guide*, pp. 158-94, Arthur, pp. 74-77, and Beecher, *Seven Lectures to Young Men,* pp. 172-89. Also mentioned by these authors in this context were such activities as bearbaiting, shooting matches and cards.

22. Beecher, *Seven Lectures to Young Men*, pp. 178, 189.

23. Alcott, *The Young Man's Guide*, pp. 166-167.

24. Ibid., p. 159. Also see Arthur, p. 76 who warns his readers about seeking amusements as a means of "killing time." Such a decision "must enervate instead of [strengthen] the mind, and will inevitably hinder any young man from rising into distinguished positions of usefulness in society."

25. See Morantz, pp. 490-507 for a useful and brief discussion of the health reform movement. My reading of the role of sport in relation to aspects of this movement is based on a number of sources including the *Journal of Health* and the work of specific individuals, most notably Charles Caldwell, M.D., *Thoughts on Physical Education: Being a Discourse Delivered to a Convention of Teachers in Lexington, Kentucky on the sixth and seventh of November 1833* (Boston, 1834), and S.R. Calthrop, *Lecture on Physical Developments and its Relationship to Mental and Spiritual Development* (August, 1858). Also see Betts, "American Medical Thought," and "Mind and Body in Early American Thought," which clearly establishes the connection between health reform and interest in sport.

26. Caldwell, pp. 4, 22.

27. Calthrop, pp. 9-10. Michael Rogin, *Fathers and Children: Andrew Jackson and the Subjugation of the American Indian* (New York, 1976) clearly shows the concern of mid-nineteenth century American leaders over their inability to live up to the standards of the Founding Fathers.

28. Calthrop, p. 14.

29. Caldwell, pp. 13-16. Also see Betts, "Mind and Body in Early American Thought," p. 798.

30. Caldwell, p. 16.

31. For other examples see William P. Dewees, *A Treatise on the Physical and Medical Treatment of Children* (Philadelphia, 1842), pp. 228-40 and *The Journal of Health*, vol. IV (Feb., 1833), 161-65.

32. Caldwell, pp. 59-61.

33. Ibid., p.64.

34. Calthrop, p. 19, Caldwell, p. 61.

35. Calthrop, p. 19. For a witty and interesting statement of similar ideas see Thomas Wentworth Higginson, "Saints and Their Bodies," *Atlantic Monthly* (March, 1858), pp. 582-95.

36. Caldwell, pp. 91-92.

37. Calthrop, p. 21.

38. Works examined included William Clarke, *The Boy's Own Book, A Complete Encyclopedia of All the Diversions, Athletic, Scientific, and Recreative of Boyhood and Youth* (Boston, 1829); Robin Carver, *The Book of Sports* (Boston, 1834); Pierce Egan, *Sporting Anecdotes* (Philadelphia, 1822); Frank Forester, *Field Sports of the United States* (New York, 1856); _____, *The Complete Manual for Young Sportsmen* (New York, 1856); Paul Preston, *Book of Gymnastics or Sports for Youth* (Boston, n.d.); Horatio Smith, *Festivals, Games, and Amusements* (New York, 1831); *Children's Amusements* (New York, 1820), *The Boy's Book of Sports* (New Haven, 1839); *The Boy's Own Book of Amusements and Instruction* (Providence, 1843); *The Boy's Treasury of Sports, Pastimes, and Recreations,* fourth edition (New York, n.d.); and *Juvenile Pastimes* (New York, 1830). I also looked at several juvenile magazines including *The Juvenile Miscellany* (Boston, 1826) and the *Juvenile Gazette* (Providence, 1819).

39. Other books on field sports included William Elliott, *Carolina Sports by Land and Water* (New York, 1859) and E.J. Lewis, *Hints to Sportsmen* (Philadelphia, 1851).

40. *Juvenile Pastimes,* pp. 3-5.

41. *Children's Amusements,* p. 26.

42. Forester, *The Complete Manual for Young Sportsmen,* p. 29. The title page of Clarke's book contained the following poem. "A playground is an emblem of the world. /Its gamesome boys are men in miniature:/The most important action of the man/May find its parody 'mong childhood's sports;/And life itself, when longest, happiest, _____/ In boyhood's brief and jocund holiday."

43. Carver, pp. 61-63.

44. Forester, *Field Sports of the United States.*

45. Carver, pp. 83, 153-54.

46. *New York Weekly Herald,* May 17, 1845.

47. For an interesting discussion of rural popular sports of the lower classes in eighteenth and nineteenth century English society and the impact of the demands of an industrialized society on them, se Robert W. Malcolmnson, *Popular Recreations in English Society, 1700-1850* (London, 1973).

48. Joel Spring. "Mass Culture and School Sports," *History of Education Quarterly,* (Winter, 1974), 483-98, argues persuasively that aspects of mass sports in the United States during these years, including the spread of interscholastic sports on all levels and the popularity of college football and professional baseball as spectator sports, signified a conservative attempt "to maintain the existing social order" by controlling the frustrations of the working class and diverting them from disrupting society. Obviously this was not the only factor at work in precipitating what some historians have called a "sports explosion" in the late 19th and early 20th centuries. The commercial prospects inherent in the promotion of mass sports and the desire of the wealthy to define their status in part by their exclusive participation in certain sporting activities also influenced events. My point is that in the antebellum period, both in terms of actual developments in sport and in terms of the audience toward whom arguments in favor of sport were directed, there was no attempt to control a group or class considered to be subordinate. What I am describing is an effort by middle class reformers to shape the values of members of their own class in ways that would permit them to continue their involvement in the expression of a capitalist society while at the same time perceiving and encouraging a sense of order and stability. Not surprisingly, or-

ganized sport in these years, as evidenced by urban baseball clubs, college sport and the growth of spectator sport tended to be controlled by and aimed predominantly at middle and upper class audiences, in part as a means of giving such people a sense of status and place in society in which such distinctions were becoming more difficult to establish. For other explanations about the growth of sport in the late 19th century see Benjamin Rader, "The Quest for Subcommittees and the Rise of American Sport," *American Quarterly* 29 (Fall, 1977) 355-69, and Dale A. Somers, *The Rise of Sport in New Orleans, 1850-1900* (Baton Rouge, 1972).

• • •

Suggestions for Further Reading:

Barnett, Robert C., "The Development of Wrestling in the United States, 1607-1865," *The Physical Educator,* XXXV, 2 (May, 1978), 87-90.

Bennett, Bruce, "Sports in the South up to 1865," *Quest,* XXVII (Winter, 1977), 4-17.

_____, "The Making of Round Hill School," *Quest,* IV (April, 1965), 53-64.

Berryman, Jack. W., "The Tenuous Attempts of Americans to 'Catch Up with John Bull': Specialty Magazines and Sporing Journalism, 1800-1835," *Canadian Journal of History of Sport and Physical Education,* X (May, 1979), 40-61.

Betts, John R., "American Medical Thought on Exercise as the Road to Health, 1820-1860," *Bulletin of the History of Medicine,* XLV (1971), 138-145.

Brynn, Soeren Stewart, "Some Sports in Pittsburgh During the National Period, 1775-1860," *Western Pennsylvania Historical Magazine,* LI, 4 (October, 1968), 345-363; LII, 1 (January, 1969), 57-79.

Fielding, Lawrence W., "Gay and Happy Still: Holiday Sport in the Army of the Potomac," *Maryland Historian,* VII (Spring, 1976), 19-32.

_____, "Reflections from the Sport Mirror: Selected Treatments of Civil War Sport," *Journal of Sport History,* II, 2 (Fall, 1975), 132-144.

_____, "Sport: The Meter Stick of the Civil War Soldier," *Canadian Journal of Sport and Physical Education,* IX (May, 1978), 1-18.

_____, "War and Trifles: Sport in the Shadows of Civil War Army Life," *Journal of Sport History,* IV (Summer, 1977), 151-168.

Holliman, Jennis, *American Sports, 1785-1835* (Durham, NC: Seeman Press, 1931; reprint, Philadelphia: Porcupine Press, 1975).

Lewis, Guy M. "The Muscular Christianity Movement," *Journal of Health, Physical Education and Recreation,* XXXVII (May, 1966), 27-28, 42.

Lucas, John A. "A Prelude to the Rise of Sport: Antebellum America, 1850-1860," *Quest*, XI (December, 1968), 50-57.

Moss, George, "The Long Distance Runners of Antebellum America," *Journal of Popular Culture*, VIII, 2 (Fall, 1974), 370-382.

Park, Roberta, "The Attitudes of Leading New England Transcendentalists Toward Healthful Exercise, Active Recreations and Proper Care of the Body: 1830-1860," *Journal of Sport History*, IV (Spring, 1977), 34-50.

_____, "Harmony and Cooperation: Attitudes Towards Physical Education and Recreation in Utopian Social Thoughts and American Communitarian Experiments, 1825-1865," *Research Quarterly*, XLV (October, 1974), 276-292.

Wiggins, David K. "Good Times on the Old Plantation: Popular Recreations of the Black Slave in Antebellum South, 1810-1860," *Journal of Sport History*, IV (Fall, 1977), 260-284.

_____, "The Play of Slave Children in the Plantation Communities of the Old South, 1820-1860," *Journal of Sport History*, VII (Summer, 1980), 21-39.

_____, "Sport and Popular Pastimes: Shadow of the Slave-quarter," *Canadian Journal of History of Sport and Physical Education*, XI (May, 1980), 61-88.

_____, "Work, Leisure and Sport in America: The British Traveler's Image, 1839-1869," *Canadian Journal of History of Sport*, XIII (May, 1982), 28-60.

AMERICAN SPORTSWOMEN
IN THE 19TH CENTURY

Margery A. Bulger

Tracing the sporting habits of American women throughout the nineteenth century, Margery Bulger sees their activity closely tied to prevailing societal values affecting the role of women. Prior to the Civil War, these provided few opportunities for female athletes. The corsets that inhibited their physical movements symbolized the rigid social mores that restricted their identity to the home and its obligations. Protected from the unruliness associated with participation in sport, yet, paradoxically, credited with adding a sense of respectability to those few sporting events that tolerated their presence as spectators, women related to sport not only as they might have wished, but as men allowed.

The expanding variety, opportunity and social context of women's sports after the Civil War paralleled their struggle for equality, freedom and independence. As sports became more physically demanding, athletic fashions became less confining. The development of such team sports as basketball and field hockey provided an outlet for their competitive energies and the mutual reinforcement of their athletic interests. Women's colleges endorsed the ideas of Catherine Beecher and other advocates of physical exercise and early included recreational sports in their curricula.

The bicycle craze of the 1890s was a fitting symbol of a century's progress for women in sport. The "democratic" bicycle broke through the class barriers that had restricted participation levels and provided a leisure time activity that was enjoyable, accessible and healthful. Despite the fears raised by some that the bicycle "would be the ruination of the home" because it encouraged mothers to the wheel rather than to the care of their children and husbands, societal attitudes more accepting of women's athletics insured growth of such activity on the eve of the new century.

An American woman's place during the 18th and early 19th centuries was without question at home. Her recreation consisted of sewing circles, church suppers, arranging flowers and pouring tea. American customs, values and attitudes were strongly influenced by the English, and in 1748 Lord Chesterfield expressed a view of women that was subscribed to by most American men and women will into the 19th century. "Women," he argued,

> are to be regarded as children of a larger growth; ... a man of sense only trifles with them, plays with them, humours and flatters them ...; but he neither consults nor trusts them with serious matters; though he often makes them believe he does both.[1]

No American democrat of the 19th century would have called the female sex inferior or unequal. Her place was only different, and because by nature she was pure, gentle and charming, she was to be protected from the rough and tumble world of work, politics and sport. Wifehood and motherhood were considered the purpose of woman's being, and for a woman to be interested in her own pleasures and self-fulfillment was against the nature of "true womanhood." In the early 1800s society had great antipathy to ladies in gigs, all skating was strictly forbidden, it was absolutely unheard of to ride to the hounds, and sliding was permitted only if a lady had a gentleman to support her on each side. Should she violate the code, her fate was clear. "We would not marry a downright, thoroughgoing, hurdle jumping, racing pace, fox-hunting lady, if she had the planet Jupiter for her portion."[2] Such threats to athletically inclined women were common in the magazines and newspapers of the time, and it is little wonder that women hesitated to partake of the sporting life.

Even for gentlemen there were very few organized sports before the Civil War. Most sports took place in the cities, and, like the English, America's interest in sports was casual and non-competitive. Gentlemen of the upper-class were members of the yachting, cricket and baseball clubs, and horse racing was extremely popular as were the field sports of hawking and fox hunting. The lower and middle class men were more likely to spend their leisure activities which required less time and money; animal baiting, prize fighting and betting on professional runners. Some women were spectators at these events, and particularly at the horse race courses elaborate preparations were taken to make them comfortable. By the 1830s, ladies' stands at the races were common. The gentlemen frequently encouraged the women to be spectators because they believed it gave a sense of respectability to sport and served to rid it of evil influences.

The first sport to become acceptable for women as participants was horseback riding. *The American Farmer,* the *Spirit of the Times,* and *Godey's Lady's Book* all commented on horsemanship for ladies.

The American Farmer was the earliest American periodical to include sports information, and by 1828 the editors were encouraging women to ride, providing they were not too manly about it:

> This is a graceful accomplishment for a lady, says Major Noah, and we are pleased to see it cultivated by their taking lessons ... We have not, however, been able to discover the reason why a lady preparing to "witch the world with horsemanship," should think right to comparison herself, with a heavy riding habit and a man's hat ... if it requires a change of dress, it does not demand one so very heroic and masculine.[3]

It was allowable for a female to ride a horse as long as she preserved her feminine character for grace and delicacy.[4]

Godey's Lady's Book was first published in 1830, and soon it was read by more women than any other periodical of the time, reaching a circulation of 150,000 before the Civil War. Although primarily a magazine of literature and poetry, instruction for horsemanship and dancing appeared in the very first issues.[5] Proper women were instructed to ride side-saddle attired in feminine clothing, with a groom nearby to help with mounting. Racing and riding to the hounds were expressly frowned upon, but there is evidence that at least some women were bold enough to take up these sports. John Allen writing in the American Farmer in 1830 said: "We do not, while thus admiring a lady on horseback, recommended that she should be able to keep up with the hounds in a stag or fox chase, like Lady ———; nor run races for high bets, like Mrs. Thornton."[6]

Women in the South rode more than their Northern sisters, although there were riding academies in New York and Boston. By the 1850s it was a fairly common sight to see women riding at the agricultural fairs throughout the country. The earliest journal to report these equestrian events was the *New York Clipper,* founded in 1853 by Frank Queen. In 1858 the *Clipper* reported on the Ladies Equestrian Convention noting that "there were upwards of four thousand persons assembled to witness it ... and the most sanguine of the projectors must have found the result to exceed his expectations."[7]

It should not be assumed that American women were unique when they began horseback riding. Women throughout the world had been riding horses for centuries. In medieval times Englishwomen had been very fond of the sport. They went hawking, shot rabbits with bows and arrows, and hunted stag. An English publication on the history of women on horseback concluded that medieval "women were not only experts at falconry—which was practised on horseback—but they even excelled the men in their knowledge and skill of the great sport of the time."[8] 19th century American women did not participate in falconry nor did they hunt on horseback, but they did ride for pleasure and occasionally they raced for a wager.

Pedestrianism or foot racing enjoyed a period of great popularity in the 1840s and 1850s. Although not acceptable to the "ladies of society," some women did compete in foot racing both in America and England. *The New York Clipper* reported in 1853 that Kate Irvine, an American, who in 1852 had walked 500 miles in 500 consecutive hours at Aston Cross Grounds in Birmingham ... "has commenced a fresh engagement of walking 580 ... There was a strong muster to see her start."[9]

The *American Farmer*, quoting the *Glasgow Herald*, reported a pedestrian match of 15 miles between an American woman and a man. During the first eight miles the woman led, but eventually she was passed and lost. The man had announced that if he was beaten by a woman, he would never again revisit his paternal mansion.[10]

Some women even became professional runners. Madamoiselle Eugenie La Fosse of Paris, Miss Lucy Reynolds of Liverpool, and "the fleet and celebrated Indian squaw Ba-Tu-uch-o-ua-ra, of the Cherokee tribe," agreed to race in Jackson Square in New Orleans for a set of jewelry.[11]

Throughout the 1850s, *The Clipper* continued to encourage athletic activities for women, and a few women ventured beyond horseback riding and pedestrianism. "Good for Miss Curtis, she gave a good specimen of rifle practice at a shooting gallery in Saratoga last week."[12] "Let them go a fishing," wrote the *Clipper* editor, "anything to draw our women from the everlasting, treadmill round of kitchen, pantry, and sitting room."[13]

Antebellum American women were not know for their robust good health and English visitors were often critical of their poor posture and lack of energy. Catherine Beecher, a pioneer educator, was one of the earliest and most influential leaders to stress the value of exercise for women. As early as 1827, Beecher hired an English lady to teach what later became known as calisthenics at the Hartford Female Seminary. In 1847 she included advice on exercise in lectures on women's rights,[14] and in 1856 she published a book entitled *Physiology and Calisthenics*.[15]

The ladies' department of the *American Farmer* suggested more exercise for girls and women and recommended trundling a hoop, battledore and trap-door for girls under twelve years of age. "For girls above the age of twelve," the magazine ascribed, "such exercises may not be allowable, except under particular circumstances of privacy."[16] Women were warned that all exercise should be done with extreme caution, for when the body is "too much exercised, it likewise is apt to produce ganglions on the ankle joints of delicate girls, as wind galls are produced on the legs of young horses who are too soon or too much worked."[17]

Prior to the Civil War, Victorian society dictated that American women should seek their exercise from walking, a little dancing, and possibly horseback riding (side saddle, and usually very tightly corsetted). Limited by restrictive dress and rigid social mores, there was very little the female athlete could do. Baseball, cricket and yachting required more physical effort than women thought they could withstand; cockfighting and animal baiting were gambled sports and not considered appropriate; croquet and archery were scarcely known before the 1860s; and tennis, golf and the bicycle had not yet appeared.

During the Civil War, most sporting activity for both men and women ceased. Many of the gentlemen's yachting clubs, gymnastic societies and baseball and cricket teams dissolved very shortly after the beginning of the war. When the war ended in 1865, there began a rapid growth in organized sport. Rising industrialism and a move toward a more urban society resulted in sport becoming less casual and more commercial. Horse racing, boxing, baseball and professional running were soon organized as spectator sports. Athletics began to be more democratic. Baseball, for instance, had been introduced and played by aristocratic males in the 1840s and 1850s, but in the 1860s it became the game for everyone. There were even some attempts to organize women's professional baseball teams. In New Orleans in 1879 one authority noted that "a large crowd of miscellaneous people went to the Fair Grounds to watch a team of girls who refused to play until each received ten dollars."[18] A man named Harry H. Freeman tried sponsoring a women's travelling baseball team in the 1860s, but he was accused of recruiting girls for a profession much older than baseball.[19] The insinuation that women baseball players were prostitutes was probably not uncommon in the 19th century. Women who played "men's sports," especially where they could be seen, were labeled as loose and vulgar, and very few were willing to sacrifice their reputations for the sake of sport.

Baseball was also played in the women's colleges and here it was somewhat more respectable, for the girls were usually protected from public view while they played. There was a Laurel Baseball Club at Vassar College in 1866 and match games were played every Saturday afternoon.[20] In 1897, Sophia Richardson reminisced about her undergraduate days at Vassar:

About twenty years ago, when I was a freshman, seven or eight baseball clubs suddenly came into being, spontaneously as it seemed, but I think they owed their existence to a few quiet suggestions from a resident physician, wise beyond her generation. The public so far as it knew of our playing was shocked.[21]

Croquet was the first new sport introduced after the Civil War, and it soon became popular among women. Unlike the men, the ladies did not yet compete in tournaments, but croquet did serve to get the ladies out of doors, and for the first time men and women were able to participate in a sport together.

Industrialization brought more wealth and more leisure to more Americans, and middle and upper-class women experienced more freedom than they had ever known. They began to expand their interests to activities outside of the home, and, as new sports were introduced, the women were often the first and most enthusiastic participants.

An Englishman, James L. Plimpton, invented roller skating and soon both ice skating and roller skating became fashionable activities for women. Bowling was another popular sport with the ladies. Originally bowling was played with nine pins. In an attempt to eliminate gamblers, Connecticut outlawed bowling at 9 pins; so a tenth pin was added and the sport continued—much to the pleasure of women in all classes of society. *The New York Clipper* in 1868 reported that a woman had bowled a 300 and a 290 game on the same night.[22]

Archery was probably the first organized, competitive sport for women. Men and women had been using the bow and arrow for target practice in the 1840s and '50s, but in 1859 a woman wrote to Frank Queen, editor of the *New York Clipper*, and inquired where she might buy archery equipment.

> I have for some time been sorely puzzled to find out what particular amusement ladies might with propriety indulge in, of which, however, my mind was relieved in your mention of archery ... When I am sufficiently expert and I have taught my lady friends, (at least as many of them who are not too modest) I shall endeavor to get up a tournament.[23]

By 1877 tournament archery had become popular, and in 1879 the National Archery Association was formed and the first national tournament was held. Women were included as members of most of the Archery Clubs from the beginning and participated in the tournaments wearing their club colors. In fact the colors appear to have overshadowed other considerations.

> Our only really serious difficulty (in organizing a club) was in selecting bows for the ladies. It did not matter so to them what the weight of the bow was, or the kind of wood it was made of, or its general usefulness, or its price, so long as the color of the plush on the handle matched the costume of the owner, and it

really did bother us to find the necessary shades of color in plush handles.[24]

A table showing the number of men and women participants in the early National Archery Championships was presented in *Outing* in 1884. There were twenty females and fifty-four males in the first tournament held in 1879.[25] Archery was a very social sport, and for most women the sociability far out-weighed the competition, but the reported scores indicate that at least some of the women were fairly serious about winning. The National Tournament for women consisted of the National Round (24 arrows at 50 yards and 48 arrows at 60 yards), shot twice. Henry Hall, reminiscing about the growth of archery, reported in 1887 that, "I have not at hand data as to the best National rounds by women: but if I remember correctly both Mrs. Hornblow and Mrs. Marshall have reached nearly to 800, and Mrs. Legh once scored 867."[26]

The game of lawn tennis, an outdoor game derived from court tennis, made its way from France to England, and in 1873, Major Walton Clopton Wingfield had a Christmas party and for the occasion printed a pamphlet called "The Major's Game of Lawn Tennis, Dedicated to the Party assembled in Nantclwyd in December, 1873." Thus were the first rules of lawn tennis published.[27] Lawn tennis was soon introduced to America and by the 1880s women were playing the game at many of the private clubs in the country. In seeking exercise and recreation there were few proper sports a woman could choose from, but tennis became one of them. It was the one fairly vigorous athletic game a woman could enjoy without being subjected to insinuations of rompishness.

Most sports historians now agree that it was a woman, Mary Outerbridge, who first introduced lawn tennis to America in 1874. In 1887, Charles E. Clay completed an early history of the Staten Island Cricket Club:

> As far as I have been able to learn, there appear to be two somewhat conflicting traditions relating to the introduction of lawn tennis, and my gallantry to the fair sex, as well as the preponderance of corroborative evidence, compels me to say, that I am inclined to support a story as ascribes the advent of this distinguished game ... to the enterprise of a lady.[28]

Malcolm D. Whitman, author of *Tennis Origins and Mysteries* and the winner of the National Tennis Championship in 1898, 1899 and 1900, proved through an examination of the official customs records and travel documents that Outerbridge returned to New York from Bermuda on February 2, 1874, equipped with tennis racquets and balls. She convinced her brother and the other male members of the Staten Island

Cricket and Baseball Club (the ladies club had not yet come into existence) to lay out a lawn tennis court in the spring of 1874.[29] Two different dates have been claimed for a "first" court in Nahant, Massachusetts, but both are later than the spring of 1874.

Lawn tennis continued to grow in popularity throughout the 1880s and 1890s, but until 1888 there were few tournaments open to women. Their long skirts, tight corsets and large hats prevented them from making the game physically demanding. Several writers of the time, principally men, tried to encourage the women to be more active in their tennis. Writing in 1883, one journalist chided the clubs:

> None of the clubs that hold open tournaments admit ladies to membership ... That such should be the case, there is not adequate reason ... It has been objected that ladies would not like the publicity that would attach to their appearance as contestants in open tournament. American ladies, now and for several years past, do and have taken part in open competitions in archery ... The fact is that archery, like tennis, is too refined a sport to offer any attractions to the more vulgar elements of society.[30]

John Habberton, in an article in *Outing* in 1885, was the earliest writer in this periodical to encourage the women to become more competitive in sports, so that they might realize some physical development:

> Of all womanly recreations out-of-doors there is most hope in lawn tennis; there would be more—a great deal more— if the game were as popular for purposes of exercise; as it is for bringing the young people of both sexes together ... however, it is useless to expect them (ladies) to dress as they should to enjoy the fullest possibilities of physical exercise. Once in a while a red-cheeked, bright-eyed girl may be seen completely absorbed in the game and dressed so as to give her arms and lungs full play, but...he advent of man...causes a woman to quickly encase herself in the feminine substitute for a strait-jacket.[31]

By 1888 women were involved in tournament tennis, although society was likely to frown if they played too hard or too well. Writers like Henry Slocum cautioned the women not to become too skillful. "In the opinion of some impartial critics the woman who is unfortunate enough to defeat all others and win a tournament 'plays just like a man,' and is too ungraceful for anything."[32] It was considered unladylike and dangerous to play with vigor, and it was universally accepted that the gentler sex should play the game differently from the men. "It does not seem impossible," remarked Slocum,

> that a woman should be able to smash and smash skillfully too. But can she learn to smash, volley and play all of the other difficult strokes of lawn tennis without sacrificing a certain amount of grace? The question is a serious one for tennis could become deprived of that feature which has distinctly marked it as the most refined and unprofessional of all the athletic games.[33]

In 1888 the United States National Lawn Tennis Association for the first time formally recognized a women's championship tournament. The tournament was held in Philadelphia where Bertha Townsend easily defeated U.F. Hansell for the championship. Townsend successfully defended her title in 1889 and became known as the best lady tennis player in America. Women had a national tournament and America had a lady tennis champion, but American women remained far behind their English counterparts in aggressiveness and skill on the court.

Lawn tennis was by no means a universal sport among American women. Playing tennis was limited to those socially advantaged women who could afford to play and who were accepted into the private clubs. The game was important in the development of women's sports, however because it gave them, for the first time, a sport with a potential for fast vigorous physical activity. Prior to lawn tennis, the only activities open to women were horseback riding, a little rowing, archery and croquet. At this time gymnasiums for women were almost unknown, and the woman's bicycle and the game of golf had not yet made their way to America.

The calibre of play among women tennis players was severely limited by social custom and by the type of costume they wore. As late as 1901 the recommended dress for women players was a skirt six to eight inches above the ankles. In one of the first published books on women's sports, Parmly Paret wrote that, "It is much wiser to play without corsets, although it must be admitted that few women do."[34] One of the early and most influential leaders to advocate dress reform for the athletic woman was Dudley A. Sargent of Harvard. He researched the effect of the corset on the physical performance of women and wrote extensively on the subject. "When we reflect," observed Dr. Sargent,

> that women has constricted her body for centuries, we believe that to this fashion alone is due much of her failure to realize her best opportunities for [physical] development ... the girls' corsets must be taken off ... As to skirts—what shall we say of

them? They have hampered the progress of civilized women for
three thousand years ... during exercise the skirt should be worn
to the knee, or should be changed to the bloomer.[35]

As more and more women took to sports, their fashions slowly
began to change. Women needed greater freedom of movement so they
began to shorten their skirts, wear fewer petticoats, and the more daring
even removed their corsets.

In addition to introducing the sport to America, women can
claim one other first in tennis. In 1905 May Sutton, wearing less clothing
than was considered appropriate, became the first American (male or
female) to win at Wimbledon, England. That was significant because it
was not until 1920, when "Big Bill" Tilden won the singles title, that an
American man was successful at this tournament.

In the mid-1880s a marvel of technology appeared that was
extremely important to the growth of women's sports. A chain-driven
vehicle known as the "safety" bicycle was developed and women
everywhere fell prey to the wheel. The bicycle craze lasted only about ten
years, but it was an important agent of social change, especially for
middle-class women. Limited by money, social status and the lack of
leisure time, many women were denied the opportunities to participate in
archery, tennis and croquet, but they were soon bicycling by the
thousands. It was also as a result of the bicycle that women's fashions
began to change quickly. The bulky skirt was soon replaced by divided
skirts and bloomers. Manufacturers everywhere began to create the
"bicycle costume," which was soon used for other out-of-door activities,
and American women experienced a higher sense of independence,
mobility and freedom than they had ever known.

Prior to the invention of the "safety," very few women had
chanced riding the "ordinary" bicycle with its huge front driving wheel,
but they did ride the tricycle. In 1885 two articles appeared in *Outing*[36] on
the sport of tricycling for ladies, and in 1888, in the same periodical,
there was a first person report of "The Ladies Eastern Tricycle Tour from
Merrimac to Naumkeag."[37] As was true with tennis and archery, tricycling
was an activity for the socially elite. Most tricycling was sponsored by
clubs, and the machines were very expensive and beyond the means of
most middle class women. The "woman's safety," however, made
bicycling less of a sport for specialists and the privileged few and more of
a leisure time activity for the masses. As a result of the bicycle it became
possible for women of all ages and all walks of life to participate in an
activity equally with men.

The sport's literature of the time began to reflect this change in the
leisure habits of women, and although most of it was supportive there were
many who were opposed to cycling by ladies. Initially the medical

profession was non-committed, but as more and more women began to ride, "there was a solemn wagging of grey beards and a low pitched murmur of 'grave consequences' to be anticipated."[38]

> There were fears that the bicycle would be the ruination of the home. While the ladies were out wheeling, who would take care of the children? There were others who claimed that riding the bicycle was making women muscular and masculine. Writing in 1899, Dr. Arabella Kenealy made a strong claim that it was against women's nature to be muscular and that women everywhere were losing their charm as a result of the "bicycle face" (a face of muscular tension). "Her movements are muscular and less womanly," asserted Dr. Kenealy, where they had been quiet and graceful, now they are abrupt and direct. Her voice is louder, her tones assertive ... All that I urge is that what she does she shall doe in a womanly way ... All that I would warn her against is the error into which she has been temporarily led, the error of supposing there is any nobler sphere than that of home.[39]

An angry reply to Dr. Kenealy's article appeared one month later. L. Ormiston Chant argued that the development of muscle did not suddenly bring about a radical change in character, and "turn a conscientious unselfish girl into a cold and unfeeling lump of human clay."[40] Chant was wise beyond her time when she claimed that muscular development did not result in a woman becoming more manly, but rather it emphasized the sex differences, and that the most beautiful bodies, both male and female, were to be found in Barnum and Bailey's acrobats.[41] Chant concluded her attack on Dr. Kenealy's position with an observation that is as appropriate for the women's rights movement of the 1980s as it was eighty years ago.

> In conclusion, it is to be hoped that "modern woman" will go on her way in spite of all the scolding and denunciation the unmodern woman hurls at her from time to time. There will doubtless always be the rude and unruly folk in all ranks and conditions of life—but it is a pity to fall into the unscientific mistake of generalizing from a few individual cases, and dignifying these with the big name of prototype ... So let us modern women take heart of grace, and go on doing the best we can to develop muscular vigor, along with a sneaking fondness for frills and pleating, and an openly avowed adhesion to the Eternal Baby, and its father.[42]

It was undoubtedly the bicycle craze of the 1890s that caused more people than ever to question the role of women in athletics. Their participation was no longer confined to the privacy of clubs. They came out on the roadways for everyone to see.

In the early 1890s golf became popular in America and it was especially suited to the "genteel nature" of women. They took an interest in the game from the beginning and the development of golf in America owes a great deal to the significant role they played in the organization and maintenance of the growing number of golf clubs. From the beginning almost all of the clubs admitted women, and at least one, the Shinnecock Hills Club in New York, laid a nine hole course for women only. On December 22, 1894 a call went out for a general meeting of golf clubs to which five clubs responded and formed the United States Golf Association.

The first U.S.G.A. Women's Championship was held in 1895 at the Meadow Brook Club, Long Island. Mrs. C.S. Brown was the winner, shooting 132 for 18 holes. For the next three years—1896, 1897, 1998—the championship was won by Beatrix Hoyt, a pioneer in the achievement of excellence in sport, and America's first great woman golfer. Her prowess was described in print: "Miss Hoyt can outdrive, on the average, seven out of ten of her ordinary masculine rivals. She has acquired the knack of getting the ball away clean and can count upon an average distance of one hundred and twenty to one hundred and sixty yards."[43] Hoyt was typical of the young and fashionable women who participated in golf. She was the grand-daughter of Salmon P. Chase, Secretary of the Treasury under President Lincoln and later Chief Justice of the United States. She was the niece of a United States Senator, and her father had sufficient money and social standing to allow him to retire early.[44] When Beatrix Hoyt died in 1961 at the age of 82, her obituary in the *New York Times* reported that "she was only sixteen years old, in leg-of-mutton sleeves, wearing a long skirt and with her hair in pigtails, when she smashed through her first National Championship in 1896."[45] Hoyt was one of only four women to win the National Championship three times, and she was the first woman to qualify for the tournament with a score under 100. In the 1896 tournament Hoyt shot a qualifying round of 95.[46]

The playing of tennis and golf took place chiefly at country clubs and because of this they received far more publicity than other sporting activities, but by the 1890s women were involved in a wide variety of other outdoor activities. There is evidence that many women hunted, fished, sailed, fenced and bowled. In the spring and summer of 1890, the following titles appeared in *Outing*: "Women and Their Guns,"[47] "Bowling for Women,"[48] "A New Hand at the Rod,"[49] and "Ladies at the Helm."[50] American women were constantly being told that they needed to catch up with their English sisters in pursuing out-of-doors sports, and such articles encouraged them to do so. Almost any sport was open to them as long as they retained their "feminine dignity." F.C. Sumichrost in an article encouraging women to take up sailing, editorialized:

> In a word, nearly every sport pursued by men has become in the present day more or less a favorite with the ladies: and as far as these sports do not overtax their strength and the pursuit of them does not involve any loss of that grace and charm of femininity which when all is said and done is the crown and glory of woman, there can be no valid reason given why ladies should not be encouraged to benefit themselves by frequent open-air life.[51]

Women's sports throughout the 19th century were largely confined to those in the upper classes of society, but following the Civil War the so-called "gentlemen's sports" became more democratic. Horse racing and baseball became popular pastimes for all classes, and the upper classes failed to monopolize many of the new sports, including American football and roller skating. Sport after sport fell to the professional and the amateurs. The concept of the gentleman sportsman who played solely for pleasure was in jeopardy. In an attempt to preserve the amateur status of sport, men began forming athletic clubs, which in turn led to the formulation of the Amateur Athletic Union in 1888. In the early days of these clubs, women were not permitted membership, but it was the custom to send out notices to the men to bring the ladies with them to the club games, "in order that athletics might be made as respectable as they were in England."[52]

By the 1890s the athletic clubs began to build facilities for women. One of the first was the Berkeley Ladies Athletic Club in New York. This club was an outgrowth of the well known Berkeley Athletic Club, "a club," said the *Fortnightly Review*, "which counts the best men in New York among the members. These gentlemen, wishing their wives and daughters to have gymnastic training ... came together and set on foot the project of a ladies branch at a cost of $200,000."[53] The ladies club was very well equipped with baths, bowling alleys, a gymnasium fitted for gymnastic training, and private dressing rooms with maids in attendance. It was quite the thing to belong to the Berkeley.

In 1894, twenty years after Mary Outerbridge had introduced lawn tennis to the Staten Island Cricket Club, women finally got a clubhouse of their own, and the *New York Times* reported the dedication in the following manner:

The formal opening of the pretty clubhouse of the Staten Island Ladies Club, occurred this afternoon. More than 300 well known Staten Island people were present and the affair proved one of the most successful ever held under the auspices of the club. Luncheon was served in a tent on the lawn, while an orchestra provided music for dancing, the smooth turf of the tennis courts serving as a ballroom.[54]

These athletic clubs played an important role in the development of women's sports. It became fashionable to be athletic. The clubs were ultra-exclusive, and memberships were expensive and restricted to the very rich, and along with the simultaneous development of collegiate sports for women, these clubs helped free the American woman from the confining aspects of Victorian society by giving respectability to physical fitness and athletics.

The early women's colleges included exercise and gymnastics as a part of the curriculum. Mary Lyon, the founder of Mount Holyoke Seminary, was recommending physical exercise for women as early as 1837. In the very first Mount Holyoke catalogue an hour a day of domestic duties was required. Lyon justified these duties as a means of saving money and as a method for furnishing the students with some daily exercise. "Regularity of exercise," said Lyon, "promotes health as surely as does systematic study."[55] In all the colleges the primary reason for teaching exercise was to cure physical defects and promote good health so the girls could better withstand the mental rigors of study. A typical class in physical training involved the rhythmical exercises of Swedish gymnastics of calisthenics based on Lewis's work.

In 1865 Vassar College opened, and Matthew Vassar considered physical training one of the fundamentals in the education of women. Facilities were provided for gymnastic activities, bowling, and horseback riding. It was also at Vassar College that the first instruction in activities other than calisthenics and gymnastics was given. The 1865 Vassar catalogue described the program thusly:

In addition to the ordinary system of school calisthenics ... the plan of the college includes instruction in Swimming, Skating, and Gardening ... A beautifully tended pond on the premises is available for boating in the summer and skating in the winter. A suitable portion of each day is set aside for physical exercise and every young lady is required to observe it as one of her college duties.[56]

As other colleges opened their doors to women, similar programs in physical training were established, and some of these followed Vassar's lead and began including sports and games as a part of the curriculum.

In the early 1890s at least three factors combined to change the focus of college physical education programs. First, the sports craze had hit America and more and more girls were entering college with experience in games. They soon became bored with the dull routine of the college exercise programs. Second, basketball was invented. And third, the psychology of G. Stanley Hall, Edward Thorndyke and John Dewey was emphasizing that learning should be fun and interesting.

The two sports which became most popular with college women were tennis and basketball. These games introduced a competitive element into the women's sports that had not been present in the boating, skating and walking activities of previous years. As a result of this increased interest in sports, women's athletic associations were organized to sponsor events, and in the 1890s bicycle clubs, walking clubs, tennis and boating clubs were numerous.

In 1891, when the game of basketball was invented by Dr. James Naismith of the Springfield Training School, it was enthusiastically received by women. In 1892 Smith College introduced basketball for women, and soon there were basketball clubs at most of the women's colleges. Basketball was the first *team* game played by any significant number of women. There had been some earlier attempts to organize women's baseball and women did play doubles in tennis, but the concept of team play was completely new to them. Hence in the earlier days of basketball it was very common for a girl to simply hold the ball until she was able to try for a goal. It never occurred to her to pass it to a teammate.[57]

It was as much to encourage teamwork as to prevent fatigue and roughness that basketball rules were revised for women. In 1899 a committee of collegiate directors of women's physical education adopted a standardized set of rules for basketball. In the revised rules the court was divided into three equal parts: forwards and guards played in the end section and the centers in the middle section. Girls could dribble the ball only three times in succession, and the ball could not be snatched or taken away from any player's hands. No guarding could be done over the body of an opponent who had the ball, nor could the ball be held longer than three seconds. This committee was the first attempt to control women's sports in colleges, and they set a pattern which was to be followed for other sports, namely, to revise the game rules so the events did not become too physically demanding or too rough.

Arguments for and against the advisability of women playing "men's basketball" continued well into the 20th century. Generally, it was the college directors of physical education who most strongly supported the revised rules. "Under the men's rules," they argued, "our girls were not

successful. They became exhausted before time was called, due to the
excitement of the game ... and since each player is limited to a certain
territory, severe strain is alleviated.[58] Those opposed to the women's
rules asserted:

> Nothing can be more harmful than to have players straining
> across the lines in every conceivable position trying to maintain
> their balance. This is an unnatural expression, without joy or
> exhilaration, while running freely for a ball contains both ...
> The girl's rules also prevent team work. While more persons can
> play, they frequently do little more than stand around in each
> other's way.[59]

In the colleges and most of the secondary schools the revised
rules won out, and women's basketball was born. There is little doubt that
college women readily endorsed this new sport. Writing in 1898 about
sports at Wellesley College, Jeannette Marks noted that:

> Basketball has become such a popular sport that even the
> members of the faculty have taken it up. In the evening, after
> dinner, strange shadows may be seen flitting to and fo before
> the gymnasium windows. This pedagogical team has threatened
> to play the students someday.[60]

The College athletic associations began to organize field days for
competition in basketball, track and field, and other activities. This
marked the beginning of intercollegiate competition for women. The
female directors of physical education, especially in the Eastern colleges,
were generally opposed to this competition. "Among other reasons,"
they declared,

> it is thought that the strain on the players would be too great;
> that the tendency would be too narrow rather than to increase
> the number of players by raising the standard of excellence of
> play and discouraging the less expert players; also that interc-
> lass contests afford all the advantages of intercollegiate games
> without the objectionable feature of the latter.[61]

While basketball continued to thrive, college women were
introduced to another team game in the early 1900s. The English game of
field hockey was presented to the girls of Vassar College by Constance
Applebee in 1901. While there is evidence that field hockey was played in
this country before the arrival of Applebee, it was largely through her
efforts that the game became so popular at the Eastern women's colleges.

Prior to 1901 field hockey was played by men at the Springfield Training School and Dr. J.H. McCurdy of the Springfield school, in writing of the game, said: "The men at Springfield first played the game of field hockey in 1897. Regarding where field hockey was first played in this country—(by women) the girls at Mount Holyoke College, had begun playing the game, I think, before Miss Applebee's arrival in this country."[62] Following a demonstration of the game at the Harvard Summer School of 1901, Applebee was invited to teach field hockey at Vassar College. Later she gave instruction at Smith, Bryn Mawr, Radcliffe and Mount Holyoke. In 1922, Applebee opened her famous Mount Pocono Hockey Camp. Field hockey never achieved the national popularity of basketball, and it was almost the exclusive property of women in colleges or in the fashionable hockey clubs located on the Eastern seaboard.

By the turn of the century, college women were engaging in tennis, basketball, field hockey, rowing, winter sports, track and field, and aquatic carnivals. The college curricula offered a variety of sports instruction, and the athletic associations were sponsoring inter-school and inter-class competition. The coeds of the 1890s pursued athletic competition with moderation, but they did begin to count accomplishment in sports almost as important as French or music.

When the 19th century ended American women enjoyed a freer life. They could ride a horse without the services of a groom; they could straddle a horse; they could run, cycle and take part in a great variety of athletic games without being less a woman. This growth of women's athletics coincided closely with women's struggle for equality, freedom and independence. More and more women had begun to take charge of their own lives and their own bodies. They were interested in controlling the size of their families, and by 1850 the birth rate had fallen twenty percent below the figure for 1800.[63] Early feminists such as Susan Anthony, Lucretia Mott and Elizabeth Cady Stanton had urged women to become better educated and to take a more active role in public affairs. During this year of reform there were major changes in the behavior and thoughts of women and as they broke out of the confines of home life and entered the public arena, they turned to sport as one avenue of freedom.

The opposition to women in sport began to diminish in the immediate post-Civil War period when several new, less physically demanding sports were introduced. By 1876 it was proper and even fashionable to play croquet, shoot the bow and arrow, and tap the ball back and forth on the lawn tennis court. But it was the bicycle craze of the 1890s that had the most profound effect on women's sports movement. By 1896, thousands of American women were wheeling. As they became more vigorous and aggressive, their skirts began to shorten and their corsets began to disappear. Women were finally free to engage in a more varied and strenuous sports life.

The women pursued these new athletics with "feminine charm and dignity" and participation generally was limited to those with money, social status and leisure. Shortly after the Civil War, the upper classes had lost their hold on baseball, horse racing and billiards, but the democratization of "women's sports," golf, tennis and archery, came much later. These sports required expensive equipment and membership in private clubs and thus they remained the exclusive property of the upper classes. By 1900 the cycling fad had ended, and its disappearance resulted in a decrease in outdoor life for great numbers of women. Golf and tennis, the aristocrats of sport, did not take the place of the democratic bicycle. Sports for women in rural America and for those who worked in the factories did not show any significant growth until the 20th century.

Sports gave 19th century women the chance to demonstrate the physical side of their nature, and although they universally believed that better health was the primary and only reason to play, women soon discovered that self-fulfillment, confidence and self-esteem were other outcomes of sport. Athletics also served as an opportunity for women to see themselves as individuals instead of subordinates. It might well be concluded that when women took up tennis and golf and the bicycle, they not only improved their health, but they also made a great stride toward real emancipation.

• • •

Notes

1. "Female Education," *Godey's Lady's Book* 3 (1890), 29.
2. Sylvanus Swanquill, "Feminine Fox Hunters," *New York Sporting Magazine and Annals of American and English Turf* (1834), 505-6, in J. Holliman, *American Sports, 1785-1835* (Durham, NC: Seeman Press, 1931), p. 163.
3. "Riding on Horseback," *American Farmer* 10 (June 1928), 95.
4. John Allen, "Ladies on Horseback," *American Farmer* 12 (June 1830), 94.
5. *Godey's Lady's Book* 1 (1830), 33-34, 146-148.
6. Allen, "Ladies on Horseback," p. 94.
7. *New York Clipper*, 18 Sept. 1850, p, 170.
8. "Women on Horseback," *Women's World* (London: Cassell and Co., 1899), p. 228.
9. *New York Clipper*, 18 June 1853, p. 181.
10. *American Farmer* 4 (Jan. 10, 1923), 415.
11. "Spirit of the Times," 8 June 1850 in Dale Somers, *The Rise of Sports in New Orleans, 1850-1900* (Baton Rouge: Louisiana State Univ. Press, 1972), p. 62.
12. *New York Clipper*, 1 Aug. 1857, p. 114.

13. *New York Clipper*, 8 Aug. 1857, p. 146.

14. Catharine E. Beecher, "The Evils Suffered by American Women and American Children: the Causes and the Remedy." An address prepared by Miss Beecher and delibered by her brother to meetings of ladies in New York and other cities (New York: Harper & Bros., 1847).

15. Elizabeth Mae Harveson, *Catharine Esther Beecher, Pioneer Educator* (Lancaster, PA: Science Press Printing Co., 1932; reprinted by the Arno Press and *The New York Times,* 1969), p. 50.

16. "Of the Exercises Most Conducive to Health in Girls and Young Women," *American Farmer* 9 (Oct. 26, 1827), 254.

17. Ibid.

18. Somers, *The Rise of Sports in New Orleans,* 1850-1900, p. 118.

19. Ibid., p. 119.

20. Harriet Ballentine, *The History of Physical Training at Vassar College* (Poughkeepsie, NY: Lansing & Bros., N.D.), p. 9.

21. Sophia Foster Richardson, "Tendencies in Athletics for Women in Colleges and Universities," *Popular Science Monthly* 50 (Feb. 1897), 517.

22. *New York Clipper*, 20 Sept. 1868, p. 148.

23. *New York Clipper,* 28 May 1858, p. 44.

24. Maumee, "Modern Archery in America," *Outing* 4 (June 1884), 35.

25. Ibid.

26. Henry Hall, *The Tribune Book of Open Air Sports* (New York Tribune, 1887), p. 15.

27. Robet Henderson, *Ball, Bat and Bishop* (New York: Rockport Press Inc., 1947), p. 125.

28. C.E. Clay, "The Staten Island Cricket and Baseball Club," *Outing* 11 (Nov. 1887), 104.

29. Malcomb Whitman, *Tennis, Origins and Mysteries* (New York: The Derrydale Press, 1932), pp. 118-132.

30. Alfred B. Starey, "Lawn Tennis in America," *The Wheelman Illustrated* 2 (Sept. 1883), 467-68.

31. John Habberton, "Open-Air Recreation for Women," *Outing* 7 (Nov. 1885), 330.

32. Henry Slocum, "Lawn Tennis as a Game for Women," *Outing* 14 (July 1889), 289.

33. Ibid., p. 298.

34. Parmley Paret, *The Women's Book of Sports* (New York: D. Appleton & Co., 1901), p. 41.

35. D.A. Sargent, "The Physical Development of Women," *Scribner's Magazine* 5 (Jan.-June, 1889), 181, 184.

36. Minna Caroline Smith, "The Tricycle for American Women," *Outing* 5 (March 1885), 423-26, "A Lady-Like Pastime," *Outing* 5 (March 1885), 462.

37. "'Daisie,' The Ladies Eastern Tricycle Tour," *Outing* 3 (Dec. 1888), 260-65.

38. W.H. Fenton, M.D., "A Medical View of Cycling for Ladies," *Living Age* CCIX (June 1896), p. 806.

39. Arabella Kenealy, "Woman as an Athlete," *Living Age* 221 (May 1899), 367.

40. L. Ormiston Chant, "Woman as an Athlete, a Reply to Dr. Arabella Kenealy," *Living Age* 221 (June 1899), 802.

41. Ibid., p. 803.

42. Ibid., p. 806.

43. Sutphen W.C. Van Tassell, "The Golfing Woman," *Outlook* 62 (June 1899), 251.

44. *New York Times*, 25 April 1905, p. 11.

45. *New York Times*, 12 August 1963, p. 29.

46. Ibid.

47. Margaret Bisland, "Women and Their Guns," *Outing* 15 (December 1889), 225-229.

48. "Bowling for Women," *Outing* 16, (April 1890), 117-21.

49. C.R.C., "A New Hand at the Rod," *Outing* 16 (June 1890), 117-21.

50. F.C. Sumichrast, "Ladies at the Helm," *Outing*, 164-88.

51. Ibid., p. 185.

52. Duncan Edwards, "Life at the Athletic Clubs," *Scribner's Magazine* 18 (July 1895), 14.

53. Elizabeth Cynthia Barney, "The American Sportswomen," *Fortnightly Review* 62 (August 1894), 268.

54. *New York Times*, 2 June 1894, p. 8.

55. B.B. Gilchrist, *The Life of Mary Lyon* (New York: Houghton Mifflin, 1910), cited in Dorothy Ainsworth, *The History of Physical Education in Colleges for Women* (New York: Barnes, 1930), p. 13.

56. Ballentine, *The History of Physical Training at Vassar College*, p. 6.

57. Paret, *The Women's Book of Sports*, p. 91.

58. Gertrude Dudley and Frances Kellor, *Athletic Games in the Education of Women* (New York: Holt, 1909), p. 181.

59. Ibid., p. 183.

60. Jeannette Marks, "Outdoor Life at Wellesley College," *Outing* 2 (May 1898), 118.

61. Richardson, "Tendencies in Athletics for Women in Colleges and Universities," p. 521.

62. Ballentine, *The History of Physical Education at Vassar College*, p.17.

63. Carl Degler, "Concern on the Part of Women for Themselves as Individuals Rather than Subordinates is the Key to the History of Women," *The Stanford Observer* (Jan. 1979), p.3.

• • •

Suggestions for Further Reading:

Barney, Elizabeth C., "The American Sportswoman," *Fortnightly Review*, LXII (August, 1894), 263-277.

Bissell, Mary T. "Athletics for City Girls," *Popular Science Monthly*, XLVI (December, 1894), 145-153.

Coffey, Margaret A., "The Sportswoman—Then and Now," *Journal of Health, Physical Education and Recreation*, XXXVI (February, 1965), 38-41, 50.

Gerber, Ellen W. et al., *The American Woman in Sport*, (Reading, MA: Addison-Wesley, 1974).

Lumpkin, Angela, "The Growth of National Women's Tennis, 1904-1940," *Quest*, XXVII (Winter, 1977), 47-53.

Oglesby, Carole A., ed., *Women and Sport: From Myth to Reality* (Philadelphia: Lea and Febiger, 1978).

Park, Roberta J., "'Embodied Selves': The Rise and Development of Concern for Physical Education, Active Games and Recreation Among American Women, 1776-1865," *Journal of Sport History,* V (Summer, 1978), 5-41.

Remley, Mary Lou, "Women and Competitive Athletics," *The Maryland Historian,* IV, 2 (Fall, 1973), 88-94.

Richardson, Sophia E., "Tendencies in Athletics for Women in Colleges and Universities," *Popular Science Monthly,* I (February, 1897), 517-526.

Robincheaux, Laura, "An Analysis of Attitudes Towards Women Athletics in the U.S. in the Early Twentieth Century," *Canadian Journal of History of Sport and Physical Education,* VI (May, 1975), 12-22.

Smith, Ronald A., "The Rise of Basketball for Women in Colleges," *Canadian Journal of History of Sport and Physical Education,* I (December, 1970), 18-36.

Toohey, D. Margaret and Betty V. Edmondson, "An Historical Perspective on Beliefs About Women's Health Issues Which Had an Impact on Attitudes Toward Women's Sport Participation in the Nineteenth Century," North American Society for Sports History, *Proceedings* (1980), 40 ff.

Vertinsky, Patricia, "Sexual Equality and the Legacy of Catherine Beecher," *Journal of Sport History,* VI, 1 (Spring, 1979), 38-49.

THE FIRST MODERN SPORT IN AMERICA: HARNESS RACING IN NEW YORK CITY 1825-1870

Melvin L. Adelman

Tracing the growth of trotting in New York City from the anti-thoroughbred racing legislation of the early nineteenth century to the formation of the National Trotting Association in 1869, Melvin Adelman makes a case for the emergence of modern sporting patterns in this country before the Civil War. This interpretation runs counter to the prevailing notion that the pre-war era saw only limited sporting activity. As Frederic Paxson argued, for example, the rise of sport in America only occurred in the three decades preceding 1900.

Noting the characteristics of premodern and modern ideal sporting types, Adelman claims that harness racing emerged as the nation's leading spectator sport by mid-century. Benefiting from a growth in commercialized amusements that the urban and economic expansion of the period made possible, trotting enjoyed a reputation as a sport particularly suited for the American temperament. Hailed for its democratic and utilitarian features, it increasingly attracted favorable coverage by the sporting press, experienced widespread public support, and saw more orderly processes develop in the breeding of trotting horses and the governance of the sport.

Beyond the interpretive merits of this article, it reflects the contributions to American history that have been made by scholars who not only pursue topics outside of the mainstream of historical study but who also reside in academic departments not necessarily known or respected for historical scholarship. Adelman wrote this piece as an assistant professor in the Department of Physical Education at the University of Illinois, Chicago Circle. His work underscores the critical role that the discipline of physical education, a principal emphasis of which is sport in its various dimensions, including history, has played in helping to focus attention on sport history scholarship. Physical educators, or, more accurately, sport historians like Adelman working in physical education, were the first to organize scholarly congresses and symposia that specifically treated sport history themes, to publish a professional scholarly journal devoted to those themes, and to form national and international organizations of professionals whose chief research interests and efforts related to sport history investigation. Their work, subject to the same standards of evaluation and criticism that govern other forms of historical scholarship, can be cited without hesitation or apology.

Historians have assigned the rise of sport in America to the last three decades of the nineteenth century. Although they found antecedents to this development in the antebellum period, especially during the 1850s, they presented the era as one of limited sporting activity.[1] This perspective of the pre-Civil War years is unfortunately based on only a handful of studies and most of these examine the changing attitudes towards athletics.[2] The sporting patterns in New York City between 1820 and 1870 revealed, however, a much more active sporting life than heretofore thought to have existed at that time. Far from mere prefigurings, the framework of modern sport was established during this half century.[3]

The modernization of harness racing between 1825 and 1870 exemplifies the growth and transformation of sport during this period. An examination of the modernization of trotting[4] can proceed by employing two ideal sporting types: one premodern and the other modern.[5] These ideal sporting types need not be perfect representations of actual historical stages, but they may be distinguished by six polar characteristics (see Table 1). The modernization of sport entails the movement of the activity in the direction of the modern ideal type. This movement is generally, although not always, accompanied by a shift in the playing arena from an open to a close one, the increasing presence of spectators and the commercialization of the sport.

Prior to 1825, harness racing was a premodern sport. Trotting consisted primarily of informal road contests which took place mainly in the northeastern section of the country. The sport was unorganized, lacked standardized rules, attracted limited public attention and possessed no permanent records. By 1870, harness racing had become a modern sport. The creation of the National Trotting Association in that year indicates the development of harness racing into a highly organized sport, with fairly uniform rules and with contests taking place throughout the country. The modernization of trotting is further illustrated by the coverage harness racing received in the daily and sporting press, the emergence of statistics and records and the appearance in 1871 of the first stud book devoted exclusively to trotting. Finally, harness racing emerged as the first sport to be successfully commercialized. By the mid-nineteenth century, trotting replaced thoroughbred racing as this country's number one spectator sport. Not until after the Civil War did base-ball challenge the supreme position of trotting; but by 1870, if not for awhile longer, harness racing remained the nation's leading spectator sport.

Table 1

The Characteristics of Premodern and Modern Ideal Sporting Types

Premodern Sport	Modern Sport
1. ORGANIZATION - is either non-existent or at best informal and sporadic. Contests are arranged by individuals directly or indirectly (e.g., tavern-owners, bettors) involved.	1. ORGANIZATION - formal organizations, institutionally differentiated at the local, regional and national level.
2. RULES - are simple, unwritten and based upon local customs and traditions. Variations exist from locale to locale.	2. RULES - are formal, standardized and written. Rules are rationally and pragmatically worked out and legitimated by organizational means.
3. COMPETITION - locally meaningful contests only; no chance for national reputation.	3. COMPETITION - national and international superimposed on local contests; chance to establish national and international reputation.
4. ROLE DIFFERENTIATION - low role differentiation among participants and loose distinction between playing and spectating roles.	4. ROLE DIFFERENTIATION -high role differentiation; emergence of specialists (professionals) and strict distinctions between playing and spectating roles.
5. PUBLIC INFORMATION - is limited, local and oral.	5. PUBLIC INFORMATION - is re–ported on a regular basis in local newspapers, as well as national sporting journals. The appearance of specialized magazines, guidebooks, etc.
6. STATISTICS AND RECORDS - non-existent.	6. STATISTICS AND RECORDS - are kept, published on a regular basis and are considered important measure of achievement. Records are sanctioned by national associations.

The contention that harness racing was the first modern sport in America does not mean that it was the initial sport to assume modern characteristics. Thoroughbred racing began to modernize during the eighteenth century when permanent jockey clubs were established. The modernization of this sport reached its pre-Civil War peak during the 1830s when the sport enjoyed a period of unprecedented growth and prosperity. By the mid-1840s, however, the process grounded to a halt when the sport collapsed throughout the North. With horse racing confined mainly to the South during the subsequent two decades, the modernization of the sport remained dormant until the revival of thoroughbred racing in the North in the years immediately following the Civil War. By 1870, nevertheless, the gestalt of horse racing was not as yet modern despite the significant steps in this direction during the antebellum period.[6]

Conversely, the claims that harness racing had become a modern sport by 1870 does not mean to suggest that the modernization of trotting was complete by this date. Rather a key point of this article is that a certain stage is reached as a sport moves along the continuum from the pre-modern to the modern ideal form in which modern characteristics are sufficiently present to shape the structure and direction of the sport. At this juncture, the sport presents a modern configuration, one which shares more in common with its future than its premodern past. It is in this sense that harness racing had become America's first modern sport by 1870.

Harness racing conjures up a rural image, the sport of the county fair. Trotting was, however, an urban product. The sport first emerged on urban roads and developed its most salient modern characteristics in the city. New York played a more critical role in the development of harness racing than any other city. As early as 1832, the *Spirit of the Times* recognized that New York was the premier city in the breeding and training of trotting horses. Nearly a quarter of a century later, one frequent correspondent to this sporting journal maintained that trotting was indigenous to the Empire City and that there were "more fine horses here than can be found any where else in the world."[7] The importance of New York to the growth of the sport did not derive solely from the concentration of the best stock in the metropolitan region. New York was the hub of harness racing throughout the period of 1825 to 1870. In the nation's most populated city, there were more trotting tracks, more races, including a disproportionate number of the leading contests, and more prize money offered than in any other place in the country. Equally significant, the characteristics of modern harness racing initially appeared in New York. Here the sport was first organized and commercialized. As a result, New York set the pattern that was to be followed on a national scale.[8]

I.

Harness racing emerged as a popular pastime in New York and in other parts of the northeast in the first quarter of the nineteenth century.[9] Sport historians have maintained that the growth of trotting was directly related to the anti-racing legislation passed by several northern states, including New York State, during this era. Denied the race course, lovers of fast horses took to the "natural track"—the highway. While the road was ill suited for the feet of the running horse, it was the natural home of the trotter. "It is no accident," a leading historian of the sport contended, "that the racing of trotters began in regions where horses could be 'raced' only in defiance of law."[10]

New York State's anti-racing law, passed in 1802, neither directly nor indirectly influenced the growth of trotting in the Empire City. As enforcement had been lax, horsemen did not have to take to the road as a substitute for the prohibited race course.[11] Rather, trotting emerged at this time because improvements in the roads now made the sport possible. One historian noted that "it was only natural that the speed of the harness horse found its first testing ground upon the smooth hard roads whose networks radiated from the northeastern cities ... especially those of the Boston-New York-Philadelphia regions."[12]

Sportsmen began racing their "roadsters" (as street trotters came to be called) because it provided them with an amusement which was convenient, participatory and relatively inexpensive. Third Avenue quickly emerged as New York's major trotting area. Beginning outside the residential portion of the city at that time, the approximately five mile road was perfectly suited for these informal trials of speed. In close proximity to the homes of the horsemen, it was a convenient location for these contests which started upon the completion of the day's work and which usually lasted until dark. Moreover, numerous taverns dotted the highway where reinsmen could stop, arrange contests and discuss the latest sporting developments.[13]

These impromptu contests appealed to the city's horsemen because the allowed personal participation. Unlike the thoroughbred racing, where the owner and the rider of the horse had long been separated, trotting permitted the sportsman to demonstrate the prowess of his horse, as well as his own skill as reinsman. Finally, the pastime did not require the capital outlay of thoroughbred racing. The trotter was not a "pure breed," but rather a horse drawn from the common stock that had the ability to trot. The plebian horses that engaged in these road races, moreover, were almost always used by their owners in their day-to-day activities.[14]

Although early nineteenth century trotting consisted almost exclusively of these impromptu contests, permanent structures began to emerge. The first trotting tracks in the New York metropolitan region were mere extensions of the courses used for thoroughbred racing. The most significant of these tracks was located in Harlem and the first recorded performance by an American trotter took place there in 1806. Several years later, the first track constructed exclusively for trotting was built in Harlem next to the Red House Tavern. The course was the major resort for the Third Avenue road racing crowd and the track was probably constructed for their benefit. While racing took place on both courses, these tracks remained essentially training grounds for the city's roadsters.[15]

More formalized matches, either on the city's roads or tracks, were a natural outgrowth of the impromptu races, or "brushes" as they were called, which took place on Gotham's streets. Since the press paid scant attention to these matches information exists on only a few of them. Probably the most important took place in 1818 when William Jones of Long Island, a prominent horseman, wagered Colonel Bond of Maryland a thousand dollars that he could produce a horse that would trot a mile in less than three minutes. The race caused great excitement among the city's sporting crowd. With odds against success, a horse named *Boston Pony* accomplished the feat in just less than the required time.[16]

The formation of the New York Trotting Club (NYTC) in the Winter of 1824-25 marks the first critical step in the modernization of harness racing.[17] The first organized trotting club in America, there is no information on its members, although most were probably drawn from the men who raced their roadsters on Third Avenue and other roads in the New York metropolitan region. The creation of the NYTC was inspired by the success thoroughbred racing had enjoyed in New York after the State revoked its anti-racing legislation in 1821. The NYTC drew its objectives and methods heavily from the experience of horse racing. Similar to the racing organization of its sister sport, the NYTC justified its association on utilitarian grounds (the sport's contribution to the improvement of the breed); instituted regular meetings twice yearly; and, constructed a race course (in Centerville, Long Island) to facilitate the growth of the sport.[18]

Trotting in New York made significant advances as both a participatory and spectator sport in the two decades following the formation of the NYTC. In 1835, the *Spirit* noted that the "number of fast horses for which our city is so celebrated is steadily accumulating." With some exaggeration, one contemporary observer claimed that "there was scarcely a gentleman in New York who did not own one or two fast (trotting) horses."[19] The rising cost of good roadsters further indicated the increasing appeal of the sport. During the 1830s, the price of the best trotting horses doubled.[20] In addition, trotting races on the city's tracks, especially the major ones, generated considerable excitement among New York's sporting crowd. In 1838, the *New York Herald* reported that the contest between *Dutchman* and *Ratner* created "as much interest in our city and neighborhood" as the intersectional horse race between *John Bascombe* and *Post Boy* held in New York two years earlier.[21]

The emerging commercialization of trotting most accurately dramatizes the growth of the sport. By the mid-1830s, entrepreneurs began to tap the public interest in harness races that took place on New York's streets and tracks. The experience of the Beacon Course in nearby Hoboken, New Jersey illustrates the early introduction of the profit motive into trotting. This course was constructed in 1837 for thoroughbred racing. When the sport proved unprofitable the following year, the proprietors of the track started to promote harness racing for the sole purpose of reaping the financial rewards from the gate receipts. By the early 1840s, businessmen had replaced the original sponsors of trotting—the road runners and their associations—as the major promoters of the sport.[22]

Although organized trotting made important progress in its first twenty years, it continued to take a back seat to horse racing. The coverage harness racing received in the press defined the secondary status of this turf sport. While trotting won the polite endorsement of New York newspapers, reports of races, even important ones, remained limited. Similarly, harness racing won the approval of sports editors John Stuart Skinner and Cadwallader Colden, but their monthly journals were devoted almost exclusively to thoroughbred racing and provided only the barest summaries and details of the developments on the trotting track. Only William T. Porter's *Spirit* paid any significant attention to trotting and even there the extent of the coverage did not correspond to the growth of the sport.

II.

As thoroughbred racing collapsed throughout the North in the decade following the Depression of 1837, the sporting press took increasing note of the activities of the trotting horse. By the early 1840s, they suggested that the "ugly duckling" had become the legitimate rival of her more respected sister. In 1847, the *Herald* pointed out that "for several years past, trotting has been gradually taking the precedence of running in this country; while one specie of amusement has been going into decay, the other has risen to heights never before attained."[23]

Contemporaries claimed that the corresponding fates of the two turf sports were closely linked to the characteristics associated with the two different horses. In contrast to the aristocratic and foreign thoroughbred, the trotter was perceived as the democratic, utilitarian, and, by logical extension, the American horse. Implicit was the belief that harness racing surpassed horse racing as the leading turf sport because it more accurately captured the spirit of the American experience.

Henry W. Herbert (better known as Frank Forester) recognized the close connection between the nature of the horses and the popularity of the respective sports. Since cost restricted the ownership of thoroughbreds to wealthy men, horse racing could never be a popular sport. By contrast, the trotter was common to all and the "most truly characteristic and national type of horse" in America. In this country, the transplanted Englishman concluded, trotting "is the people's sport, the people's pastime, and consequently, is, and will be, supported by the people."[24]

This perspective provides a good starting point in understanding the maturation of trotting if such terms as democratic, utilitarian and even American are broadly conceived. While contemporaries grossly exaggerated the extent to which the masses owned trotters, ownership of these plebian and relatively inexpensive horses was far more widespread than thoroughbreds.[25] Precise data on the owners of trotting horses in New York is non-existent, but available information does permit a profile to be logically deduced. The evidence indicates that only a small number of trotting men came from the "upper crust."[26] Conversely, the cost and upkeep of trotting horses were still sufficiently high to generally exclude individuals who fell below the middle class. While broad parameters still exist, it appears that trotting owners came from the more prosperous segments of the middle class—men who lived a comfortable, but hardly opulent, lifestyle. Nevertheless, individuals of more moderate means could still own a roadster as a result of the limited price of the horse and their usage in daily activities. This was particularly the case for men working in New York's various food markets. Their involvement in harness racing gave credence to the common adage that "a butcher rides a trotter" often used to illustrate the democratic nature of the horse."[27]

The fortunes of the two turf sports, the *Herald* repeatedly insisted, were connected to their utilitarian functions. The decline of horse racing stemmed from the fact that the thoroughbred had little practical benefit. The newspaper conceded that trotting "may not be attended with all the high zest and excitement" of running races, but it is "a more useful sport, as the qualities in the horse which it is calculated to develop are more intimately connected with the daily business of life.[28] The growth of harness racing did reflect shifting patterns of travel. With the improvement of roads and wagons, the driving horse increasingly replaced the saddle horse as the basic means of convoy in the northeastern and Middle Atlantic states. As one scholar pointed out, there was "a direct correlation between the improved modes of transportation and their popular manifestations seen on the trotting track."[29]

Since Americans believed that the true nature of the trotter—democratic and utilitarian—could only be developed in this country, they perceived the trotter as a native product although they were familiar with English antecedents. In 1853, the *Herald* wrote, "We are the first who have attached particular importance to the breeding of trotting horses, and in this respect ... have shown the practical nature of our character."[30] These assumptions may be passed of as American chauvinism, but the contention that both the horse and the sport were indigenous products does contain merit. Harness racing had been a popular pastime in England, but its emergence as a sport first occurred in the United States.[31]. Similarly, the establishment of a distinct breed of trotting race horse was an American creation, although this process was not completed until the late nineteenth century. More significantly, it was the perception of the trotter as the American horse, more than the reality, which was of critical importance to the growth of the sport. While harness racing never wrapped itself in the flag to the extent that baseball did, nationalistic overtones gave trotting a sanction absent in horse racing.[32] Oliver Wendell Holmes, Sr. captured these sentiments. He noted that the running horse was a gambling toy, but the trotting horse was a useful animal. Furthermore, "horse racing is not a republican institution; horse-trotting is."[33]

While the contemporary explanation provides a starting point, other critical factors must also be examined if a comprehensive analysis of the maturation of trotting is to be constructed. Trotting's supreme position in the turf world can be more productively analyzed in terms of three interacting forces: the increasing potential for commercialized amusements made possible by urban and economic expansion; the greater susceptibility of trotting to commercialization than any of its sporting counterparts; and, the more innovative nature of trotting.

The absence of surplus wealth and concentrated populations traditionally restricted the development of commercialized amusements. During the antebellum period, these two major barriers began to dissolve under the impact of urban and economic growth. The expanding economy throughout these years not only produced a significant rise in wealth, but, more importantly, broadened the availability of discretionary income among a wider segment of the population. The concentration of large numbers of permanent institutions devoted to commercialized amusements.[34] These newer forms of popular entertainment shared three essential properties: they were cheaper, depended on volume, and appealed to a wider segment of the populace. While commercialized amusements increased throughout the first four decades of the nineteenth century, their numbers multiplied rapidly in the two decades preceding the Civil War. As one scholar pointed out, commercialized amusements underwent "an expansion of new proportions" during the lengthy era of general prosperity between 1843 and 1860.[35]

The plebian character of the trotter and its relatively inexpensive price made the sport more susceptible to commercialization. Since the trotter cost less than the thoroughbred, the prize money offered by track proprietors did not have to be as great for the owners of the trotters to cover their cost and make a profit. As late as 1860, purses in New York rarely exceeded $250 and contests could be run for as low as $10. The stakes were naturally higher in match or privately arranged races. By the 1850s, a few contests went for as much as five thousand dollars per side. In general, however, the amounts fell below that which existed for similar kinds of thoroughbred races. Clearly one does not find anything comparable to the stakes placed on the major intersectional thoroughbred contest, such as between *Eclipse* and *Henry* or *Boston* and *Fashion*, or for that matter the money that could be won in horse racing's larger sweepstake races.

The nature of the trotter facilitated the commercialization of the sport by making more races possible. Whereas a good thoroughbred might race six or seven times a year, the more durable trotter started at least twice as many races annually. Furthermore, a trotter's career lasted longer, many racing into their teens. More importantly, the trotter came from the common horse stock. Consequently, there were simply more of them to race. The impact of the greater numbers can be seen in terms of the respective racing sessions in New York. There were at most three weeks of thoroughbred racing in the city annually; but hardly a week would pass, except in the winter months, without a trotting match taking place somewhere in the New York metropolitan region.

Finally, harness racing was not bogged down in the "aristocratic" trappings which characterized horse racing. In 1843, the *Spirit* recognized that trotting men were more innovative and aggressive than their horse racing counterparts. As a result of their greater "enterprise, industry and go *aheadiveness*," the sporting journal predicted, harness racing "will soon be a formidable rival to thoroughbred racing in the North." Nearly a quarter of a century later, *Turf, Field and Farm*, essentially a thoroughbred journal, gave the same basic reasons and used exactly the same words in explaining the greater popularity in harness racing.[36]

Trotting was more innovative than horse racing in two critical ways. The first was a product of the different social backgrounds of those involved in the respective sports. Engaged in thoroughbred racing were wealthy men and/or people from established families. Most of the owners of trotting horses and the proprietors of trotting tracks, however, appear to have been middle class in origin. The different social origins affected the entire tone of the two turf sports. While thoroughbred racing was run for and by the upper class, harness racing enticed a broader segment of the populace. The commercially minded proprietors of trotting tracks catered more readily to all ticket holders than those involved in their sister sport. One does not find connected with trotting complaints of exclusiveness, aristocracy and snobbishness levelled by the press against the leaders of thoroughbred racing. As a leading sporting journal noted, "Racing will never succeed in New York until it and its attended arrangements are put on a more democratic basis—something approaching the order of the first class trotting races. Then, like the trots, it will get the support of the people."[37]

In addition, trotting was more innovative because the comparatively new sport was not inhibited by tradition. By the 1840s, horse racing in America had a long heritage on how a thoroughbred race should be conducted. The absence of institutional confinements made it easier for trotting to adjust to commercialization. Similar to their horse racing counterparts, trotting men initially valued a horse which combined speed and endurance. Early trotting contests were raced in heats from one to five miles. By the early 1840s, trotting men broke with this pattern. Most major contests were not one mile heats with the winner required to win three heats. Since the new system placed less strain on the trotter, the horse could race more frequently and thereby more races were possible. Furthermore, harness racing contests took place in a wider variety of styles, giving the sport greater diversity and interest.

Harness racing surged to the forefront of not only the turf world, but modern sport in general, because more than any other sport of the day it captured the flow of the American experience. In common with other forms of popular entertainment, the emergence of trotting as a spectator sport was a product of the two dynamic forces—urbanization and economic expansion—transforming and modernizing American life. The impact of these agents of change would have been far less had not trotting possessed properties which predisposed it towards commercialization. Here the nature of the horse played a critical role. Of equal significance was the fact that those who governed trotting, at least from the standpoint of sport, internalized the values of modern society. As such, they put a greater premium on innovation rather than tradition, and cash rather than class.

III.

Harness racing progressed rapidly as a popular spectator sport both in New York and throughout the country in the two decades preceding the Civil War. While the changes in the social and economic conditions, discussed in the previous section, created the setting for the growth of the sport, performers attracted the crowds. During the early years of organized trotting, numerous horses left their mark on the history of sport, but it was *Lady Suffolk* who set the standard of excellence and was the sport's first hero.[38] The fifteen year career of *Lady Suffolk* (1838-1853), moreover, illustrates the condition and development of trotting during this period.

Foaled in 1833, *Lady Suffolk* was bred by Leonard Lawrence of Suffolk County, Long Island, from whence she drew her name. The *Lady* was a descendent of imported *Messenger*, the founding father of the American trotter, but no preparation was made for a trotting career.[39] As a weanling she was sold for $60, then resold as a two year old for $90. At age four she was pulling a butcher or oyster cart when David Bryan purchased her for $112.50 for use in his livery stable. The prowess of the horse went undiscovered until none other than William T. Porter by chance rented her for a tour of the Long Island tracks. The editor of the *Spirit* was impressed with the *Lady's* speed and good gait. He told Bryan that she had too much potential as a racer to be wasted in his stable. In the spring of 1838, Bryan entered the *Lady* in her first race. The "Old Grey Mare," as she was later affectionately called, completed the mile contest in three minutes flat, winning the fabulous sum of eleven dollars.

Bryan owned *Lady Suffolk* until his death in 1851. Of Irish or Celtic origin, little is known of his background, save for his previous occupation. It is clear, however, that Bryan was the embodiment of the professional ethic which came to dominate the sport. As one historian wrote, "For Bryan, his *Lady Suffolk* , the most loved as well as the most admired horse of her time, was not, first and foremost, a sporting animal—she was a mint of money, a nugget of rich metal to be melted by him in the heat of competition and struck off into dollars."[40] Bryan raced his grey mare mainly in the New York metropolitan area because this is where he lived and, even more importantly, because the city's courses provided the best financial opportunities. Similar to other professional trotting men of his day, however, Bryan campaigned with *Lady Suffolk* on the growing number of tracks throughout the country, going as far west as St. Louis and as far south as New Orleans.

Bryan had the reputation of being a poor reinsman and he placed excessive demands on *Lady Suffolk* . Nevertheless, he was an unqualified success by the new professional standards. He entered the *Lady* in 162 races and won between $35,000 and $60,000.[41] The ability of *Lady Suffolk* to achieve victory, despite the clumsy and inept driving of her owner, derived from her saintly patience, an unbreakable spirit and a remarkable endurance. At age nineteen, her last full year on the turf, the Old Grey Mare demonstrated her tremendous stamina by coming to the start twelve times.

Harness racing had emerged as the nation's leading spectator sport by the time *Lady Suffolk* was retired in the early 1850s. During this decade, the sport emerged as an integral part of the county fair and the public's desire to see harness races resulted in the creation of an ever increasing number of trotting tracks throughout the country. By 1858, one sporting journal estimated that over seventy trotting courses existed in America.[42]

Expanding coverage of harness racing corresponded with its growth. In New York, the daily newspapers naturally focused on contests within the metropolitan region, but the city-based sporting journals reported on races throughout the country. While trotting men had always been preoccupied with "time" as a measure of their horses' abilities and performances, statistics and records took on new importance when horsemen began touring the increasing number of tracks in search of fame and fortune. That these measurements served the interest of track promoters and fans of the sport was to a large extent responsible for their expanding value. Since a trotter might visit a city only one a year, proprietors of the courses could use the statistical reputation of a horse to encourage people to come see the race even though they may have never seen him perform. Similarly, statistics nourished fan interest by providing them with a method of evaluating a horse in the absence of personal observation or witnessing the horse race on only a handful of occasions.

Trotting men were not only familiar with unsurpassed performances, but were already cognizant of the concept of the record. In 1860, for example, *Flora Temple*, who succeeded *Lady Suffolk* as the "princess of the turf," sought to break *Dutchman's* record (7:32.5) for three miles. Since "the watch never breaks and never tires," *Wilkes' Spirit of the Times* reported, the effort of *Flora Temple* (eventually unsuccessful) to surpass the time of the then dead horse evoked considerable speculation and discussion.[43]

New York continued to dominate the development of harness racing even though the sport expanded nationally. At least seven trotting tracks existed in the metropolitan region, with three—Union, Fashion and Centerville Courses—hosting first class contests. More significantly, with the ever increasing importance of gate receipts, trotting in the Empire City drew the largest number of spectators. Between six and eight thousand spectators were usually present at each of the four to six leading matches held annually. However, when *Flora Temple* raced, attendance could jump into double figures. Within a period of seventeen days in 1859, her contests with *Ethan Allen* and then *Princess* drew crowds of 12,000 and 20,000, respectively.

The growth of harness racing as a sports spectacle did not occur without problems. As the commercial and professional ethic came to dominate the sport, suspicions of irregularities on the trotting track markedly increased. The question of the integrity of harness racing produced the first extensive discussion and concern about the honesty of professional-commercial sport. Cries of foul play on the New York tracks were already heard as early as the 1830s. The *Spirit* claimed that the public are beginning to express concern about the improprieties on the trotting track and insisted that men of character must immediately rule off the track those who disgrace the sport or else the "trotting course and everything pertaining them must 'go to pot.'"[44]

While complaints of irregularities persisted, the city's sporting press began to repeat these charges vociferously only in the 1850s. Fundamentally these statements did not vary from the theme, solution and dire predictions offered by the *Spirit* over a decade earlier. In 1857, the *New York Times* asserted that many owners of fast trotters would not allow their horses to compete in races since the courses had "fallen under the control of men who made use of them to subserve their own private interest."[45]

During the next two decades, the New York press emphatically argued that the fixing of races was a common practice.[46] So often were the charges made that by their sheer numbers this argument becomes a compelling one. Yet was it accurate? It would be naive to assume that no races were rigged, but the claims of widespread manipulation of contests seems grossly exaggerated. Evidence of these "clandestine arrangements" are significantly lacking. It is not surprising, therefore, that the arguments develop a predictable rhythm and break down into vague generalities. In contrast to the contention of rampant wrongdoings, I was impressed at the number of times the favorite, and especially the outstanding horses, won.[47] Clearly, many of the assertions, which at times border on the incredulous, can be cast aside as sensationalist journalism.[48] From time to time, moreover, statements in the press not only challenged the prevailing view, but often contradicted previous beliefs.[49]

The rise of the "manipulation theory" derived from three inter-related factors: the non-existence of investigative commissions; the nature of professional sport and the attitude towards professional athletes; and the primitive concept of "upset." In absence of effective investigating commissions as we know them today, charges of irregularities were rarely examined. The lack of this critical institutional structure for the governance of sport facilitated the growth of rumor and innuendo and made personal judgment the sole criteria in deciding the honesty of a race. The case brought against James Eoff illustrates the obvious drawbacks of such a method in determining the integrity of a contest. In 1859, *Princess*, a California mare, was the first horse to make the trip from the West Coast to New York. With little time to recoup from the long journey, she was matched against *Flora Temple*. Hiram Woodruff, the leading antebellum reinsman and a spectator at the contest, wrote that ninety-five percent of the huge crowd felt that *Princess* lost because Eoff, her jockey, pulled the mare. So vociferous was the cry of "fix" that the Union Jockey Club, a thoroughbred organization which owned the course where the race took place, held a rare investigation. There Eoff claimed that the California mare tired because she had not recovered from her trip and could not be pushed any harder. Woodruff felt the explanation was a plausible and truthful one. He further pointed out that not one of the many people who felt the race had been thrown came forward to substantiate their charge.[50]

The nature of professional athletics made creditable the assertion that races were fixed. Since the major purpose of the contest for the professional athlete is to make money, what guarantees exist that he would not manipulate the event to maximize profit? A certain class bias against the professional athlete accentuated the suspicions inherent within the professional system. While no monolithic view of either the professional athlete or professional athletics existed, the prevailing attitude was that the public was assured honest contests only when the "better class" governed the sport.[51]

The strong temptations confronting the professional athlete went far in explaining why the press so vehemently opposed what was known as "hippodroming"—the making of contests for the sole purpose of splitting the gate receipts (in contrast to racing for stakes and purses). With no money depending on the outcome, and therefore with no incentive to win, these "concocted affairs" were perfect races to rig. As the *New York Clipper* pointed out, "many matches advertised for heavy stakes are merely for 'gate money' and so arranged that the winners are known to the 'initiated' before the event ever took place."[52]

The suspicions of wrongdoing were justifiably heightened by the less than candid policy of track promoters in billing what was essentially an exhibition" as a match race for large stakes. This less than honest practice does not prove, however, that the contests were fixed. In 1860, the *Spirit* conceded that hippodroming had become a method of scheduling races, but it doubted "if there is one-tenth part of the rascality on a trotting track that many people suppose."[53]

The development of hippodroming was a legitimate response to the financial considerations of both the owners of the horses and the proprietors of the courses rather than being the product of evil intent. Woodruff claimed that *Flora Temple* caused the new system. In a class by herself, the mare "could not get a match on even terms, and was excluded from all purses."[54] It is unlikely that *Flora Temple* or any other horse initiated hippodroming. Instead it emerged from the inadequacy of the prevalent winner-take-all system.[55] The new arrangements made it possible for a horse to be defeated and the owner still be able to cover part of his cost and possibly emerge with a profit. Consequently, it gradually facilitated an expansion in both the number of trotters and races. Equally important for the proprietors, it guaranteed the presence of the super horses that drew the huge crowds. "No matter how these 'little arrangements' are concocted," the *Clipper* was forced to conclude, "It is but fair to say that generally made interesting races, and in a way the spectators are pleased."[56]

The most striking fact about the literature of the day was the primitive understanding of the concept of "upset." Nineteenth century writers were conscious that luck played a factor in the outcome of athletic contests and that the more talented performer did not always win. On most occasions when the favorite lost, however, the press and the public offered some excuse for his defeat. As I perceive it, the concept of upset does not automatically entail that luck played a part in the underdog winning, although it may and often does. Rather it is premised on the realization that on certain occasions a competitor can achieve a level of performance which is not his usual standard and quite possibly may never be reached again.

Today it is axiomatic that on any given day any professional athlete or team could defeat any other professional athlete or team. Over the

years, the vicissitudes of sport have sufficiently demonstrated the validity
of this idea. The legitimacy of even the most unbelievable developments
go unquestioned. Jargon ridden as this perspective has become in our
mass communication sporting world, the internalization of this view by
the fan and the press alike is mandatory if the integrity of professional
sport is to be accepted. Precisely because such an attitude was absent in
the early days of professional sport any unexpected occurrence frequently
became translated into "fix."[57]

Serious doubts must be raised of the prevalent view that
widespread manipulation of races followed on the heels of the growth of
professional-commercial harness racing. While dishonest contests occurred in New York, they were the exception rather than the rule.
Nevertheless, professionalization did significantly alter the character of
these contests. The emphasis of amateur turfmen on style and
sportsmanship yielded to the sole objective of success as jockies adopted
tricks and tactics which if not outright violations of the rules permitted the
drivers to get all he could within them. Such practices were often chas-
tised and contributed to the belief that there was a lack of propriety on the
trotting track; but they foreshadowed the pattern which emerged in all
professional sports. As one historian pointed out, these techniques were
consistent with the dominant American values "in that it was results that
counted, not how hard you tried or how sportingly you behaved."[58]

IV.

While commercialization became harness racing's leading characteristic by the 1850s, informal trials of speed persisted on New York's
streets. With the growth of the city, however, severe restrictions began to
be placed on the roadster. By the early 1860s, New York's road runners
had moved from Third Avenue to Harlem Lane in the upper part of
Manhattan. This location shortly began to succumb to the forces of
progress. Dismayed by the prospect of the loss of New York's last good
driving area, the editor of *Wilkes' Spirit* believed that it "was incumbent
upon the city's authorities to supply the vacancy created by the occupation
of Harlem Lane." As the headquarters of the fast trotter, anything less, he
suggested, "would be a national loss, as well as a municipal sham and
disgrace."[59]

The call for government intervention might be considered a "far
sighted" approach, but trotting men took steps more typical of the period.
They established private organizations which brought or rented their own
tracks. Unlike earlier trotting or jockey clubs, these organizations did not
sponsor public or private races, although club members could and probably did arrange contests amongst themselves and their guests. Rather,
they were formed to perpetuate an informal pastime no longer possible in

the more formalized urban setting.[60] The first of these clubs was the Elm Park Pleasure Grounds Association established in the late 1850s. The majority of the 400 members were prosperous businessmen, although there were a handful of men of considerable wealth, most notably Cornelius Vanderbilt and Robert Bonner.[61]

Of New York's road drivers, none had a more dramatic impact on the development of harness racing than Robert Bonner. Born in Londonderry, Ireland in 1824, Bonner amassed his fortune by the time he was thirty as the owner of the *New York Ledger*, a weekly family journal.[62] In 1856, his physician advised him to find an outdoor recreation for health reasons. Bonner then bought a horse and began driving it on New York's speedways. There he had a few brushes with Vanderbilt. What emerged was a friendly rivalry between these two for the ownership of the best trotters. The Bonner-Vanderbilt duel, a leading turf historian insisted, "marked the beginning of a change that provided the sport not only with strong financial backing but an efficient leadership."[63] While the confrontation between the steamship and newspaper magnates did not initiate a new era, it symbolized and gave impetus to an already existing process.

In the battle between the two giants, Bonner emerged as the king of the road. He spent lavishly in purchasing some of the best trotters of his era. Between 1859 and 1870, Bonner bought thirteen horses at a total cost of $162,000. His prize purchase was *Dexter*, clearly the number one trotter of his day. By the time he retired in 1890, the newspaper magnate had spent nearly half a million dollars for his horses, including $40,000 each for his stars *Maud S.* and *Pocahontas*.[64]

Bonner's reputation as a horseman did not derive solely from his ownership of possibly the largest and best stable. A more significant reason, as the *New York Tribune* pointed out, was that he "did more to lift the trotting horse from disrepute to respectability than any other man."[65] According to the universally accepted perspective, prior to Bonner's involvement, acceptable society viewed the owners of trotting horses as fast men "who spent their afternoons trotting from tavern to tavern ... (and) had too much money in their pockets."[66] Bonner was the critical figure in altering this negative impression. A man of unimpeachable character, the strict Scotch-Presbyterian did not smoke, drink or swear. Moreover, he so violently opposed gambling that he refused to enter his horses in public places. Consequently, Bonner could bring a dignity to the sport that other wealthy *nouveaux*, such as the salty Vanderbilt, never could. Through Bonner's influence, the ownership of trotting horses won an acceptable position in society, with the result that "Men of affairs, men of money, men of social position began to buy trotters, drive them on the road and even enter them for races on the public tracks."[67]

That the possession of trotting horses gradually achieved greater respectability in New York society when men of wealth became involved in the sport is undeniable as it was almost inevitable. This development did not emerge from a shift in the attitude of the city's "upper crust," but rather from a shift in its composition. As older elites gave way to the onslaught of new wealth, they lost their position as the arbiters of culture. The ascending group, from whom trotting men were overwhelmingly drawn, dictated from its new position the acceptability of its own activity.[68] The increasing involvement of New York's affluent in trotting, therefore, can be understood against the background of what a leading scholar of New York elites described as the plutocratic nature of the city's high society. Since New York society was easily accessible to the newly risen who were uncertain of the traditions and prerogatives of their new class and status, it produced an elite structure which encouraged the pursuit of publicity and created a fashionable style of conspicuous luxury. Although these traits did not emerge as the dominant characteristics of New York society until the late 1870s, they were strongly present among the city's elite even prior to the Civil War.[69]

Nouveaux riches New Yorkers became involved in trotting, as they would in other sports, as a means of status confirmation. Interesting differences existed, however, between trotting and other sporting activities. In the prevailing pattern, new wealth asserted its position by patronizing those sports which had an upper class heritage and/or could be afforded only by men of wealth. In the early years of trotting, the sport shared none of these characteristics. To function as other upper class sports, therefore, exclusiveness had to be created. Two interrelated processes accomplished this transformation: the purchasing of the best trotters at lavish prices and the rationalization of the breeding industry.

The willingness of wealthy men to pay premium prices resulted in their monopoly of the best trotters by the 1870s.[70] The soaring cost of trotters was in part a product of the growth of the sport and the increasing number of bidders for what was a relatively fixed market; there can be only a few champions per period. However, the law of supply and demand, important though it may be, does not explain the surge in prices. For example, Bonner bought *Dexter* in 1867 for the increditable sum of $33,000 even though his seller, George Trussle of Chicago, had paid only $14,000 for the horse two years earlier. Another subtle but significant reason therefore existed for the rising cost. The fabulous sums trotting horses attracted was a critical part of the status game. To have obtained the best horses at anything less than these fantastic sums would have not satisfied the needs of these *parvenus* to demonstrate their wealth and status.

The rationalizations of the breeding industry further encouraged the concentration of good trotting horses in the hands of the wealthy. In the mid-nineteenth century, this business required little capital, organization or promotion. Some attention was paid to pedigree; however, lineage was usually guesswork, if not outright falsification. The small scale on which the business was run was not conducive to finely selective breeding, but its random nature had the valuable result of diffusing the blood of the best stock widely throughout the country. This haphazard method, one historian noted, "contributed to the sport a delightful element of uncertainty, discovery and surprise, the satisfaction of making something out of nothing." This business enabled David Bryan and William M. Rysdyk, a former farm hand, to make their fame and fortune from their horses *Lady Suffolk* and *Hambletonian*, respectively, at a cost of less than $250 for the two horses.[71]

Within two or three decades, small breeders yielded to the larger stables owned by wealthy men for pleasure, profit or both. These well capitalized stock farms gathered the best trotters. Similar to other American industries in the latter part of the nineteenth century, the concentration of talent and wealth permitted the breeding of trotting horses to become a more rationalized process. For the small breeder, the swift trotter was essentially a sideline, although an important one, to the general stud services his horses provided. Above all, the major objective was the procreation of the race and the overall improvement of the breed. In the large stables, speed was the sole objective. Using innovative techniques, the big farms "became laboratories of speed." As one turf historian concluded, "A system of breeding that had diffused the qualities of the best sires so widely through the common horse stock was replaced by a system more narrowly concentrated but for that reason more likely to produce exceptional results."[72]

During the 1870s, four more critical steps were taken to rationalize the breeding industry: (1) the creation of the first turf register devoted exclusively to the trotting horse (1871); (2) the appearance of the first sporting journal, *Wallace's Monthly Magazine,* concerned primarily with trotting affairs (1875); (3) the formation of the National Association of Trotting Horse Breeders (1876); and, (4) the establishment of a standard breed of trotting horse (1879).[73] By the end of this decade, the rationalization of the breeding industry solidified the ownership of the leading trotters in the hands of wealthy men. Unable to compete with the big farms, the horses of the smaller breeders found themselves confined to tracks at county fairs. The day that a horse could be removed from a butcher's cart and become a world's champion was relegated to dime novels and serials in popular magazines.

Neither the shift in the social composition of the owners of trotting horses not changes in the breeding industry undermined the popularity of harness racing. Since the initial growth of the sport was strongly linked to the inexpensive cost of the trotter and its broadly based ownership, why did trotting continue to enjoy widespread popular appeal in the aftermath of these profound alterations? The persistent perception of the trotter as the democratic and utilitarian horse, despite the changes, played a contributory role. As late as 1884, one newspaper insisted that

the "millionaire horsemen with their mammoth establishments and invested thousands, represent but a small fraction of the money employed
in this special industry."[74] While the contention that the average farmer
was the backbone of the sport was inaccurate, the tremendous growth of
harness racing at the county fair, with its rural connotations, did give the
sport a democratic aura.[75]

The symbiotic relationship which already developed between the
growth of harness racing, the changes in the breeding industry and the
commercialization of the sport was an even more important factor. This
linkage made it virtually impossible for the wealthy owners of trotters to
create a sport run solely for their own class. While considerations of status
contributed to elite involvement in this sport, financial concerns, for the
overwhelming majority of these turfmen, were always present.[76] To offset
the surging cost of trotting horses required a corresponding expansion of
the economic side of the sport. Consequently, trotting me continued to
welcome the public and their money from gate receipts and gambling as a
means of defraying their expenses and making a profit.[77] The ongoing
willingness of harness racing to cater to a broad segment of the population
resulted in the perpetuation of trotting as the "people's pastime."

V.

Harness racing underwent tremendous growth as a commercial-
spectator sport in New York in the 1860s. The outbreak of the Civil War
brought a brief pause to the general prosperity of the sport, but things
were back into full swing by the Fall of 1862. During the following year,
trotting in New York appeared to be one continuous stream of match
races. Symbolized by a series of six races, each for $5,000, between
General Butler and *George Patchen*. These match races attracted large
audiences to the various courses. By 1864, the *Clipper* noted that the previous season was "Successful beyond precedent, alike in the quantity and
quality of the sport which it produced."[78]

More significant for the overall development of trotting than
these glamorous races was the increasing size of the purses given by the
proprietors and clubs of the various tracks. The prize money tendered at
the Fashion Course, for example, more than tripled, increasing fro
$3,750 to $11,500, in the years between 1862 and 1870. By the start of the
1870s, the aggregate sum of the purses offered by New York's three leading
tracks during their weekly sessions exceeded $25,000. In addition, the
proprietors scheduled other purse contests from time to time.[79] Races
which went for no more than $250 during the 1850s, and were run for
about $1,000 by the early 1860s, could go for as much as $5,000 by the end
of the decade.

An increase in the number of horses coming to the start corresponded with the rise in prize money. Whereas four horses rarely entered a race in the 1850s, this had become the norm by the early 1860s and it was not uncommon to find as many as seven horses in a contest. When there were 78 entries for the ten races held at the Fashion Course in 1964, one sporting journal called it by far the greatest number ever known for a regular meeting.[80] To facilitate the growing number of horses, the proprietors of the courses adopted the policy of sweepstake racing, long used in horse racing, with nominations to these contests sometimes coming as much as a year in advance.

The rapid expansion of harness racing not only in New York but throughout the nation during this decade, and especially after the Civil War, gave rise to several problems. According to the press, the most serious one remained the specter of the "fix." Calling upon the proprietors of the courses to cleanse and reform trotting of its evil elements, they continued to prognosticate dire consequences if their advice went unheeded.[81] Nevertheless, no significant action was taken until the Naragansett (RI) Trotting Association called a convention of track operators in late 1869. Meeting in New York the following February, delegates from forty-six tracks in fifteen states established the National Trotting Association for the Promotion of the Interest of the Trotting Turf, later simplified to the National Trotting Association (NTA).

The dual objectives of the NTA were the creation of uniform government and the prevention of punishment of fraud. To facilitate the former goal, the NTA adopted rules which would be used at all tracks in the association. To expedite the later aim, the NTA attempted to buttress the power of local authorities by creating a board of appeals which would rule on all kinds of infractions. To give muscle to this court, it made the suspension on one track applicable to all courses within the federation.[82]

Turf historians have accepted the desire to reform the evils of the turf as the major factor behind the creation of the NTA. Although they recognized the need for changes in the institutional structure of harness racing, they perceived this development as a means to the larger end.[83] Since the contemporary press and these historians grossly exaggerated the degree to which races were fixed, the lofty ideals assigned by these writers much be questioned. At the time of the creation of the NTA, in fact, several individuals asked how the proprietors of the courses, who had at least tacitly accepted the fraudulent behavior even though they may not have been responsible for it, were going to lead a reform movement. Interestingly, the right of track operators to represent the "trotting fraternity" at this convention was based on their vested economic interest in the sport."[84]

The formation of the NTA can be more appropriately examined as a response to what were the major problems of the turf: the inefficiency of uncoordinated local organizations and local rules to meet the needs of the proprietors of the courses and the owners of the horses. As early as 1858, *Porter's Spirit of the Times*, noting the growth of the sport, called for the creation of a national organization to govern harness racing.[85] Only with the tremendous expansion of trotting in the years following the Civil War, however, did the extant institutional structures of harness racing become incapable of meeting the requirements of the sport. Far from being a means to an end, the new institutions were ends in themselves. The creation of the NTA, to borrow a popular historical phrase, was part of harness racing's "search for order."

Trotting had long been governed solely by local rules. This system did not prove excessively unwieldy when harness racing depended mainly on match races or consisted of contests with small fields comprised largely of neighborhood horses. With the growth of the sport, the older rules became inoperative. In 1862, the Fashion Course rewrote their rules to adjust to the more numerous starters. Such a simple matter as the positioning of the horses on the track prior to each heat, heretofore left to the individual driver, now had to be codified. Moreover, races began to be handicapped to maintain competitive balance between the increasing number of trotters present on the course. In the early 1860s, New York tracks began handicapping by weight, but not until the next decade was the more efficient system of time-classification introduced. The increase in the number of tracks throughout the country was far more significant in producing homogeneity in the rules. To facilitate the easy movement of horses from course to course, standardization of the rules and regulations became necessary.[86]

The NTA drew heavily on the experience of the New York tracks. Since the leading sporting journals were located in Manhattan, New York's rules were the ones published and therefore practiced on a goodly number of courses throughout the country even prior to the convention.[87] Moreover, Isaiah Rynders, the only New Yorker on the one man committee designated to draft the NTA's regulations, was the chairman of this group. John L. Cassady, a delegate at the convention and a leading commentator on the trotting scene, maintained that Rynders was the busiest and most influential member at the convention.[88]

Rynders' presence and influence in the creation of the NTA raises further questions of those who viewed this association as a reform movement led by men in "white hats." A former Mississippi river boat gambler, the founder of the notorious Empire Club, a major New York gang, an active and influential member of Tammany Hall and a leading "shoulder hitter," he was the man, the *Times* claimed, who was most responsible for the "organized system of terrorism and ruffianism in city politics." Clearly, Rynders was the prototype (gambler, ruffian) of the individual who the press frequently complained wielded undo and a negative influence on the sport.[89] If this was the man who was leading the reform, it may be asked from whom were they reforming the turf?

Besides the necessity of uniform rules, the expansion of harness racing made it imperative that the various tracks be coordinated. For New York's major courses it was not so much a question of the need to synchronize their respective schedules as it was the growing competition from the increasing number of tracks emerging outside of Manhattan. With these courses offering good prize money to attract top notch horses to their meetings, even New York lacked the financial resources to meet the combined competition of these tracks. While New York remained the sport's capital, the virtual monopoly it had of the best horses in former days was undermined. In the years immediately following the Civil War, the proprietors of the turf in Gotham were forces to abandon their policy of arranging purses races throughout the year and adopted a more compact racing season.[90] To guarantee the presence of the best talent, the enlarged market necessitated the creation of some form of systematic scheduling to avoid conflicting engagements.[91]

The subsequent development of the NTA goes beyond the scope of this article. Clearly greater research into this organization, as with all phases of harness racing, is necessary. Nevertheless, the perspective drawn from the experience of New York raises questions concerning the traditional view of the formation of this federation. While New York track operators paid lip service to the need to reform the turf, the desire for order, and thereby profit, motivated them to join the national association. Through collective action they could coordinate the activities of the expanding sport, as well as buttress local authority. While the institutional reform checked some of the persistent problems confronting the turf, they were a product of pragmatic, rather than moral, objectives.[92]

The formation of the NTA symbolized the transformation of harness racing from a premodern to a modern sport. In contrast to the informal road contests which took place in the northeastern section of the country a half century earlier, harness racing evolved into a highly organized sport, with relatively uniform rules and with contests taking place in all sections of the nation. The emergence of a trotting literature (stud books and *Wallace's Monthly Magazine*) and developments in the breeding industry (the formation of the National Association of Trotting Horse Breeders and the creation of a standard breed) in the 1870s further demonstrate the centralizing and modernizing forces at work in the sport. By this decade, one social historian noted, harness racing "had grown to such mammoth proportions and won a greater share of the public attention than any other public pastime which contributed to the enjoyment of the people."

• • •

Notes

1. For the general review of the sporting patterns of nineteenth century America, see John R. Betts, *America's Sporting Heritage*, 1850-1950 (Reading, MA: Addison-Wesley, 1974), pp. 10-246; John A Krout, *Annals of American Sport* (New Haven: Yale University Press, 1929); Foster R. Dulles, *A History of Recreation: America Learns to Play*, 2nd ed. (New York: Appleton-Century-Crofts, 1965), pp. 84-99, 136-47, 182-99, 223-29; John A. Lucas and Ronald A. Smith, *Saga of American Sport* (Philadelphia: Les and Febiger, 1978), pp. 55-302; Dale A. Somers, *The Rise of Sport in New Orleans* (Baton Rouge: Louisiana State University Press, 1972); Frederic L. Paxson, "The Rise of Sport," *Mississippi Valley Historical Review*, 4 (Sept., 1917), 143-68.

2. For studies dealing with the changing attitudes towards athletics during the antebellum period, see John R. Betts, "Mind and Body in Early American Thought," *Journal of American History*, 54 (Mar., 1968), 797-805; Guy M. Lewis, "The Muscular Christianity Movement," *Journal of Health, Physical Education and Recreation*, 37 (May, 1966), 27-28, 42; John A. Lucas, "A Prelude to the Rise of Sport: Antebellum America, 1850-1860," *Quest* 11 (Dec., 1968), 50-57; Roberta J. Park, "'Embodied Selves': The Rise and Development of Concern for Physical Education, Active Games and Recreation Among American Women, 1776-1865," *Journal of Sport History*, 5 (Summer, 1978), 5-41; Arthur C. Cole, "Our Sporting Grandfathers: The Cult of Athletics at Its Source," *Atlantic Monthly*, 110 (July, 1932), 88-96. For other works touching on this period, see Jennie Holliman, *American Sport, 1785-1835* (Durham, NC: Seeman Press, 1931); Sorern S. Brynn, "Some Sports in Pittsburgh During the National Period," *Western Pennsylvania Historical Magazine*, Part 1, 51 (October, 1968), 345-68, Part II (Jan. 1969), 57-59.

3. Melvin L. Adelman, "The Development of Modern Athletics: Sport in New York City, 1820-1870," (Unpublished Ph.D. dissertation: University of Illinois, 1980).

4. For the purpose of simplicity and convenience the terms "trotting" and "harness racing" will be used interchangeably, although technically there are differences between the two. Trotting is a style of racing and may occur "in saddle" (the dominant form until the 1840s) or in harness. Harness racing is a method of racing and consists of trotting and pacing gaits.

5. My thoughts on the characteristics of premodern and modern ideal sporting types were influenced by Eric Dunning. "The Structural-Functional Properties of Folk Games and Modern Sport," *Sportwissenschaft*, 3 (Jahrgang, 1978), 215-38; Allen Guttmann, *From Ritual to Record, The Nature of Modern Sports* (New York: Columbia University Press, 1978), pp. 15-55. For a discussion of the usage of ideal sporting types, see Alan G. Ingham, "Methodology in the Society of Sport: From Symptoms of Malaise to Weber for a Cure," *Quest*, 31 (1979), 198-211. Also of value was Richard D. Brown, *Modernization: The Transformation of American Life, 1600-1865* (New York: Hill and Wang, 1976), pp. 3-22.

6. For the limited commercialization and modernization of horse racing prior to 1870, see Adelman, "Modern Athletics," pp. 74-77, 162-65.

7. *Spirit of the Times* 1 (May 12, 1832),26; (Mar. 8, 1856), 38.

8. I recognize that an essential characteristic of modern sport is its national dimension. Nevertheless, the evolution of sport from pre-modern to modern can be revealed at a local level. While this paper focuses mainly on the changing pattern of harness racing in New York, I have united, when necessary, my discussion of trotting there with similar developments taking place nationally.

9. For the development of harness racing during the first quarter of the nineteenth century, see Dwight Akers, *Drivers Up: The Story of American Harness Racing* (New York: G.P. Putnam's Sons, 1938), pp. 27-36.

10. Ibid., p. 29 (27-30); Holliman, *American Sport*, p. 121; John Hervey, *The American Trotter* (New York: Coward McCann, 1947), p. 27.

11. For the continuation of horse racing in New York, see John Hervey, *Racing in America, 1665-1865,* 2 vols., (New York: The Jockey Club, 1944), 1: 136-40, 253-60; Adelman, "Modern Athletics," p. 33. The anti-racing legislation also prohibited trotting and pacing. See *Laws of New York, 25th Session* (Albany, 1802), pp. 69-70. That bill prohibited these sports illustrates that New Yorkers were familiar with them even prior to the nineteenth century. Nevertheless, there is no evidence that the sport enjoyed any degree of popularity prior to 1800.

12. Hervey, *American Trotter,* p. 19.

13. For a discussion of racing and taverns on Third Avenue, see Akers, *Drivers Up,* pp. 30-31; Abram C. Dayton, *Last Days of Knickerbocker Life in New York* (New York: G.P. Putnam's Sons, 1897), pp. 237-58; Charles Astor Bristed, *The Upper Ten Thousands: Sketches of American Society* (New York: Stringer and Townsend, 1852), pp. 23-24; *American Turf Register and Sporting Magazine* 8 (Sept., 1836), 41.

14. Until the creation of the Standard-bred light harness horse in 1879, the trotter was a "mongrel horse" although certain well recognized families, such as the Morgans, Bellfounders and Messangers, emerged in the second quarter of the nineteenth century. Consequently, the trotting horse during this period was at best "a group of horse families that had a common characteristic, their ability to trot" [Akers, *Drivers Up,* pp. 106-9; Hervey, *American Trotter,* p. 12).

15. Frank A. Wrench, *Harness Horse Racing in the United States and Canada* (New York: D. Van Nostrand, 1948), p. 21; Hervey, *American Trotter,* pp. 21-22; Akers, *Drivers Up,* p. 28; Dayton, *Last Days,* pp. 245-60. As late as 1847, the Harlem Course was still viewed as the beginners school for the city's roadsters. See *New York Herald,* 28 April, 1847.

16. Thomas Floyd-Jones, *Backward Glances: Reminiscence of An Old New Yorker* (Somerville, NJ: Unionist Gazette Association, 1941), p. 71; Akers, *Drivers Up,* p. 13; Hervey, *American Trotter,* pp. 22-23.

17. For the formation of the NYTC, see Akers, *Drivers Up,* pp. 37-38; Drout, *Annals,* p. 48; Holliman, *American Sports,* p. 122. Johan Huizinga saw the creation of permanent organizations as the starting point of modern sport. See his *Homo Ludens: A Study of the Play Element In Culture* (Boston: Beacon Press, 1955), p. 196.

18. For the relationship between the formation of the NYTC and the re-emergence of horse racing in New York after 1821, see the speech of the president of the NYTC. *New York Evening Post,* 20 May 1825. For the parallel developments in horse racing in New York, see Adelman, "Modern Athletics," pp. 38-39.

19. *Spirit* 5 (Dec. 12, 1835); Henry W. Herbst, *Frank Forester's Horse and Horsemanship of the United States and the British Providence of North America,* 2 vols., (New York: Stringer and Townsend, 1857), 2, 158. Also see *Turf Register* (Sept., 1836), 41; Dayton, *Last Days,* pp. 245-47; Akers, *Drivers Up,* pp. 59-60.

20. Peter C. Welch, *Track and Road: The American Trotting Horse, A Visual Record 1820-1900* From the Harry T. Peters "America On Stone" Lithographs Collection (Washington, D.C.: Smithsonian Institute Press, 1967), p. 18.

21. *Herald,* 11 Oct. 1838. For popularity of trotting as a spectator sport, also see *Post,* 19 Sept. 1832; *Spirit,* 1 (Sept. 15, 1832), 11 (July 31, 1841) 258; *New York Spectator,* 9 Oct., 1829. *New York American,* 2 Oct. 1832. For discussion of

the race between Post Boys and John Bascombe, see Hervey, *Racing in America*, 2: 117-119.

22. For the experience of the Beacon Course, see Adelman, "Modern Athletics," pp. 56-57; Hervey, *Racing in America*, 2:99-100, 103. Harry B. Weiss and Grace M. Weiss, *Early Sports and Pastimes in New Jersey* (Trenton: The Pass Time Press, 1960), p. 124. Also see Akers, *Drivers Up*, p. 152.

23. *Herald*, 28 April 1847. Also see *Turf Register* 14 (Apr. 1843), 227; *Spirit* 13 (Mar. 18, 1843), 25. For the decline of thoroughbred racing in New York and throughout the North following the Depression of 1837, see Adelman, "Modern Athletics," pp. 57-64; Hervey, *Racing in America* 2, pp. 153-54.

24. Herbert, *Frank Forester's* 2: 123, 126-27. Also see, *Turf Register* 14 (April 1843), 216-17; *Turf, Field and Farm* 4 (June 12, 1867), 387.

25. In contrast to the view that the trotter was the horse of the masses, only one New Yorker in thirty in 1826 even owned a horse and by 1853 this ratio increased to only one in twenty-three. For figures, see *Herald* 25, Apr. 1853.

26. Frank Forester maintained that prior to 1840 (or before commercialization), trotting was "as completely in the hands of gentlemen sportsmen, as the turf proper." [Herbert, *Frank Forester's*, 2: 158]. The evidence does not confirm this thesis. While the owners of thoroughbreds in the New York metropolitan region were from wealthy and/or eminent families, only three New Yorkers actively involved in trotting came from the city's upper crust. To make this assessment the names of individuals involved in trotting were extracted from the newspapers and then checked against Edward Pessen's list of the wealthiest New Yorkers in 1828 and 1845. For this list, see his article "The Wealthiest New Yorkers of the Jacksonian Era: A New List," *New York Historical Society Quarterly*, 53 (April, 1970), 155-72. For the social composition of thoroughbred men in New York between 1821 and 1845, see Adelman, "Modern Athletics," pp. 66-67.

27. For the involvement of men in New York's various food markets with trotting, see Floyd-Jones, *Backward Glances*, p. 9.

28. *Herald*, 16 May, 25 April, 1849, 30 May 1848, 21 June 1853, 4, 10 June 1859, 15 Mar. 1869.

29. Welsh, *Track and Road*, p. 75.

30. *Herald* 25, April 1853.

31. For the differences in the development of harness racing in the United States and England, see Hervey, *American Trotter*, p. 19.

32. For the view of the trotter as an American development, see Robert Bonner, "Papers," Box 12, 19 Feb. 1895, New York Public Library, Hervey, *American Trotter*, p. 20. Akers, *Drivers Up*, p. 29. Harness racing also never suffered from the religious opposition which checked the growth of horse racing in various regions of the country. See ibid., p. 29; Peter C. Welsh, "The American Trotter," *American Heritage*, 23 (Dec., 1966), 31.

33. For Holmes' statement, see Lucas and Smith, *Saga*, p. 93.

34. For the urbanization of America during the antebellum period, see Charles N. Glaab and A. Theodore Brown, *A History of Urban America* (New York: Macmillan, 1967), p. 26; Blake McKelvey, *American Urbanization: A Comparative Perspective* (Glenview, Ill: Scott, Foreman & Co., 1973), p. 14. For changing economic developments during this period, see George R. Taylor, *The Transportation Revolution, 1815-1860* (New York: Harper and Row, 1968); Douglass C. North, *Growth and Welfare in the American Past: A New Economic History* (Englewood Cliffs, NJ: Prentice-Hall, 1966), pp. 75-89. Stuart Bruchey, *The Roots of American Economic Growth, 1607-1861* (New York: Harper and Row, 1965), pp. 141-207.

35. Arthur H. Cole, "Perspectives on Leisure-Time Business," *Explorations in Entrepreneurial History*, 2nd series, 1 (Summer, 1964), 23, 27-8. It

would be erroneous to perceive these commercialized "popular" amusements as being "mass institutions. Rarely were they patronized by large number of men from the working class. Their support was overwhelmingly drawn from the middle class.

36. *Spirit* 13 (Mar. 18, 1843), 25; *Turf, Field and Farm* 4 (June 22, 1867), 387.

37. *Porter's Spirit of the Times* 1 (Oct. 25, 1856), 132.

38. For the career of *Lady Suffolk*, see John Hervey, *The Old Grey Mare of Long Island* (New York: Derrydale Press, 1936); Hiram Woodruff, *The Trotting Horse of America, How To Train and Drive Him, with Reminiscences of The Trotting Turf*. Edit. by Charles J. Foster. 19th ed. (Philadelphia: Porter and Coates, 1874), pp. 211-47; Akers, *Drivers Up*, pp. 49-56.

39. For the impact of Messenger on American trotting, see Hervey, *American Trotter*, pp. 28-43. Akers, *Drivers Up*, p. 26.

40. Akers, *Drivers Up*, p. 49. Bryan's continual ownership of *Lady Suffolk* was a rarity. During this period most trotters, including some of the best horses, passed through several owners during their careers.

41. For Bryan's reputation as a reinsman and his demands on *Lady Suffolk*, see Akers, *Drivers Up*, p. 50. By comparing earnings, numbers of races and miles raced of *Lady Suffolk* and the three competitors in the intersectional horse races of the 1840s—*Fashion, Boston,* and *Peytonia*—the differences between trotting and thoroughbred racing can be illustrated. In a nine year career, *Fashion* won $41,500, by winning 32 out of 36 races. In eight years, *Boston* was triumphant in 40 of his 45 contests winning $51,700. *Peytonia* won $62,400, although no figures were available for the length of her career or the number of her victories. Furthermore, *Fashion* raced no more than 260 miles and *Boston* no more than 324 miles during their careers. (Both probably raced much less). By contrast, *Lady Suffolk* ran at least 500 miles and quite possibly as much as 800 miles. The figures on thoroughbreds were drawn from Hervey, *Racing in America* 2, 175-76, 217-19, 299.

42. *Porter's Spirit* 3 (Jan. 23, 1858), 329. For the emergence of harness racing at the county fair, see Betts, *Sporting Heritage*, pp. 34-36; Akers, *Driver's Up*, pp. 105-8; Welsh, "The Trotter," p. 31.

43. Wilkes' *Spirit of the Times* 3 (Sept. 22, 1860), 54; (Oct.6 1860): 76. For the career of *Flora Temple*, see Woodruff, *Trotting Horse*, pp. 247-335. Akers, *Drivers Up*, pp. 78-89.

44. *Spirit* 7 (Oct. 21, 1837), 284.

45. *New York Times*, 16 April 1857.

46. For the complaints of irregularities on the trotting track between 1850 and 1870, see *New York Clipper* 1 (June 25, 1853), (Mar. 25, 1854), 5 (Sept. 26, 1857), 117; 7 (June 25, 1859), 74; 6 (Apr. 9, 1859), 402; 9 (Aug. 10, 1861), 130; (Aug. 31, 1861), 154; 17 (Nov. 20, 1869), 258; *Herald*, 17 Sept. 1853, 4 June 1859, 3 Aug. 1860, 25 Sept., 3 Oct., 11 Nov., 1869, *Times* 5 June 1863; *Wilkes' Spirit* 2 (Aug. 13, 1860), 360; 4 (Aug. 10, 1861), 36; 5 (Nov. 23, 1861), 184; (Dec. 7, 1861), 213; 6 (June 21, 1862), 249; (Aug. 2, 1862), 344; 7 (Nov. 8, 1862), 153; 14 (July 7, 1866), 297.

47. Restrictions of time did not permit me to investigate the accuracy of this impression, but the performance of four leading trotters—*Lady Suffolk, Flora Temple, Dexter* and *Goldsmith Maid*—during this period provides some insights. Of these trotters, Dexter won 92 percent of his races, *Flora Temple* 84.82 percent and *Goldsmith Maid* 79.8 percent. These outstanding records minimize the number of opportunities that they could have thrown a race and gives credence to the belief that their defeats were the product of other factors. On the other hand, *Lady Suffolk* won 54.9 percent of her races. Her record could be blamed on Bryan's mismanagement of the horse, but no one will question his integrity. "Money

grubber though he was," Akers noted, Bryan "was too jealous of his grey mare's reputation ever to throw a race." [*Drivers Up*, p. 154]. In contrast to the above horse, *George Wilkes*, a trotter of outstanding potential and in turn an immensely successful progenitor, won 39.15 percent of his races. Such a poor performance record could give credence to Hervey's contention that he "was manipulated in the most discretable way was an open secret." Nevertheless, the same historian brought compelling evidence that his poor record could be explained as a product of other factors. He noted that *George Wilkes'* owners made great demands on the horse and that the horse regularly performed stud service in conjunction with his trotting campaigns. Furthermore, many of his defeats came at the expense of the leading trotters of his day. FInally, *George Wilkes* had a notorious reputation as a quitter and sulker, a point which this scholar readily accepts as valid [*American Trotter*, p. 106-8]. The winning percentages were drawn from the records in ibid., pp. 453-61.

48. In his work on harness racing, Akers devoted an entire chapter, entitled "Sharps and Flats," to the crisis of fixing of races created for the sport. Nevertheless, he conceded that "Not all races, probably not most of them, were dishonestly driven ... Much of the ugly gossip could be set down as the malicious imagination of fanatics who looked upon racing and betting as vices." Despite the presence of this brief statement, Akers left the impression, through the choice of his chapter title and the disproportionate amount of space devoted to the fixing of races, that he believed that the manipulation of contests was a widespread practice on trotting tracks. [*Drivers Up*, ch. 11]. Harold Seymour is also guilty of the same type of analysis in his treatment of corruption in baseball. See his *Baseball, The Early Years* (New York: Oxford University Press, 1960), pp. 52-54. For a different view of duplicity on the diamond, see Adelman, "Modern Athletics," pp. 412-420.

49. *Spirit* 30 (July 28, 1860), 298; *Turf, Field and Farm* 5 (Nov. 30, 1867), 338; *Herald* 6 Apr. 1860.

50. Woodruff, *Trotting Horse*, pp. 296-98. For a somewhat similar incident, see ibid., pp. 262-63.

51. In contrast to trotting, there were almost no charges of fixing contests in thoroughbred racing in New York between 1820 and 1870 even though jockies were professional athletes and large amounts of money depended on the outcome. Upper class control of the sport was largely responsible for the different attitudes.

52. *Clipper* 6 (APr. 9, 1859), 402; 1 (Mar. 25, 1854), 7 (June 25, 1859), 74; *Wilkes' Spirit* 2 (Aug. 11, 1860), 356; *Herald* 4 June 1859, 6 Apr., 3 Aug. 1860.

53. *Spirit* 30 (July 28, 1860), 298. While the *Spirit* did not believe that races were fixed, it nevertheless opposed races for gate money.

54. Woodruff, *Trotting Horse*, p. 288.

55. Unlike today, where the purses are divided, albeit unequally, among a certain number of horses, the winners, in the overwhelming number of races, were rewarded the entire purse in the antebellum period. Both thoroughbreds and trotting men recognized the economic problems created by this system as early as the 1830s; however, this method of reward continued to prevail in both turf sports until after the Civil War.

56. *Clipper* 7 (July 16, 1859), 103.

57. Nothing more coherently indicates that nineteenth century writers did not understand the concept of "upset" than the absence in their works of any term which resembles in any way the meaning the term has today.

58. Seymour, *Baseball*, p. 60. For the changing style of professional drivers, see Akers, *Drivers Up*, p. 152.

59. *Wilkes' Spirit* 12 (Mar. 25, 1865), 57; (Mar. 18, 1865), 41; (Mar. 11, 1865), 24. For road racing in New York between 1850 and 1870, see Akers, *Drivers Up,* pp. 90-92; Krout, *Annals,* p. 55, Wheaton J. Lane, *Commodore Vanderbilt, An Epic of the Steam Age* (New York: Alfred A Knopf, 1942), pp. 162-63. *Clipper* 18 (Apr. 16, 1870), 13.

60. For discussion of this theme, see Adelman, "Modern Athletics," pp. 639-6440, 709-710.

61. While there is no comprehensive list of EPPGA members, there was a register book for the year 1859-1860. It is perfectly clear that not all the signees of this book were members of the club; one being Senator Stephen Douglas of Illinois. Nevertheless, the repetition of names does not indicate that the majority were. The occupation of these members were then examined in the New York City directories. Data could be found on 53 members. Of this group, 25 (47.1%) were either merchants or brokers. Twenty-three (43.3%) other members engaged in service occupations with the majority of this group (12) associated with the food and drink industry. Of the remaining five, three were lawyers and two were clerks. Biographical data on these turfmen was unfortunately limited, but what evidence does exist indicates that they originated mainly from the middle class. In only one case was a member the son of an upper-middle class New Yorker and it is perfectly evident that none of the EPPGA members came from the city's upper class. While more data is still necessary, the evidence tends to support the earlier contention that New York's road runner came mainly from the prosperous segments of the middle class. For the register book, see *Elm Park Pleasure Garden Association,* "Visitors Book," New York Historical Society.

62. For background material on Bonner, see his own "Scrapbook of Newspaper Clippings, 1850-1899," 2 vols., New York Public Library, Stanwood Cobb, *The Magnificent Partnership* (New York: Vintage Press, 1945); Charles Morris (ed.), *Makers of New York* (Philadelphia: L.R. Hamersly, 1895), p. 236. Notices of Bonner's death (July 6, 1899) can probably be found in every major American newspaper.

63. Akers, *Drivers Up,* p. 95. For the Bonner-Vanderbilt battle, see ibid., pp. 90-104; Lane, *Commodore Vanderbilt,* p. 163; Adelman, "Modern Athletics," 112-113.

64. Bonner, "Papers," v.1, p. 66; Hervey, *American Trotter,* p. 77; Akers, Drivers Up, p. 95.

65. *New York Tribune,* 7 July 1899.

66. Akers, *Drivers Up,* p. 93; Lane, *Commodore Vanderbilt,* p. 164. While New York's upper crust were never supporters of trotting, it is doubtful that its opposition to either the sport or trotting men was as monolithic as these writers suggested. See Dayton, *Last Days,* pp. 237-58; Bristed, *Upper Ten Thousands,* pp. 23-24.

67. Akers, *Drivers Up,* p. 95.

68. I found only one individual involved in trotting prior to 1870 (excluding the three noted in the 1830s, see fn. 26) who was a descendant of the city's antebellum elite. The lone case, George B. Alley, moreover, was not a product of the new respectability the ownership of trotting horses won. Involved with trotting prior to Bonner, Alley was "one of the most prominent patrons of the trotter in the Metropolis, if not the foremost among them all" between 1850 and 1870. [Hervey, *American Trotter,* p. 131]. For biographical material on Alley, see *Times,* 17 Oct. 1883.

69. For a discussion of New York elites, see Frederic C. Jaher, "Style with Status: High Society in Late Nineteenth-Century New York," in *The Rich, the Well-Born, and the Powerful: Elites and Upper Classes in History* (Urbana, IL: University of Illinois Press, 1973), pp. 258-84; idem., "Nineteenth-Century Elites in Boston

and New York," *Journal of Social History*, 6 (Fall, 1972), 32-77. For the view that New York's upper class during the antebellum period was a stable group, see Edward Pessen, *Riches, Class and Power Before the Civil War* (Lexington, MA: D.C. Heath, 1973), pp. 84-85, 146. For criticism of this view, see Whitman Ridgway, "Measuring Wealth and Power in Antebellum America: A Review Essay," *Historical Methods Newsletter*, 8 (Mar., 1975), 75; Frederic C. Jaher, "Elites and Equality in Antebellum America," *Reviews in American History*, 2 (Mar., 1974), 86-87.

70. John Elderken, "Turf and Trotting Horse of America," in *Every Horse Owner's Cyclopedia*, edit. by Robert McClure (Philadelphia, 1872), p. 53, quoted in *Welsh, Track and Road*, p. 18; Akers, *Drivers Up*, pp. 168-69.

71. Akers, *Drivers Up*, p. 105. For the story of William M. Rysdyk and *Hambletonian*, see ibid., 115-119; Hervey, *American Trotter*, pp. 44-88.

72. Akers, *Drivers Up*, pp. 168-69.

73. For a very good discussion of these developments, see Hervey, *American Trotter*, pp. 277-92.

74. The quote can be found in Betts, *Sporting Heritage*, p. 145. For the persistence of the utilitarian argument, see Adelman, "Modern Athletics," pp. 118-120.

75. For the tremendous popularity of harness racing at county fairs in the immediate post-Civil War years, see Betts, *Sporting Heritage*, p. 144.

76. Until recently historians have designated wealthy participants in athletics as "sportsmen." The inference they expected to be drawn from this term was that these rich men eschewed financial considerations and were involved in sport solely for its own sake. The evidence on New York turfmen, both thoroughbred and trotting, between 1820 and 1870 testifies to the inaccuracy of this impression. While many of these turfmen did not feel compelled to profit from their involvement, they were not out to lose money either. When they could no longer cover their costs, as had been the case with the owners of the thoroughbreds in New York in the 1840s, their involvement in the sport ceased. For further discussion of this theme, see Adelman, "Modern Athletics," pp. 65-68. For other recent challenges to the traditional view, see Steven A. Riess, "The Baseball Magnate and Urban Politics in the Progressive Era, 1895-1920." *Journal of Sport History*, 1 (Spring, 1974), 41-62; Jonathan Brower, "Professional Sports Team Ownership: Fun, Profit and Ideology of the Power Elite," *Journal of Sport and Social Issues*, (1976), 16-51.

77. As early as 1862, the proprietor of the Fashion Course sold to a gambling "auctioneer" the right to handle all the betting on the track. For this privilege, the "pool seller," as these gamblers were called, paid the proprietor a flat fee. See *Times* 24 July 1862. For a discussion of the "pooling system" of wagering, see William H.P. Robertson, *A History of Thoroughbred Racing in America* (Englewood Cliffs, NJ: Prentice-Hall, 1964), pp. 93-94.

78. *Clipper* 12 (Dec. 17, 1864), 282; 11 (June 6, 1863), 63; *Herald* 11 Sept. 1862; *Times* 11 Sept. 1862, 16 Oct. 1864, 8 Sept. 1865; *Wilkes' Spirit* 8 (May 2, 1863), 140. 10 (July 16, 1864), 313; 11 (Oct. 8, 1864), 78-79; 12 (Apr. 29, 1865), 132-133.

79. For the figures, see *Times* 18 Mar. 1862; *Wilkes' Spirit* 22 (Apr. 16, 1870).

80. *Wilkes' Spirit* 10 (Mar. 26, 1864), 56.

81. *Clipper* 17 (Nov. 20, 1869), 258; 9 (Aug. 10, 1861), 130; (Aug. 31, 1861), 154; *Herald*, 6 Apr. 1860, 25 Sept., 9, 17 Nov. 1869; *Times* 5 June 1863; *Wilkes' Spirit* 2 (Aug. 11, 1860), 360; 4 (Aug. 10, 1861), 36; 7 (Nov. 8, 1862), 153; 14 (July 7, 1866), 297.

82. *National Association for the Promotion of the Interest of The Trotting Turf, Rules and Regulations Adopted February 4, 1870* (Providence Press, 1870),

p. 19; John Hervey, "American Harness Horse and Horsemen," in *American Harness Racing* (New York: Ralph F. Hartenstein, 1948), p.32.

83. Hervey, "American Harness Horse," p. 32. *Wrench, Harness Horse Racing*, pp.16-18; Akers, *Drivers Up*, pp. 161-66.

84. *Wilkes' Spirit* 21 (Jan. 29, 1870), 370-1.

85. *Porter's Spirit* 3 (Jan. 23, 1858), 370.

86. *Wilkes' Spirit* 21 (Jan 29, 1870), 370; *Times* 12 June 1862. For a discussion of the emergence of the time-classification system, see Akers, *Drivers Up*, pp. 138-39.

87. For the publication of the New York rules, see *Spirit* 8 (Apr. 21, 1838), 80; 11 (Jan. 29, 1842), 569; 13 (June 3, 1843), 156; 18 (May 6, 1848), 128. Dale Somers informs us that the New Orleans Trotting and Pacing Club adopted the rules used at the Beacon Course. See his, *Rise of Sport*, p. 35.

88. *Wilkes' Spirit* 22 (Feb. 26, 1870), 20-21. John L. Cassady wrote under the name of "Larkin."

89. *Times*, 14 Jan. 1885. For additional information on Rynders and his political involvement, see Alexander B. Callow, Jr., *The Tweed Ring* (New York: Oxford University Press, 1966), p. 58; Herbert Asbury, *The Gangs of New York: An Informal History of the Underworld* (New York: Capricorn Books, 1970), pp. 43-44. Rynders was not the only man of this "ilk" to have sporting associations with the "better class." John Morrissey—the one time heavyweight champion, casino operator and member of the notorious Tweed Ring—and the creme-de-la-creme of New York society were co-partners in establishing racing in Saratoga, New York in 1863. For this connection, see Hugh Bradley, *Such Was Saratoga* (New York: Doubleday, Doran and Co., 1950), pp. 142-45. Bernard Livingston, *Their Turf: America's Horsey Set and Its Princely Dynasties* (New York: Arbor House, 1973), pp. 229-30.

90. *Wilkes' Spirit* 19 (Jan. 30, 1869), 377; *Times* 31 Jan. 1870. The newer racing schedule affected only purse races. Match races, sweepstakes and some specially arranged contests continued to be held throughout the year.

91. I have found no evidence that the NTA in 1870 or afterwards emerged with a *formal* racing calendar. Nevertheless, the creation of systematic schedules, through the federation of local trotting clubs began in the 1870s. The first and by far the most important of these associations was the Grand Circuit established in 1873. The success of this organization "led local associations elsewhere to form similar combinations." In time, an organizational pattern emerged that remains in existence today, "In a truer sense than before, harness racing became a 'national sport.'" [Akers, *Drivers Up*, p. 141].

92. It is significant to note that Akers conceded that the NTA did not immediately succeed in reforming the trotting turf even though he judged the organization's effort to cleans the sport of its abuses an overall success [*Drivers Up*, pp. 164-65].

93. Marshall B. Davidson, *Life in America*, 2 vols. (Boston: Houghton Mifflin, 1951), 2:35.

• • •

Suggestions for Further Reading:

Akers, Dwight, *Drivers Up: The Story of American Harness Racing* (New
     York: Putnam's, 1938).
Berryman, Jack W., "John S. Skinner's *American Farmer.* Breeding and
     Racing the Maryland 'Blood Horse,' 1819-1829," *Maryland
     Historical Magazine,* LXXVI (Summer, 1981), 159-173.
Betts, John R., "Agricultural Fairs and the Rise of Harness Racing,"
     Agricultural History, XXVII (April, 1953), 71-75.
Cunningham, John T., "Queen of the Turf," *New Jersey History,* XCVI
     (Spring-Summer, 1978), 43-48.
Hervey, John, *The American Trotter* (New York: Coward McCann, 1947).
_____, *Racing in America, 1665-1865,* Vol. II (New York:
     Jockey Club, 1944).
MacLeod, Duncan, "Racing to War: Antebellum Match Races Between
     the North and the South," *Southern Exposure,* VII, 3 (Fall, 1979),
     7-13.
Struna, Nancy L., "The North-South Races: American Thoroughbred
     Racing in Transition," *Journal of Sport History,* VIII, 2
     (Summer, 1981), 28-57.
Welsh, Peter C. "The American Trotter," *American Heritage,* XXIII
     (December, 1966), 31 ff.
Wrench, Frank A., *Harness Horse Racing in the United States and
     Canada* (New York: Van Nostrand, 1948).

THE QUEST FOR SUBCOMMUNITIES
AND THE RISE OF AMERICAN SPORT

Benjamin G. Rader

In focusing on the "take-off" stage of organized sport in America, that is, the period in the mid-nineteenth century when sport emerged as a force within the nation's social structure, Benjamin Rader offers an interpretation that is more than must another variation on the new social safety-valve theory which Frederick Paxson first advanced. Rader emphasizes that the quest of certain groups to establish subcommunities within the larger society provided a framework for their own identity, an expression of shared interests, and an explanation for the rise of sport.

Stemming from a tradition of voluntary associationism that had already become a striking feature of American society by the early nineteenth century, sport organizations initially had either an ethnic or status direction. Nationality, religious beliefs, and language were some of the factors that bound immigrant groups together in forming separate ethnic communities. The Scottish Caledonian clubs and the German Turner societies, for example, used sport to coalesce and preserve traditional cultural patterns. The track and field competitions of the former and the physical training programs of the latter soon crossed ethnic boundaries and achieved a broad appeal among both native-born and other hyphenated Americans who took over the immigrant's sports and transformed them to meet their own needs. For native Americans, in particular, status communities of varying degrees of exclusivity and focus (yachting, racquet sports, cricket, baseball and "athletic," or track and field) emerged as counterparts to the ethnic associations and another means to deal with the demands of an emerging urban-industrial society.

Although Rader focuses on those voluntary sport organizations which tended to be central to the formation of ethnic and status communities, he acknowledges in concluding that sport could supplement other institutions or associations, for example, churches, schools, and labor unions, that were also important to community existence. In these contexts, sport could provide a commonality of purpose and identity that overcame socio-economic, racial, ethnic and religious differences. Sport, as an instrument of local, regional, and even national community consciousness, flows from this transcendent appeal.

One of the most intriguing problems for the sport historian is to account for the relationship between the American social structure and the "take off" stage of organized sport in the United States.[1] We still know little about why sport arose in the latter half of the nineteenth century. Equally obscure are the relationships of sport to groups and individuals within American society. What social functions, either latent or manifest, did sport perform during the take-off stage? This essay contends that a quest for subcommunities in the nineteenth century furnishes an important key to understanding the rise of American sport. As earlier communities based on small geographic areas—typically agricultural villages—declined or were undermined, Americans turned to new forms of community. Sport clubs, as one type of voluntary association, became one of the basic means by which certain groups sought to establish subcommunities within the larger society.

As early as the 1830s voluntary associations had become a striking feature of American society. Tocqueville observed that "In no country in the world has the principle of association been more successfully used or applied to a greater multitude of objects than in America ..."[2] A contemporary of Tocqueville believed that since Americans had destroyed "classes, and corporate bodies of every kind, and come to simple direct individualism," the vacuum had been filled by the "production of voluntary organizations to an immense extent." Although many of the organizations of the 1830s were temporary, designed to accomplish only a specific purpose, they provided a "noble and expansive feeling which identifies self with community."[3] Max Weber summed up the transcendent importance of voluntary organizations to American society. "In the past and up to the very present," wrote Weber, "it has been a characteristic precisely of the specifically American democracy that it did *not* constitute a formless sand heap of individuals, but rather a buzzing complex of strictly elusive, yet voluntary associations."[4] The clubs could sort out persons according to any criteria they chose: it might be common interests, sex, ethnicity, occupation, religion, status, or a combination thereof. Likeminded men found in voluntary organizations a milieu in which they could counter the impersonality of the burgeoning cities.

The voluntary association became one of several means by which Americans sought to replace the old village community with new subcommunities. In addition to voluntary societies, important considerations for determining the membership of a subcommunity could be living in a particular neighborhood, belonging to a certain religious denomination, and attending specific educational institutions. For example, essential to becoming a member of a high status community might be living in a section of the city with others of a similar income range, sharing a common ethnicity and religious preference (native-born American and Protestant Episcopal), and attending the "right" schools (a New England boarding school and an Ivy League College). Birth into an old family continued to provide a person with advantages in obtaining membership in a status community, but less so than it had in the eighteenth century.

Of special interest for the rise of sport was the quest for two types of subcommunities: ethnic and status. (When prefaced by "status" or "ethnic," the use of the term "subcommunity" is redundant and thus community" will be substituted.) The ethnic community usually arose from contradictory forces of acceptance and rejection of the immigrant by the majority society. The status community, by contrast, was a product of status equals who wanted to close their ranks from those they considered inferior. Several tests can be applied to determine whether a sport club was integral to the quest for ethnic or status communities: the adoption of exclusionary membership policies, the promotion of other activities besides sport, the development of appropriate symbols which facilitated communication between members, and the belief, either implicit or explicit, that sport participation was useful in socializing youth.

Since sport per se was not threatening to deeply held persona beliefs and yet provided a milieu for fellowship and common purpose, the sport club was an attractive alternative to other forms of voluntary associations. Athletic activity, which is necessarily subordinated to rules, encouraged a temporary equality between members. The equality of play strengthened the bonds between members who might be divided by personal values.[5] The sport club could be easily transformed into a multi-faceted social agency. It could also be an instrument for social exclusion; for the socialization of youth, and for disciplining the behavior of its members. In short the sport club assumed some of the traditional functions of the church, the state, and the geographic community. Almost incidentally the sport club of the nineteenth century provided a tremendous impetus to the growth of American sport.

• • •

The need of immigrant groups to form separate ethnic communities depended upon a host of variables including their nationality, religious beliefs, language, and status. The majority society of native-born Americans (hereafter referred to as native-Americans) was less likely to discriminate against immigrants who were most like themselves. Immigrants from England, Scotland, and Wales tended to assimilate more rapidly than those from other parts of Europe. The history of nineteenth century sport clubs reflected the process of acculturation by distinctive ethnic groups. The Scottish Caledonian clubs, for example, functioned briefly as an ethnic community. But as Scottish immigration declined and the Scots adopted the native-American culture, the need for an ethnic community subsided. The German Turner societies began as ethnic communities, and as the club members assimilated they sometimes became status communities.[6]

The Scottish Caledonian clubs may have been the most significant ethnic community in encouraging the growth of nineteenth-century American sport. Extending back into the mists of Scottish history, rural communities had held annual track and field games. Beginning in the 1850s these games began to provide one of the bases for organizing Caledonian clubs in America. Wherever a few Scots settled, they usually founded a Caledonian club; eventually they formed well over 100 clubs. In 1887, for example, the *Scottish-American Journal* reported that "A Caledonian Club has been organized at Great Falls Montana, with a membership of 37 enthusiastic Scots."[7] The clubs restricted membership to persons of Scottish birth or descent.

Although the evidence is not conclusive, it appears that the Caledonian clubs functioned as a major agency for the formation of a Scottish ethnic community in many American cities. The purposes of the clubs, as one of the founders of the Boston organization put it, was to perpetuate "the manners and customs, literature, the Highland costume and the athletic games of Scotland, as practiced by our forefathers."[8] Apart from sport, the clubs sponsored extensive social activities such as dinners, dancing, and bagpipe playing. In short the clubs provided a sense of community in a strange society.

Native-born Americans exhibited an unexpected enthusiasm for the annual Caledonian games. Huge crowds, upwards to 20,000 in New York City, turned out to view competition in footracing, tug o' war, hurdling, jumping, pole vaulting, hammer throwing, and shot-putting. The clubs quickly recognized the potential for financial gain. They opened competition to all athletes regardless of nationality or race, charged admission, and offered lucrative prizes to winners. From the 1850s to the mid-1870s the Caledonians were the most important promoters of track and field in the country. The success of the games helped to stimulate the formation of the native-American athletic clubs (in this era "athletic" was synonymous with track and field) and the growth of inter-collegiate track and field. In fact, by the 1880s the wealthy native-American clubs had seized basic control of American track and field from the Caledonians. The Caledonians then began to decline rapidly as promoters of sport, but they continued to serve as the focal point of Scottish communities. With the slackening of Scottish immigration and the rapid assimilation of Scots into American society, most of the clubs disappeared by the turn of the twentieth century. Most of the Scots no longer felt a compelling need for a distinctive ethnic community.

Unlike the Scottish Caledonian clubs, the Turner societies had first been organized in their native land. In reaction to the rule of Napoleon, the power of the German aristocracy, and the disunity of the German States, Friedrick Ludwig Jahn formed the first Turner society in

Berlin in 1811. From the start, the Turners had a strong ideological cast. By establishing universal education and a systematic program of gymnastics (the latter modeled after the ancient Greeks), Jahn hoped to create a united Germany ruled by the people. Young men of the middle class—petty officials, intellectuals, journalists, and students—flocked to Jahn's new society. The Revolution of 1848 brought disaster for the Turners in Germany; many of them emigrated to the United States.[9]

The Turner immigrants faced a different challenge in America, since the Americans had already achieved several of the Turner goals. The United States had no hereditary aristocracy to combat, and a representative democracy was accepted as the ideal political form. Yet the Turners were utopian, free-thinking, and socialistic. They sought an organic community. American individualism ran counter to their deepest social instincts. They also arrived during the heyday of the Know-Nothing movement. Though the nativists directed their energies primarily at the Catholic Church and Irish immigrants, the Turners bore the brunt of mob action in several American cities. Perhaps even more crucial in driving the Turners together was the fierce antagonism they experienced from the "church" Germans. The haughty anticlericalism and superior cultural achievements of the turners made it impossible for them to find refuge in the larger German ethnic communities. Consequently, the Turner societies formed distinctive subcommunities in many American cities, sharply separated from those Germans whose lives centered around their churches.

Even prior to the immigration of the Forty-Eighters, the Turners had begun to influence American thinking about the human body and the relationship of the body to the rest of man's being. The Turners initiated America's first physical training programs. In 1826, Carl Follen, who was called to teach German literature at Harvard, organized the first college gymnasium modeled after the Jahn system. A year earlier Francis Lieber, a famous encyclopedist, was appointed as the first director of the Tremont Gymnasium in Boston. And Carl Beck, a Latin teacher, founded a gymnastics program at Round Hill School.

Shortly after their arrival in the New World the Forty-Eighters began to organize Turner societies. Friedrich Hecker, a hero of the Revolution in Baden, erected a gymnasium in Cincinnati in 1849 to cultivate "rational training, both physical and intellectual." The Turner halls provided a complete social center with lectures, libraries, and usually a bar. Here the Turners tried to preserve the speech, songs, and customs of the Fatherland, often forming separate militia companies. In 1851 the Turners held a national gymnastics festival in Philadelphia. This competitive event became an annual affair, with gymnasts from over 150 societies participating. After the Civil War the Turners abandoned most of their radical political program and assimilated rapidly into the host society, but they continued to agitate for their physical training program.

One of the striking features of the Chicago World's Fair of 1893 was a mass exercise performed by 4,000 German-American members of the national *Turnerbund.* In 1898 the United States Commissioner of Education declared that the introduction of school gymnastics in Chicago, Kansas City, Cleveland, Denver, Indianapolis, St. Louis, Milwaukee, Cincinnati, St. Paul, and San Francisco was due to the Turners and that "the directors of physical education [in these cities] are graduates of the Seminary or Normal School of the North American Turnerbund."[10]

The examples of the Caledonian clubs and the Turner societies by no means exhaust the involvement of ethnic communities in sport. Both the Irish parishes and Irish volunteer fire departments sponsored and promoted athletics. Ironically, as late as the 1920s, a French-Canadian faction in Woonsocket, Rhode Island "resorted to the archetypical American game [baseball]" as a means of preserving their community from the forces of assimilation.[11] While sport should not be considered a necessary precondition for the existence of any of the nineteenth-century ethnic communities, it often helped coalesce and preserve traditional cultural patterns. Sport seemed to assist in blurring economic and ideological differences within the community. In turn, of course, the ethnic communities encouraged the rise of sport. In the cases of both the Caledonians and the Turners, native-Americans eventually took over the immigrants' sports and transformed them to meet their own needs.

• • •

Many native-American groups in the nineteenth century tried to cope with the new urban industrial society by forming subcommunities based on status. The socially exclusive club became the main agency of status ascription. As automatic social deference declined in the nineteenth century, the number of private clubs ballooned. These clubs capitalized on the indefinite social differentiations of American society; they tried to promote a specific style of life that would exclude outsiders. The style usually included a code of honor, a proper mode of dress and speech, education at the "right" schools, pursuit of the appropriate sports, and a host of in-group behavioral nuances. The exclusive club, then, provided "an intricate web of primary group milieux which [gave] ... form and structure to an otherwise impersonal urban society of secondary groups."[12]

The private clubs served as accurate barometers of different levels of nineteenth-century status communities. At the apex of the status structure in large American cities were the metropolitan men's clubs, such as the Philadelphia Club founded in 1835, the Union (1836) and the Century Clubs (1847) in New York, and the Somerset in Boston (1851). The members of these clubs came to dominate the social and economic life of their respective cities. Usually composed of older men, these clubs did not promote sport. After the Civil War the Union Leagues, centers of Republican respectability, and the University clubs, composed of the graduates of prestigious colleges, ranged slightly below the patrician metropolitan clubs. Neither the University clubs nor Union Leagues considered sport an important part of club life. On the third rung of the upper status layer of the American club structure were the athletic clubs organized in the late nineteenth century. These clubs originated with younger men who shared a common interest in sports. In due time the athletic, cricket (in Philadelphia), racquet, and yacht clubs became important instruments of status ascription and sometimes served as stepping stones to memberships in the metropolitan clubs.[13]

Yacht clubs were one of the first voluntary sport organizations to be formed by an upper-status group. John C. Stevens, scion of a wealthy New York family and former president of the prestigious Union Club, founded the New York Yacht Club in 1844. A "succession of gentlemen ranking high in the social and financial circles" of the city soon joined the club.[14] Among them was William R. Travers, later the leading promoter of the New York Athletic Club. The club erected an elaborate facility at the Elysian Fields, a part of Stevens' estate at Hoboken, New Jersey. Each year the clubs sponsored a regatta off the clubhouse promontory. Apart from owning plush yachts, club members had to pay dues of $40 the first year and $25 thereafter. The club prescribed expensive uniforms for members and sponsored regular balls and social cruises to Newport, Rhode Island, Bar Harbor, Maine, and other nearby wealthy summer resorts. In 1851 Stevens, with his yacht *America*, defeated 18 British yachts at the Isle of Wight, to win a coveted cup donated by the Royal Yacht Squadron; in 1857 he gave the cup to the New York Yacht club on the condition that it would be "a perpetual challenge cup for friendly competition between foreign countries." By 1893 six international matches had been held for the America's Cup, all incidentally won by American yachts. By the 1890s every major eastern seaboard city had its exclusive yacht club.

The first baseball clubs occupied a position somewhere near the bottom of the upper status structure, ranking below the status achieved by the yacht clubs or the metropolitan athletic clubs. The membership of the New York Knickerbocker baseball club, organized in 1845, included young professionals, merchants, and white collar workers. As Harold Seymour noted, they were not simply interested in playing baseball. "They were primarily a social club with a distinctly exclusive flavor —somewhat similar to what country clubs represented in the 1920s and 1930s ..."[15] Membership was limited to forty, applicants could be blackballed, and the club insisted on strict rules of proper conduct. Since the club held contests every Monday and Thursday, those without a substantial amount of leisure time were automatically excluded. Players who failed to appear for the contests could be fined. The club held a large banquet after each game and sponsored festive social affairs in the off season. Club members, Seymour wrote, "were more expert with the knife and fork at post-game banquets than with bat and ball on the diamond."[16] The Knickerbocker baseball club provided both a means by which its members could distinguish themselves from the urban masses and a setting for close interpersonal relationships between men of similar tastes and social understanding.

The early clubs which imitated the Knickerbockers tried to prevent baseball from becoming a mass commercial spectacle. In 1858 they organized the National Association of Baseball Players to stop the creeping commercialism which was invading the sport. By 1860 about 60 clubs had joined the Association, which "clung to the notion that baseball ought to be a gentleman's game. For this reason amateurism was applauded, and participants were expected to be persons of means and local standing."[17] The clubs scheduled outside contests only with teams that enjoyed equal social stature. Influenced by the English notion that sport should be an exclusive prerogative of gentlemen, club members were supposed to be magnanimous in victory and friendly in defeat. After contests the home club usually gave a large banquet for the visitors.

Baseball clubs survived only briefly as effective agencies of status communities. Since baseball could be played relatively quickly in any open space, and since it required inexpensive equipment, from the 1850s on it became a favorite sport of the lower and middle classes. Seymour found that in the decade of the 1850s in New York City there were clubs composed exclusively of fire companies, policemen, barkeepers, dairymen, school teachers, physicians, and even clergymen. The social decorum of the game changed dramatically. The clubs began to charge admission and divide the receipts among their best players. Betting, cheering, and general rowdyism (sometimes leading to riots) became commonplace. The "founding" clubs either folded or sometimes took up another sport. Baseball would never again be suited for the needs of those who were striving to form high status communities. The sport did, however, serve as a mechanism for the perpetuation of occupational identities.

Organized in the post-Civil War era, the metropolitan athletic clubs were far more socially prestigious than the early baseball clubs.[18] The founders of the athletic clubs were usually wealthy young men who enjoyed track and field competition. At first they did not conceive of their clubs in terms of social exclusiveness but in terms of the common congeniality and sporting interests of the members. Professional athletes, gamblers, and "rowdies" tended to dominate the existing world of track and field. Drawing upon the English sporting heritage, the clubs began to draw rigid distinctions between amateur and professional athletes by the mid-1880s. By becoming champions of the amateur code of athletics, they, in effect, were able to bar lower-income persons from participation in the track and field competition which they sponsored.[19]

The athletic clubs provided the major stimulus to the growth of amateur athletics. The New York Athletic Club (NYAC), the first and most prestigious of the clubs, began sponsoring open track and field meets in 1868. By special invitation the New York Caledonian Club participated, allegedly making it an "international match—American against Scotland."[20] In the 1870s NYAC expanded its activities by building the first cinder track in the country at Mott Haven and sponsoring the first national amateur championships in track and field (1876), swimming (1877), boxing (1878), and wrestling (1878). In 1879, eight of the exclusive clubs formed the National Association of Amateur Athletes of America, to which NYAC transferred the annual track and field championships. By 1883 there were some 150 athletic clubs in the United States and each usually held at least one annual competition. In 1888 the National Association foundered on attempts to define and enforce the amateur code. A few of the affiliated clubs formed the Amateur Athletic Union. Composed of the most exclusive clubs, the union claimed jurisdiction over more than 40 sports and rigorously enforced the amateur code in the contests that it sponsored. Until the formation of the National Collegiate Athletic Association in 1905, the union and its collegiate affiliates dominated all amateur sport of championship quality.

Metropolitan athletic clubs became an important link in a web of associations that constituted elite status communities. For example, William R. Travers, long-time president of the New York Athletic Club, belonged to 27 social clubs including New York's two most prestigious men's clubs. The athletic clubs excluded from membership all except those near the top of the social hierarchy. Ironically, as the clubs became more effective agencies of community formation, they tended to lose their emphasis on sport. Usually they opened their doors to the entire family, they built special facilities for women, and they began to sponsoring dazzling balls and banquets. By the 1880s and 1890s only a few of the members were top-flight athletes; most of the members either were too old to play, were occasional athletes, or did not engage in competition at all. Frederick W. Janssen, a member of the Staten Island Athletic Club and an active athlete, rued the tendency of the clubs to become social centers:

> The social element in clubs is like "dry rot" and eats into the vitals of athletic clubs, and soon causes them to fail in the purpose for which they were organized ... Palatial club houses are erected at great cost and money is spent in adorning them that, if used to beautify athletic grounds and improve tracks, would cause a wide-spread interest in athletic sports and further the development of the wind and muscles of American youth.[21]

The tendency noted by Janssen was irreversible, for the social functions performed by the clubs had become more important to the members than athletic competition.

The metropolitan athletic clubs were forerunners of the great country club movement of the twentieth century. Unlike athletic clubs, country clubs became havens for those seeking to establish status communities in the suburbs and smaller cities. While golf was not the initial reason for forming the first country clubs, it became the most potent agency for the spread of the clubs throughout the nation. Beginning in 1888 with the formation of the St. Andrews Golf Club of Yonkers, New York, golf slowly invaded the wealthy suburban areas of New York, Boston, Philadelphia, and Chicago. In 1894 both St. Andrews and the Newport Golf Club scheduled national amateur championships; the formation of the Amateur Golf Association of the United States in 1894 eliminated the confusion. With but few exceptions, a reporter wrote in 1898, golf "is a sport restricted to the richer classes in this country."[22] Until the 1920s golf continued to have a highly select following.

Sport clubs, such as the country clubs, were far less significant as constituents of status communities in England than in the United States. The contrasts between the functions of the clubs were sharply drawn by George Birmingham, an Englishman:

> There are also all over England clubs especially devoted to particular objects, golf clubs, yacht clubs, and so forth. In these clubs members are drawn together by their interest in a common pursuit, and are forced into some kind of acquaintanceship. But these are very different in spirit and intention from the American country club. It exists as a kind of center of the social life of the neighborhood. Sport is encouraged by these clubs for the sake of general sociability. In England sociability is a by-product of an interest in sport.

> The country club at Tuxedo [New York] is not perhaps the oldest, but it is one of the oldest institutions of its kind in America. At the proper time of year there are dances, and a debutante acquires, I believe, a certain prestige by "coming out" at one of them. But the club exists primarily as a social center of Tuxedo. It is in one way the ideal, the perfect country club. It not only fosters, it regulates and governs the social life of the place.[23]

In addition to the early baseball, yacht, metropolitan athletic, and country clubs, several other voluntary sport organizations served as instruments of status communities. The Philadelphia cricket clubs and the racquet clubs of the large cities were as socially prestigious as the metropolitan athletic clubs. The history of these clubs followed a pattern similar to the athletic clubs. Cricket as a sport in Philadelphia, for example, declined when the clubs assumed larger social functions. For a time, several of the Philadelphia cricket clubs became major centers of lawn tennis. But in the 1920s, when lawn tennis began to move out of the network of the exclusive clubs, the cricket clubs no longer furnished players of championship quality.[24]

Lawn tennis first flourished in Newport, Rhode Island, a summer resort of the very rich. In Newport, the nation's wealthiest families constructed huge palaces of stone for summer homes and entertained each other lavishly. Dixon Wectore has written that "Other than social consciousness, the only bond which drew this summer colony together was sport—which might consist of sailing around Block Island, or having cocktails upon one's steam yacht reached by motor-boat from the landing of the New York Yacht Club, or bathing at Bailey's Beach or the Gooseberry Island Club, or tennis on the Casino courts."[25] The posh Newport Casino Club, built by James Gordon Bennett, Jr., publisher of the New York *Herald*, became the home of the United States National Lawn Tennis Association (1881) and was the site of the national championships until 1913 when the tournament was moved to Forest Hills, New York. Lawn tennis long remained a sport dominated by clubs of impeccably high status aspirations.

The sponsorship of tennis and golf by the elite clubs expanded the opportunities for women to participate in sport. Many of the first tennis courts were built specifically for the wives and daughters of club members. During the first decades of the development of American tennis, many observers believed that tennis would remain primarily a sport for women. In the early years the women preferred doubles to singles, possibly because they were encumbered by bustles and full-length skirts. Women held a few tournaments as early as 1881 and in 1886 they scheduled the first women's national tennis championships. The task of breaking the sex barrier in golf was more difficult. In the closing years of the nineteenth century the golf clubs along the Atlantic Coast began reluctantly to set aside the links on certain afternoons for female players. Only 13 women participated in the first national tournament held on the Meadowbrook course on Long Island in 1895. In 1898, H.L. Fitz Patrick announced, probably prematurely, that "the American golf girl has arrived!"[26] Golfing women helped initiate a more liberated style of dress; by 1898 a few brave ladies were playing without hats and with elbow-length sleeves. But, compared to me, the number of women athletes remained exceedingly small. Most of the women engaged only in the social life of the clubs.

Within a limited context and for a short time the collegiate athletic associations represented a quest for subcommunities. In the 1880s, as newly enriched groups sought a college education as a means of achieving a social position commensurate with their wealth, college enrollments spurted upwards. The academic degree, particularly from an Ivy League school, was a passport to polite society. But the new students found themselves confronted with a large number of strangers, often a boring curriculum and uninspired teaching, and few opportunities for social intercourse except through sedate literary and oratorical societies. In response to this unexciting, impersonal academic setting, they formed a vast array of clubs, fraternities, and athletic associations. Athletic associations usually opened their doors to any student who was athletically talented. Because of this membership policy, the associations probably served as less satisfactory subcommunity agencies than did the other collegiate social clubs. At any rate, in the 1890s the associations began to collapse as independent student-run clubs. Colleges hired professional coaches, seized control of athletics from the students, and transformed intercollegiate sports into commercial ventures.[27]

This essay has focused on voluntary sport organizations which tended to be central to the formation of either ethnic or status communities. Neighborhoods and persons with common occupations or religious preferences formed a host of smaller sport clubs in the nineteenth century. Since these clubs rarely had elaborate athletic facilities nor seemed to be concerned about social activities other than sport, they were apparently not as important as agencies of community formation. Yet they should not be neglected as a dimension of the general nineteenth-century quest for communities. Sport could supplement other institutions or associations that were more vital to the existence of communities. Some of the churches, for example, apparently found that sponsoring an athletic team bound their membership closer together and reinforced common values. Some skilled craftsmen found in sport a means by which they could distinguish themselves more clearly from ordinary workingmen. School sports, particularly in the twentieth century, helped give an identity and common purpose to many neighborhoods, towns, and cities which were otherwise divided by class, race, ethnicity, and religious differences. In a larger, less tangible sense, mass sporting spectacles may have been an aspect of a search for a city-wide, regional, or even national communities.

• • •

Notes

1. Little progress has been made in analyzing the relationship between the sport "takeoff" and the American social structure since Frederick L. Paxson's "The Rise of Sport," *Mississippi Valley Historical Review*, 4 (Sept., 1917), 144-68. Paxson's main argument was that sport provided a new social safety valve which replaced the one closed by the frontier. Recent historical treatments of the sport revolution tend to accept this thesis. See for example, Dale A. Somers, *The Rise of Sports in New Orleans, 1850-1900* (Baton Rouge: Louisiana State Univ. Press, 1972), 275-76, and John R. Betts, *America's Sporting Heritage, 1850-1950* (Reading, MA: Addison-Wesley, 1974), 178. Neither author elaborates on Paxson's article, although Somers suggests several other relationships between sport and society. Paul Hoch, in his neo-Marxian appraisal of contemporary American sport, *Rip Off the Big Game: The Exploitation of Sports by the Power Elite* (Garden City, NY: Anchor Books, 1972), provides a version of the safety valve thesis by arguing that a "power elite" made sport into an opiate of the masses. See also the analysis of Joel H. Spring in "Mass Culture and School Sports," *History of Education Quarterly*, 14 (Winter 1974), 483-500. Spring found that at the turn of the century, proponents of organized sport in the schools believed that athletics was a useful means of social control. This may in part account for Paxson's formulation of the thesis and its continued acceptance.

2. Alexis de Tocqueville, *Democracy in America*, Phillips Bradley, ed. (New York: Alfred A. Knopf, 1951), Vol, 2, 191.

3. Quoted in Walter S. Glazer, "Participation and Power: Voluntary Associations and the Functional Organization in Cincinnati in 1840," *Historical Methods Newsletter*, 5 (Sept. 1972), 153.

4. H.H. Gerth and C. Wright Mills, trans. and eds. *From Max Weber: Essays in Sociology* (New York: Oxford Univ. Press, 1958), 310. Another important dimension of the quest for subcommunities was the formation of fraternal organizations in the nineteenth century. See Charles W. Ferguson, *Fifty Million Brothers: A Panorama of American Lodges and Clubs* (New York: Farrar and Rhinehart, 1937), and Noel P. Gist, *Secret Societies: A Cultural Study of Fraternalism in the United States* (Columbia, MO: Univ. of Missouri Press, 1940). Fraternal organizations did not formally promote sport. Perhaps the most popular voluntary organizations of all were American churches, many of which eventually promoted some form of sport. For a general treatment, see Sidney E. Mead, *The Lively Experiment: The Shaping of Christianity in America* (New York: Harper and Row, 1963).

5. For this idea I am indebted to Hugh Dalziel Duncan, *Communication and the Social Order* (London: Oxford Univ. Press, 1962), esp. 334-37. See also Michael Novak, *The Joy of Sports: End Zones, Bases, Baskets, Balls, and the Consecration of the American Spirit* (New York: Basic Books, 1976), 132-41.

6. For an example of the transition of a Turner group from an ethnic to a status community, see Noel Iverson, *Germania, U.S.A.: Social Change in New Ulm, Minnesota* (Minneapolis: Univ. of Minnesota Press, 1966).

7. Quoted in Gerald Redmond, *The Caledonian Games in Nineteenth-Century America* (Rutherford, NJ: Fairleigh Dickinson Univ. Press, 1971), 45. On the clubs also see Rowland Tappan Berthoff, *British Immigrants in Industrial America, 1790-1950* (Cambridge, MA: Harvard Univ. Press, 1953), 151-52, 167-68, 179.

8. Quoted in Redmond, *The Caledonian Games*, 39.

9. See esp. A.E. Zucker, ed., *The Forty-Eighters: Political Refugees of the German Revolution of 1848* (New York: Columbia Univ. Press, 1950).

10. Quoted in ibid., 109. Equally interesting as sport organizations that promoted ethnic communities were the Czech Sokols. Eventually some 184 Sokols were organized in the United States. Most had buildings in which calisthenics, gymnastics, athletic contests, singing, and other activities took place. Training in the Sokol system included the Czech youth and women as well as men. See *Panorama: A Historical Review of Czechs and Slovaks in the United States of America* (Cicero, IL: Czechoslovak National Council of America, 1970), 133-52.

11. Richard Sorrel, "Sports and Franco-Americans in Woonsocket, 1870-1930," *Rhode Island History,* 31 (Fall 1972), 112. Sorrel believes that sport both encouraged and discouraged the acculturation of the French Canadians in Woonsocket.

12. E. Digby Baltzell, *Philadelphia Gentlemen: The Making of a National Upper Class* (New York: Free Press, 1958), 335.

13. The "muscular" Christianity movement appears to have prepared the way for the increased interest of the upper status communities in sport. The movement fought the traditional interest of the upper status communities in sport. The movement fought the traditional Puritan attitudes toward sport and provided a rationale for participation in athletics. Most of the advocates of muscular Christianity were Protestant Episcopal clerics; not coincidentally, a disproportionate percentage of those who belonged to the status elite were members of the Protestant Episcopal Church. See Guy Lewis, "The Muscular Christianity Movement," *Journal of Health, Physical Education and Recreation,* 37 (May 1966), 27-28, 42, and John A Lucas, "A Prelude to the Rise of SPort: Ante-Bellum America, 1850-1860," *Quest,* 11 (Dec. 1968), 50-57.

14. Charles A. Peverelly, *The Book of American Pastimes: Containing a History of the Principal Base Ball, Cricket, Rowing, and Yachting Clubs of the United States* (New York: pub. by author, 1866), 19. Prior to the Civil War, Stevens was a pioneer in many early sporting ventures. See *National Cyclopedia of American Biography,* Vol. 1 (New York: James T. White, 1893), 447.

15. Harold Seymour, *Baseball: The Early Years* (New York: Oxford Univ. Press, 1960), 15. Seymour found that "among some fifty-odd names on their roster from 1845 to 1860 were 17 merchants, 12 clerks, 5 brokers, 4 professional men, 2 insurance men, a bank teller, a 'Segar Dealer,' one hatter, a cooperage owner, a stationer, a United States Marshall, and several 'gentlemen.'"

16. Ibid.

17. David Quentin Voigt, *American Baseball: From Gentleman's Sport to the Commissioner System* (Norman: Univ. of Oklahoma Press, 1966), 9.

18. See especially Joe D. Willis and Richard G. Wettan, "Social Stratification in New York City Athletic Clubs, 1865-1915," *Journal of Sport History,* 3 (Spring, 1976), 45-63 and Somers, *The Rise of Sport in New Orleans,* chap. 11.

19. As an introduction to the topic of the amateur code see Arnold Flath, *A History of Relations Between the National Collegiate Athletic Association and the Amateur Athletic Union of the United States, 1905-1963* (Champaign, IL: Stipes, 1964) and Robert Korsgaard, "A History of the Amateur Athletic Union of the United States," Ed.D. project, Teachers College, Columbia University, 1952). Accusations that the amateur code discriminated against working class athletes exasperated Caspar Whitney, the dignified sports editor of *Harper's Weekly,* "And what drivelling talk is all this that prates of ignoring the poor 'laborer,'" wrote Whitney, "... and wants to drag him into our sport, putting him under restrictions with which he has no sympathy, and paying him for the time he may lose from his trade! What sporting 'Coxeyism' is this that has neither rhyme nor reason to war-

rant it serious consideration by intelligent mankind? Caspar W. Whitney, *A Sporting Pilgrimage* (New York: Harper and Brothers, 1895), 208.

20. Frederick W. Janssen, *History of American Amateur Athletics* (New York: Charles R. Bourne, 1885), 35.

21. Quoted in Willis and Wettan, "Social Stratification," 52.

22. H.L. FitzPatrick, "Golf and the American Glrl," *Outing*, 33 (Dec. 1898), 294-95. For the golf facilities of the major cities see a series of articles in *Outing*, 34 (May-Aug., 1899), 129-42, 260-68, 354-65, 443-57.

23. George Birmingham, "The American at Home and in His Club," in Henry Steele Commager, ed., *America in Perspective* (New York: New American Library, 1947), 175. See also Caspar W. Whitney, "Evolution of the Country Club," in Neil Harris, ed., *The Land of Contrasts, 1880-1901* (New York: George Braziller, 1970), 134-46 and Robert Dunn, "The Country Club: A National Expression," *Outing*, 47 (Nov. 1905), 160-74. Unfortunately no adequate history of American country clubs exists.

24. Baltzell, *Philadelphia Gentlemen*, 358-61 and John A. Lester, ed., *A Century of Philadelphia Cricket* (Philadelphia: Univ. of Pennsylvania Press, 1951).

25. Dixon Wector, *The Saga of American Society: A Record of Social Aspiration, 1607-1937* (New York: Charles Scribner's Sons, 1937), 457.

26. Fitzpatrick, "Golf and the American Girl," 294. For a survey of women in nineteenth-century sport see Ellen W. Gerber, et al., *The American Woman in Sport* (Reading, MA: Addison-Wesley, 1974).

27. See Harold J. Savage, et al., *American College Athletics* (New York: Carnegie Educational Foundation, 1929) 3-33, and Guy Maxton Lewis, "The American Intercollegiate Football Spectacle, 1869-1917," Diss. Univ. of Maryland, 1965. Apparently collegiate football did establish a sense of community among the student body. In 1906 President Hadley of Yale reported that football had taken "hold of the emotions of the student body in such a way as to make class distinctions relatively unimportant" and had made "the students get together in the old-fashioned democratic way." Arthur Twining Hadley, "Wealth and Democracy in American Colleges," *Harper's Monthly*, 113 (Aug. 1906), 452. For a similar view, see Eugene L. Richards, "Intercollegiate Athletics and Faculty Control," *Outing*, 26 (July 1895), 325-28.

• • •

Suggestions for Further Reading:

Barney, Robert K., "German Turners in American Domestic Crisis," *Stadion*, IV (1978), 344-357.

Danforth, Brian, "Hoboken and the Affluent New Yorker's Search for Recreation," *New Jersey History*, XCV (Autumn, 1977), 133-144.

Danhoff, Eric, "The Struggle for Control of Amateur Track and Field in the United States," *Canadian Journal of History of Sport and Physical Education*, VI (May, 1975), 43-85.

Jable, J. Thomas, "The Birth of Professional Football: Pittsburgh Athletic Clubs Ring in Professionals in 1892," *Western Pennsylvania Historical Magazine*, LXII (April, 1979), 136-147.

Pesavento, Wilma, J., "Sport and Recreation in the Pullman Experiment, 1880-1900," *Journal of Sport History*, IX (Summer, 1982), 38-62.

Redmond, Gerald, *The Caledonian Games in Nineteenth Century America* (Rutherford, NJ: Fairleigh Dickinson University Press, 1971).

Schleppi, John R., "'It Pays': John H. Patterson and Industrial Recreation at the National Cash Register Company," *Journal of Sport History*, VI (Winter, 1979), 20-28.

Sorrell, Richard S., "Sports and Franco-Americans in Woonsocket, 1870-1930," *Rhode Island History*, XXXI, 4 (November, 1972), 117-126.

Wettan, Richard G., and Joe D. Willis, "L.E. Myers, 'World's Greatest Runner'," *Journal of Sport History*, II, 2 (Fall, 1975), 93-111.

_____, "Effect of New York's Athletic Club on America's Athletic Governance," *Research Quarterly*, XLVII (October, 1976), 499-505.

_____, "Social Stratification in New York City's Athletic Clubs, 1865-1915," *Journal of Sport History*, III (Spring, 1975), 45-76.

_____, "Social Stratification in the New York Athletic Club: A Preliminary Analysis of the Impact of the Club on Amateur Sport in Late Nineteenth Century America," *Canadian Journal of History of Sport and Physical Education*, VII (May, 1976), 41-53.

AMERICA'S FIRST INTERCOLLEGIATE SPORT: THE REGATTAS FROM 1852 TO 1875

Guy M. Lewis

In the following essay, Guy Lewis examines the beginnings of inter-collegiate athletic competition in the United States. The 1852 boat race between crews from Harvard and Yale dramatically altered the status of sport on American campuses and introduced an element of collegiate life that had assumed immense proportions by the end of the nineteenth century.

Lewis discusses the process whereby both college students and the public accepted the outcome of the racing competition as a measure of an institution's prestige. Within a few years of the initial regatta, several eastern colleges had joined Harvard and Yale in establishing organizations and introducing training procedures to support their crews. Assisted by administrators who appreciated the reputation of victorious crews, and aided by alumni giving and student subscriptions, collegiate crews improved their equipment and facilities in the quest for a competitive edge and new oarsmen.

Voluntary associations of representatives from the competing schools emerged to promote the sport, ensure the best possible financial arrangements with the public and private groups that wished to sponsor the racing spectacles, and mediate disputes over eligibility, professionalism, and fouls. The intercollegiate regatta became the leading event of the day and "an indispensable part of the college scene." The values and practices which accompanied its growth were in many respects the precursors of all that was to follow in the rise of intercollegiate sport.

Intercollegiate athletic competition was unknown in the United States prior to the 1852 boat race between crews from Harvard and Yale, but by 1875 the regattas were the most important aspect of student life at many of the leading colleges in the East. The birth of intercollegiate athletics was not the natural result of the appearance of sport on the campus, because college boys had participated in ball games and other contests requiring strength and skill since early Colonial days. Nor did the first contest create a sufficient amount of interest among the students to ensure the permanence of the practice. Rather, America's first intercollegiate sport was the product of a number of interrelated forces.

The students at Harvard and Yale were primarily responsible for the developments which led to the establishment of intercollegiate rowing in the East. They participated in the first context, staged dual meets when students at other schools had no interest in competitive athletics, and promoted and organized the first union regattas. Public and student attention focused upon the Yale-Harvard races because the crews were from the nation's two leading institutions. As newspaper and magazine editors increased their coverage of the contests, many Americans came to accept the result of each race as the measure of an institution's prestige. The emergence of this value standard led to an increase in the number of schools entering crews in the regattas. It also prompted students, faculty members, alumni, and administrators to assist the crew members in their pursuit of victory. Other factors that contributed to the rise of intercollegiate rowing were the activities of foreign and domestic oarsmen, the ineptitude of faculties and administrators in dealing with the emerging phenomenon, and the enterprise of men with commercial interests.

Review of Literature

Chronicles of the regattas exist in ample quantity but in each case the writers were more interested in recording factual information about the events than in attempting to identify and evaluate the impact of developments upon the sport. *Red Top: Reminiscences of Harvard Rowing* (5), *A History of Yale Athletics* (6), and *The Story of the Yale-Harvard Race, 1852-1912* (12), are excellent descriptive accounts of crew at Yale and Harvard, the leading institutions in the promotion of sport during the early period. In addition to these, *A History of Rowing in America* (7) and *American Rowing: Its Backgrounds and Traditions* (8) are more general in scope but the focus of each is upon the outcome of the regattas, the competitors, equipment, and training.

Colonial and Antebellum Boating

Boat racing, one of the earliest competitive sports conducted in America, was by mid-century the leading spectator event in the country. Whale boat races were held in the Cape Cod area in 1765 (4), and contests between boats pulled by slaves were sources of entertainment for Southern aristocrats (3). By the 1850s, organized clubs were conducting regattas along the Atlantic seaboard from Charleston, South Carolina, to Portland, Maine, and in such other locations as New Orleans, Louisville, St. Louis, Pittsburgh, Chicago, and Detroit (3).

Early Collegiate Boating

The students at Yale organized the first collegiate boat club in America after William J. Weeks purchased a boat in the spring of 1843. One year later, a group of Harvard undergraduates formed a boat club. Weeks was probably influenced by the activities of the New York crews, and the displays of prowess by the Chelsea oarsmen evidently attracted the attention of the Harvard boys.

By 1850 there were several clubs on both campuses, but the members were more interested in social intercourse than competitive sport (9). Boating at Harvard almost came to an end in 1850 when the faculty placed a ban upon the formation of new clubs because one of the crews had created a disturbance while on a visit to Boston (11).

First Intercollegiate Race

The edict had reduced the number of operational boats to one by the spring of 1852, when the Yale boys invited the Harvard students to engage in a series of regattas on New Hampshire's Lake Winnipesaukee. The proposal for America's first intercollegiate context came from a railroad superintendent who was willing to defray all expenses and include a two-week vacation for the participants, in exchange for the attention the events would focus on an area serviced by his company, but there was little interest in competitive boating. Had it not been for the efforts of James M. Whiton and Joseph M. Brown the crewmen would have refused the offer (40).

Preparations for the races included some rowing by one of Yale's three crews, the black-leading of boat bottoms, and a pastry-free diet on the day of the first contest. Most of the boys spent their time fishing and exploring the region. The entire affair was regarded by the crewmen as a "jolly lark" (22).

While the participants displayed no concern over the outcome of the impending contests, officials of the railroad company were determined to make the events a profitable business venture. Bright red circulars were distributed throughout the region and the time schedules of excursion trains and steamers appeared in newspaper advertisements. The committee of arrangements engaged the Concord Mechanics' Brass Band to contribute to the desired festive spirit of the occasion and invited the area's most prominent political figures to attend the first event, General Franklin Pierce, New Hampshire's favorite son and Democratic candidate for the presidency of the United States, and Judge Josiah G. Abbott of the Massachusetts Supreme Court.

At 11 a.m. on August 3, 1852, the officials conducted a "scratch" race, and in the afternoon approximately one thousand spectators gathered at Centre Harbor to see the race, in which the Harvard crew defeated the two Yale boats. The first place prize was a pair of mounted black-walnut oars with silver ornamentation (33).

The boys spent the following eight days vacationing in the area, and it was this aspect of the trip that most interested them. In their minds, the entire affair was "a frolic without a sequel," and nothing about the attitude or behavior of the boys suggested that the loss had reduced Yale's prestige, nor had victory raised Harvard's. Only a brief mention of the affair, no names or description, appeared in the first issue of the *Yale Literary Magazine* published after the race, and the world outside the campus was even less excited about the event. A correspondent for the *New York Tribune* predicted that while the race was a relief from the all-absorbing subject of politics, intercollegiate sport would "make little stir in the busy world" (37).

The 1855 Regatta

Yale's six clubs united in June of 1853 to form the Navy, which staged its first commencement regatta a few weeks later. Because of faculty restrictions there were no intercollegiate contests in 1853 and 1854, but late in June of 1855, Harvard accepted another challenge from Yale. There was some apprehension about the outcome of the contest at Cambridge because "it was believed that defeat had stimulated the Yale men to the purchase of finer boats and renewed practice in rowing" (36). The concern over the outcome of the contest was not unanimous because at least one Harvard boatman was far more excited about the existence of six clubs with more than one hundred students rowing during the pleasant evenings and the red and blue jackets than he was about the contest at Springfield, Massachusetts.

Harvard again defeated Yale and won the prize set of colors presented by the citizens of Springfield. There was a question of eligibility, but the Yale crewmen decided to allow a graduate of the class of 1853 to serve as coxswain of one of the Harvard crews.

The First Union Regatta, 1859

The proposal to resume the intercollegiate regattas in 1858 came from a Harvard student who was disturbed over the fact that American correspondents in reporting the Oxford-Cambridge race expressed "lugubrious lament for the entire disregard of exercise among Americans." They always, he wrote, establish a "gloomy parallel between the physical vigor of English and American Students" (20). In response to his suggestion for creation of a regatta in which crews from all the colleges in New England would compete for honors, representatives from Harvard, Yale, Brown, and Trinity met in New Haven on May 26, 1858.

The delegates formed the College Regatta Association and, after considering offers from the towns of Springfield and Worcester, Massachusetts, voted to stage the contest in Springfield on July 23, 1858. The event did not take place due to the accidental drowning of a Yale crewman during a practice session a few days prior to the scheduled race.

In addition to the stimulus the regattas gave to boating at Yale and Harvard, they also were largely responsible for the formation of clubs on other campuses. In 1854, the boys at Pennsylvania formed a university barge club and two years later Trinity and Dartmouth had crews. The following hear, the boys at Brown revived the sport; the club organized during the 1840s had failed to interest the students. Columbia's first boat club appeared in 1858.

On February 23, 1859, delegates from Trinity, Brown, Yale, and Harvard assembled at Brown University in Providence, Rhode Island. They decided to stage a union regatta on Lake Quinsigamond, Worcester, Massachusetts, on July 26, 1859, after a committee of citizens convinced them that their lake was a more favorable location for the regatta than the Connecticut River.

Preparations for the 1859 regatta were more elaborate than those for previous races. The Yale boys purchased a shell from James McKay, the famous boat builder, and crews at both schools underwent an intensive training program. A reporter noted that the Yale crew "is running faster, eating more and rawer food, which we hope will not be all in vain" (24).

Of the 15 to 20 thousand spectators present for the event, a large number were from New York City, and many of New England's towns and villages were represented by delegations. Harvard's crew defeated the boats from Yale and Brown in the College Union Regatta, but the following day, Yale won the $100 prize and Harvard the second prize of $75 in the City Regatta.

The growth of spectator interest in the contests and the emphasis on winning was due largely to the activities of the reporters and editors. In 1852, the accounts of the race were not more than a few inches in length in either the public or student publications, but in 1859 the editor of the *New York Herald* considered the event the leading news item of the day and, consequently, devoted three and one-half front page columns to the report of the regatta. In the article the reporter listed the college crews according to the amount of prestige each possessed in boating. After Yale's victory in the City Regatta, one reporter thought it necessary to remind his readers that the victor was still a "little in the rear of Harvard and its *machinery* for education ..." (35).

Harvard again defeated Brown and Yale in the 1860 College Union Regatta at Worcester and on the following day won the City Regatta. The Yale crewmen contended that one Harvard boat had purposely fouled their boat in order to assure a Harvard victory. The exuberant

Harvard students did not wait for the decision on the foul before celebrating the victories. They honored the oarsmen with speeches, floral wreathes, and a parade up and down the halls of the banner-laden hotel. Beyond all control, the celebrants met the police in a pitched battle, after which the wild throng took over the town. Doors and signs were torn from business establishments and were used as fuel for a huge bonfire. Songs and cheers proclaimed Harvard's triumphs as the city waited for the peace of morning throughout the long night (31). When news of the disturbance reached New Haven, the faculty decreed that no race could be held during term time. Because of this, there was a cessation in intercollegiate activity until 1864.

The Civil War had little effect upon the boating activities of the Yale students, but at Harvard there was a noticeable decrease in the amount of participation in all sports. In 1860 the students at Yale reorganized the Navy. They adopted the plan employed at Cambridge University in which college boat clubs were admitted into membership rather than class crews. Two years later, the Navy constructed a boat house, the first such college facility. The commander raised $1,000 among the undergraduates and $150 from the alumni. Two professors signed a note at the Townsend City Savings Bank for the remainder of the money; the total cost was $3,400 (1).

The Yale-Harvard Races, 1864-1870

Yale's faculty revoked the ban on regattas during term time in 1864, and the school's commodore promptly sent a challenge to Harvard, which Horatio G. Curtis accepted in behalf of the university crew. The leaders agreed to stage the contest in Worcester after the city officials assured them that the 1860 disturbance would not prohibit a cordial welcome.

In early June of 1864, the clubs at Harvard revived the university regatta for the purpose of promoting manly sport in general and rowing in particular and to improve the proficiency of the university crew. The Harvard students were certain that the training would "enable old Harvard, not only this summer, but forever after, to maintain against all comers her claim to the championship of the Colleges" (25).

Crewmen at Yale were determined to make the "coolness of the announcement of the last number [after the 1860 race] of the *Harvard Magazine* of 'the annual victory of the Harvard boats in the College Union Regatta,' at least ill timed if not unnecessary" (28). Wilbur R. Bacon assumed responsibility for the development of the crew and closely supervised the intensive workouts for two and one-half months prior to the race. During the final four-week period, the crew was under the direction of William Wood, the first professional trainer employed by a college club.

Yale defeated Harvard for the first time in a collegiate contest. Elated students proposed that the administration employ Wood to superintend the department of physical education, and Professor Cyrus Nothrop, who later, as president of the University of Minnesota, developed a vigorous intercollegiate program at that institution, led the faculty, student and alumni celebration that took place around the large tent erected for the assembly. The enterprising Nothrop capitalized on the spirit of the occasion and conducted a successful drive for funds to retire the mortgage on the boat house. The graduates were in a generous mood because everyone associated with Yale was satisfied that the outcome of the regatta was "sacredly connected with the glory of Alma Mater herself" (16). It was also obvious to those outside the academic world that the character of the race had changed. One observer remarked: "But alas! the stream that bears the contestants of these days is one of blood, and no friendly hands meet at the close of conflict ..." (29).

The following year, the Yale crew, again under the direction of Bacon and Wood, defeated Harvard. The loss brought much criticism of the training procedure and rowing style of the Harvard crew.

William Blaikie, a former Harvard crewman, in the fall of 1865, instituted a new training plan at his school. He and his associates contributed their time and energy to the cause of a winning crew without remuneration. Blaikie made a thorough study of the English stroke and decided that the use of backs and legs, as well as the arms, made it a more effective style than the one employed by Americans. A series of Harvard victories over Yale followed the adoption of the Blaikie plan.

Yale attempted to counter the effectiveness of Blaikie's innovations by reorganizing the Navy so that greater emphasis could be placed on the training of the university crew. Two new positions, president of the Navy and captain of the university crew, replaced the abolished commodore's post. The captain's sole responsibility was to prepare the crew for intercollegiate competition.

A decision dispute which resulted in the curtailment of Yale-Harvard relations for one year erupted at the conclusion of the 1870 race. Yale's boat crossed the finish line first but later the judges, after considerable deliberation, decided that it had fouled the Harvard boat at the turn stake. When they presented the first place award to Harvard, disorder broke out among segments of the 15 thousand spectators.

The issue was debated in the public and student press throughout the year. Harvard partisans felt that the blame for the unpleasantries belonged to Yale since Yale insisted upon retaining the service of a professional oarsman. One writer charged that members of the Yale faculty encouraged winning at any cost, in the belief that victorious crews had a positive effect upon enrollment (21). In rebuttal, Yale students argued that Worcester was an undesirable place to stage a contest because residents were partial to Harvard and the necessity of a turning race increased the chance of a foul (14).

A number of American college boys were attracted to rowing as a result of the Harvard-Oxford race over the Putney-Northlake course on August 27, 1869. The Harvard club, aware of interest on other campuses in competitive rowing, invited Yale, Massachusetts Agricultural College (University of Massachusetts), Brown, and Bowdoin to send representatives to a meeting at the Massasoit House in Springfield Massachusetts. Yale refused to participate in the conference but delegates from other institutions met on April 15, 1871, and formed the Rowing Association of American Colleges.

The Revival of the Union Regatta

Yale's boatmen persisted in their efforts to persuade Harvard to engage in dual competition. In June, a Harvard student concluded that "the question of having a union college regatta might as well be settled now as at any other time. There is not a college man near us that has not some boating aspirations" and Yale is both "foolish" and "ridiculous" not to recognize the association (15). Despite the sentiment in favor of the union regatta, the Yale crewmen remained at home in 1871.

On July 21, 1871, on the Ingleside course near Springfield, Massachusetts, Massachusetts Agricultural College defeated Brown and Harvard for the Rowing Association championship. The victory of the "bucolics" over the "intellectuals," wrote a Harvard student, "was a bitter pill for us to swallow ..." (26). But, at Massachusetts Agricultural, celebrations began as soon as President William S. Clark shouted the news, "We've won! We've won!" to the students he passed as he drove his horse-drawn carriage at full speed through the campus to the administration building (2). The triumph was ample reward for students determined to earn respect for their institution and a testament to the coaching skill of Josh Ward, the professional oarsman who had trained the crew.

The success of Massachusetts Agricultural encouraged Amherst, Bowdoin, and Williams to enter the 1872 regatta. Yale also acknowledged the popularity of the union affair and sent a crew to the competition. John Biglin, a professional oarsman, trained the Amherst boys in their successful bid for the 1872 college championship. Encouraged by the triumph of Amherst, crews from six new colleges joined the ranks of those that were attempting to gain recognition through a regatta victory. The new entries swelled the number of colleges participating in the 1873 Rowing Association Regatta at Springfield to eleven.

In the controversial diagonal finish-line race of 1873, the Harvard shell crossed the line first but officials later discovered that the crew had not pulled the full distance since the line was on an angle. Pros and cons of the decision were discussed in public and student newspapers throughout much of the following year. The boys at Yale generally ignored the issue and focused their attention upon the construction of a new $15,000 boat house, but members of the Rowing Association, especially those from Harvard, were convinced that professional trainers were responsible for the evident decay in values. At Harvard's insistence, the association voted to forbid the employment of professional coaches.

The Fully Developed Spectacle, Saratoga in 1874 and 1875

John Morrissey, one of the developers of Saratoga Lake, included sport in his plan to popularize the lake. In 1871, Morrissey made the country at large aware of Saratoga when he sponsored a contest between British and American boatmen for $5,000 in prize money. The successful venture influenced Morrissey to offer members of the Rowing Association increased social opportunities and generous expense allotments for the crews if they would hold the 1874 regatta on Saratoga Lake. Funds for the promotional scheme were secured from the following sources: $1,500 from Renssalaer and Saratoga railroad companies, $500 from each large hotel, and $40 from each member of the Saratoga Rowing Association (38).

Many of the 30 thousand spectators, which included President Ulysses S. Grant, also participated in the week-long schedule of social and sporting events. Things were conducted on such a lavish scale that James G. Bennett, Jr., owner of the New York *Herald,* prophesied that in time "the regatta at Saratoga will be national in character and as full of general interest as the Oxford and Cambridge contest in England" (39). He made the event a must for those with social aspirations when he observed that the city was "crowded by the 'elite' of American society ..." (39).

The captains of Yale and Harvard entered foul claims against each other but the officials decided to disallow both allegations. While Yale and Harvard partisans debated the issue, Columbia's victorious crew returned to New York where the members received a tremendous welcome at Grand Central Station. Following this, a band led a parade to the campus where Professor Barnard congratulated crew members on their accomplishment and thanked them for the luster their act had "shed upon the name of Columbia College. You have done more," he said, "to make Columbia known than all your predecessors because little was known about Columbia one month ago but today wherever the telegraph cable extends, the existence of Columbia College is known and respected" (30).

Delegates from the nine colleges represented in the 1874 regatta, Columbia, Cornell, Dartmouth, Harvard, Trinity, Williams, Yale, Princeton, and Wesleyan, met at Hartford, Connecticut, to make arrangements for the 1875 event. They decided to extend voting rights to Brown, but denied Amherst the same privilege. After considerable debate over applications for membership, the size of the event being the major objection, Union, Hamilton, and Rutgers were admitted to the association. The representatives considered proposals from the commander of the Schuylkill Navy at Philadelphia and delegations from New London, Connecticut, and Saratoga. The Philadelphia representative wanted the association to hold the 1876 regatta in conjunction with the Exposition. New London's mayor and the Saratoga delegation placed bids for the 1875 regatta. After evaluating the presentations of both groups, association delegates decided that unless the Saratoga group agreed to a number of specific commitments they would accept the offer of New London's mayor. The conditions were that the Saratoga sponsors must provide free transportation for boats and crews, boat houses, steamers for the referee and judges, awards, buoyed lanes, and "the ordinary provisions for the entertainment of the students and their friends by a grand complimentary ball" (17). The Saratoga delegation gained the right to stage the 1875 regatta when it pledged to fulfill the demands of the Association.

On July 14, 1875, Cornell defeated crews from twelve other colleges for the championship. Overjoyed spectators rushed, fully clothed, into the water to greet the crewmen. In Ithaca, minutes after receipt of the news, every bell in town was pealing, and exploding firecrackers filled the air with noise and smoke. President Andrew D. White ordered the head of the Military Department to add the noise of cannon fire to the celebration. He then broke into the bell tower and contributed such sounds as he could make on the recently installed (but undedicated) chimes, an act for which he was severely criticized. Ithaca residents provided the crew members with a palace car for their return trip and honored them with a parade down the city's gaily decorated main street. At the campus entrance, students, under the supervision of Professor John E. Sweet, had constructed a 50-foot high wooden arch. It was covered with evergreen boughs, surmounted by a rowing shell and crossed oars, and bore the inscription, "Good Boys" (13).

President White declared that one hundred thousand dollars could have purchased the amount of publicity the victory gained for the university. In recognition of the importance of the accomplishment, he cancelled a $1,100 note the university held against the Navy. White "charged it to advertising" (10).

White had made several contributions to the victory. He abolished the practice of requiring the boys to labor on the farms as a source of physical activity. White insisted that athletics were more beneficial and, furthermore, properly directed intercollegiate sport would contribute to the institution's reputation. In an effort to encourage the aspiring crewmen, he made them a gift of a new cedar shell in 1873. White's estimation of the public's interest in the regattas was based on fact. The New York Exchange experienced an "exceedingly" dull day on the eve of the 1874 regatta because "pool betting [on the race] formed the principal business of the afternoon, and in this distraction the market gradually 'slumped' off, closing at about the lowest point of the day" (32).

The 1875 event was the most newsworthy item of the day. Owners of the *Herald* and *Harper's Weekly* had constructed a 30-foot tower on the highest point overlooking the lake. Staff writers, photographers, illustrators, and telegraphers from both publications, equipped with field glasses and a high-powered telescope, reported the details in the even as they took place. In hotel lobbies, clubs, telegraph offices, and on the streets outside the newspaper offices in New York, Boston, and other cities, hundreds of persons gathered to receive instantaneous reports from the tower at Saratoga.

Feature articles about the regatta appeared in New York newspapers two weeks prior to the event, and the *Herald's* report of the race occupied two and one-half pages; it included an illustration-photograph of the positions of the shells at the finish line, and the headline across the top of the front page, "The University Regatta," was a newspaper first. One of the many reports of the regatta which appeared in *Harper's Weekly* contained sketches and photographs of the event and individual portraits of the Cornell crew.

It was evident that because of the publicity students felt that victory did enhance the prestige of an institution. Remarks in an article published in the Yale *Courant* in which the author took exception to the idea offended the editor of Cornell's *Era*. He wrote:

> It must be rather galling to one of The First Colleges in This Country to be vanquished by a "smaller college," so we shall have to make allowances for those after-thoughts of the *Courant*. Let them wrap themselves up in the mantle of their dignity and "wax great" in the sense of their superiority. We are glad that they have accumulated glory enough in times past where with they may shine for ages to come, without troubling themselves about present efforts for success ...
>
> Such sneers as those in the *Courant* are unable to prevent the people of this country from seeing that the *prestige* gained by being a "venerable institution" is not everything, and that *work done* is the only enduring claim to greatness. (18)

Following the 1875 regatta, the big question among the crewmen was whether or not Yale and Harvard would withdraw from the association. Harvard had been instrumental in establishing the union regatta, but Yale had never favored the plan and, in fact, refused to participate in the first one. Leaders at Yale wanted dual meets so that spectator interest would be equally divided, not spread out over a large field of contestants. Many Harvard students felt that withdrawal would lead to severe and justified criticism of the college. Reasons given for this position were as follows: (a) Harvard founded the union regatta; (b) Harvard had never won a university race; (c) it would be said that "having found that the fresh-water colleges can beat us, and anxious to regain our lost prestige, [we] resort to this expedient to create a spurious enthusiasm in our favor;" and (d) Harvard would be sneered at as snobbish "for aping the English—the standard fling at Harvard—in attempting to establish an American Oxford-Cantab race in the face of victorious opponents" (27).

A vote of the University Boat Club officially withdrew Yale from the association on December 21, 1875. Student sentiment at Harvard favored withdrawal but a review board composed of the Executive Committee of the University Boat Club and a group of interested graduates decided that Harvard should remain in the association until after the 1876 race (23).

Although the editor of Cornell's newspaper attempted to ridicule the decision, it was evident that, with the action, the association had lost its two most important members. He labeled the reasons for withdrawal "trumped-up" and "ludicrous" and cynically stated that in the future there would be a Rowing Association race for the championship of the American colleges and a contest between Harvard and Yale for the championship of Harvard and Yale. The editor did admit that association colleges would "lose the prestige which such renowned institutions as Yale and Harvard give to their annual races" (19).

With the withdrawal of Harvard and Yale from the Rowing Association of American Colleges, the first phase in the development of intercollegiate crew in the United States came to an end. During this formative period, 1852-1875, the yearly regatta became an indispensable part of the college scene. The acceptance of competitive rowing by the colleges in the East was a gradual process in which the pursuit of prestige served to transform a simple and ephemeral pastime into a well-organized and established institution. Students, administrators, faculty members, alumni, and businessmen, in the absence of constructive action by college officials, contributed to the rise of the spectacle. The example of native and foreign crewmen was also a factor in the emergence of rowing, but, in the final analysis, the intercollegiate regatta was largely the product of publicity and the activities of the undergraduates at Harvard and Yale.

• • •

Notes

1. Bagg, Lyman H., *Four Years at Yale* (New Haven: Charles C. Chatfield, 1871).

2. Bowker, William H., *The Old Guard; The Famous Faculty of Four; The Mission and Future of the College; Its Debt to Amherst College, Harvard College and Other Institutions* (Boston: Wright and Potter, 1908).

3. Dulles, Foster Rhea. *A History of Recreation: America Learns to Play* (New York: Appleton-Century-Crofts, 1965).

4. Hackensmith, Charles William, *History of Physical Education* (New York: Harper & Row, 1966).

5. Herrick, Robert F., ed., *Red Top: Reminiscences of Harvard Rowing* (Cambridge: Harvard University Press, 1948).

6. Hurd, Richard M., *A History of Yale Athletics* (New Haven: R.M. Hurd, 1888).

7. Johnson, Robert B., *A History of Rowing in America* (Milwaukee: Corbit and Johnson, 1871).

8. Kelley, Robert F., *American Rowing: Its Background and Tradition* (New York: G.P. Putnams, 1932).

9. Morrison, Samuel E., *Three Centuries of Harvard* (Cambridge: Harvard University Press, 1942).

10. Rogers, Walter P., *Andrew D. White and the Modern University* (Ithaca: Cornell University Press, 1942).

11. Vaille, F.O. and Clark, H.A., *The Harvard Book*, II (Cambridge: Welch, Bigelow, 1875).

12. Wellman, James, and Peet, Walter B., *The Story of the Yale-Harvard Race, 1852-1912.* (New York: Harper and Brothers, 1912).

13. Young, C.V.P., *The Cornell Navy* (Ithaca: Taylor and Carpenter, 1907).

Magazines

14. "Boating," *Harvard Advocate*, 10:24, October 14, 1870.

15. "The Boating Imbroglio," *Harvard Advocate*, 11:136-37; June 9, 1871.

16. "The College Regatta," *Yale Literary Magazine*, 30:10-14; October, 1864.

17. "Convention of the Intercollegiate Rowing Association," *Harvard Advocate*, 18:120-22; January 15, 1875.

18. "Editorial," *Cornell Era*, 8:17; October 1, 1875.

19. "Editorial," *Cornell Era*, 8:97; January 14, 1876.

20. "Editor's Table," *Harvard Magazine*, 4:178-80; May, 1858.

21. "Exchanges," *Harvard Advocate*, 10:10-12; October 14, 1870.

22. "The Harvard and Yale Regatta of 1852," *Yale Literary Magazine*, 18:39-40; October, 1852.

23. "Items," *Harvard Advocate*, 20:98; January 10, 1876.

24. "Memorabilia Yalensia," *Yale Literary Magazine*, 24: 427-30; August, 1859.

25. "The Regattas," *Harvard Magazine*, 10:327-31; July, 1864.

26. "Victory in Defeat," *Harvard Advocate*, 12:7; October, 1871.

27. "The Week," *Harvard Advocate*, 20:1-3; October 1, 1875.

28. "Worcester Regatta," *Yale Literary Magazine,* 26:36-40; September, 1860.

Newspapers

29. "The College Union Regatta," *New York Tribune,* July 30, 1864.
30. "Columbia's Heroes," *New York Herald,* July 22, 1874.
31. "The Days of the Regattas at Worcester," *New York Tribune,* July 27, 1860.
32. "Financial and Commercial," *New York Herald,* July 17, 1874.
33. "The Great College Boat Race," *New Haven Daily Palladium,* August 6, 1852.
34. "Muscle of the Colleges," *New York Herald,* July 27, 1859.
35. "The Regatta," *Worcester Palladium,* August 3, 1859.
36. "Regatta on the Connecticut River," *New York Herald,* July 24, 1855.
37. "Regattas on Lake Winnepiseogee," *New York Tribune,* August 10, 1852.
38. "Saratoga," *New York Herald,* July 15, 1874.
39. "The Saratoga Regatta," Editorial, *New York Herald,* July 15, 1874.

Pamphlet

40. *The First Intercollegiate Regatta,* August 3, 1852. Pamphlet issued at dinner commemorating the event, December 10, 1902, at the University Club, New York.

• • •

Suggestions for Further Reading:

Blanchard, John A., *The H Book of Harvard Athletics, 1852-1922* (Cambridge, MA: Harvard University Press, 1923).

Bledstein, Burton J., *The Culture of Professionalism: The Middle Class and the Development of Higher Education in America* (New York: W.W. Norton, 1976).

Chu, Donald, "The American Conception of Higher Education and the Formal Incorporation of Intercollegiate Sport," *Quest,* XXXIV, 1 (1982), 53-71.

_____, "Origins of the Connection of Physical Education and Athletics at the American University: An Organization Interpretation," *Journal of Sport and Social Issues,* III, 1 (1979), 22-32.

DeMartini, Joseph R., "Student Culture as a Change Agent in American Higher Education: An Illustration from the Nineteenth Century," *Journal of Social History,* IX (Summer, 1976), 526-541.

Kelley, Robert F., *American Rowing: Its Background and Traditions* (New York: Putnam's, 1932).

Lawson, Hal A. and Alan G. Ingham, "Conflicting Ideologies Concerning the University and Intercollegiate Athletics: Harper and Hutchins at Chicago, 1892-1940," *Journal of Sport History*, VII, 3 (Winter, 1980), 37-67.

Lewis, Guy M., "The Beginning of Organized Collegiate Sport," *American Quarterly*, XXII (Summer, 1970), 222-229.

_____, "Enterprise on the Campus: Developments in Intercollegiate Sport and Higher Education, 1875-1939" in Bruce L. Bennett, ed., *The History of Physical Education and Sport* (Chicago: The Athletic Institute, 1972), 53-66.

Matthews, Joseph J., "The First Harvard-Oxford Race," *New England Quarterly*, XXXIII (March, 1960), 74-82.

Ray, Harold L. "Chautauque: Early Showcase for Physical Education," *Journal of Health, Physical Education and Recreation*, XXXIII (November, 1962), 37-41, 69.

Savage, Howard J., *American College Athletics* (New York: Carnegie Foundation for the Advancement of Teaching, Bulletin No. 23, 1929).

Smith, Michael D., "Origins of Faculty Attitudes Toward Intercollegiate Athletics: The University of Wisconsin," *Canadian Journal of History of Sport and Physical Education*, II, 2 (December, 1971), 61-72.

Smith, Ronald A., "Athletics in the Wisconsin State University System, 1867-1913," *Wisconsin Magazine of History*, LV, 1 (Autumn, 1971), 2-22.

VanWyck, Clarence, "Harvard Summer School Physical Education, 1887-1932," *Research Quarterly*, XIII (December 1942), 403-431.

Veysey, Laurence R., *The Emergence of the American University* (Chicago: University of Chicago Press, 1974).

Walker, Francis A., "College Athletics," *Harvard Graduates' Magazine*, II (September, 1893), 1-18.

THE TECHNOLOGICAL REVOLUTION AND THE RISE OF SPORT, 1850-1900

John R. Betts

In this pioneering analysis of the development of modern sport in America, John Betts explores the impact of the technological environment upon the extent and nature of sporting activity. Emphasizing the close relationship of technology and social change, Betts plays down the role of individuals in sport history and Frederic Paxson's notion that sport developed as a "safety-valve" to the increased urbanization and industrialization of the late nineteenth century. "Sport," he concludes, "was as much a product of industrialization as it was an antidote to it."

Although Betts acknowledges that some formal sporting activity occurred in the ante-bellum period, it generally lacked the organization, publicity, commercial and competitive appeals, and participation levels to have a major impact on the nation's social habits. Invention provided an impetus to these factors and changed the face of sport as it did every other institution in the new technological society. Beginning with the steamboat in the 1820s, Betts demonstrates the influence of such developments as the railroad, telegraph, penny press, sewing machine, electric light, street car, camera, vulcanization of rubber, bicycle, automobile, and mass production technology on the sporting ways and interests of the American people.

Betts concedes that "the technological revolution is not the sole determining factor in the rise of sport." Neither, for that matter, are the manifestations of the revolution which he highlights a complete inventory of the technology that boosted sports participation and spectatorship. The influence of construction technology and its effect on stadium facilities, for example, may have been as significant a development during the period that Betts covers as television and cable have become in our own time. This essay does not constitute a comprehensive survey of the topic, but it does provide a provocative interpretation and an analytic framework for further study.

The roots of our sporting heritage lie in the horse racing and fox hunting of the colonial era, but the main features of modern sport appeared only in the middle years of the nineteenth century.[1] Organization, journalistic exploitation, commercialization, intercommunity competition, and sundry other developments increased rapidly after 1850 as the agrarian nature of sport gave way gradually to the influences of urbanization and industrialization. Just as the Industrial Revolution was to alter the interests, habits, and pursuits of all classes of society, it was to leave a distinct impress on the development of sport.

Many other factors were responsible for the directions taken by sport in the half century from 1850 to 1900. Continuing rural influences, the decline of Puritan orthodoxy, the English athletic movement, the immigrant, frontier traditions of manliness and strength, and the contributions of energetic sportsmen were to have a significant effect on the sporting scene. Industrialization and urbanization, however, were more fundamentally responsible for the changes and developments in sport during the next generation than any other cause. Manufacturers, seeking cheap labor, encouraged immigration; factories were most efficiently run in larger towns and cities; urban masses, missing the rustic pleasures of hunting and fishing, were won to the support of commercialized entertainment and spectator sports; the emergence of a commercial aristocracy and a laboring class resulted in distinctions every bit as strong in sport as in other social matters; and the urgency of physical exercise as life became more sedentary was readily recognized.

The revolution in manufacturing methods, which had such profound social consequences for the American way of life, derived from a powerful inventive spirit which flourished throughout the nineteenth century. From England and western Europe we borrowed many mechanical innovations and most of our scientific theory, but Americans demonstrated a native ability soon recognized everywhere as "Yankee ingenuity." These inventions were to revolutionize transportation, communication, manufacturing, finance, and all the many facets of economic life. Although the tendency in narrating the history of sport has been to emphasize the role of individuals, the changing social scene was of equal importance in directing sport into the channels it eventually took in modern society. The impact of invention had a decisive influence on the rise of sport in the latter half of the century. By 1900 sport had attained an unprecedented prominence in the daily lives of millions of Americans, and this remarkable development had been achieved part through the steamboat, the railroad, the telegraph, the penny press, the electric light, the streetcar, the camera, the bicycle, the automobile, and the mass production of sporting goods.

The transformation of the United States from a rural-agrarian to an urban-industrial society, of course, affected the development of sport in other ways. Urbanization brought forth the need for commercialized spectator sports, while industrialization gradually provided the standard of living and leisure time so vital to the support of all forms of recreation. But it is the relationship of invention to sport, and that alone, which constitutes the theme of his study.

Early American interest in outdoor exercise was largely confined to hunting, fishing, horse racing, field sports, and the informal games of the local schoolyard. As the nation became more commercially minded in the decades after the War of 1812, many of those who lived in rapidly growing cities became concerned over the sedentary habits of clerks, office workers, and businessmen. In the years before 1850 there emerged a limited interest in rowing, running, prize fighting, cricket, fencing, and similar activities, but the only organized sport which excited the minds of most Americans was the turf. A more general interest in horse racing appeared in the 1820s and 1830s, and many jockey clubs held meetings attended by throngs of spectators in their carriages and barouches.[2]

From the early years of the century steamboat captains engaged in racing on the Hudson, Ohio, Mississippi, and other rivers, and the steamboat served as a common carrier of sports crowds. By the 1850s it became an indispensable means of transport to the races along the eastern seaboard and in the Mississippi Valley. As one of the first products of the age of steam it played a significant role in the rise of the turf and outdoor games.[3]

In the years preceding the Civil War the turf was also encouraged by the development of a railroad network. As early as 1838 Wade Hampton was transporting race horses to Charleston by rail;[4] in 1839 the Nashville Railroad was carrying New Orleans crowds to the Metairie Course;[5] in 1842 the Long Island Railroad was already suffering the abuse of irate passengers swarming to the races; and three years later it carried some 30,000 passengers to the *Fashion-Peytona* race at more than fifty cents each.[6] Kentucky became the leading breeding center for thoroughbreds and Louisville could announce in 1851: "Lexington, Georgetown, Frankfort, Paris and other towns in this State, are now but a short ride from our city by railroad conveyance. Horses can come from Lexington here in five hours."[7] The famous trotter *Flora Temple* began barnstorming tours; racing and trotting benefited from the cooperation of railroad lines; and "speed trials" at agricultural fairs during the 1850s were attended by excursionists.[8] Other outdoor sports also profited from the interest shown by certain lines. When excitement over rowing began to catch on in the late 1830s the first boat shipped west of the Appalachians went by way of the Erie Canal.[9] It was a railroad, however, which encouraged the holding of the first intercollegiate rowing race between Harvard and Yale in 1852.[10] Baseball clubs were organized throughout the East and Midwest during the decade and the National Association of Base Ball Players was formed in 1857, soon after both sections had been connected by rail. Chicago had its first baseball team in 1856, two years after it was linked by rail to Baltimore, Maryland, and Portland, Maine. In 1860 the Excelsior Club of Brooklyn made a tour of upper New York state. Most of the early prize fights were held along the rivers served by steamboats; the Harlem Railroad carried fight crowds in the early 1850s to the Awful Gardiner-William Hastings (*alias* Dublin Tricks) match sixty miles north of New York City and to a highly publicized championship fight at Boston Four Corners, New York;[11] and the John Morrissey-John Heanan match on the Canadian shore near Niagara Falls in 1858 was advertised by the Erie Railroad.[12]

The Civil War failed to halt turf meetings and outdoor recreation in the North. It was, however, only with the return of peace that the nation felt a new sporting impulse and began to give enthusiastic support to the turf, the diamond, the ring, and other outdoor activities. The game of baseball, spreading from cities to towns and villages, became a national fad, and matches were scheduled with distant communities. A tournament at Rockford, Illinois, in 1866 was attended by teams from Detroit, Milwaukee, Dubuque, and Chicago.[13] In 1869 Harry Wright's Cincinnati Red Stockings were able to make a memorable transcontinental tour from Maine to California; a New Orleans club visited Memphis, St. Louis, and Cincinnati; and eastern teams condescended to travel as far west as the Queen City. The Erie line offered to convey a New Orleans club, then visiting Cincinnati, to New York and return at half-fare rates. When the Cincinnati Red Stockings made their tour by boat, local lines, and the Union Pacific in 1869 it was reported: "The boys have received every attention from the officers of different roads ... At all the stations groups stare us almost out of countenance, having heard of the successful exploits of the Club through telegrams of the Western Associated Press."[14]

Baseball clubs made use of the rapidly expanding network of the 1870s, and the organization of the National League in 1876 was only possible with the continued development of connecting lines. In the 1886 edition of Spalding's Official Base Ball Guide the Michigan Central advertised: "The cities that have representative clubs contesting for the championship pennant this year are—Chicago, Boston, New York, Washington, Kansas City, Detroit, St. Louis and Philadelphia. All of these cities are joined together by the MICHIGAN CENTRAL Railroad. This road has enjoyed almost a monopoly of Base Ball travel in former years." Throughout the 1870s and 1880s the expanding railroad network played an indispensable role in the popularization of the "national game."[15]

A widespread interest in thoroughbred and trotting races also was in great part sustained by railroad expansion. In 1866 the Harlem, Rensselaer and Saratoga Railroad Company, realizing the advantage of encouraging the racing public, arranged to convey race horses at cost by express train from New York to Saratoga. *Turf, Field and Farm* pointed to the need for better transportation arrangements and predicted, "The completion of the Pacific Railroad will not be without effect upon the blood stock interests of the great West."[16] Jerome Park, Long Branch, and Gravesend catered to New York crowds, Baltimore attracted huge throngs of sportsmen, and in California racing was encouraged by the building of lines into the interior of the state. In the 1870s western turfmen began sending their horses by rail to eastern tracks, the Grand Circuit linked Hartford, Springfield, Poughkeepsie, and Utica with Rochester, Buffalo, and Cleveland, and racing associations formed in virtually every section. When Mollie McCarthy and Ten Broeck raced in Louisville in 1877, "Masses of strangers arrived by train, extra trains and steamboats." People from "all over the land" attended Kentucky Derby in 1885, the City Council declared a holiday, and sixteen carloads of horses were sent from Nashville to Louisville.[17] Agricultural fairs, with the cooperation of numerous companies, drew thousands to their fairground tracks, and the railroads encouraged intersectional meetings by introducing special horse cars in the middle eighties.[18]

In the decades after the Civil War an apologetic but curious public acquired a "deplorable" interest in prize fighting, and railroad officials were not slow to capitalize on the crowd appeal of pugilism despite its illegality. When Mike McCoole met Aaron Jones in 1867 at Busenbark Station, Ohio, "Tickets were openly sold for excursion trains to the bout" and sporting men from the East were in attendance, while another McCoole fight in 1869 encouraged the lines to run specials from Cincinnati and other nearby cities.[19] After 1881 John L. Sullivan, the notorious "Boston Strong Boy," went on grand tours of the athletic clubs, opera houses, and theaters of the country, his fights in the New Orleans area with Paddy Ryan, Jake Kilrain, and James J. Corbett luring fans who jammed the passenger coaches. When the Great John L. met Kilrain near Richburg, Mississippi, in 1889, the Northeastern Railroad carried a tumultous crowd from New Orleans to the site, even though Governor Robert Lowry of Mississippi issued a proclamation against the affair and called out armed guards to prevent any invasion of the state. After the brawl the Governor requested the attorney general "to begin proceedings to forfeit the charter of the Northeastern railroad."[20] Railroad companies expressed only a minor concern for such sporadic events, it is true, but the prize ring was greatly aided by their cooperation.[21]

Poor connections, uncomfortable cars, and the absence of lines in rural sections remained a problem for some years.[22] Many of the difficulties and inconveniences of travel remained throughout these expansive years of railroading, but all sports were encouraged by the improved transportation of the post-bellum era. Immediately after the war a New York crew visited Pittsburgh to participate in a regatta held on the Monongahela River.[23] The first intercollegiate football game between Rutgers and Princeton was attended by a groups of students riding the train pulled by "the jerky little engine that steamed out of Princeton on that memorable morning of November 6, 1869."[24]   Intercollegiate athletics depended on railroad service for carrying teams and supporters to football, baseball, and rowing, as well as track and field contests.

Harvard's crack baseball team made the first grand tour in 1870, "the most brilliant in the history of college baseball," according to Henry Chadwick almost two decades later.   Playing both amateur and professional clubs, Harvard won a majority of the games played in New Haven, Troy, Utica, Syracuse, Oswego (Canada), Buffalo, Cleveland, Cincinnati, Louisville, Chicago, Milwaukee, Indianapolis, Washington, Baltimore, Philadelphia, New York, and Brooklyn.[25]   Amateur and professional cycling races were held throughout the country,[26] while rod and gun enthusiasts relied on branch lines into rural preserves.[27]   By the closing years of the century virtually every realm of sport had shared in the powerful impact of the railroad on American life.

Almost contemporaneous with the development of a continental railroad system came the diffusion of telegraph lines throughout the nation.   From its invention in 1844 the electric telegraph rapidly assumed a significant role in the dissemination of news.[28]   When the Magnetic Telegraph Company's line reached New York, James Gordon Bennett's *Herald* and Horace Greeley's *Tribune* installed apparatus in 1846.   Direct contact was made between the East and New Orleans two years later, largely to meet the urgent demand for quicker news from the Mexican War front.   By 1861 San Francisco was connected by wire with the Atlantic coast, and throughout the war years use of the telegraph was extended in military operations.

During the pioneer years telegraphic messages were both costly and brief, and sports events were reported on a limited scale.   One of the first reports by wire was that of the Tom Hyer-Yankee Sullivan brawl at Rock Point, Maryland, in 1849.   A New York dispatch read, "We hope never to have to record a similar case of brutality in this country," and even Greeley, an inveterate foe of the prize ring, permitted the printing of dispatches of this brutal encounter.   Interest was not confined to Baltimore, Philadelphia and New York, for some newspapers in the West noticed it.   In the next decade several fights were widely reported by telegraph.   When Morrissey and Heanan fought for the American championship in Canada in 1858, anxious crowds waited at Western Union offices for the news; when Heanan met Tom Sayers in England two years later the news was spread by wire after it was brought to America by the *Vanderbilt.*[29]   Horse racing and yachting news was less novel and less sensational, but *Lady Suffolk's* appearance on the course at the Rochester, New York, fair in 1851, the victory of Commodore John Cox Stevens' yacht *America* at Cowes in the same year, and the exciting trotting races of the decade were given extensive wire coverage.[30]   When *Lexington* met *Lecomte* at New Orleans in 1855, however, there seems to have been little reporting of the race in the North.   Newspapers of that section were primarily concerned in that year with the trouble in Kansas, the rise of the Republican party, the heat of the abolitionist crusade, and the public furor over the murder of pugilist William Poole.

The expansion of sporting news in ensuing years was directly related to the more general usage of telegraphy, which made possible instantaneous reporting of ball games, horse races, prize fights, yachting regattas, and other events. Box scores, betting odds, and all kinds of messages were relayed from one city to another, and by 1870 daily reports were published in many metropolitan papers. In that year the steamboat race of the *Natchez* and the *Robert E. Lee* was reported throughout the country in one of the most extensive telegraphic accounts of any non-political event prior to that time.[31] Not only did the newspapers make a practice of publishing daily messages from all corners of the sporting world, but crowds formed around Western Union offices during any important contest.[32] When the Associated Press sent its representatives in 1889 to the Sullivan-Kilrain fight in New Orleans, reporters appeared from "every prominent journal in the Union," and Western Union was said to have employed 50 operators to handle 208,000 words of specials following the fight. Poolrooms and saloons were often equipped with receiving sets to keep customers and bettors posted on baseball scores and track results, while newspapers set up bulletin boards for the crowds to linger around.[33] And the business transactions of sporting clubs and associations were often carried on by wire.

Sport had emerged into such a popular topic of conversation that newspapers rapidly expanded their coverage in the 1880s and 1890s, relying in great part on messages sent over the lines from distant points. Among the leaders in this field during these formative years of "yellow journalism" were such New York papers as Bennett's *Herald*, Charles Dana's *Sun*, and Joseph Pulitzer's *World.* The sports page was not solely the result of improvements in telegraphy, however, for popular interest had encouraged the employment of specialists who were extremely quick, as were the publishers, to capitalize on the news value of sporting events. Chicago produced the pioneers in baseball writing in such masters of breezy slang and grotesque humor as Leonard Washburne, Charles Seymour, and Finley Peter Dunne. Cincinnati newspapers, staffed by experts like Henry Weldon, O.P. Caylor, and Byron (Ban) Johnson, were among the most authoritative journals in the diamond world. In 1895, when William Randolph Hearst invaded the New York field and brought the *Journal*, he immediately brought in western writers and, within a few years, developed the first sports section.[34] The telegraph retained its functional importance in recording daily box scores and racing statistics, but it was no longer the one indispensable factor it had been in earlier decades.

The Atlantic cable, successfully laid in 1866 by Cyrus Field, had overcome the mid-century handicap of reporting two- or -three weeks-old

English sporting news. At the end of that year James Gordon Bennett, Jr. with the aid of the Associated Press, featured cable dispatches of the great ocean race. When the Harvard crew rowed against Oxford in a highly publicized race in 1869, "the result was flashed through the Atlantic cable as to reach New York about a quarter past one, while the news reached the Pacific Coast about nine o'clock, enabling many of the San Franciscans to discuss the subject at their breakfast tables, and swallow the defeat with their coffee!"[35] The combination of cable and telegraph aroused a deeper interest in international sport. Nor must be ignore that forerunner of the modern radio, the wireless which was demonstrated publicly in America for the first time in the yacht races of 1899. From Samuel F.B. Morse to Guglielmo Marconi the revolution in communication had encouraged the rise of sport.

Public interest in sport was also aroused by the enlarged format and greater circulation achieved by numerous inventions which revolutionized the printing process. By 1830 the Napier double-cylinder press was imported from England and developed by R. Hoe and Company, printing those cheap and sensational papers which were the first to feature horse races, prize fights, and foot races—the New York *Sun*, the New York *Transcript*, and the Philadelphia *Public Ledger*.[36] James Gordon Bennett, Sr., recognized the value of catering to the whims of the masses and occasionally featured turf reporting in the *Herald* of the 1840's.[37] In 1846 the Hoe type-revolving cylinder press was introduced by the *Public Ledger*, enabling newspaper publishers, after improvements were made in the machine, to print 20,000 sheets an hour.[38] Other inventions facilitated the mass publication of the daily paper, making possible the sensationalized editions of Bennett, Pulitzer, and Hearst.[39] With the arrival of the new journalism of the 1880s, sporting news rapidly became a featured part of the metropolitan press.[40].

Publishers also aided in the popularization of outdoor sport throughout this whole era. From the 1830s onward sporting books appeared, the most famous of prewar authors being Henry William Herbert, whose illustrious pseudonym was Frank Forester. After the Civil War cheap methods of publication gave a great stimulus to the dime novel and the athletic almanac. While the vast majority of the thrillers and shockers concerned the Wild West or city crime, athletic stories and manuals were put out by Beadle & Adams, the leading publisher of the paper-backed dime novel.[41] After the establishment of A.G. Spalding & Brothers the *Spalding Guide* developed into the leading authority on rules of play, and all sorts of handbooks were included in the Spalding Library of Athletic Sports. The New York Clipper began publishing a theatrical and sporting *Clipper Almanac* in the 1870s, while newspapers like the New York *World*, the New York *Tribune*, the Chicago Daily *News*, the Washington *Post*, and the Brooklyn *Daily Eagle* issued almanacs listing athletic and racing records and sporting news. Richard Kyle Fox of the *National Police*

Gazette published *Fox's Athletic Library* and sporting annuals. By the end of the century book publication had grown to astronomic proportions when compared to the Civil War era, and the Outing Publishing Company issued more than a hundred titles on angling, canoeing, yachting, mountain climbing, hunting, shooting, trapping, camping, cycling, and athletics.

A few dime novels had taken up the athletic theme in the 1870s, but more mature stories like Mark Sibley Severance's *Hammersmith: His Harvard Days* (1878), Noah Brooks' *Our Baseball Club* (1884), and, of course, Thomas Hughes' English classics, *Tom Brown at Rugby* and *Tom Brown at Oxford*, were responsible for the rising desire for sports fiction. By the 1890s a demand for boys' athletic stories was met in the voluminous outpouring of the heroic sporting achievements of Gilbert Patten's "Frank Merriwell."[42] Along with the newspaper and the sporting journal the field of publishing, with its improved techniques and expanded output, did much to attract attention to athletics at the turn of the century.

Much of the angling and hunting equipment and horseman's supplies came from England in the colonial era, but in the years before and after the American Revolution several dealers in sporting wares appeared in Philadelphia, New York, and Boston. From the early years of the nineteenth century merchants and gunsmiths in Kentucky supplied the settlers west of the Appalachian range.[43] Field sports were still enjoyed mainly by schoolboys and sportsmen with their simple rods in the 1840s and 1850s, but from the 1830s onward fishing and hunting purely for recreation developed into a sporting fad, the end of which is not in sight. Charles Hallock, noted sportsman, conservationist, and journalist of the post Civil War era recalled how the rural folk of Hampshire County, Massachusetts, responded to a visiting sportsman of the 1840's who brought with him a set of highly finished rods, reels, and fly-fishing equipment.

> Ah! those were the halcyon days. No railroads disturbed the quiet seclusion of that mountain nook ... Twice a week an old fashioned coach dragged heavily up the hill into the hamlet and halted in front of the house which was at once post-office, tavern, and miscellaneous store ... One day it brought a passenger ... He carried a leather hand-bag and a handful of rods in a case. The village *quidnuncs* said he was a surveyor. He allowed he was from Troy and had "come to go a-fishing." From that stranger I took my first lesson in fly-fishing.[44]

By the 1850s the manufacture of cricket bats and stumps, billiard tables, archery equipment, guns, fishing tackle, and other sporting accessories was carried on by a host of individual craftsmen and by such concerns as J.W. Brunswick & Brothers of Cincinnati, Bassler of Boston,

Conroy's of New York, and John Krider's "Sportsmen's Depot" in Philadelphia.

Mass-production methods of manufacture were still in their infancy in post-Civil War decades, but the factory system became ever more deeply entrenched. While the sporting goods business never attained any great economic importance in the nineteenth century,[45] much of the popularity for athletic games and outdoor recreation was due to standardized manufacturing of baseball equipment, bicycles, billiard tables, sporting rifles, fishing rods, and various other items.[46] Although most American youths played with restitched balls and a minimum of paraphernalia, college athletes, cycling enthusiasts, and professional ballplayers popularized the products of George B. Ellard of Cincinnati, Peck & Snyder of New York, and other concerns.[47]

By the end of the century A.G. Spalding & Brothers was the nationally recognized leader in this field. As a renowned pitcher for the Boston and Chicago clubs and then as the promoter of the latter, Albert Spalding had turned to the merchandizing of athletic goods in 1876.[48] One of the most avid sponsors of the national game, he branched out into varied sports in the 1880s, and acquired a virtual monopoly over athletic goods by absorbing A.J. Reach Company in 1885, Wright and Ditson in 1892, as well as Peck & Snyder and other firms. By 1887 the Spalding "Official League" baseball had been adopted by the National League, the Western League, the New England League, the International League, and various college conferences, and balls were offered to the public ranging in price from 5 cents to $1.50. To gain an even greater ascendency over his rivals A.G. Spalding published a wide range of guides in *Spalding's Library of Athletic Sports*, in which his wares were not only advertised but those of rivals were derided as inferior.

The sewing machine was one of many inventions which made possible the more uniform equipment of the last decades of the century when local leagues and national associations took shape throughout the United States. Canoeing and camping were other diversions which gave rise to the manufacture of sporting goods on an ever larger scale. In the latter years of the century the mail order house and the department store began to feature sporting goods. Macy's of New York began with ice skates, velocipedes, bathing suits, and beach equipment in 1872, although all sporting goods were sold by the toy department. By 1902, with the addition of numerous other items, a separate department was established. Sears, Roebuck and Company, meanwhile, devoted more than eighty pages of its 1895 catalogue to weapons and fishing equipment, and within a decade not only hunting and fishing equipment but also bicycles, boxing gloves, baseball paraphernalia, and sleds were featured.[49]

When Thomas A. Edison developed the incandescent bulb in 1879 he inaugurated a new era in the social life of our cities. Although the first dynamo was built within two years, gas lighting did not give way immediately, and the crowds which jammed the old Madison Square Garden in New York in 1883 to see John L. Sullivan fight Herbert Slade still had to cope not only with the smoke-filled air but also with the blue gas fumes. The Garden had already installed some electric lights, however. At a six-day professional walking match in 1882 the cloud of tobacco smoke was so thick that "even the electric lights" had "a hard struggle to assert their superior brilliancy" over the gas jets. Even "the noisy yell of programme, candy, fruit and peanut venders who filled the air with the vilest discord" failed to discourage the crowd, according to a philosophically minded reporter who wondered what Herbert Spencer would think of "the peculiar phase of idiocy in the American character" which drew thousands of men and women to midnight pedestrian contests.[50]

Within a few years electric lighting and more comfortable accommodations helped lure players and spectators alike to Y.M.C.A.s, athletic clubs, regimental armories, school and college gymnasiums, as well as sports arenas. In 1885, at the third annual Horse Show in Madison Square Garden, handsomely dressed sportswomen reveled in the arena, "gaudy with festoons of racing flags and brilliant streamers, lighted at night by hundreds of electric lights," while visitors to the brilliantly lighted New York Athletic Club agreed that "fine surroundings will not do an athlete any harm."[51] The indoor prize fight, walking contest, wrestling match, and horse show were a far cry from the crude atmosphere of early indoor sport. In 1890 carnivals were held at the Massachusetts Mechanics' Association by the Boston Athletic Association and at the new Madison Square Garden in New York by the Staten Island Athletic Club; the horse show attracted fashionable New Yorkers to the Garden; and indoor baseball, already popular in Chicago, was taken up in New York's regimental armories.[52] A decade of electrification, paralleling improvements in transportation and communication, had elevated and purified the atmosphere of sport. The saloon brawls of pugilists in the 1850s and 1860s were gradually abandoned for the organized matches of the 1880s and 1890s. At the time of the Sullivan-Corbett fight in the New Orleans Olympic Club in 1892, an observer wrote in the Chicago *Daily Tribune,* September 8, 1892: "Now men travel to great boxing contests in vestibule limited trains; they sleep at the best hotels ... and when the time for the contest arrives they find themselves in a grand, brilliantly lighted arena."

Basketball and volleyball, originating in the Y.M.C.A. in 1892 and 1895, were both developed to meet the need for indoor sport on winter evenings. The rapid construction of college gymnasiums and the building of more luxurious clubhouses after the middle eighties stemmed in great part from the superior appointments and more brilliant lighting available for athletic games, and much of the urban appeal of indoor sport was directly attributable to the revolution which electric lighting made in the night life of the metropolis.

Electrification, which transformed everything from home gadgets and domestic lighting to power machinery and launches, exerted an influence on the course of sport through the development of rapid transit systems in cities from coast to coast. Horse-drawn cars had carried the burden of traffic since the 1850s, but the electric streetcar assumed an entirely new role in opening up suburban areas and the countryside to the pent-up city populace. Soon after the Richmond, Virginia, experiment of 1888, the streetcar began to acquaint large numbers of city dwellers with the race track and the ball diamond.[53] Experimental lines had been laid even earlier in the decade, and Chicago crowds going to the races at Washington Park in 1887 were jammed on "the grip," one reporter noting the "perpetual stream of track slang," the prodding and pushing, and the annoying delay when it was announced that "the cable has busted."[54] Trolley parks, many of which included baseball diamonds, were promoted by the transit companies; ball teams were encouraged by these same concerns through gifts of land or grandstands; and the crowds flocked to week-end games on the cars.[55] At the turn of the century the popular interest in athletic games in thousands of towns and cities was stimulated to a high degree by the extension of rapid transit systems, a development which may possibly have been as significant in the growth of local sport as the automobile was to be in the development of intercommunity rivalries.

Numerous inventions and improvements applied to sport were of varying importance: the stop watch, the percussion cap, the streamlined sulky, barbed wire, the safety cycle, ball bearings, and artificial ice for skating rinks, among others. Improved implements often popularized and revolutionized the style of a sport, as in the invention of the sliding seat of the rowing shell, the introduction of the rubber-wound gutta-percha ball which necessitated the lengthening of golf courses, and the universal acceptance of the catcher's mask.

Vulcanization of rubber by Charles Goodyear in the 1830s led to the development of elastic and resilient rubber balls in the following decade, and eventually influenced the development of golf and tennis balls as well as other sporting apparel and equipment. The pneumatic tire, developed by Dr. John Boyd Dunlop of Belfast, Ireland, in 1888, revolutionized cycling and harness racing in the next decade. Equipped with pneumatic tires, the sulky abandoned its old highwheeler style, and the trotter and pacer found it made for smoother movement on the track. Sulky drivers reduced the mile record of 2:08.75 by *Maud S.* with an old highwheeler to 1:58.50 by *Lou Dillon* in 1903 with a "bicycle sulky." According to W.H. Gocher, a racing authority, the innovation of pneumatic tires and the streamlining of the sulky cut five to seven seconds from former records, which was "more than the breeding had done in a dozen years."[56] The pneumatic tire, introduced by racing cyclists and sulky drivers, went on to play a much more vital role in the rise of the automobile industry and the spectacular appeal of auto racing.

The camera also came to the aid of sport in the decades following the Civil War. Professional photography had developed rapidly in the middle period of the century, but nature lovers became devotees of the camera only when its bulkiness and weight were eliminated in the closing years of the century. Development of the Eastman Kodak after 1888 found a mass market as thousands of Americans put it to personal and commercial use. Pictoral and sporting magazines which had been printing woodcuts since the prewar era began to introduce many pictures taken from photographs, and in the late 1880s and early 1890s actual photographic prints of athletes and outdoor sportsmen came into common usage. *Harper's Weekly, Leslie's Illustrated Weekly, Illustrated American,* and the *National Police Gazette* featured photography, and by the end of the century the vast majority of their pictures were camera studies.[57] Newspapers recognized the circulation value of half-tone prints, but because of paper and technical problems they were used sparsely until the New York *Times* published an illustrated Sunday supplement in 1896, soon to be imitated by the New York *Tribune* and the Chicago *Tribune*. The year 1897 saw the half-tone illustration become a regular feature of metropolitan newspapers, rapidly eliminating the age-old reliance on woodcuts. At the turn of the century sport was available in visual form to millions who heretofore had little knowledge of athletics and outdoor games.[58]

It was in 1872 that Eadweard Muybridge made the first successful attempt "to secure an illusion of motion by photography." With the help of Leland Stanford, already a noted turfman, he set out to prove whether "a trotting horse at one point in its gait left the ground entirely."[59] By establishing a battery of cameras the movements of the horse were successively photographed, and Muybridge later turned his technique to "the gallop of dogs, the flight of birds, and the performance of athletes." In his monumental study entitled *Animal Locomotion* (1887) he included thousands of pictures of horses, athletes, and other living subjects, demonstrating "the work and play of men, women and children of all ages; how pitchers throw the baseball, how batters hit it, and how athletes move their bodies in record-breaking contests."[60] Muybridge is considered only one among a number of pioneers of the motion picture, but his pictures had presented possibly the best illusion of motion prior to the development of flexible celluloid film. A host of experimenters gradually evolved principles and techniques in the late 1880s which gave birth to the true motion picture. Woodville Latham and his two sons made a four-minute film of the price fight between Young Griffo and Battling Barnett in 1895, showing it on a large screen for an audience, an event which has been called "the first flickering, commercial motion picture."[61] When Bob Fitzsimmons won the heavyweight championship from James J.

Corbett at Carson City, Nevada, in 1897, the fight was photographed for public distribution. With the increasing popularity in succeeding years of the newsreel, the short subject, and an occasional feature film, the motion picture came to rival the photograph in spreading the gospel of sport.[62]

When sport began to mature into a business of some importance and thousands of organizations throughout the country joined leagues, associations, racing circuits, and national administrative bodies, it became necessary to utilize on a large scale the telephone, the typewriter, and all the other instruments so vital to the commercial world. Even the phonograph, at first considered a business device but soon devoted to popular music, came to have an indirect influence, recording for public entertainment such songs as "Daisy Bell," "Casey at the Bat," "Slide, Kelly, Slide," and, early in the present century, the theme song of the national pastime, "Take Me Out to the Ball Game." All of these instruments created a great revolution in communication, and they contributed significantly to the expansion of sport on a national scale.

The bicycle, still an important means of transport in Europe but something of a casualty of the machine age in the United States, also had an important role. After its demonstration at the Philadelphia Centennial, an interest was ignited which grew rapidly in the 1880s and flamed into an obsession in the 1890s.[63] Clubs, cycling associations, and racing meets were sponsored everywhere in these years, and the League of American Wheelmen served as a spearhead for many of the reforms in fashions, good roads, and outdoor exercise. Albert H. Pope was merely the foremost among many manufacturers fo the "velocipede" which became so popular among women's clubs, temperance groups, professional men, and, at the turn of the century, in the business world and among the trades. Contemporary observers speculated on the social benefits to be derived from the cycle, especially in enticing women to the pleasures of outdoor exercise. Bicycling was discussed by ministers and physicians, it was considered as a weapon in future wars, police squads in some cities were mounted on wheels, mail carriers utilized it, and many thought it would revolutionize society.[64]

As a branch of American industry the bicycle was reputed to have developed into a $100,000,000 business in the 1890s. Mass-production techniques were introduced, Iver Johnson's Arms and Cycle Works advertising "Every part interchangeable and exact." The Indiana Bicycle Company, home of the Waverly cycle, maintained a huge factory in Indianapolis and claimed to be the most perfect and complete plant in the world: "We employ the highest mechanical skill and the best labor-saving machinery that ample capital can provide. Our methods of construction are along the latest and most approved lines of mechanical work."[65]

Much of the publicity given to competing manufacturers centered around the mechanical improvements and the speed records of their products. Between 1878 and 1896 the mile record was lowered from 3:57 to 1:55.20. While recognizing the effect of better riding styles, methodical training, improved tracks, and the art of pacemaking, one critic contended, "The prime factor ... is the improvement of the vehicle itself. The racing machine of 1878 was a heavy, crude, cumbersome affair, while the modern bicycle, less than one-sixth its weight, equipped with scientifically calculated gearing, pneumatic tires, and friction annihilators, represents much of the difference."[66] Roger Burlingame has pointed out the impact of the bicycle on the health, recreation, business, and the social life of the American people, and on the manufacture of the cycle he claimed that "it introduced certain technical principles which were carried on into the motor car, notably ball bearings, hub-breaking and the tangential spoke."[67] Little did cycling enthusiasts realize that in these same years a much more revolutionary vehicle, destined to transform our way of life, was about to make its dramatic appearance on the national scene.

One of the last inventions which the nineteenth century brought forth for the conquest of time and distance was the automobile. During the 1890s the Haynes, Duryea, Ford, Stanley Steamer, Packard, and Locomobile came out in quick succession, and the Pierce Arrow, Cadillac, and Buick were to follow in the next several years.[68] Manufacturers of bicycles had already turned to the construction of the motor car in a number of instances. As early as 1895 Herman H. Kohlsaat, publisher of the Chicago *Times-Herald*, sponsored the first automobile race on American soil. One of the features of this contest, run through a snowstorm and won by Charles Duryea, was the enhanced reputation achieved for the gasoline motor, which had not yet been recognized as the proper source of motor power. A number of European races inspired American drivers to take to the racecourse, and the experimental value of endurance or speed contests was immediately recognized by pioneer manufacturers. Nor were they slow to see the publicity value of races featured by the newspapers.[69]

Henry Ford "was bewitched by Duryea's feat," and he "devoured reports on the subject which appeared in the newspapers and magazines of the day." When other leading carbuilders sought financial backing for their racers, Ford determined to win supremacy on the track. After defeating Alexander Winton in a race at Detroit in 1902, "Ford's prowess as a 'speed demon' began to appear in the columns of the widely circulated trade journal *Horseless Age*."[70] In later years he was to contend, "I never thought anything of racing, but the public refused to consider the automobile in any light other than as a fast toy. Therefore later we had to race. The industry was held back by this initial racing slant, for the attention of the makers was diverted to making fast rather than good cars." The victory over Winton was his first race, "and it brought advertising of the only kind that people cared to read." Bowing to public opinion, he was determined "to make an automobile that would be known wherever speed was known," and he set to work installing four cylinders in his famous "999." Developing 80 horse power, this machine was so frightening, even to its builders, that the fearless Barney Oldfield was hired for the race. Oldfield had only a tiller with which to drive, since there were no steering wheels, but this professional cyclist who had never driven a car established a new record and helped put Ford back on his feet. The financial support of Alex Y. Malcomson, an admirer of "999," gave him a new start: "A week after the race I formed the Ford Motor Company."[71]

The next few years witnessed the establishment of Automobile Club of America races, sport clubs in the American Automobile Association, the Vanderbilt Cup, and the Glidden Tour. Reporting on the third annual Glidden Tour in 1906, *Scientific American* defended American cars, heretofore considered inferior to European models: "Above all else, the tour has demonstrated that American machines will stand fast driving on rough forest roads without serious damage to the cars or their mechanism. Engine and gear troubles have practically disappeared, and the only things that are to be feared are the breakage of springs and axles and the giving out of tires. Numerous shock-absorbers were tried out and found wanting in this test; and were it not for pneumatic tires, which have been greatly improved during the past two years, such a tour would be impossible of accomplishment."[72]

The Newport social season featured racing, Daytona Beach soon became a center for speed trials, and tracks were built in various parts of the nation, the first of which may have been Narragansett Park in 1896.[73] Not until the years just prior to World War I did auto racing attain a truly national popularity with the establishment of the Indianapolis Speedway, but the emphasis on speed and endurance in these early years spurred manufacturers to build ever faster models and advertisers to feature the record performances of each car. Henry Ford had long since lost interest, while the Buick racing team was discontinued in 1915. By then mass production had turned the emphasis toward design, comfort, and economy. Racing was not abandoned and manufacturers still featured endurance tests in later years, but the heated rivalry between pioneer builders had become a thing of the past.[74]

Technological developments in the latter half of the nineteenth century transformed the social habits of the Western World, and sport was but one of many institutions which felt their full impact. Fashions, foods, journalism, home appliances, commercialized entertainment, architecture, and city planning were only a few of the facets of life which underwent rapid change as transportation and communication were revolutionized and as new materials were made available. There are those who stress the thesis that sport is a direct reaction against the mechanization, the division of labor, and the standardization of life in a machine civilization,[75] and this may in part be true, but sport in nineteenth-century America was as much a product of industrialization as it was an antidote to it. While athletics and outdoor recreation were sought as a release from the confinements of city life, industrialization and the urban movement was, of course, greatly enhanced by the revolutionary transformation in communication, transportation, agriculture, and industrialization.[76]

The first symptoms of the impact of invention on nineteenth century sports are to be found in the steamboat of the ante-bellum era. An intensification of interest in horse racing during the 1820s and 1830s was only a prelude to the sporting excitement over yachting, prize fighting, rowing, running, cricket, and baseball of the 1840s and 1850s. By this time the railroad was opening up new opportunities for hunters, anglers, and athletic teams, and it was the railroad, of all the inventions of the century, which gave the greatest impetus to the intercommunity rivalries in sport. The telegraph and the penny press opened the gates to a rising tide of sporting journalism; the sewing machine and the factory system revolutionized the manufacturing of sporting goods; the electric light and rapid transit further demonstrated the impact of electrification; inventions like the Kodak camera, the motion picture, and the pneumatic tire stimulated various fields of sport; and the bicycle and automobile gave additional evidence to the effect of the transportation revolution on the sporting impulse of the latter half of the century. Toward the end of the century the rapidity with which one invention followed another demonstrated the increasingly close relationship of technology and social change. No one can deny the significance of sportsmen, athletes, journalists, and pioneers in many organizations, and no one can disregard the multiple forces transforming the social scene. The technological revolution is not the sole determining factor in the rise of sport, but to ignore its influence would result only in a more or less superficial understanding of the history of one of the prominent social institutions of modern America.

• • •

Notes

1. Among the most useful works to be consulted on early American sport are John A. Krout, *Annals of American Sport* (New Haven, 1929); Jennie Holliman, *American Sports, 1785-1835* (Durham, 1931); Foster R. Dulles, *America Learns to Play: A History of Popular Recreation, 1607-1940* (New York, 1940); Robert B. Weaver, *Amusements and Sports in American Life* (Chicago, 1939); and Herbert Manchester, *Four Centuries of Sport in America, 1490-1890* (New York,

1931). For certain aspects of ante-bellum sport, see Arthur M. Schlesinger and Dixon R. Fox (eds.), *A History of American Life*, 13 vols. (New York, 1927-1948).

2. See the *New York American*, May 27, 1823; *New Orleans Daily Picayune*, March 27, 1839; *New York Weekly Herald*, May 17, 1845, July 11, 1849; and accounts of many races in the *Spirit of the Times* (New York) for prewar years. In an era when bridges were more the exception than the rule the ferry was an indispensable means of transportation. See, for example, Kenneth Roberts and Anna Mr. Roberts (eds.), *Moreau de St. Méry's American Journey, 1793-1798* (Garden City, 1947), 173; *New York American*, May 27, 1823.

3. For examples of the steamboat in early sport, see the *New York Herald*, June 17, 1849; *Wilkes' Spirit of the Times* (New York), XII (August 5, 1865), 380; *New Orleans Daily Picayune*, December 1, 1855, December 10, 1859; *Spirit of the Times*, XX (June 19, 1869), 276; *New York World*, June 19, 1869. When the passenger lines began converting to steam in the Civil War era, the development of international sport was facilitated to a considerable degree. In the latter decades of the century the steam yacht became the vogue among American millionaires.

4. John Hervey, *Racing in America, 1665-1865*, 2 vols. (New York, 1944), II, 101.

5. *New Orleans Daily Picayune*, March 27, 1839.

6. *American Turf Register and Sporting Magazine* (Baltimore, XIII (July, 1843), 367; *New York Daily Tribune*, May 14, 1845).

7. *Spirit of the Times*, XXI (July 12, 1851), 246.

8. Albert L. Demaree, *The American Agricultural Press, 1819-1860* (New York, 1941), 203-204. Specific instances of such aid can be found in the *Cultivator* (Albany), IX (March, 1842), 50; *American Agriculturalist* (New York), II (October 16, 1843), 258; *New York Daily Tribune*, September 18, 1851; *Transactions of the Illinois State Agricultural Society* (Springfield), I, 1853-54 (1855), 6; II, 1856-57 (1857), 24-32; *Report and Proceedings of the Iowa State Agricultural Society* ... October, 1855 (Fairfield, 1856), 24; *Fifth Report of the Indiana State Board of Agriculture ... For the Year 1856* (Indianapolis, 1858), 34, 482-83; *Kentucky Farmer* (Frankfort), I (July, 1858), 12; *Wisconsin Farmer* and *North-Western Cultivator* (Madison), IX (October, 1857), 873; XI (October, 1859), 386-87; *Springfield Weekly Illinois State Journal*, September 5, 19, 1860. The "ploughing matches" of the ante-bellum era attracted large crowds seeking both entertainment and the latest improvements in agricultural implements.

9. Samuel Crowther and Arthur Ruhl, *Rowing and Track Athletics* (New York, 1905), 11.

10. James N. Elkins, superintendent of the Boston, Concord and Montreal Railroad, agreed to pay all transportation costs for the crews and their equipment to the New Hampshire lake where the race was to be held. Robert F. Kelley, *American Rowing: Its Background and Traditions* (New York, 1932), 100-101.

11. *New York Daily Times*, October 13, 1853; *Boston Advertiser*, October 14, 1853.

12. *New York Herald*, October 23, 1858.

13. *Wilkes' Spirit of the Times*, XIV (July 7, 1866), 294. More rural areas felt the impact somewhat later, Warrenton, Mississippi, holding a tourney in 1885 to which special trains were sent. *New Orleans Daily Picayune*, July 19, 1885.

14. *New York World*, August 21, 1869; *Cincinnati Commercial*, September 22, 1869; *San Francisco Evening Bulletin*, October 5, 1869. Their use of Pullman cars set a precedent in sports circles. Advertising by local lines for an approaching game appeared in the *Cincinnati Commercial*, August 24, 1869.

15. See *Spalding's Official Base Ball Guide* (New York, 1886), appendix. The Memphis Reds Base Ball Association sent a printed circular to Harry Wright of

the Boston team in 1877 in which it stressed the reduced rates to any club visiting St. Louis or Louisville. *Harry Wright Correspondence,* 7 vols., I (1865-1877), 40, *Spalding Baseball Collection* (New York Public Library). In the 1880s enthusiastic crowds turned out to the railroad station to welcome home the victorious nines. *Frank Leslie's Boys' and Girls' Weekly* (New York), XXXV (October 6, 1883), 174; *New York Sun,* September 7, 1886.

16. *Turf, Field and Farm* (New York), I (September 2, 1865), 69; VIII (May 28, 1869), 344.

17. *Wilkes' Spirit of the Times,* XIV (May 19, 1866), 185; *San Francisco Evening Bulletin,* October 15, 1869; *Baltimore American and Commercial Advertiser,* October 25, 1877; *New Orleans Daily Picayune,* April 20, 1884, May 9, 15, 1885; Charles E. Trevathan, *The American Thoroughbred* (New York, 1905), 371.

18. *New York World,* April 29, 1884.

19. Alexander Johnston, *Ten—And Out! The Complete Story of the Prize Ring in America* (New York, 1947), 42-43.

20. Dunbar Rowland (ed.), *Encyclopedia of Mississippi History,* 2 vols. (Madison, 1907), II, 142; *St. Paul and Minneapolis Pioneer Press,* February 8, 1882; *New Orleans Daily Picayune,* August 6, 1885; *New York Sun,* May 12, 1886.

21. Railroad interest in sport was illustrated by the *New York Railroad Gazette*: Horse-racing tracks of the violest [*sic.*] character are encouraged (indirectly, it may be) in more than one case by railroads normally law-abiding. Sunday excursions patronized chiefly by roughs who conduct baseball games of a character condemned by all decent people are morally the same as prize fights in kind though not in degree." Quoted in the *New Orleans Daily Picayune,* August 6, 1885).

22. For illustrations of the difficulties of railroad travel, see the *Walter Camp Correspondence,* Box 64 (Yale University Library, New Haven).

23. *Wilkes' Spirit of the Times,* XIII (October 14, 1865), 102.

24. Parke H. Davis, Football, *The American Intercollegiate Game* (New York, 1911), 45.

25. *Outing* (New York), XII (August, 1888), 407-408.

26. By the 1890s many railroads carried bicycles as free freight and professional cyclists could tour their National Circuit in luxury cars. *New York Journal,* September 18, 1897.

27. Scores of railroads in every section of the country served those seeking to hunt or fish in the rustic countryside. See, particularly, Charles Hallock (ed.), *The Sportsman's Gazeteer and General Guide* (New York, 1877), Pt. II, 1-182. See also the Chicago and Northwestern Railway advertisement in the *Spirit of the Times,* XCII (August 19, 1876), 53.

28. For the early development of the telegraph, see James D. Reid, *The Telegraph in America and Morse Memorial* (New York, 1887); Waldemar Kaempffert (ed.), *A Popular History of American Invention,* 2 vols., (New York, 1924); and Robert L. Thompson, *Wiring a Continent: The History of the Telegraph Industry in the United States, 1832-1866* (Princeton, 1947).

29. *Boston Daily Journal,* February 7, 8, 9, 1849; *New York Daily Tribune,* February 8, 9, 1849; *Milwaukee Sentinel and Gazette,* February 10, 1849; *Boston Daily Courier,* October 21, 1858; New York Times, October 21, 1858; *New Orleans Daily Picayune,* May 6, 7, June 29, 1860; *Nashville Daily News,* April 29, 1860.

30. *New York Daily Tribune,* September 19, 1851; *Natchez Courier,* September 19, 1851.

31. *New Orleans Daily Picayune,* July 6, 1870.

32. Ibid., See also *New York Times,* October 21, 1858; *Harper's Weekly* (New York), XXVII (October 13, 1883), 654.

33. Oliver Gramling, *AP: The Story of the News* (New York, 1940), 232; *New Orleans Daily Picayune*, July 10, 1889. For poolrooms, saloons, and bulletin boards, see the *New York Sun*, October 6, 1878; *New York Herald*, February 7, 1882; *New Orleans Daily Picayune*, May 17, 1884, July 6, 1885; *New York World*, September 8, 1892. Also see *Harper's Weekly*, XXVII (October 13, 1883), 654; XXXVI (April 2, December 17, 1892), 319, 324, 1210. Henry L. Mencken, in *Happy Days, 1880-1892* (New York, 1940), 225, nostalgically recalled how, since there were few sporting "extras" in Baltimore in the 1880s, "the high-toned saloons of the town catered to the [baseball] fans by putting in telegraph operators who wrote the scores on blackboards."

34. The *New York Transcript* and the *Sun* sensationalized the news as early as the 1830s and began reporting prize fights. James Gordon Bennett's *Herald* exploited sporting interest in pre-Civil War years and his son continued to do so in the period following the war. Magazines which capitalized on sport included the *American Turf Register* and *Sporting Magazine*, the *Spirit of the Times*, the *New York Clipper* and the *National Police Gazette* (New York), as well as a host of fishing and hunting journals. Through the 1880s and 1890s the *New York Sun* and the *World* competed for the sporting public, only to be outdone by the *Journal* at the end of the century. Among the prominent writers of the era were Henry Chadwick, Timothy Murnane, Harry Weldon, Harry C. Palmer, Al Spink, Sam Crane, Walter Camp, Caspar Whitney, and Charles Dryden. See William H. Nugent, "The Sports Section," *American Mercury* (New York), XVI (February, 1929), 329-38; and Hugh Fullerton, "The Fellows Who Made the Game," *Saturday Evening Post* (Philadelphia), CC (April 21, 1928), 18 ff.

35. *New York Herald*, December 30, 31, 1866; *Cincinnati Commercial*, August 24, 28, 1869; *Frank Leslie's Illustrated Newspaper* (New York), XXIX (September 28, 1869), 2.

36. The origins of the penny presss are ably discussed in Willard G. Bleyer, *Main Currents in the History of American Journalism* (Boston, 1927), 154-84; and in Frank L. Mott, *American Journalism, A History* (New York, 1941), 228-52.

37. Bleyer, *History of American Journalism*, 197, 209; Alfred M. Lee, *The Daily Newspaper in America* (New York, 1937), 611; *New York Weekly Herald*, May 15, 17, 1845, and *Herald* files for the 1840s.

38. Bleyer, *History of American Journalism*, 394.

39. Ibid., 394-98.

40. Joseph Pulitzer's *New York World* began an intensive exploitation of sport as a front-page attraction almost immediately after its purchase in 1883, and by the following year first-page accounts of pedestrian matches, dog shows, and similar topics became regular features.

41. Albert Johannsen, *The House of Beadle and Adams and its Dime and Nickel Novel: The Story of a Vanished Literature*, 2 vols. (Norman, 1950), I, 260, 377-79.

42. John L. Cutler, *Gilbert Patten and His Frank Merriwell Saga*, University of Maine *Studies* (Orono), Ser. II, No. 31 (1934).

43. Charles E. Goodspeed, *Angling in America: Its Early History and Literature* (Boston, 1939), 285 ff.

44. Charles Hallock, *The Fishing Tourist: Angler's Guide and Reference Book* (New York, 1873), 198.

45. In 1900 the value of sporting goods manufactured was only $3,628,496. United States Bureau of the Census, *Statistical Abstract of the United States* (Washington, 1909), 188.

46. See the *Spirit of the Times*, XX (May 4, 1850), 130; *Natchez Courier*, November 26, 1850; *Madison Daily State Journal*, March 26, 1855; *New Orleans*

Daily Picayune, April 4, 1856. As midwestern merchants began to purchase large stocks from the East, John Krider advertised widely. *Madison Daily State Journal,* April 13, 1855. Michael Phelan, who in 1854 developed an indiarubber cushion permitting sharp edges on billiard tables, joined with Hugh W. Collender in forming Phelan and Collender, the leading billiards manufacterer until the organization of the Brunswick-Balke-Collender Company in 1884. Gymnastic apparatus, created by Dudley A. Sargent and other physical educators, was featured by many dealers, while the readers of *American Angler* (New York), *Forest and Stream* (New York), and other sporting journals were kept informed of the latest models of rifles, shotguns, and fishing rods and reels.

47. George B. Ellard, who sponsored the Red Stockings, advertised his store as "Base Ball Headquarters" and "Base Ball Depot," and the "Best Stock in the West." *Cincinnati Commercial,* August 24, 1869. Other merchandisers included Horsman's Base Ball and Croquet Emporium in New York and John H. Mann of the same city. Peck and Snyder began dealing in baseball equipment in 1865 and by the 1880's claimed to be the largest seller of sporting goods.

48. Moses King (ed.), *King's Handbook of the United States* (Buffalo, 1891), 232; Arthur Bartlett, *Baseball and Mr. Spalding: The History and Romance of Baseball* (New York: 1951), *passim., Fortune* (New York), II (August, 1930), 62 ff.; Arthur Bartlett, "They're Just Wild About Sports," *Saturday Evening Post,* CCXXII (December 24, 1949), 31 ff.; *Spalding's Official Base Ball Guide for 1887* (New York and Chicago, 1887), *passim.*

49. It was on mass manufacture of baseballs and uniforms that Spalding gained such a leading position in the sporting goods field. Since the business was restricted in these early years certain difficulties had to be overcome. To make the most out of manufacturing bats Spalding bought his own lumber mill in Michigan, while Albert Pope received little sympathy from the rolling mills in his first years of manufacturing bicycles. *Wheelman* (Boston), I (October, 1882), 71. For department and mailorder stores, see Ralph M. Hower, *History of Macy's of New York, 1858-1919* (Cambridge, 1946), 103, 162, 234-35, 239; Boris Emmet and John C. Jeuck, *Catalogues and Counters: A History of Sears, Roebuck and Company* (Chicago, 1950), 38; David L. Cohn, *The Good Old Days* (New York, 1940), 443-60.

50. *New York Herald,* October 23, 1882; *New York Sun,* August 7, 1883. The introduction of electric lighting in theaters was discussed, while the opposition of gas companies was recognized. *Scientific American, Supplement* (New York), XVI (November 10, 1883), 6535-36.

51. *Harper's Weekly,* XXIX (February 14, November 14, 1885), 109, 743.

52. See ibid., XXXIV (March 1, 8, 1890), 169, 171, 179. A new Madison Square Garden with the most modern facilities was built in the years 1887-1890; The California Athletic Club in San Francisco featured a "powerful electric arc light" over its ring; and electric lights in the Manhattan Athletic Club's new gymnasium in 1890 "shed a dazzling whiteness," Ibid., XXXIV (April 5, 1890), 263-64; *New York Daily Tribune,* November 2, 30, 1890.

53. After the completion of the Richmond line rapid transit spread throughout the country. Although in 1890 there were only 144 electric railways in a national total of 789 street lines, by 1899 there were 50,600 electric cars in operation as contrasted to only 1,500 horse cars. Gilson Willets, et al., *Workers of the Nation,* 2 vols. (New York: 1903), I, 498. For the suburban influence, see the *Street Railway Journal* (New York), XVIII (November 23, 1901), 760-61.

54. *Chicago Tribune,* July 5, 1887.

55. *Street Railway Journal,* XI (April, 1895), 232; XII (May, November, 1896), 317,319, 708; *Cosmopolitan* (New York), XXXIII (July, 1902), 266; *Collier's*

(New York), CXXV (May, 1950), 85; Oscar Handlin, *This Was America* (Cambridge, 1949), 374; *New Orleans Daily Picayune*, February 27, 1899.

56. W.H. Gocher, *Trotalong* (Hartford, 1928), 190.

57. Robert Taft, *Photography and the American Scene: A Social History, 1839-1889* (New York, 1938), 441.

58. Photography developed throughout the nineteenth century as an adjunct of the science of chemistry. Chemical and mechanical innovations were also responsible for the improvements of prints and all kinds of reproductions. Woodcuts were featured in the press, engravings were sold widely, and lithographs were found in the most rural home. Nathaniel Currier (later Currier & Ives) published hunting, fishing, pugilistic, baseball, rowing, yachting, sleighing, skating, trotting, and racing scenes for more than half a century. Cheap prints, calendars, and varied reproductions of sporting scenes did much to popularize the famous turf champions and sporting heroes of the era. See Harry T. Peters, *Currier & Ives: Printmakers to the American People* (Garden City, 1942).

59. Frank L. Dyer and Thomas C. Martin, *Edison: His Life and Inventions*, 2 vols. (New York, 1910), II, 534-35.

60. Kaempffert, *Popular History of American Inventions*, I, 425.

61. Lloyd Morris, *Not So Long Ago* (New York, 1949), 24.

62. The pioneer years of the motion picture industry are described by numerous other works, among them Deems Taylor, *A Pictorial History of the Movies* (New York, 1943), 1-6; Leslie Wood, *The Miracle of the Movies* (London, 1947), 66 ff.; George S. Bryan, *Edison: The Man and His Work* (Garden City, 1926), 184-94; Josef M. Eder, *History of Photography*, trans. by Edward Epstean (New York, 1945), 495 ff; Taft, *Photography and the American Scene*, 405-12; Morris, *Not So Long Ago*, 1-35.

63. There was a brief craze in 1869, during which year, according to Albert H. Pope, "more than a thousand inventions were patented for the perfection and improvement of the velocipede." *Wheelman*, I (October, 1882), 70. Interest declined, however, until the Philadelphia celebration of 1876. Although race meetings and cycling clubs were widely reported in the 1880s, there were only 83 repair establishments in 1890 and the value of products in bicycle and tricycle repairs was only about $300,000. By 1900 there were 6,378 repair shops and the value in repairs exceeded $13,000,000. United States Bureau of the Census, *Statistical Abstract of the United States* (Washington, 1904), 516.

64. For summaries of the impact of the bicycle, see E. Benjamin Andrews, *History of the Last Quarter-Century in the United States, 1870-1895*, 2 vols. (New York, 1896), II, 289-90; Arthur M. Schlesinger, *The Rise of the City, 1878-1898* (New York, 1933), 312-14; Roger Burlingame, *Engines of Democracy: Inventions and Society in Mature America* (New York, 1940), 369-74.

65. *Harper's Weekly*, XL (APril 11, 1896), 365. It is interesting that the "father of scientific management," Frederick W. Taylor, a tennis champion and golf devotee, was said to have learned through sport "the value of the minute analysis of motions, the importance of methodological selection and training, the worth of time study and of standards based on rigorously exact observation." Charles De Fréminville, "How Taylor Introduced the Scientific Method Into Management of the Shop," *Critical Essays on Scientific Management, Taylor Society Bulletin* (New York), X (February, 1925), Pt. II, 32. Mass-production techniques, however, were only partially responsible for the outpouring of athletic goods which began to win wider markets at the turn of the century. The manufacture of baseball bats remained a highly specialized trade, while Scotch artisans who came to the United States maintained the personalized nature of their craft as makers of golf clubs. Despite the great improvements in gun manufacture, Elisha J. Lewis asserted in 1871 that there were thousands of miserable guns on the mar-

ket: "The reason of this is that our mechanics have so many tastes and fancies to please, owing principally to the ignorance of those who order fowling pieces, that they have adopted no generally-acknowledged standard of style to guide them in the getting up of guns suitable for certain kinds of sport." Elisha J. Lewis, *The American Sportsman* (Philadelphia, 1871), 435. Although numerous industries had taken up the principle of interchangeable parts, mass-production techniques were to come to the fore only with the assembly lines of Henry Ford and the automobile industry in the years before World War I.

66. *Harper's Weekly*, XL (April 11, 1896), 366.

67. Burlingame, *Engines of Democracy: Inventions and Society in Mature America*, 3.

68. Herbert O. Duncan, *World on Wheels*, 2 vols. (Paris, 1927), II, 919 ff.

69. Lawrence H. Seltzer, *A Financial History of the American Automobile Industry* (Boston, 1928), 91; Pierre Sauvestre, *Histoire de L'Automobile* (Paris, 1907), passim.; Ralph C. Epstein, *The Automobile Industry, Its Economic and Commercial Development* (Chicago, 1928), 154; Reginald M. Cleveland and S.T. Williamson, *The Road Is Yours* (New York, 1951), 175-76, 194-97.

70. Keith Sward, *The Legend of Henry Ford* (New York, 1948), 14.

71. Henry Ford and Samuel Crowther, *My Life and Work* (Garden City, 1927), 36-37, 50-51).

72. *Scientific American*, XCV (August 11, 1906), 95.

73. G.F. Baright, "Automobiles and Automobile Races at Newport," *Independent* (New York), LIV (June 5, 1902), 1368.

74. In these years the motorcycle and the motorboat also created interest, Sir Alfred Harmsworth (later Lord Northcliffe) establishing the Harmsworth Trophy for international competition in 1903. Air races also won widespread publicity in the press from 1910 onward. Glenn H. Curtiss achieved an enviable reputation as an aviator, newspapers sponsored air meets, and considerable attention was given to the "new sport of the air." Ibid., LXIX (November 3, 1910), 999.

75. Lewis Mumford, *Technics and Civilization* (New York, 1934), 303-305; Arnold J. Toynbee, *A Study of History*, 6 vols. (London, 1934-1939), IV, 242-43.

76. Technological developments throughout the business world transformed the pattern of city life. The electric elevator and improvements in the manufacture of steel made possible the skyscrapers of Chicago and New York in the late 1880s. Concentration of the business community in the central part of the city was increased also by the telephone switchboard and other instruments of communication. Less and less open land remained for the youth living in the heart of the metropolis, and it was to meet this challenge that the Y.M.C.A., the settlement house, the institutional church, the boys' club, and other agencies expanded their athletic facilities. The playground movement and the public park grew out of the necessity for recreational areas for city dwellers, and public authorities early in the twentieth century began to rope off streets for children at play. The subway, the streetcar, and the automobile made possible the accelerated trend toward suburban development, where the open lot or planned play area offered better opportunities to participate in sport. The more general implications of the impact of the technological revolution on society, already considered by several outstanding scholars, are not discussed here, the principle aim of this study being to describe the interrelationship of sport and invention in the latter half of the nineteenth century. Although the account of the auto slightly transgressed the limits of this study, it was felt necessary to give it an abbreviated treatment. The twentieth century, and the role of improved sporting equipment, rac-

ing and training devices, the radio, television, improved highways, and bus and air transport, would require an equally extensive study.

• • •

Suggestions for Further Reading:

Bennett, Bruce L., "Sports in the South Since 1865," *Quest*, XXXI, 1 (1979), 123-144.

Betts, John R., "Sporting Journalism in Nineteenth Century America," *American Quarterly*, V (Spring, 1953), 39-56.

Cavallo, Dominick, *Muscles and Morals: Organized Playgrounds and Urban Reform, 1880-1920* (Philadelphia: University of Pennsylvania Press, 1981).

Hardy, Stephen, "The City and the Rise of American Sport: 1820-1920," *Exercise and Sport Sciences Reviews*, IX (1981), 183-219.

_____, *How Boston Played: Sport, Recreation and Community, 1865-1915* (Boston: Northeastern University Press, 1982).

_____, "'Parks for the People':   Reforming Boston Park System, 1870-1915," *Journal of Sport History*, VII, 3 (Winter, 1980), 5-24.

McArthur, Benjamin, "The Chicago Playground Movement," *Social Science Review*, XLIX (September, 1975), 376-395.

Mrozek, Donald J., *Sport and American Mentality, 1880-1910* (Knoxville, TN: University of Tennessee Press, 1983).

Rosenzweig, Roy, "Middle Class Parks and Working-Class Play: The Struggle Over Recreational Space in Worcester, Massachusetts, 1870-1910," *Radical History Review*, XXI (Fall, 1979), 31-46.

Shergold, Peter R., "The Growth of American Spectator Sport: A Technological Perspective" in Richard Cashman and Michael McKernan, eds., *Sport in History: The Making of Modern Sporting History* (Queensland, Australia: University of Queensland Press, 1979), 21-42.

Somers, Dale A., *The Rise of Sports in New Orleans: 1850-1900* (Baton Rouge: Louisiana State University Press, 1972).

Spring, Joel H., "Mass Culture and School Sports," *History of Education Quarterly*, XIV (Winter, 1974), 483-498.

Vincent, Ted, *Mudville's Revenge: The Rise and Fall of American Sport* (New York: Seaview Books, 1981).

BASEBALL IN SAINT LOUIS, 1867-1875:
AN HISTORICAL CASE STUDY IN CIVIC PRIDE

Gregg Lee Carter

Urban America, both as a setting for the development of sport and as an influence on its transformation, is central to the rise of American sport and its study. For Frederic Paxson, sport was the urban safety valve. This interpretation continues to influence sport historians who see sport somewhat paradoxically as a reaction against the unpleasant features of the city and as a product of the advantages of urban life. The relationship between sport and urban culture is also manifest in the processes of immigrant assimilation, community definition and identity, social control and order.

In the late nineteenth century, American cities began to use sport to attract attention and to boost their images. Western cities, in particular, feeling the need to demonstrate that they were no longer frontier outposts but rather sophisticated communities equal to the best in the East, promoted sport as a symbol of their success. As Gregg Carter examines in this article, St. Louis turned to baseball in order to elevate its overall status and to dramatize its rivalry with Chicago "for the economic and cultural supremacy of the Midwest." To the extent that baseball epitomized such aspects of American culture as drive, determination and spirit, a St. Louis victory over Chicago on the playing field forged civic pride and bolstered a competitive self-image. Although citizens of the "Mound City" initially pinned their hopes for baseball success on native sons, they did not hesitate too long to "import" professionals once they realized that this was the way to victory. Community pride, it seemed, could display considerable flexibility, not unrelated to results on the scoreboard.

A Tale of Two Cities—A.D. 2000
By Jack Frost

A village, once, of low degree,
A city's rival tried to be.
The city now in triumph stands.
The village—leveled to the sands.

This mournful tale's designed to tell
How, like the frog who tried to swell
Until he'd be an ox in size,
Soon burst this town of many lies.

From out her miasmatic smells
One morn came nine athletic swells,
Who would their humbler rivals meet,
And crush them with a sore defeat.

They met these rivals on the green;
They ne'er were more surprised, I ween,
For though they hard and harder fought,
Their puny efforts counted *naught.*

Again they met—but, while, you know,
Brains fed on lake fish larger grow,
And while to man great use they've been,
A game of ball they cannot win.

As lions, came this buffer crew,
Intending mighty deeds to do;
Like badly beaten fowls they went,
With feathers drooping, crushed and bent.

This little village seemed accursed;
Soon all her gaudy bubbles burst.
She proved what me thought her before,
A wind-bag burgh—and nothing more.

Where this wretched village stood
Now stands a sign of painted wood,
On it these words: "Upon this spot
Chicago stood, but now stands not;
Her time soon came, she had to go;
A victim, she, of too much blow.[1]

The history of the community image of St. Louis in the last half of the nineteenth century is the story of a city whose self-conception poorly resembled reality. St. Louis conceived herself as continuing to be the premiere trade center on the Mississippi Valley. Furthermore, the same characteristics that had made her the commercial capital of the Midwest were to shape St. Louis into *the* great city of the country before the twentieth century dawned. Prophetic faith in the destiny of the "Mound City" reached its climax in the writings of Lagan Uriah Reavis between 1867 and 1881. Using specious arguments, Reavis reasoned that St. Louis' river and geographical location, climate, population, social institutions, business leadership, railways, and surrounding natural resources made her the logical economic capital of not only the United States but also of the world.[2]

Yet, in reality the "Mound City" was not the leading commercial center of the Midwest. To be sure, antebellum St. Louis could, relatively speaking, truthfully describe herself as the "New York of the West." However, dramatically afflicted by the Union blockade during the Civil War and controlled by conservative business leaders thereafter, St. Louis permanently lost her position to Chicago as the premiere trading center and metropolis of the mid-continent market area during the late 1860s and 1870s.[3]

Continually striving to maintain her mythic self-image, postbellum St. Louis began to manipulate every possible symbol that could both denigrate Chicago and dub her "The Future Great City of the World." Ludicrous as it may seem, baseball became one of these symbols. When St. Louis defeated Chicago on the diamond, her pride swelled. Her victory was just another testimony "to the supremacy of the Western city with the greatest population, the most flourishing trade, and the biggest bridge ..."[4]

An examination of the contemporary local newspaper columns on baseball reveals that they contain not only more expressions of the intense rivalry between the two cities, but also reflected the "Mound City" residents' use of baseball as a symbol in the preservation of St. Louis' over-aggrandized self-conception. These phenomena became fully evident for the first time in May of 1875. On May 6th the St. Louis Browns defeated the Chicago White Stockings ten to zero before a crowd of ten thousand spectators. The St. Louis *Dispatch* reported that "the entire city" took great interest in the contest, and that after the game:

> Everywhere, the excitement regarding the great victory was most intense. In hotel, shop, restaurant, bar room, in the home circle and on the street, but little was talked of save the terrific "poultieling" the Browns had administered the Chicago Whites ...[5]

The St. Louis *Republican* smugly placed the victory in perspective to the greater Chicago-St. Louis rivalry by propounding:

Time was when Chicago had an excellent base ball club, the best in the West, but that was before St. Louis decided to make an appearance on the diamond field and there, as everywhere else, attest her supremacy ...

And the *Republican* added editorially:

St. Louis is happy. Chicago has not only been beaten at baseball, but outrageously beaten. With all the bragging of that boastful city ... the result only illustrates once more the old truth that bluster does not always win. In this, as other things, St. Louis proves stronger ... Chicago came, saw, and was conquered.[6]

The St. Louis *Democrat* sustained both the *Dispatch*'s and the *Republican*'s reports by stating:

WE HAVE MET THE ENEMY AND THEY ARE OURS ... For some time past those who know the merits of the game of ball, and those, also who had not the remotest conception as to how it was played ... have been agitated concerning the coming of the Chicago "White Stockings" and their first meeting with the brown hosed players of St. Louis. The prestige gained by the Whites in the past has not been ignored by any means ... But the presumption that the Brown Stockings would be completely demoralized and wiped out of existence after the first game with the club from the Lake City would have been most reasonable,on the part of a stranger, after hearing the average Chicago man state the case ... Time has told a different story, and the shoe is changed to the other foot.[7]

The Chicago newspapers reported that St. Louis was "in the seventh heaven of happiness" as a result of the May 6th game.[8] They were also quick to point out how St. Louis was "contemptibly" using her victory as a symbol of general supremacy. The Chicago *Tribune* noted how St. Louisans apparently believed that "the fate of the cities had been decided by eighteen hired men."[9] The Chicago *Times* was even more sardonic and attempted to sarcastically quell St. Louis' jubilation:

ST.LOUIS TRIUMPH: The solace that we find in the discomfiture of St. Louis over the sale of the great bridge, makes it hardly admirable to indulge in words of self-congratulation within one week after the great game of base ball. The overpowering sense of shame that reference to that unfortunate game must always bring to any Chicago man is in some degree lightened by reflection upon the commercial triumph we have often gained over St. Louis; but the stain and disgrace are by no means removed. In mere matters of business we have had our own way. St. Louis did not care particularly to interfere, or at least laterierd too late. But all that is nothing beside this defeat at base ball. It was fondly supposed in Chicago that every preparation had been made to ensure a victory. The time devoted to preliminary arrangements was ample. For weeks nothing was talked of in business circles save the approaching contest which was to decide the question of superiority between the two cities in the most intellectual, refined and progressive pursuit ever entered upon by man. The excitement became intense a few days before the game, and culminated when the first reports were received. When the result was announced deep gloom settled upon the city. Friends refused to recognize friends, lovers became estranged, and business was suspended. All Chicago went to the funeral, and the time, since then has dragged wearily along, as though it were no object to live longer in the world.

In view of this appalling misfortune, it is some slight relief to think how speedily the great bridge, over which St. Louis held one of the grandest celebrations of the day, passed into Chicago hands. Not that the bridge is of any great value, but since Chicago must in time manage the entire business of St. Louis, it was well to secure control of this way of approach. It will avoid trouble and complications on all sides, and indeed was a great benefit to St. Louis, by enabling her to escape paying for the fireworks consumed at the time of the inauguration of the bridge. This little triumph is not alluded to as a matter that should offset the base ball defeat, but merely as something that renders the defeat endurable. We have no desire to interrupt the rejoicing now going on in the Mound city. It is right and proper that her citizens should feel proud of an achievement that places her at once in the front rank of brains and culture. Whatever envy we may feel shall be carefully concealed, and there shall be no manifestation of the pain we experience. There shall be nothing to mar the rejoicing of happy St. Louis, peerless among the cities of the west, in everything ... Let jealousy be kept down, and let there be one instance at least of unalloyed happiness in the world. If ever a victor deserved a perfect triumph St. Louis deserves it now. It is not in our hearts to interfere with her reward.[10]

That Chicago easily recognized St. Louis' manipulation of base-ball to sustain her self-image is not surprising. Nevertheless, the impor-tant question dawns, "Why did St. Louis use *baseball?*" What were the characteristics of the game which allowed it to be employed in such a fashion?

First the game of baseball was *competitive.* Such a trait made it readily adaptable into the greater matrix of the St. Louis-Chicago compe-tition. Next, baseball was *salient.* It was unnecessary to peruse the com-plex data of the financial pages or to hypothesize on the comparative re-sources of each community; everyone concerned could literally see the contest. Furthermore, attention drawn to baseball victories over the "Lake City" permitted St. Louis to temporarily avoid the stark reality of her eco-nomic inferiority to Chicago. Closely related to baseball's saliency was its *simplicity.* The diamond game pitted St. Louis against Chicago in a con-flict which had an undeniable and single victor.[11] In short, the baseball field was a comprehensible microcosm of the St. Louis-Chicago rivalry that was readily amenable to the promotion of civic pride.

All of the previously quoted passages have been concerned with St. Louis' first professional baseball team, the "Brown Stockings," and its games with the Chicago White Stockings in May of 1875. Chicago had or-ganized her professional nine in 1870; and from that date until May of 1875, the White Stockings had thoroughly drubbed every St.Louis amateur challenger.[12] In light of this fact, the question arises as to why St. Louis waited so long to organize a professional club.

As early as 1867, the local newspapers were using their baseball columns to rail at Chicago and make invidious comparisons between the two cities. In July of 1867 the Chicago Excelsior-Washington, D.C. Nationals game occasioned the following comments from the *Daily Missouri Democrat:*

> We understand that the beating was pretty heavy on the Excelsiors, the Chicagoans backing their men with their purses to an extent to which they seldom venture. They thought they had a "dead sure thing" on the Nationals. The event took all the conceit out of their minds, and relieved them of large sums of money. The score was 49 to 4! What a defeat! Chicago was more terribly whitewashed than any other city, and hides its di-minished head in the tunnel under the lake. It could not, how-ever, be reasonably expected that nine men who live on "blue beef" and breathe the odors of the Chicago river, can compete in base ball with an equal number from a healthy country like the District of Columbia.[13]

And as early as 1871, the *Democrat* recognized that St. Louis was being continually subjected to "inglorious" defeats at the hands of Chicago and other eastern teams because she lacked a professional nine:

... the interest in base ball matters has been on the ebb in this city for a year or two past, as in fact has been the case in every part of the country where the playing has been left to purely amateur organizations. The cause in the decline is natural, and can be accounted for by reasons which are, perhaps, apparent to all in any way familiar with the game ... the superiority in almost every case of visiting nines, entirely or in part composed of professionals, has exercised a depressing influence on the home organizations, which are obliged to sustain defeats because they are altogether made up of amateurs.[14]

Yet, it was not until the fall of 1874 that St. Louis businessmen undertook the organization of a professional club. Paradoxically, one of the impelling forces in the organization of this nine—the preservation of the proud self-image of St. Louis—was also one of the influences that retarded its formation until September of 1874.[15]

It is convenient to view this influence as a form of civic pride rooted in St. Louis' *genius loci;* the Latin term which denotes "the body of associations connected with, or inspirations that may be derived from" a specific locality. One of the reasons why St. Louis fought the formation of a professional team was that no successful professional organization could reasonably be expected to consist of totally local players. St. Louis' pride would not permit the adoption of a team whose players were not native, or at least long-time residents.

The first indication that local pride would be pitted against the creation of a St. Louis professional nine appeared in the Democrat's report of an upcoming Philadelphia professional-St. Louis amateur team game in June of 1868:

In all their games thusfar in the West the Philadelphia Athletics have succeeded in vanquishing their opponents, and it remains to be seen whether they will likewise bear away trophies from St. Louis. The closest contests have been in Cincinnati, where they defeated the Buckeye club on Friday last by a score of 22 to 8 and the Cincicinnati [sic] on the day following by 20 to 13. These two Western clubs, however, are said to be mainly composed of "professional" players who have recently been "imported" from the East, and it is not wonderful that their games should have been so nearly equal. But in St. Louis the Athletics will be pitted against pure unadulterated Western muscle—the Union nine being composed solely of young men who have been born and reared in St. Louis ...[16]

After a local team lost to the Brooklyn Atlantics later in the same month, the *Democrat* lamented:

> ... we consider the defeat discreditable to St. Louis. That our boys can do better we are satisfied, but somehow they always lose their grip when playing with professionals. Western muscle is certainly as good as Eastern, and we yet hope to be able to record the fact that a St. Louis nine has successfully competed with the crack players sent out from New York, Philadelphia, and Washington. *All that is necessary* is practice and a close study of the fine points of the game.[17]

And later in the 1868 season, the same newspaper let it be known how it felt about using non-St. Louisans on a local nine:

> We see by a telegraphic dispatch that the Chicago Excelsiors "went for" the Cincinnatis a day or two since, but the "imported" material in the latter was too much for our sucker friends. We say "sucker" but in fact it is rather a misnomer, as a large pro-portion of the Excelsior club is made up of players who hail from the Eastern States. It *is* rather a good joke, calling the match at Cincinnati a contest between Cincinnati and Chicago. When our Lake City friends come to St. Louis they will find in the Union nine none but Western material; and if our boys succeed in beating their visitors (which they hope and we believe they will do) we shall certainly claim the victory for St. Louis muscle.[18]

"The Empires" and other local amateur clubs "bade fair to redeem the reputation of St. Louis" against professional teams to no avail.[19] By 1871, St. Louis might concede that her best clubs ranked only "with the very first nonprofessional organizations in the country," but as late as the fall of 1872, hope still continued that the local teams would "play well enough to justify them in inviting the best professional nines in the coun-try to St. Louis."[20] At the beginning of the 1873 season the *Democrat* ex-horted "the St. Louis boys to practice constantly if they desired to main-tain their city's reputation."[21] But by 1874, it was finally realized that "the Future Great City" would find "it impossible to gather base ball laurels against Chicago" and other cities unless St. Louis had a professional club.[22]

In response, J.B.C. Lucas and other local businessmen began the organization of a team that would "bring the championship pennant to St.

Louis;" and they founded the St. Louis (Professional) Base Ball Association in September, 1874.[23] However, the temper of St. Louis *genius loci* lingered. The *Democrat* reported in October of 1874 that the St. Louis "Empires intend to get up a team next season that will walk away with the new St. Louis professional club, if composed of *imported* players."[24] Despite the threat, when the Brown Stockings announced their roster for the 1875 season, not a single St. Louisan was to be found on the team. St. Louis' pride was hurt. The *Democrat* was quick to point out that all of the players were "imported" and complained:

> ... it will be noticed, and with regret, we think, that there is not one single player from this city on the nine. There are a great many excellent ball tossers in our midst, and the directors of the new club might have put in just one St. Louis boy,even if he had to play as an "assistant to a substitute."[25]

In reaction to this situation, a first-rate local amateur club, the Red Stockings, decided to turn professional.[26] Again the *Democrat* expressed the connection that St. Louis made between her *genius loci* and the quality of her native baseball players, by laconically remarking in February of 1875:

> Yesterday's Republican thinks that the St. Louis Reds cannot do better than to secure Mack, formerly of the Philadelphia club, to play second base for them. The Reds do not intend to go into the transportation business to secure players.[27]

Thus, when the 1875 baseball season opened, St. Louis had two professional teams—of which the Browns were unquestionably the better talented. But to which club would the city give her major support? Would it go to the superior nine or to the team composed entirely of "St. Louis boys?"

Events between opening day on May 6th, and June 26th shaped the final decision. By the latter date, the Brown Stockings had won twelve and lost five, including victories over Chicago and the major eastern teams (Boston, Hartford, New York, and Philadelphia); whereas the Red Stockings had accrued a 1 and 13 record (losing to all the major eastern teams *and* Chicago). On that date both the Red Stockings and the Brown Stockings had games scheduled. The next day the *Globe-Democrat* reported that "3,000 spectators" attended the Browns-Washington game, but only "a very small crowd was present" at the Reds-Hartford contest. Before the end of July, 1875, the Red Stockings would fold as a professional corporation.

Prior to the first Brown Stocking game of the 1875 season,the St. Louis Daily Times had wisely predicted:

The St. Louis "Browns" are composed of what some of our contemporaries are pleased to call "imported players;" a slight
prejudice on this account exists against them; in time this feeling will rapidly give way. Not a professional club in the country,
with the exception of the Red Stocking club of St. Louis, is composed entirely of local players, but several localities grow to take
the same interest in their men, and give them their full sympa-
thies.[28]

A *Missouri Republican* baseball writer probably summed up the
driving force behind St. Louis' decision to whole-heartedly adopt the
Brown Stockings as "our boys," when he introduced his report of a game
by postulating, "Success is the standard of all merit upon earth ..."[29] The
desire to put a winning nine on the field at all costs had finally overcome
the temper of the "Mound City's" pride in her *genius loci.* But both forces
had the same source; St. Louis drive to maintain her civic self-image.

In the final analysis, the present article may be viewed as part of
the greater study of the community image of nineteenth-century St. Louis.
During much of that century, the self-image of the "Mound City" revolved, to a great extent, around her rivalry with Chicago for the economic and cultural supremacy of the Midwest. Convinced of her inevitable greatness, St. Louis could not bear to see Chicago inexorably
develop into the economic capital of the region in the decades
immediately following the Civil War. In the continuing drive to maintain
her mythic self-conception, St. Louis began to manipulate every possible
symbol that would proclaim her to be "the Future Great City of the World."
As the descriptions and hyperbole of the contemporary newspaper
accounts demonstrated, baseball became one of these symbols.

• • •

Notes

        1. This poem was printed in the *St. Louis Democrat,* May 15, 1875. It was
prompted by the two victories of the St. Louis Brown Stockings over the Chicago
White Stockings.
        2. See Logan Uriah Reavis, *The New Republic or the Transition Complete,
with an Approaching Change of National Empire, Based on the Commercial and
Industrial Expansion of the Great West , St. Louis: The Future Great City of the
World* (St. Louis, 1870)—between 1870 and 1880, this book went through at least
eight printings, including one in German; *The Railways and River Systems of the
City of St. Louis, with a brief statement of facts designed to demonstrate that St.
Louis is rapidly becoming the Food Distributing Center of the North American
Continent* (St. Louis, 1879); *The Commonwealth of Missouri, or the Empire State of*

the American Union (London, 1880). In July of 1869 Reavis was hired by the National Capital Convention committee to publicize St. Louis' bid for the national capital, which inspired his *Pamphlet for the People: Containing Facts and Arguments in favor of The Removal of the National Capital* (St. Louis, 1871). The attempt by St. Louisans to get the national capital moved to the "Mound City" can be viewed as another expression of their mythic conception of St. Louis; see Olynthus B. Clark, "The Bid of the West for the National Capital," *Mississippi Valley Historical Association: Proceedings*, Vol. III (1909-1910), 214-290. In chapter IV of his *Community Image in the History of Saint Louis and Kansas City* (Unpublished Ph.D. dissertation, U. of Missouri, 1969), Donald Oster notes that until 1884, the Reavis image of St. Louis seems to have been fairly well accepted by most St. Louisans.

3. See Catherine Virginia Soraghan, *The History of St. Louis: 1865-1876* (Unpublished A.M. thesis, Washington University, 1936), chap. V; and Wyatt Winton Belcher, *The Economic Rivalry Between St. Louis and Chicago: 1850-1880* (New York, 1947). In addition, Belcher notes that, "One of the principal reasons why the prophecies of future greatness for St. Louis did not come to pass was that the people thought that no special efforts were necessary, since these prophecies would fulfill themselves automatically" (15).

4. From the report by the *St. Louis Republican* on May 7, 1875, of the St. Louis-Chicago professional game.

5. *St. Louis Dispatch*, May 7, 1875.

6. *St. Louis Republican*, May 7, 1875.

7. *St. Louis Democrat*, May 7, 1875.

8. *Chicago Tribune*, May 7, 1875. Reprinted in the *St. Louis Democrat, St. Louis Daily Globe*, and *St. Louis Republican*, May 8, 1875.

9. *Chicago Times*, May 7, 1875.

10. *Chicago Times*, May 8, 1875. Reprinted in the St. Louis Daily Times, May 11, 1875.

11. However, it might be noted that when St. Louis lost to Chicago, she had a hard time giving the "city of divorces" an "undeniable" victory. Note the lame excuse given by the *Democrat* on April 30, 1874, when the St. Louis Empires lost to the Chicago White Stockings in 1874:

> Today the Empires intend to hunt out the best bats that can be found in the city, and show the Chicago boys in next Friday's game that they know a thing or two. To get good bats they will have to send East, as the bats in St. Louis are not considered first-class. Had the Whites allowed the Empires the use of their bats yesterday, the game would have turned out differently. Namrog and Seward had to use broken bats from the second inning to the close of the game. Of course the Empires had no claim to the visitors bats; but it is the first time that a professional club ever refused to let the St. Louis clubs use them.

Unfortunately, the next day the *Democrat* was forced to retract its feeble reprieve for the Empires:

> It seems that our reporter was misinformed about St. Louis bats not being first class. The Chicago White Stockings purchased a dozen bats in this city, each player picking out his own bat and marking his name on it. The Empires bought a dozen a month ago, but most of them gave out by the terrific batting of the State Championships ... (*St. Louis Democrat*, May 1, 1874).

12. Actually, Chicago had always played St. Louis with professional or "semi-professional" teams. The Chicago Excelsiors, a semi-professional club, defeated St. Louis nines in September and October of 1868. The White Stockings decimated several "Mound City" clubs in the spring of 1870, and again in 1874 (see

the *Daily Missouri Democrat* and/or *St. Louis Democrat*, September 24, 1868; October 6, 1868; April 30-May 2, 1870; April 18-May 9, 1874; September 12, 1874; *St. Louis Republican*, *St. Louis Daily Times*, and *St. Louis Daily Globe*, April 18-May 9, 1874. The White Stockings were disbanded from early 18761 through 1873.

13. *Daily Missouri Democrat*, July 29, 1867.

14. *Missouri Democrat*, July 31, 1871.

15. Of course, there were other influences that prevented the earlier formation of a professional club. One of these was certainly a moralistic impulse against the gambling usually associated with professional sport. On June 30, 1870, the *Missouri Democrat* reprinted comments by the *Philadelphia Public Record* concerning the National game and gambling:

> An advertisement appeared in yesterday's journals to the effect that at certain and specific places "pools" would be "sold" for the match between the famous "professionals" clubs known respectively as the Redstockings and Athletics. Now we ask what is this but gambling? The whole game of base ball "professionals" is a fraud upon the public, and places this so-called National game upon the exact level of mere money-making shows ...

Another retarding influence on the early creation of a professional team was St. Louis' lack of daring businessmen. Wyatt Belcher notes that "Chicago's business leaders were more energetic and more astute than those of St. Louis, and it was largely this that enabled Chicago first to overtake St. Louis as a commercial rival, and then to advance rapidly ahead of that city." Belcher continues, "The ruling characteristic of St. Louis businessmen was their conservatism. They were not imaginative men ... They believed in the old adage, 'Attend to your own business and it will attend to you.'" (see Belcher, 114-115).

16. *Daily Missouri Democrat*, June 14, 1868.

17. Ibid., June 29, 1868.

18. Ibid., September 24, 1868.

19. Ibid., May 1, 1870.

20. Ibid., September 23, 11872.

21. *St. Louis Democrat*, April 22, 18973.

22. *St. Louis Daily Globe*, May 1, 1874. There were a few expressions of a desire to organize a professional nine in St. Louis well before 1874. In a letter to the *"Editors Missouri Democrat"* on June 24, 1869, one observer pleaded:

> Why cannot St. Louis have a good base ball club? I ask the above question for the reason that I have not taken up a newspaper for the past week without reading an account of the "victories" of the Cincinnati club—the famous "Red Stockings"—now on a tour to the principal Eastern cities ... Now why can't St. Louis support a good club as well as Cincinnati? I think she *can* and out to. Your city is far ahead of Cincinnati in everyting else: why not be at *least* her equal in base ball matters? ... I write this because I take interest in your beautiful city, and do not want to see her lag behind in anything.

In August of 1873 the *Democrat* commented that the games in St. Louis between the Boston Red Stockings and several local clubs might "do a great deal towards the organization of professional nines in the West next season." (*St. Louis Democrat*, August 10, 1873). But sentiments such as the preceding could not override St. Louis' pride rooted in the temper of her *genius loci* until the fall of 1874.

23. *St. Louis Daily Globe*, September 20, 1874; see also the *St. Louis Democrat*, September 30, 1874; *St. Louis Daily Times*, September 23, 1874, and September 30, 1874.

24. *St. Louis Democrat*, October 11, 1874.

25. Ibid., November 21, 1874.
26. Ibid., February 16, 1875.
27. Ibid., February 16, 1875.
28. *St. Louis Daily Times*, May 5, 1875. It should be noted that the baseball writer of the *Times*, William C. Steigers, was also a major stockholder in the Brown Stockings corporation.
29. *Missouri Republican*, August 16, 1868.

• • •

Suggestions for Further Reading:

Adelman, Melvin L., "The First Baseball Game, the First Newspaper References to Baseball, and the New York Club: A Note on the Early History of Baseball," *Journal of Sport History*, VII, 3 (Winter, 1980), 132-135.

Barney, Robert K., "Of Rails and Red Stockings: Episodes in the Expansion of the National Pastime in the American West," *Journal of the West*, XVII, 3 (July, 1978), 61-70.

Bartlett, Arthur, *Baseball and Mr. Spalding: The History and Romance of Baseball* (New York: Farrar, Strauss and Young, 1951).

Coffin, Tristam, *The Old Ball Game: Baseball in Folklore and Fiction* (New York: Harder and Harder, 1971).

Daniel, W. Harrison, "The Rage in the Hill City: The Beginnings of Baseball in Lynchburg," *Virginia Cavalcade*, XXVIII, 4 (Spring, 1979), 186-191.

Evans, Harold C., "Baseball in Kansas, 1867-1940," *Kansas Historical Quarterly*, IX, 2 (May, 1940), 175-193.

Freedman, Stephen, "The Baseball Fad in Chicago, 1865-1870: An Exploration of the Role of Sport in the Nineteenth-Century City," *Journal of Sport History*, V, 2 (summer, 1978), 42-64.

Hage, G.S., "Games People Played: Sports in Minnesota Daily Newspapers, 1860-1890," *Minnesota History*, XLVII (Winter, 1981), 321-328.

Jensen, Harry, Jr., "The Public Acceptance of Sports in Dallas, 1880-1930," *Journal of Sport History*, VI, 3 (Winter, 1979), 5-19.

Levine, Peter, *A.G. Spalding and the Rise of Baseball* (New York: Oxford University Press, 1985).

Monroe, Cecil, "The Rise of Baseball in Minnesota," *Minnesota History*, XIX (June, 1938), 162-181.

Murdock, Eugene C., *Mighty Casey: All American* (Westport, CT: Greenwood Press, 1984).

Northam, Janet A. and Jack W. Berryman, "Sport and Urban Boosterism in the Pacific Northwest: Seattle's Alaska-Yukon-Pacific

Exposition, 1909," *Journal of the West*, XVII, 3 (July, 1978), 53-59.

Seymour, Harold, *Baseball*, 2 vols. (New York: Oxford University Press, 1960, 1971).

_____, "How Baseball Began," *New York Historical Society Quarterly*, XL, 4 (October, 1956), 369-385.

Smith, Robert P., "Heroes and Hurrahs: Sport in Brooklyn, 1890-1898," *Journal of Long Island History*, XI (Spring, 1975), 7-21.

Spalding, Albert G., *America's National Game* (New York: American Sports Publishing Company, 1911).

Stern, Joseph S., Sr., "The Team That Couldn't Be Beat: The Red Stockings of 1869," *Cincinnati Historical Society Bulletin*, XXVII, 1 (1969), 25-41.

Tyrrell, Ian, "The Emergence of Modern American Baseball c. 1850-1880" in Richard Cashman and Michael McKernan, eds., *Sport in History: The Making of Modern Sporting History* (St. Lucia, Queensland, Australia: University of Queensland Press, 1979), 21-42.

Voigt, David, *American Baseball*, 3 vols. (Norman, OK: University of Oklahoma Press, 1966, 1970, 1982).

_____, "America's First Red Scare—The Cincinnati Reds of 1869," *Ohio History*, LXXVIII, 1 (1969), 13-24.

_____, "The Boston Red Stockings: The Birth of Major League Baseball," *New England Quarterly*, XLIII 4 (December, 1970), 531-549.

Wallop, Douglas, *Baseball* (New York: Norton, 1969).

FOOTBALL IN AMERICA:
A STUDY IN CULTURE DIFFUSION

David Riesman
Reuel Denney

Published in 1951, the following essay still retains much of its value in explaining the involvement of intercollegiate football with several elemental themes in American life. Acknowledging the "semi"-professional nature of the intercollegiate game, the authors focus on the relationship between American football and its English origins and argue that the game that evolved in this country reflected societal values and patterns that were distinctly American. Among the themes that they explore are the increased costs and specialization of the game, its ethnic and class consciousness, audience identification, and the processes of defining, limiting, and conventionalizing its symbolic representations of violence. In each case, rules and rituals developed for American football that institutionalized these characteristics and clearly set the sport apart from its English counterparts, rugby and soccer.

Since 1951, of course, college football has grown dramatically in scale. Television contracts for the 1986 season exceeded $500 million, yet only a few dozen football programs throughout the country actually make money for their institutions. The vulnerability that comes with bigness, which Riesman and Denney observed, is manifested in recruiting violations, "point-shaving" scandals, ludicrous notions of the "student-athlete" concept, rabid boosterism, and a "win-at-any-cost" mentality. It would be ironic, indeed, if the excesses that accompany the game, rather than the game itself, now serve to reflect the culture of which football is a part. Just as football has been an agent of culture diffusion, the growth of the game in this country has extended the diffusion factor beyond the playing fields.

On October 9, 1951, Assistant Attorney General Graham Morrison instituted an anti-trust action against a number of universities on account of their efforts to limit TV broadcasts of their games—efforts dictated by the terrible burdens of what we might speak of as "industrialized football." This action occurred only a few weeks after the scandal of the West Point student firings, which, along with the William and Mary palace revolution, indicated that football was indeed reaching another crisis in its adaptation to the ever-changing American environment. Small colleges such as Milligan—a church-supported school in the mountains of Eastern Tennessee—were discovering that football was now so mechanized that they could no longer afford the necessary entry fee for machinery and personnel. Last year, Milligan spent $17,000, or two-thirds of its whole athletic budget—and did not get it all back in the box-office net. Football had come to resemble other industries or mechanized farms, into which a new firm could not move by relying on an institutional lifetime of patient saving and plowing back of profits, but only by large corporate investment. The production of a team involves the heavy overhead and staff personnel characteristic of high-capital, functionally rationalized industries, as the result of successive changes in the game since its post-Civil-War diffusion from England.[1]

It would be wrong, however, to assert that football has become an impersonal market phenomenon. Rather, its rationalization as a sport and as a spectacle has served to bring out more openly the part it plays in the ethnic, class, and characterological struggles of our time—meaning, by "characterological struggle," the conflict between different styles of life. The ethnic significance of football is immediately suggested by the shift in the typical origins of player-names on the All-American Football Teams since 1889. In 1889, all but one of the names (Heffelfinger) suggested Anglo-Saxon origins. The first name after that of Heffelfinger to suggest non-Anglo-Saxon origin recruitment was that of Murphy, at Yale, in 1895. After 1895, it was a rare All-American team that did not include at least one Irishman (Daly, Hogan, Rafferty, Shevlin); and the years before the turn of the century saw entrance of the Jew. On the 1904 team appeared Pierkarski of Pennsylvania. By 1927, names like Casey, Kipke, Oosterbaan, Koppisch, Garbisch, and Friedman were appearing on the All-American list with as much frequency as names like Channing, Adams, and Ames in the 1890s.

While such a tally does little more than document a shift that most observers have already recognized in American football, it raises questions that are probably not answerable merely in terms of ethnic origins of players. There is an element of class identification running through American football since its earliest days, and the ethnic origins of players contain ample invitations to the making of theory about the class dimensions of football. Most observers would be inclined to agree that the arrival of names like Kelley and Kipke on the annual All-American list was taken by the Flanagans and the Webers as the achievement of a lower-class aspiration to be among the best at an upper-class sport. The question remains: what did the achievement mean? What did it mean at different stages in the development of the game? Hasn't the meaning worn off in the fifty-odd years, the roughly two generations since Heffelfinger and Murphy made the grade?

There are many ways to begin an answer to such questions, and here we can open only a few lines of investigation. Our method is to study the interrelations between changes in the rules of the game (since the first intercollegiate contest: Rutgers, 6 goals—Princeton, 4 goals, in 1869) and to analyze the parallel changes in football strategy and ethos. All these developments are to be seen as part of a configuration that includes changes in coaching, in the training of players, and in the no less essential training of the mass audience.

Since football is a cultural inheritance from England, such an analysis may be made in the perspective of other studies in cultural diffusion and variation. Just as the French have transformed American telephone etiquette while retaining some of its recognizable physical features, so Americans have transformed the games of Europe even when, as in track or tennis, the formalities appear to be unaltered. Even within the Western industrial culture, there are great varieties, on a class and national basis, in the games, rules, strategy, etiquette, and audience structures of sport. In the case of college football—we shall leave aside the symbolically less important professional game—the documentation of sportswriters (themselves a potent factor in change) allows us to trace the stages of development.

II

A study of Anatolian peasants now under way at the Bureau of Applied Social Research indicates that these highly tradition-bound people cannot grasp the abstractness of modern sports. They lack the enterprise, in their fatalistic village cultures, to see why people want to knock themselves out for sportsmanship's remote ideals; they cannot link such rituals, even by remote analogy, with their own. These peasants are similarly unable to be caught up in modern politics, or to find anything meaningful in the Voice of America. Nevertheless, football itself, like so many other games with balls and goals, originated in a peasant culture.

Football, in the earliest English form, was called the Dane's Head and it was played in the tenth and eleventh centuries as a contest in kicking a ball between towns. The legend is that the first ball was a skull, and only later a cow's bladder. In some cases, the goals were the towns themselves, so that a team entering a village might have pushed the ball several miles en route. King Henry II (1154-89) proscribed the game, on the ground that it interfered with archery practice. Played in Dublin even after the ban, football did not become respectable or legal until an edict of James I reinstated it. The reason was perhaps less ideological than practical: firearms had obsoleted the art of bowmanship.

During the following century, football as played by British schoolboys became formalized, but did not change its fundamental pattern of forceful kicking. In 1823, Ellis of Rugby made the mistake of picking up the ball and running with it toward the goal. All concerned thought it was a mistake: Ellis was sheepish, his captain apologetic. The mistake turned into innovation when it was decided that a running rule might make for an interesting game. The localism, pluralism, and studied casualness of English sports made it possible to try it out without securing universal assent—three or four purely local variants of football, football-hazing and "wall games" are still played in various English schools. Rugby adopted "Rugby" in 1841, several years after bridge had helped to popularize it.[2]

This establishment of the running or Rugby game, as contrasted with the earlier, kicking game, had several important results. One was that the old-style players banded themselves together for the defense of their game, and formed the London Football Association (1863). This name, abbreviated to "Assoc," appears to have been the starting point for the neologism, "Soccer," the name that the kicking game now goes by in many parts of the English-speaking world. A second result was that the English, having found a new game, continued to play it without tight rules until the Rugby Union of 1871. As we shall see, this had its effects on the American game, the third and most important result of Ellis' "mistake," of course, was that he laid the foundations for everything fundamental about the American game between about 1869 and the introduction of the forward pass. (The forward pass is still illegal in Rugby and closely related football games.)

III

In the Colonial period and right down to the Civil War, Americans played variants on the kicking football game on their town greens and schoolyards. After the war, Yale and Harvard served as the culturally receptive importers of the English game. Harvard, meeting McGill in a game of Rugby football in 1874, brought the sport to the attention of collegiate circles and the press—two identifications important for the whole future development of the game. But if Harvard was an opinion leader, Yale was a technological one. A Yale student who had studied at Rugby was instrumental in persuading Yale men to play the Rugby game and was, therefore, responsible for some of Yale's early leadership in the sport.

It happened in the following way, according to Walter Camp and Lorin F. Deland.[3] The faculty in 1860, for reasons unknown, put a stop to interclass matches of the pre-Rugby variety. "During the following years, until 1870, football was practically dead at Yale. The class of '72, however, was very fond of athletic sports, and participated especially in long hare and hound runs. The revival of football was due in a large measure to Mr. D.S. Schaft, formerly of Rugby School, who entered the class of '73 and succeeded in making the sport popular among his classmates, and eventually formed an association which sent challenges to the other classes."

Soon after the period described by Camp, it became clear that American players, having tasted the "running" game, were willing to give up the soccer form. It became equally clear that they either did not want to, or could not, play Rugby according to the British rules. "The American players found in this code [English Rugby Rules] many uncertain and knotty points which caused much trouble in their game, especially as they had no traditions, or older and more experienced players, to whom they could turn for the necessary explanations," says Camp. An example of such a problem was English rule number nine:

"A touchdown is when a player, putting his hand on the ball in touch or in goal, stops it so that it remains dead, or fairly so."

The ambiguity of the phrase "fairly so" was increased by the statement in rule number eight that the ball is dead "when it rests absolutely motionless on the ground."

Camp's description of these early difficulties is intensely interesting to the student of cultural diffusion not only because of what Camp observed about the situation, but also because of what he neglected to observe. Consider the fact that the development of Rugby rules in England was accomplished by admitting into the rules something that we would call a legal fiction. While an offensive runner was permitted to carry the ball, the condition of his doing so was that he should *happen* to be standing behind the swaying "scrum" (the tangled players) at the moment the ball popped back out to him. An intentional "heel out" of the ball was not permitted; and the British rules of the mid-nineteenth century appear to take it for granted that the difference between an intentional and an unintentional heel-out would be clear to everyone. Ellis' mistake became institutionalized—but still as a mistake. This aspect of Rugby rule-making had important implications for the American game.

British players, according to tradition as well as according to rules, could be expected to tolerate such ambiguity as that of the heel-out rule just as they tolerated the ambiguity of the "dead" ball. They could be expected to tolerate it not only because of their personal part in developing new rules but (a point we shall return to) because they had an audience with specific knowledge of the traditions to assist them. In America it was quite another matter to solve such problems. No Muzafer Sherif was present[4] to solidify the perceptions of "nearly so," and the emotional tone for resolving such question without recurrent dispute could not be improvised. Rather, however, than dropping the Rugby game at that point, because of intolerance for the ambiguities involved, an effort was undertaken, at once systematic and gradual, to fill in by formal procedures the vacuum of etiquette and, in general, to adapt the game to its new cultural home.

The upshot of American procedure was to assign players to the legalized task of picking up and tossing the ball back out of scrimmage. This in turn created the role of the center, and the centering operation. This in turn led to a variety of problems in defining the situation as one of "scrimmage" or "non-scrimmage," and the whole question of the legality of passing the ball back to intended runners. American football never really solved these problems until it turned its attention, in 1880, to a definition of the scrimmage itself. The unpredictable English "scrum" or scramble for a free ball was abandoned, and a crude line of scrimmage was constructed across the field. Play was set in motion by snapping the ball. Meanwhile Americans became impatient with long retention of the ball by one side. It was possible for a team that was ahead in score to adopt tactics that would insure its retention of the ball until the end of the period. By the introduction of a minimum yardage-gain rule in 1882, the rulemakers assured the frequent interchange of the ball between sides.

The effect of this change was to dramatize the offensive-defensive symmetry of the scrimmage line, to locate it sharply in time ("downs"), and to focus attention not only on the snapping of the ball, but also on the problem of "offside" players. In the English game, with no spatially and temporally delimited "line of scrimmage," the offside player was penalized only by making him neutral in action until he could move to a position back of the position of the ball. In the American game, the new focus on centering, on a scrimmage line, and on yardage and downs, created the need for a better offside rule. From that need developed offside rules that even in the early years resembled the rules of today. American rulemakers were logically extending a native development when they decided to draw an imaginary line through the ball before it had been centered, to call this the "line of scrimmage," and to make this line, rather than the moving ball itself, the offside limit in the goalward motion of offensive players. At first, lined-up players of the two sides were allowed to stand and wrestle with each other while waiting for the ball to be centered; only later was a neutral zone introduced between the opposing lines.

Even with such a brief summary of the rule changes, we are in a position to see the operation of certain recurrent modes or patterns of adaptation. The adaptation begins with the acceptance of a single pivotal innovation (running with the ball). The problems of adaptation begin with the realization that this single innovation has been uprooted from a rich context of meaningful rules and traditions, and does not work well in their absence. Still more complex problems of adaptation develop when it is realized that the incompleteness of the adaptation will not be solved by a reference to the pristine rules. In the first place, the rules are not pristine (the English rules were in the process of development themselves). In the second place, the tradition of interpreting them is not present in experienced players. In the third place, even if it were, it might not be adaptable to the social character and mood of the adapters.

Let us put it this way. The Americans, in order to solve the heel-out problem, set in motion a redesign of the game that led ultimately to timed centering from a temporarily fixed line of scrimmage. Emphasis completely shifted from the kicking game; it also shifted away from the combined kicking and running possible under Rugby rules; it shifted almost entirely in the direction of an emphasis on ball-carrying. Meanwhile, to achieve this emphasis, the game made itself vulnerable to slowdowns caused by one team's retention of the ball. It not only lost the fluidity of the original game, but ran up against a pronounced American taste for action in sports, visible action. There is evidence that even if players had not objected to such slowdowns, the spectators would have raised a shout. The yardage rule was the way this crisis was met. This, in turn, led to an emphasis on mass play, and helped to create the early twentieth-century problems of football. But before we consider this step in the game's development we must turn to examine certain factors in the sport's audience reception.

IV

A problem posed for the student of cultural diffusion at this point can be stated as follows: What factor or factors appear to have been most influential in creating an American game possessing not only nationally distinct rules, but also rules having a specific flavor of intense legality about many a point of procedure left more or less up in the air by the British game?

We can now go beyond the rule-making aspect of the game and assert that the chief factor was the importance of the need to standardize rules to supply an ever-widening collegiate field of competition, along with the audience is implied. The English rule-makers, it appears, dealt with a situation in which amateur play was restricted to a fairly limited number of collegians and institutions. The power of localism was such that many an informality was tolerated, and intended to be tolerated, in the rules and their interpretation. American football appeared on the American campus at the beginning of a long period in which intercollegiate and interclass sportsmanship was a problem of ever-widening social participation and concern. Football etiquette itself was in the making. Thus, it appears that when early American teams met, differences of opinion could not be resolved between captains in rapid-fire agreement or penny-tossing as was the case in Britain. American teams did not delegate to their captains the role of powerful comrade-in-antagonism with opposing captains, or, if they did, they felt that such responsibilities were too grave.[5]

Into just such situations football players thrust all of the force of their democratic social ideologies, all their prejudice in favor of equalitarian and codified inter-player attitudes. Undoubtedly, similar considerations also influenced the audience. Mark Benney, a British sociologist who is familiar with the games played on both sides of the Atlantic, points out that, whereas the American game was developed in and for a student group, the English game was played before quite large crowds who, from a class standpoint, were less homogeneous than the players themselves, though they were as well informed as the latter in the "law" of the game. Rugby football was seldom played by the proletariat; it was simply enjoyed as a spectacle.

Held by the critical fascination the British upper strata had for the lower strata, the audience was often hardly more interested in the result of the game than in judging the players as "gentlemen in action." "The players," Mr. Benney writes, "had to demonstrate that they were sportsmen, that they could 'take it;' and above all they had to inculcate the (politically important) ideology that legality was more important than power." The audience was, then, analogous to the skilled English jury at law, ready to be impressed by obedience to the traditional legal ritual and form, and intolerant of "bad form" in their "betters." The early Yale games, played before a tiny, nonpaying audience, lacked any equivalent incentive to agree on a class-based ritual of "good form," and when the audiences came later on, their attitude towards upper-class sportsmanship was much more ambivalent—they had played the game too, and they were unwilling to subordinate themselves to a collegiate aristocracy who would thereby have been held to norms of correctness. The apparent legalism of many American arguments over the rules would strike British observers as simply a verbal power-play.

Such differences in the relation of the game to the audience, on this side of the Atlantic, undoubtedly speeded the development of the specifically American variant. Native, too, are the visual and temporal properties of the game as it developed even before 1900: its choreography could be enjoyed, if not always understood, by non-experts, and its atomistic pattern in time and space could seem natural to audiences accustomed to such patterns in other foci of the national life. The midfield dramatization of line against line, the recurrent starting and stopping of field action around the timed snapping of a ball, the trend to a formalized division of labor between backfield and line, above all, perhaps, the increasingly precise synchronization of men in motion—these developments make it seem plausible to suggest that the whole procedural rationalization of the game which we have described was not unwelcome to

Americans, and that it fitted in with other aspects of their industrial folkways.

Spurred by interest in the analysis of the athletic motions of men and animals, Eadweard Muybridge was setting out his movie-like action shorts of the body motion (more preoccupied even than Vesalius or da Vinci with the detailed anatomy of movement)[6] at about the same time that Coach Woodruff at Pennsylvania (1894) was exploring the possibilities for momentum play: linemen swinging into motion before the ball is snapped, with the offensive team, forming a wedge, charging toward an opposition held waiting by the offside rule. In Philadelphia, the painter Eakins, self-consciously following the tenets of Naturalism and his own literal American tradition, was painted the oarsmen of the Schuylkill. Nearby, at the Midvale plant of the American Steel Company, efficiency expert Frederick Winslow Taylor was experimenting with motion study and incentive pay geared to small measurable changes in output—pay that would spur but never soften the workman.[7]

Since we do not believe in historical inevitability, nor in the necessary homogeneity of a culture, we do not suggest that the American game of football developed as it did out of cultural compulsion and could not have gone off in quite different directions. Indeed, the very effectiveness of momentum play, as a mode of bulldozing the defense, led eventually to the rule that the line must refrain from motion before the ball is snapped. For the bulldozing led, or was thought to lead, to a great increase injuries. And while these were first coped with by Walter Camp's training table (his men had their choice of beefsteak or mutton for dinner, to be washed down with milk, ale, or sherry), the public outcry soon forced further rule changes, designed to soften the game. After a particularly bloody battle between Pennsylvania and Swarthmore in 1905, President Roosevelt himself took a hand and insisted on reform.[8]

Camp's colleague at Yale, William Graham Sumner, may well have smiled wryly at this. Sumner was exhorting his students to "get capital," and cautioning them against the vices of sympathy and reformism—a theme which as given innumerable academes a good living since—while Camp was exhorting his to harden themselves, to be stern and unafraid. In spite of them both, the reformers won out; but the end of momentum play was not the end of momentum. Rather, with an ingenuity that still dazzles, the game was gentled and at the same time speeded by a new rule favoring the forward pass. But before going on to see what changed this introduced, let us note the differences between the subjects of Sumner's and Camp's exhortations on the one hand, and Taylor's on the other.

Frederick Taylor, as his writings show, was already coming up against a work force increasingly drawn from non-Protestant lands, and seeking to engender in them a YMCA-morality, whereas Camp was inculcating the same morality into young men of undiluted Anglo-Saxon stock and middle- to upper-class origins. Not for another fifty years would the sons of Midvale prove harder, though fed on kale or spaghetti, and only intermittently, than the sons of Yale. Meanwhile, the sons of Yale had learned to spend summers as tracklayers or wheat harvesters in an effort to enlarge their stamina, moral toughness, and cross-class adventures.

Nevertheless, certain basic resemblances between the purposes of Taylor and those of Sumner and Camp are clearly present. By contrast with the British, the Americans demonstrated a high degree of interest in winning games and winning one's way to high production goals. The Americans, as in so many other matters, were clearly concerned with the competitive spirit that new rules might provoke and control. (British sports, like British industry, seemed to take it for more for granted that competition will exist even if one does not set up an ideology for it.) Much of this seems to rest in the paradoxical belief of Americans that competition is natural—but only if it is constantly recreated by artificial systems of social rules that direct energies into it.

Back of the attitudes expressed in Taylor, Sumner, and Camp we can feel the pressure no only of a theory of competition, but also a theory of the emotional tones that ought to go along with competition. It is apparent from the brutality scandals of 1905 that President Roosevelt reacted against roughhouse not so much because it was physical violence, but for two related reasons. The first and openly implied reason was that it was connected with an unsportsmanlike attitude. The second, unacknowledged, reason was that Americans fear and enjoy their aggression at the same time, and thus have difficulty in pinning down the inner meanings of external violence. The game of Rugby as now played in England is probably as physically injurious as American football was at the turn of the century. By contrast, American attitudes toward football demonstrate a forceful need to define, limit, and conventionalize the symbolism of violence in sports.

If we look back now at England, we see a game in which shouted signals and silent counting of timed movements are unknown—a game that seems to Americans to wander in an amorphous and disorderly roughhouse. Rugby, in the very home of the industrial revolution, seems pre-industrial, seems like one of the many feudal survivals that urbanization and industrialization have altered but not destroyed. The English game, moreover, seems not to have developed anyone like Camp, the Judge Gary of football (as Rockne was to be its Henry Ford): Camp was a sparkplug in efforts to codify inter-collegiate rules; he was often the head of the important committees. His training table, furthermore, was one of the signs of the slow rise in "overhead" expense—a rise which, rather like the water in United States Steel Stock, assumed that abundance was forthcoming and bailing out probable, as against the British need for parsimony. But at the same time the rise in costs undoubtedly made American football more vulnerable than ever to public-relations considerations: the "gate" could not be damned.

V

This public relations issue in the game first appears in the actions of the rules committee of 1906—the introduction of the legalized forward pass in order to open up the game and reduce brutal power play. Between 1906 and 1913 the issue was generally treated as a problem centered about players and their coaches, and thus took the form of an appeal to principles rather than to audiences. However, the development of the high audience appeal that we shall show unfolding after 1913 was not autonomous and unheralded. If public relations became a dominant factor by 1915, when the University of Pittsburgh introduced numbers for players in order to spur the sale of programs, it had its roots in the 1905-13 period. The rules committee of 1906, by its defensive action on roughhouse rules, had already implicitly acknowledged a broad public vested interest in the ethos of the game. Let us turn to look at the speed with which football was soon permeated by broad social meanings unanticipated by the founders of the sport.

By 1913, the eve of the First World War, innovation in American industry had ceased to be the prerogative of Baptist, Calvinist, and North of Ireland tycoons. Giannini was starting his Bank of America; the Jews were entering the movies and the garment hegemonies. Yet these were exceptions, and the second generation of immigrants, taught in America to be dissatisfied with the manual work their fathers did, were seldom finding the easy paths of ascent promised in success literature. Where, for one thing, were they to go to college? If they sought to enter the older eastern institutions, would they face a social struggle? Such anxieties probably contributed to the fact that the game of boyish and spirited brawn played at the eastern centers of intellect and cultivation was to be overthrown by the new game of craft and field maneuver that got its first rehearsal at the hands of two second-generation poor boys attending little-known Notre Dame.

The more significant of the two boys, Knute Rockne, was, to be sure, of Danish Protestant descent and only later became a Catholic. During their summer vacation jobs as lifeguards on Lake Michigan, Rockne and Gus Dorais decided to work as a passing team. Playing West Point early in the season of 1913, they put on the first demonstration of the spiral pass that makes scientific use of the difference in shape between the round ball used in the kicking game and the oval that gradually replaced it when ball-carrying began. As the first players to exploit the legal pass, they rolled up a surprise victory over the Army. One of the effects of the national change in rules was to bring the second-generation boys of the early twentieth century to the front, with a craft innovation that added new elements of surprise, "system" and skull-session to a game that had once revolved about an ethos of brawn plus character-building.

With the ethnic shift, appears to have come a shift in type of hero. The work-minded glamor of an all-'round craftsman like Jim Thorpe gave way to the people minded glamor of backfield generals organizing deceptive forays into enemy territory—of course, the older martial virtues are not so much ruled out as partially incorporated in the new image. In saying this, it must not be forgotten, as sports columnist Red Smith has pointed out, that the fictional Yale hero, Frank Merriwell, is openly and shamelessly represented as a dirty player in the first chapters of his career. But the difference is that his deviation from standard sportsmanship consisted largely of slugging, not of premeditated wiliness. In fact, the Yale era, even into Camp's reign, was characterized by a game played youthfully, with little attention to the player's prestige outside college circles. Again, the second-generationers mark a change. A variety of sources, including letters to the sports page, indicate that a Notre Dame victory became representational in a way a Yale or Harvard victory never was, and no Irish or Polish boy on the team could escape the symbolism. And by the self-confirming process, the Yale or Harvard showing became symbolic in turn, and the game could never be returned, short of intra-muralization, to the players themselves and their earlier age of innocent dirtiness.[10] The heterogeneity of America which had made it impossible to play the Rugby game at Yale had finally had its effect in transforming the meaning of the game to a point where Arnold of Rugby might have difficulty in drawing the right moral or any moral from it. Its "ideal types" had undergone a deep and widespread characterological change.

For the second-generation boy, with his father's muscles but not his father's motives, football soon became a means to career ascent. So was racketeering, but football gave acceptance, too—acceptance into the democratic fraternity of the entertainment world where performance counts and ethnic origin is hardly a handicap. Moreover, Americans as onlookers welcomed the anti-traditional innovations of a Rockne, and admired the trick that worked, whatever the opposing team and alumni may have thought about the effort involved. One wonders whether Rockne and Dorais may not have gotten a particular pleasure from their craftiness by thinking of it as a counter-image to the stereotype of muscle-men applied to their fathers.

It was in 1915, at about the same time that the newcomers perfected their passing game, that the recruitment of players began in earnest. Without such recruitment, the game could not have served as a career route for many of the second generation who would not have had the cash or impetus to make the class jump that college involved.[11]

The development of the open and rationalized game has led step by step not only to the T formation, but also to the two-platoon system. These innovations call for a very different relationship among the players than was the case under the older star system. For the game is now a co-operative enterprise in which mistakes are too costly—to the head coach, the budget, even the college itself—to be left to individual initiative. At least at one institution, an anthropologist has been called in to study the morale problems of the home team, and to help in the scouting of opposing teams. To the learning of Taylor, there has been added that of Mayo, and coaches are conscious of the need to be group-dynamics leaders rather than old-line straw bosses.

Today, the semi-professionalized player, fully conscious of how many peoples' living depends on them, cannot be exhorted by Frank Merriwell appeals, but needs to be "handled." And the signals are no longer the barks of the first Camp-trained quarterback—hardly more differentiated than a folk dance caller—but are cues of great subtlety and mathematical precision for situations planned in advance with camera shots and character fill-ins of the opposing team. James Worthy and other advocates of a span of control beyond the usual half-dozen of the older military and executive manuals might find support for their views in the way an eleven is managed. Industrial, military, and football teamwork have all a common cultural frame.

Yet it would be too simple to say that football has ceased to be a game for its players, and has become an industry, or a training for industry. In the American culture as a whole, no sharp line exists between work and play, and in some respects the more work-like an activity becomes, the more it can successfully conceal elements of playfulness.[12] Just because the sophisticated "amateur" of today does *not* have his manhood at stake in the antique do-or-die fashion (though his manhood may be involved), in very ambivalent ways, in his more generalized role as athlete and teammate), there can be a relaxation of certain older demands and a more detached enjoyment of perfection of play irrespective of partisanship.

The role of football tutor to the audience has been pushed heavily onto radio and TV announcers (some of whom will doubtless be mobile into the higher-status role of commentators on politics or symphony broadcasts). The managerial coalescence of local betting pools into several big oceans has also contributed to the audience stake in the game. Yet all that has so far been said does not wholly explain alumnus and subway-alumnus loyalties. It may be that we have to read into this interest of the older age groups a much more general aspect of American behavior: the pious and near-compulsory devotion of the older folks to whatever the younger folks are alleged to find important. The tension between the generations doubtless contributes to the hysterical note of solemnity in the efforts of some older age groups to control the ethics of the game, partly perhaps as a displacement of their Kinsey-belabored efforts to control youthful sexuality.

And this problem in turn leads to questions about the high percentage of women in the American football audience, compared with that of any other country, and the high salience of women in football as compared with baseball imagery (in recent American football films, girls have been singled out as the most influential section of the spectators). The presence of these women heightens the sexual impact of everything in and around the game, from shoulderpads to the star system, as the popular folklore of the game recognizes. Although women are not expected to attend baseball games, when they do attend they are expected to understand them and to acquire, if not a "male" attitude, at least something approaching companionship on a basis of equality with their male escorts.[13]

For all its involvement with such elemental themes in American life, it may be that football has reached the apex of its audience appeal. With bigness comes vulnerability: "inter-industry" competition is invited, and so are rising costs—the players, though not yet unionized, learn early in high school their market value and, like Jim in Huckleberry Finn, take pride in it.[14] The educators' counter-reformation cannot be laughed off. With the lack of ethnic worlds to conquer, we may soon find the now-decorous Irish of the Midwest embarrassed by Notre Dame's unbroken victories. Perhaps the period of innovation which began in 1823 at Rugby has about come to an end in the United States, with large changes likely to result only if the game is used as a device for acculturation to America, not by the vanishing stream of immigrants to that country, but by the rest of the world that will seek the secret of American victories on the playing fields of South Bend.

● ● ●

Notes

1. The growing scale of college football is indicated by its dollar place in the American leisure economy. In 1929, out of $4.3 billion in recreation expenditures by Americans, the college football gate accounted for $22 million. In 1950, out of $11.2 billion in such expenditures, it accounted for $103 million. While something less than 1% of the total United States recreation account, college football had ten times the gross income of professional football. The 1950 gate of $103 million suggests that a total capital of at least $2 billion is invested in the college football industry. The revenue figures, above, of course, do not include the invisible subsidization of football, nor do they hint the place that football pools occupy in the American betting economy.

2. A commemorative stone at Rugby reads as follows:

This stone
commemorates the exploit of
William Webb Ellis
who with a fine disregard for the rules of
football, as played in his time,
first took the ball in his arms and ran with it,
thus originating the distinctive feature of
the rugby game
A.D. 1823

3. Walter Camp and Lorin F. Deland, *Football* (Boston: Houghton Mifflin Co., 1896).

4. Cf., his *An Outline of Social Psychology* (New York: Harper & Brothers, 1948), pp. 93-182.

5. "Fifty years ago arguments followed almost every decision the referee made. The whole team took part, so that half the time the officials scarcely knew who was captain. The player who was a good linguist was always a priceless asset." John W. Heisman, who played for both Brown and Penn in the 1890s, quoted in Frank G. Menke, *Encyclopedia of Sports* (New York: A.S. Barnes Co, 1944), p. 293.

6. Sigfried Giedion, *Mechanization Takes Command* (New York: Oxford University Press, 1948), pp. 21-27.

7. In view of the prejudice against "Taylorism" today, shared by men and management as well as intellectuals, let us record our admiration for Taylor's achievement, our belief that he was less insensitive to psychological factors than is often claimed, and more "humane" in many ways than his no less manipulative, self-consciously psychological successors.

8. "In a 1905 game between Pennsylvania and Swarthmore, the Pennsy slogan was 'Stop Bob Maxwell,' one of the greatest linesmen of all time. He was a mighty man, with amazing ability to roll back enemy plunges. The Penn players, realizing that Maxwell was a menace to their chances for victory, took 'dead aim' at him throughout the furious play.

"Maxwell stuck it out, but when he tottered off the field, his face was a bloody wreck. Some photographer snapped him, and the photo of the mangled Maxwell, appearing in a newspaper, caught the attention of the then President Roosevelt. It so angered him, that he issued an ultimatum that if rough play in football was not immediately ruled out, he would abolish it by executive edict." Frank G. Menke, *Encyclopedia of Sports.*

Notice here the influence of two historical factors on football development: one, the occupancy of the White House in 1905 by the first President of the United States who was a self-conscious patron of youth, sport, and the arts; two, the relative awareness in 1905 of photographic sports coverage. Widespread increased photographic coverage of popular culture was the direct result of the newspaper policies of William Randolph Hearst, beginning about 1895.

9. "After the church, football is the best thing we have," Rockne.

10. One of us, while a Harvard undergraduate, sought with several friends to heal the breach between Harvard and Princeton—a breach whose bitterness could hardly be credited today. The Harvards believed Princeton played dirty—it certainly won handily in those years of the 20's—while Princetonians believed themselves snubbed by Harvards as crude parvenus trying to make a trio out of the Harvard-Yale duo. The diplomatic problems involved in seeking to repair these status slights and scars were a microcosm of the Congress of Westphalia or Vienna—whether the Harvard or Princeton athletic directors should enter the room first was an issue. A leak to the Hearst press destroyed our efforts,

as alumni pressure forced denials of any attempt to resume relations, but the compromise formulas worked out were eventually accepted, about the time that the University of Chicago "solved" the problem of the intellectual school by withdrawing from the game altogether.

11. See George Saxon, "Immigrant Culture in a Stratified Society," *Modern Review*, II, No. 2, February 1948.

12. See David Riesman (with the collaboration of Reuel Denney and Nathan Glazer), *The Lonely Crowd* (New Haven: Yale University Press, 1950), chapters 15, 17.

13. Anthropologist Ray Birdwhistell convincingly argues that football players play with an eye to their prestige among teammates, other football players, and other men.

14. Their pride varies to some extent with their place on the team. Linemen, with the exception of ends, have lower status than backfield men. Many players believe that backfields are consciously or unconsciously recruited from higher social strata than linemen.

• • •

Suggestions for Further Reading

Berryman, Jack W., "Early Black Leadership in Collegiate Football: Massachusetts as a Pioneer," *Historical Journal of Massachusetts*, IX (June, 1981), 17-28.

Cady, Edwin H., *The Big Game: College Sports and American Life* (Knoxville, TN: University of Tennessee Press, 1978).

Cunningham, John, "Not a Coward on Either Side," *New Jersey History*, XCVI (Autumn-Winter, 1978), 99-104.

Dains, Mary K., "University of Missouri Football: The First Decade," *Missouri Historical Review*, LXX (October, 1975), 20-54.

Kaye, Ivan N., *Good Clean Violence: A History of College Football* (Philadelphia: Lippincott, 1973).

Leckie, Robert, *The Story of Football* (New York: Random Youse, 1965).

Lewis, Guy M., "Theodore Roosevelt's Role in the 1905 Football Controversy," *Research Quarterly*, XL (December, 1969), 717-724.

Martin, John Stuart, "Walter Camp and His Gridiron Game," *American Heritage*, XII, 6 (October, 1961), 50-55 ff.

Moore, John Hammond, "Football's Ugly Decades, 1893-1913," *Smithsonian Journal of History*, II, 3 (Fall, 1957), 49-68.

Sack, Allen L., "Yale 29-Harvard 4: The Professionalization of College Football," *Quest*, XIX (1973), 24-34.

_____, and David L. Westby, "The Commercialization and Functional Rationalization of College Football," *Journal of*

Higher Education, XLVI, 6 (November-December, 1976), 625-647.

Shapiro, Beth J., "John Hannah and the Growth of Big-Time Inter-collegiate Athletics at Michigan State University," *Journal of Sport History*, X, 3 (Winter, 1983), 26-40.

Smith, Ronald A., "Harvard and Columbia and a Reconsideration of the 1905-06 Football Crisis," *Journal of Sport History*, VIII, 3 (Winter, 1981), 5-19.

Stagg, Amos A. and Wesley W. Sterit, *Touchdown!* (New York: Longmans, Green, 1927).

Synnott, Marcia G., "The 'Big Three' and the Harvard-Princeton Football Break, 1926-1934," *Journal of Sport History*, III (Summer, 1976), 188-202.

Watterson, John S., III, "The Football Crisis of 1909-1910: The Response of the Eastern 'Big Three'," *Journal of Sport History*, VIII, 1 (Spring, 1981), 33-49.

PROGRESS AND FLIGHT:
AN INTERPRETATION OF THE
AMERICAN CYCLE CRAZE OF THE 1890s

Richard Harmond

In the mid-1890s a cycle craze swept across the nation. What once had been considered only a toy (and a dangerous one at that) attracting 150,000 or so "wheelmen" in 1890, the bicycle claimed nearly 10 million American riders by the end of the decade. Hailed as a great mechanical marvel, praised for its contributions to physical fitness and emotional well-being, and supported by aggressive advertising and merchandising campaigns, the bicycle had become an influential force in our national life.

As Richard Harmond explores in this essay, the bicycle also represented "a major expression of current beliefs and fears." The cycle, particularly the safer, lighter, more comfortable and more affordable machine that had replaced the ordinary or high wheeler by 1892, had a paradoxical attraction. As a symbol of nineteenth century technological advancement, the bicycle represented the forces of inventive progress. As a means of flight from the consequences of such progress, it offered the rider escape and the opportunity to restore himself for facing the tensions and disruptions of an increasingly mechanized and industrialized society.

Serving both progressive wants and desires and simultaneously gratifying escapist tendencies, the bicycle ushered in a new era of sporting activity. In one sense, the cycle craze benefited from an activist mood that the aggressive nationalism, expressive music and literature, and liberating social norms of the day inspired. In another, the bicycle was a "democratic" vehicle that crossed class lines (but not racial, despite the racing accomplishments of Marshall W. "Major" Taylor, the champion black cyclist from Indianapolis), encouraged wide recreational participation, and stimulated competitive interests.

The machine cannot be divorced from its larger social pattern; for it is this pattern that gives it meaning and purpose. Every period of civilization carries within it the insignificant refuse of past technologies and the important germs of new ones; but the center of growth lies within its own complex. (Lewis Mumford, *Technics and Civilization*, p. 110-11.)

As the nineteenth century neared its close, Americans had good reason to celebrate the technological accomplishments of the past several generations. Conveyor belts and interchangeable parts had sharply altered the system of production; the reaper and other farm machines had expanded enormously the output of food; the steam engine had revolutionized long distance transportation on water and land; and the utilization of electricity was transforming methods of communication, lighting and local travel. For a people who tended to measure progress in quantitative terms, especially by an improvement in physical well-being, an increase in utility, or a growth in power and speed, the mechanical advances of the nineteenth century were truly dazzling.[1]

There was another side to the story, though, for the material progress wrought by machines had been costly. Within a brief span, as history measures time, technology had changed the United States from a rustic, primitive land to an industrial giant.[2] That shift, involving as it did great social and economic dislocations, required extensive and often wrenching adjustments on the part of the populace. During the 1890s the process of adjustment became particularly painful.

It was no coincidence that the bicycle rose to popularity at this time. Some years before, because it had been difficult and even hazardous to manipulate, Americans had built up a prejudice against the bicycle. But after the appearance of the safety bicycle, their prejudice subsided. Once this was accomplished, Americans discovered the bicycle to be a craft of speed and liberation, as well as an efficient and highly useful device. At the same time, the vehicle enabled them to escape some of the less desirable conditions associated with their technologically oriented society. And it was this paradoxical attraction of the bicycle—as an instance of inventive progress and as a means of flight from the consequences of such progress—which substantially explains the great cycle craze of the years between 1893-96.

I

There is no question about the heightened interest, even the fervor, with which Americans greeted the bicycle in the mid-1890s, though it had not always been a widely popular vehicle. We should not forget that less than a decade earlier, in the era of the ordinary, enthusiasm for the bicycle was distinctly limited. Indeed, in those days the general public entertained serious reservations about the wheel.

The object of these negative sentiments, the ordinary or high wheeler, was the standard bicycle in the years before the rise of the safety. With its tubular steel frame, ball bearings, and hollow or spongy tires, the ordinary of the mid-1880s was a vast technical improvement over the "bone shaker," a vehicle which had exhausted the patience and vigor or riders in the late 1860s.[3] Unfortunately, the high wheeler was hard to master and dangerous to use. The prospective rider usually devoted weeks of effort and endured frequent spills acquiring the knack of mounting the vehicle; and he often spent further months of practice becoming a proficient cyclist.[4]

Nor was this the limit of his trials. Once confident of his ability to remain aloft, the rider ventured out to confront the challenges of the highway (if, that is, his locality permitted him on the highway). Gliding along, perched warily over the large front wheel of his cycle, he had to be prepared for several dangers. Among these might be the frightened reaction to his approach of a bicycle-shy horse, harassment from prankish youngsters or the malicious determination of a teamster to drive him off the road. A more common occurrence was for the cyclist to hear a "help" and a "bound" and, turning, see "some large fearless dog" rushing after him. Besides these risks, the rider also continually had to be alert for a jarring encounter with a rock or some other obstruction in the road, which could send him hurtling over the handle bars of his rather unstable vehicle.[5]

All in all, wheeling in the 1880s had its drawbacks. "The greatest wonder to me," one rider aptly recalled, was "that not more cyclers who rode high wheelers were killed." We can readily appreciate why the hazards of riding the ordinary were, according to another contemporary, "commonly imagined to be about the same as those which beset the professional tightrope walker."[6]

Nevertheless, the ordinary had its hardy band of devotees. To those bold and persistent men who were able to manipulate it, the high wheeler was a source of healthy outdoor exercise, pleasure and, if need be, transportation.[7] But the number of such riders, though it grew steadily, was never large and clearly had a limit. Bicycling in the 1880s was an activity restricted to athletically inclined men. Most probably it would have remained so had the ordinary not been supplanted.[8]

Even as those youthful athletes rode about, proud and high on their ordinaries, ingenious men were at work devising a machine for the average person. As early as the 1870s, but more especially in the years 1885-90, the cumulative achievements of a group of largely European inventors resulted in a bicycle that was at once safe to ride and relatively easy to pedal. Its notable features included the tubular construction and ball bearings of the ordinary, along with two equal-sized wheels (thus eliminating headers), chain-gear drive, a diamond-shaped frame and pneumatic tires. This, of course, was the safety bicycle, and it was quickly made available to the American public.[9]

Americans did not, however, become an eager army of buyers. In the first place, early models of the safety were subject to criticisms. The machine was, for instance, quite heavy, some versions weighing seventy pounds or more. The pneumatic tire was also considered overly puncture-prone.[10] Moreover (and the difficulties just mentioned did not help matters here), because of real or vicarious experiences with the old high wheeler, people remained suspicious of any kind of a bicycle.[11] Lastly, at a list price of $125 or more for top grade models, the new vehicle was expensive and seemingly beyond the means of a large part of the public.

All of these problems would have to be resolved before there could be any real boom in bicycling. In one way or another—beginning with the safety's design—the cycle industry did meet them successfully, and, in the process, climbed from obscurity to industrial eminence.[12]

The evolution of the bicycle between 1890 and 1895, though less dramatic than during the previous half decade, was nonetheless impressive. In 1891-1892 an improved pneumatic tire was placed on the market, and well before the end of the latter year it had demonstrated its superiority over the rival cushion tire. The attributes of the new tire were essential to the further development of the safety. Because it reduced rolling friction, the air-filled tire added to a vehicle's speed; and because it absorbed road shock, the tire not only increased riding comfort, but also enabled manufacturers to cut back on the weight of the bicycle. By 1893 the machine had dropped to thirty-five pounds, and over the course of the next two years it shed another ten to twelve pounds. Moreover, inventors and engineers made other useful changes in the cycle, such as the installation of more effective coaster brake and the substitution of wooden for metal rims. By the mid-1890s the American bicycle had reached a stage where the *Scientific American* could describe it as "the most beautiful mechanism, and the lightest and easiest running of any wheel manufactured in any country."[13]

The emergence of a safe and, at the same time, light and comfortable machine did much to overcome popular suspicion of the wheel. Equally effective in combating current skepticism was a wide-ranging promotional campaign. The bicycle industry, seeking to infuse wheeling with a sense of excitement and adventure, supported racing tournaments and subsidized top speed riders.[14] Concomitantly, the industry launched an advertising campaign so extensive that, in the opinion of one scholar, it stimulated advertising in other fields. Bicycle interests allocated thousands of dollars annually to instruct the public about the lightness, swiftness, strength and beauty of their product. Some of this sum was spent on catalogues and posters, but most of the money went for advertisements which appeared in trade periodicals (of which at one time there were over eighty), as well as the big daily newspapers and the better magazines. In return, by running editorials and regular columns on the wheel, plus special articles by bicycle enthusiasts and medical men, the presses and magazines made cycling an increasingly more respectable activity.[15]

For anyone convinced by what he read in his favorite daily or magazine, but perhaps slightly hesitant about facing the road alone, companionship was available in a variety of cycling clubs. Riders might sign up with the League of American Wheelmen, a large national organization which, like the American Automobile Association of another era, defended the rights and promoted the broader interests (with special emphasis on better roads) of the riding fraternity. Or, if the League did not seem suitable, a cyclist could enlist in one of the numerous local touring-social clubs that were springing up in cities and towns across the land.[16]

Advertising and clubs by themselves were not enough, however, for there was still the obstacle of price. To overcome this hurdle, the cycle trade presented the clientele with options and inducements.

To start with, the customer was not limited to the top grade machines listed at $125 and above. He might also shop around among the medium grades, with prices ranging between $85 and $100; or he might select from among the low grades, marked at about $50. The careful buyer knew, too, that all of these prices were subject to change. He realized, for example, that as a result of overproduction, manufacturers and dealers periodically hawked their wares at sharply reduced prices. And, if he followed trade matters closely, he was aware that, because of the if of mass production techniques in the manufacture of bicycles, the drift of prices was downward.[17]

Again, the patron, if he wished, could make his purchase on the installment plan. He also expected the retailer to give him a liberal trade-in allowance on his old machine. This widely established practice, in turn, laid the basis for a thriving second-hand business, where adequate bicycles were placed within reach of those earning modest incomes.[18]

As we can see today, installment buying, trade-ins and the larger engineering and promotional effort of which these were a part, had their intended result. Statistics and some relevant contemporary observations suggest as much. In 1890, at the dawn of the modern bicycle age, there were only about 150,000 riders in the United States. But the new safety began to prove so attractive to segments of the public that in 1891 a columnist for *Sporting Life* felt confident enough to predict that "wheeling is going to be the universal sport." The following year, a writer in the *American Athlete* asserted that bicycling "in the slang vernacular," had "'caught on,'" and some months later an editorial in the same magazine declared with assurance that the possibilities ahead for cycling were "practically immeasurable judged by the occurrences of the past few years."[19]

Such optimism was well founded. While estimates vary, it seems likely that by 1893 there were close to a million riders in the United States.[20] The old prejudice against the bicycle, as commentators recognized, had finally been overcome.[21] Any lingering doubts on this score were dispelled in the summer of 1894 as society people took to the safety, and cycling became a "marked feature of the Newport season." Moreover, society was joined on wheels by a flock of literary and public figures, including E.L. Godkin, Richard Harding Davis, Owen Wister, Frances Willard, Lillian Russell, Justice Edward D. White of the Supreme Court and Speaker of the House Thomas B. Reed.[22]

And so, with cycling taking on a life and style of its own, the silent steed entered the halcyon years of the mid-1890s. This was a time when it appeared that no one "article of use, pleasure, or sport," in the words of the *American Wheelman*, had ever before retained "such a hold on popular approval, popular taste, or popular fancy as the bicycle." Across the land adults of all ages and both sexes surrendered to the bicycle passion, although it was in the urban-suburban complexes of the northeast and midwest that the largest body of riders was to be found.[23] By 1896, as the cycle craze reached its peak, there were probably four million riders in America. This was a striking figure when compared with the 150,000 or so cyclists of 1890.[24]

In the meantime, the bicycle, once reviled as a dangerous toy, became the subject of songs, poetry, fiction and earnest social commentary. Talk of its being something of a fad was generally dismissed. More commonly, the safety was credited with initiating "a new era in the means of passenger transportation." More than that, it was seen as a "new power" discovered by the human race, and "as a new social force," even a "revolutionary" social force which "could not be abandoned without turning the social progress of the world backward." With characteristic understatement, the *Times* summarized the dominant view by announcing that the wheel had "come to stay," and was to be "one of the powerful elements in shaping social habits.[25]

In the long run, these pronouncements turned out to be somewhat overblown; but at the time they represented the very real popularity and importance which the bicycle had attained in the America of the mid-1890s.

II

Advertising and aggressive merchandising undoubtedly sold a lot of bicycles, but the safety achieved its enormous popularity both for what it proferred and for what it came to represent. On the one hand, the safety promised its riders the pleasures and advantages of speed, good health, greater freedom of movement and utility. On the other hand, it beckoned to them to ride swiftly away from their problems and fears. In short, the bicycle was both a mechanism of progress and a vehicle of flight.

It was not strange that Americans had come to associate speed with the progress of civilization. A mobile, energetic and enterprising people, they knew that swift transportation and communication had been indispensable to the unification and exploitation of their huge and productive land. They had also witnessed the material achievements of such rapidly functioning devices as the sewing machine, typewriter and high-speed press. It may be, too, that, at a different level of consciousness, speed and the closely related desire to save time had become important goals to Americans because, as a people, they were increasingly more concerned with temporal events, rather than those which were to take place in eternity. At any rate, by the 1890s Americans were captivated by the idea of speed, and much of the attraction of the bicycle stemmed from the fact that the vehicle was able to actualize this idea in a highly gratifying fashion.[26]

Riding a bicycle was obviously a pleasurable activity. Since the men and women of the 1890s belonged to the first and *last* generation of adults to learn how to cycle, their initial sense of delight stemmed from encountering a new and exciting kind of motion. One rider vividly related his earliest experience with this new form of motion. He was a trainee at an indoor cycling school in New York; the experience the cyclist describes is after a difficult and frustrating lesson.

> Toward the end of my session I discovered that I didn't have to keep a tight rein or to be constantly trying to bend the handlebars, and then, all of a sudden, I was going round and round the place, not pushing pedals, but flying. My world took on a new aspect. I was master, or about to become master of the the poetry of motion, of what began to seem there and then the most fascinating and exhilarating method of locomotion that man has ever invented.[27]

As a rider developed more skill and confidence, and as his wheel became "a mechanism of life, the cyclist's other self in steel and rubber," his fascination and exhilaration grew apace. To the joy of motion was now added the delight of a new and "fresh sense of power," which the cyclist received from his relatively effortless passage along the road. Pedaling on, at an "easy and rapid" clip, the rider might be "lifted out" of himself, "up, up from the body that drags." Or, he may have quickened his pace, given himself up to "jolly abandon," and undergone the zestful thrill which inheres in fast and risky flight.[28] In the case of some riders, speed became an irresistible temptation. Contemporaries labelled as "scorchers" those consumed by this passion.

If cycling offered the psychic pleasures of motion and speed, it also conferred other more measurable benefits. One of the most important of these, in the opinion of medical men, was a firm and healthy body.

Doctors and others who studied the subject had grown deeply concerned about the effects which the spreading pattern of sedentary living was having on the population's physical condition. Through most of the nation's history, these authorities asserted, the average American had received all of the exercise he needed in his daily round of chores on the farm or in the shop. "Civilization itself was a gym," as a writer in *Outing* pointed out. But as the nineteenth century progressed, and the wilderness was tamed and cities were established, greater numbers of people began to earn their livelihoods at less physically demanding tasks in factories, offices and stores. Life grew softer in other ways, too. Trolley cars, for example, induced city dwellers to walk less and elevators relieved them of the necessity of climbing stairs. By 1890, according to one alarmed observer, this easier scheme of living had produced a generation of people "prematurely aged," and possessing "easily prostrated physiques."[29]

The medical men of the 1880s and 1890s concluded that exercise was essential to offset the physically debilitating effects of the sedentary life.[30] Hence, they urged Americans to compensate for the missing muscular effort of their forefathers with various forms of artificial activity. And most doctors agreed that among the best of such activities was cycling, for it exercised not only the legs but also the upper parts of the body and, performed regularly and moderately, strengthened the heart and lungs. Moreover, wheeling was fun, exposed the participant to the open air, and engendered "a feeling of brain rest and mental refreshment."[31]

The medical endorsement of cycling played its part in encouraging people to take up the sport. But it is equally apparent that the safety bicycle itself had a very large role in winning converts to what one historian of the Gilded Age calls "the new gospel of physical activity."[32] As a doctor, in a paper read before the New York Academy of Medicine in December, 1894, suggested, the safety was "probably the greatest factor" influencing the extension of the doctrine of physical culture in nineteenth-century America.[33]

This was particularly evident in the case of women. Most medical men contended that physical recreation was every bit as necessary for women as it was for men.[34] Yet an "old and convential belief," as one lady phrased it, had long limited women's participation in energetic outdoor activities. By the closing decade of the nineteenth century a little progress had been made against this "deep-rooted prejudice." Women, for instance, participated in such sports as archery, tennis, croquet and golf. But these activities had not acquired anything resembling a mass appeal.[35] The generality of women needed an easily learned, enjoyable, outdoor exercise which, at the same time, did not tax their strength nor seriously breach current standards of decorum. Cycling met these conditions. Not surprisingly, then, American women, who had been "starving for sunshine, fresh air"and some sport "to keep their bodies healthy and robust," took eagerly to the wheel. And thus began the widespread participation of women in outdoor athletics.[36]

Not that controversy was absent from the encounter between women and the wheel. The safety was charged with the responsibility of "leading young and innocent girls into ruin and disgrace," and with having women assume an "immodest posture." But the strongest objections centered on the bicycle costume which, in the opinion of one typical critic, invited improper remarks from "the depraved and immoral."[37] If some guardians of public virtue cried out in alarm, however, their protests had little effect on the ladies or, for that matter, the general public. Moreover, doctors and leaders of the women's rights movement, enthusiastic cyclists, doffed their confining whalebone corsets, and donned shorter dresses, split skirts and even bloomers. By doing so these riders conquered their inhibitions, improved their health, and enlarged their sense of physical freedom. Without planning it that way, they also advanced the cause of dress reform by making a rational, freer-flowing garb more commonplace.[38]

Many riders, men and women alike, learned that cycling could be much more than a pleasurable and healthy activity. They found that their wheels furnished them with a novel and, in some ways, an unrivaled form of transportation. It was true that cyclists could not surpass the steam railway in speed of locomotion, and they had to make a sustained effort to equal the electric trolley, which averaged about 15 miles per hour. Still, on smooth, level road they could take sprints of up to 25 miles per hour. Then, too unlike railroad and trolley passengers, bicycle riders did not have to pay fares or wrestle with jostling crowds; and above all, they were neither bound by time schedules nor confined to fixed routes. They were independent travelers.[39]

Only the horse offered an independence of movement comparable to the bicycle, though on several counts the silent steed was clearly superior to the neighing one. Since a good horse cost about $150 (without a carriage), and another $25 or so each month for upkeep, a safety was far cheaper to own than a horse. Moreover, the practiced cyclist could travel at the same, or even a faster rate of speed, and go much farther than the individual lumbering along in a horse-drawn buggy. And, when the cyclist reached his destination, he did not have to feed water and bed down his silent steed. He simply picked up his safety and parked it inside the doorway.[40]

Where the roads permitted, cyclists could travel as their mood or mission dictated. Many chose to roam over the world around them.

Riders skipped religious services—and thus incurred clerical wrath—to spend their Sundays touring the countryside. People took their vacations on wheels. Some visited neighboring states, and others, more distant parts of their native land. A few even sailed for Europe and, arriving there, set out on their bicycles to explore, in leisurely and independent fashion, the landscape and historic sites of the Old World.[41]

By putting Americans on the move, the bicycle opened up new vistas to its users. This was especially so in the case of young people from culturally limited small towns. One cyclist recalled this of his youth:

> On the bicycle you could go where you pleased, fixing your own schedule. It took you to "the city" to attend a theater matinee and be back home in time for the evening meal. Soon after I owned a bicycle I rode with two other boys the sixteen miles from our Ohio town to Dayton and, at a cost of fifty cents for a seat in the peanut gallery, saw Joseph Jefferson in *Rip Van Winkle*, the first good actor any of us had ever seen. That was *living*. Our horizons were broadening.[42]

Others unearthed more practical uses for this new mode of transportation. Thousands of people, some of whom lived in the suburbs, rode back and forth to work each day on their bicycles. Ministers, doctors and salesmen made their calls on wheels. Botanists and geologists found the safety a valuable aid in their field work; while artists, photographers, park commissioners, sanitation foremen, letter carriers, tradesmen and delivery boys, among others, used the vehicle to facilitate their tasks.[43]

With so many pedaling about, New York and other cities established mounted police squads to run down scorchers and bicycling burglars. The men attached to these squads were also adept at capturing runaway horses. ' Theodore Roosevelt, who was a New York City Police Commissioner in the mid-1890s, observed that the members of that city's bicycle detail

> soon grew to show not only extraordinary proficiency on the wheel, but extraordinary daring. They frequently stopped runaways, wheeling alongside of them, and grasping the horses while going at full speed; and, what was even more remarkable, they managed not only to overtake but to jump into the vehicle and capture, on to or three different occasions, men who were guilty of reckless driving, and who fought violently in resisting arrest ...[44]

As the foregoing discussion indicates, the modern bicycle was a highly versatile device. In an age of utility this alone would have been sufficient to have it counted among the era's distinctive mechanical improvements. But the safety's identification with the forces of progress involved much more than its mere usefulness to the professions, business and government. To contemporaries, it was bettering the people's physical well-being, unifying the nation by breaking down regional and cultural barriers, acting as "the advance agent of personal freedom in locomotion an din costuming," and, most significantly, satisfying the American love of speed. No wonder the wheel was ranked with the great inventions of the age.[45]

To those fascinated by new machines, as most Americans were, the bicycle was even something of a symbol of nineteenth-century technological advancement. As a cycling book of he time presented the situation, an "individual starting out with a twenty-five pound machine, a light cyclometer, a small bicycle clock, and a compact camera" was indeed a "most wonderful example of the world's progressiveness." In a more philosophical vein, the *Scientific American*, impressed with its speed and power, saw the lithe, two-wheeled machine as "one expression of the great world struggle of mind to overcome the inertia of matter."[46]

Coursing through the cycling literature, however, was another less compelling, but nonetheless insistent theme—escape. The very technological progress which the bicycle typified had brought about a tension-prone, and sometimes strife-torn, industrialized society, and the wheel seemed to assure cyclists an opportunity for forgetfulness and flight.

There were few who protested the opinion of a contemporary that "nervousness" was the characteristic malady of the American nation.[47] It was not considered accidental, either, that this nervousness had appeared after several decades of unprecedented technological change or that the condition seemed to be such a marked feature of urban life. Economist David A. Wells, for instance, suggested that the replacement of the slow-moving letter by electrical communication had so accelerated the decision making process of businessmen, that the increased mental and emotional pressure on them had led to an alarming rise in nervous and physical disorders. The *Chicago Tribune*, surveying a broader range of mechanical innovations, remarked that it was the American's "fate to live in an age when railways, telegraphs and fifty other inventions" had added "immeasurably to the wear and tear of the individual and separate units of society." Approaching the matter from a slightly different angle, a Harvard professor explained that his was an age of progress, but that the price had been high. This could be seen, he went on, in the big cities where civilization was most advanced, but where life was most rapid and intense. These urban centers, he believed, were "like so many great furnaces," consuming their inhabitants "in order to keep the machinery of our complex social organism in motion."[48]

There was no dearth of advice for the nerve-wracked Americans of the "great furnaces." Cycling restored one's "confidence and cheerfulness," advised a physician, and caused the future once again to look

"bright and full of hope." Or, as the author of *Hygienic Bicycling* informed his readers, on wheels "all morbid thoughts take their flight."
Others offered similar counsel.[49] A Boston clergyman, for example, in
an address entitled the "Mission of the Bicycle," spoke to his Sunday congregation.

> We long to lay aside the dignity of manhood and womanhood,
> to flee away for a few hours from the serious business of life, but
> there is no escape.
>
> But suppose you own a wheel. There is your escape. There is
> your instrument of fun and frolic, and you can take your dignity
> along. The time for the duties of the day is over. You mount
> your silent steed, and there is motion and speed and change of
> scenery; there is forgetfulness, for the time, of cares and duties;
> you glide along, and lo! you are at the summit of the hill.
>
> You place your feet on the coasters and glide away toward the
> base, and you are a boy again sliding down hill, only you have
> no sled to draw up, for you ride both ways. Before you know it
> laughter comes back. Sunshine fills the soul. The cares of life,
> and its duties thereafter are cushioned with the pneumatic tires,
> and the fun of youth becomes projected through our maturer
> years. Try it, and you will say that the half has never been
> told.[50]

Devotees of the wheel also reminded overwrought insomniacs
that bicycling was a "nerve calming medicine," and a "sweet restorer" and
inducer of "nature's sweetest restorer—dreamless sleep." It may even be
that for some cyclists, scorching—referred to by a disgusted Englishman
as "cyclomania"—was a form of escape.[51]

A physical relief from the tensions of society was one benefit. A
number of cyclists, though, looked to nature for peace of mind. They
mounted bicycles, fled the city's "'maddening crowd,'" and headed for the
country. Once there, miles from "so-called civilization," they refreshed
themselves with the sights and smells of green fields, brightly colored
flowers and stretches of shadowy woods.[52]. One poet wrote thusly of the
bicycle:

> Care-worn city clerks it hurries off to
>   natures' fairest scenes
> Flower decked meads and, trellised hop-grounds;
>   babbling brooks and village greens.
> Round-backed artisans it bears, too, from
>   the small and stuffy room,
> To the lanes where trailing roses all the
>   summer air perfumes;

And it makes them grow forgetful of the
   stifling, man-made town,
As they Climb the breezy roadway o'er
   the swelling, God-made down.[53]

In more prosaic fashion, the Pope Company—the largest of the American bicycle manufacturers—explained the benefits of wheels in one of its cycling catalogues.

The man of sedentary habits throws off the confinements of the office, and seeks relief in an enjoyment of nature. To ride into the country with ever-changing scenery, and to breathe the healthy air is fraught with enjoyment. The nerves are relieved, and sound health and sleep is promoted.[54]

Inasmuch as cyclists were able to ride away from their problems and themselves, the wheel acted as an emotional palliative. Though far from a unique occurrence—one thinks, for example, of the motion picture projector—it was no small achievement for a machine to be the means by which people temporarily delivered themselves from the disruptions and stresses of a machine-based society.[55]

Yet some contemporaries seemed more impressed with the bicycle as a possible harmonizer of economic class differences. Perhaps there was something to this. The bicycle craze had hardly begun when, in the spring of 1893, the country was hit by a financial panic which soon deepened into the worst depression in American history. Over the next three years the nation was staggered by labor violence, clashes between troops and workers and a farmers' revolt that culminated in the divisive McKinley-Bryan campaign of 1896. These were bitter years for America, and men talked gloomily about the future of the country.[56] Then the crisis passed. By 1897 the economy had revived, Populism had petered out, and a political peace settled on the land. But during the years 1893-96—a period which coincided with the cycle craze—there were those who insisted that the bicycle had been a mechanism of stabilization.

The ability to own and drive a carriage was a distinguishing feature of the well-to-do urban resident in late nineteenth-century America—and, as such, beyond the reach of the masses. On the other hand, people in the most moderate circumstances scrimped and saved to buy bicycles.[57] They recognized that they then possessed a means of recreation and transportation which surpassed the horse and trap. And should a rich man purchase a safety, he was no better than anyone else on the road. He had to exert the same physical effort to move his machine and face the same road conditions as other riders, and, at a distance or from the rear, his expensive new wheel was indistinguishable from a poor man's second-hand vehicle.

This was why some observers referred to the bicycle as the "great leveler," or as a democratic machine.[58] Here also was one reason why the safety may have served as an agent of social peace in the mid-1890s. Thus, John D. Long, President McKinley's Secretary of the Navy, declared that,

> The bicycle is the great safety of modern days. The man who owns a bicycle rides his own steed. He throws his dust in the face of the man in the carriage, so that it is no longer pleasant to ride in a coach and four.[59]

Contemporaries believed, too, that possession of a bicycle gave its owner an opportunity to develop a new and diverting set of interests. A poor man, said Senator George Frisbie Hoar of Massachusetts, used his safety for transportation as well as exercise, and from his machine derived "innocent, healthy and harmless recreation." Moreover, as other suggested, ownership of bicycles admitted rich and poor alike to a new social class—the freemasonry of the wheel. ("There were but two classes of people," explained a contemporary, "those who rode and those who wanted to.") On the road, people from different social strata exchanged friendly greetings, and at rest they might chat about bicycles and related matters.[60]

The safety, according to a columnist of *Bicycling World*, had "made all men brothers." This was claiming too much. But it does seem clear, as a writer in the *Chicago Times Herald* remarked, that the bicycle had cheered "the spirit of man" in a time of economic depression. That we recall the 1890s as gay rather than grim is singular evidence of this observation.[61]

III

The time arrived, however, when adult Americans no longer looked to the safety to cheer their spirits. The cycle craze reached its high point in 1896 when the bicycle industry produced about a million vehicles. The following year manufacturers turned out over a million machines, but twice as many of these vehicles as the year before were shipped for sale abroad. Even better indices of somewhat lessened zeal for the wheel were the reduced coverage given to cycling in the press and magazines, the demise of many of the trade journals (in late 1897, for example, three of the big Chicago bicycle magazines consolidated), and the increasing involvement of prominent bicycle manufacturers in the development of a power-driven horseless carriage.[62]

Between 1898 and 1900, the interest of the American public in the bicycle continued to ebb. The industry manufactured at the rate of a million or more machines annually, but a growing portion of these went into the export trade. By 1901, according to one writer, Americans had even stopped discussing the safety. Three years later the industry's output had fallen to about 225,000 vehicles. The safety remained a factor in adult transportation for a few years more; but the bicycle era had clearly come to an end in the United States.[63] Why was this?

The bicycle won its popularity in part because it had indulged escapist impulses. Its tenure as a vehicle of flight was short-lived, however. To a certain extent this may have been because the feverish class hostility of the mid-1890s subsided with the return of better times and the decline of Populism. Whatever the state of the economy, of course, the stresses and demands of urban-industrial life persisted. But in the Spanish-American War, perhaps those seeking an emotional release from contemporary pressures came upon a more exciting outlet than cycling. As Lewis Mumford argues interestingly in his *Technics and Civilization*, nothing rivals warfare as a release from the tedium and tension of a mechanistic society.[64]

A weightier consideration was the inability of the bicycle to maintain its place as a progressive machine. For a few years, one cyclist remembered, the safety had fulfilled "the ever-growing desire for greater and greater speed." But by the opening of the new century, people realized that the horseless carriage was superior in this category. Had not a steam-powered vehicle—capable of doing a mile in a minute and four seconds—paced the great Negro cyclist, Major Taylor, when he set the world record for a mile in one minute and nineteen seconds?[65] While it would be some years before the average American could afford an automobile, to a people enamored of speed the bicycle began to seem old-fashioned.

So, though the bicycle had answered the vague longing for a time-saving, distance-conquering, independent mode of transportation, in doing this it had also "whetted" the public appetite for wheeled contrivances." The bicycle, as inventor Hiram P. Maxim pointed out, created a demand which it could no longer satisfy. "A mechanically propelled vehicle was wanted instead of a foot-propelled one," he wrote, "and we now know that the automobile was the answer."[66]

In this, as in so many other respects, the bicycle had prepared the way for the automobile. The safety, a perceptive contemporary remarked in *Outing*, was "but a single part in a great and widespread movement in transportation which it was in point of time at least, privileged to lead."[67]

The same point could as validly be made about woman's rights and popular recreation, as about transportation. In the long view, the bicycle was only one among many factors promoting the cause of dress reform and female equality. And those who wanted outdoor exercises, or an activity to counter nervous strain, had an increasing variety of sports to choose from in twentieth-century America.[68]

The bicycle had risen from its lowly status as a toy to its lofty station as a mechanical marvel because it had served progressive wants and desires and gratified escapist tendencies. By World War I, no longer able or at least no longer needed to fill these roles, the bicycle returned to its earlier place as an American toy. But it would be a mistake on this account to take lightly the safety's earlier prominence. In the mid-1890s the safety bicycle was an influential force in our national life and, what seems of greater note, a major expression of current beliefs and fears.

• • •

Notes

1. Henry Steele Commager, *The American Mind* (New Haven: Yale University Press, 1950), pp. 5-8; Victor C. Ferkiss, *Technological Man: The Myth and the Reality* (New York: George Braziller, 1969), pp. 11, 66. For some contemporary statements, see *Scientific American*, LXXV (July-December, 1896), 50-51, *Century Magazine*, LII (May-October, 1896), 152; David A. Wells, *Recent Economic Changes* (New York and London: D. Appleton and Company, 1889), pp. 67, 370, 366; *North American Review*, CLXI (September, 1895), 299; Edward W. Byrn, T*he Progress of Invention* (New York: Russell and Russell, 1900), pp. 4-6; *Munsey's Magazine*, XXIV (October, 1900-March, 1901), 36,40.

2. Leo Marx, *The Machine in the Garden: Technology and the Pastoral Ideal in America* (New York: Oxford University Press, 1064), p. 343.

3. C.F. Caunter, *The History and Development of Cycles* (Part I; London: Her Majesty's Stationary Office, 1955), pp. 15-17, 20; *Sewanee Review*, V (1897), 50.

4. Robert P. Scott, *Cycling Art, Energy and Locomotion* (Philadelphia: J.B. Lippincott Company, 1889), p. 118; D.B. Landis, "Evolution of the Bicycle and its History in Lancaster County," *Historical Papers and Addresses of the Lancaster County Historical Society*, XXXV (1931), 283-84; *Wheel and Cycling Trade Review*, II (August, 1888-February, 1889), 285-433.

5. Charles E. Pratt, *The American Bicycler: A Manual* (Boston: Houghton, Osgood and Company, 1879), pp. 106, 124, 125; *The Wheel*, May 15, 1885; *Outing*, I, (October, 1882-March, 1883), 5i; Hannibal Coons, "Bicycles Built for All," *Holiday*, IV (July, 1948), 83; Fred H. Colvin, *60 Years with Men and Machines* (New York and London: McGraw Hill Book Company, Inc., 1947), p. 87.

6. *Bicycling World*, XXV (September, 1892-March, 1893), 214; *Century Magazine*, LII (May-October, 1896), 785.

7. *Outing*, I (October, 1882-March, 1883), 204; *Chautauquan*, VIII (October, 1887-July, 1888), 458-59; Colvin, *60 Years with Men and Machines*, pp. 13-14.

8. Foster Rhea Dulles, *America Learns to Play* (New York & London: D. Appleton-Century Company, 1940), p. 194; *The Living Age*, CCXVII (April-June, 1898), 856; Chauncey M. Depew, ed., *One Hundred Years of American Commerce* (New York: D.O. Haynes and Company, 1895), p. 551.

9. Caunter, *History of Cycles*, pp. 33-37; Waldemar Kaempffert, ed., *A Popular History of American Inventions*, 2 vols. (New York & London: Charles Scribner's Sons, 1924), I, 141.

10. Henry Clyde, *Pleasure-Cycling* (Boston: Little, Brown and Company, 1895), p. 46; *Twelfth Census of the United States*, X (1900), 332.

11. Cf., *infra.*, note 21.

12. *Scientific American*, LXXIV (January-June, 1986), 4; LXXVII (July-December, 1897), 292; *Fifty Years of Schwinn-Built Bicycles* (Chicago: Arnold Schwinn and Company, 1945) p. 28. In 1890, the bicycle industry consisted of a few dozen shops and factories, employing 1700 people, and with invested capital of some two million dollars. By 1895 the industry was made up of over 300 shops and factories, employing 25,000 people and an invested capital in exces of twenty million dollars. Between 1890 and 1896 Americans spent over one hundred million dollars for bicycles.

13. *Twelfth Census*, X, 332-34; *Scientific American*, LXXIV (January-June, 1896), 2.

14. On the ties between bicycle manufacturers and racing, see the remarks by the President of the League of American Wheelmen in *Wheel and Cycling Trade Review*, XIV (November 2, 1894), 23.

15. James P. Wood, *The Story of Advertising* (New York: The Ronald Press Company, 1958), pp. 283, 276078; *Wheel and Cycling Trade Review*, IX (June 10, 1892), 18; *American Wheelman*, VIII (October 29, 1896), 38; XI (February 3, 1897), 14; *American Athlete*, XII (July 21, 1893), 51.

16. *Outing*, XXX (April-September, 1897), 341-51, 488-94.

17. *Wheel and Cycling Trade Review*, XI (June 16, 1893), 38; *Bicycling World* XXXVIII October-November, 1898), 81; Kaempffert, ed., *Popular History of Inventions*, I, 141; *New York Tribune*, August 8, 1897, p. 6. Thus, in 1895 the top grades were generally reduced to $100, and two years later the price of these models was cut another $25.

18. Wood, *Story of Advertising*, p. 282; *Wheel and Cycling Trade Review*, X (February 17, 1893), 44; *Bicycling World*, XXV (September, 1892-March, 1893), 432; XXXI (May-November, 1895), 677; Clyde, *Pleasure Cycling*, p. 45.

19. *Bicycling World*, XXII (October, 1890-April, 1891), 239; *Sporting Life*, XVI (March 21, 1891), 10; *American Athlete*, IX (June 10, 1892), 489; X (December 9, 1892), 403.

20. *American Athlete*, XI (March 31, 1893), 285.

21. *Wheel and Cycling Trade Review*, XI (March 3, 1893), 27; *Bicycling World*, XXVIII (December, 1893-May, 1894), 579; *New York Times*, January 5, 1896, p. 25.

22. *Scribner's Magazine*, XVII (January-June, 1895), 704-06; "Monthly Record," *Outing*, XXVI (April-September, 1895), 1; *The Critic*, XXIV (New Series: July-December, 1895), 107, 226-28.

23. *American Wheelman*, VIII (July 2, 1896), 25; Arthur Judson Palmer, *Riding High: The Story of the Bicycle* (New York: E.P. Dutton, 1956), p. 113.

24. *Bicycling World*, XXXIII (July 10, 1896), 26; *Scientific American*, LXXV (July-December, 1896), 69; *New York Herald*, quoted in *Literary Digest*, XIII (1896), 196.

25. *The Outlook*, LI (January-June, 1895), 1006; *Bicycling World*, XXXI (May-November, 1895), 137; *The Forum*, XXI (March-August, 1896), 680; *Harper's Weekly* XL (January-June, 1896), 370; *Century Magazine*, L (May-October, 1895), 374; XLIX (November, 1894-April, 1895) 306; *New York Times*, June 21, 1896, p. 4.

26. *Cosmopolitan*, XXXIII (May-October, 1902), 136, 131; Roger Burlingame, *Engines of Democracy* (New York and London: Charles Scribner's Sons, 1940), pp. 360, 372.

27. *Scribner's Monthly,* LXVII (January-June, 1920), 635.

28. *Outing,* XXIX (October, 1896-March, 1897), 516; Clyde, *Pleasure-Cycling,* p. 28; *Scientific American,* LXXX (January-June, 1899), 292; *American Athlete,* X (October 14, 1892), 278; *Harper's Weekly,* XL (January-June, 1896), 353.

29. *Atlantic Monthly,* XC (October, 1902), 534; *Outing,* XXXII (April-September, 1898), 383; *North American Review,* CLII (January-June, 1891), 682-83; *Lippincott's Monthly Magazine,* XLV (January-June, 1890), 617.

30. *Journal of the Franklin Institute,* CXXXIV (July-December, 1892), 230-35; Hospital, as quoted in *Scientific American,* LX (January-June, 1889), 185; *Wheel and Cycling Trade Review,* V (February-August, 1890), 34.

31. *New York Times,* May 21, 1893, p. 12; *Scribner's Magazine,* XVII (January-June, 1895), 708-12; *Scientific American,* LXXII (January-June, 1895), 5.

32. Arthur M. Schlesinger, Sr., *The Rise of the City, 1878-1898* (New York: The MacMillan Company, 1938), p. 316.

33. As quoted in Luther H. Porter, *Cycling for Health and Pleasure* (New York: Dodd, Mead and Company, 1895), p. 182. See also, Arthur Train, *Puritan's Progress* (New York: Charles Scribner's Sons, 1931), p. 400.

34. *Journal of Social Science,* XXII (June, 1887), 46-47; *Literary Digest,* XI (May-October, 1895), 637; XIII (1896), 455-56.

35. *Outlook,* LII (July-December, 1895), 349; *Nineteenth Century,* XXXIX (April-June, 1896), 797; Schlesinger, *Rise of the City,* p. 318; Train, *Puritan's Progress,* p. 300.

36. *Bicycling World,* XXXVI (December 17, 1897), 19; Henry Collis Brown, *In the Golden Nineties* (Hastings-On-Hudson: Valentine's Manual, Inc., 1928), pp. 48-49.

37. *Literary Digest,* XIII (1896), 361; *Bicycling World,* XXXV (July 23, 1897), 5; Dr. C.E. Nash, *Historical and Humorous Sketches of the Donkey, Horse and Bicycle* (Little Rock: Press of Tunnah and Pittard, 1896), p. 200; *New York Times,* May 16, 1899, p. 1.

38. *New York Tribune,* May 12, 1895, p. 6; *Outlook,* LIII (January-June, 1896), 752; *Century Magazine,* LIV (May-December, 1897), 473; *Cosmopolitan,* XIX (May-October, 1895), 394; *Bicycling World,* XXVI (January 14, 1898), 8; Andrew Sinclair, *The Better Half: The Emancipation of the American Woman* (New York: Harper and Row, 1965), p. 107; Dulles, *America Learns to Play,* pp. 266-67.

39. Hiram Percy Maxim, *Horseless Carriage Days* (New York: Dover Publications, Inc., 1962), pp. 1-2; *Wheel and Cycling Trade Review,* XIII (August 3, 1894), 17.

40. *Bicycling World,* XXX (November, 1894-May, 1895), 957; *Harper's Weekly,* XL (January-June, 1896), 354; Burlingame, *Engines of Democracy,* p. 372).

41. *The Forum,* XXI (March-August, 1896), 682; *Bicycling World,* XXXIII (May 29, 1896), 11; *The Arena,* VI (1892), 582; *The Living Age,* CCXIV (July, August, September, 1897), 714.

42. Fred C. Kelly, "The Great Bicycle Craze," *American Heritage,* VIII (December, 1956), 70.

43. *Bicycling World,* XXX (November, 1894-May, 1895), 957; *Century Magazine,* XLIX (November, 1894-April, 1895), 50.

44. *Bicycling World,* XXXV (September 10, 1897), 13; *American Wheelman,* VIII (September 17, 1896), 41; *Scientific American,* LXXIV (January-June, 1896), 291; *Theodore Roosevelt, An Autobiography* (New York: Charles Scribner's Sons, 1925), pp. 182-83.

45. *Bicycling World,* XXXIV (May 7, 1897), 17; *Scribner's Magazine,* XIX (January-June, 1896), 783; *Munsey's Magazine,* XV (April-September, 1896), 131.

46. W.S. Beekman and C.W. Willis, *Cycle Gleanings* (Boston: Press of Skinner, Bartlett and Company, 1894), pp. 10-11; *Scientific American*, LXXX (January-June, 1899), 292.

47. *McClure's Magazine*, II (December, 1893-May, 1894), 305; Schlesinger, *Rise of the City*, p. 433.

48. Wells, *Recent Economic Changes*, p. 350; *Chicago Tribune*, quoted in Current Literature, XV (January-June, 1894), 521; *North American Review*, CLXIV (January-June, 1897), 559-60.

49. George B. Bradley, M.D., *Why Should We Cycle?* (New York, 1895), p. 6; H.C. Clark, *Hygenic Bicycling* (Delaware City, Delaware, 1897), p. 12; *Wheel and Cycling Trade Review*, XL (June 9, 1893), 24; *Universal Medical Magazine*, quoted in Bicycling World, XXV (September, 1892-March, 1893), 256; *British Medical Journal*, quoted in *Literary Digest*, XII (December, 1895-April, 1896), 377.

50. *Wheel and Cycling Trade Review*, XI (May 5, 1893), 30.

51. *Harper's Weekly*, XXXIV (July-December, 1890), 686; Porter, *Cycling for Health and Pleasure*, p. 11; *Bicycling World*, XXX (June 26, 1896), II; *The Living Age*, CCXV (October, November, December, 1897), 470-72.

52. Edmond Redmond, ed., *The Bards and the Bicycle* (New York: M.F. Mansfield, 1897), p. 33; *Scribner's Magazine*, XVII (January-June, 1895), 702; *Bicycling World*, XXXI (May-November, 1895), 53, 93.

53. Redmond, ed., *Bards and Bicycle*, pp. 129-30.

54. *Columbia Bicycles* (Pope Manufacturing Company, 1892), p. 38.

55. While this account focuses on America, it should be recalled that during the 1890s the bicycle was also popular in Britain and on the continent—and for some of the same reasons. Nor is this surprising. The United States and the advanced Western nations shared many of the same values (such as utilitarianism), and were undergoing a similar process of urbanization and industrialization. Stressing this latter point, John Higham has argued that in both America and Europe during the 1890s a boom in sports and recreation, and a heightened interest in nature attest to a common reaction to the constraints of urban-industrial life. See John Higham, "The Reorientation of American Culture in the 1890s," in John Weiss, ed., *The Origins of Modern Consciousness* (Wayne State University Press, 1956), pp. 27-29, 32-33.

Higham has also suggested, however, that this reaction expressed itself in a somewhat different fashion on this side of the Atlantic. He notes, for instance, the lead taken by the United States in sports as well as the unusual ferocity found in American sports. It seems likely, too, that the widespread fascination with speed was peculiar to the American scene. But until a full analysis is undertaken of the bicycle in a cross-cultural setting, any remarks on the vehicle's comparative attractions must necessarily remain tentative.

56. Ray Ginger, *Age of Excess: The United States from 1877 to 1914* (New York: The Macmillan Company, 1965), p. 158.

57. Blake McKelvey, *The Urbanization of America, 1860-1915* (Rutgers University Press, 1963), p. 187; Mark Sullivan, *Our Times: The United States, 1900-1925*, 6 vols. (New York and London: Charles Scribner's Sons, 1925-35), I, 243.

58. *Century Magazine*, XLIX (November, 1894-April, 1895), 306; *Bicycling World*, XXXII (May 15, 1896), 11; *Detroit Free Press*, quoted in Literary Digest, XIII (1896), 197; *Wheel and Cycling Trade Review*, XX (September 17, 1897), 36.

59. *New York Times*, June 3, 1899, p. 6.

60. *Cosmopolitan*, XIX (May-October, 1895), 394; *American Athlete*, XII (December 29, 1893), 539; *Harper's Weekly*, XLVIII (January-June, 1904), 906; *Lippincott's Magazine*, XLIX (January-June, 1892), 605; Kelly, "Great Bicycle Craze," loc.cit., p. 73; *Scribner's Magazine*, LXVII (January-June, 1920), 636.

61. *Bicycling World*, XXXIV (July-December, 1896), 69; *Bicycling World*, XXXVII (September 16, 1898), 20; XXXVI (April 8, 1898), 29; Kaempffert, ed., *Popular History of American Inventions*, I, 142.

63. *Scientific American*, LXXXII (January-June, 1900), 5; *Thirteenth Census of the United States*, VIII (1910), 475; *Twelfth Census*, X, 328; Victor C. Clark, *History of Manufactures in the United States*, 3 vols. (New York: McGraw-Hill Book Company, Inc., 1929), III, 156; *The Bookman*, XIII (March-August, 1901), 425; *Fifty Years of Schwinn-Built Bicycles*, p. 55.

64. Lewis Mumford, *Technics and Civilization* (New York: Harcourt, Brace and Company, 1934), pp. 309-10.

65. Andrew W. Gillette, "The Bicycle Era in Colorado," *Colorado Magazine*, X (November, 1933), 213; New York Evening Sun, January 24, 1900.

66. *The Horseless Age*, I (November, 1895), 8; Maxim, *Horseless Carriage Days*, pp. 4-5.

67. *Outing*, XXXV (October, 1899-March 1900), 641. For a summary of the numerous mechanical connections between the bicycle and the automobile, see Allan Nevins, *Ford: The Times, The Man, The Company* (New York: Charles Scribner's Sons, 1954), pp. 186-90.

68. Frederick W. Cozens and Florence Scovil Stumpf, *Sports in American Life* (Chicago: The University of Chicago Press, 1953), pp. 28-29, 215ff.

• • •

Suggestions for Further Reading

Aronsson, S.H., "The Sociology of the Bicycle," *Social Forces*, XXX (1952).

Higham, John, "The Reorientation of American Culture in the 1890's" in Higham, *Writing America's History: Essays on Modern Scholarship*(Bloomington,IN:Indiana Univ.Press,1970), 73-102.

Kelly, Fred C., "The Great Bicycle Craze," *American Heritage*, VII (December, 1956).

KIrshcner, Don S., "The Perils of Pleasure: Commercial Recreation, Social Disorder and Moral Reform in the Progressive Era," *American Studies*, XXI (Fall, 1980), 27-42.

Purdy, S.B., "Of Time, Motion, and Motor Racing," *Journal of American Studies*, IV, 3 (Fall, 1981), 93-103.

Smith, Robert A., *A Social History of the Bicycle: Its Early Life and Times in America* (New York: American Heritage, 1972).

Taylor, Marshall W. "Major," *The Fastest Bicycle Rider in the World* (Battleboro, VT: Green-Stephen, 1972).

Tobin, Gary A., "The Bicycle Boom of the 1890's: The Development of Private Transportation and the Birth of Modern Tourism," *Journal of Popular Culture*, VII (Spring, 1974), 838-849.

RACE AND ETHNICITY IN
AMERICAN BASEBALL, 1900-1919

Steven A. Riess

As Steven Riess, the author of the following essay, explores in his recent book, *Touching Base: Professional Baseball in American Culture in the Progressive Era* (Westport, CT: Greenwood Press, 1980), one of the principal explanations for baseball's surge in popularity in the early decades of the twentieth century was that the game seemingly "touched base with more themes in American life and society than anything else at the time." The American ideals and "realities" that the game purportedly symbolized included the country's native origins, agrarian heritage, ethnic assimilationism, social democracy, individualism, and rags-to-riches opportunism. In a country quick to embrace fact and fiction in the name of national pride with equal enthusiasm and, often, little discrimination, baseball provides a useful paradigm for exploring the relationship between myth and reality and understanding the society which embraces its manifestations.

Riess focuses on one aspect of the conventional wisdom of the day, namely, the notion that professional baseball provided an excellent opportunity for ambitious, hard-working athletes from impoverished backgrounds to realize upward social mobility. He tests this premise through examining the racial and ethnic composition of major league player rosters. Although his analysis produces a picture in sharp contrast to the equalitarian images of baseball's promoters, it is one very much in line with the nativism and racism of the day and the barriers they formed to the promise of the game and American life.

Not surprisingly, some ethnic groups assimilated more smoothly than others and entered the ranks of professional baseball more rapidly. As the social status of the game improved, second and third-generation Germans and Irish dominated the player rosters along with old stock Americans of Anglo-Saxon lineage. Newer immigrant groups, especially from eastern and southern Europe, gained only token representation on the playing fields. This was more, however, than that which black Americans achieved. Although American Indians and light skinned

247

Cubans occasionally made it to the majors, blacks did not. The segrega-
tionist ideology of the Progressive Era frustrated black socio-economic
mobility through sport just as it locked them into a caste structure within
their own land. The door remained closed until 1947 when Jackie
Robinson put on the uniform of the Brooklyn Dodgers.

Conventional wisdom has long held that professional baseball
has been an excellent source of upward mobility for the ambitious, hard-
working athlete. Baseball was said to recruit its players on a democratic
basis, regardless of ethnicity or other factors. Like the entertainment industry, boxing, crime, politics, or even the church, baseball was viewed
as an excellent opportunity for impoverished, uneducated youths who
had no social contacts to help them get started in a career. A test of that
conventional wisdom is to see whether or not baseball has indeed been a
source of mobility for the downtrodden in the cities by examining the
ethnicity of major league ballplayers in the first two decades of the
twentieth century.

By the turn of the century, professional baseball was becoming a
well-paying high prestige occupation. Wages averaged $2,000 at a time
when the average worker earned under $700 a year and was higher than the
pay of many professionals. Rookies usually earned $1,200, although one
Harvard man began at $4,000. By 1910, several players and managers
were earning salaries in excess of $10,000. In addition, a successful player
could make more money by using his fame to get endorsements and to
obtain easy off-season work. The high wages and the lifestyle of the professional ballplayer attracted a large number of middle class sons to the
occupation. The improved social status of the sport was reflected by the
player's education: one-fourth of the major leaguers had attended college
compared to under five percent for other men their age. Ballplayers were
also beginning to be welcomed at the finest hotels, to travel in polite
society,and to marry respectable, well-educated middle class girls.[1]

Baseball attracted its recruits from its young fans. Fans who attended baseball games were supposedly from all social and economic
groups. But in reality, most spectators were white-collar men who had the
time to go to the ball parks since games were played in the middle of the
afternoon, usually Monday through Saturday. Nonmanual workers could
put in a full day at the office, ride the streetcar or trolley to the ballfield,
enjoy a two hour game, and still get home in time for dinner. Blue-collar
fans were much more restricted. The average unskilled man worked fifty-
five hours a week, which meant that he could not see a game unless he took
off from work. Sunday was his only day off, but Sunday baseball was widely

prohibited in 1900. In addition, the ten cents for carfare and fifty cents for a ticket became quite expensive to a man earning less than two dollars a day. The fans would become much more democratic after World War I when workers' wages rose substantially at the same time that working hours dropped, and when Sunday baseball was played in the large eastern cities.[2]

Harold Seymour has asserted, on the basis of limited evidence, that most working class fans in the nineteenth century were either of native descent or second-generation Irish and Germans who bought cheap bleacher seats. These fans probably had jobs with unusual workings hours, e.g., bakers; had short working days, such as construction workers; or had their day off during the week, as would policemen or firemen. Club owners tried to interest German-Americans in their sport by placing advertisements in German language newspapers, and by providing beer and Sunday games in heavily German cities like St. Louis and Cincinnati. Irishmen who frequented games were thought to be merchants, off-duty policemen, bartenders, porters, clerks, or expressmen. Irish interest in the national pastime was so great that certain sections of ball parks appeared to be exclusively patronized by them, such as "Burkeville" at the Polo Grounds, or the "Kerry Patch" at St. Louis' Sportsman's Park.[3]

These working class spectators assimilated into the dominant American culture and had actively participated in baseball rituals since childhood. Blue-collar fans were prominent mainly in western towns which had Sunday baseball. These fans often took their young sons to the ball park as a kind of ritual passage into boyhood. They seldom brought their wives whose place was in the kitchen.[4] James T. Farrell recalled in *My Baseball Diary* what baseball's influence was like on a growing poor Irish boy:

> Obviously, because I was born on the South Side of Chicago, I became a White Sox fan. Since baseball took such a strong hold upon me, it permeated my boyish thoughts and dreams. It became a consuming enthusiasm, a part of my dream or fantasy world. The conversations about baseball which I sometimes heard at home, the nostalgic recollections of players who have passed out of active play, the talk of players' names in an almost legendary way, all this was part of an oral tradition of baseball passed on to me, mainly in the home, during the early years of this century. It was a treat to a little boy to be taken to a ball game and also to sit while his elders talked of the game. Along with this, my elders approved of my interest in baseball and encouraged me ... Baseball was a means of awakening for me, an emergence from babyhood into the period of being a little boy ... (pp. 29-30).

Baseball was one of the few topics of conversation men could intelligently and confidently discuss with other men or their own children. It provided a common experience which helped transcend differences among people.

New immigrants from Austria-Hungary, Italy, and Russia did not become baseball fans. They were primarily concerned with the problems of earning a living and sustaining their traditions in the new world, not in assimilating the normative behavior patterns of the new society. They worked at the arduous and poorest paying jobs, and had little time left over for diversions. What leisure time they had was spent at ethnic clubs or ethnic taverns meeting and talking with others of similar backgrounds. Occasionally a newcomer might try to Americanize himself by learning about such American institutions as baseball and boxing. In Abraham Cahan's short novel, *Yekl, A Tale of the New York Ghetto,* Jake the tailor is ridiculed by his fellow workers for devoting so much attention to a child's game.

Little attention was paid to baseball or to other American sports in the foreign language newspapers which were interested in their ethnic group's welfare in the United States and their homeland.[5] When a sports item did appear in these newspapers, it involved ethnic pride. In Chicago, where people of foreign parentage comprised nearly seventy-eight per cent of the population in 1890, the Czech press often printed the results of the Bohemian-sponsored amateur baseball leagues. The Czechs took pride in their young men who became professional baseball players, and the editors of *Denni Hlasatel* looked to the day when every major league club would have at least one Czech on its roster.[6] A newspaper helping its readers acculturate might occasionally try to introduce them to baseball. Abraham Cahan's *Jewish Daily Forward,* (New York), printed an article in 1907 entitled "The Fundamentals of Baseball Explained to Non-Sports," which was accompanied by a diagram of the Polo Grounds.[7]

Despite the lack of interest shown by the new immigrants, professional baseball actively sought ballplayers from these ethnic groups. Chicago teams recruited Slavic players in order to attract the interest of the large Czech and Polish communities there. Most Slavic major leaguers spent at least part of their careers in Chicago. In New York, the Giants made notable efforts to discover Jewish athletes who would attract the attention of middle class Jews moving into Washington Heights neighborhood where the Polo Grounds was located. In 1916 they signed Benny Kauff, the star of the Federal League who, it turned out, was of Slavic origin. Seven years later, the Giants signed Moses Solomon but he failed to make the team.[8]

Although the immigrants were not interested in the national pastime, their sons took up baseball learning to play it in school and on city streets. Youngsters memorized the statistical accomplishments of their heroes and debated the comparative prowess of their idols. The cost of a ball game was usually too great for a ghetto youth, but if his interest was keen enough, he might get in without paying. On occasions professional teams distributed free tickets to youth groups like the YMCA, the Boy Scouts, or settlement houses. But there were other ways: finding baseballs hit out of the ball park, clearing trash in the stands before game time, sneaking into the park, watching the game through a knothole in the fence, or just waiting at the ticket entrance in hopes that a spectator might have an extra pasteboard, or a ballplayer would give away an unneeded pass.[9] In the 1890s Morris Raphael Cohen would walk from his home to the nearby Brooklyn baseball park, then located in Brownsville, and watch a game through a hole in the fence. Cohen was an ardent fan, but he almost never saw a game inside the park.[10] Young Harry Golden was able to attend ball games during summer in the early 1900s because of the job he shared with friends delivering pretzels to the Polo Grounds for a quarter plus carfare. On the day when he brought the pretzels, he would arrive at ten o'clock and lounge in the clubhouse until the game started, running errands for the New York Giants players. After the game he returned home to the lower East Side in time to sell his evening newspapers to the workers on their way home.[11]

Black Americans viewed baseball quite differently from the new immigrants from Eastern and Southern Europe. Blacks were familiar with baseball and enjoyed attending ball games. But they were barred from participating in professional baseball. Black athletes had been professional ballplayers in the nineteenth century, and the Walker brothers had even played in the major leagues in 1884 for Toledo, but racial prejudice forced the Blacks out of Organized Baseball in the 1890s. As a result, Blacks formed their own semiprofessional teams.[12]

Black fans attended professional and semiprofessional games in all parts of the country. In northern cities they would sit wherever they pleased, but usually were restricted to the bleachers because of the expense of other locations. Southern franchises made special arrangements to segregate their Black supporters by providing them with a separate entrance and their own seating area. However, it is unlikely that many Blacks went to professional ball games because of the cost. The average Black New Yorker in 1900 working as a servant or laborer earned $4 to $6 a week.[13]

Most Black baseball fans attended the semiprofessional games played by Black teams. The best Black clubs toured the country, playing both Black and White teams. Sometimes their opposition included major league stars.[14] These games were also popular with White fans, and on occasions the White spectators outnumbered the Blacks.[15] Home games were generally scheduled on Sundays in readily accessible fields: the New York's Harlem Oval, which seated 2,600 and was located at 142nd Street and Lenox Avenue; Chicago's Schorling Park, which held 4,000 and was situated at 39th and Shields on the perimeter of the Black belt.[16] The New

York promoters had to circumvent the penal codes which prohibited Sunday baseball by selling programs instead of tickets. A bleacher seat cost a quarter, and a grandstand seat fifty cents.[17] Leading Black teams like the Leland Giants, the Chicago American Giants, the Lincoln Giants, or the Philadelphia Giants were so popular that they played a number of games each year at the larger major league parks. In 1911 four Black teams played a doubleheader at the Polo Grounds which attracted 13,000 even though fans were charged the same high prices demanded by the New York Giants at their home games.

THE ETHNIC BACKGROUND OF BASEBALL PLAYERS

In the nineteenth century, most of the professional baseball players were either native-born Americans or of Irish or German descent. This continued during the first decades of the twentieth century. The single change in ethnic composition was the increasing percentage of native White American athletes entering the sport as it became respectable and well-paying. Over 90 percent of the professional players in the early 1900s belonged to these groups. Although young men of recent immigrant stock, mainly Russian Jews and Italians, achieved fame and even dominance in boxing, only a handful succeeded in professional baseball.[18]

Baseball was a good source of social mobility for Irishmen. Irish-Americans generally had difficulty improving their lot. While many nineteenth century German immigrants arrived in America with a trade or capital to purchase a farm, Irish newcomers arrived unprepared for their new environment except that they could speak English. Irishmen had little alternative but to take the lowest paying jobs requiring muscle power. A recent study of social mobility in Boston indicates that in 1890 just 10 percent of the Irish Americans did worse in advancing themselves than other White ethnic groups. For instance, of the second-generation Irish Bostonians born in the period 1860-79, 38 percent were white-collar, while of the Yankees and second-generation British and Western Europeans, over 50 percent were white-collar. The Boston Irish's lack of success was exemplified by the concentration of blue-collar Irishmen in the least skilled jobs.[19] Irishmen completely dominated the boxing ring in the last half of the nineteenth century. One-half of the sixteen world champions in the 1890s were of Irish extraction. This dominance declined somewhat in the early 1900s; yet, eight of the twenty-six champions crowned between 1900 and 1910 were Irish.

Baseball was a popular sport in the northeastern cities where the Irish immigrants settled, and many second-generation Irish played baseball, usually on teams sponsored by saloons or political clubs. The most proficient players were recruited to play professionally, and some eventually made the major leagues. Their example encouraged other Irish youths to seek a career in professional baseball. Their parents encouraged baseball as a career. This attitude differed markedly from the attitudes of nineteenth century middle class parents who abhorred the idea of their sons becoming professional ballplayers.[20]

The Irish dominance of baseball was reflected in the claim of one expert that approximately one-third of the major leaguers in the early 1890s were of Irish extraction.[21] While many had names which were apparently of Irish origin, to characterize them all as Irish is a mistake. Many of them were probably of Scotch-Irish descent. Nevertheless, the public saw baseball as Irish dominated. Some observers were asserting that by the 1910s that the Irish domination had ended, replaced by native white Americans who were attracted to the then national pastime by its improving pay and prestige. Grantland Rice disagreed with those journalists who found the Irish influence declining. Irishmen filled eleven of the sixteen managerial posts in the American and National Leagues in 1915.[22]

In the twentieth century, the number of major league players of German and Irish origins were approximately equal, and together they outnumbered the native-born players who were the single largest group. Germans were the largest immigrant group int he nineteenth century, and they quickly assimilated into the mainstream of American society. German migrants were much more geographically mobile than the Irish and did not remain in their ports of entry, but moved into the heartland. They were also much more socially mobile. In Boston, 27 percent of the German newcomers held white-collar jobs in 1890 compared to 10 percent of the Irish. Many German migrants arrived with skills acquired in the old country or with money saved to purchase farms. The class difference between first-generation Germans and Irish continued into the second-generation, with 52 percent of the Germans in white-collar jobs, compared to 38 percent of the Irish. However vertical mobility rates between second-generation Germans and Irish of the same social class were nearly identical.[23]

Despite the relative success of the German migrants, their sons and grandsons were strongly attracted to professional baseball as a career. Middle class sons found it a good way to maintain their status, and lower class Germans saw in baseball a chance to improve their social rank. The same thoughts probably went through the minds of Irish and native American youths of similar class backgrounds.

In terms of recruitment patterns, there was some difference between Germans and Irish. There appears to have been more college educated Irishmen than Germans in the major leagues, but the evidence is too sketchy to be certain. Poor youths with athletic skills could obtain financial compensation for participating in college sports. But whether or not poor Irishmen were more likely than indigent Germans to take this route to success is something we just don't know and which requires further research.

Although baseball presented itself as a democratic sport which was an important factor in assimilating immigrants, only a handful of the major leaguers were new immigrants from Eastern or Southern Europe. An examination of the ethnic background of rookies in selected years indicates that in the period 1901-1906 there were five Bohemian, two Jewish, and no Italian first-year men. In 1910 there were no rookies from any of these groups, and in 1920 there was one Bohemian and two Italians out of 133. Veterans resented their presence. They were worried these newcomers might take their jobs, force down salary levels, and destroy the prestige of their occupation. Many fans apparently wanted to see the sport distinctly American, and jeered and belittled players of recent immigrant stock. Contemporary explanations for the absence of the new ethnics occasionally had racist overtones, such as the *New York Tribune's* suggestion that these newcomers lacked the courage necessary to stand firmly in the batter's box and take a strong swing at the ball.[24]

The immigrants whose absence was probably most discussed were the Jews. Although by 1900 they already comprised a sizable percentage of the population in cities like New York and Chicago, there were few Jews in professional baseball. This trend has continued to the present day. The first Jewish major leaguers were Nick Bertonstock and Lip Pike who played in the NAPBBP in 1871, but in the next seventy years they were succeeded by some fifty-five others. Jewish absence was particularly noteworthy since many baseball owners and officials were Jewish. Louis Kramer was founder of the American Association and its president in 1891. Nathan Menderson was president of the Cincinnati Reds from 1882 to 1890. In the next twenty years other baseball magnates of Jewish descent included Barney Dreyfuss of the Pittsburgh Pirates, Andrew Freedman of the Giants, Julius Fleischmann of the Reds, and Judge Harry Goldman, and the brothers Moses and Sidney Frank, of the Baltimore Orioles.[25] Baseball was viewed as a low prestige enterprise, and the old business elite shunned it for more respectable investments. Their absence provided opportunities for Jews and non-WASPs to make money and gain status. The experience of these club owners was similar to that of the Jewish furriers, jewelers, and nickelodeon operators who built up the film industry.[26]

Mass Jewish migration to America from Russia and Austria-Hungary began in the 1880s and lasted until the start of World War I. These immigrants were far better prepared for city life in the United States than peasant newcomers had already been exposed to urban society in Europe and they brought with them more skills, a tradition for entrepreneurship, and a profound respect for education. Jewish newcomers were quite successful. By 1910, one-fourth of the Jews in Boston had white-collar jobs, a success story similar to that of the British immigrants

of the previous generation. Most Jewish nonmanual workers were ped-
dlers earning small incomes, but it was a job which entailed risk taking and
developed business skills which would be important for the group's future.
Italian immigrants, by comparison, did more poorly than their Jewish
contemporaries. Just 12 percent of the Italian immigrant generation held
white-collar jobs, a record similar to the Irish immigrants of the late
nineteenth century.

Ambitious second-generation Jews who lacked the capital or initiative to start a small business, or were poorly educated, might seek other
avenues of social mobility in crime, entertainment, or professional athletics, particularly boxing. These were many of the same avenues for advancement that prior downtrodden groups like the Irish had taken.
Boxing was a natural occupation for ghetto youngsters to enter since it was
related to their day-to-day experiences. It was a functional skill, important for boys to learn if they wished to survive in the urban jungle. Jewish
boys coming home from school were often set upon by roving gangs of
Irish or Italian toughs, and it was necessary that they learn to defend
themselves. This street fight training prepared youngsters for careers as
policemen, criminals, or boxers.[27]

Jewish parents vigorously opposed the pugilistic ambitions of
their sons but family qualms often gave way to the paycheck which boxers
brought home to help support the family. At first only a handful of Jews
fought the ring, but once a few like Leach Cross, a man who fought to pay
his way through dental school, and Abe Attell, the world lightweight
champion, achieved widespread fame, they became models for the
younger to emulate. They were regarded as race heroes defending the
honor of the Jewish people and proving to the world that the Jewish male
was not meek and cowardly. Three of the nineteen American world
champions in the 1910s were Jewish, equal to the number of Irish and
German champions. In the next decade, 17.5 percent (7) of the champions were Jewish, placing them third behind the Italians and the Irish.
They were second to the Italians in the 1930s with 14.3 percent (8).[28]

Contemporary sportswriters were puzzled by the dearth of Jews in
professional baseball while they were so prominent in boxing. In 1903,
Barry McCormick noted in the St. Louis Republic, "He [the Jew] is athletic
enough and the great number of Jewish boxers show that he is adept at one
kind of sport at least." However, McCormick could only identify two Jews,
Barney Pelty and Harry Kane, in the major leagues.[29] Baseball did not fit
well into the Jewish immigrant's experience. Jews living in the crowded
Lower East Side of New York had little opportunity to play baseball and
become sufficiently proficient. Space was at a premium with the population density reaching 500,000 per square mile. Furthermore, young Jews
had little leisure time to spend playing baseball because they either
worked full time, or attended school and worked afterwards. Most of their
spare time came at night when it was too late to play baseball and possible

to go to a settlement house or a gymnasium to learn the fundamentals of boxing.[30]

The few Jewish major leaguers encountered discrimination. Several altered their names to hide their ethnic background and protect themselves against unfair treatment. Seven major leaguers with the surname Cohen changed it to such nondescript names as Kane, Bohne, and Ewing. Johnny Kling and Jacob Henry Azt, who were thought to be Jewish, but were actually German, received considerable abuse from colleagues who believed they were Jewish.[31]

Baseball magnates in Chicago and New York where there were large Jewish populations wanted to hire Jewish ballplayers because they would attract their fellow Jews to the ball parks. The New York Giants made special efforts in the late 1910s to recruit a Jewish star since the surrounding Washington Heights neighborhood was rapidly becoming a Jewish community. When the Federal League folded before the start of the 1916 season, Giants' owner Harry Hempstead signed a number of its best players including the league's star Benny Kauff, who was widely believed to be Jewish although he was actually Slavic. In 1923, a local Jewish youth, Moses Solomon, put in a brief appearance with the Giants. Three years later, the team purchased a highly regarded minor leaguer named Andy Cohen to replace the great Rogers Hornsby who had just been traded to St. Louis. Cohen was publicized by the New York press as a ghetto youth making good. However, they were far off the mark because Cohen had been born in Baltimore, raised in Waco, Texas, and educated at the University of Alabama, hardly a Lower East Side environment. Cohen never fulfilled the Giants' high expectations, and lasted just three years in the majors.[32]

The majority of the Jewish ballplayers did not come from New York, but from towns in the hinterland. Harry Kane was born in Hamburg, Arkansas, and others were from towns like Atlanta, Farmington, Missouri, and Middleport, Ohio. These athletes were far removed from ghettoized Jewish influences, and probably assimilated into the mainstream American culture which approved of baseball more quickly than did Jews raised in Brownsville or the Lower East Side where the sport was widely castigated as a children's game played by men in short pants. Moreover, there was space to play baseball and more opportunities to become proficient at it in communities that were less crowded than New York's Jewish neighborhoods.[33]

Besides the Jews, the other major, new immigrant groups were the Italians and Slavs who began migrating to the United States *en masse* in the 1880s, settling primarily in the northeastern and midwestern cities. They came without skills or capital, and had to take the lowest skilled, poorest paying jobs. The first generation Italians and Slavs did not display the same entrepreneurial bent as the Jewish contemporaries nor did they have the same respect for education. They took their children out of school at early ages and put them to work in factories and mines to help supplement the family income.   Consequently, second-generation Italians and Slavs were not as well prepared as their Jewish peers to move up into white-collar jobs.[34]

Opportunities were available to the poor, unlettered second-generation Italians and Slavs in such well-paying, but low prestige occupations as crime, entertainment and boxing, positions which the respectable middle class shunned.   In their poverty-stricken communities, the only people who ever had fat bankrolls were generally either criminals or pugilists, and they became role models to the youngsters who idolized them.   Many Slavic and Italian young men became boxers, taking advantage of the skills they learned in the streets.   They received training at settlement houses, private gymnasiums, and church sponsored athletic facilities.   The first Polish world champion boxer was Stanley Ketchell in 1907, and Pete Herman, the first Italian champion, was crowned in 1917. Italians became very prominent in professional boxing, and between 1920 and 1955 there were more Italian boxing champions than from any other ethnic group.[35]

However in the first third of the century, few Italians or Slavs entered professional baseball.   The first Polish batting champion was Al Simmons in 1930 and the first Italian was Ernie Lombardi in 1938.   Like the Jewish immigrants, these newcomers lived in crowded tenement communities where there was limited space available for parks which made it difficult for their sons to play baseball. Also, most of their leisure time came after dark when it was too late to play baseball.

The most successful of the new immigrant groups in professional baseball were the Czechs. Bohemian immigrants in Chicago and the industrial towns of Pennsylvania and Ohio founded athletic clubs so they could continue playing their traditional sports. These clubs often sponsored baseball leagues since the national pastime was popular among the second-generation and it was a good way to keep Czech youngsters tied to their heritage. Many watched the Bohemian teams compete on Sundays, and the results were reported in the Czech press and occasionally even in the big city dailies. Bohemian amateur clubs in Chicago contributed several players to the major leagues in the 1910s.

The underrepresentation of Italian and Slavic players continued until the latter part of the 1930s. In 1929, for example, only four regulars among the five major league teams in New York and Chicago were of recent immigrant stock, and two of them were Jewish. As late as 1935, *Who's Who in the National League* indicated indicated that there were just four Italians and two Slavs on the combined rosters of the Brooklyn Dodgers, the New York Giants, and the Chicago Cubs.[36]

American Indians were far more prominent and successful in professional baseball than the new immigrants in the first two decades of the century. The first Indian major leaguer was Lou Sockalexis who played for Cleveland from 1897 to 1899, and he was followed by about thirty other players of Indian descent in the next twenty years. Indian major leaguers were given a disproportionate amount of attention in the press because their presence was so surprising and out of the ordinary, and because certain of the Indian ballplayers like Chief Meyers and Chief Bender happened to be outstanding performers. Baseball's propagandists publicized the Indian backgrounds of these major leaguers as proof of the sport's democratic recruitment policies.[37]

Indians were attracted to professional baseball because they believed it was an occupation free from racial prejudice, where talent alone would determine their ultimate success. As Chief Bender noted,

> The reason I went into baseball as a profession was that when I left school [Dartmouth], baseball offered me the best opportunity both for money and advancement that I could see. I adopted it because I played baseball better than I could do anything else, because the life and the game appealed to me and because there was so little of racial prejudice in the game ... There has been scarcely a trace of sentiment against me on account of birth. I have been treated the same as the other men.[38]

Cubans were another ethnic group prominent in baseball during the Progressive Era. Although the Cuban Esteban Bellan played in the NAPBBP in 1871, the island was not really exploited as a source of ballplayers until the 1910s. Baseball was a popular sport in Cuba, and visiting Cuban teams toured the Northeast in the early 1900s playing semipro seams. In the meantime, a different major league club visited Cuba each year to play exhibition games against local stalwarts. Major league players and managers, particularly Calvin Griffith of the Reds, were impressed by the quality of baseball they saw there, and in 1911 Griffith began signing Cubans to major league contracts. By 1915 there were at least five Cubans in the majors and eleven more in the minors.[39]

The matter of race was a big problem in recruiting Cubans. Unlike the U.S., little if any racial prejudice existed in Cuba, and Blacks and Whites were given equal opportunities there. Many star players were Black but professional scouts could not sign them because of racial barriers in the United States. American magnates were careful to point out that the Cubans they did sign were White Spaniards ("Castilians"), well-to-do, and from superior family backgrounds. Veteran American players were not happy with the Cuban invasion, fearing they would take jobs away from them and cause a drop in prevailing salaries by accepting lower wages. However, the veteran players did not have much to fear from Cubans, or even Indians, for that matter, since only a handful became professional athletes, and fewer still made the major leagues. Indeed, these two groups together comprised less than two percent of the major leaguers from 1900 to 1920.[40]

Asians and Blacks were completely excluded from professional baseball even though the sport claimed to select its players solely on the basis of talent. Their absence reflected American racial prejudices. Except for Hawaiians, few Asians played baseball. A minor crisis did occur in 1915 when an Oriental of great promise was discovered by Frank Chance, manager of the Los Angeles team in the Pacific Coast League. Chance wanted to sign him to a contract but feared the wrath of his ballplayers and the antipathy of West Coast fans.[41]

The exclusion of Blacks was far more significant because they presented a real threat to White baseball players. About thirty Blacks had actually played in Organized Baseball in the nineteenth century before the racial barrier were drawn shut. The first Black professional ballplayer was John W. ("Bud") Fowler who played for New Castle, Pennsylvania in 1872. Twelve years later, Moses Fleetwood Walker, a former student at Oberlin and Michigan, became the first Afro-American in the major leagues when he signed to play with Toledo of the American Association.[42]

The fate of the pioneer Black players was not a happy tale for they were poorly treated by both their teammates and the fans. In 1889, *Sporting News* surveyed the dismal situation, noting that "race prejudice exists in professional baseball ranks to a marked degree, and the unfortunate son of Africa who makes his living as a member of a team of White professionals has a rocky road to travel."[43] White players refused to socialize with their Black teammates, and tried to force them out of the sport. Negroes were given poor coaching, sliding runners tried to spike them, and pitchers tried to hit them. Spectators were equally ill-disposed to Black athletes, insulting them and threatening their lives. Late in the 1884 season, Toledo's manager received a letter from Richmond a few weeks before a scheduled three game series there:

> We the undersigned do hereby warn you not to put up Walker the negro catcher the evenings that you play in Richmond, as we could mention the names of 75 determined men who have sworn to mob Walker if he comes on the grounds in a suit. We hope you will listen to our words of warning, so that there will be no trouble; but if you do not there certainly will be. We only write this to prevent much bloodshed, as you alone can prevent.[44]

After 1898 there were no Black players in Organized Baseball. An unwritten policy developed among baseball magnates who agreed not to sign any Blacks. The principal challenge to that pact was aborted during spring training in 1901 when Giant manager John J. McGraw tried to pass off the Black star Charles Grant as an Indian. However, Charles Comiskey recognized Grant.[45] A minor challenge to the racist policies arose in 1910 when a new association known as the United States League was established outside the jurisdiction of Organized Baseball with franchises in Baltimore, Brooklyn, Boston, Newark, Patterson, Philadelphia, Providence, and Trenton. The league promised to hire any able athlete regardless of race or background, and it was reported that three of the first one hundred players signed by the circuit were Black. However, this experiment in biracial athletics was short-lived, for the league collapsed almost immediately after the start of its season.[46]

Excluded from Organized Baseball, Blacks organized their own semiprofessional teams and leagues. The quality of play among the best clubs was high. Black teams often played all-star aggregates of White major leaguers on Sundays during the summer or in the fall after their season ended.   White players and managers were occasionally quoted in newspapers praising the abilities of the Black players they competed against at home and in Cuba.[47] A *St. Louis Post-Dispatch* reporter stated that the Black ballplayers were actually superior to their White counterparts:

> It is in baseball that the descendants of Ham is at his athletic best. Less removed from the anthropoid ape, he gets down on ground balls better, springs higher for liners, has a stronger and surer grip, and gets in and out of base on all fours in a way that makes the higher product of evolution look like a bush leaguer.[48]

He predicted that Whites would eventually be superceded in baseball as they had been in boxing.

Most of the Black semiprofessionals came from the South. They worked as railroad porters, waiters, or government employees and played baseball on the weekends. A few had college experience. The best athletes made baseball a full-time job. They played for teams like the Chicago Giants who played baseball twelve months a year, touring the Northeast or Midwest in the summer, and then playing in a California winter league or at a Florida hotel where they entertained guests. The touring teams played up to 200 games a year, traveling by modest means, staying at whatever hotels would admit them, and getting paid on an irregular basis. One Black magnate estimated that the average Black player in the early 1900s was paid $466 for the season compared to $571 for minor leaguers and $2,000 for major leaguers. The leading historian of Black baseball estimates that the typical black ballplayer in the 1910s was paid $40 to $75 a month while stars received $105. The highest reported salary was paid the great John Henry Lloyd, who earned $250 a month in 1917. The athletes who played baseball on a full-time basis received compensation comparable to that of Black letter carriers or school teachers. Some of the stars were better paid than school principals.

Nevertheless, Black ballplayers were not highly regarded by the Black middle class which considered them unrespectable and irresponsible, and they were barred from better Black homes.[49]

Most profits from Black baseball ended up in White hands. Nearly all the Black clubs were owned by White men, and the semiprofessional teams scheduled their games through a White booking agency which forced the few Black owners to accede to disadvantageous terms if they wished to get any games. Nat Strong, the head of the agency, had a great deal of power, and prevented teams that refused to do business on his terms from getting ball games. In 1909 he led the fight to oust cafe proprietor John W. Connors, then the only Afro-American owner of a Black New York baseball club, out of the sport. Connors had refused to accept Strong's stipulations granting him a fixed guarantee rather than the typical and more profitable terms which called for a percentage of the gate.

After World War I, an effort was initiated to wrestle control of Black baseball away from White domination. The movement was led by Rube Foster, a former star pitcher, who had become the owner of his own semiprofessional club. Foster felt that since the players and two-thirds of the spectators at Negro games were Black, the profits from the ball games should stay in Black hands. In 1920 he organized the Negro National Baseball League with franchises in eight cities, all owned and operated by Blacks. Foster further hoped that his Black association could create ancillary jobs for Blacks as scouts, umpires, clerks, secretaries, and other occupations needed to support a baseball enterprise.[50]

Black ballplayers hoped that the day was not too distant when they would be welcomed into Organized Baseball and paid the high salaries of major leaguers. These athletes pinned their hopes on the successes of Cubans and Indians in the major leagues, for the Blacks hoped their presence indicated a liberalized attitude towards men of color, foreshadowing their own admission into professional baseball. The advancement of light skinned Cubans was watched with particular interest by players and by journalists like Lester Walton, sports editor of the *New York Age*, one of the principal Black newspapers of the day. Walton wrote at the end of the 1911 season:

> With the admission of Cubans of a darker hue in the two big leagues it would then be easy for colored players who are citizens of this country to get into fast company. Until the public gets accustomed to seeing Negroes on big league teams, the colored players should keep their mouths shut and pass for Cubans.[51]

The dreams of these Black ballplayers were not fulfilled for another generation, until after World War II when Jackie Robinson was chosen by Branch Rickey to break the color barrier. In 1963 the proportion of black Americans in the big leagues reached 10 percent, approximately their share of the national population. By 1972, their percentage had nearly doubled to 18.8 percent. Another 8.7 percent were black Latins. Yet there are relatively few Black fringe players, there are few Black executives, and only one Black manager, Frank Robinson. Aaron Rosenblatt has demonstrated rather convincingly that a Black player has to hit about twenty points higher than a White bench-warmer to remain on the squad.[52]

The historic experience of blacks in baseball was in no way similar to that of the White immigrants. Second- and third-generation Germans and Irish were prominent on major league rosters from the earliest days of professional baseball, and while the new immigrants were poorly represented until World War II, they had an equal chance to become major leaguers once they were assimilated. Even Cubans and Indians were accepted in Organized Baseball. But baseball's democratic ideology did not extend to Black Americans, who were completely excluded from professional baseball because of racial prejudice. This semi-official policy existed although experts acknowledged the quality of the best Black ballplayers. Unlike the foreign-born immigrants who had to learn about various American institutions like baseball, Blacks constituted a readily available but unused source of talent for professional baseball during the Progressive Era.

• • •

Notes

1. David Q. Voigt, *American Baseball*, vol. 2, *From the Commissioner System to Continental Expansion* (Norman, 1971), p. 65; James Youtsler, *Labor's Wage Policies in the Twentieth Century* (New York, 1956), pp. 38-39; Steven A. Riess, "Professional Baseball and American Culture in the Progressive Era, Myths and Realities, with Special Emphasis on Atlanta, Chicago, and New York," (Ph.D. diss., University of Chicago, 1974), 253-56, 258.

2. For a detailed study of the spectators in the early twentieth century, see Riess, "Professional Baseball," 35-66.

3. Harold Seymour, Baseball, vol. 1, *The Early Years* (New York, 1960), pp. 327-28; David Q. Voigt, *American Baseball*, vol. 1, *From Gentleman's Sport to the Commissioner System* (Norman, 1966), p. 178; *St. Louis Dispatch,* June 16, 1883.

4. Photographs of bleachers scenes almost never revealed women seated there, although they were seen in grandstand shots. See Albert G. Spalding, *America's National Game* (New York, 1911), p. 502 ff., for a wide panoramic view of the bleachers completely filled without any women and compare it to other photographs there which depict grandstand crowds. These photographs show many women seated there, wearing the fashionable bonnets of the day.

5. My conclusions on this matter are drawn from Federal Writers Project, Illinois, *Chicago Foreign Language Press Survey*, typescript (Chicago, 1942),

Special Collections, University of Chicago Library (hereafter cited as CFLPS). For a very biased and derogatory view of one ethnic group and their interest in American culture, see Kenneth D. Miller, *The Czecho-Slovaks in America* (New York, 1922), pp. 98-99.

6. See, e.g., *Svornost*, April 8, 1890, CFLPS; Denni Hlasatel, September 16, 1911, CFLPS.

7. Ande Manners, *Poor Cousins* (New York, 1972), p. 278.

8. Harold Seymour, *Baseball*, vol. 2, The Golden Years (New York, 1971), p. 83; *Harry Golden, For 2¢ Plain* (New York, 1959), pp. 227-29.

9. Seymour, *Baseball*, 2:61.

10. Morris Raphael Cohen, *A Dreamer's Journey: The Autobiography of Morris Raphael Cohen* (Boston, 1949), pp. 80-81.

11. Harry Golden, *The Right Time: An Autobiography* (New York, 1969), p. 54.

12. The best study of the subject is Robert Peterson, *Only the Ball Was White* (Englewood Cliffs, 1970).

13. Gilbert Osofsky, *Harlem: The Making of a Ghetto, Negro New York, 1890-1930* (New York, 1968), p. 16, see also W.E.B. DuBois, *The Philadelphia Negro* (Philadelphia, 1899), pp. 133-37.

14. See, e.g., *New York Age*, October 31, 1912; August 28, October 2, 1913; Peterson, *Only the Ball Was White*, p. 66.

15. *New York Age*, June 29, 1911. In the South, segregated seating was provided for white spectators. *Atlanta Constitution*, July 23, 1902; July 15, 1919.

16. *Chicago Daily News*, January 25, 1911; *New York Age*, July 20, 1911; *Broad Ax*, May 18, 1912. Schorling eventually increased the capacity of his park to 9,000. Peterson, *Only the Ball Was White*, p. 108.

17. Peterson, *Only the Ball Was White*, p. 70. The *Broad Ax* ran advertisements in the spring and summer of 1910 stating that the price of tickets to the Leland Giants' park at 69th and Wentworth on the South Side of Chicago was 25¢, 35¢, and 50¢. Youths were charged fifteen cents. See also *Broad Ax*, April 15, 1911.

18. *New York Times*, July 20, 1919; Thomas J. Jenkins, "Changes in Ethnic and Racial Representation Among Professional Boxers: A Study in Ethnic Succession," (M.A. thesis, University of Chicago, 1955), pp. 15, 21; S. Kirson Weinberg and Henry Avond, "The Occupational Culture of the Boxer," *American Journal of Sociology*, 57 (March, 1952): 460-69.

19. Stephen Thernstrom, *The Other Bostonians: Poverty and Progress in the American Metropolis, 1880-1970* (Cambridge, MA, 1973), pp. 131-32.

20. Lawrence S. Ritter, ed., *The Glory of Their Times* (New York, 1966), p. 37.

21. *Sporting News*, October 8, 1892.

22. *New York Tribune*, February 24, 25, March 4, 8, 26, 1915. As late as 1923, Fred Lieb estimated that one-half of the players and three-fourths of the stars were Irish. See Fred Lieb, "Baseball—The Nation's Melting Pot," *Baseball Magazine*, 21 (August, 1923): 393-95. On the difficulty of trying to ascetain people's ethnic identity from their names, see William F. Obgurn and Clark Tibbitts, "A Memorandum on the Nativity of Certain Criminal Classes Engaged in Organized Crime, and of Certain Related Criminal and Non-Criminal Groups in Chicago" (Unpublished manuscript, July 30, 1930), pp. 142-45, in *Charles E. Merriam Papers, Special Collections*, University of Chicago Library.

23. Thernstrom, *Other Bostonians*, pp. 132, 134.

24. *New York Tribune*, September 28, 1918. See also *Constitution*, March 6, 1910; Irving Leitner, *Baseball, Diamond in the Rough* (New York, NY, 1972), p. 205. For an opposite view, see *New York Tribune*, March 9, 1915.

25. Joseph Gerstein, "Anti-Semitism in Baseball," *Jewish Life*, 6 (July, 1952): 21-22; Stanley B. Frank, *The Jew in Sports* (New York, 1936), pp. 75-91; *Encyclopaedia Judaica*, 1st ed., s.v. "Sports."

26. Ben B. Seidman, *The Potentates* (New York, 1971), pp. 260-61.

27. Mark Haller, "Organized Crime in Urban Society: Chicago in the Twentieth Century," *Journal of Social History*, 5 (Winter, 1971-72): 221-27; Daniel Bell, *The End of Ideology* (Glencoe, Illinois, 1960), pp. 127-50.

28. Jenkins, "Professional Boxers," pp. 85-89.

29. Quoted in *Cincinnati Enquirer*, November 17, 1903; see also *Sporting News*, June 13, 1897; Frederick C. Lane, "Why Not More Jewish Ball Players?" *Baseball Magazine*, 36 (January, 1926): 341.

30. Frederick C. Lane, "He Can Talk Baseball in Ten Languages," Ibid., 40 (March, 1928): 440.

31. Gerstein, "Anti-Semitism in Baseball," pp. 21-22; Seymour, *Baseball*, 2: 82-83; Lieb, "Baseball—The Nation's Melting Pot," p. 395; Golden, *The Right Time*, p. 55; *Encyclopaedia Judaica*, s.v. "Sports."

32. Samuel S. Merin, "A Close-Up of Andy Cohen," *Baseball Magazine*, 41 (July, 1928): 358; *Sporting News*, April 26, 1928; Golden, *Right Time*, P. 55; Allen, *Dodgers and Giants*, p. 122; Seymour, *Baseball*, 2:83.

33. Compiled from the *Baseball Encyclopedia: The Complete and Official Record of Major League Baseball* (New York, 1969).

34. Thernstrom, *Other Bostonians*, pp. 135-37; 162-63, 168-72; Bell, *End of Ideology*, pp. 127-50.

35. Jenkins, "Professional Boxers," pp. 15, 98.

36. Data on players taken from Harold Johnson, *Who's Who in the National League, 1935* (Chicago, 1935). A spot-check of rosters appearing in the *Baseball Encyclopedia* from 1925 through 1935 further indicate the absence of these newcomers. Their surnames were easy to spot, although some might have been missed because they anglicized their names.

37. "Indians Who Played in the Big Leagues," *Baseball Magazine*, 27 (July, 1921): 355; Seymour, *Baseball*, 2:81-82.

38. *Chicago Daily News*, October 19, 1910.

39. *Atlanta Constitution*, January 10, 1909; January 2, 1916; *New York Tribune*, December 3, 1909; December 26, 1911; April 15, 1917; New York Age, December 8, 22, 1910; Seymour, *Baseball*, 2:85-88.

40. *New York Tribune*, October 13, 1912; February 26, 1914.

41. *Chicago Daily News*, November 27, 1915. In another incident, Walter McCredie, manager of Portland in the Pacific Coast League, tried to put a Chinese-Hawaiian player on his roster, but had to release him because the other players objected to him. *Chicago Defender*, January 16, 1915. For an excellent analysis of racial discrimination in baseball, see Gerald W. Scully, "Discrimination: The Case of Baseball," in *Government and the Sports Business*, ed., Roger G. Noll (Washington, 1974), pp. 221-273.

42. Peterson, *Only the Ball Was White*, pp. 18, 23.

43. Ibid., p. 41.

44. Ibid., p. 23.

45. Ibid., pp. 54-56.

46. *Constitution*, March 4, 1910; *New York Age*, March 10, 1910.

47. See, e.g., *New York Age*, January 26, 1911; January 11, 1919.

48. Ibid., September 28, 1911.

49. Ibid. Jack Johnson was then world heavyweight champion.

50. *New York Age*, June 18, 1918; *Chicago Defender*, April 19, October 4, 1919. At first the umpires at black games were always white, even though most spectators were black, and Olympic Park, the main playing field, was located at

136th Street and Fifth Avenue in Harlem. *New York Age,* August 5, 1912; *Chicago Defender,* October 9, 1920.

    51. *New York Age,* September 28, 1911.

    52. Ralph Andreano, *No Joy in Mudville* (New York, Cambridge, MA, 1965), p. 138; Lacy J. Banks, "How Much is a Player Worth?" *Ebony,* 17 (June, 1972), p. 153-62; Aaron Rosenblatt, "Negroes in Baseball: The Failure of Success," *Transaction Magazine,* 4 (September, 1967): 51-54.

· · ·

Suggestions for Further Reading

Brashler, William, *Josh Gibson: A Life in the Negro Leagues* (New York: Harper & Row, 1978).

_____, "Looking for Josh Gibson," *Esquire,* LXXXIX (February, 1978), 104-108 ff.

Gelber, Steven M., "'Their Hands Are All Out Playing': Business and Amateur Baseball, 1845-1917," *Journal of Sport History,* XI, i (Spring, 1984), 5-27.

_____, "Working at Playing: The Culture of the Work Place and the Rise of Baseball," *Journal of Social History,* XVI (June, 1983), 3-20.

Gerstein, Joseph, "Anti-Semitism in Baseball," *Jewish Life,* VI (July, 1952), 21-22.

Holway, John, *Voices from the Great Black Baseball Leagues* (New York: Dodd, Mead and Co., 1975).

Lewis, Guy M., "World War I and the Emergence of Sport for the Masses," *The Maryland Historian,* IV, 2 (Fall, 1973), 109-122.

Mormino, Gary Ross, "The Playing Fields of St. Louis: Italian Immigrants and Sports, 1925-1941," *Journal of Sport History,* IX (Summer, 1982), 5-19.

Murdock, Eugene, *Ben Johnson: Czar of Baseball* (Westport, CT: Greenwood Press, 1982).

_____, "The Tragedy of Ben Johnson," *Journal of Sport History,* I ,1 (Spring, 1974), 26-40.

Peterson, Robert, *Only the Ball Was White* (Englewood Cliffs, NJ: Prentice-Hall, 1970).

Reiss, Steven, "The Baseball Magnates and Urban Politics in the Progressive Era, 1895-1920," *Journal of Sport History,* I, 1, (Spring, 1974), 3-25.

_____, "Baseball Myths, Baseball Reality, and the Social Functions of Baseball in Progressive America," *Stadion,* III, 2 (1977), 273-311.

_____, "Professional Baseball and Social Mobility," *Journal of Interdisciplinary History*, XI, 2 (Autumn, 1980), 235-250.

_____, "Professional Sunday Baseball: A Study in Social Reform, 1892-1934," *The Maryland Historian*, IV, 2 (Fall, 1973), 95-108.

_____, *Touching Base: Professional Baseball and American Culture in the Progressive Era* (Westport, CT: Greenwood Press, 1980).

Sander, David, "Only the Ball Was White," *Journal of Popular Culture*, V, 1 (1971), 243-245.

Whorton, James C., "Muscular Vegetarianism: The Debate Over Diet and Athletic Performance in the Progressive Era," *Journal of Sport History*, VIII, 2 (Summer, 1981), 58-75.

Wiggins, David K., "Isaac Murphy: Black Hero in Nineteenth Century American Sport, 1861-1896," *Canadian Journal of History of Sport and Physical Education*, X (May, 1979), 15-32.

JACK DEMPSEY:
AN AMERICAN HERO IN THE 1920s

Randy Roberts

American sport celebrated its coming of age in the 1920s through introducing a new brand of hero to the national stage—the sports star. Here were figures who captured the public's fancy on the strength of individual prowess and performance that bore little resemblance to the familiar patterns of hero-making. For unlike the "idols of production," who hailed from the traditional worlds of politics, business, science and industry, the new "idols of consumption" were products of the news media and the world of entertainment. These were situational heroes—created in one day's headlines, undone in another's. In the process, consensus faded on the nature of heroic standards.

In the 1920s, the "Golden Age of American Sport," however, produced several sports figures who had remarkable staying power in the public's favor. They are important to study because they give us clues to the dynamics of hero-worship and identity. In a gallery that included Red Grange, Bill Tilden, Bobby Jones and Walter Hagen, foremost among them was probably Babe Ruth. But while every major American sport had its idolized champion in the decade, no athlete rivaled boxer Jack Dempsey in capturing media attention and fan interest on those occasions when he fought for the heavyweight crown.

As Randy Roberts explains in this article, "Dempsey the image" was more important than "Dempsey the man." Tracing the "Manassa Mauler"'s career from his pounding of Jess Willard in 1919 to win the heavyweight title to his loss to Gene Tunney in 1926, Roberts focuses on the way in which each of Dempsey's title defenses "became a platform from which to debate issues central to the 1920s." The pre-fight hype engineered by promoter Tex Rickard and manager Jack Kearns for the 1921 bout with French war hero Georges Carpentier, for example, focused as much on moral and social issues as it did on the boxing skills and contrasting styles of the pugilists. The Dempsey image, molded by paintings and the cinema in addition to the print media, emphasized aggressiveness, directness, decisiveness and coarseness. It was unmistakably a low-brow image, without the hedonism of Ruth, but appealing to essentially the same audience—the working class Americans who cheered their heroes' ability to take action (literally) with their own hands and to revitalize the traditional dream of success.

On the Fourth of July, 1919, as the temperature climbed to 114°, a nation said to be "surfeited with fighting and bloodshed" mustered 20,000 sanguinary spectators to the shores of Maumee Bay, just outside Toledo, Ohio, to witness what they hoped would be more fighting and bloodshed. They were not disappointed. For under that blazing sun, a brine-hardened, tan Jack Dempsey beat a flabby and aging Jess Willard into submission in three rounds. A New York *Times* reporter asserted that the crowd could find no enjoyment in watching a man receive cuts around both eyes, have six teeth forcibly removed, and absorb blows which swelled the right side of his face to twice its normal size.[1] Yet, the wild cheering and excitement which pulsed through the capacity crowd refuted the reporter's claim.[2] The timeless axiom that nothing arouses public interest as quickly as a good fight was demonstrated in full. And for the next eight years, the aphorism would hold again and again for Dempsey's bouts.

From 1919 to 1927, Jack Dempsey was a celebrated figure. Newspapers mapped his varied movements, and the magazines ranging from the middle-class *Saturday Evening Post* and *Collier's* to the more highbrow *New Republic* and the *American Mercury* carried articles on him. Crowds totaling over 500,000 saw his title fights, while millions more heard those bouts which were broadcasted over radio.[3] In eight years, Dempsey earned more than ten million dollars.[4] Certainly a man who could become as popular as Dempsey and earn as much money as he did deserves scholarly attention. Yet, Dempsey's impact on America has been all but ignored by historians.[5] Like most sports topics, the history of Dempsey's career has fallen by default into the hands of myth-makers. The following pages attempt to go beyond mere mythology to view Dempsey as a facet of complex society rather than as a part of a circumscribed legend.

Discussing the impact of Muhammed Ali on American life in the 1960s, Eldridge Cleaver gave a cogent glimpse into the relationship between boxing and society when he wrote that "the boxing ring is the ultimate focus of masculinity in America, the two-fisted testing ground of manhood, and the heavyweight champion, as a symbol, is the real Mr. America."[6] Cleaver's view of the heavyweight champion as a national symbolic hero was not original with him. A 1921 editorial in the *New Republic* noted that Dempsey represented the ideal hero image to youths who had "a small verbal repertory but a large stock of scowls and blows."[7] Eleven years earlier, the heavyweight crown was viewed as the symbol of racial dominance. Discussing the upcoming title bout between black champion Jack Johnson and white ex-champion Jim Jeffries, columnist Max Balthazar wrote:

Can the huge white man, the California grizzly ... beat down the wonderful black and restore to the Caucasians the crown of elemental greatness as measured by strength of blow, power of heart and being, and, withal, that cunning or keenness that denotes mental as well as physical superiority.[8]

And even before 1910, as John Higham illustrated, the "heavyweight champions loomed large among American folk heroes."[9]

The dynamic impact of boxing champions and other popular folk heroes upon American life has been given serious attention by a number of psychologists, sociologists, and folklorists. Paul Meadows has noted that "the [popular] hero ... may be utilized to typify the whole culture or perhaps some aspects of it. He may be thought of as an index to the national mind or spirit."[10] Representing the ethnocentric attitudes of a culture, national heroes are "what they always have been, the measure of the range of our values."[11] Like Meadows, Orrin E. Klapp emphasizes that the popular hero in America "expresses out characteristic values. [He] reveals not only the traits we admire but also our field of interest."[12] But the function of a hero such as Dempsey does more than simply characterize a social milieu. As a popular hero, he helps to perpetuate certain collective values and to nourish and maintain certain socially necessary sentiments.[13] Thus the popular hero serves a dual function: he both reflects the collective psychology of a society at a given time and acts to reinforce necessary social values.[14]

In an age of mass communications, heroes can be arbitrarily produced and widely diffused in a short time.[15] Sidney Hook has accurately observed that whoever controls the microphones and printing presses of a society can create a synthetic hero overnight.[16] In the case of an athletic personality, the sports section of newspapers and magazines is the instrumental tool in forming a hero. And more often than not, the image of a sports hero that a periodical forms is the one which is most compatible with its readers. As Harry Edwards has noted, public opinion studies continually demonstrate that people will neither buy nor read that with which they disagree. Americans, Edwards observes, "tend to read only what reinforces their own attitudes."[17] Thus, if a newspaper or magazine continually emphasizes that a hero is kind, gentle, and truthful, it is safe to assume that this is what the readers want to believe about the hero.

As with most popular heroes, Dempsey the man was less important than Dempsey the image. The Dempsey image was dynamic, for at no time between 1919 and 1926 was it static. Forces and issues of the 1920s affected it and, as will be illustrated, his image underwent a considerable metamorphosis between his victory over Willard in 1919 and his defeat at the hands of Gene Tunney in 1926. But always the image would reflect the social and intellectual milieu which gave rise to it.

As early as 1921, it was noted that Americans' attitude toward Jack Dempsey lacked a "sense of proportion."[18] Boxing, a sport previously

discredited in America, was by 1921 legalized and accepted as entertainment for all classes and both sexes. Why did a deplored sport become a
national passion? Furthermore, why did Jack Dempsey become a national hero when the former world's heavyweight champion, Jess Willard, had
barely been known?

Part of the "lack of proportion" toward boxing stemmed from the
nation's World War I experience. The martial spirit of wartime carried
over into the sports world and caused a renaissance of boxing in the
United States.[19] The U.S. Army taught boxing to the World War I dough-
boy. According to the army's rationale, boxing served a dual function: it
was excellent training for learning how to use a bayonet, and it relieved
the tensions of camp life. In one camp alone 30,000 men received boxing
lessons, and inter-camp competition spurred interest from the generals
down to the privates.[20]

When the war ended the interest in boxing did not decline. In
fact, boxing gained even more popularity in the post-war decade, and
legislation was passed to legalize the sport in most of the states.[21] The
man most directly responsible for the amazing rise in post-World War I
boxing was Jack Dempsey. It was his career, his quick knockouts, which
attracted the public's attention to boxing in the 1920s.

Dempsey's status as a hero was built on only a handful of matches.
An examination of Dempsey's fighting record prior to his winning the
heavyweight crown in 1919 hardly reveals the unbeatable superman of
popular fantasy. Only two years before Dempsey made his reputation by
defeating Willard, he had been knocked out by "Fireman" Jim Flynn in less
than one round, and less than a year before he won the title he had been
humiliated by a fat little sailor named Willie Meehan.[22] Dempsey's
knockout average, a popular yardstick for measuring relative punching
ability, is only .613, well below that of such horrendous performers as
Floyd Patterson and Primo Carnera and only a few points above Tommy
Burns, the man considered by most ring historians as the worst heavyweight champion.[23] Therefore, considerably more went into the making
of the Dempsey legend than just a fighting record.

To understand the nature of Dempsey's reputation as the
"Manassa Mauler," one must return to the shores of the Maumee Bay on
that stifling hot July the Fourth, 1919. Dempsey entered the ring that day
as the unquestionable underdog. His 6 ft. 1 in. and 189 pound frame was
dwarfed by Jess Willard, the "Pattawatomie Giant" who stood 6 ft. 3 in. and
weighed in excess of 250 pounds. Yet, Dempsey won, and in winning he
punished his opponent to a degree he would never again equal.[24] After
the fight, it was reasoned that any boxer who could inflict such damage
must be in some way superhuman. The Dempsey legend was launched.
Public acceptance was complete; in one bout Dempsey gained the fighting reputation which would remain virtually unaltered for the remainder
of his career.[25]

Dempsey's emergence as a popular hero follows exactly the pattern of the typical "conquering hero" which Klapp has outlined.[26] All the major characteristics are present: Dempsey moved from relatively obscure social status to the rank of a hero by one spectacular demonstration of inordinate ability, and immediately a mythical interpretation of him arose.[27] Yet, as Klapp illustrates, a hero cannot emerge from a social vacuum; he is created to meet real emotional needs of a society.[28] So too, Dempsey acted as a point of social reorientation during the turbulent years of 1919-1920. With race riots erupting in cities throughout the United States and the Red Scare claiming victims by the hundreds, Dempsey seemed like something stable, something people could depend on.

The news media was quick to portray Dempsey as a person who represented all which America had long esteemed. His mere physical description exuded traditional values. To the New York *Times*, Dempsey was "modest, with boyish simplicity" and "refuses to indulge in broggadocia"; he was also seen as a "model of clean living ... a gentleman from head to toes," and a person who loves children.[29] Further proof of Dempsey's adherence to the traditional American virtues can be seen in his first reported action after the Willard bout. He quickly send off the following telegram: "Dear Mother: Won in third round. Received your wire. Will be home as soon as possible. Love and Kisses. Jack."[30]

Labor Day, 1920, saw the Dempsey myth buttressed by another quick knockout and more all-American deeds. In his first title defense, he defeated Billy Miske in a bout held at Benton Harbor, Michigan. While it is entirely possible that Miske may have been a worthy contender had he not been dying of Bright's disease, Dempsey was depicted as reaching his humanitarian zenith when he sent his friend into a state of unconsciousness in the third round.[31] Not only was Dempsey portrayed as a humanitarian inside the ring, he was also seen as a kind-hearted soul outside the ropes. Again, it was the New York *Times* which furnished the best example of the ingredients which went into the making of the Dempsey myth. They printed a heart-warming story of how before the fight a cute little girl had presented Dempsey with a kiss and a four-leaf clover, which he kept in his glove.[32] This type of story could only add to the growing adulation of Dempsey.

The printing press was not the only mass media force which molded the popular image of Dempsey. The visual arts—painting, drama, and the cinema—were also active in its formulation. For the first time in America, painters in the twenties began to find boxing a suitable subject for their canvasses. George Bellows could find "no more dramatic clash in nature than the fury and the ruthlessness of combat within the ropes."[33] In his painting Dempsey and Firpo, Bellows graphically captures the importance Dempsey had to the lives of people in the 1920s. Commenting on the pictures of Dempsey by such artists as Bellows and Alonzo Victor

Lewis, a New York *World* writer applauded their effort, stating that since Dempsey had the "native grace, physical beauty, and prowess which has fired the imagination of the world," he should by all means be preserve don canvas.[34]

While painting captured and preserved the drama of Dempsey's life, it influenced the actual molding of the Dempsey myth only indirectly. After all, few of Dempsey's most ardent followers either saw or understood the paintings. However, the cinema did play a direct role. Millions of people went to movies, and the melodramas which Dempsey starred in were highly profitable. By the art of the make-up man, Dempsey was transformed from the "foremost demonstrator of modified murder" into a "somewhat sheepish and harmless looking young man who makes moon faces at the heroines and pats the hand of a tubercular stage mother."[35] In all ways, Dempsey was cast in a role to epitomize the traditional values which the news media emphasized. W.O. McGeehan, the leading New York *Herald Tribune* sports columnist, wrote that a Dempsey movie was always of high moral quality:

> There is nothing in them to bring the blush of shame to the most sensitive cheek ... Of course there is a hint of what they call "sex" in these films. But it is handled with a delicacy that would even get by the judge who maintained that all literature should be denatured to suit a seminary girl of the mid-Victorian period. Mr. Jack Dempsey does not make love with the brazenness of a Valentino. His love-making is repressed. Mr. Dempsey merely looks at the "goil." He does not manhandle her. There are no shameless petting parties in this clean and wholesome Dempsey film. The Dempsey "movies" are safe and sane, and will get by any censor.[36]

Thus the motion picture industry reinforced the image of Dempsey that was presented in the news media. In a time of change and flux, Dempsey was portrayed as a stable force. Whether he was composing a telegram to his mother, kissing cute little girls, or making his "mooncalf expression" at older "goils," Dempsey was always seen in the light of past values and time-honored traditions.

The only serious obstacle which threatened to block this hero-making process was Dempsey's fight with Georges Carpentier, or, as his name was anglicized, "Gorgeous Car-painter."[37] Few ring battles have more dramatically symbolized the conflict of the values and issues of a given time. That the bout held a symbolic importance was clearly recognized at the time of the fight. A *New Republic* editorial warned specifically against forcing a boxer into becoming a representative symbol.[38] The public, the editorial observed, "took the fight as an orgy of sentimentality, and twisted Carpentier into a figure which the realities of this attractive prize-fighter do not support."[39] On the international level, the *Neue Zurcher Zeitung,* a liberal Swiss daily, said the bout symbolized the fact that "the young democratic giant—as dramatically incorporated in Dempsey's powerful, brutal, natural strength, born of the American West ... has become the master of the world."[40]

The central issue which animated the contest was each fighter's war record. Throughout World War I, Dempsey had done his fighting in the rings of the West Coast rather than in the trenches of France. Jack "Doc" Kearns, Dempsey's manager, offered the explanation that Dempsey, under "work or fight" orders, had decided he could best serve his country by working in the shipyards in Seattle.[41] In justifying his action, Dempsey said that since government had not instructed him to join the army, he was just following orders.[42] However, the issue could not easily be evaded. A New York *Times* editorial clearly dramatized the larger moral issue at stake:

> Dempsey says that he is not a draft dodger. Technical facts sustain him. His adherents assert that his negative patriotism, negative action, brings him forth from the slacker shadows and puts him, head up and dauntless, in the clear light of noble duty, nobly done ... Dempsey, whose profession is fighting, whose living is combat, whose fame is battle; Dempsey six feet one of strength, in the glowing splendor of youth, a man fashioned by nature as an athlete and a warrior—Dempsey did not go to the war, while weak-armed, strong-hearted clerks reeled under pack and rifle; while middle-aged men with families volunteered; while America asked for its manhood. Dempsey did not go to France to do battle for forty-eight states, but is ready now to go for four hundred thousand dollars. Our greatest fighter sidestepped our greatest fight. There rests the reason for the Dempsey chorus of dispraise.[43]

Dempsey's war record was brought into a sharper focus when compared to the record of Georges Carpentier, his French opponent. When the war started in August, 1914, Carpentier joined the French Air Force as a pilot.[44] During the war, he was twice wounded by shrapnel, once in the right foot and once in the head, and he was twice decorated, with the Croix de Guerre and the *Medaille Militaire.*[45] Thus the fight pitted the "slacker" against the military hero. Emphasizing this theme, a *Literary Digest* story observed that "one of the two men ... has a war-record made in the trenches; the other has a war-record which was made far in the rear of the fighting line. Georges Carpentier pulled off the gloves, picked up the bayonet, faced the German shells, and won the war-cross of gallantry in action; Jack Dempsey dropped his mitts to handle tools in a shipyard."[46]

Yet as central as the war question was, there were other issues which further complicated matters. Dempsey, for the most part, was a known quantity. Except for his amorphous stand on the war, he seemed quintessentially American. The Dempsey myth was certainly established and widely understood by the summer of 1921. Carpentier, on the other hand, was both physically and symbolically foreign. He came from France and neither spoke nor wanted to speak English.[47] Everything about him seemed somehow too flashy, too foreign. In shades of Valentino, he was described as being a "tall, slender, urban, and debonair young exquisite."[48] His tastes were portrayed as being strictly aristocratic. Owning over 200 suits and changing clothes six or eight times a day, Carpentier was always the height of fashion.[49] In his leisure time, he enjoyed fast cars, billiards, bridge, serious plays, highbrow literature, opera, and dancing.[50] Thus although he liked movies and Charlie Chaplin—illustrating that he was "not too bright or good for human nature's daily food"—Carpentier was most assuredly not the representative of traditional values that Dempsey was.[51]

Viewing the two boxers, the American public was faced with a perplexing dilemma: Carpentier was a war hero but he also was a foreigner, while the American, Dempsey, was a draft dodger. Obviously, this was not an easy choice to make. Intellectuals on both sides of the Atlantic came out overwhelmingly for Carpentier.[52] But the support the masses had to offer was split. The American Legion adopted a resolution condemning Dempsey as a draft dodger and appropriated money to bet on Carpentier.[53] Reacting to the American Legion's stand, the Veterans of Foreign Wars of Atlantic City pledged their support of Dempsey. Justifying their stand, a leader said, "We look on Dempsey as the American champion going into the ring to uphold America's title of supremacy in a game at which it has excelled for generations."[54]

After he had chosen his favorite, the American fan could only sit back and watch the pre-fight build-up, which was, in fact, spectacular. Newspapers and magazines in both the United States and Europe printed daily articles about the fight. The inordinate amount of press space devoted to the fight went neither unnoticed nor unquestioned in foreign countries. Both the London *Times* and the *Manchester Guardian* noted that the American people had lost all "sense of proportion" regarding the bout.[55] In tiny, neutral Switzerland, the *Neue Zurche Zeitung* wrote that "one tenth of this interest of the press-power concentrated upon this event would have easily put the United States into the League of Nations ... America is more engaged by this event than by the Versailles peace or by the greatest European revolution."[56] Even in the Far East, the fight gained newspaper coverage. The *Japan Times* claimed that American fight promoters were insensitive to Eastern feeling because they scheduled the Dempsey-Carpentier match for Saturday, July 2, which meant the fight would be held on Sunday, Japanese time.[57] Furthermore, the paper was incensed that the bout monopolized "the telegraph and cable lines to the exclusion of debates and decisions that will influence the sections of the larger part of mankind for years to come."[58]

If foreign papers mapped every undulation of the fighters' lives, the American press detailed every sweat pore Dempsey and Carpentier opened while training. This was no mere flirtation with the combatants; the press was quite serious in their coverage of the pre-fight events. For weeks before the bout, the *New York Times*, St. Louis *Post-Dispatch*, New Orleans *Times-Picayune,* and New York *Tribune* carried front page stories about the fighters. In the newspapers, the match was also used as a catalyst for selling consumer goods. For example, the New Orleans *Times-Picayune* ran a full-page advertisement entitled, "The 'Fight of the Century' Will End in Round??" Each of twelve stores picked a round; if the bout ended in round one, the Delta Lumber Company would give five dollars reduction on the first purchase made on July 4, 1921; or, if the fight ended in round two, A.B.S. Falling Hair and Dandruff Remedy would sell thirty 60¢ bottles at one-half price.[59] Nor were the newspapers the only mass media platform which showed excessive interest in the affair. Magazines of every nature, from the highbrow to the lowbrow, also demonstrated an inordinate interest in the two men. Magazines made the bout subject to psychological interpretation, literary speculation, and religious controversy.[60] Indeed, by the time of the fight, it is hard to imagine a single sector of American life which had not in one way or another expressed an interest in the outcome.

The stage was thus set for the fight. On July 2, 1921, the attention of millions of people around the world focused on a ring at Boyle's Thirty Acres in Jersey City, New Jersey. As a financial experiment, the fight was an unqualified success: 80,183 people paid $1,789,238 to see the fight in person.[61] As an outstanding sports event, the fight left much to be desired; Dempsey weathered a mild attack in the second round and knocked Carpentier out in the fourth round. But as uneventful as the actual fighting was, the press reported on it as if it were the only news fit to print. Even a newspaper as traditionally conservative in its treatment of sports as the New York *Times* announced the result of the bout in three streamer headlines running all the way across its first page.[62] Nothing but information about the fight covered most of the first thirteen pages of the *Times.* An exception to this was a small article entitled, "Harding Ends War." The war was the same one Dempsey had sidestepped, but in the carnival mood which prevailed after the fight no one seemed interested in the war issue anymore. Dempsey had won. The American champion, albeit one with certain defects, had triumphed over the European champion. Public opinion, as reflected in the press, seemed satisfied.

In the wake of the Carpentier fray, Dempsey was once again placed in a pantheon reserved only for unblemished idols. The *Japan Times* wrote that Dempsey's name was far better known that Lloyd George's and thousands of boys would "rather be Dempsey ... than be the President of the United States or the greatest force in the world of finance, art, or letters."[63] Francis Hackett, writer for the *New Republic*, noted that Dempsey was not cruel, humiliating, or brutal: "He was simply superior."[64] Many writers echoed the same views, while still other journalists continued the adulation on a higher, symbolic level. P.W. Wilson, for example, wrote that too often men think only in terms of politics, theologies, and economic systems; yet Dempsey's victory declared to everyone that "it is, ultimately, the man who counts. His food, his muscles, his habit, his frame of mind, his morale, matter infinitely to the whole world."[65]

Of more interest than the praise for Dempsey was what the fight's result represented to American society. On one level, the ministers of America saw the fight, as Dr. John Roach Straton said, as clear proof that "we have relapsed into paganism."[66] A cross section of surveyed ministers generally agreed with Straton. But to others, the affair represented less a shift toward barbarism than an indication of the weakening of the power of the pulpit. According to the New Haven *Journal-Courier*, the masses were no longer content to follow blindly the moral precepts of the "intemperate guardians of other people's business," whose methods were "intemperate and insolent, overbearing and dictatorial."[67]

If the fight highlighted a conflict in the moral predilections of society, it certainly demonstrated a growing rift between the "highbrows" and "lowbrows." It has been illustrated that the rich and more educated people interested in boxing had been for Carpentier. From Heywood Broun in America to George Bernard Shaw in Europe, writers for the more selective magazines had gone to their thesauruses searching for better adjectives to describe Carpentier. Also, from the readiness of the public to forget the war issue, one suspects that among the literary inarticulate Dempsey always had strong support. By 1921, many people were beginning to question American involvement in the Great War. War idealism had been diminished by the Red Scare and race riots of 1919, and the Wilsonian rationale for war had been undermined by the League fight in America. Nowhere was the disillusionment by the masses more clearly portrayed than in the following editorial in the St. Louis *Post-Dispatch*:

The highbrows have had their day. They have wrangled over world peace and protection against future war for nearly three years, and they have accomplished neither. They have left no brain cell unagitated to resume the turning of the economic wheels, but in vain. Now, let us see what the lowbrows have done. In gate receipts alone they have shaken into circulation $1,600,000 from the pockets of people who have been holding back on the monopoly game. Of this, $400,000 is going into the Federal Treasury, where it will pay for a coat of paint and possi-

bly a big gun or two on one of our sorely needed new battleships
... A Dempsey-Carpentier fight in every state ... would put the
old doldrums on the blink.[68]

Thus the Dempsey-Carpentier bout was more than an athletic
contest between two men. It also became a platform for debates over
grave moral, social, and political issues, debates which were central to the
1920s.

Dempsey's victory over Carpentier ended the debate over his war
record. Free from this albatross, his popularity took a sharp turn upward.
Twice in 1923 he defended his title, and both fights received banner
treatment by the major American newspapers.[69] As a public hero,
Dempsey became a lucrative commodity. One Florida land firm paid
him $10,000 a day for shaking hands with prospective buyers. Falling into
the land craze himself, Dempsey claimed he was in on the "ground floor"
of a five million dollar land deal.[70] Yet if the 1923 bouts increased his
value as a public commodity, they also highlight different social themes
which span the 1920s.

Tommy Gibbons became the first of Dempsey's 1923 opponents.
In an actionless bout which lasted fifteen dreary rounds, Dempsey edged
out a victory. Dull though the actual fighting was, the match generated a
storm of controversy. The issue which precipitated the conflict was
money. Before the 1920s athletes had not been paid what the public
considered outrageous amounts of money for performing their particular
skill. For instance, when John L. Sullivan became the first heavyweight
champion by virtue of his 1892 defeat of Paddy Ryan, he was paid only five
thousand dollars.[71] In the 1920s however, the price went up. Sports became "big business," and no sport more so than boxing. Throughout the
1920s, the large purses Dempsey won caused discussion. According to a
San Francisco *Chronicle* editorialist, the money involved in the
Dempsey-Gibbons bout indicated that professional boxing had lost "all
sense of proportion."[72] To the New Haven *Journal-Courier*, the money
paid the champion was "a study of national degeneracy."[73] Even the
Christian Science Monitor, a newspaper which rarely devoted space to
sports coverage, noted that war veterans must "wonder at the national
temperament that leaves them to shift as best they may for a livelihood,
while giving $500,000 and unbounded adulation to a pugilist who carefully
avoided the trenches."[74]

While the money issue dominated the Gibbons affair, Dempsey's
second fight of 1923 raised the topic of nationalism. Once again, as in the
Carpentier fight, Dempsey was challenged by a foreigner; this time it was
the Argentinian, Luis Angel Firpo. After two rounds of furious action,
which saw Firpo knocked down eight times and Dempsey beaten out of the
ring, the champion saved his title by knocking his adversary out. But to
the news media, the fight was more than just a sensational display of

punching power. They transformed Dempsey's fistic victory into a victory for Americanism. Bruce Bliven, a writer for the *New Republic,* went to the fight to see the "Nordic race defend itself against the Latin ..."[75] More to the point was an editorial in the *Brooklyn Eagle.* "One shudders," the editorialist wrote, "to think of what might have happened to the Monroe Doctrine if Firpo had won. Today it is safe to say that South America has more respect for us than ever before. If Europe would only send over a first class challenger, Mr. Dempsey might do something to restore American prestige abroad."[76] The Dempsey corollary to the Monroe Doctrine may come as a surprise to diplomatic historians, but to an America concerned over its own image, Dempsey, both as a moral reflection and an international interpreter, was seen as a bold reaffirmation of Americanism.

After the Firpo bout of September 14, 1923, Dempsey rested. Not until three years later, September 23, 1926, would he defend his title again. In part, these were years of ballyhoo, meant for the titillation of the public. Newspapers, serious and sensational alike, were caught up in the process. The New York *Times* printed a challenge to Dempsey from Prince Mohammed Ali Ibrahim of Egypt. Ali's trainer, Blink McCloskey, said the prince had a blow called the "Pyramid punch" that "lands with the force of a falling pyramid and knocks a rival stiffer than a sphinx."[77] But these were also serious years, for a profound atmosphere of racism hung over the surface ballyhoo excitement. Harry Wills, the major heavyweight contender, constantly clamored for a title match, but because he was black he was refused the fight. Indeed, Dempsey's first public statement after he had destroyed Willard in 1919 was that he would not under any circumstances pay attention to a "Negro challenger."[78] True to his word, he never did. And, for the most part, the press and New York Boxing Commission never seriously tried to stage the fight.[79]

When official and public pressure did force Dempsey to fight again, he chose Gene Tunney. Literally and symbolically, this was a match of contrasts. Dempsey, the crude, wild-swinging mauler inside the ring, lived a life of action outside the ring. But always, he maintained his attachments with his followers. He joked and talked with them; he always seemed one of the "boys."[80] While he had his troubles—the draft issue, divorces, moral improprieties—the public always seemed to forgive him. Like the proverbial "bad little boy," Dempsey was viewed as basically good, no matter what wrong he did.

By contrast, Tunney was smooth inside the ring and socially polished outside the ropes. No draft issue clouded his past. An ex-marine, Tunney had not waited to be drafted to serve his country during the war.[81] And no personal scandals shaded his career. One observer wrote: "Tunney looks and acts clean. His private life ... has been above reproach ... Socially, Tunney is a charming, cultured gentleman ..."[82] To the press as a whole, no single person in sports better illustrated the virtue in American society than Tunney. As a New York *Times* editorialist wrote:

> Tunney should make an ideal heavyweight champion. He has a flawless record; he did his first fighting for his country, then he fought for himself. Of unblemished character, representing the highest ideals in American manhood, an example for the younger generation, modest, retiring, unassessing, well read and educated—he combines every desirable characteristic.[83]

Surely, then, the public would be delighted if Tunney defeated Dempsey.

Yet the lines are seldom this clearly drawn. Even in sports, which by their very nature lend themselves to black and white issues, the conflicts are not so tightly constructed. While on the surface Tunney seemed perfect to succeed Dempsey in capturing the public's imagination, the process was by no means that simple. For however ideal Tunney seemed, there was in his character a tragic flaw: he just did not seem truly American. To the masses, Tunney represented something as foreign as Carpentier. Tunney, who had lectured on Shakespeare before Professor Wendell Phelp's class at Yale, who went on walking trips in Europe with Thornton Wilder, who married a socially prominent woman, and who regarded the public with a lofty indifference, was certainly viewed as antiathletic, if not downright anti-American, by the masses.[84]

Tunney's tragic flaw was seen during the 1920s. Heywood Broun, writing for the *Nation*, noted that while Tunney was enormously popular with the "wise public which came to boxing matches on passes," he had "not touched the heart of America."[85] James J. Corbett, an ex-heavyweight champion who was unpopular in his own time as a titleholder, warned Tunney that if he did not show he was part of the "common people" he would never be popular.[86] But Tunney ignored all advice. He continued to speak in metaphors which only further alienated the public. Unlike Dempsey, whose crude manners and aggressive fighting style people could easily identify with, Tunney had always remained above the public's love.

The actual fight was never in doubt. Tunney, full of grace and polish, out-pointed Dempsey with little trouble.[87] Dempsey's career as heavyweight champion had ended. Yet even in defeat, he continued to express the sentiments which had made him a popular hero. Striking a humbly nationalistic pose, Dempsey said, "I have no alibis to offer. I lost to a good man, an American—a man who speaks the English language. I have no alibis."[88] This was the style of language the public loved to hear, and when it was gone boxing as a sport lost the fantastic popularity it had enjoyed from 1919 to 1926.

Dempsey's loss to Tunney signified an end to the Golden Age of boxing. It also marked the symbolic death of one of the greatest heroes of the 1920s. Neither Babe Ruth nor Bobby Jones commanded the press space that Dempsey did. But the question remains: What did Dempsey mean to or represent about the 1920s? It has been shown that the career of Jack Dempsey encompassed more than just his fights. Each fight became symbolically something larger. Each became a platform from which to debate issues central to the 1920s. War issues, race questions, cultural schisms, and nationalistic impulses all found their way into Dempsey's fights. No newspaper or magazine was above using some aspect of Dempsey's career to demonstrate symbolically some facet of a social, political, or economic issue.

More importantly, Dempsey, the hero, tells us something about the temperament of the 1920s. Roderick Nach, in *The Nervous Generation: American Thought 1917-1930*, wrote that "Ideas change with glacial slowness. A new attitude may appear and gain strength, but the older one does not automatically disappear."[89] This concept is of paramount importance in understanding the influence of Dempsey. While the 1920s may have seen something of what Frederick Lewis Allen called "the revolution in manners and morals," the old virtues were not stifled. When the masses wanted a hero, they chose a fighter who had been characterized as a possessor of the traditional mores, and not a fighter who symbolized the "lost generation." Just as the public showed support for the timeless American virtues by making Gene Stratton-Porter the preeminent popular novelist of the 1920s, they voiced their acceptance of the old American ways by their adherence to the Dempsey myth.[90]

• • •

Notes

1. *New York Times*, July 5, 1919, p.1.

2. John Lardner, *White Hopes and Other Tigers* (NY, 1951), pp. 58-59.

3. Nat Loubet, et al., *The 1973 Ring Boxing Encyclopedia and Record* (New York, 1973), pp. 86-87; Frederick Lewis Allen, *Only Yesterday: An Informal History of the 1920s* (New York, 1964), pp. 174-75. In the second Dempsey-Tunny bout alone some 145,000 paid over $2,600,000 to see the match and over 40,000,000 heard the fight over the radio.

4. Loubet, *Ring Record Book*, p. 81-82.

5. One finds occasional references such as that by Robert K. Murray, *Red Scare: A Study of National Hysteria, 1919-1920* (New York, 1964), p. 241, that "A growing public interest in post war sports ... helped take the nation's mind off bolshevism as attention drifted from the antics of Lusk and Palmer to those of Jack Dempsey and Babe Ruth."

6. Eldridge Cleaver, *Soul on Ice* (New York, 1968), p. 85.

7. "Carpentier: A Symbol," *The New Republic*, July 20, 1921, p. 206.

8. *Omaha Evening World-Herald*, July 1, 1910, p. 11.

9. John Higham, *Writing American History: Essays on Modern Scholarship* (Bloomington, 1972), p. 80.

10. Paul Meadows, "Some Notes on the Social Psychology of the Hero," *Southwestern Social Science Quarterly*, XXVI (1945), 239.

11. Ibid., 239.

12. Orrin E. Klapp, "Hero Worship in America," *American Sociological Review*, XIV (1949), 62. Klapp has written a great deal on this subject. The reader might consult other works by him which include Heroes, *Villains, and Fools: The Changing American Character* (Englewood Cliffs, NJ: 1962), pp. 95-124; Symbolic Leaders: *Public Dramas and Public Men* (Chicago, 1964), pp. 211-64; "Creation of Popular Heroes," *American Journal of Sociology*, LIV (1948), 135-41; "Heroes, Villains, and Fools, as Agent of Social Control," *American Sociological Review*, XIX (1954), 56-62; and "The Folk Hero," *Journal of American Folklore*, LVII (1949), 17-25.

13. Klapp, "Heroes, Villains, & Fools, as Agents of Social Control," p. 62.

14. Klapp, "Creation of Popular Heroes," p. 141.

15. Sidney Hook, *The Hero in History: A Study in Limitations and Possibility* (New York, 1943), Chapter 1; Klapp, "Creation of Popular Heroes," p. 139; Harry Edwards, "Sports and the Mass Media," in Marie M. Hart (ed.), *Sport in the Socio-Cultural Process* (Dubuque, IA, 1972), pp. 363-368; and Leonard Shuter, *The Jocks* (New York, 1969), p. 131.

16. Hook, *The Hero in History*, p. 10.

17. Edwards, "Sports and the Mass Media," *Sport in the Socio-Cultural Process*, p. 365.

18. *The Times* (London), July 2, 1921, p. 13.

19. It is interesting to note that the previous high point of boxing in the United States had occurred during the middle to late 1890s. Its zenith was reached at approximately the same time as the Spanish-American War, when Jim Jeffries won the title in 1899.

20. Thomas Foster, "Why Our Soldiers Learn to Box," *Outing*, May, 1918, pp. 114-16.

21. The single most important piece of boxing legislation was the Walker Law which went into effect on May 24, 1920. Under this New York State law, boxing was permitted. Bouts could be scheduled for up to fifteen rounds, and decisions could be given. The law also provided for a commission to be established to supervise the sport. The Walker Law has served as the pattern for world wide boxing since it was passed. For a history of New York boxing laws, see Loubet, *Ring Record Book*, p. 129.

22. "Dempsey and the Fat Sailor," *Boxing Illustrated and Boxing Encyclopedia* (New York: Ring Book Shop, 1964), p. 614.

24. The Dempsey-Willard bout has been clouded by controversy ever since the day of the fight. It was rumored shortly after the fight that Dempsey's gloves were "loaded." Dempsey's manager, Jack "Doc" Kearns, substantiated these claims in an article entitled "He Didn't Know the Gloves Were Loaded," *Sports Illustrated*, January 13, 1964, pp. 48-56. According to Kearns, he had bet $10,000 at ten to one odds that Dempsey would win the title fight in less than one round. In order to guarantee a victory, he had Dempsey's hands soaked in plaster of paris. The mere fact that Dempsey never again inflicted such a devastating battering to an opponent lends validity to Kearn's assertion. However, an article by John Hollis, "Were Dempsey's Fists Loaded in Toledo?" *Boxing Illustrated and Wrestling News*, May, 1964, pp. 10-24, reaches the opposite conclusion. Hollis applied the plaster of paris as Kearns allegedly had and found it simply would not dry.

25. *New York Times*, September 14, 1919, p. 6.

26. Klapp, "Creation of Popular Heroes," p. 136; Klapp, "Hero Worship in America," p. 55.

27. Ibid.

28. Klapp, "Creation of Popular Heroes," p. 135.

29. *New York Times*, July 5, 1919, p. 5.

30. Ibid., p. 2.

31. Miske died shortly after the bout but supposedly always thought well of Dempsey for giving him one last big payday. On his deathbed, Miske was reported to have gasped: "Tell Jack thanks. Tell him thanks from Bill." It is stories like this, read by thousands, which help to keep the Dempsey myth alive today. See Michael A. Glick, "Boxing's Tender Side," *Boxing Illustrated and Wrestling News*, December, 1958, pp. 34-35.

32. *New York Times*, September 7, 1920, p. 13.

33. John Betts, "Organized Sports in Industrial America," (unpublished Ph.D. dissertation, 1951), pp. 398-399. When Bellows died in 1925, he had already established himself as the greatest American artist of the ring. Introducing Georges Carpentier (1921) and Dempsey-Firpo (1923) successfully capture the dynamic impact of Dempsey and boxing.

34. "Jack Dempsey in Oil," *The Literary Digest*, August 18, 1923, p. 34.

35. *New York Herald Tribune*, June 5, 1924, p. 17; "Dempsey as a Movie Actor," *The Literary Digest*, June 21, 1924, pp. 61-63.

36. *New York Herald Tribune*, June 5, 1924, p. 17. For a review of Dempsey on the stage, see G.J. Nathan, "Dempsey as an Actor," *The American Mercury*, November 1928, pp. 377-78. Stressing the effeminacy of most professional actors, Nathan wrote that "Mr. Dempsey may not be much of an actor, but his worst enemy certainly cannot accuse him of belonging to the court of Titania."

37. "Carpentier, From Pit-Boy to Esthete of the 'Boxer,'" *The Literary Digest*, June 11, 1922, p. 34.

38. "Carpentier: A Symbol," *The New Republic*, pp. 206-07.

39. Ibid., p. 207.

40. "First Civilization vs. Sword Civilization," *The Living Age*, September 24, 1921, p. 774.

41. *New York Times*, February 28, 1920, p. 6.

42. Ibid., January 23, 1920, p. 14.

43. Ibid., January 26, 1920, p. 8.

44. "Did 'Psychic' Power Aid Brown When Carpentier Licked Beckett?" *The Literary Digest*, January 17, 1920, p. 127.

45. "Georges Carpentier—Gentleman, Athlete, and Connaisseur of the 'Boxe,'" ibid., April 17, 1920, p. 130; *New York Times*, June 10, 1921, p. 15.

46. "War-Record of Dempsey," *The Literary Digest*, February 14, 1920, p. 122.

47. Georges Carpentier-Gentleman, Athlete, and Connoisseur of the 'Boxe,'" *The Literary Digest*, pp. 130-36.

48. Ibid., p. 130.

49. Ibid., pp. 33-34.

50. Ibid., pp. 130-36; "Carpentier, From Pit-Boy to Esthete of the 'Box,'" ibid., p. 39. As a dancer Carpentier was said to be unsurpassed.

51. "Georges Carpentier-Gentleman, Athlete, and Connoisseur of the 'Boxe,'" ibid., p. 133.

52. For the views of the intellectuals who were interested in boxing, see Arnold Bennett, "The Great Prize Fight," *The Living Age*, January 24, 1920, pp. 124-17; Francis Hackett, "The Carpentier Fight: Bennett vs. Shaw," *The New Republic*, January 14, 1920, pp. 198-200; Francis Hackett, "Dempsey-Carpentier," ibid., July

13, 1921, pp. 185-87; Heywood Broun, "Mr. Dempsey's Five Foot Shelf," *The Bookman*, August 1921, pp. 521-24; "Boswell Takes Dr. Samuel Johnson to the Beckett-Carpentier Fight," *The Literary Digest*, January 17, 1920, pp. 127-28; and "Shaw called a 'Colossal Joke' as a Prize-Fight Reporter," ibid., April 17, 1920, pp. 146-48.

53. *New York Times*, January 14, 1920, p. 24; "War Record of Dempsey," *The Literary Digest*, p. 124.

54. *New York Times*, May 18, 1921, p. 14.

55. *The Times* (London), July 2, 1921, p. 13; *The Manchester Guardian*, July 2, 1921, p.8.

56. "First Civilization vs. Sword Civilization," The Living Age, pp. 773-74. The daily went on to say, "People greedily read every scrap of information, every prophecy and speculation, published regarding the coming fight, every detail of the biography of the contestants, their weight, physical condition, health, and programme of daily acts." From all indications this seems fairly accurate.

57. *The Japan Times*, July 2, 1921, p. 2.

58. Ibid., July 4, 1921, p. 4.

59. *New Orleans Times Picayune*, July 1, 1921, p. 13.

60. P.W. Wilson, "The Big Prize-Fight Psychologically Considered," *Current Opinion*, August 1921, pp. 172-75. Heywood Broun, "Mr. Dempsey's Five Foot Shelf." The Bookman, pp. 512,-24; "'Carbuncle' of Boyle's Thirty Acres," *The Literary Digest*, July 30, 1921, pp. 31-32.

61. Loubet, *Ring Record Book*, p. 86.

62. *New York Times*, July 3, 1921, p. 1; Allen, *Only Yesterday*, p. 174. *The Times* is by no means unique in this respect.

63. *The Japan Times*, July 4, 1921, p. 4.

64. Francis Hackett, *The New Republic*, p. 187.

65. P.W. Wilson, "The Big Prize-Fight Psychologically Considered," *Current Opinion*, August 1921, p. 175.

66. "'Carbuncle' of Boyle's Thirty Acres," *The Literary Digest*, p. 31.

67. Ibid., pp. 31-32.

68. *St. Louis Post-Dispatch*, July 2, 1921, p. 14.

69. See the July 5, 1923, and September 15, 1923, issues of the *New York Times*, *San Francisco Chronicle*, *New Orleans Times-Picayune*, *St. Louis Post-Dispatch*, and *New York Herald Tribune*.

70. *New York Times*, January 29, 1926, p. 24.

71. Loubet, *Ring Record Book*, p. 81.

72. *San Francisco Chronicle*, July 6, 1923, p. 22.

73. "Moralizing on the Million-Dollar Fight," *The Literary Digest*, October 6, 1923, p. 36.

74. Ibid., p. 35. These disputers over the sum of money an athlete should or should not receive illustrates an interesting paradox at work in the 1920's. Clearly, the increased amount of public attention and mass media coverage devoted to sporting events created a situation where athletes could gain exorbitant sums of money. By gaining so much money, the athlete then came under public and media attack because he seemed to threaten the moral posture (i.e., "sports sake") of sports. This paradox is certainly seen in Dempsey's career. See New York Times editorial "The Welfare of Boxing," September 8, 1922, p. 12; and "From Homer to Hearst," *The Outlook*, July 18, 1923, pp. 401-02.

75. Bruce Bliven, "Arc Lights and Blood: Ringside Notes at the Dempsey-Firpo Fight," *The New Republic*, September, 26, 1923, p. 125.

76. "'Big Business' of Prize Fighting," *The Literary Digest*, October 13, 1923, p. 62.

77. *New York Times*, March 4, 1924, p. 14.

78. Ibid., July 6, 1919, p. 17.

79. The issue of racism in boxing in the 1920s is a constant one; Wills from 1919 to 1926 was always the number one contender. But a full discussion of it is out of the range of the present paper. Suffice it to say, "they [Dempsey and Wills] never fought because Tex Richard refused to promote it." (Correspondence with Nat Fleisher, November 3, 1972.).

80. Fleisher, *Jack Dempsey*, pp. 149-60.

81. "Lieutenant Tunney, The Pride of the Marines," *The Literary Digest*, October 16, 1926, pp. 42-46.

82. Ibid., p. 44.

83. *New York Times*, Sept. 27, 1926, p. 18.

84. Allen, *Only Yesterday*, p. 175.

85. Heywood Broun, "It Seems to Heywood Broun," *The Nation*, August 8, 1928, p. 125.

86. "Corbett to Tunney on 'How to Win the Mob,'" *The Literary Digest*, January 14, p. 125.

87. *New York Times*, September 24, 1926, p. 1.

88. Ibid.

89. Roderick Nash, *The Nervous Generation: American Thought, 1917-1930* (Chicago: Rand McNally and Company, 1970), pp. 41-42.

90. Ibid., p. 137.

● ● ●

Suggestions for Further Reading:

Allen, Frederick Lewis, *Only Yesterday: An Informal History of the 1920s* (New York: Harper and Row, 1931).

Carter, Paul, *The Twenties in America* (New York: Crowell, 1968).

Danzig, Allison and Peter Brandwein, eds., *Sport's Golden Age: A Close-up of the Fabulous Twenties* (New York: Harper and Row, 1948).

Dempsey, Jack, *Round by Round: An Autobiography* (New York: McGraw Hill, 1940).

Farr, Finis, *Black Champion: The Life and Times of Jack Johnson* (New York: Scribner's, 1964).

Fleischer, Nat, *Jack Dempsey* (New Rochelle, NY: Arlington House, 1970).

Gallico, Paul, *The Golden People* (Garden City, NY: Doubleday, 1965).

Gilmore, Al-Tony, *Bad Nigger! The National Impact of Jack Johnson* (Pt. Washington, NY: Kennikat, 1975).

_____, "Jack Johnson: A Magnificent Black Anachronism of the Early Twentieth Century," *Journal of Social and Behavioral Sciences,* XIX (Winter, 1973), 35-43.

_____, "Jack Johnson and White Women: The National Impact, 1912-1913," *Journal of Negro History*, LVIII, 1 (January, 1973), 18-38.

_____, "Jack Johnson, the Man and His Times," *Journal of Popular Culture*, VI, 3 (Spring, 1973), 496-506.

Kearns, Jack "Doc" and Oscar Fraley, *The Million Dollar Gate* (New York: Macmillan, 1966).

Leuchtenburg, William E., *The Perils of Prosperity, 1914-1932* (Chicago: University of Chicago Press, 1958).

McCallum, John D., *The World Heavyweight Boxing Championship: A History* (Radnor, PA: Chilton, 1974).

Reising, Robert, "Jim Thorpe: Multi-Cultural Hero," *Indian Historian* VII, 4 (1974), 14-16.

Roberts, Randy, "Heavyweight Champion Jack Johnson: His Omaha Image, a Public Reaction Study," *Nebraska History*, LVII (Summer, 1976), 226-241.

_____, *Jack Dempsey: The Manassa Mauler* (Baton Rouge: L.S.U. Press, 1979).

_____, *Papa Jack: Jack Johnson and the Era of White Hopes* (New York: Free Press, 1983).

Weinberg, S. Kirson and Henry Arond, "The Occupational Culture of the Boxer," *American Journal of Sociology*, LVII (March, 1952), 460-469.

Weston, Stanley, *Heavyweight Champions from Sullivan to Ali* (New York: Ace, 1976).

THE BABE ON BALANCE

Marshall Smelser

"No other person outside public life," declares Marshall Smelser in the following assessment of Babe Ruth, "so stirred our imaginations and captured our affections." His magnificent talent and enthusiasm for the game, his zest for the good life, and his propitious arrival on the national scene just when baseball was struggling to regain its moral health after the Black Sox scandal of 1919 and to escape the low-scoring doldrums of the "scientific" game which had characterized play up until his time combined to account for Ruth's success and popularity.

Although the Babe played the game perhaps better than anyone before or since, his appeal transcended athletic achievement. His symbolic importance is as endearing as his playing record. He satisfied the psychological and social needs of a significant following who cheered his exploits both on and off the field. Like other athletes who flourished in the 1920s, Ruth served a compensatory cultural function. Having achieved fame and fortune through individual talent and effort that seemed to overcome an increasingly bureaucratic, systematic, and complicated world, Ruth revived visions of the American dream, celebrated the erosion of Victorian morality, and disdained notions of individual powerlessness. Through his example, he reflected a popular nostalgia for an imaginary America and offered an antidote to the longing and confusion that many had in an era of changing values and fading ideals.

A product of the mass media and the fickle world of entertainment, Ruth has faced the difficult task of sustaining public favor. Yet, he has survived the years and his biographers very well. The outpouring of works in the 1970s on the Babe's life and times indicate that he has lost none of his fascination and freshness. Smelser's portrait finds Ruth eminently placed in the right spot at the right time. He is also firmly ensconced in the annals of American sport and the folk heritage of the country.

Babe Ruth's success depended on his constitution and his temperament, but it also owed much to the accident of timing. If he had come to New York before the First World War he would have played with a weakly financed team much less able and popular than the Giants. He came to New York when the Yankees had rich, ambitious owners who were able to make the most of the interest he stirred. The result was a rising zest for public spectacles, and Ruth rose with the flood, in just the right place. From 1920 to 1932 there was a stormy excitement over baseball unknown before or since. The only rival idols of baseball heroes were college football players and, occasionally, boxers. A career like Ruth's is no longer possible. Today baseball has the lively competition of professional football, hockey, golf, and basketball, which split the popular interest. Imagine concentrating the popular feeling for the darlings of basketball, hockey, and football entirely on baseball heroes, and mostly on Babe Ruth. That's the way it was in the 1920s. Where Ruth stood was the center of the world of games. As the most cursory reading of the 1920 sports pages shows, his feat of hitting fifty-four home runs in 1920 was deliriously exciting.

No one was more persistently popular, not even Lindbergh. The press used hundreds of tons of extra newsprint to tell of Lindbergh, but the story ran out in a few years. Babe Ruth's story went on and on. He met an elemental need of the crowd. Every hero must have his human flaw which he shares with his followers. In Ruth it was hedonism, as exaggerated in folklore and fable. If he had been nothing more than an exceptional batter, he would have been respected, but he attracted more than respect. The public love of Ruth approached idolatry, and his reputed carnality was necessary to the folk-hero pattern. As Waite Hoyt said, he was "the kind of bad boy it is easy to forgive." He fit the public image of what a highly paid ballplayer *ought* to be, and, if he didn't really fit, the people wished to believe any legend that would shape the image. (They still do.) The combination of great skill on the field and a shared flaw off the field made him the most admired and theatrical man in the game.

He made money. Salaries, plus a bonus in the early twenties, and a percentage of club exhibition games paid him about a million dollars. World Series shares and barnstorming profits made him perhaps another half million. Many kinds of what we might call celebrity income also brought in about a half million. In real purchasing power, the only athletic heroes who have done better are a few heavyweight boxing champions and Pele, the Brazilian soccer player.

It is hard to think of him as doing anything else with his life. If he could have started earlier in golf, say as a caddie, he might have made as much as twenty-five thousand dollars a year, which was a high annual income for a golf professional in his time. With his nearly perfect physical coordination, he could no doubt have become a mechanically excellent pianist, but he showed no artistic tastes. Boxing had no money-ceiling at the time, but the company and the game itself were dangerous, and he did not have the kind of killer spirit necessary. Football was not then profitable. It had to be baseball.

People like to think he would have played even better if he were playing today, but the only advantage today's batters have is that American League fences, according to a calculation suggested by Cleveland Amory, are closer, on the average, by about twenty-four feet. This advantage is offset by all-night flying, less regular hours, the creation of the specialized relief pitcher, and the inferiority of the lighting for night games. Furthermore, Ruth didn't have to compete with blacks.

Ruth's last photographs have made him seem a freak carved out of blubber with no ability except to hit the ball a long way. Red Smith said what most expert witnesses felt: "The truth is that he was the complete ball player, certainly one of the greatest and maybe the one best of all time." Ruth seems to have been tailored to the game. We can list very few serious rivals for the adjective "best." Smith's word "complete" is the key word. Ruth could have been in the big leagues a long time at every position except second base, shortstop, and third base, positions in which left-handed throwers are handicapped. For example, only two pitchers in the Hall of Fame (Whitey Ford and Lefty Grove) have better won-lost percentages than Ruth's. His many-sidedness was so dazzling that if it were supported only by oral tradition, apart from baseball's great heap of numbers called statistics, young people would snicker at the Ruth stories of their elders. Every art form has its greatest practitioner. Every art form also has able men who say there is *one* way to perform (the one way changes from time to time) and set down the rules. In each case the greatest practitioner first excelled according to the rules, then threw them away and soared higher. Ruth pitched conventionally, and as peer of the best, in 1915, 1916, and 1917, but found one position two confining. He went on to prove he could do almost everything else better than almost everybody else. The collaboration of Ed Barrow and Babe Ruth in converting a pitcher to a master of the whole game was the most influential single act in baseball history since the decision to pitch overhand instead of underhand.

To rate one player as the best is, of course, to place a high value on opinion. True, the pitching strategy of managers in Ruth's day differed from today's, and for the worse. But we can fairly contrast him with his contemporaries. After 1919, while in his prime, he was incomparable. There is no doubt at all that he was the best in his own time.

Ty Cobb's name naturally comes to mind, but Ruth could have done anything Cobb did, if he chose to do it, except steal as many bases. Branch Rickey, perhaps baseball's only true intellectual, saw Ruth as "a rational conservative in play as compared to Cobb." Cobb would often risk games in order to shine, but Ruth never. Ruth's risks were risks to snatch victory. We don't much dwell on Ruth as man thinking, but thinking is not some kind of juggler's trick or a special exercise of the consciously literate. A man thinking is a man completely attending to something he is doing. In the ball game (although almost nowhere else) Ruth qualified as Homo sapiens.

He was, even more, an instinctive player. The leaping spirit of life that animated Ruth's play can solve many a game puzzle which reason is too slow to solve.

Hercules, the Greek patron of athletes, was usually pictured as a man carrying a club. Whether civilized man is man the tool-user, or man the time-keeper, or man the fuel-burner (as anthropologists debate) the oldest graphic symbol of civilization is said to be the club-carrying man. That is what Ruth was. Despite his pitching and fielding records, we remember him as the man with the club, primitive but successful, the fundamental man who was victor over everything. Like Hercules, he satisfied the feeling of the people of his time that there was practically nothing a man couldn't do if he was strong enough and had a big enough stick.

There is an old saw that says, "You can't win 'em all." Babe Ruth at bat seemed to be asking, "Why not?"

> Ruth filled the parks by developing the home run into a hit of exciting elegance. For almost two decades he battered fences with such regularity that baseball's basic structure was eventually pounded into a different shape. —Lee Allen

The explosive popularity of Babe Ruth in 1919 and 1920 marked the division between quite different styles of play. The characteristic elements of the earlier style were the bunt, the hit-and-run play, and the stolen base. In 1911 the total of stolen bases in both leagues was 3,394; in 1951 it was 863. The new idea was to clutter the bases with runners who waited for a long hit to bring them home in a group. But not only batting and running changed. Pitchers had to work more carefully, pitching to alleged weaknesses, preferring to walk batters rather than to chance the home run.

The earlier game was consciously dedicated to the nineteenth-century god Science. To bunt, to steal, to hit-and-run were explicitly called "scientific" baseball in the first decade of this century, by which time the religion of Science had trickled down to the popular culture. Babe Ruth, the iconoclast, showed the fans they need not believe in the old god—that baseball was for fun, not for a moral duty.

Ruth and those who tried to play as he played prompted changes in the rules, equipment, and strategy. If one Ruth could fill a park, wouldn't sixteen Ruths fill sixteen parks? The ball became livelier and the pitcher was forbidden to spit on it. Even welterweight infielders now had bats with heavy barrels and thin handles. The successors of those pitchers who were kins of diamonds from 1900 to 1920 faced the painful fact that slight .220 hitters could wreck winning games in late innings by swinging for the fences.

The change was not universally welcomed. For those who liked baseball as a game played with a sphere and a cylinder, blending the sport of gymnastics with geometry, it made the game much too dependent on strength. The new game has also somewhat lowered the standard of outfield play, since almost none of the annual three thousand home runs requires any response on the field. But the people, by buying tickets in greater proportion, showed they liked what had happened. It is still true that an advertised duel between two leading pitchers may sell an extra ten thousand tickets. Nevertheless, a 1—0 loss for the home team, pitched by a pair of journeymen, will please the crowd less than a 16-15 win.

You can't keep Ty Cobb's name out of this kind of discussion. It is only fair to the intelligent, flexible, and neurotic Cobb to say that if he had first appeared in 1925 instead of 1905, he would have been as great a player, but a different kind.

As it was, the earlier game was the Cobb game; the later was the Ruth game. Cobb hit roughly as many home runs as Ruth stole bases, which is the simple formula of the change. Their value to their teams, on the scoreboard, was about equal. Cobb was worth 170 runs per season, Ruth 167 (based on runs scored, plus runs batted in, minus home runs, divided by seasons of play). But Cobb did his work coldly and craftily while Ruth played loosely and joyously, and the happy big bang sold a lot more tickets than Cobb's foxiness did. Ruth was the first man who seemed capable of breaking up the ball game every day he played. "Did he hit one today?" became a national household question.

We often read that Babe Ruth "saved baseball" at the time of the 1919 Black Sox scandal (exposed in 1920) by reviving interest in the game. That is not quite accurate. His twenty-nine home runs of 1919 and his fifty-four of 1920 eclipsed the scandal, blocked it out of the minds of the *Volk*, so that the miscreants got about a tenth of the attention they would have had in, say, 1910. What he did for baseball was to enliven it so that the trend of attendance was reversed. From 1910 to 1918 baseball attendance did not increase as rapidly as the population. From 1919 to 1930 attendance increased at a much greater rate than did the population. Until we know some other cause we may credit the Ruth game with turning the figures around.

Despite his relatively high salaries, Ruth was a bargain for the Yankees. At his peak he was worth from a third of a million to half a million dollars to franchise. To baseball as an industry, his value was simply incalculable. We can only say that every club benefited from the greater popularity of the game. His presence with the Yankees, according to their ablest scout, Paul Krichell, also had a good deal to do with the success of the Yankees in winning twenty-two pennants after Ruth left the team.   In the days when the recruiting of beginners was an auction and not a kind of lottery, the Yankees found it easier to sign promising rookies because they all wanted to be Yankees. The American League profited in the same way. By outdrawing the National League, every American League club was better off, and therefore better able to outbid National League rivals for young talent. (This advantage lasted until the National League earned the gratitude of blacks by breaking down the skin-color barrier).

Babe Ruth is better remembered than his contemporary presidents Harding, Coolidge, Hoover, better than his contemporary ethical hero Lindbergh, better than the foxy hero Cobb. He needs no rescue from oblivion. Proofs of his lasting fame are everywhere, as a few instances will show:

—An organized baseball program for boys too old for Little League and too young for American Legion junior baseball, called the Little Bigger League, changed its name in 1953 to the Babe Ruth League and, with Claire Ruth's help, has been flourishing ever since.

—As of this writing, the city of Baltimore is renovating Pius Shamberger's house, where George Ruth was born and lived for a few days, in order to make it a Babe Ruth shrine.

—The National Commemorative Society, which commissions souvenir silver medals, polled its members in 1968, asking whose memory should be perpetuated on the 1969 medal. Babe Ruth won over Alexander Hamilton by a score of 760 to 724.

—*Der Sport Brockhaus; alles vom Sport von A-Z* (Wiesbaden, 1971) gave Ruth seven lines (with three errors of fact) and a portrait.

—In the part of Israel's "youth woodland" called the "freedom forest for Soviet Jewry," an ex-New Yorker named Jeff Shaya planted a tree in 1972 to memorialize Babe Ruth.

This list could be much longer.

Another kind of evidence is the interest of collectors. Dr. Helen Cripe of the American Antiquarian Society, studying the public sales of Americana, found in the catalogs of well-known dealers seventeen pieces of Ruthiana listed in the years 1963-1973, at prices from $6.50 to $250.00. Advertisements in the *Antique Trader* (Summer 1973) give us a relative evaluation: three Mickey Mouse watches of 1931, from $95 to $135, and one Babe Ruth watch at $110.

Babe Ruth's fame is grounded on firm achievement. A baseball player can't hide mistakes or clumsiness; he stands alone and naked. There is no way to build up an ordinary player artificially into a great player for very long. A few hot dogs become well known, but their days of true popularity are few. Ruth was even more than a great player, he was a fold hero. He didn't have all the qualities Thomas Carlyle insisted a hero must have (nor has Mickey Mouse), but he still gets from ordinary people most of the homage Carlyle said was due a hero.

His fame will last. Once a living legend persists from the first generation into the third generation, that legend is secure and durable. Captain John Smith made it; John Rolfe is rarely spoken of. Abraham Lincoln is remembered; Douglas is recalled, if ever, only as Lincoln's foil. Babe Ruth's name draws crowds of small boys to the Ruth exhibit at Cooperstown. Do many small boys beg to visit Lindbergh's trophies in St. Louis or Grant's tomb in New York?

> A man may be very imperfect and yet worth a good deal.
> —Anthony Trollope, *Framley Parsonage*

Babe Ruth could not know the real world as obscure people know it. After living his formative years in a kind of monastery for boys, he leaped into a heroic place as a winner on winning teams. He never saw anything anonymously; it was all shown to him from where he stood on his pedestal. The ordinary person's world, how it worked, what it looked like, what it did to people, he couldn't know. Which may explain his fellow feeling for people institutionalized in artificial worlds—orphanages, hospitals, prisons.

He became a normal person by working to be normal. It was a hard struggle for him to become an acceptable member of society, partly because of his physical endowment. His appetites were strong, and his muscular urges even stronger. Driven by his make-up to satisfy his gut and to use his muscles more than he used his mental powers, he was initially out of balance. With effort he became what we call normal by the age of thirty. If he had had less human sympathy and even greater physical strength, he might have been in a state of permanent emotional disturbance. But his generosity and affections were as large as his hungers and his need to use his muscles.

It is rather sad that he never learned how typical a man he was. A reading of his memoirs and a study of his behavior raise the suspicion that he thought of himself as a kind of freak. Yet in every American cigar store, pool hall, barber shop, bar and grill, during his glory times, were specimens much like him—lacking only the ability to play baseball well.

Ruth had all of our faults, yet had the material success most Americans would like to have. Never did he try to be anything he was not; he never spoke on a subject he was unqualified to speak on, expect in reply to interviewers' questions, and rarely even then. The ballplayer was larger than the man. His mind was empty of practically everything but baseball, and packed tight with baseball. He never said a banal thing about baseball except in situations contrived by press agents, where he echoed the puritan bosh about the uplifting gifts of sport—platitudes he had heard others use, *pro forma*, with apparent success. Except when cornered in that way, he was intellectually honest.

Did his manner of life hurt his play? The matter of keeping in shape for baseball has in it a deal of superstition. Inborn ability to make catlike movements is far more important than precise weight. Only in long games and double-headers does overweight take its price. He may have neglected to keep in condition, but that wasn't what killed him. Up to the age of thirty he tried hard to support the deathless belief of many, that pleasure is happiness. Stories of the sins of popular heroes certainly grasp the attention of readers; so much has been written about Ruth's very ordinary and rather tiresome hedonism (but never with names, places, dates) that one is convinced there must be a real need to believe him a glutton who played best with a hangover. It reduces him to a smaller moral size so that some people can feel superior in some way to the otherwise titanic figure. And, as John McCabe well noted in his life of George M. Cohan, America sees itself as "Peck's Bad Boy," rough and hard to rule but instinctively doing good because it knows what is right. Ruth *had* to be a bad boy to be the paramount American. As Tristam Coffin said, "The hero must have a bit of the fool in him."

The record contradicts Ruth's reputation for self-destructive gluttony. As of 1972, only sixty-one out of ten thousand ballplayers had played twenty full seasons in the major leagues. Ruth was one who played twenty full seasons, and parts of two others. Whatever he did, it didn't destroy him as a player or a person.

Babe Ruth was driven by ambition and love. The ambition was to be the most successful baseball player, and the standard of success was the salary. Having money, he saw no reason not to enjoy it. He was driven by love in the same sense of an urge to do good, which he saw in two ways—as being kind to the helpless and as not hurting people on purpose. He was good at both. The home runs and the dollars are famous, but we overlook the absence of permanent enemies and the number of people who knew him well and loved him.

With most professional athletes, play is work. With Ruth, play was play. And it was his life. Was his life trivial? Because the Greeks taught us that what is universally popular is literally vulgar and ignoble, we think the business leader, the statesman, and the soldier are really living, while the athlete is wasting his and our time. (Euripides, for one, was very rough on athletes on this point; he had competing theaters to fill.) But there is a certain nobility in uniting mind and body in acts that need their perfect harmony. There is no need to apologize for athletes. The body is disorganized stimuli, gnawing hungers, and some unsystematic goals. The athlete makes it over into something controlled and directed toward its own excellence. If the mind merely lives in the body as a fish lives in a bowl, it would be folly to spend much time and effort to perfect the bowl.

But man is mind and body in one, and the great athlete is a complete man who has found the limits of adventure within the bounds of the rules of his kind of play. That is not trivial.

Only in constant action was his constant certainty found. He will throw a longer shadow as time recedes. —John Cornford, *A Memoir*

Babe Ruth lived only fifty-three years, but not all shortened lives are unfinished lives. Some are well rounded off, and end at a proper time. Since we have no reason to think he could have been a successful manager, and he had no other serious interest than baseball, we may say his was a finished, complete life. He was born at precisely the right time; it is hard to see how he could have been eminent if born earlier, or unique if born later. In the judgment of the people, no ballplayer has succeeded him. More than that, all others have diminished while he has grown. At the first election to the Hall of Fame in 1936, he ranked third. At mid-century, the Associated Press poll ranked him first over Cobb as the greatest ballplayer int he previous fifty years. In 1969, the centennial year of professional baseball, the Baseball Writers Association of America and the baseball broadcasters voted him the best player in the history of the game. They were nearly all strangers to him personally. Somehow that fact seems to add credibility to Babe Ruth's history; one feels like saying it really *did* happen.

A puzzled dramatic critic, in 1948, asked Babe Ruth's close friend, the sportswriter Dan Daniel, why Ruth should have a funeral unlike any before in New York (or, one may add, since) and more obituary space than any New Yorker ever had, more memorializing than proposed for presidents, or scientists, or warriors. "Why all this? What did this man Ruth do? What did he have, to merit this?"

To answer, a generation later: he is our Hercules, our Samson, Beowulf, Siegfried. No other person outside public life so stirred our imaginations and captured our affections.

• • •

Suggestions for Further Reading:

Asinof, Eliot, *Eight Men Out: The Black Sox and the 1919 World Series* (New York: Holt, Rinehard and Winston, 1963).
Creamer, Robert W. *Babe: The Legend Comes to Life* (New York: Simon and Schuster, 1974).

Crepeau, Richard C. *Baseball: America's Diamond Mind, 1919-1941* (Orlando: University Presses of Florida, 1980).

Jable, J. Thomas, "Sunday Sport Comes to Pennsylvania: Professional Baseball and Football Triumph Over the Commonwealth's Archaic Blue Laws, 1919-1933," *Research Quarterly*, XLVII (October, 1976), 357-365.

Lucas, John A., "The Unholy Experiment—Professional Baseball's Struggle Against Pennsylvania's Sunday Blue Laws, 1926-1934," *Pennsylvania History*, XXXVIII, 2 (April, 1971), 163-175.

Luhrs, Victor, *The Great Baseball Mystery* (New York: Barnes, 1966).

McGuire, Bonnie, "Babe Ruth," *New York Folklore Quarterly*, I, 1&2 (1975), 97-107.

Meany, Tom, *Babe Ruth* (New York: 1947).

Ruth, Babe and Bob Considine, *The Babe Ruth Story* (New York: Scholastic Books, 1969).

Ruth, Claire Hodgson and Bill Slocum, *The Babe and I* (Englewood Cliffs, NJ: Prentice-Hall, 1959).

Smelser, Marshall, *The Life That Ruth Built* (New York: Quadrangle, 1975).

Smith, Dean, "The Black Sox Scandal," *American History Illustrated*, XI (January, 1977), 16-24.

Smith, Robert, *Babe Ruth's America* (New York: Crowell, 1974).

Sobol, Ken, *Babe Ruth and the American Dream* (New York: Ballantine, 1974).

Wagenheim, Ken, *Babe Ruth: His Life and Legend* (New York: Praeger, 1974).

MULTIFARIOUS HERO:
JOE LOUIS, AMERICAN SOCIETY
AND RACE RELATIONS
DURING WORLD CRISIS, 1935-1945

Dominic J. Capeci, Jr. & Martha Wilkerson

The interaction between sport and society can be marked in the development and appeal of certain sports, values ascribed to them, and uses made of them. As we have seen with Jack Dempsey and Babe Ruth, it can also be measured in the careers of individual sports figures. Throughout the 1930s and World War II years, no American sport personality exemplified this relationship more than Joe Louis and none—perhaps before or since—had so many roles assigned to him in representing the needs of a society in crisis at home and abroad.

Louis rescued boxing form a period of little public interest and an undistinguished line of heavyweight champions following Gene Tunney's retirement in 1928. His rematch with German champion Max Schmeling in 1938 thrust Louis into the role of standardbearer of freedom *vs.* fascism in a fight that symbolized the international and interracial tensions of the day. Unlike Jack Johnson, the controversial black heavyweight titlist during the Progressive era, the "Brown Bomber" presented a non-threatening image to whites and gained their respect as "a credit to his race." For black Americans, Louis was a source of inspiration and hope, a hero who had persevered and triumphed.

In this article, Dominic Capeci and Martha Wilkerson explore the "multifarious" dimensions of Louis' heroic stature. They find it rooted in the diverse needs of the society which embraced him and the transcendent quality of his own appeal. "More hero than leader, defining no ideology, presenting no strategy and organizing no constituency," Louis combined enormous ring skill, a capacity for personal growth, and a significant amount of ambiguity to become the people's choice.

        In an effort to interpret race relations during the 1930s and 1940s,
historians have tussled with the interaction of the individual and society.
Some have focused on leaders, others on organizations and events; all
have demonstrated stirrings of change in the depression decade and, especially, the war years.[1] Yet few have studied heroes, those who cast light
on how citizens perceive "the essence of themselves" and on the social
milieu in which they live.[2] More than any other hero, heavyweight boxer
Joe Louis loomed large from 1934 to 1945, a time when Afro-Americans
encountered severe hardships, challenged racial mores, and laid foundations for future advances. Amidst both the hostile racism and reform
spirit of the Great Depression, he exemplified black perseverance: God,
wrote novelist Ernest Gaines, sent Joe to lift "the colored people's heart."[3]
More surprising, he emerged an American hero in the Second World War
because of the dramatic impact of Nazism on racial attitudes. In each
period, he and his admirers inspired, nurtured and reinforced one
another, resulting in his playing several, sometimes contradictory—indeed, multifarious—roles. As a black man in a racist
environment, his remarkable transition from race champion to national
idol signaled the interplay of the individual, society, and changing times:
as much as any leader, organization or event, his experience provides
insights into this watershed period of race relations.

        Born May 13, 1914, the son of sharecroppers Lily Reese and
Munrow Barrow, Louis grew up near Lafayette, Alabama with his seven
brothers and sisters.[4] He was happy despite his father's early separation
from the family and the confines of segregation. After his family migrated
to Detroit in 1926, he engaged in high jinks and street fights but never ran
afoul of the law. Introduced to boxing by a friend in 1932, he fell in love
with the sport, the environment and, most of all, the thoughts of money
and respect that came to those in the ghetto who hit hard and moved
quick. He turned professional by his twentieth birthday.

        Louis was enormously influenced by a handful of people. Earthly
and religious, his mother taught him to "trust in God, work hard and hope
for the best;" she said "a good name" was "better than money" and encouraged him to be somebody.[5] The aspiring, courageous and decent
lives that she and her second husband, Pat Brooks, lived impressed young
Louis. Managers John Roxborough and Julien Black echoed this message
of black dignity. Aware of the resentment triggered by Jack Johnson, the
first black heavyweight champion (who challenged racial mores and fled
conviction for violating the Mann Act), they instructed Louis in clean living and sportsmanlike conduct; Jack Blackburn, Louis' trainer and father-
like confidant, constantly berated "that fool nigger with his white woman,
acting like he owned the world."[6] Marva Trotter, whom Louis married in
1935, also reinforced his drive for excellence. Black and supportive, all
assisted Louis through his early life, a time of "increased vulnerability and
heightened potential."[7]

Between his initiation as a professional boxer in 1934 and his rematch with Max Schmeling in 1938, Louis captured the imagination of blacks everywhere. In the throes of economic crisis, when white citizens displayed racial intolerance, when white leaders approached civil rights with "political calculus" and when white liberals, North and South, ignored society's deep-seated, institutionalized anti-black attitude, Louis appeared messianic; as black leadership became more aggressive and black masses more aware, he dramatized their struggle between good and evil."[8] After he defeated Primo Carnera in 1935, for example, Harlem residents poured through the streets "shouting, clapping, laughing, and even crying."[9] Given black opposition to Mussolini's invasion of Ethiopia, they celebrated more than a boxing match. Louis seemed invincible in the ring, recording thirty-five wins, twenty-nine knockouts and one loss to Schmeling in 1936 before becoming champion the following year.[10] Graceful, quick and powerful at 6' 1 1/2", 200 pounds, he annihilated all comers, permitting admirers vicarious victories, "even dreams of vengeance," over white society.[11] As significantly, he seemed both Superman and Little Man, greater than his supporters yet acceptable to them; he challenged stereotypes, instilled hope and provided models for racial advancement.[12] Galahad-like, fighting clean and complimenting opponents, he enhanced black respectability; inarticulate and untutored, having stammered as a youth and never advancing beyond sixth grade, he appealed to those—waifs and highbrows alike—who understood action as eloquence and poise as bearing. Whether fighting in the ring or starring in "The Spirit of Youth," a thinly veiled biographic film about himself, he portrayed "black ambition without blundering into fantasy."[13] To Maya Angelou growing up in rural Arkansas, he proved that "we were the strongest people in the world."[14]

Despite sketchy evidence that segments of upper class black society played down his achievements during the mid 1930s, the overwhelming majority of blacks identified with Louis.[15] Below the Mason-Dixon line sharecroppers gathered at general stores or in the yards of white neighbors to hear the broadcast of Louis' fights.[16] They honored him with letters and song, as did Florida stevedores who celebrated his defeat of James Braddock:

Joe Louis hit him so hard he turn roun and roun
He thought he was Alabama bound, Ah, Ah[17]

Slum-locked welfare recipients helped fill Comiskey Park for that championship fight, while most residents of Chicago's South Side, Detroit's Paradise Valley and New York's Harlem huddled in small groups about their radios before reveling in the streets victoriously.[18] Elites, too, cheered Louis. Lena Horne noted that Louis "carried so many of our hopes," while Charles C. Diggs, Michigan State Senator from Detroit, convinced legislative colleagues to officially congratulate the new champion for serving as "an example and inspiration to American youth."[19]

Louis genuinely related to all segments of Black America. He always remembered his rural, southern roots. He ate blackeyed peas superstitiously on fight day and he gave money to Alabama 'relatives' who appeared on his mother's doorstep in Detroit.[20] Northern blacks knew that Louis roamed the streets of Detroit's eastside and worked at Ford Motor Company, just as they had done there or in similar settings. Perhaps most endearing, Louis organized jobless pals into the Brown Bomber Softball Team and donated to the community chest. Humble origins aside, Louis hobnobbed with celebrities. He became the darling of entertainers like Bill "Bo Jangles" Robinson, who introduced him to Hollywood. Louis meshed well with all blacks because they worshipped him for his feats and, as pointedly, for his divine mettle. In the poetry of Langston Hughes:

> Joe has sense enough to know
> He is a god
> So many gods don't know.[21]

Yet Louis enamored few whites before the mid 1930s, as racism continued relatively unabetted throughout the depression. In hometown Detroit, for instance, whites barred blacks from jobs and housing and, through the Klan-like Black Legionaires, terrorized them.[22] Occasionally, writers for publications ranging from the *New York Times* to the *Literary Digest* questioned Louis' intelligence, ridiculed his speech or stereotyped him as "kinky-haired, thick-lipped," "shuffling,"[23] If many whites "stored up" criticism "for Joe," as an NAACP official suspected, white elites embraced him.[24] Small in number, news-hungry celebrities were drawn by his fame and vote-seeking politicians by his popularity among blacks.[25] Intellectuals and liberals, who challenged white supremacy on the basis of overwhelming scientific research and fought for reform primarily along economic lines (thereby aiding blacks without confronting larger society's racist beliefs), found in Louis a powerful but unthreatening symbol of black excellence and interracial unity: "Isn't Joe Louis wonderful?" marveled author Carl Van Vechten.[26] Certainly a handful of the champion's personal friends thought so, including Joe Dimaggio and Ed Sullivan.

Inside the ring, racial attitudes began to shift. Louis' handlers knew that prejudice permeated boxing as white fighters and investors, ever mindful of Jack Johnson, denied black contenders a chance for the heavyweight title. Indeed, the color line that Jack Dempsey and promoter Tex Richard had drawn from 1919 to 1926 carried into the next decade.[27] By that time, however, boxing had fallen into disrepute, marred by scandal, ignoble champions and undesirable gunmen. Roxborough and Black recognized Louis' talent and the opportunity for personal gain and social change in this atmosphere, providing they could avoid scandal and bury the memory of Johnson. They established rules of public behavior for Louis and, in 1935, contracted with white promoter Mike Jacobs. Shrewdly, he scheduled the Carnera bout in Yankee Stadium, which exposed Louis to a known opponent in all important New York City and challenged the Madison Square Garden impresarios who ignored black fighters. The ring announcer—himself aware of the fight's social significance—reminded spectators of democratic tenets and sportsmanlike conduct.[28] For his exemplary behavior and victories over Carnera and thirteen other heavyweights that year, Louis became *Ring Magazine's* "Boxer of the Year" and the Associated Press' "Athlete of the Year," even rank-and-file white boxing fans and southern white journalists considered this 'well-behaved' 'good nigger' as 'the savior of a dying sport.'"[29]

Publicly Louis embodied the Galahad image promoted by his handlers. He brought dignity to the race, but he did not comprehend fully the plight of black people. Before the Carnera fight, when blacks envisioned him a savior capable of humiliating the symbol of Mussolini's Ethiopian invasion, Louis heard the name of Back-to-Africa advocate Marcus Garvey for the first time.[30] Rather than serve as a race symbol, however, he desired to make money and party "with pretty girls." He devastated Carnera and four other opponents; he became cocky and out of shape, losing the first Schmeling fight by a knockout. Crestfallen and disturbed that blacks took his defeat to Hitler's henchman personally, Louis returned home to nurse his pride and his wounds.

Only twenty-four when winning the title, he understandably failed to grasp his relationship with black society. Publicly the paragon, privately he played with the Brown Bombers against the approval of his managers who feared possible injury; he engaged in numerous sexual encounters and love affairs, sometimes with white women.[31] He received double messages from Roxborough and Black, who directed him never to be photographed with white ladies, but said nothing about dating them. Perhaps he emulated Roxborough, who acted legitimate publicly while operating numbers privately; success drew approval despite black awareness of shady activities.[32] Outwardly, Louis became the person his mother desired and the image his handlers forged.[33]

Louis' personal growth accompanied the national shift from depression to war. Between 1937 and 1941, particularly as a result of the Schmeling rematch, he and Afro-Americans gained confidence. They both smarted over the first bout, which cast doubt on his title and their manhood. In addition, the rise of Hitler abroad placed discrimination at home in bold relief and stimulated black protest for civil rights.[34] Nazism also revealed racism as "an unmitigated evil," forcing white society to question its own moral integrity.[35] In this milieu, black and white citizens alike placed the second Louis-Schmeling fight in an international, racial context: American democracy v. Arian supremacy; even President Franklin D. Roosevelt sent for Louis, felt his biceps and reminded: "Joe, we're depending on those muscles for America."[36] On June 22, 1938, seventy-thousand partisan fans filled Yankee Stadium to see the fight, while many, many more listened to it on the radio. When Louis smashed Schmeling to the canvas four times amidst forty-one blows, delivering the K.O. at 2:04 of round one, celebrations occurred everywhere.[37]

The victory greatly affected Louis, who became more sure of himself and at ease with others. He fully understood, possibly for the first time, his meaning for and commitment to black society. No longer isolated, he saw beyond family, friends, and personal pride a broader version of people and things black; "If I every do anything to disgrace my race," he remarked later, "I hope to die."[38] Louis' triumph also appealed to white society's patriotism and need, outside of the South, to appear racially moral in the face of its Nazi-like values.[39] As an integrative force, he seemed capable of bringing the races together along commonly held ideals and against common enemies without challenging basic conditions of black life. In fact, sixty-four percent of all radio owners in the nation listened to the rematch—a figure only exceeded in this internationally tense period by two presidential broadcasts.[40]

Louis' mass appeal spread in 1939 and 1940, bringing him greater recognition. He drew honors from *Ring Magazine*—"Boxer of the Year" for the third time in six years—and the Schomburg Collection of the New York Public Library and the Association for the Study of Negro Life and History for improving race relations.[41] Aware of his phenomenal popularity, particularly among blacks and white liberals, political brokers sought his support. In the hotly contested presidential campaign of 1940, Roosevelt's advisers shared NAACP spokesman Walter F. White's belief that northern black voters could decide the election.[42] Hence, they invited Louis to "thank the President for increasing Negro participation in defense" and "to offer his own services."[43] Such might parry criticism of Roosevelt seeking a third term, appeals by challenger Wendell Willkie for black ballots and pressure by black leaders for desegregation in the armed services and defense industries.

Nevertheless presidential aids sensed potential "dangers" and cancelled the Roosevelt-Louis meeting.[44] Doubtless the dangers consisted of John Roxborough and his brother, Charles, a prominent Michigan figure in the Republican Party, who persuaded (more likely instructed) Louis to be "in Willkie's corner."[45] During the crucial, closing days of the campaign, Republicans used him as Democrats had hoped to. He stumped in Chicago, St. Louis and New York, noting Roosevelt's failure to support an anti-lynching bill or get blacks off the WPA rolls; he predicted Willkie would "win by a knockout" and "help my people."[46] One concerned Democrat suggested a broadcast by vocalist Marian Anderson "to offset Joe Louis' influence."[47] Michigan State Senator Diggs, however, assured Roosevelt that "the overwhelming majority" of black voters realized his record and Louis' political ignorance.[48] Diggs proved accurate, for blacks disregarded their hero's preference because it challenged their dreams for equal opportunity, which Roosevelt, however paternalistically continued to act upon. Indeed, worried by Willkie's bid for black support, which included the strongest civil rights plank in political party history, Roosevelt followed the counsel of civil rights advocates and, among other concessions, promoted Colonel Benjamin O. Davis the first black brigadier general and appointed William H. Hastie civilian aide to the Secretary of War.[49] Such was enough for blacks to place Louis in context and consider Roosevelt—in Willkie's phrase—"the Champ" of things political. Having to choose between heroes and a Republican Party which had not been responsive, they voted according to New Deal and wartime realities.

Louis retained his heroic stature, nonetheless. His endorsement of Willkie appeared orchestrated by someone selfishly willing to sell "this otherwise good boy down the river."[50] As significantly he remained humble in defeat: "I never alibi after a fight."[51] And he quickly returned to the ring, easily defending his title for the twelfth time against Al McCoy in December. Sportswriter James P. Dawson hailed him as "the greatest 'fighting' champion" ever in the heavyweight class.[52] His elevation to truly national status was in the offing.

Such began to occur during 1941, a crucial year for Louis and society. As world war intensified abroad, so did black militancy and white soul-searching at home. Black leaders, faced with the dilemma of opposing the Axis while protesting homegrown racism, unveiled the Double V campaign for the purpose of channeling black frustrations into positive, patriotic actions.[53] By simultaneously seeking victory on two fronts—over foreign and domestic foes—they hoped to bolster black morale and promote racial equality; by linking the struggles and stimulating black defense of the country, they avoided charges of treason and claimed first-class citizenship. White leaders, meanwhile, understood the meaning of Nazism for white supremacy in the United States and the resistance by larger society to any suggestion of changes in the *status quo*.[54] Rather than chance alienating whites and hindering preparedness, they played up democratic rhetoric and, when forced by black pressure, compromised on symbolically important issues involving the armed forces and defense industries without fundamentally altering basic conditions.[55] In this context, Louis' forthcoming boxing feats served both personal and societal purposes. He mirrored the aggressiveness of the black masses and the patriotism of their leaders, bringing respect to the race; he embodied the fighting spirit and the interracial symbolism needed by white citizens and leaders during world crisis.[56]

Between January and June, he defended the championship monthly, keeping himself before the press and public. He fought Red Burman, Gus Dorazio, Abe Simon, Tony Musto and Buddy Baer, in what some called the bum-a-month campaign, before meeting Billie Conn in an historic bout. No fight since the Schmeling rematch generated such excitement; Louis experienced difficulty defeating some of the "bums" and Conn, the 175 pound light heavyweight champion, entered as the underdog. Indeed, controversy swirled over whether Louis was slipping.[57]

On June 18, 54,487 people, including noted businessmen, politicians, "stars of stage and screen," and 700 sportswriters filled the Polo Grounds.[58] Most of them rooted for Conn, the cocky Irishman from Pittsburgh who spotted the Dark Destroyer twenty-five pounds and fought "a brand of battle" few expected. They supported Conn, local reporters opined, because of his dashing underdog appeal rather than his race; Louis believed otherwise, later referring to Conn as a 'white hope.'[59] No doubt both factors influenced the crowd, but after twelve spirited rounds by Conn, which left Louis "bewildered, dazed, and on his way to a decisive defeat," the champion rallied.[60] In the thirteenth round Conn, whose speed thus far carried the fight, ceased to box and threw a long left hook; Louis seized the opening, stunning his opponent with a devastating right cross followed by a fusillade of "crushing fire" with both hands "savagely, thudding home." Conn crumbled, ending one of the greatest heavyweight battles ever.

Louis re-emerged even more heroic and popular among both races. Blacks in Harlem celebrated his victory according to formula: "shouting, dancing, pelting each other with torn paper."[61] Whites who saw, heard or read about the match understood the epic dimension of Louis. His loss of speed, which probably reflected the smaller challenger's quickness more than the champion's aging, and come-from-behind win signaled human imperfection; but his courage throughout the bout and his awesome power and skill in the final round revealed god-like invincibility.[62] His stepping back when Conn slipped in the tenth round (instead of attacking at a time when he was losing the championship), his praise for Conn as "an excellent ring general" and his admission of having declined as a fighter bespoke near-spiritual grace. To the faithful, like Alabama-born actress Tallulah Bankhead, Louis loomed as one of the three greatest men in the nation.[63]

Even great men face difficulties, as Louis and his admirers discovered. In July, Marva filed for divorce. She charged "extreme and repeated cruelty" and estimated Louis' annual income from boxing at $250,000.[64] Over the next six weeks, reporters publicized their private relations and extravagant life style. In mid August they reconciled and, despite Marva's allegations that Joe acted ungodly by striking her, the champion remained as popular as ever. Maybe black fans believed the rumor that Marva had been "cutting some capers" with a prominent doctor while white supporters probably identified with the soft-spoken, magnanimous Louis they knew publicly.[65] Moreover, everyone could deduce from the reconciliation that charges of brutality were exaggerated. And all expected heroes who fight their way to the top to be wealthy.

Having weathered six title defenses, Conn's near win and marital problems, Louis now fought Lou Nova and re-established his own indisputable supremacy. In predictable ritual, 56,549 persons jammed into the Polo Grounds on September 29 to see the champion drop Nova "like a deflated balloon" in the sixth round.[66] Celebrities abounded, including one-time paramour Sonjia Henie and former challenger Billie Conn; even Roosevelt rearranged his travel schedule to hear the fight broadcast. In the aftermath, the *New York Times* editorialized anew about Louis' infallibility, and Detroit promoters planned a "White Hope" tournament to find the next challenger.[67]

Increased renown continued to bring Louis into contact with black leaders and organizations, but his managers always stood between them. Detroit Urban Leaguer John C. Dancy, whose agency benefitted from Louis' generosity and who knew the champion well enough to pass along the request of others, observed that Roxborough handled all business matters.[68] On occasion Walter F. White thanked Louis for helping the association financially, requested his autographed photo or reprimanded journalists depicting him as "exceedingly stupid."[70] Black and Roxborough, nevertheless, protected Louis from controversial racial issues.

They permitted him more exposure in race relations as times changed, but continued to shield him from militant protest. Aware of the strident Double V effort by White and others, Black and Roxborough aligned Louis with the more conservative, gradualistic National Urban League and Federal Council of the Churches of Christ. Hence he participated in the League's radio program on vocational education and, more significantly, solicited funds for the Council's Department of Race Relations.[71] "The hardest fight I ever had was against prejudice and discrimination," he informed Roosevelt in a request for money. Ironically, executive aides—doubtlessly smarting from the President recently having been forced by A. Philip Randolph and White to create the Fair Employment Practices Committee—suspected "the Italian hand" of White behind Louis' solicitation and advised against a contribution.[72] They misunderstood completely, because "in times like these" White believed in a "more dynamic and direct approach" to racial problems than efforts at Christian education.[73] Obviously displeased, he recognized the champion's right to place his assistance where he believed it would do "the most good."

As the national emergency bound Louis and society more closely together, White thought Louis could best serve Afro-America in the armed forces. In the fall of 1941, he knew of the champion's 1-A classification and of increased violence between black servicemen and white citizens, police and soldiers.[74]   Behind the scenes he contacted Black and Roxborough, Eleanor Roosevelt and military authorities, negotiating the possibility of commissioning Louis in the Army's Morale Division.[75] Apparently all endorsed his proposal, particularly Army commanders who had no other plans for controlling interracial conflict and imagined Louis capable of boosting black emotions.[76]   White, of course, envisioned the champion as both a morale builder for blacks and an integrator for whites. One of the few blacks known and respected by both races, Louis could serve the Double V strategy by encouraging black participation and exemplifying black patriotism at a time when blacks appeared indifferent to the war and whites seemed vulnerable to civil rights propaganda.   He fit the needs of black leaders, white liberals and War Department officials.

For this reason, White became alarmed over Louis' image. His influential assistant, Roy Wilkins, warned that public reaction would be "very unfavorable" if Louis somehow avoided the draft.[77] People might resent his enormous income, widely publicized at $2,000,000 in seven years of professional fighting, and compare him with Jack Dempsey, who evoked near lasting criticism for refusing to serve in the last war. Instead they would be "greatly impressed" if Louis entered the service as "a private just like Joe Doakes earning $18 a week"; by not accepting "some soft berth" made possible "through pull with Army higher-ups," he could follow the examples of Hank Greenberg, Winthrop Rockefeller and other famous, wealthy individuals. White agreed with Wilkins and pressed the twenty-seven year old champion and his managers to squelch the story that talk of military service had been ballyhoo for the Nova bout.[78] And if Louis' age would prevent him from being called, White urged that he volunteer.

Black and Roxborough had other plans, however, indicating the limited influence of White and other leaders of themselves and their fighter. They opted for the draft and delayed Louis' November induction by signing a rematch with Buddy Baer. They arranged for Louis and promoter Jacobs to donate their purses for this twentieth title defense to the Navy Relief Society.[79] Such generosity and patriotism enhanced the champion's image and future, as well as their own and boxing's. It also brought raves from whites and sparked debate among Double V-minded blacks aware of the Navy's discrimination.[80] Perhaps realizing the futility of stopping the bout, White complimented Louis for acting "far bigger than the Navy" and hoped his example might influence its policy of relegating blacks to messmen status.[81] He played on this theme in the wake of Japan's attack on Pearl Harbor; since "the unqualified support" of every citizen was needed in this national peril, he lectured leading editors, it was time to get rid of prejudice.[82] He later organized NAACP Youth Councils to distribute leaflets to fight fans entering Madison Square Garden and asked Senator Arthur Clapper of Kansas to write the *New York Times*, appealing for the removal of discrimination at "the psychological moment" of the bout.[83]

Louis held firm to his commitment despite some black criticism. Many things were wrong with America, he agreed, "but Hitler won't fix them."[84] When asked by reporters why risk his million dollar championship for nothing, he corrected: "I ain't fighting for nothing. I am fighting for my country." On January 9, in "a flag-draped setting" hyped by the prefight rhetoric of Wendell Willkie, Louis destroyed Baer in round one, donated $47,000 to the Navy Relief Society and received praise from some blacks for having drawn "loop rings" around "ding-donging and complaining" leaders.[85]

Three days after the Baer match Louis passed the Army physical, ending the civilian period more popular than ever before. According to the Springarn Medal nomination for the NAACP's highest award, his clean life, unprecedented title defenses and Navy relief bout won the "respect of Americans and of people the world over."[86] By displaying traits—particularly love of country—admired by larger society, he conformed increasingly to its criteria for heroes; by enhancing his own and black esteem, while ignoring Double V protest, he avoided having to choose one race and set of ideas over another.[87] Honors came to him from all quarters, including the Edward J. Neil Trophy for outstanding contribution to boxing.[88] He also inspired suggestions that naval units bear his name and songs and posters that celebrated his patriotism.[89]

Although set in motion by the war crisis, his transition from sports hero to super patriot lay ahead. Some whites still perceived Louis as a great champion, nothing more; they denied him the Springarn Medal for this reason. Anticipating strong backing for Louis and Randolph, White inquired about the possibility of naming two recipients of the award.[90] Such was impossible and Randolph emerged as the Springarn Medal Committee's choice because he appealed to everyone, while the champion faced adamant opposition from white minister John Haynes Holmes of The Community Church in New York City.[91] Holmes admired Louis' ability, his "sense of propriety, personal honor and public spirit." Yet he considered boxing "bestial and degrading," appealing to base instincts; those concerned with the "serious business of life" should neither admire nor recognize it. Out of touch with Afro-America and large segments of white society, the Park Avenue clergyman nevertheless represented those who, for similar racial reasons, envisioned Louis as no more than an athlete.

Once Louis entered military service, this view of him eroded and, between 1942 and 1945, he became a national symbol. His physical on January 12 and assignment to Company C at Camp Upton, Long Island drew praise from reporters. Joining the service and being unable to fit into the uniform of "an ordinary man," enhanced his image and instilled national confidence.[92] United States Senator Prentiss M. Brown of

Michigan lauded his enlistment, which bandleader Lucky Millander memorialized in "Joe Louis Is a Mighty Man."[93] Few, if any, citizens realized how his managers stalled induction for months or how he awaited formal notice rather than volunteer. Instead they believed that he chose freely to forsake luxury, jeopardize life and defend America; they knew of discriminatory military practices and of his segregated unit, making his action even more impressive. Indeed, the *New York Times* editor reminded readers resentful of war taxes of the champion's contribution.[94]

Even before completing basic training, Louis boosted the war effort by agreeing to speak for the Navy Relief Society. Before 20,000 persons on March 10, he stood erect in uniform and dismissed the idea of doing more than any other "redblooded American."[95] Everyone would do their part, he predicted, and "we'll win 'cause we are on God's side." His words stunned the Madison Square Garden crowd momentarily, then jubilation: tears, laughter, applause, stamping, whistles. Louis' simple, touching greatness explained columnist Bill Corum, could make him "a symbol" in troubled times. Indeed, he envisioned the global struggle a holy crusade, called it "God's War" and, in the process, fulfilled Roosevelt's request that newsmen find a name for the conflagration. Public relations consultant Carl Byoir celebrated the champion in "Joe Louis Named the War," a poem widely circulated, nationally broadcasted and praised by the President.[96] He wrote that unlike others who fought and claimed "God is on our side," Louis spoke more modestly and reverently of being on God's side, drawing the war's name out of his humanity and "out of some instinct that reaches back":

> Back through all the struggle of mankind
> To establish the rights
> That we are fighting to keep now.[97]

Louis' influence continued well into the war as long as writers Sammy Cahn and Jule Styne highlighted his memorable words in "Keep Your Powder Dry."[98]

Fascination grew for Louis as he defined the crisis evangelically. Such beckoned black participation by challenging the argument that this was "a white man's war"; such soothed white consciences by engendering moral self-worth in a racist society fighting for democracy. Blacks understood what Louis meant by being on God's side, but did whites? Given "the downright oppression" in America, "The holier than thou attitude" expressed by some white writers about the champion's statement struck one black cleric as "sinful."[99] Whether or not whites took the opportunity offered by war "to get on God's side," Louis again bridged racial lines and continued to appear saintly.

He returned to Madison Square Garden on March 27 for another title defense. The event replicated that staged for the Navy Relief Society.[100]

Flags, speeches and government figures abounded, including Under Secretary of War Robert Patterson who extolled Louis' patriotism over national and short wave broadcasts. Civilians and combat soldiers listened as Louis dispatched Abe Simon in six rounds, donating his purse of $64,950 to the Army Emergency Relief Organization. Magnanimous as ever, he treated black G.I.s to almost $3,000 worth of fight tickets.

Just as the military officials exploited Louis' commercial and patriotic value, so did black organizations. National Urban Leaguers hoped to capitalize on the Simon bout by raising funds for their programs to place blacks in war jobs. They sought permission from Louis' managers for one hundred girls of both races to solicit contributions from fans while distributing match books which bore the message that defense and democracy necessitated the training and hiring of all Americans.[101] Despite cooperation from Louis' handlers, the request never received approval.[102] That project failing, NUL officials asked that Louis sign letters intended for potential contributors. This was the moment, executive secretary Lester B. Granger acknowledged, when "Joe's assistance could be of inestimable value."[103]

Military authorities also realized Louis' worth. Placing the champion in special services, they dampened charges of favoritism by treating him routinely. He completed boot camp, rose to corporal and spoke unplaintively of needing to work harder for sergeant's chevrons.[104] A model soldier, he delighted Army personnel who assigned him several roles.

During and immediately after basic training, Louis stimulated the sale of defense bonds. Black disabled veterans in Milwaukee planned their drive around "Joe Louis Day," while he spoke before a predominantly black gathering of 20,000 hometown Detroiters who bought bonds totalling $275,000.[105] Officials and private citizens requested his appearance at bond selling rallies in New York and Memphis, claiming that such would increase sales and boost black morale.[106] All agreed with the Hutchinson, Kansas, correspondent that Louis stirred "the flame of patriotism" in the hearts of his people.[107] Much the same might have been said about his impact on whites, at least the 65,000 patrons at the Tam O'Shanter golf tournament who purchased $933,000 worth of bonds at Louis' urgings.[108]

Representatives of labor, academe and mass organizations also requested Louis' services. Members of Ford Local 600 desired his presence at their patriotic rally, and Malcolm S. MacLean of Hampton Institute recommended he visit black colleges and uplift R.O.T.C. students with his simple talks that "weigh a ton."[109] More pointedly for race relations, White solicited Louis for NAACP-sponsored events; he believed the champion would help the association achieve an "affirmative note."[110] Only the United Automobile Workers' request appears to have been acted upon favorably by government officials, who preferred direct control of Louis' activities.

Military leaders, too understood the value of Louis as morale builder and, especially during his first year of duty, image-maker. He promoted the service by appearing in the film "This is the Army," speaking on the broadcast "Army Hour" and participating in "I am an American Day."[111] In every instance he waxed patriotic: "this fight's the biggest ... I [have] ever been in, and ... I haven't any doubts about helping to win." Later, in the face of the Los Angeles and Detroit race riots, the War Department moved to bolster blacks and educate whites, using clips of Louis in a widely shown docu-drama "The Negro Soldier."[112]

Army officials also arranged for Louis to tour military camps in the United States beginning August 30, 1943. Over the next four months the champion boxed before thousands of soldiers. He visited the G.I.s in hospitals, lectured on good health and sparred two or three rounds daily. Shortly thereafter he visited the British Isles, France, Italy and North Africa, returning home in October of 1944. In all, he traveled fourteen months, covered 30,000 miles, entertained 2,000,000 troops and fought nearly 200 exhibition bouts overseas.[113] Servicemen flocked to watch him fight, "exchange quips,act in skits or just talk." Most appreciative were the wounded, one of whom begged to have his eyes unbandaged so he could see the champion and, having his wish fulfilled, exclaimed: "This is the happiest I've been"[114] Doubtless Louis provided "invaluable service" to the Army.[115]

Most black spokesmen and white officials also recognized Louis' potential to incite, however unintended, yet check violence. Even as the champion's prestige grew among whites in the early 1940s, interracial conflict sprang from his victories over Conn and Baer in locales as far removed as Detroit and Gurdon, Arkansas.[116] Clearly Louis instilled pride, even assertiveness in some blacks, which many whites perceived as a threat to the racial status quo. "Since Joe Louis became so prominent every Negro goes around strutting his stuff," complained one Michigander.[117] Exactly because of the champion's influence among blacks, leaders of both races sought his assistance to curb discord. Following the spring riots of 1943 in Los Angeles, Detroit and elsewhere, Roosevelt supposedly sent Louis as goodwill emissary to Pittsburgh, "the most sensitive spot for another outbreak."[118] Disorder came instead to New York where Mayor Fiorello H. LaGuardia recruited celebrities to circulate through Harlem appealing for peace.[119] He called for Louis, who was out of town. Frightened by the specter of race war, scores of municipal officials created interracial committees, northern and southern liberals worked to "keep the lid on" and White sought Louis' participation in race relation programs.[120] Black editors retreating from direct action admonished rioters, particularly in Harlem where blacks ignited the disorder, and invoked Louis' example and words: "you cannot expect to win a fight by hitting foul blows."[121]

Louis himself struck "fair" punches for Afro-America. Besides promoting social control over black soldiers and civilians, he helped integrate society and change racial attitudes. Although organized protest lay behind Roosevelt's ordering the placement of black sailors in all naval branches, black newsmen and white officials agreed that Louis' benefit bout for the Navy Relief Society contributed to moving the race beyond messmen duty.[122] Neither black pressure nor Louis' magnanimity integrated the Navy but, judged one editor, "he slapped Jim Crow in the face."[123] He weakened the segregated structure of civilian and military society elsewhere: expressing dissatisfaction at bond rallies; integrating promotional golf tournaments; boxing with soldiers of both races before integrated audiences only. Indeed, while the Army used Louis to promote its image and the war effort, he turned the tables on more than one occasion; he informed 20,000 Detroiters that if given defense jobs and "an even break in the Army," blacks "would show the world how to win this war."[124]

When pressed by circumstances, he protested publicly. He ignored a 'White Only' sign in the bus depot of Camp Sibert, Alabama (which resulted in his and Sugar Ray Robinson's arrest) and questioned Jim Crow theater seats in Salisbury, England.[125] More often he inquired privately as to why blacks of Jackie Robinson's athletic ability and education could neither play for post football teams nor attend Officer's Candidate School (OCS). Later Louis exaggerated his significance in correcting some of these wrongs. Rather than single-handedly desegregating buses on Army posts, for example, his arrest merely reflected one of innumerable incidents of racial friction and low morale that dictated new policy; hence on July 8, 1944 the military command adopted the procedure of Brigadier General George Horkan of Camp Lee, Virginia, who provided sufficient vehicles, on a first come, first-served basis for all soldiers traveling between post and town.[126] Nevertheless Louis assisted in bringing about minor, though far from insignificant alterations. Robinson did play some football for Fort Riley, Kansas, and enter OCS, attributing the latter to Louis' efforts.[127] Certainly the champion's intervention in Robinson's behalf and his exhibitions with soldiers of both races "helped broaden the base of athletic competition of many posts."[128] He also might have been instrumental in Robinson going to OCS, but Robinson's ability and education must have been significant in themselves; in any case, military opposition to training more than token numbers of black officers continued throughout the war.[129] Not as assertively, consistently, dramatically or effectively as many others, Louis interacted with racist institutions and turbulent times to advance the struggle for equality.

Such occurred for several reasons. In the service Louis found himself alone, making "all kinds of decisions,"[130] While he completed basic training, Black faced charges and Roxborough served time for running numbers and, pushing Louis to his emotional depths, Blackburn died.

Military duty kept him, his mother and Marva apart, and ongoing marital problems ended in divorce two years later. Stripped of his guardians, Louis seemed more independent and concerned about racial justice, particularly for black soldiers and friends like Robinson. The war atmosphere affected him as well, for everyone from Roosevelt to Double V advocates espoused democratic principles. He became sensitized, fighting relief bouts, selling bonds and bolstering morale while witnessing discrimination in the Army; he believed that all servicemen should be treated identically "as American soldiers."[131] Perhaps worldwide fame also influenced him. French Tunisians asked every black soldier if he was the champion and a Soviet general looked for the man he had heard so much about: "No, not Eisenhower," he informed a CBS correspondent, "Joe Louis."[132] Despite being more independent, sensitive and popular than ever before, he rebelled rarely.

During the last months of war, Louis continued the model soldier, contemplated civilian life and basked in accolades. From his return to the United States in October 1944 until his discharge a year later, he visited defense plants to spur production or integrate labor forces.[133] He modestly parried efforts by admirers, like Congressman Adam Clayton Powell, Jr., to promote him from technical sergeant (his rank for "excellent work overseas") to second lieutenant.[134] He joked about buying several civilian suits in "every color, except brown," but, not wanting special treatment, preferred staying in uniform until victory.[135] He looked forward to boxing again, as did fans who believed him still capable of defending the title with "one hand."[136] Neither had long to wait, for he mustered out of the Army on October 1 amidst great fanfare. Receiving the Legion of Merit "for exceptionally meritorious conduct in the performance of outstanding services" abroad, he expressed characteristic gratitude.[137] A medal and a military review, the presence of a brigadier general and national broadcast coverage of the ceremony signified Louis' extraordinary prominence.

Quickly he returned to civilian life, as memories of his "meritorious conduct" lingered on and helped Americans adjust to peace. Many read Margery Miller's *Joe Louis: American* and news stories of "the nice things Joe has done."[138] They expressed pride in Louis for his character, his inspiration when "the Great War came" and his willingness to die so the nation might live.[139] Certainly citizens of both races associated themselves, their courage and commitment in the face of disaster with the champion who represented "the best ideals of Americanism."[140] With victory in hand and reconstruction ahead, they again saw in him what they wanted to see in themselves: excellence.

Louis and society, then, interacted throughout the world crisis, helping to define one another. Initially, he made most blacks "unafraid of tomorrow" and some whites receptive to changing times.[141] Such was made possible by his awesome fistic skill and attractive human qualities;

by his handlers, who understood—in the estimation of one white gradu-
alist—"inter-racial relations and human psychology"; by black newsmen
hungry for copy and their readers equally hungry for heroes; and by white
promoters seeking profits and honest trainers wanting scandal-free
bouts.[142] His politically symbolic victory over Carnera and Schmeling
brought increasing respect from whites and near universal decent treatment from daily presses.[143] His olympian demeanor and patriotic action
thrust him into more historically significant and internationally prominent roles.

Preparedness and war engendered instability and heightened societal needs for someone of Louis' stature, a hero capable of pulling everyone into "a framework of comprehensibility and control."[144] In
providing this function, he touched on "the range of values in society:"
patriotism and protest, continuity and change.[145] His enormous appeal
and growth occurred because he identified himself with blacks personally
and with all citizens representatively; he reflected both cultures and
became their champion in and out of the ring.[146] Most importantly, he
threatened neither race and unwittingly nurtured the status quo; one
observer, expressing the feelings of many, extolled Louis for always
having done "the right thing."[147] He pleased various segments of both
communities who played on his prestige as a means to manipulate public
behavior: black editors desiring democratic advances without rebellion,
southern newsmen taking aim at Hitler without hitting Jim Crow targets,
government officials seeking racial peace without social justice, white
liberals wanting moral integrity without social changes and white citizens
striving for respectability without recognizing black grievances.[148]
Occasionally, he stepped out of character and challenged
discrimination, but only in military life and only very tentatively.

Genuinely the people's choice, Louis possess that quality—"divine
grace"—characteristic of heroic leadership.[149] He emerged more hero
than leader, defining no ideology, presenting no strategy and organizing
no constituency. Yet his historical significance lay in the symbolism he
represented for black and white societies, their ideologies, their struggles
and their "assurances of success."[150] Traditionally, most prominent
blacks "have been primarily spokesmen, symbolic leaders and
propagandists, rather than individuals with a solid organizational
base."[151] In his own way and for different racial constituencies, Louis
functioned in all of these categories, played more than theatric parts in
the life-and-death drama of war and educated countrymen in decency
and democracy. He also marked the transition from earlier, one-dimensional paragons to contemporary, many-faceted heroes who undertake
several functions and reveal themselves "warts and all."[152] He laid, in a
white admirer's words, "a red rose on Abe Lincoln's grave;" he became,
from a black perspective, America's David.[153] When Billy Conn wished
he could have the heavyweight crown, Louis joshed that he had it for

twelve rounds of their fight but"didn't exactly know what to do with it!"[154] The same cannot be said of Joe Louis, multifarious hero of a society at war.

•   •   •

Notes

1. Harvard Sitkoff, "'No More Moanin'": Black Rights History in the 1970s," *Prologue: The Journal of the National Archives,* XI (Summer 1979): 84-86 for the historiography of race relations. See also Richard Polenberg, *War and Society: The United States, 1941-1945* (Philadelphia, 1972), 99-130 and John Morton Blum, *V Was for Victory: Politics and American Culture During World War II* (New York, 1976), 182-220 for this interpretation.

2. A.O. Edmonds, *Joe Louis* (Grand Rapids, 1973); Lawrence W. Levine, *Black Culture and Black Consciousness: Afro-American Folk Thought from Slavery to Freedom* (New York, 1977), 420-40 and Jeffrey T. Sammons, "Boxing as a Reflection of Society: The Southern Reaction to Joe Lewis," *Journal of Popular Culture,* 16 (Spring, 1983), 23-33, respectively. For notable exceptions which provide a broad overview, the meaning of Louis for blacks during the depression and for white Southerners from 1934 to 1941: Al Tony Gilmore, "The Black Southerner's Response to the Southern System of Race Relations: 1900 to Post-World War II" in Robert Haws, ed., *The Age of Segregation: Race Relations in the South, 1890-1945* (Jackson, MS, 1978), 73 for the quotation.

3. Quoted in Gilmore, ibid., 74.

4. Joe Louis (with Edna and Art Rust, Jr.), *Joe Louis: My Life* (New York, 1978), 3-33 and 93 for information in this paragraph (hereafter cited as Louis, *My Life*). See also Joe Louis, *My Life Story* (New York, 1947), for his initial, very guarded and somewhat misleading autobiography (hereafter cited as Louis, *Story*). A comparison of these autobiographies reveals much about the champion's self-image and development at different stages of life.

5. Quoted in Margery Miller, *Joe Louis, American* (New York, 1945), 12. Louis, *My Life,* 5 and 19.

6. Al Tony Gilmore, *Bad Nigger! The National Impact of Jack Johnson* (Port Washington, NY, 1975), for the Johnson story. Louis, *My Life,* 38-39 for Roxborough's and Black's instructions, and 36 for Blackburn's quotation. Caswell Adams, "Introducing the New Joe Louis," *Saturday Evening Post,* May 10, 1941, 107. John C. Dancy to Ross Pascoe, Jan. 16, 1946, Reel 11. *Detroit Urban League Papers,* microfilm edition thereafter cited as DULP); Louis, *My Life,* 176 and 185 for the significance of the handlers.

7. Christopher F. Monte, *Beneath the Mask: An Introduction to Theories of Personality* (2nd ed: New York, 1980), 224-62. For a summary of Erik H. Erikson's psychoanalytic ego psychology: Erik H. Erikson, "Reflections on Dr. Borg's Life Cycle," in his *Adulthood* (New York, 1978), 5 for the quotation which is applicable to Louis.

8. Nancy J. Weiss, *The National Urban League* (New York, 1974), 266 for "political calculus"; Robert L. Zangrando, *The NAACP Crusade Against Lynching, 1909-1950* (Philadelphia, 1980), 98-165 for an example of it; John B. Kirby, *Black Americans in the Roosevelt Era: Liberalism and Race* (Knoxville, 1980), 218-35 and Morton Sosna, *In Search of the Silent South: Southern Liberals and the Race Issue* (New York, 1977), 60-63 for white liberals; Jeremiah Wilson Moses, *Black Messiahs and Uncle Toms* (University Park, PA, 1982). For Louis as messiah: Harvard

Sitkoff, *A New Deal for Blacks: The Emergence of Civil Rights as a National Issue* (New York, 1978), 261-62. For black leaders: August Meier and Elliot Rudwick, *Black Detroit and the Rise of the UAW* (New York, 1979), 35-107. For black awareness: Martha Wilkerson and Richard A. Dodder, "Toward a Model of Collective Conscience and Sport in Modern Societies," *International Journal of Sport Psychology*, 13 (1982), 272 for the quotation.

9. Roi Ottley, *'New World A-Coming': Inside Black America* (New York, 1943), 188.

10. Louis, *My Life*, 270-77 for these and all other statistics regarding Louis' boxing record.

11. Orrin E. Kapp, "Heroes, Villains, and Fools as Agents of Social Control," *American Sociological Review*, XIX (Feb., 1954), 61. For the interpretation which is applicable to Louis, Lena Horne and Richard Schickel, *Lena* (Garden City, NY, 1965), 75 for the quotation.

12. Dixon Wecter, *The Hero in America: A Chronicle of Hero-Worship* (Ann Arbor, MI, 1941), 7 and 11. For the interpretation which is applicable to Louis: Ottley, 'New World A-Coming,' 189.

13. Thomas Cripps, *Slow Fade to Black: The Negro in American Film, 1900-1942* (New York, 1977), 339.

14. Maya Angelou, *I Know Why the Caged Bird Sings* (New York, 1969), 129.

15. Alexander J. Young, Jr. "Joe Louis, Symbol: 1933-1949" (unpublished Ph.D. diss. University of Maryland, 1968), 83 for evidence of black elite reservation about Louis.

16. Angelou, *I Know Why the Caged Bird Sings* (New York, 1969), 129; Mark D. Coburn, "America's Great Black Hope," *American Heritage* 29 (Oct. 1978), 91.

17. Young, "Joe Louis, Symbol," 82-83. For the letters, Levine, *Black Culture and Black Consciousness*, 437 for the lyrics.

18. Louis, *My Life*, 114 and 119; Miller, *Louis*, 109; Levine, *Black Culture and Black Consciousness*, 436.

19. Horne and Schickel, *Lena*, 75; Senate Resolution No. 39, *Journal of the Senate of the State of Michigan 1937 Regular Session*, 1641, Michigan State Library, Lansing, Michigan.

20. Young, "Joe Louis, Symbol," 103. For the diet, Louis, *My Life*, 121. For the 'relatives' and 52, 67, 74, and 80 for information in this paragraph.

21. Langston Hughes, "Joe Louis" in Ruth Miller, ed., *Black American Literature* (New York, 1971), 550.

22. Alan Clive, *State of War: Michigan in World War II* (Ann Arbor, MI, 1979), 11.

23. Coburn, "America's Great Black Hope," 88 for the *New York Times* reference and the *Literary Digest* quotations.

24. Walter White to Earl Brown, June 19, 1940, Box 365, *National Association for the Advancement of Colored People Papers* (General Office Files, 1940-1955), Manuscript Collection, Library of Congress, Washington, D.C., thereinafter cited as NAACP).

25. Young, "Joe Louis, Symbol," 104, 116, and 113.

26. Sitkoff, *A New Deal for Blacks*, 190-215. For intellectuals: Kirby, *Black Americans in the Roosevelt Era*, 218-35 and Sosna, *In Search of the Silent South*, 63. For the liberals: Cripps, *Slow Fade to Black*, 257 for the quotation.

27. Randy Roberts, "Jack Dempsey: An American Hero in the 1920s," *Journal of Popular Culture*, 8 (Fall, 1974); 420 and n. 79; Roberts, *Jack Dempsey: The Manassa Mauler* (Baton Rouge, LA, 1979) for Dempsey's life.

28. Young, "Joe Louis, Symbol," 120; George Hutchinson, "The Black Athletes' Contribution Towards Social Change in the United States" (unpublished Ph.D. diss., United States International University, 1977), 86 for a similar announcement at the Max Baer fight.

29. Miller, *Louis*, 35; Young, "Joe Louis, Symbol," 42; Edmonds, *Joe Louis*, 40; Sammons, "Boxing as a Reflection of Society," 26.

30. Louis, *My Life*, 58, 63, 90-91 and 118-19 for information in this paragraph.

31. Ibid., 65, 66-67, 81-83, 182-83 and 39 for information in this paragraph.

32. Roxborough appeared Robin Hood-like to unemployed blacks: Louis, *My Life*, 29-30. That Black, Blackburn and he had police records partly explains their attraction to the masses and entrepreneurs, who recognized shady dealings as an avenue for upward mobility in a society of limited opportunities. David M. Katzman, *Before the Ghetto, Black Detroit in the Nineteenth Century* (Chicago, 1973), 171-74 and Allan Spear, *Black Chicago: The Making of a Negro Ghetto, 1890-1920* (Chicago, 1967), 71 and 76-78. Their criminal activities aside, some professionals admired the all-black composition of "Joe Louis and Co.": *Detroit Tribune*, June 22, 1940, 12.

33. Earl Brown, "Joe Louis the Champion, Idol of His Race, Sets a Good Example of Conduct," *Life*, June 17, 1940, 52. Marshall W. Fishwick, *American Heroes, Myth and Reality* (Westport, CT, 1954), 228-29 for the contention that "skillful and faithful manipulators" lay behind all heroes, creating "a mythical image and a second life for them." Parts of Louis' image and life—his humanitarianism, for example—were genuine, however.

34. Richard M. Dalfiume, "The 'Forgotten Years' of the Negro Revolution," *The Journal of American History*, LV (June, 1968), 90-106.

35. Peter J. Kellog, "Civil Rights Consciousness in the 1940s," *The Historian*, XLII (Nov. 1979), 31.

36. Jack Orr, "The Black Boxer: Exclusion and Ascendance" in John T. Talamani and Charles H. Page, *Sport and Society* (Boston, 1973), 241; quoted in Louis, *My Life*, 137 and 141 for the following statistic.

37. Young, "Joe Louis, Symbol," 130.

38. Erik H. Erikson, *Childhood and Society*, (2nd ed., New York, 1963), 263-66. For the concepts of isolation and intimacy, Edwin R. Embree, *Thirteen Against the Odds* (New York, 1944), 237 for the quotation.

39. Kellogg, "Civil Rights Consciousness in the 1940s," 33; Sammons, "Boxing as a Reflection of Society," 30.

40. *Time*, Sept., 29, 1949, 60.

41. *Amsterdam News* (New York), Jan. 6, 1940, p. 15; *New York Times*, Feb. 14, 1940, 13.

42. Walter White, *A Man Called White: The Autobiography of Walter White* (New York, 1948), 187-88.

43. Memo to Roberta Barrows (from H.K.), September 23, 1940 and Edwin M. Watson to Julian Rainey, Sept. 25, 1940, Box 13, OF 300, *Franklin D. Roosevelt Papers*, Roosevelt Library, Hyde Park, New York (thereafter cited as FDRP).

44. *Oscar R. Ewing to Edwin M. Watson*, Sept. 28, 1940, ibid.

45. Quoted in *New York Times*, Oct. 27, 1940, 37; Louis, *My Life*, 158-59 for his version of the endorsement.

46. *New York Times*, Oct. 31, 1940, 18; Oct. 27, 1940, 37 for the quotations, and Nov. 5, 1940, 21.

47. Anonymous telegram to Roosevelt, Nov. 2, 1940, OF 4884, FDRP.

48. Digg's telegram to Roosevelt, Nov. 1, 1940, OF93, FDRP.

49. Sitkoff, *A New Deal for Blacks*, 303-09; Herbert Parmet, *Never Again: A President Runs for a Third Term* (New York, 1968) for the election results.

50. Diggs telegram to Roosevelt, Nov. 1, 1940, OF93, FDRP.

51. Quoted in Miller, *Louis*, 133.

52. *New York Times*, Jan 31, 1941, 22.

53. Lee Finkle, "The Conservative Aims of Militant Rhetoric: Black Protest During World War II," *The Journal of American History*, LX (Dec. 1973), 702-04 and *Forum for Protest: The Black Press During World War II* (Rutherford, NJ, 1975), 88-128.

54. Neil A. Wynn, *The Afro-American and the Second World War* (New York, 1976), 99 and 108-09.

55. WIlliam H. Harris, *The Harder We Run: Black Workers Since the Civil War* (New York, 1982), 117 and James A. Neuchterlein, "The Politics of Civil Rights, the FEPC, 1941-1946," *Prologue: The Journal of the National Archives*, X (Fall, 1978), 171-91 regarding Randolph, Roosevelt and the Fair Employment Practices Committee.

56. Clarence Williams to the NAACP, Jan. 3, 1942, Box 549, NAACP; Walter H. Jacobs to Roosevelt, Nov., 14, 1941. Box 100, PPF-9-J.FDRP.

57. Bill White to the Editor, *New York Times*, May 31, 1941, 18; John Kieran, "Sports of the Times," *New York Times*, June 18, 1941, 26.

58. *New York Times*, June 18, 1941, 27 and June 19, 1941, 1 for the following quotation, and 27.

59. *New York Times*, June 20, 1941, 25; Louis, *My Life*, 167.

60. *New York Times*, June 20, 1941, 25 for these quotations, and June 19, 1941, 1 for the following quotations and description of the fight.

61. *New York Times*, June 19, 1941, 27.

62. Ibid., June 19, 1941, 27 and June 20, 1941, 25 for information in this and the next sentence.

63. *Pittsburgh Courier*, Feb. 28, 1982, 1. Roosevelt and Willkie being the other greatest men.

64. *New York Times*, July 3, 1941, 21; July 10, 1941, 21. For Marva's quotation, Aug. 19, 1941, 23 and Aug. 20, 1941, 21 for information in this paragraph.

65. John C. Dancy to Presley S. Winfield, Aug. 12, 1941, Box 1, John C. Dancy Papers, *Michigan Historical Collections*, Bentley Historical Library, Ann Arbor, Michigan (hereafter cited as JCDP).

66. *New York Times*, Sept. 30, 1941, 1. For the statistic and quotation and 29 for information in the following sentence, Louis, *My Life*, 81 for reference to the Louis-Henie affair.

67. *New York Times*, Oct. 1, 1941, 20; *Detroit Tribune*, Oct. 4, 1941, 7.

68. John C. Dancy, *Sand Against the Wind: The Memoirs of John C. Dancy* (Detroit, 1966), 186-88; Dancy to Julia Black, Oct. 3, 1941, Box 1, JCDP.

69. White to Louis, Roxborough and Black, Dec. 12, 1941, Box 365, NAACP.

70. White to Louis, Feb. 16, 1940 and Feb. 24, 1940, Box 365, NAACP; White to Editor, *Life*, June 18, 1940, for the quotation, and White to Earl Brown, June 19, 1940, Box 365, NAACP regarding the latter's "Joe Louis the Champion, Idol of His Race, Sets a Good Example of Conduct," *Life*, June 17, 1940, 50.

71. Guichard Parris and Lester Brooks, *Blacks in the City: A History of the National Urban League* (Boston, 1971), 312; Louis to Roosevelt, Sept. 27, 1941, OF 93, FDRP.

72. Memorandum for Watson (from S.T.E.), Oct. 2, 1941, Box 5, OF 93, FDRP. Black militancy aside, Roosevelt must have recalled Louis' opposition to his re-election before informing the champion that he donated to relief organiza-

tions of broader scope. Edwin W. Watson to Louis, Oct. 7, 1941, Box 5, OF 93, FDRP.

73. White to Robert D. Kohn, Oct. 7, 1941, Box 365, NAACP.

74. *New York Times*, Sept. 10, 1941, 31; Richard M. Dalfiume, *Desegregation of the U.S. Armed Forces Fighting on Two Fronts, 1939-1953* (Columbia, MO, 1969), 64-68.

75. White to Eleanor Roosevelt, Sept. 22, 1941 and White to Louis, Roxborough and Black, Oct. 3, 1941, Box 365, NAACP.

76. Brigadier General F.H. Osborn to White, Oct. 1, 1941, Box 365, NAACP.

77. Memorandum to White (from Wilkins), Oct. 3, 1941, Box 365, NAACP.

78. White to Louis, Roxborough and Black, Oct. 3, 1941, Box 365, NAACP.

79. *New York Times*, Nov. 13, 1941, 39 and Dec. 17, 1941. Baer agreed to donate two and one half percent of his share to the society.

80. *Pittsburgh Courier*, Dec. 6, 1941, 17 and Dec. 13, 1941, 17.

81. White telegram to *Pittsburgh Courier*, Nov. 15, 1941, Box 365, NAACP.

82. White to Editor, *New York Times*, Dec. 15, 1941, Box 365, NAACP. He sent an identical letter to several New York dailies, which was published by at least one newspaper, the *Herald Tribune*.

83. Madison S. Jones, Jr. to Edna Scott, n.d., Memorandum to Miss Crump (from Mr. Morrow), Jan. 9, 1942 and Memorandum to Mrs. Bowman (from Distribution Committee), Jan. 19, 1942, Box 365, NAACP. Regarding the leaflets, White to Clapper, Jan. 2, 1942, ibid., for the quotation.

84. Quoted in "Our Joe," an unidentified press clipping, n.d., Box 549, NAACP.

85. *New York Times*, Jan. 10, 1942, 19. *Amsterdam News*, Jan. 17, 1942, 1; *Pittsburg Courier*, Feb. 28, 1942, 5.

86. Memorandum (from the Secretary of the Springarn Medal), Jan. 26, 1942, Box 549, NAACP.

87. Wecter, *The Hero in America*, 1-16, 476-91 for the majority's criteria for heroes. Erik H. Erikson, *Young Man Luther: A Study in Psychoanalysis and History* (New York, 1958), 259 for the theory of meshing with different groups and ideas.

88. *Pittsburgh Courier*, Jan. 3, 1942, 16; Feb. 14, 1942, 3; and Jan. 10, 1942, 17.

89. Spencer Page to Roosevelt, Jan. 15, 1942, OF 4884, FDRP, *Pittsburg Courier*, Jan. 31, 1942, 20 and Feb. 7, 1942, 11 for the song and poster. The Boxing Writers Association of New York presented the Neil trophy.

90. White to Arthur B. Springarn, Jan. 22, 1942 and Springarn to White, Jan. 23, 1942, Box 549, NAACP.

91. Holmes to White, Jan. 27, 1942, Box 549, NAACP.

92. *Amsterdam News*, Jan. 17, 1942, 1 and 3.

93. *Detroit Tribune*, Jan. 17, 1942, 1; *Pittsburgh Courier*, Jan. 31, 1942, 20.

94. Miller, *Louis*, 163.

95. *Pittsburgh Courier*, March 21, 1942, 17 and May 16, 1942, 17 for information in this paragraph; some reporters, including the Courier's misquoted Louis in their original stories.

96. Roosevelt to Byoir, May 4, 1942 and Byoir, "Joe Louis Named the War," PPF 2176, FDRP; Edward Anthony to Arthur B. Springarn, May 5, 1942, Box 365, NAACP.

97. Byoir guessed that Louis found inspiration in his great grandfather, no doubt a slave, but columnist W. K. Kelsey opined that "consciously or uncon-

sciously" he paraphrased Lincoln, who reputedly said something similar to a Southern delegation during the Civil War. However, Louis credited bandleader friend Lucky Millander for helping formulate ideas for the benefit speech. Byoir, "Joe Louis Named the War," *Detroit News*, March 22, 1941, 6; Louis, *My Life*, 1973-74.

98. *Michigan Chronicle*, Nov. 11, 1944, 14.

99. Ibid., June 20, 1942, 6.

100. *New York Times*, March 28, 1942, 12; *Pittsburgh Courier*, April 4, 1942, 17; Louis, *My Life*, 174.

101. Lester B. Granger to Dancy, March 6, 1942, and Dancy to John Roxborough, March 6, 1942, Reel 10, DULP.

102. Dancy to Lester B. Granger, March 9, 1942 and Ann Tanneyhill to John Roxborough, March 21, 1942, Reel 10, DULP.

103. Granger to John Roxborough, March 30, 1942, Reel 10, DULP.

104. *Pittsburgh Courier*, March 21, 1942, 20. *Michigan Chronicle*, June 6, 1942, 13. Privately, the Army favored Louis with passes for Blackburn's funeral, his daughter's birth and his wife's debut as a singer; Louis, *Story*, 159, 166 and 168.

105. *Pittsburgh Courier*, March 28, 1942, 16; *Michigan Chronicle*, June 6, 1942, 1.

106. Summer A. Sirtl to Roosevelt, June 2, 1942. OF 4884 and Benjamin F. Bell, Jr., telegram to Roosevelt, Sept. 6, 1943, OF 4408 FDRP.

107. Quoted in Memo (from M.H. McIntyre), July 11, 1942, OF 4884, FDRP.

108. *Detroit News*, July 20, 1943, 19 and July 31, 1943, 14.

109. Victor G. Reuther to John Gallo, March 11, 1942, Box 31. *United Automobile War Policy Collection*, Archives of Labor and Urban Affairs, Detroit, Michigan; MacLean to Marvin H. McIntyre, Nov. 20, 1942, Box 7, OF 93, FDRP.

110. White to Charles Poletti, April 30, 1043, Box 248, NAACP.

111. *Pittsburgh Courier*, April 11, 1942, 20 and *Detroit News*, June 11, 1943, 29; *Michigan Chronicle*, May 16, 1942, 12 for the broadcast and following quotations: "Headliners," *New York Times Magazine*, May 24, 1942, 19.

112. Wynn, *The Afro-American and the Second World War*, 30 and 83.

113. *New York Times*, Oct. 11, 1944, 25 for statistics and the following quotation, and Sept. 24, 1945, 32.

114. Quoted in Miller, *Louis*, 179.

115. *Michigan Chronicle*, Oct. 28, 1944, 15 for the quotation of Col. Joe Triner, former chairman of the Illinois Boxing Commission.

116. *Detroit Tribune*, June 28, 1941, 3; *Pittsburgh Courier*, Feb. 21, 1942, 11.

117. B.M. Merrill to Edward J. Jeffries, Jr. March 2, 1942, Box 9, *Mayor's Papers, Burton Historical Collection*, Detroit Public Library, Detroit, Michigan.

118. Military Intelligence Division, War Department, "Race Riots," Aug. 5, 1943, Box 18, Record Group 319. Washington National Records Center, Suitland, Maryland (hereafter cited as WNRC). It is unclear whether Louis visited Pittsburgh.

119. Dominic J. Capeci, Jr., *The Harlem Riot of 1943* (Philadelphia, 1977), 104 for LaGuardia following White's advice.

120. Sitkoff, "Racial Militancy and Interracial Violence in the Second World War," 678-79 and Donald R. McCoy and Richard T. Ruetten, "Towards Equality: Blacks in the United States During the Second World War," in A.C. Hepburn, ed., *Minorities in History* (New York, 1979), 148 for conflicting views of the significance of these committees; Sosna, *In Search of the Silent South*, 108 for Jonathan Daniel's quotation, White to John Roxborough, Aug. 18, 1943, Box 365, NAACP.

121. Finkle, "The Conservative Aims of Militant Rhetoric," 711; *Michigan Chronicle*, Aug. 7, 1943, 1 for the Louis Martin's quotation.

122. Dalfiume, *Desegregation of the U.S. Armed Forces*, 54-55 and 101; *Detroit Tribune*, April 11, 1942, 1 and *Pittsburgh Courier*, April 18, 1942, 16; Special Services Division, Office of War Information, "Negro Organizations and the War Effort," April 28, 1942, Box 1843, Record Group, 44, WNRC.

123. *Michigan Chronicle*, May 23, 1942, 4.

124. Ibid., June 6, 1942, 2.

125. Louis, *My Life*, 185-86 for his view of the depot and theater incidents, and 177-79 for his recollections of the Jackie Robinson episode below, Sugar Ray Robinson (with Dave Anderson), and Sugar Ray (New York, 1970, 122-24 and W.C. Heinz, *Once They Heard Cheers* (New York, 1979), 305-06 for their being provoked by a white Military Policeman at Camp Sibert.

126. Ulysses G. Lee, Jr., *The United States Army in World War II: Special Studies: The Employment of Negro Troops* (Washington, D.C.), 323-34 (thereafter cited as *The Employment of Negro Troops*).

127. Jackie Robinson, *I Never Had It Made* (New York, 1972), 25 and 28-29.

128. Lee, *The Employment of Negro Troops*, 307.

129. Ibid., 203-204, 211, 270-74 and Dalfiume, *Desegregation of the U.S. Armed Forces*, 63-74 for military policy.

130. Louis, *My Life*, 180-81.

131. Louis, *Story*, 169.

132. *AfroAmerican* (Baltimore), May 22, 1943, 24; *Michigan Chronicle*, May 29, 1944, 7 for the quotation.

133. *New York Times*, Oct. 24, 1944, 14; Ottley, '*New World A-Coming*,' 299.

134. *New York Times*, March 8, 1945, 16 and April 10, 1945, 23.

135. *Michigan Chronicle*, April 7, 1945, 7; *New York Times*, July 16, 1945, 6.

136. *New York Times*, Aug. 15, 1945, 22; *Michigan Chronicle*, March 3, 1945, 4 for the quotation of Ford employee Arthur Mitchell of Detroit.

137. *New York Times*, Sept. 24, 1945, 32.

138. Bernard B. Perry to White, Sept. 18, 1945, Box 365, NAACP; J.H. Eliashon to Dancy, Jan. 22, 1946, Reel 11, DULP.

139. Elijah P. Marrs to White, April 29, 1946, Box 91, NAACP for an example.

140. Adam Clayton Powell, Jr. to Roosevelt, March 6, 1945, OF 4884, FDRP.

141. Ottley, '*New World A-Coming*,' 190 for the quotation; William Harrison to White, Oct. 19, 1941, Box 549, NAACP.

142. Guy Wells to James E. Shepard, April 22, 1942, Box 24, *Howard W. Odum Papers Southern Historical Collection*, Wilson Library, Chapel Hill, North Carolina; St. Clair Drake and Horace R. Cayton, Black Metropolis: A Study of Negro Life in a Northern City (rev. ed.: New York, 1962), II, 403 for an example—Chicago Defender, 1933-38—of the overwhelming coverage of Louis by black newspapers. Young, "Joe Louis, Symbol," 104.

143. White to Editor, *Life*, June 18, 1940, Box 365, NAACP.

144. Sidney Hook, *The Hero in History: A Study in Limitation and Possibility* (New York, 1943), 12; Kapp, "Heroes, Villains, and Fools as Agents of Social Control," 57 for the quotation.

145. Eldon E. Snyder and Elmer Spreitzer, *Social Aspects of Sports* (Englewood Cliffs, NJ: 1978), 31.

146. Erik H. Erikson, *Gandhi's Truth: On the Origins of Militant Nonviolence* (New York, 1969), 266 and Identity: *Youth and Crisis* (New York, 1968), 31-32, respectively, for the theories of individual group identity and cultural consolidation.

147. Carl Rowan, "Nonsense about Joe" (Springfield, MO) *Leader and Press*, April 2, 1981, 5-A; John Kieran, "A Champion All the Way," *Opportunity Journal of Negro Life*, XX (Feb. 1942), 48.

148. William J. Goode, *The Celebration of Heroes' Prestige as a Control System* (Berkeley, CA, 1978), 1-2 and 10 for this theory. One federal official even suggested that Louis ask black civilians to rid themselves of venereal disease as "a patriotic measure"; J.M. Ragland to White, May 12, 1942, Box 365, NAACP.

149. James MacGregor Burns, *Leadership* (New York, 1978), 243.

150. Edmonds, Joe Louis, 86 for Louis as a symbol. Lewis M. Killian and Ralph H. Turner, *Collective Behavior* (Englewood Cliffs, NJ, 1957), 465 for the quotation. John Williams Ward, "The Meaning of Lindbergh's Flight," *American Quarterly*, X (Spring 1958), 3-16 for the best example of the significance of heroism that does not imply leadership.

151. August Meier and Elliot Rudwick, *Along the Color Line: Explorations in the Black Experience* (Urbana, 1976), 2.

152. Marshall Fishwick, "Prologue" in his. Ray B. Brown and Michael T. Marsden, eds., *Heroes in Popular Culture* (Bowling Green, Ohio, 1972), 7 for characteristics of old and modern heroes; Louis presented an exemplary image but played numerous roles, thereby bridging the qualities of past and future heroes.

153. *New York Times*, Oct. 12, 1942, 12 for the quotation of James J. Walker, and May 13, 1979, v. 3 for the Reverend Jesse Jackson's view of Louis as David-like.

154. Quoted in Young, "Joe Louis, Symbol," 110.

• • •

Suggestions for Further Reading

Anderson, Jervis, "Balck Heavies," *American Scholar*, XLVII (Summer, 1978), 387-395.

Coburn, Mark D., "America's Great Black Hope," *American Heritage*, XXIX, 6 (October-November, 1978), 82-91.

Davis, Lenwood, comp., *Joe Louis: A Bibliography of Articles, Books, Pamphlets, Records, and Archival Materials* (Westport, CT: Greenwood Press, 1983).

Edmonds, Anthony O., *Joe Louis* (Grand Rapids: Eerdemans, 1973).

_____, "The Second Louis-Schmeling Fight: Sport, Symbol and Culture," *Journal of Popular Culture*, VII, 1 (Summer, 1973), 42-50.

Kelley, W.G., "Jackie Robinson and the Press," *Journalism Quarterly*, LIII (Spring, 1976), 137-139.

Kirby, John B., *Black Americans in the Roosevelt Era: Liberalism and Race* (Knoxville: University of Tennessee Press, 1980).

Louis, Joe, *My Life Story*, (New York:, 1947).

———— with Edna and Art Rust, Jr., *Joe Louis: My Life* (New York:, 1978).

Miller, Margery, *Joe Louis: American* (New York, 1945).

Nagler, Barney, *The Brown Bomber* (New York: World, 1972).

Orr, Jack, "The Black Boxer: Exclusion and Ascendance" in John T. Talamini and Charles H. Page, eds., *Sport and Society* (Boston: Little, Brown, 1973).

Rosenblatt, Aaron, "Negroes in Baseball: The Failure of Success," *Transaction*, IV (1967), 51-53.

Sammons, Jeffrey T., "Boxing as a Reflection of Society: The Southern Reaction to Joe Louis," *Journal of Popular Culture*, XXVI (Spring, 1983), 23-33.

Smith, Ronald A., "The Paul Robeson-Jackie Robinson Saga and a Political Collusion," *Journal of Sport History*, VI (Summer, 1979), 5-27.

Tygiel, Jules, *Baseball's Great Experiment: Jackie Robinson and His Legacy* (New York: Oxford University Press, 1983).

Wiggins, David K., "Wendell Smith, the *Pittsburgh Courier-Journal* and the Campaign to Include Blacks in Organized Baseball, 1933-1945," *Journal of Sport History*, X, 2 (Summer, 1983), 5-29.

Weaver, Bill L., "The Black Press and the Assault on Professional Baseball's 'Color Line,' October, 1945-April, 1947," *Phylon*, XL (Winter, 1979), 303-317.

Young, James V. and Arthur F. McClure, *Remembering Their Glory: Sports Heroes of the 1940's* (Cranbury, NJ: A.S. Barnes, 1977).

INTERCOLLEGIATE ATHLETIC SERVITUDE: A CASE STUDY OF THE BLACK ILLINI STUDENT-ATHLETES 1931-1967

Donald Spivey & Thomas A. Jones

They vie for nearly one hundred national championships on three levels of competition under the auspices of four separate coordinating associations. Before matriculation they are the prizes in recruiting efforts which spare neither expense nor energy nor hyperbole to win their signatures on letters of intent. Throughout their undergraduate years, they are among the most visible on campus. They are subjected to the unique pressures that only public performance in competition brings. And upon graduation—for those who do graduate—they are a source of institutional pride and accomplishment. Yet, there are few characters on the American collegiate scene, or perhaps in all American sport, who evoke images more startling in their contrast than the student-athlete.

On one end of the spectrum is the compelling ideal implicit within the phrase "student athlete." Here is the young man or woman who has mastered both the rigors of a particular sport and the demands of a legitimate academic program of study. On the other end is the individual who suffers the devastating stereotype "dumb jock." Although a substantial middle ground may exist between the two images, the portrait of the latter is so pervasive that it has had a slanderous effect on the whole corpus of student-athletes.

The following essay provides a glimpse into the world of the student-athlete and the sources of this negative imagery. In focusing on black athletes at the University of Illinois, it reveals patterns of exploitation, racism, and irresponsibility that go well beyond the campus of this Big Ten institution. The authors particularly emphasize that the athletic scholarship experience for the great majority of the black Illini failed to deliver on two key points—a college degree and a professional sports career. Only 35% of the athletes in this study earned their degrees; 6% made it to the pros. As shocking as these figures seem to be, they are actually above national averages. Four years after entering college in 1977, only 18% of black male athletes across the country had graduated. The odds against a young black athlete making it as a professional are placed by Berkeley sociologist Harry Edwards at 20,000 to 1.

Intercollegiate athletics has become, and likely will remain, an important and institutionalized component of higher education in this country. The black Illini situation reflects its disgraceful elements. Whether or not intercollegiate sport can overcome this record and be both big and moral at the same time remains to be seen. The student-athlete as either a noble and attractive ideal or a shameful and deceptive fraud hangs in the balance.

Young black men from relatively poor socio-economic backgrounds have entered some of the most prestigious universities in this country largely because they were sought out for their athletic ability. Athletic scholarships have usually provided the financial means for these student-athletes to attend college. Because of this fact there exists the widespread assumption that these grants provided one of the few, if not only, means for black athletes to attend college, obtain a degree, and go on to improve their basic life situation. However, in more cases than not, this assumption masks the realities of being a black student-athlete on most of the nation's college and university campuses. Student-athletes in general, and black student-athletes in particular, often find it difficult to cope with the dual elements of the student-athlete role.[1] The quest for university prestige when coupled with the lure of an income-producing intercollegiate sports program intensifies the desire for winning teams. The desire to win at whatever the cost has resulted in the development of sports programs in major conferences such as the Big Ten, Big Eight, Southeast, and Southwest that order the student-athlete's role as an athlete before his role as a student. What happens to blacks in this near professional setting of major intercollegiate sports is the focus of this study.

WHO WILL GRADUATE

There is a substantial amount of descriptive literature which graphically details the many problems facing blacks within the intercollegiate sports arena.[2] In spite of this store of information, there is a paucity of data on the academic success of black student-athletes as indicated by their rate of graduation from the same colleges and universities which were so intent on securing the services of their athletic talents. In this paper we shall examine the case of the University of Illinois, a member of the Big Ten Conference, with respect to the graduation patterns of black student athletes. Specifically, we investigate the percentage of black Illinois student-athletes who obtain a degree; compare black student-athletes academically with white student-athletes; and, compare student-athletes academically with student-non-athletes.

Two hundred and twenty-seven blacks received athletic scholarships to the University of Illinois from 1937 through 1967: football, 156; track, 51; basketball, 18; fencing, 2; baseball, wrestling, swimming, tennis, golf and ice-hockey, 0. Sixty-five percent of the black Illini student-athletes failed to graduate.[3] While we found no substantial difference between the major and minor sports athletes in terms of entrance examination scores and high school class rank, black Illini participating in football and basketball, the two most remunerative sports for Illinois, have a higher academic attrition rate than their counterparts in the track and fencing programs. Edwards concludes that the black athlete in the predominantly white school is first, foremost, and sometimes only, an athletic commodity, and therefore, is "expected to 'sleep, eat, and drink' athletics."[4] It is our supposition that the other factors discussed below are exacerbated by the fact that black athletes on the major teams are expected to spend what amounts to a disproportionate share of each day in activities devoted to their sport. This in turn leaves little time for academic pursuits.[5]

TABLE 1

Percent of University of Illinois Black and White Athletes and Non-athletes Who Received Degrees,[a] (N's in parenthesis)

	Black Athletes				Black Non-Athletes[b]	White Athletes[c]	White Non-Athletes[d]
	Football	Track	Basketball	Fencing			
Pre-1950	56.0	50.0	n.a	n.a	43.0	66.0	51.0
1950-1959	26.0	46.0	100.00	n.a	44.0	48.0	59.0
1960-1967	22.0	50.0	29.0	50.0	55.0	48.0	65.0
Total Percent	29.0	47.0	38.0	50.0	49.0	53.0	59.0
Total N	(35)	(23)	(6)	(1)	(80)	(89)	(202)

[a] Source: *Report of the University of Illinois Board of Trustees,* 1937-1972; University of Illinois Archives, "The Negro Student Files," 1941-1972; University of Illinois, *Student-Staff Directory,* 1937-1972. All percentages are rounded.
[b] Random Sampling (N = 200).
[c] Random Sampling (N = 200).
[d] Random Sampling (N = 500).

ACT SCORES AND CLASS RANK

Utilizing American College Testing and Scholarship Aptitude Test scores, and high school class rank, the Big Ten Conference of the National Collegiate Athletic Association conducted research in 1961 to develop prediction equations for assessing the prospective student-athlete's chances of obtaining a "passing" (2.0 or C) grade point average during the first year at those universities composing the Conference. The results indicate that a student entering the University of Illinois with an ACT composite score of 25 and high school class rank in the seventieth percentile has a 50 percent chance of achieving a first year G.P.A. of 2.0.[6] Ninety-six percent of the black Illini student-athletes for whom we have data fall below the predicted success quotients.

Comparison of the mean of ACT composite scores and class rank of blacks entering the University of Illinois on a sports scholarship reveals a gross deficiency in preparation for college. Although black Illini student-athletes are from the upper third of their respective high schools and white student-athletes rank lower, it must be noted that 47 percent of the black student-athletes are from Chicago and primarily from inner city, black, ghetto schools.[7] The fact that black student-athletes ranked in the upper third of their high school graduating class, yet had achieved substandard ACT scores may be taken as an indication of the inferiority of their high school preparation for academic competition in college.

Athletic department personnel are cognizant of the black athlete's deficiency in academic preparation, and often counsel him to take those courses which are more likely to keep him eligible to compete than move him toward graduation. The black athlete is usually advised that he can get the grades and remain eligible by majoring in physical education[8]—advice followed by 66 percent of the black Illini student-athletes. The college of Physical Education, however, has one of the highest attrition rates on the Illinois campus. Moreover, the flunk-out rate for black Illini athletes far exceeds the University's general academic attrition rate.[9] It may well be that no "easy" courses exist at the University of Illinois, especially for those students who lack adequate academic preparation.

TABLE 2

Mean for American College Testing (ACT) Composite Score and
Class Rank of Black and White Athletes and Nonathletes
Entering the University of Illinois[a]
(N's in parenthesis)

	ACT Composite Score	Class Rank (Percentile)
Athletes		
Black	18	70
White (N = 200)[b]	23	59
Non-Athletes		
Black (N = 200)[b]	23	84
White (N - 500)[b]	27	81

[a] Source: Office of the Registrar, University of Illinois.
[b] Random Sampling.

TABLE 3

Distribution by Percentage of Black and White Athletes and Nonathletes
Residing in the East North Central Region Prior to Enrollment
at the University of Illinois, 1937-1972[a]
(N's in parenthesis)

	Black Athletes (215)	White Athletes[b] (200)	Black Non- athletes[c] (188)	White Non- athletes[d] (490)
East North Central	66.0	69.0	61.0	94.0
Illinois	61.0	53.0	53.0	90.0
Chicago	47.0	28.0	25.0	21.0
Inner City Chicago	46.0	17.0	12.0	6.0

[a] Source: University of Illinois, *Student-Staff Directory*, 1937-1972;
University of Illinois Archives, "The Negro Student Files," 1941-1972. The
percentages for each area are computed for the total area, not excluding
smaller regional categories. All percentages are rounded.
[b] Random Sampling (N = 200).
[c] Random Sampling (N = 200).
[d] Random Sampling (N = 500).

TABLE 4

Percentile Distribution by College of Enrollment of Black and White
Athletes and Nonathletes at the University of Illinois, 1937-1972[a]

College Enrolled	Black Athletes (217)	White Athletes[b] (196)	Black Non-athletes[c] (181)	White Non-athletes[d] (471)
Agriculture	1.0	6.0	1.0	13.0
Aviation	n.a.	1.0	1.0	.4
Commerce	8.0	5.0	8.0	8.0
Communications	n.a.	1.0	4.0	9.0
Education	1.0	6.0	33.0	7.0
Engineering	5.0	6.0	2.0	17.0
Fine & Applied Arts	4.0	5.0	4.0	13.0
Liberal Arts & Sciences	15.0	40.0	38.0	31.0
Physical Education	66.0	33.0	9.0	3.0

[a] Source: University of Illinois, *Student-Staff Directory*, 1937-1972;
University of Illinois Archives, "The Negro Student Files," 1941-1972. All
percentages are rounded.
[b] Random Sampling (N = 200).
[c] Random Sampling (N = 200).
[d] Random Sampling (N = 500).

PREJUDICE AS A DETRIMENTAL FORCE

The existence of racial prejudice within the University's academic, athletic and social environments further diminished the probability of
a black student-athlete graduating from the University of Illinois. There is
no reason to believe that a pleasant campus environment is an essential
ingredient in fostering academic success. Such an environment does not
exist for blacks at the University of Illinois.

The University of Illinois Athletic Association maintained a policy of racial exclusion until 1931 when Earl A. Jameson made a brief appearance on the track team.[10] However, it was not until 1937, during the
coaching tenure of Robert Zuppke, that Illinois' most prestigious sport,
football, was integrated when Alphonse Anders became the first black to
participate on that team and the first black recipient of an athletic

scholarship to Illinois. Anders lasted only two seasons.[11] Jameson and Anders, like other black athletes during the Zuppke era at the University of Illinois, encountered a pattern of discrimination typical of that to be found in practically every secondary school, college, university, and professional athletic team throughout the United States. Many black athletes of potential star caliber became frustrated and often simply stopped trying to compete.[12]

An Illinois undergraduate, Jean Knapp, in 1946 reported, "Negroes are not allowed on baseball, basketball, tennis,and swimming teams."[13] This policy continued until 1957 when two blacks who later became outstanding performers for Illinois, Mannie Jackson and Govoner Vaughn, gained admission into the basketball program. The "color line" against athletic participation began to disappear but this was only one barrier with which blacks had to contend.

The social environment at the University of Illinois had ill effects upon some black student-athletes. Recalling the difficulties, Claude "Buddy" Young, a track and football star for the Illini in the 1940's, said "few social outlets" existed for "black athletes and this made academic production impossible."[14]

As an additional burden, barred from university housing, blacks walked miles to and from campus.[15] Black athlete William Willis complained of the difficulties due to discrimination in housing. "We [black students] live so far from campus that," Willis lamented, "it is really difficult to walk back and forth so far three or four times a day ... I live in a private home now, and we just don't get along with the owners too well."[16] Discrimination in campus housing ceased in 1955.[17] Social problems and related frustrations, however, continued.

Jesse L. Jackson, now the Rev. Jesse L. Jackson and leading civil rights activist, attended the University of Illinois on a sports scholarship in the late 1950s. He was disgruntled by the separatism then imposed on blacks. "While the white guys were out there partying with the girls on the weekends," Jackson reminisced, "the blacks sat in their dorm drinking Coke and playing cards." Jackson became so disgusted that he quit at the end of his freshman year. He secured a scholarship to North Carolina Agricultural and Technical State University, an all-black school where he excelled as a football star, an honor student and president of the student body.[18]

Black Illini athletes who could deal with the problems of campus life still had to survive the prejudices of coaches, teammates and alumni. For example, it is usual for players who make the first team to "start" games. Nevertheless, before the 1960s, black Illini were often denied their right to start. "After earning a position on the first team," black former All-American Bill Burrell reflected on his years with Illinois' football program from 1956 to 1960, "blacks were seldom allowed to start in the game ... The Alumni Association had much influence on the makeup of the

starting lineup. I actually made All-American from the second-team."
Burrell added: "The coaches were prejudiced as were most of the players.
There were a lot of conflicts ..."[19]

Some positions on collegiate and professional teams are designated "white only." In Illini sports, one position reserved traditionally for
whites is quarterback. For one year, 1958, the Illini had a talented black
quarterback in Mel Myers—their first, and so far, only black quarterback.
William Y. Smith, a prominent leader of Urbana-Champaign's black
community and a close friend of Myers, recalled that Mel Myers never
played on the first team, and, according to Smith, suffered insulting racial
innuendos from white teammates and sports fans who resented a black
playing quarterback. In addition, Smith believed, during scrimmages the
defense played its roughest when Myers was on offense.[20]

Efforts to hinder blacks from progressing in collegiate and
professional sports are well known.[21] When blacks attained success there
were attempts to minimize their accomplishments by means of racial
stereotyping which belittled individual achievements.[22] Simon and
Carey, in their investigation of alleged racial discrimination against black
Illini athletes in 1963, found that blacks complained about the stereotypes
("Uncle Tom" jokes) and hostile attitude of coaches, teammates, instruc-
tors, and white students. The athletes said they had been "humiliated by
teachers, coaches, other athletes, and white students."[23] According to
their report, most black Illini athletes "believe that the Athletic
Association and the Department of Physical Education give them lower
grades than they deserve, prevent them from gaining recognition in
certain sports, and police their social activities."[24]

Reports indicate that the Athletic Association did police the social activities of its black athletes. The most severely sanctioned social
activity was interracial dating. In 1963, three black athletes at the
University of Illinois confronted a black graduate student and told him
that a member of the Athletic Association had "urged them to stop dating
or being seen with white girls."[25] To fight this racial discrimination, the
athletes solicited the Urbana-Champaign chapter of the NAACP for assistance and within days the entire university community was in an uproar.
The issue soon was dropped, however. The three blacks backed down
from their stand because of pressure brought upon them by their
coaches.[26]

One Illinois policy for recruitment and maintenance of athletes
raised some fundamental questions about racial policies in the sixties. In
their zeal to recruit superior talent, Illinois coaches, with the assistance of
influential alumni, had initiated a lavish recruitment fund which would
also provide the prospect with money in excess of his scholarship once
the prospect became an Illini.

On December 22, 1966, Mel Brewer, then Assistant Athletic
Director of the University of Illinois, disclosed to the Commissioner of

the NCAA the existence of this fund established for the purpose of distributing improper financial aid to the University's athletes. The violations of NCAA rules, uncovered as a result of the disclosure and subsequent investigation, became known as the Illinois "Slush Fund" scandal. The fact that a "Slush Fund" existed should have surprised no one familiar with how "Big Time" intercollegiate sports operate. But the racial questions of probability, student responsibility, and discrimination deserve attention here. First, is it probable that only eight Illinois athletes received improper funds and that Illinois was the only university guilty of the infraction? Second, should student-athletes be punished for accepting money from a lucrative enterprise in which their actions are sanctioned under direct authority of their coaches? Third, the decision rendered by the NCAA barred eight Illinois players from ever competing in the Association; seven of the eight were blacks.[27]

For the black Illini in the late sixties problems persisted. In our interviews with blacks who had participated in sports at Illinois during this period, we heard numerous complaints: about "stacking," where a number of blacks are placed in competition for the same position; about local sports commentators biased in favor of white athletes; and about the Athletic Association's polity of recruiting a limited number of blacks in order not to exceed "the quota."[28]

In 1970 and 1971 a number of small conferences of educators, coaches and athletic directors were held to consider the plight of black athletes at major white universities.[29] These conferences generated attention to the problems of black collegiate athletes. On March 7, 1972, three Michigan State University black professors sent a list of complaints to Big Ten Commissioner Wayne Duke stressing: "The primary purpose for attending a university should be to get an education and not to play sports." This priority "should be the case for both black and white athletes. However, because of the importance of athletics to the university ... the role of the athlete is seen as more important than the role of the student."[30] So far, nothing has resulted from the Michigan State professors' efforts.

CONCLUSION

The athletic scholarship was, in the final analysis, of minor benefit to the vast majority of black Illini recipients. Black Illini student-athletes had, as ascertained from our interviews, two basic goals: (1) obtain a degree and (2) play professional sports. Sixty-five percent, however, failed to earn a degree and only 14 advanced to a career in professional sports.[31] The limited accomplishments were predictable, when viewed in retrospect. Entering the University of Illinois with deficient scholastic preparation they then had to cope with the negative aspects of the athletic, academic and social environments. It is a tremendous feat that even a small percentage of black athletes successfully completed the academic and sport programs. Further research is needed to assess whether the conditions blacks faced at Illinois were or are typical for black participants in "Big Time" intercollegiate sports throughout the country. We hope that this paper serves to stimulate both interest and research in that direction.

• • •

Notes

1. Jack Scott, *The Athletic Revolution* (New York: The Free Press, 1971), pp. 40-41, 178-202, 204-214; See John Underwood, "The Desperate Coach," *Sports Illustrated* (August 25, 1969), pp. 66-76; Harry Edwards, *Sociology of Sport* (Illinois: The Dorsey Press, 1973), pp. 175-182; An excellent analysis of the economic functioning of major intercollegiate sport programs is given in James Koch, "The Economics of 'Big Time' Intercollegiate Athletics," *Social Science Quarterly*, 52 (Sept., 1971), pp. 248-260.

2. Some of the most important works are: Harry Edwards, *The Revolt of the Black Athlete* (New York: The Free Press, 1969); Jack Olsen, *The Black Athlete: A Shameful Story* (New York: Time-Life Books, 1968); William Russell, *Go Up for Glory* (New York: Coward-McCann, 1966); Jesse Owens, *Blackthink: My Life as Black Man and White Man* (New York: William Morrow and Company, 1970); James P. Terzian and Jim Benagh, *The Jimmy Brown Story* (New York: Julian Messner, 1964); Jack Orr, *The Black Athlete* (New York: The Lion Press, 1969); and Edwin B. Henderson, *The Negro in Sport* (Washington, D.C.: Associated Publishers, 1949).

3. We distinguish between non-scholarship athletes, and those recruited and recipient of an athletic scholarship. This is an important distinction for there is a small percentage of "walk-on" athletes who in fact participate on the teams but they are not a true reflection of the operative system and, therefore, have been omitted. Our figures also included only those black Illini athletes prior to 1968, since the average time it takes a student to graduate from Illinois is approximately 4.5 years.

4. Edwards, *Revolt of the Black Athlete*, p. 9.

5. The athletes participating in football and basketball spend an average of four to five hours a day in athletics (and this does not include the time an individual athlete may spend daily recuperating from practice) which usually, on either a formal or informal basis, continues throughout the entire year.

6. University Examination Service, State University of Iowa, *A Study of Selected Measures as Predictors of Academic success at Institutions of the Western Conference*, Report No. 2, Results—Part II (Iowa: State University of Iowa, 1961), pp. 4,7,8.

7. We checked the high schools of black athletes recruited from Chicago with the *Illinois Directory of Public Elementary and Secondary Schools in Selected Districts* (1970). Over 90 percent of those black athletes had attended all-black, ghetto schools. For further discussion along this line see *Integrated Education*, 9 (Sept.-Oct., 1971), pp. 4-67; and Geraldine F. Johnson, "Metropolitan Tests: Inappropriate for ESEA Pupils," Ibid., 9 (Nov.-Dec., 1971), pp. 22-42.

8. William A. Ruffer, 'Symposium on Problems of the Black Athlete,"
Journal of Health, Physical Education and Recreation, (Feb., 1971), p. 12; Robert
L. Green, Joseph R. McMillan, and Thomas S. Gunnings, "Blacks in the Big Ten,"
Integrated Education, 10 (May-June, 1972), p. 34.

9. See *University of Illinois Office of Admissions and Records,* "Number
and Percentage of Total Enrollment Placed on Probation or Dropped for Poor
Scholarship," *Confidential Reports, 1948-1972* (mimeographed). Cited for comparative reference by permission of the University of Illinois.

10. University of Illinois Athletic Association, "Track," 1931, Publicity
Office Files of the University of Illinois Athletic Association.

11. Ibid., "Football," 1937-1940.

12. John Smith, interview, University of Illinois, March 10, 1972. Smith
attended Illinois as an undergraduate in the late 1930's. He was an initiator of the
"Symposium on Problems of the Black Athlete," in 1970, and is now Instructor in
the Department of Physical Education at the University of Illinois.

13. Jean Knapp, "The University of Illinois and Its Negroes," *The Green
Cauldron* (University of Illinois Archives, April 12, 1946), p. 12.

14. WCIA, "Interview with Claude 'Buddy' Young," October 4, 1967.

15. Catherine Hunt, "The University of Illinois and the Drive for Negro
Equality, 1945-1951," Unpub., Grad. Seminar paper (University of Illinois Archives,
1966), pp. 30-33.

16. *Daily Illini,* October 29, 1949, p. 4.

17. Hunt, "Drive for Negro Equality," p. 43.

18. "Jesse Jackson, One Leader Among Many," *Time,* (April, 6, 1970), p.
21.

19. William Burrell, interview, Aurora, Illinois, May 2, 1972.

20. William Y. Smith, interview, Champaign, Illinois, April 14, 1972; on
the question of discriminatroy practices pertaining to player-positions see John
W. Loy and Joseph F. Elvogue, "Racial Segregation in American Sport,"
International Review of Sport Sociology, 5 (1970), pp. 5-25.

21. See Michael Govan, "The Emergence of the Black Athlete in
America," *The Black Scholar,* 3 (November, 1971), pp. 16-28.

22. Such stereotypical justifications were: Blacks are superior sprinters
because of *anatomical peculiarities,* excellent football players as a result of *natural ability,* great basketball players due to the fact they're *born with rhythm.* "Sure
he is a superb high jumper and broad-jumper, he's part ape." For discussion, see
Edwards, *Sociology of Sport,* pp. 190-197.

An indication of the University of Illinois Athletic Association's racism,
which often took a subtle form, is a 1960 official release by the publicity office
concerning the abilities of Marshall Starks, who gained the most yards on the
football team during its 1959 season. The title of the release read: "Marshall
Starks, Illinois Leading Ground Gainer Last Year, Had Deal With Local Barbecue-
House." It may have been true that "Starks had agreement with local barbecue-
house that for each touchdown he ran, he would receive a slab of barbecued
ribs." What is of greater interest is that the publicity release was limited to a discussion of the connection between Starks and barbecued ribs. University of
Illinois Athletic Association, "Football," 1960, Publicity Office Files of the
University of Illinois Athletic Association.

23. Rita James Simon and James W. Carey, "The Phantom Racist: Alleged
Discrimination against Negro Athletes at Illinois Raised Broader Issues that
Remain Unsolved," *Transaction,* 4 (Nov., 1966), p. 6.

24. Ibid., p. 10.

25. Ibid., p. 5.

26. Ibid., p. 11; the athletic establishments can exert influence over their athletes' social and political activities. For discussion pertaining to this point see Koch, "Economics of 'Big-Time' Intercollegiate Athletics," pp. 254-255.

27. See *Illinois Joint Legislative Committee, Report to the Seventy-Fifth General Assembly* (1968), Exhibits No. 4 and 17, pp. 3-17, 53-65.

28. Lawrence Jordan, Norris Coleman, and David Jackson, interview, University of Illinois, April 5, 1972; Carl Glover, telephone interview, Charleston, South Carolina, April 6, 1972; Melvin Blair, interview, University of Illinois, April 12, 13, 1972; Willie Smith, interview, Chicago, April 10, 1972; Timothy Beamer, telephone interview, New York, April 24, 1972; Cyril Pinder, telephone interview, Chicago, April 25, 1972. Six other black Illini athletes made similar remarks but asked that their names be withheld.

29. The most prolific of these conferences was the "Symposium on Problems of the Black Athlete," held December 5, 1970, at Indiana State University.

30. Green, et al., "Blacks in the Big Ten," p. 33.

31. See Roger L. Treat, *The Official Encyclopedia of Football* (New York: A.S. Barnes and Co., 1970); Zander Hollander, *The Modern Encyclopedia of Basketball* (New York: Four Winds Press, 1973); and Hy Turkin and S.C. Thompson, *The Official Encyclopedia of Baseball* (New York: A.S. Barnes and Co., 1972). Nine black Illini in football and five in basketball went on to play professional sports.

• • •

Suggestions for Further Reading

Atwell, Robert, et al., *The Money Game: Financing Collegiate Athletics* (Washington: American Council on Education, 1980).

Behee, John, *Hail to the Victors! Black Athletes at the University of Michigan* (Ann Arbor: Swenk-Tuttle Press, 1974).

Benaugh, Jim, *Making It to #1: How College Football and Basketball Teams Get There* (New York: 1976).

Brown, Roscoe C., Jr., "The Black Gladiator—The Major Force in Modern American Sport," *76th Annual Proceedings of the National College Physical Education Association for Men* (January, 1973), 43-50.

Dillard, S., "A Speck in the Crowd: Black Athletes on White Campuses," *Journal fof Physical Education and Recreation*, XLVIII (1945), 66-68.

Durso, Joseph, *The Sports Factory: An Investigation into College Sports* (New York: Quadrangle, 1975).

Edwards, Harry, *The Revolt of the Black Athlete* (NY: Free Press, 1969).

_____, "Sport Within the Veil: The Triumphs, Tragedies and Challenges of Afro-American Involvement," *Annals of the American Academy of Political and Social Science*, 445 (1979), 116-127.

Evans, J. Robert, *Blowing the Whistle on Intercollegiate Athletics* (Chicago: 1974).

Green, R.L. and G.S. Smith, T.S. Gunnings, J.H. McMillan, "Black Athletes: Educational, Economic and Political Considerations," *Journal of Non-White Concerns*, III, 1 (1974), 6-38.

Hanford, George H., *The Need for a National Study of Collegiate Athletics: A Report to the American Council on Education* (New York: Carnegie Corporation and Ford Foundation, 1974).

Koch, James V., "The Economics of Big Time Intercollegiate Athletics," *Social Science Quarterly*, LII (September, 1971), 248-260.

Lapchick, Richard E., *Broken Promises: Racism in American Sports* (New York: St. Martins/Marek, 1984).

Loy, John, and Joseph F. McElvogue, "Racial Segregation in American Sport," *International Review of Sport Sociology*, V (1970), 5-23.

McCallum, John D., *Big Ten Football Since 1895* (Radnor, PA: Chilton, 1976).

_____ and Charles H. Pearson, *College Football, USA, 1869-1972* (Greenwich, CT: Hall of Fame Publications, 1972).

Olsen, Jack, *The Black Athlete: A Shameful Story*, (NY: Time-Life, 1969).

Rosen, Charles, *The Scandals of '51* (New York: 1978).

Scott, Jack, *The Athletic Revolution* (New York: Free Press, 1971).

Shaw, Gary, *Meat on the Hoof* (New York: Dell, 1973).

Underwood, John, *The Death of an American Game: The Crisis in Football* (Boston: Little, Brown, 1979).

_____, "The Writing is on the Wall," *Sports Illustrated*, LIV (May 19, 1980), 36 ff.

Wolf, David, *Foul! The Connie Hawkins Story* (New York: Holt, Rinehart and Winston, 1972).

Zingg, Paul J., "What Next for the Student-Athlete?" *The Educational Forum*, XLVI, 3 (Spring, 1982), 283-293.

"NICE GIRLS DON'T SWEAT"
WOMEN IN AMERICAN SPORT[1]

William H. Beezley
Joseph P.Hobbs

The history of women in American sport parallels closely the role of women in our society. Constrained by a nineteenth century "cult of true womanhood," that defined their life according to a virtuous code of piety, purity, submissiveness and domesticity, women faced great social, psychological and legal barriers to sports participation. As William Beezley and Joseph Hobbs show in the following essay, Victorian notions that women's sports should be neither strenuous nor spectator-oriented dominated concepts of athletic participation and competition for women well into the twentieth century. Even when things began to change in the 1960s—spurred on by a revived feminist movement, international competition with the Soviets particularly in track and field, increased economic power and leisure capital for women, and various legislative and court mandates, especially Title IX of the 1972 Education Amendments Act—sexual discrimination and disparity continued to mark American sport.

Although women's sports are clearly in transition, the pace is hardly blinding. The authors point to differentials in prize money and earnings for male and female athletes in the same sport, athletic budgets for men's and women's intercollegiate sports programs, media coverage, and the academic study of sport as examples of the second-class treatment that women's sports receive. Moreover, the outlook for women's athletics is not particularly rosy. In an era when nearly 70% of men's intercollegiate athletic programs lose money and over 80% of football programs are not self-supporting, it is unlikely that women's programs will benefit in a big way on the campus. Except for a few individual sports, like golf and tennis, and the Olympics every four years, collegiate programs offer the best opportunities for women's athletics. If these opportunities remain static or, worse, fade, then the status of women's sports will not improve.

Beezley and Hobbs suggest that an attitudinal change effecting definitions and measurements of achievement in sport might benefit both men's and women's athletics. It seems clear, though, that the most important attitudinal changes that are needed to improve the role of women in sport are those that go beyond the fields of play.

Why do women want to participate in organized sport? The literature grows daily on the unsavory aspects of sport—winning at all costs, cheating, gambling, recruiting violations, injuries, drugs, exploitation of athletes, the increasing resemblance of sport to the larger society where the individual is unrecognizable and unimportant. But the literature also grows on the value of sport for teaching discipline, competitiveness and teamwork, and bringing relaxation and healthful exercise to participants and entertainment for spectators.[2] For women, as for other excluded groups such as immigrants, sport seems an important avenue to full citizenship, and an escape from the status of house slave on an isolated "plantation."

To begin with, let us consider the efforts to provide participation in sport for college women. Lydia Huntley Signourney in some 2000 articles and 60 books exhorted women toward emancipation.[3] Organized physical training and sports in higher education was still some 20 years away, yet some educators in the antebellum period acted on their belief that women in school needed exercise. For example, Mary Lyon, the founder of Mount Holyoke College, was not alone in including physical education as part of woman's education. Although southern female education continued to be centered in the home during the antebellum period, over 200 private schools were founded and some school curricula required physical activities. Wesleyan Female College, along with others, even provided indoor recreation rooms for use during inclement weather.[4] These physical educators would provide a mixed, indeed controversial, legacy. They did not urge that young women compete with men in sport or anything else. They accepted and encouraged the notion of women's place—mother and housekeeper. They prescribed exercise that would not make young women "ungraceful" and "unlady-like" but instead would make and keep them healthy enough to fulfill their given role in society. Catherine Beecher's *Course of Calisthenics for Young Ladies* set out activities that for many became a model.[5] And so educated young women participated in calisthenics, walks, dancing, horseback riding and other activities, but they were not to enter the man's world.

Nevertheless, as collegiate sport organized in the last half of the 19th century, women began to compete, as did men, in intercollegiate basketball, volleyball, and field hockey.[6] The pioneers had their difficulties: Lynn Emergy, at the 1979 meeting of the NASSH, in a paper entitled

"The First Intercollegiate Contest for Women: Basketball, April 4, 1896," recounted how it was.[7] The game was between the University of California, Berkeley, and Stanford University. No men were allowed to attend. The young women were, after all, playing in bloomers and might even be sweating, sights not to be witnessed by men who were not blood relatives. All went well until one of the baskets needed to be repaired. Because only men could use tools, two male laborers were called in to make repairs. At the sight of the men, the Berkeley team screamed and hid in a corner. But Stanford, according to Emery, "paid scant attention to the men and moved indifferently to a convenient area where they assumed becoming postures of ease." The Berkeley team behaved more conventionally; newspaper accounts dealt primarily not with the athletic abilities of the players, but with their "pleasing appearance and becoming actions."

As the skill of college women in sport increased, so did competition. This development, coupled with the growing accomplishments and publicity of other women's sports figures in the early 20th century, caused a reaction of alarm among many, including the intellectual heirs of those female physical educators of the early 19th century. They did not want women to enter this man's world of competition. As these physical educators looked around in the 1920s, they saw other disquieting signs: the suffragette who talked of women voting as a bloc since they had now acquired the franchise, and the flapper who not only indulged in but actually talked about sex, drank in public with men and showed her legs. The next thing one knew, women would want to take off their bulky sport clothes and show most of their bodies to be able to run better, swim better or shoot baskets better. And so began what Barbara Jane Walder has called "Mrs. Hoover's Holy War on Athletics." Mrs. Hoover was Lou Henry Hoover, wife of then Secretary of Commerce Herbert Hoover. Mrs. Hoover and others succeeded in reducing intercollegiate competition as we know it today from a still small percentage of colleges to nearly none by 1930. What competition remained occurred on play days and sports days and through telegraphic meets. High level competition was discouraged.[8]

By the end of World War II, however, about one third of eastern colleges had intercollegiate athletics for women. But although practice changed, principle remained intact until the late 1960s, when, as part of the second feminist wave of the 20th century, a new generation of physical educators insisted that woman's place was wherever she wanted to be. Intercollegiate competition among women increased dramatically.

Today's students of college physical education for women do not simply write off the founding mothers as Aunt Janes. Instead, they point out the dangers of being too present-minded when looking at the past. Ellen Gerber reminds us that the perceived mission at that time was to provide physical activity for all women instead of today's emphasis on equality of opportunity, especially in quality programs.[9] If such women had flown the ideological flag of equality, they might well have not made the gains they did.

From the myriad of organizations overseeing college women's athletics came a National Commission on Intercollegiate Sports. This commission established national Intercollegiate Championships in the late 1960s in Gymnastics, Golf, Track and Field, Swimming, Volleyball and Badminton. This proliferation of championships demanded a strong, unified body to give direction and governance to women's athletic programs, and in 1972 the AIAW (Association for Intercollegiate Athletics for Women) was founded.

The AIAW hoped to bring about more intense and higher level competition while avoiding the abuses threatening men's college athletics. The AIAW placed strong restrictions on recruiting and took other steps to avoid cheating on transcripts and recruiting, exploitation of students and too much emphasis on commercialism.[10] The AIAW's hope for a separate but equal and purer existence than the governing body of male college athletics, the NCAA (National Collegiate Athletic Association), received a rude reception from the sister body. The NCAA fought the growth of women's programs, but the number of women participating in collegiate competition continued to grow. This pressure, intensified by aid from the federal government, resulted in the NCAA's decision: If you can't lick them, take them over. In January 1980 the NCAA established women's championships in five sports for Divisions II and III, the smaller colleges, and in January 1981 the NCAA established women's championships in twelve sports for Division I, the major colleges.[11] Where the NCAA will take women's athletics, only Walter Byers knows.

Of perhaps even greater impact on women's sports in educational institutions is something known as Title IX. Section 901(a) of Title IX of the Education Amendments Act of 1972 brought women's education under the protection of the Civil Rights Act of 1964. It reads: "No person in the United States shall on the basis of sex, be excluded from participation in, be denied the benefits of, or be subjected to discrimination under any education program or activity receiving federal financial assistance."[12]

Sports was obviously an area in which education discriminated by gender. Funding for competitive sports for women was estimated to be less than one percent of that provided for men's programs. Some women opposed certain aspects of the act, fearing that athletic scholarships and related things would pervert women's athletics. Men, however, acting through the NCAA, provided the major opposition. Father Edmund M. Joyce, executive vice president of Notre Dame, condemned the bill's guidelines on equal spending for men and women as "asinine." Small wonder: in 1978, Notre Dame had a total scholarship budget of just under one million dollars for male athletes, and nothing for women athletes.[13]

The federal government has been slow in formulating policy to implement the act and to this date passive in its actual implementation. Even now, the NCAA has a class action suit which argues that athletic departments are self-sufficient and therefore the federal government cannot decide how they must spend their self-generated funds. In a recent separate case a federal district judge in Michigan ruled that colleges and public schools do not have to provide equal expenditures for men and women if a particular sport in question does not receive federal assistance.[14]

Despite the resistance by the NCAA and confusion from the federal government, participation by high school and college women in sport continues to grow. For example, in 1971-72 there were 95 AIAW college track teams; in 1977-78, 424. In 1973, 7,292 high schools had girls' track teams with 178,209 participants; in 1977-8, 13,789 high schools sponsored over 466,000 participants.[15] These statistics and others reflect the efforts of educators and government officials as well as the determination of a generation of more confident young women not to surrender the world of sport simply because of gender. Shortly after Fr. Joyce of Notre Dame denounced Title IX, NEW Secretary Joseph Califano was Notre Dame's graduation speaker. He was greeted by a silent protest against Title IX by the seniors, some of whom had "IX" taped to their graduation caps. It is rumored that Califano then talked to the President of Notre Dame. In any event, the next semester Notre Dame produced $80,000 for women's athletic scholarships—only a start, but a beginning.[16]

The experience of women in collegiate sport is mirrored in the larger history of women in sport—a start from near zero, some change amidst great opposition, a way yet to go. Women's growing involvement was influenced by factors that were changing a rural agrarian nation—a nation seen as homogeneous, governed by an unchanging orthodoxy—into a dynamic modern nation which, in acknowledging its diversity, made more difficult the imposition of an orthodoxy.

Developments in transportation and communication, along with continuing technological breakthroughs, brought from mid-19th century on a new America and along with it, new and modern sports.[17]

Women's place and possibilities were affected by all aspects of the New America, but developments such as labor-saving home appliances and better birth control devices would give women more leisure time. Conceivably, women would both need exercise and have time for it. Industrial might brought a new kind of total war. The factories needed workers, and women were increasingly an available and always cheap source of labor. Wars against the bad guys raised questions about bad practices at home.

Within this context, then, women inched into the man's world of sport. John A. Lucas and Ronald A. Smith, in *Saga of American Sport* (probably to date the best overall history), maintain that three questions summarize women's place in sport. In the 1890s, the question most frequently asked was, "Should a lady ride a bicycle?" In the 1920s, it was, "Shall women compete in highly competitive athletics?" In the 1960s and '70s we asked, "Shall women have equal opportunity with men to compete in athletics at all levels?"[18]

"Should a lady ride a bicycle?" In order to ride a bicycle without killing herself, a woman had to hike a skirt. Rising hemlines could lead to just about anything. We know now it did.[19] Women and men now played together at croquet, proving correct those good souls who had opposed women playing croquet at all, on the grounds that such activity would debase women and society.[20] Mary E. Outerbridge of Staten Island introduced tennis to the United States in 1874. Angela Lumpkin of UNC-Chapel Hill has shown the consequences.[21] Women played daintily for a while but eventually adopted "male" tactics. They dressed in an appropriately modest manner at first but then—simply to play better—wore fewer clothes. Despite all these efforts and subsequent gains, women remained second class citizens during the 19th century.

Yet things were moving the way of those who were not white Anglo-Saxon males. In a burgeoning economy, jobs had to be filled. At the start of the 20th century millions of immigrants arrived, and they were coming, not from north and west Europe, but from south and east Europe. New and different immigrants meant new and different ways of living, and a new, necessarily more egalitarian ethic would have to be adopted in an economy that depended for growth on everyone—not just WASPs—buying things.

Despite strong opposition, women began to compete in the Olympics, beginning in 1900 with golf and tennis.[22] The New York Female Giants played softball. Even more amazingly, a woman, Helene Britton, in 1911 inherited ownership of baseball's St. Louis Cardinals and, despite intense opposition, remained owner for 6 years.[23] The changing status of women in the first two decades of the century culminated in the passage of the 19th Amendment, bringing national suffrage to women in 1920. And so Eleanora Sears—who, bred in Boston's upper class, played sports with an attitude and vigor thought at the time to be only masculine, and who at age 44 was still good enough to win the 1928 National Women's Singles Championship in squash[24]—had company early in the century.

In the 1920s technological innovations and scientific management doubled productivity.[25] Workers benefited both at home and in the factory. Leisure time and more money meant that people could go out to be entertained by, among other things, sporting events. George E. Mowry, in *The Twenties*, acknowledges that among the reasons for the spectacular rise of professional sports in the 1920s were the new leisure time of the masses, increased living standards, and the new means of creating through ballyhoo:

But perhaps as important as all of these other factors was the instinctive need of a rapidly growing collectivized society for individual expression. On the battlefield, in the factory production line, at home in a city apartment, and increasingly even in the business world the individual was becoming lost in a welter in the hive. The sporting field was one of the few remaining areas of pure individual expression where success or failure depended precisely upon individual physical and intellectual prowess. And if the masses themselves could not or would not participate directly, they could at least, by a process of identification, salute the old virtues.[26]

The decade of the 1920s was indeed the Golden Age of American Sports, and women were part of it. Glenna Collett was the first woman to break 80 for a round of 18 holes of golf. Gertrude Ederle in 1926 became the first woman to swim the English Channel and her time of 14 hours and 23 minutes bettered the existing male record by two hours. Helen Wills, Little Miss Poker Face, dominated tennis. Margaret Gisolo even broke the gender rules barrier in American Legion Junior Baseball before the Legion changed its rules. But Gisolo's brief career at least raised questions about the prevailing belief that females could not compete equally with male peers.[27] Floretta McCutcheon in 1922, at age 39, defeated the long reigning male bowling champion, Jimmy Smith, in a 3 game set, 704-687.[28] Women's play in the 1920s became more intense: losers got angry.

Yet the 1920s proved not to be the liberation of workers or women. Worker's wages did not rise nearly so much as corporate profits, and women were still clustered in individual or dual sports such as swimming, golf and tennis. Team sports were not really acceptable—thus the triumph of Mrs. Hoover and the anti-competitive movement. The feminine mystique, aided by the sudden and dramatic Great Depression of the 1930s, persisted despite the vote and despite the flapper. A woman's place was in the home and not in the job market competing with those who were the breadwinners.

And so, despite the efforts of women like Babe Zaharias—who set world records in the 1932 Olympics and changed the style of play in women's golf[29]—a woman's world on the eve of World War II was still a very small one. The 1940 census showed twenty-five percent of women gainfully employed—nearly the same percentage as in 1910. In addition, most women who entered the labor force in the 1920s and '30s went into areas traditionally defined as women's work. Middle class women still had to choose between a career and marriage.

World War II changed nearly everything and nearly everyone, including women.[30] Economic prosperity, spurred by technological innovation, solved the Great Depression. It brought full employment, even more massive government intervention in our lives, and America the self-appointed responsibility of leadership of the free world. Women went to work—married women went to work and performed jobs requiring skills and/or physical strengths. There was hardly a job they did not fill. All of this was accepted because it was necessary to defeat the Axis. After the war, however, women continued to work. The economy was prospering and there was room for women. Jobs opened up, not in the manufacturing sector, where resistance to women's participation was strongest, but in the service area. Two incomes became increasingly necessary for a family to keep up with the middle-class Joneses, and women went into the labor force under the traditional banner of helping out, not a flag that demanded equality. Attitudes changed more slowly. It would be unrealistic to believe that as soon as numbers of married women began to work they would demand equal treatment. And yet the fact that they were working would become an essential condition in women's lives. In the 1950s, the country rested after the turbulence of the 1930s and '40s. By the 1960s, the country was ready for a new period of activism.

The civil rights movement was the catalyst for all groups tired of seeing a good life on TV which they could not share. Thus, in the 1960s, when Betty Friedan and others raised again an ideological alternative to "a woman's place is in the home," the appeal made sense, because there was not a huge gap between the reality of women's lives and the rhetoric of women's place.

And so the feminist movement surged again in many forms. Organizationally there were moderates such as NOW (The National Organization of Women) and there were radicals such as cell groups in SDS (Students for a Democratic Society) and independent organizations such as WITCH (Women's International Terrorist Conspiracy from Hell). Tactics varied as well: direct action such as boycotts, naming a sheep as a counter Miss America in 1968, establishing day care centers and abortion clinics and providing alternatives to children's books that contained sexual stereotypes. Congress responded with the Equal Pay Act of 1963, Title VII of the Civil Rights Act of 1964, and Title IX in 1972. Finally, the movement came together in support of a proposal to amend the Constitution, a proposal that had first been introduced in Congress in 1923. In March, 1972, the Congress passed and sent to the states the proposed Equal Rights Amendment, the substantial part of which reads: "Equality of rights under the law shall not be denied or abridged by the United States or by any State on account of sex." The proposed amendment swept through a couple of dozen of the required 38 states almost immediately,[31] before finally failing to receive the required number of state approvals before the extended time period ran out.

The Supreme Court also moved. Until 1971, every legislatively drawn gender line was accepted by the Court.[32] For example, the Court as recently as 1961 had upheld a state law that placed women on juries only if they volunteered (that decision was not overturned by the Court until

1974).[33]   Beginning in 1971 the court began to question the legitimacy of distinction by gender in many areas.[34]

Individual women also forced change by entering male preserves. The female percentage of lawyers, bank managers, physicians, accountants, and bus drivers increased dramatically, although in no instance to majority status. Female workers rose from thirty-four percent of the labor force in 1950 to over fifty percent in 1980.[35] 1980 alone saw the first women graduates of the military academies, the first female military test parachutist, the first female head of a Hollywood motion picture studio, the first woman elected to the policy making council of the AFL-CIO, and the first woman elected to receive the highest award of the Radio-Television News Directors' Association. In 1980 women received some twenty-eight percent of the 31,200 doctorates awarded in the U.S. as compared to some ten percent in 1965.[36] A woman or a man could now drive a truck or cry.

And yet, problems remained in all these areas. The ERA stalled because of opposition from women and men. The Supreme Court continued to uphold some distinctions by gender. Traditionally female jobs continued to be dominated by women. The gap between the median earning of men and women remained as great as ever; as in 1960, women's earnings continued to be about sixty percent of those of men.[37] Sociologists began talking of the feminization of poverty. The lack of child care centers and means for collecting child support payments, and the lack of access to good jobs are bringing poverty among female-headed families to the point where the majority of all poor families is now headed by a woman. Some experts contend that the proportion of the poor who are in female-headed families may comprise one hundred percent within twenty years.[38].

The story of women in American sport since World War II is similar to the story of other women.[39]   Participation increased dramatically, but not until the late 1960s did women begin to demand such things as equal prize money in tennis tournaments or equal PE facilities. But, as in other areas, the pioneers in participation must be given due credit.

Some competed against other women. In the Olympics, track and field stars like Wilma Rudolph and Wyomia Tyus continued to lower women's times so dramatically that even the most diehard male chauvinist could no longer be certain that women could never run as fast as men. Women's times in the marathon became so close to men's that the Olympics finally decided to add the event for women in 1984. Basketball continued to be an area of competition for women. UCLA signalled one effect of Title IX by becoming the first major college to win the women's collegiate championship. The success of collegians such as Nancy Leiberman led in 1978 to the formation of the Women's Professional Basketball League. Tennis and golf continued to be the most prominent sports. Golfers Mickey Wright and Kathy Withworth dominated the tour in the 1960s, and Nancy Lopez won purses in the 1970s that were actually respectable. In tennis, Maureen Conally and Doris Hard were great players, and Althea Gibson smashed tennis' color barrier. But it took Billie Jean King to demand successfully that women's prize monies be of the magnitude that players of the 1970s such as Christ Evert and Tracy Austin won. Small wonder that in 1980 when the inaugural dinner of the Women's Sports Hall of Fame was held, King was among the first nine women inducted into the hall.[40]

Alongside traditional activities, women moved into new areas of sport. The All-American Girls Baseball League was formed in 1943 and continued through the early 1950s, albeit with chaperones and an emphasis on decorum.[41] Little girls played baseball in Little League. Kathy Kusner in 1961 became the first woman in 10 years to join the U.S. Equestrian team—champion in the only Olympic sport where men and women competed against each other. In 1968 she became the first woman in the U.S. to be granted a jockey license. Soon both Mary Bacon and Robyn Smith were riding horses and winning against men. Suzy Chaffee skied to victory in the open competition in the world championships, hot dog or free-style. Others drove cars to victories against men: Donna Mae Mims in 1964 won the Class II (Imported 2 seater) sports car club of America championship in a bright pink Austin-Healey Sprite. Shirley (Cha-Cha) Muldowney in 1977 won the Top Fuel title in the Summer nationals drag racing championships. Janet Guthrie drove in the Indianapolis 500. On the golf tour, a tournament was established in which man/woman duos competed. Bronwin Russell in 1980 became the first female caddy in the U.S. Open Men's tournament. Betsy Rawls in that same tournament became the first female to serve as a rules official. Leonore Modell in 1964, at age 14, became the youngest person ever to swim the English Channel. And the list is growing.

Some women enlarged their area of sport by competing against other women but in areas reserved for men. National Championships were established for women in rodeo and weightlifting. Other women formed rugby teams. And not only are women in their own locker room, but some women journalists are demanding entrance to male locker rooms.[42] Where will it end?

Where indeed! Women in sport have come a long way. Not long ago dictionaries defined biography as the history of lives of men. Women, in challenging this definition, have called into question the attribute—gender—which, along with race and class, has served as a key reference point for individual identity and American society's organization. As such, the movement is by definition controversial.

Some worry whether women should be imprisoned in what Robert Lipsyute calls *Sportsworld*,[43] where the emphasis on winning causes a perversion of what sport should be and where the athlete is exploited almost beyond belief. Some studies argue that a clear majority of professional basketball and football players do not have college degrees, even though they went to college four years. Why should women's athletics imitate the depersonalization, drugs, violence, cheating, and the rest that seems to pervade men's sports? Already there are prominent cases of cheating.[44]

The response to this criticism is that sports can be fun, a release of tension, a source of self-confidence and health, and provide the satisfaction of challenge, discipline and accountability. In any event, by allowing athletes to be women, we have allowed athletes to be other things as well; some athletes are male, some female, some tall, some short, some heterosexual, some homosexual. And all are capitalists like the rest of us.

Women have at best advanced from the back of the bus only to the middle. Their second-class citizenship is apparent in many ways. For example, last year Tom Watson, the leading male golfer, won $530,800; Beth Daniel, the leading female golfer, won $231,000, less than fifty percent of Watson's earnings, and golf and tennis are the nearest to parity for male and female athletes.[45] College athletic budgets remain much lower for women than men. Media coverage of women's sport is but a tiny fraction of coverage for men. The same disparity occurs in the academic study of sport.[46]

So for both scholars and journalists, the term "athlete" continues to mean male. Do you read of the Wolfpack men's basketball team? No, but you do read of the Wolfpack women's basketball team. At least they are not called Wolfpackettes, as our female colleagues are not called historianettes. Where is it written that athletes are supposed to be male? The Dallas Cowboy Cheerleaders have gotten more exposure—if you will pardon the term—on national television, including prime time, than all of women's sports put together. We don't object to the Dallas Cheerleaders, but we do wonder why we cannot be given a chance to learn to appreciate other examples of the athletic skills of women. *Sports Illustrated,* founded in 1954, put out its first bathing suit issue (this means pictures of women) shortly thereafter. The bathing suit issues are among the most popular. Recently a magazine funded by *Newsweek* arose to challenge *Sports Illustrated: Inside Sports.* Sure enough, it was a bathing suit issue—and it was this cover, jokingly but openly challenging *Sport's Illustrated*'s bathing suits—that *Newsweek* ran as a full page ad for the magazine.[47]

Why must women's accomplishments in sport be measured by definitions concocted by men, even as noted in the title of this paper? Can you imagine a paper on "men in sport"? Why not try to have the best of both worlds? Despite setbacks, the direction of women's involvement in our society is clear; they'll not go back to bedroom and kitchen alone. Let's make the best of it and develop a new *zeitgeist*. Perhaps, for example, college women could show college men what basketball is: a game of joy, of movement toward the basket, of rigorous exercise, of incredible displays of individual skills and coordinated team efforts. The task will be difficult because the men play a game called keepaway in which the coaches "strategize" ways to keep the young men from getting tired, having fun or even sweating. But women could give it a try.

The notion of "everybody knows" is a chimerical one. In *Sports Illustrated*'s review of 1954, the only women depicted were cheerleaders. Now there is nothing wrong with being a cheerleader or a housewife or a secretary. But in 1954 "everybody knew" those jobs and a few others were the only ones women were capable of performing. But we believe now that the world of women ought to be a choice not a mandate. What everybody knows, in short, has changed. Fundamental economic and technological developments, coupled with the courage and skill of human beings, have enlarged woman's world. Women have more options now. This has made the world more uncertain; it was nice to know that a person defined by gender had to get the cup of coffee. On the other hand, if whoever gets a cup of coffee does so by choice, then maybe the other person won't have coffee accidentally spilled in his or her lap. Each may realize that the simple act of getting someone a cup of coffee can be an act of love. Then, perhaps all of us can accept the notion that, while some girls glow, some women sweat.

• • •

Notes

1. The statement that "Nice Girls Don't Sweat" is not original to the authors. The authors first saw it as the title of a senior history undergraduate thesis submitted to North Carolina State University April 16, 1974 by Sally Williamson. Others attest that they have known the expression for at least fifty years. John A. Lucas and Ronald A. Smith, in *Saga of American Sport* (Philadelphia: Lea & Febiger, 1978, especially in chapters 15 and 20) provide an excellent narrative summary and analysis of women in sport. For a multidisciplinary perspective on women in sport, see Ellen W. Gerber, et al., *The American Woman in Sport* (Reading, MA: Addison-Wesley, 1974). The latter work contains an excellent historical account by Ellen Gerber, which complements nicely the work by Lucas and Smith. Both historical accounts place the development of women's sport in the broader context of social, political and economic events. See also Mary L. Remley, *Women in Sport: A Guide to Information Sources* (Detroit: Gale Research Co., 1980).

2. John Underwood assesses the current debate in "A Game Plan for America," *Sports Illustrated*, 54, No. 9 (February 23, 1981), 65-80.

3. Lydia Huntley Sigourney devoted much of her life to the emancipation of women, which to her included sound physical and mental health.

4. Roxanne Albertson, "School Physical Activity Programs for Antebellum Southern Belles," *North American Society for Sport History Proceedings* (1979), p. 15.

5. Patricia Vertinsky, "Sexual Equality and the Legacy of Catherine Beecher," *Journal of Sport History,* 6, No. 1 (Spring 1979), 38-49.

6. Guy Lewis, "The Beginning of Organized Collegiate Sport," *American Quarterly,* 22, No. 2, Pt. 1 (Summer, 1970), 222-29; June A. Kennard, "Review Essay, The History of Physical Education," *Signs: Journal of Women in Culture and Society,* 2, No. 4 (Summer 1977), 835-42; Margaret A. Coffey, "The Sportswoman—Then and Now," *Journal of Health, Physical Education and Recreation,* 36 (Feb. 1965), 38-41, 50; Judith A. Davidson, "The Homosocial World of Intercollegiate Athletics," *North American Society for Sport History Proceedings* (1978), p. 32; Dewar, "The Beginnings and Directions of Ms. Basketball in North America," *North American Society for Sport History Proceedings* (1977), pp. 33-34.

7. *North American Society for Sports History Proceedings* (1979), pp. 19-20.

8. Barbara Jane Walder, "Mrs. Hoover's Holy War on Athletics," *Women Sports,* 1, No. 4 (Sept., 1974), 23-24.

9. Ellen Gerber, "The Controlled Development of Collegiate Sport for Women, 1923-1936," *Journal of Sport History,* 2, No. 1 (Spring 1979), 1-28.

10. For the birth of the AIAW, see Joanna Davenport, "The Historical Development of AIAW," *North American Society for Sport History Proceedings* (1979), pp. 35-36.

11. NCAA 'takeover' and Inevitable Power Play," *Raleigh News and Observer,* Jan. 16, 1981, p. 21. On the past and present NCAA, see Skip Applin, "The Recent Historical Development of the NCAA," and Niels Thompson, "The Present Status of the NCAA," North American Society for Sports History Proceedings (1979), 35-37.

12. "How HEW Will Measure Compliance with Title IX," *Chronicle of Higher Education* (Dec. 10, 1979), Vol. XIX, No. 15, 13-16.

13. Lisa Gubernick, "Catching Up with the Pack," *The Runner,* 3, No. 2 (Nov. 1980), 72-77.

14. Doug Tucker, "Title IX Issue Appears Headed for High Court," *Raleigh News and Observer,* Feb., 28, 1981, p. 15.

15. Gubernick, "Catching Up," *Runner,* 75.

16. Gubernick, "Catching Up," *Runner,* 72.

17. Allen Guttman, in *From Ritual to Record: The Nature of Modern Sports* (New York: Columbia University Press, 1978) assigns to modern sports seven distinct characteristics that scholars such as Max Weber and Talcott Parsons have used to describe modern society: secularism, equality of opportunity to compete and in the conditions of competition, specialization of roles, rationalization, bureaucratic organization, quantification and the quest for records. See also John R. Betts, "The Technological Revolution and the Rise of Sport, 1850-1900," *Mississippi Valley Historical Review,* XL (Sept. 1953), pp. 231-256.

18. Lucas and Smith, *Saga of American Sport,* p. 342.

19. Lucas and Smith, *Saga of American Sport,* pp. 257-61. See also D. Margaret Toohey and Betty V. Edmondson, "An Historical Perspective on Beliefs About Women's Health Issues Which had an Impact on Attitudes Toward Women's Sport Participation in the Nineteenth Century," *North American Society for Sports History Proceedings* (1980), pp. 40.

20. John Durant and Otto Bettman, *Pictoral History of American Sports—From Colonial Times to the Present* (Cranbury, NJ: A.S. Barnes, 1952, 1956, 1973), pp. 46-47.

21. Angela Lumpkin, *Women's Tennis: A Historical Documentary* (Troy, NY: Whitson Publishing Co., 1980).

22. Sheila Mitchell, "Women's Participation in the Olympic Games, 1900-1926," *Journal of Sport History*, 4, No. 2 (Summer 1977), 208-28.

23. Bill Borst, "The Matron Magnate," *Baseball Research Journal* (1977), 25-30; See also David Voigt, "Sex in Baseball: Reflections on Changing Taboos," *Journal of Popular Culture*, XII, No. 3 (Winter 1978), 389j-403.

24. Joanna Davenport, "Eleanora Randolph Sears, Pioneer in Women's Sports," *North American Society for Sport History Proceedings* (1976), p. 17 and Cleveland Amory "Boston Unique—Miss Sears," 141, *Vogue* (February 15, 1963), 81-83; and Lucas and Smith, *Saga of American Sport*, pp. 342-43.

25. William E. Leuchtenburg, *The Perils of Prosperity* (Chicago: University of Chicago Press, 1958).

26. George E. Mowry, *The Twenties: Fords, Flappers & Fanatics* (Englewood Cliffs, NJ: Prentice-Hall, 1963).

27. Tony Ladd, "The Girl Who Broke and Set the Gender Barrier in Baseball," *North American Society for Sport History Proceedings* (1978), p. 31.

28. Phyllis Ryant Ement, "Foremothers: Floretta McCutcheon," *Women Sports*, 3, No. 10 (Oct., 1976), 60-62.

29. Babe Didrikson Zaharias, *This Life I've Led* (New York: Barnes, 1955); *Current Biography* (1956), 663; *New York Times*, Sept. 28, 1956; Betty Hicks, "Foremothers: Babe Didrikson Zaharias," *Sports World*, 2, No. 11 and 12 (Nov.-Dec., 1975), 24-28, 18-25; and William Oscar Johnson and Nancy Williamson, "Babe," *Sports Illustrated*, Vol. 43, No. 14, 112-33, Vol. 43, No. 15, 48-57; Vol. 43, No. 16, 48-62.

30. William H. Chafe, *The American Woman: Her Changing Social, Economic and Political Roles, 1920-1970* (New York: Oxford, 1972). See also June Sochen, *Herstory* (Sherman Oaks, CA: Alfred Pub. Co., 1974, 1981); Lois W. Banner, *Women in Modern America—A Brief History* (New York: Harcourt Brace Jovanovich, 1974); and Peter G. Filene, *Him/Her/Self—Sex Roles in Modern America* (New York: Harcourt Brace Jovanovich, 1974).

31. For a discussion of the legal context and implications, see Ginsbur, "Gender," *Cincinnati Law Review*, 44, No. 1 (1975), pp. 1042.

32. Ginsburg, "Gender," p. 4.

33. *Hoyt v. Florida*, 368 U.S. 57 (1961).

34. *Reed v. Reed* 404 U.S. 71 (1971).

35. "Battle of the Sexes—Men Fight Back," *U.S. News and World Report*, XXIX No. 23 (Dec. 8, 1980), 50-52.

36. Associated Press, "1980 Has Been a Landmark Year for Women," *Savannah Morning News*, Dec. 22, 1980, p. 6. B.

37. "Battle of the Sexes—Men Fight Back," *U.S. News and World Report*, XXIX No. 23 (Dec. 8, 1980), 50-52.

38. Dianne Dumanoski, The Boston Globe, "Poverty Takes on a Feminine Look," in the *Raleigh News and Observer*, March 8, 1981, III., pp. 1, 6.

39. Joanna Bunker Rohrbaugh assesses the "joyous" impact on women of their growing involvement in sport in "Femininity on the Line," *Psychology Today*, 13, No. 3 (August 1979), 30-42. Letty Cottin Pogrebin assesses the impact of boys and girls playing together and concludes that both sexes would benefit by seeing females "who are not only lovers and friends, but leaders, heroes, high-scorers and champions." *Next* (Jan.-Feb. 1981), 96-101. Shelly Armitage, in "The Lady as a Jock: A Popular Culture Perspective on the Woman Athlete," *Journal of Popular Culture*, 10, No. 1 (Summer 1976), 122-132, traces the changing role models for women. Phyllis Hollander, *100 Greatest Women in Sports* (New York: Grosset & Dunlap, 1976), summarizes the career of many modern women athletes.

Harry Edwards, in "Desegregating Sexist Sport," *Intellectual Digest*, III, No. 3 (Nov. 1972), 82-83 contends that American women cannot obtain equality "until they have succeeded in overthrowing male domination of sport."

40. *Raleigh News and Observer*, Sept. 17, 1980, p. 16.

41. Merrie A. Fidler, "The All-American Girls' Baseball League, 1943-1954," *North American Society for Sport History Proceedings* (1977), pp. 35-36; W.G. Nicholson, "Women's Pro Baseball Packed the Stands," *Women Sports*, 3, No. 4 (April 1976), 22-24.

42. Bob St. John, *Landry* (Waco, TX: Word Books, 1979), 167.

43. Rober Lipsyte, *Sports World: An American Dream Land* (New York: Quadrangle, 1975).

44. See, for example, Jane Leavy, "The Saga of Rosie Ruiz," *The Washington Post*, April 27, 1980, p. N. 1.

45. *Sports Illustrated*, 54, No. 7 (Feb. 12, 1981), 112.

46. An NCSU undergraduate history major, Robert Levin, did a survey of the *Proceedings of the Meetings of the North American Society for Sport History.* He discovered that, since 1974, of the 40-50 or so papers given each year, usually only 5 or so dealt with women; of books displayed at the convention—varying year to year from below 20 to over 60—only 1 or 2 are about women. Levin found similar results in the *Journal of Sport History*, both as to articles printed and articles cited from other journals in the section "Journal Surveys." *The Journal of Sport History*, 6 No. 1 (Spring 1979)—lists only 8 books about women. Lists of recommended books by prominent scholars and journalists yield similar results. Obviously much monographic work needs to be done in the field.

47. The first issue of *Sports Illustrated* to have a bathing suit feature was Vol. 1 No. 19 of December 20, 1954. *Newsweek's* ad for *Inside Sports* was in *Newsweek* (March 28, 1981).

• • •

Suggestions for Further Reading

Bassett, Sarah, "Entitled to Equal Treatment," *Michigan Alumnus Magazine* (November, 1982), 10-12.

Bishop, Elva and Katherine Fulton, "Shooting Stars: The Heyday of Industrial Women's Basketball," *Southern Exposure*, VII, 3 (Fall, 1979), 50-56.

Boutilier, Mary A. and Lucinda SanGiovani, *The Sporting Woman* (Champaign, IL: Human Kinetics, 1983).

Davenport, Joanna, "The Women's Movement into the Olympic Games," *Journal of Health, Physical Education and Recreation*, XLIX, 3 (march, 1978), 58-60.

Gerber, Ellen, "The Controlled Development of Collegiate Sport for Women, 1923-1936," *Journal of Sport History*, VI, 1 (Spring, 1979), 1-28.

Holland, Judith R. and Carole Oglesby, "Women in Sport: The Synthesis Begins," *Annals of the American Academy of Political and Social Science*, 445 (Spetember, 1979).

Howell, Reet, ed., *Her Story in Sport: A Historical Anthology of Women in Sports* (West Point, NY: Leisure Press, 1982).

Johnson, William Oscar and Nancy P. Williamson, *"Whatta-Gal": The Babe Didrickson Story* (Boston: Little, Brown, 1977).

King, Billie Jean and Kim Chapin, *Billie Jean* (New York: Harper & Row, 1974).

Twin, Stephanie L., ed., *Out of the Bleachers: Writings on Women and Sport* (Old Westbury, NY: The Feminist Press, 1979).

Walder, Barbara Jane, "Mrs. Hoover's Holy War on Athletics," *Women Sports*, I, 4 (September, 1974), 23-24.

Zaharias, Babe Didrickson, *This Life I've Led,* (New York: Barnes, 1955).

MYTH AND METAPHOR: BASEBALL IN THE HISTORY AND LITERATURE OF AMERICAN SPORT

Paul J. Zingg

As the final selection in this volume, the following essay on baseball re-emphasizes many of the principal themes and points that tie all of the articles together. As an historiographical review, it demonstrates that baseball literature and scholarship have improved significantly, both quantitatively and qualitatively, since Jacques Barzun offered his encouraging advice in 1954. In the process, the study of baseball forms a valid reflection of sport history investigation in general.

Yet, sport history is still coming into its own. Although it has moved beyond the statistical summaries and superficial hagiographies of earlier years, it has not found its full stride. Too many gaps exist both in its study and its presentation. But, baseball, rich in heritage, resources and influence, offers the best prospects for sport history to achieve greater respect and credibility.

As the "national pastime," although no longer unchallenged in this claim, baseball links its identity and appeal to a long list of "American" ideals and values. These have been amply celebrated by baseball publicists from the days of Albert Spalding and Harry Chadwick and enshrined in the literature of the game by the likes of Mark Harris, Ring Lardner, Bernard Malamud, W.P.Kinsella, Robert Coover and Phillip Roth. Like the nation it purportedly mirrors, though, baseball often has had a hard time distinguishing between its own mythology and reality.

In claiming to be a useful paradigm for the study of American society and culture, sport history, as a whole, must also face the difficult task of separating fact and fiction. The task takes on greater significance—and frustration—in a country that insists on its own exceptionalism and delights in creating and embracing myths. In this environment, myth and reality have intersected to such a degree that they have often become one and the same. Recognizing this in our sport history will help us understand what we play and why we give it so much attention.

Heeding Jacques Barzun's advice to know "the heart and mind of America" through baseball, sport historians have made the game the focus of the best and most imaginative products of the new sport scholarship.[1] In the process they have explained and enlarged the sources of the game's attraction. These spring from baseball's claim as the oldest of the American team sports that emerged over the past century as leisure outlets for an increasingly urbanized and industrialized society. It has been a remarkably stable game, undergoing few substantive rule changes in the conduct of game play since the organization of the Cincinnati Red Stockings in 1869 as the sport's first avowed professional team.[2] The one-on-one character of the diamond game—batter against pitcher, hitter against fielder, runner against fielder—has made it a game of statistics and records as perhaps no other. Its immutable quality has allowed comparisons between players and teams throughout its existence and, through its own version of the Holy Scriptures, the newspaper box score, affords a sense of recognition for us today with the game's nineteenth century pioneers. The game even has its own archives in the National Baseball Hall of Fame, an important resource center noted for both the size and quality of its collection.

The intrinsic nature of the game offers other clues to its popularity and longevity. "Satisfying though played day after day, sufficiently complex to fascinate the poet, sufficiently obvious to please the peasant," observed Tristam Coffin, it offers a sensitive balance of physical skill, problem solving, and chance.[3] "It is," says this literary scholar and folklorist, "hard to play well, yet easy to learn. It is fun to watch, yet challenging to study."

It is also a game, which, more than any other in this country, is steeped in rich mythological currents and metaphorical contexts. The former reaches to the game's very roots with its own "creation myth." This advances the notion that baseball sprang full-bodied from the fertile mind of Abner Doubleday on a summer afternoon in Cooperstown, New York, in 1839. This provided a unique American authorship to the game from which its other myths drew sustenance.

Reflecting beliefs, that is, definitions of "reality," that have been built-up to shape or secure the convenient wishes of various constituencies, baseball's myths are charged with values, aspirations, ideals, and meanings that have a vitality of their own. This characteristic, to a certain degree, mitigates the question of their correlation to empirical fact. Like the country that celebrates it as its "national pastime," baseball has seen myth and reality merge to such an extent that they have become one and the same thing.[4] The myth-encrusted world that it represents suggests both an aspect of the game's true identity and a source of its enduring appeal. It also provides a fuller meaning to baseball's characterization as America's sport.

Baseball as a metaphor considers not only the language of the game and the extent to which it influences the way we think, look, and talk, but also the sustained imagery of the sport's season and its patterns of play. The symbolic value of baseball also emerged early. In 1889, for example, Mark Twain described the aggressive, competitive game of his day as "the very symbol, the outward and visible expression of the drive and push and rush and struggle of the raging, tearing, booming, nineteenth century." By the 1890s, elements of the game's vocabulary had already transcended the playing field and assumed different, but related, contexts in common usage. As technological advances in mass communications brought more sports to a wider listening and viewing audience, this process accelerated, often obscuring the original meaning and source of certain words and phrases.

With the emergence of a critically-acclaimed body of sports literature in recent years, enough to comprise a veritable sub-genre of American literature, baseball has reached new and old audiences who appreciate the literary possibilities of the game and its hold on the popular imagination. Through serious fiction and popular non-fiction, film, song, and theater, the game has revealed its own contours and provided a fascinating lens with which to see the society that embraces it and the many individuals who are caught up in its appeal. Let us turn now in greater detail to the notions of baseball as myth and metaphor.

Baseball's claim as the national pastime strikes home in ways that go well beyond its alleged connection to a legitimate folk heritage in the play and games of the American people. The hallowed "American tradition" it more accurately reflected in the formative years of its reputation was the spirit of capitalism. The entrepreneur who recognized the relationship between the game's growing popularity and the profits that could be gained from it was Albert G. Spalding, a former pitching star for the Rockford (Illinois) Forest Cities and the Boston Red Stockings in the 1870s, who had built a multi-million dollar sports equipment business by the end of the century. Spalding enlisted the assistance of Henry Chadwick as the chief editor of his American Sports Publishing Company to further his goals. For over two decades before his death in 1908, Chadwick served Spalding faithfully in this endeavor. Capitalizing on the new wave of nationalism that the end of the Civil War, the centennial celebration of 1876, and the imperial impulse of the 1890s brought, the pair worked tirelessly to exploit baseball as America's national game.

Their collaboration proved immensely successful. It led, in particular, to the enshrinement of Doubleday and Cooperstown as the father and cradle, respectively, of baseball's birth. Both ingredients were necessary in order to "prove" the American origins of the game and to satisfy the proclamations of Spalding and Chadwick that baseball was singularly suited to the American character. Spalding financed an historical commission, comprised of men of "high repute and undoubted knowledge of

Base Ball," that in 1907 delivered the news that proponents of the game wanted to hear. The commission identified Doubleday, a major general in the United States Army and a hero to boot at the Battle of Gettysburg, as the inventor of the game. The great moment supposedly came while he was an instructor at a local military prep school in Cooperstown. In one sweep of the "historian's pen," Doubleday was elevated into that pantheon of American military heroes, who, like George Washington, Andrew Jackson, and Ulysses S. Grant, served their country well in both war and peace.

Delighted, although one would suspect less than surprised by the commission's report, Spalding proclaimed that it had at last freed baseball "from the trammels of English traditions, customs, conventionalities."[5] Having cleansed baseball of any Old World artificiality and decadence, Spalding launched an aggressive campaign to celebrate the newly-certified "American game." In 1911, he published *America's National Game*, a book rarely equalled in the annals of sport history for its unabashed chauvinism and nationalistic bombast. "Baseball," proclaimed Spalding, is "the exponent of American Courage, Confidence, Combatism; American Dash, Discipline, Determinism; American Energy,Eagerness, Enthusiasm; American Pluck, Persistency, Performance; American Spirit, Sagacity, Success; American Vim, Vigor, Virility."[6]

But Spalding was more than just a shrewd businessman who exploited a theme in order to make a profit. He recognized the appeal of patriotism and understood the dynamics of myth-making. To a great extent, he simply plugged into a process that has been evident and accepted in many cultures, but particularly active and creative in the United States. Historical myths and legends play a crucial role in forging national identity and stimulating patriotic pride. As Friedrich von Schlegel in Germany, Ernest Renan in France, Giuseppe Mazzini in Italy, Edmund Burke and John Stuart Mill in England, and others have observed, collective traditions and a useful historical memory contribute to successful nationalism. In some cases, where the actual record may come up a little short, some selective invention—William Tell and his unerring aim or Robert Bruce and his persevering spider—can serve just as well.

Throughout their history, Americans have appeared unusually eager to embrace fact and fiction with equal enthusiasm—and often little discrimination—in the name of national pride. The "search for a useable past" in America, the need to assert the country's special qualities and unique features, indeed, its exceptionalism, has encouraged a focus "on the simple, the symbolic and the ideological."[7] Baseball fits this agenda perfectly. Artificially conceived, vigorously defended, ostentatiously celebrated, baseball is the quintessential American game.

Reflecting both the process that links myth and reality and the society that embraces its manifestations, baseball affords the historian a rich subject and an intriguing challenge. Those who now echo Barzun's advice are quick to measure the game's appeal. Steven Riess, author of *Touching Base: Professional Baseball in American Culture in the Progressive Era*, and several related articles, explains the game's rise to popularity "because it touched base with more themes in American life and society than anything else at the time."[8] Richard Crepeau, *Baseball: America's Diamond Mind, 1919-1941*, sees the importance of the study of baseball no less than providing some direction in answering Hector de Crevecoeur's enduring question, "What then is the American, this new man?"[9] Both examine the sociocultural heritage and significance of the sport and the interaction between the every-changing values of the country and those of the game. From King Kelly to Babe Ruth to Joe DiMaggio, these two works trace the evolution of America from an agrarian society to an industrial giant and the transformation of those who played the game from rugged individualists to corporate cogs. More than outstanding contributions to sport history, they are valuable resources for the sociologist and the cultural anthropologist too in the quest to better understand the country's mores, values and beliefs. Crepeau's research emphasis on *The Sporting News,* baseball's weekly trade journal, gives his work a certain one-dimensional character. However, he has creatively used that resource as no other baseball historian and has effectively demonstrated along with Riess that the diamond game has begun to smooth away some of sport history's rough methodological features.

Although scholars may be drawn to the game for a variety of reasons—Donald Mrozek argues that the insistence that baseball is so *American* "seems to automatically make it worthy of special attention."[10] —they quickly discover that the mythology that envelops it poses a common obstacle to its study. In a perceptive essay on myth-making within the American experience, Thomas Bailey observed that "myths are so essential to our culture that if they did not exist, like Voltaire's God, they would have to be invented."[11] As we have already seen, Spalding and Chadwick understood this concept well. Now those who are studying baseball's past and commenting on its present are finding out how deep the myths go and how powerful is their hold.

Two former players, Jim Bouton and Curt Flood, provide revealing lessons in the struggle with baseball's mythology. In 1970, Bouton published *Ball Four: My Life and Hard Times Throwing the Knuckleball in the Big League.*[12] It has since been followed by scores of similar books, including Bouton's own two sequels.[13] These usually dictated, ghost-written memoirs of major-leaguers recount their exploits (often barroom and bedroom) away from the playing fields and their trials (with teammates and management) in the stadium. Although Bouton's work was not the first baseball autobiography, it was at that time the best and the most controversial.[14] Baseball Commissioner Bowie Kuhn was so impressed that he promptly censured Bouton for having written it.

Beyond the details of a rather mediocre career, the book zeroes in on the central theme of baseball, namely, baseball *is* America. On that point, Bouton and his critics—largely sportswriters and broadcasters—are in agreement. That is the extent of their harmony. For the America that Bouton's baseball world reflects is neither virtuous nor fair nor tolerant. It is a game run by greedy egotists, scarred by the same racial and social tensions that affect the rest of the country, and played by individuals, who, in Bouton's pages, "became what they are, not larger than life, but perhaps if anything, a little smaller."[15]

Curt Flood challenged baseball orthodoxy in a more dramatic manner. In 1970, the all-star outfielder, claiming that his basic rights to negotiate a contract for his services on the open market would be denied, refused to be traded from the St. Louis Cardinals to the Philadelphia Phillies. Flood initiated a suit against major league baseball that challenged the legality of the reserve clause.[16] This instrument of owner collusion that, in the name of team stability and balanced competition, bound players for life to the team that first signed them, had essentially been in effect since the formation of the National League in 1876. By the late 1880s, it had become an integral part of the Standard Player's Contract. In economic terms it was a monopsony, a bargaining relationship between player and owner in which the seller (the player) was limited to only one buyer (the owner), who, in turn, set the purchase price (the salary) and used his bonded "servant" until he decided to sell, trade, or retire him.

Flood's suit did not improve his chances for enshrinement in the Hall of Fame. Fans were not particularly moved by the $100,000-a-year player characterizing himself as a "wage slave." Owners expressed outrage over an attack that they felt threatened the very fabric of the game, not to mention their profit margins. Even Philip Roth in his 1971 satirical novel on American political leadership, *Our Gang,* had the president of the United States, "Trick E. Dixon," identify Curt Flood (along with Hanoi, the Berrigan brothers, the Black Panthers, and Jane Fonda) as a likely suspect in turning the Boy Scouts of America against him.[17] By "destroying" baseball, Flood had apparently succeeded in undermining the youth of the country, as the Boy Scout "revolt" demonstrated.

The Supreme Court eventually heard *Flood v. Kuhn* (407 U.S. 258) in 1972. Ironically, the case came before the Court during the first real players' strike in baseball's history. The strike only delayed the season opener for a few weeks, but it signalled a new resolve and solidarity among the players with which the owners would henceforth have to contend. The Supreme Court, however, was not about to usher in a power shift in player-owner relations. The Court upheld the owners' argument that the reserve system brought stability to the game and, as such, represented a reasonable business practice on their part.

But the inevitable had only been delayed. Within five years, the venerable reserve clause had fallen to new challenges and legal maneuvers. Even Flood, who had declared his readiness "to go up against the system," expressed surprise at its quick collapse.[18] Jim Bouton has experienced a curious vindication in his own right. With frequent revelations of drug dealing and abuse among major league baseball players grabbing headlines and tarnishing the game's image, Bouton's version of the game's underside—midnight "sexcapades" and beer blasts—seem quite naive. The old ball game has changed.

Yet, baseball has weathered difficult transitions before. It survived franchise battles and player revolts in the late nineteenth century and emerged with the National Agreement of 1903 that restored order and provided a framework for league governance. It overcame the "Black Sox Scandal" of 1919 to build an image of moral incorruptibility and to revel in the "golden age of sport" during the 1920s.[19] In 1947, the game finally rejected its color ban when Jackie Robinson donned the uniform of the Brooklyn Dodgers. The event changed the face of the game forever, and to the extent that it helped influence an attitude more accepting of blacks as equals, it may also have helped change American society.[20]

Each of these crises has bolstered the basic mythology of the game and insured its hold on the popular imagination. In the lives and careers of those who have actually played the game, as opposed, for example, to those who have managed, organized, umpired or broadcast it, baseball provides a host of heroes as further sources of the game's appeal.[21] They also provide valuable insights to the process of hero creation.

Like the game itself, baseball's heroes must be understood in a wider social and cultural context. To the extent that the game symbolizes alleged American ideals and images (its native origins, qualities of ethnic assimilation and social interaction, individualism, rags-to-riches opportunism, primitive pastoralism, to name just a few), its heroes reflect a lingering popular nostalgia and need for them.[22] Benjamin Rader describes the "compensatory cultural function" that sports heroes served as they began to capture the public's fancy earlier in this century.[23] Achieving their fame and fortune through individual prowess and performance that seemed to overcome an increasingly bureaucratic, systematic, and complicated world, "they assisted the public in compensating for the passing of the traditional dream of success, the erosion of Victorian values, and feelings of individual powerlessness."[24]

These were a new brand of heroes. They were not, as Leo Lowenthal describes, "idols of production" from the worlds of politics, business, science and industry, but "idols of consumption," products of the mass media and the world of entertainment.[25] The American public faces a news blitz every day that crowds yesterday's heroes out of the headlines with scarcely a backward glance. As new situations create new heroes, consensus fades on the identification of heroic standards. Yet, the staying power of certain sports figures in the public's favor is unmistakable. Their charismatic presence and persistence give us clues to the process and purpose of achieving and retaining the hero's mantle. America's preeminent sports hero is, of course, a baseball player—Babe Ruth.

Earlier accounts of Ruth's life, including an autobiography and a memoir by his wife, essentially retold the legendary stories already associated with him. They represented the Babe as the classic American success story.[26] Consider his own words: "The greatest thing about this country is the wonderful fact of life that it doesn't matter which side of the tracks you were born on, or whether you're homeless or homely or friendless. The chance is still there. I know."[27] Such sentiments may elicit ridicule amidst today's prevailing cynicism, but there is no denying the enduring appeal of the man behind them.

That appeal is reflected in a recent outpouring of works on Ruth's life and times.[28] These are all significant efforts, each rising above journalistic hyperbole and tavern gossip. Like the best biography, and sport is beginning to claim a few entries in this category, they leave the thoughtful reader with the impression that not only has he been a part of something revealing, but also something important.[29]

Moving beyond the private person and the public athlete, the new studies of Ruth search in some way for the symbolic importance that his exploits on and off the playing field represented. They basically agree that Ruth was a man of immense appetite, who "lived elementally—in touch with the forces of the universe in a much more profound way than those of us who use our minds."[30] As a player, the Babe revolutionized the game by celebrating its most awesome offensive weapon, the home run. It lifted the game out of its low-scoring doldrums and fired the public's imagination. It posed a sharp contrast to a game that had become increasingly rational and scientific in its emphasis on defense. The "power" game reflected the dramatic social and cultural transformations in American life that technological advancements, international influence, and the intellectual ferment of the 1920s encouraged. As the Great Bambino brought new excitement and joy to the game, his hedonistic tastes also fascinated an America struggling to escape the memories of war and depression and anxious to throw off its inhibitions and constraints. Ruth seemed to have neither conscience nor sense of propriety. He was a breath of fresh air. The attention that he continues to receive indicates that he still is.

Other recent portraits of baseball's personalities lack the high drama that is associated with Ruth but, nevertheless, provide us with important insights into the game and those who played it.[31] The Jackie Robinson story is particularly critical to study because of the influence it may have had on the civil rights movement. This is the theme that Jules

Tygiel pursues in his work, *Baseball's Great Experiment: Jackie Robinson and His Legacy*, a study that has appeal for both popular and academic audiences. It is unclear whether Branch Rickey, the Dodger owner, promoted Robinson as an expression of his genuine support for blacks or as a response to political pressure in New York with its significant black population.[32] It is clear, though, that Robinson had his own notions of Rickey's bottom line. Noting how his teammates began to shed their initial coolness toward him, Robinson wrote: "They hadn't changed because they liked me better; they had changed because I could help fill their wallets."[33]

Robinson's career focused attention on the racial aspects of baseball and revealed the persistent patterns of the game's discriminatory past. In other baseball biographies, in particular Charles Einstein's *Willie's Time* and Kal Wagenheim's *Clemente*, additional reflections of American racial attitudes appear that take the studies and their subjects effectively beyond the bounds of sport history.[34] Einstein's memoirs, as much his own as Mays', interchanges the career of the athlete and the history of the country. It is only a twenty-three year passage, but the innocence—lingering or otherwise—that the United States lost in the era from Korea to Watergate affected sports as well. Wagenheim particularly emphasizes Clemente's socialization into Puerto Rican culture and society and the changing force of prejudice and discrimination in the United States. Both Mays and Clemente—the former less dramatically, the latter through openly supporting Curt Flood and advocating the equal treatment of blacks and Latins—understood that their responsibility to their respective racial constituencies transcended accomplishments in the ballpark. By the time of Willie's retirement in 1973 and Roberto's untimely death in 1972, much of the idealistic crust that had protected baseball from the racial tensions and social divisions that plagued the rest of the country had crumbled. Robinson, Mays, and Clemente, like Moses Fleetwood Walker in the 1880s and the scores of talented black ballplayers who exhausted their careers in the Negro leagues, knew the reality beneath the layers of baseball mythology long before it became fashionable to highlight it.

Recent studies on ethnicity in baseball also suggest that notions of the game as an agent of social integration, local pride and solidarity, and immigrant assimilation fall well short of the actual record. In this regard, Riess' work is particularly significant.[35] He refutes the democratic quality of the game from both the spectator and player perspectives and concludes that the new immigrants from eastern and southern Europe during the Progressive Era found no greater advancement in the "national pastime" than they did in other professions. Baseball's impact on the local and regional level has yet to be explored as adequately, but a promising start has been made.

Particularly noteworthy is Gary Mormino's article on Italian immigrants in St. Louis and the more comprehensive studies of Dale Somers and Stephen Hardy on New Orleans and Boston, respectively.[36] Two related and imaginative essays by Steven Gelber explore amateur baseball's relationship to the work place and suggest elements of a Marxist approach that reminds one of Paul Hoch's earlier critique of big-time sport.[37]

Baseball's other leagues—its minor, little, and long defunct Negro leagues—provide additional sources for study that further attest to the lure and lore of the diamond. Pat Jordan's two books on minor league baseball and Martin Ralbovsky's studies of the Little League world reveal that the ethos of the game exists on various levels and affects virtually all ages.[38] Ralbovsky's summary of Little League baseball, that it "is a hydra-headed enterprise devoted to (1) earning money, and (2) promoting America," has a familiar ring to it.[39] *Only the Ball Was White*, Robert Peterson's fine history of the old Negro leagues, surveys the only outlet for such great players as Josh Gibson, Luke Easter, John Henry Lloyd, and Satchel Paige before Jackie Robinson broke the "color line."[40] Among the few fist-hand accounts of life in the Negro leagues are Satchel Paige's autobiography and John Holway's *Voices from the Great Black Baseball Leagues.*[41]

The task of pulling together baseball's many eras, themes and sources into a general history of the game has produced mixed results so far. The multi-volume works of Harold Seymour and David Voigt are the most comprehensive surveys of the game's history.[42] Both describe the growth of the game in the context of American history and emphasize the mirror quality of baseball *vis-a-vis* the nation's socio-economic development. Seymour's study is probably more consistent and academically satisfying than Voigt's three volumes, although both avoid the anecdotal style that can easily entrap such efforts.

Among the best single volume histories are Lee Allen's *100 Years of Baseball*, Douglas Wallop's *Baseball: An Informal History,* and Donald Honig's *Baseball America.*[43] Allen's work is one of major inspiration to contemporary baseball historians for its focus on the theme that the history of America is baseball, and *vice versa.* Wallop and Honig do their best to sustain it. The former, who reworked Goethe's *Faust* for the diamond game in the 1954 novel *The Year the Yankees Lost the Pennant,* has written a general history to commemorate the 100th anniversary of baseball's professional beginnings.[44] Honig's latest work relies primarily on the personalities of baseball's greatest stars to tell its story, an approach that proves both lively and disappointing. His fascination with the game's heroes and legends often translates into hyperbole, which detracts from the book's meticulous research. Both Wallop and Honig adequately relate baseball to the various social, political, and cultural climates in America throughout the years they cover. Geared for a general audience, however, both books lack the rich detail of Seymour's study and the critical perspectives of less extensive, but more focused, studies like those of Riess, Creqeau, and Levine.

With few exceptions, Roger Kahn's sentimental study of the 1952-1953 Brooklyn Dodgers the most noteworthy, the histories of individual teams are not so successful and are riddled with anecdote and *cliche*.[45] The Putnam series of team histories produced in the late '40s and early '50s, although not providing an individual title of great significance, was written by some of the finest sportswriters of the era and is collectively important. Frank Graham's accounts of the Giants and Dodgers, Lee Allen's work, and Frank Lieb's contributions stand out.[46]

Two additional works in the latter vein are *The Glory of Their Times* by Lawrence Ritter and *Baseball: When the Grass Was Real* by Honig.[47] Although Ritter's is superior, they are companion pieces both chronologically and methodologically. Ritter artfully arranges his interviews with twenty players, who, gracefully and easily, narrate their reminiscences of the old ball game from 1900 to the onset of the Depression. Honig picks up the story at that point and carries it into the 1940s through the words of the eighteen ballplayers he interviewed. The semi-amateur game that some of Ritter's subjects played probably has more nostalgic appeal than the corporate profession that engaged most of Honig's athletes. That, in itself, may explain the greater appeal of Ritter's book. More likely, though, is that Ritter has set a standard for the sports memoir that avoids simpering modesty and high-minded platitude.

Moving into the realm of fiction and popular non-fiction, the metaphorical quality of baseball becomes a more conscious part of the literature. Granted, it is never too far beneath the surface in the historical accounts, a condition that book and article titles suggest in themselves.[48] But by definition metaphor transfers terminology from an object or context of ordinary designation to one that is appropriate only through implicit comparison or analogy. Historical writing hardly eschews the figurative, but it is not rooted in it to the extent, and with the freedom, that other genres possess and value.

Roger Angell's *The Summer Game*, a gathering of his eloquent *New Yorker* pieces, may be the best sports journalism since Ring Lardner and Red Smith.[49] He successfully captures the feel of selected players, games, series, and pennant races from 1961-1972 without recourse to pseudo-psychological terminology or rhapsodies about their greater meaning. Arranged in diary fashion, the book lacks the continuity and cumulative impact of *The Boys of Summer*, but, with Tom Boswell's *Why Time Begins on Opening Day*, reflects a gentle style and an unblinking eye.[50] Neither Angell nor Boswell are intent on making baseball out to be more than it is, or themselves more than they are. It is perhaps for that reason that their observations possess an honest and timeless quality. These are two books for both fans of baseball and admirers of good writing.

Donald Hall, *Fathers Playing Catch with Their Sons*, evidently believes that baseball can teach us something about how to live life.[51] Unfortunately, his book is not a successful text because he forces the theme throughout, rather than let it develop at its own pace in the mind of the reader as Angell, Boswell, and Kahn have done. Hall's notions that "baseball is a country all to itself" or that the game creates an almost indelible bond between fathers and sons and beyond are neither convincing nor clear.

Nearly one-fourth of the book is drawn from another work of his, *Dock Ellis in the Country of Baseball*, written with the controversial Pittsburgh Pirate pitcher of the 1970s.[52] The excerpts center on events surrounding a game in which Ellis deliberately hit the first three Cincinnati batters he faced with pitches. Ellis admitted in 1984 that he was on drugs at the time—a rather significant piece of information that Hall neglects to mention. Hall may claim poetic license in this omission, but it is not the only factual shortcoming of the book. He praises Boswell for his writing. It is not clear that Hall understands why.

Baseball fiction, however, enjoys the key advantage of its genre in exploring the metaphorical dimensions of the game and its language. It is a product of the imagination. Its appeal does not depend upon a conscious theme or prescribed interpretation. Its charm lies equally in folds of subtle suggestion and streams of graphic imagery. It is personal. The reader is free to conclude that baseball is like "life," or the nuclear family, or nuclear war or welfare, or any other all-encompassing simile. He is also free to conclude that baseball is, well, like—baseball.

The protagonists in American baseball fiction have grown more numerous and become more complex since Jack Keefe faced his first batter for the Chicago White Sox in Ring Lardner's *You Know Me Al* and Roy Tucker headed south for spring training with the Brooklyn Dodgers in John Tunis' *The Kid from Tomkinsville*.[53] Their company now includes the pitching ace of the New York Mammoths, Henry Wiggin, and his doomed battery-mate, Bruce Pearson; an Iowa farmer named Ray Kinsella entertaining J.D. Sallinger and the ghost of Shoeless Joe Jackson in a baseball stadium carved out of a cornfield; Henry P. Waugh and the strange world of his boardgame; and, of course, Roy Hobbs, his talents and temptations and ties with Eddie Waitkus and T.S. Elliot.[54] Yet all of these characters are bound together by the irresistable appeal of the American "types" and situations they portray and the literary exuberance that brings them to life.

Lardner's "Busher," with his goofy, self-confidence and innocence, was an American for his day. In the early years of the twentieth century, self-doubt and self-consciousness scarcely clouded the national outlook and played no part in pitcher Keefe's. Virginia Wolff even called his solecistic commentary "the voice of a continent." Malamud's "Knight"-errant is the American mythic hero of another age. Reflecting the fashionable literary cult of the obscure at mid-century, itself a product of a time of blurred values and frightening tensions, *The Natural* suggests the tragic limitations of the average American dream. Hobbs is undone as much by the choices he makes as the disillusionment he discovers. In team owner Judge Goodwill Banner, the agent of both factors that destroy Hobbs, we encounter a character whose sanctimony and perfidy is, paradoxically, neither dated nor metaphorical. *Shoeless Joe* is also about dreams and magic and life—and a quintessential North American notion that anything is possible. Reflecting the "magical realism" of Gabriel Garcia Marquez, Juan Rulfo, Julio Cortazar and other Latin American novelists whose works have contributed to the new synthesis of literature in the Western Hemisphere, W.P. Kinsella spins an extravagant fantasy about believable people in extraordinary situations. He creates a world of compelling whimsy, where baseball becomes a metaphor for religion, a symbol of the need to hold onto something, anything, in a faithless age.

Contemporary American fiction now claims an impressive corpus of works that either sustain a baseball storyline or contain key allusions to the game. David Carkeet, *The Greatest Slump of All Time*, Eric Rolfe Greenberg, *The Celebrant*, Philip Roth, *The Great American Novel*, and William Kennedy, *Billy Phelan's Greatest Game*, fit the former.[55] The latter category includes: William Kennedy, *Ironweed*, E.L. Doctorow, *Ragtime*, Ken Kesey, *One Flew Over the Cuckoo's Nest*, and Larry Woidode, *Beyond the Bedroom Wall*.[56]

Going back a little farther, one finds baseball images and subjects in the writings of Mark Twain, William Faulkner, F. Scott Fitzgerald, Sinclair Lewis, John Dos Passos, Ernest Hemingway, and J.D. Salinger.[57] The great American game has not escaped the attention of the great American *literati*.

Nor has its fictional representations been confined to the novelist's domain. Jim Steinman's musical tribute to teenage libido, "Paradise by the Dashboard Light" recorded by Meatloaf, relates the efforts of a turned-on 17 year-old to "score" after successfully making it to first, second, and third "base."[58] John C. Fogarty's "Centerfield," though, is unmatched for capturing the feel and appeal of a game he obviously knows and loves.[59]

Beat the drum, hold the phone,
The sun came out today.
We're born again,
There's new grass on the field.
Rounding third and heading for home,
It's a brown-eyed, handsome man.
Anyone can understand
The way I feel.

These are the kinds of lines that inspire big-leaguers and hot-stovers, sandloters and stick-ballers. Just ask Charlie Brown, that most resolute of all baseball fans, who, upon considering Linus' remark that "Somebody said that sports are sort of a caricature of life," responded "That's a relief. I was afraid it *was* life!"[60]

Indeed, sports may not be life, but baseball has clearly made the strongest claim to be its mirror in the United States. Study of the game has come a long way since Barzun offered his challenge. The imaginative appeal of the game has broadened considerably since Jack Keefe wrote his first letter to his buddy Al. New dimensions of inquiry now characterize its scholarship and a new appreciation of its literary possibilities enliven American fiction. As myth and metaphor, baseball conveys a sense of the place of sport in American life. Its symbols, rituals, and attraction give us clues to our belief systems, values, and behavior, not the least of which is why and how we play. Baseball is, after all, a game, an expression of our basic recreation needs. In the final analysis to overlook this point is to fail to keep one's eye upon the ball.

• • •

Notes

1. Barzun, *God's Country and Mine* (New York: Harper&Row, 1965), 159.

2. On the origins of ball games and professional play in the United States, see: Robert W. Henderson, *Bat, Ball and Bishop: The Origin of Ball Games* (New York: Rockport Press, 1947); Melvin L. Adelman, "The First Baseball Game, "The First Newspaper References to Baseball, and the New York Club: A Note on the Early History of Baseball," *Journal of Sport History*, VII, 3, (Winter, 1980), 132-135; Robert K. Barney, "Of Rails and Red Stockings: Episodes in the Expansion of the National Pastime in the American West," *Journal of the West*, XVII, 3 (July, 1978), 61-70; Harold Seymour, "How Baseball Began," *New York Historical Society Quarterly*, XL, 4 (October, 1956), 369-385; Joseph S. Stern, Sr., "The Team That Couldn't Be Beat: The Red Stockings of 1869," *Cincinnati Historical Society Bulletin*, XXVII, 1 (1969), 25-41; Ian Tyrell, "The Emergence of Modern American Baseball c. 1850-1880" in Richard Cashman and Michael McKernan, eds., *Sport in History: The Making of Modern Sporting History* (St. Lucia, Queensland, Australia: University of Queensland Press, 1979), 21-42; David Voigt, "America's First Red Scare—The Cincinnati Reds of 1869," *Ohio History*, LXXVIII, 1 (1969), 13-24, and "The Boston Red Stockings: The Birth of Major League Baseball," *New England Quarterly*, XLIII, 4 (December, 1970), 531-549. Elements of this section on baseball historiography in this article have appeared in my bibliographic essay, "Diamond in the Rough: Baseball and the Study of American Sport History," *The History Teacher*, (May, 1986), 385-403.

3. Coffin, *The Old Ball Game: Baseball in Folklore and Fiction* (New York: Harder and Harder, 1971), 13.

4. Scholars investigating other aspects of the American experience are discovering the relevance and excitement of a "mythological" approach. See, for

example: George N. Tindall, "Mythology: A New Frontier in Southern History" in Frank E. Vandiver, ed., *The Idea of the South: Pursuit of a Central Theme* (Chicago: University of Chicago Press, 1964); Oliver La Farge, "Myths That Hide the American Indian," *American Heritage Magazine*, VII (October, 1956); C. Vann Woodward, "The Anti-slavery Myth," *The American Scholar*, XXXI, 2 (Spring, 1962); William H. Goetzmann, "The Mountain Man as Jacksonian Man," *American Quarterly*, XV, 3 (Fall, 1963); Nicholas Cords, "Parson Weems, the Cherry Tree and the Patriotic Tradition" in Cords and Patrick Gerster, eds., *Myth and the American Experience* (Encino, CA: Glencoe, 1973); and Milton M. Gordon, "Assimilation in America: Theory and Reality," *Daedalus*, XC (Spring, 1961).

5. Spalding, *America's National Game* (New York: American Sports Publishing Company, 1911), 4.

6. On Spalding, see: Arthur Bartlett, *Baseball and Mr. Spalding: The History and Romance of Baseball* (New York: Farrar, Strauss and Young, 1951) and Peter Levine, *A.G. Spalding and the Rise of Baseball* (New York: Oxford University Press, 1985).

7. Henry Steele Commager, "The Search for a Usable Past," *American Heritage Magazine*, XVI, 2 (February, 1965).

8. Quoted in Paul Dsruisseaux, "'And Besides, I Grew Up Next Door to Ebbets Field,'" *The Chronicle of Higher Education* (June 8, 1983), 17.

9. Crepeau, *Baseball: America's Diamond Mind, 1919-1941* (Orlando, FL: University of Florida Press, 1980), xi.

10. Quoted in Desruisseaux, *Chronicle*, 19; *Sport and American Mentality: The Rise to Respectability, 1880-1910* (Knoxville: University of Tennessee Press, 1983).

11. Bailey, "The Mythmakers of American History," *Journal of American History*, LV (June, 1968), 5.

12. (New York: World, 1970).

13. *I'm Glad You Didn't Take It Personally* (New York: Dell, 1973) and *Ball Four, Plus Five* (New York: Stein and Day, 1981).

14. The fare before *Ball Four* included such first hand accounts as: Jim Brosnan, *The Long Season* (New York: Dell, 1961) and *Pennant Race* (New York: Harper, 1962); Ty Cobb, *Busting 'Em* (New York: E.J. Clode, 1914) and with Al Stump, *My Life in Baseball: The True Record* (New York: Doubleday, 1961); Jerome H. (Dizzy) Dean, *Dizzy Baseball* (New York: Greenberg, 1952); Jim Piersall and Al Hirschberg, *Fear Strikes Out* (New York: 1955); Joe Garagiola, *Baseball is a Funny Game* (New York: Bantam, 1962); Sandy Koufax with Ed Linn, *Koufax* (New York: Viking, 1966); and George Herman (Babe) Ruth and Bob Considine, *The Babe Ruth Story* (New York: Dutton, 1948). A sampling of more recent memoirs include: Tom Seaver with Dick Schaap, *The Perfect Game* (New York: Dutton, 1970); Willie Mays with Charles Einstein, *My Life In and Out of Baseball* (Greenwich, CT: Fawcett, 1973); Billy Martin, *Number 1* (New York: Dell, 1981); Ron Guidry and Peter Golenboch, *Guidry* (New York: Avon, 1981); Ron LeFlore and Jim Hawkins, *Breakout: From Prison to the Big League* (New York: Harper and Row, 1978); Tommy Lasorda and David Fisher, *The Artful Dodger* (New York: Arbor House, 1985); and Jimmy Piersall with Richard Whittingham, *The Truth Hurts* (New York: Contemporary Books, 1985).

15. David Halberstam, "American Notes: Baseball and the National Mythology," *Harper's Magazine*, CCXLI, 1444 (September, 1970), 24.

16. On baseball's reserve clause and the controversy surrounding Flood's challenge, see: Lee Lowenfish and Tony Lupien, *The Imperfect Diamond: The Story of Baseball's Reserve Clause and the Men Who Fought to Change It* (New York: Stein and Day, 1980); Lance E. Davis, "Self-Regulation in

Baseball, 1909-1971" in Roger Noll, ed., *Government and the Sports Business* (Washington: Brookings Institution, 1974); and Edward R. Garvey, "From Chattel to Employee: The Athletes' Quest for Freedom and Dignity," *Annals of the American Academy of Political and Social Science*, 445 (September, 1979), 91-101.

17. (New York: Random House, 1971).

18. Flood with Richard Carter, *The Way It Is* (New York: Pocket Books, 1972).

19. On the "Black Sox Scandal," see: *Eliot Asinof, Eight Men Out: The Black Sox and the 1919 World Series* (New York: Holt, Rinehart and Winston, 1963); Victor Luhrs, *The Great Baseball Mystery* (New York: Barnes, 1966); and William Veeck, Jr. with Ed Linn, *The Hustler's Handbook* (New York: Putnam's, 1965). Asinof's is the best and most comprehensive work on the subject, although Luhr offers a fresh and stimulating interpretation of the scandal. Veeck's chapter, "Harry's Diary—1919," provides some new information on the scandal and the choice of Judge Kenesaw Mountain Landis for commissioner. On the role of the biggest star in the scandal, see: Donald Gropman, *Say It Ain't So, Joe! The Story of Shoeless Joe Jackson* (Boston: Little, Brown, 1979).

20. This is the theme of Jules Tygiel's book, *Baseball's Great Experiment: Jackie Robinson and His Legacy* (New York: Oxford University Press, 1983).

21. The host of supporting characters includes: Owners— Arthur Mann, *Branch Rickey: American in Action* (Boston: Houghton-Mifflin, 1957); Bill Veeck and Ed Linn, *Veeck—As in Wreck* (New York: Putnam's, 1962); and Gustave Axelson, *"Commy": The Life Story of Charles A. Comisky* (Chicago: Reilly and Lee, 1919); Managers—Leo Durocher and Ed Linn, *Nice Guys Finish Last* (New York: Simon and Schuster, 1975); Connie Mack, *My 66 Years in the Big Leagues* (Philadelphia: Winston, 1950); Casey Stengel and Harry Paxton, *Casey at the Bat* (New York: Random House, 1962); Frank Graham, *Casey Stengel* (New York: John Day, 1958); Robert W. Creamer, *Stengel: His Life and Times* (New York: Dell, 1984); Joseph Durso, *The Days of Mr. McGraw* (Englewood Cliffs, NJ: Prentice-Hall, 1969); Blanche McGraw with Arthur Mann, *The Real McGraw* (New York: Putnam's, 1944); Umpires—Ron Luciano and David Fisher, *The Umpire Strikes Back* (New York: Bantam, 1982); Commissioners—J.G. Taylor Spink, *Judge Landis and 25 Years of Baseball* (New York: Crowell, 1947); Eugene Murdock, "The Tragedy of Ban Johnson," *Journal of Sport History*, I, 1 (Spring, 1974), 26-40, and *Ban Johnson: Czar of Baseball* (Westport, CT: Greenwood Press, 1982); and Wives—Danielle Torrez and Ken Lizotte, *High Inside: Memories of a Baseball Wife* (New York: Putnam's, 1983) and Bobbie Bouton and Nancy Marshall, *Home Games: Two Baseball Wives Speak Out* (New York: St. Martins, 1983).

22. The quest for baseball's "character" is closely tied to the search for American national character. Yet, just as the image of the game has been affected by its history and heroes, it, too, has been impossible to define with absolute precision. To a certain extent, this ambiguity is part of "the American way." Lee Coleman, "What is American: A Study of Alleged American Traits," *Social Forces*, XIX (1941), conducted a survey of the then existing large body of literature on the American character forty-six years ago and concluded that "almost every conceivable value or trait has at one time or another been imputed to American culture by authoritative observers." David M. Potter, "The Quest for National Character," in John Higham, ed., *The Reconstruction of American History* (New York: Harper and Row, 1962), further noted that "almost every explanation, from Darwinian selection to toilet-training has been advanced to account for the attributed qualities."

23. Rader, "Compensatory Sport Heroes: Ruth, Grange and Dempsey," *Journal of Popular Culture*, XVI, 4 (Spring, 1983), 11-22.

24. Rader, *American Sports: From the Age of Folk Games to the Age of Spectators* (Englewood Cliffs, NJ: Prentice-Hall, 1983), 176-177.

25. Lowenthal, *Literature, Popular Culture and Society* (Englewood Cliffs, NJ: Prentice-Hall, 1961), 109-140. Along the same lines are: Daniel J. Boorstin, *The Image: Or What Happened to the American Dream* (New York: Atheneum, 1962) and Larry May, *Screening Out the Past: The Birth of Mass Culture and the Motion Picture Industry* (New York: Oxford University Presss, 1980). Other works that comment on the rise and role of the sports hero are: Dixon Wecter, *The Hero in America: A Chronicle of Hero Worship* (Ann Arbor: University of Michigan Press, 1963); Roderick Nash, *Nervous Generation: American Thought, 1917-1930* (Chicago: Rand McNally, 1970); Ray Browne, Marshall Fishwick and Hael T. Marsden, *Heroes of Popular Culture* (Bowling Greeen, OH: Bowling Green University Popular Press, 1972); and two books by Orin E. Klapp, *Heroes, Villains, and Fools* (Englewood Cliffs, NJ: Prentice-Hall, 1962) and *Symbolic Leaders: Public Dramas and Public Men* (Chicago: Aldine, 1964).

26. Clair Hodgson Ruth and Bill Slocum, *The Babe and I* (Englewood Cliffs, NJ: Prentice-Hall, 1959); Tom Meany, *Babe Ruth* (New York: 1947); and Roger Kahn, "The Real Babe Ruth," *Esquire* (August, 1959), 27-30.

27. Ruth, *The Babe Ruth Story*, 9.

28. Robert W. Creamer, *Babe: The Legend Comes to Life* (New York: Simon and Schuster, 1974); Marshall Smelser, *The Life That Ruth Built* (New York: Quadrangle, 1975); Robert Smith, *Babe Ruth's America* (New York: Crowell, 1974); Ken Sobol, *Babe Ruth and the American Dream* (New York: Ballantine, 1974); and Kal Wagenheim, *Babe Ruth: His Life and Legend* (New York: Praeger, 1974).

29. See, for example: Randy Roberts, *Jack Dempsey: The Manassa Mauler* (Baton Rouge: L.S.U. Press, 1979) and *Papa Jack: Jack Johnson and the Era of White Hopes* (New York: Free Press, 1983); William J. Baker, *Jesse Owens: An American Life* (New York: Free Press, 1986); David Wolf, *Foul! The Connie Hawkins Story* (New York: Holt, Rinehart and Winston, 1972); Gary Shaw, *Meat on the Hoof* (New York: Dell, 1973); Dave Meggyesy, *Out of Their League* (New York: Warner, 1971); Jerry Kramer, *Instant Replay* (New York: New American Library, 1969); William Oscar Johnson and Nancy P. Williamson, *"Whatta-Gal": The Babe Didrickson Story* (Boston: Little, Brown, 1977); Billie Jean King with Kim Chapin, *Billie Jean* (New York: Harper and Row, 1974); and Frank Deford, *Big Bill Tilden: The Triumphs and the Tragedy* (New York: Simon and Schuster, 1975). Additionally, there are several studies on Joe Louis, including: Anthony O. Edmonds, *Joe Louis* (Grand Rapids: Eerdmans, 1973); Barney Nagler, *The Brown Bomber* (New York: World: 1972); and Gerald Aston, *"And a Credit to His Race"* (New York: *Saturday Review*, 1974).

30. Leverett, T. Smith, Jr. "The Babe in '74," *Journal of Sport History*, VI 2 (Summer, 1979), 72.

31. Craig Nettles and Peter Golenbock, *Balls* (New York: Putnam's, 1984); Ron Guidry and Gollenbock, *Guidry* (New York: Avon, 1981); Golenbock, *Bums: An Oral History of the Brooklyn Dodgers* (New York: Putnam's, 1984); Gene Schoor, *Yogi* (New York: Ballantine, 1985); Reggie Jackson and Mike Lupica, *Reggie* (New York: Ballantine, 1985); Thurman Munson and Martin Appel, *Thurman Munson* (New York: Ace, 1980); Ed Figueroa and Dorothy Harshman, *Yankee Stranger* (Pompano Beach, FL: Exposition Press, 1982); Lou Pinella and Maury Allen, *Sweet Lou* (New York: Putnam's, 1986); and Mickey Mantle and Herb Gluck, *The Mick* (New York: Doubleday, 1985.

32. Arthur Mann's biography of Rickey (see note 26) celebrates the owner's alleged commitment to black equality and opportunity in baseball. Less sentimental accounts that stress political and economic motivations are: Milton J. Shapiro, *Jackie Robinson of the Brooklyn Dodgers* (New York: Julian Messner, 1957) and Jay J. Coakley, *Sport in Society: Issues and Controversies* (St. Louis: Mosby, 1978). On other aspects of "breaking the color barrier" and Robinson's role, see: Ronald A. Smith, "The Paul Robeson-Jacke Robinson Saga and a Political Collision," *Journal of Sport History*, VI (Summer, 1979), 5-27; David K. Wiggins, "Wendall Smith, the *Pittsburgh Courier-Journal* and the Campaign to Include Blacks in Organized Baseball, 1933-1945," *Journal of Sport History*, X, 2 (Summer, 1983), 5-29; Bill L. Weaver, "The Black Press and the Assault on Professional Baseball's 'Color Line,' October, 1945-April, 1947," *Phylon*, XL (Winter, 1979), 303-317; and William Simons, "Jackie Robinson and the American Mind: Journalistic Perceptions of the Reintegration of Baseball," *Journal of Sport History*, XII, 1 (Spring, 1985), 39-64.

33. Robinson, *I Never Had It Made* (New York: Putnam's, 1972), 10.

35. Einstein, *Willie's Time: A Memoir of Another America* (New York: Lippincott, 1979) and Wagenheim, *Clemente* (New York: Praeger, 1973).

35. Riess, *Touching Base: Professional Baseball and American Culture in the Progressive Era* (Westport, CT: Greenwood Press, 1980). Related articles by Riess include: "The Baseball Magnates and Urban Politics in the Progressive Era, 1895-1920," *Journal of Sport History*, I, 1 (Spring, 1974), 3-25; "Baseball Myths, Baseball Reality and the Social Functions of Baseball in Progressive America," *Stadion*, III, 2 (1977), 273-311; "Professional Baseball and Social Mobility," *Journal of Interdisciplinary History*, XI, 2 (Autumn, 1980), 235-250; "Race and Ethnicity in American Baseball: 1900-1919," *Journal of Ethnic Studies*, IV, 4 (Winter, 1977), 39-55; and "Professional Sunday Baseball: A Study in Social Reform, 1892-1934," *The Maryland Historian*, IV, 2 (Fall, 1973), 95-108.

36. See, for example: Harold C. Evans, "Baseball in Kansas, 1867-1940," *Kansas Historical Society Quarterly*, IX, 2 (May, 1940), 175-193; Gregg Lee Carter, "Baseball in St. Louis, 1867-1875: An Historical Case Study of Civic Pride," *Missouri Historical Bulletin*, XXXI (July, 1975), 253-263; W. Harrison Daniel, "The Rage in the Hill City: The Beginnings of Baseball in Lynchburg," *Virginia Cavalcade*, XXVIII, 4 (Spring, 1979), 186-191; Stephen Freedman, "The Baseball Fad in Chicago, 1865-1870: An Exploration of the Role of Sport in the Nineteenth-Century City," *Journal of Sport History*, VI, 3 (Winter, 1979), 5-19; Cecil Monroe, "The Rise of Baseball in Minnesota," *Minnesota History*, XIX (June, 1938), 162-181; Robert P. Smith, "Heroes and Hurrahs: Sport in Brooklyn, 1890-1898," *Journal of Long Island History*, XI (Spring, 1975), 7-21; and Harry Anderson, "The Ancient Origins of Baseball in Milwaukee," *Milwaukee History*, VI, 2 (Summer, 1983), 42-57. More comprehensive studies include: Dale A. Somers, *The Rise of Sports in New Orleans, 1850-1900* (Baton Rouge: L.S.U. Press, 1972); Stephen Hardy, *How Boston Played: Sport, Recreation, and Community, 1865-1915* (boston: Northeastern University Press, 1982); and Melvin L. Adelman, *A Sporting Time: New York City and the Rise of Modern Athletics, 1820-70* (Urbana, IL: University of Illinois Press, 1985).

37. Gelber, "'Their Hands Are All Out Playing': Business and Amateur Baseball, 1845-1917," *Journal of Sport History*, XI, 1 (Spring, 1984), 5-27, and "Working at Playing: The Culture of the Work Place and the Rise of Baseball," *Journal of Social History*, XVI (June, 1983), 3-20; and Gary Ross Mormino, "The Playing Fields of St. Louis: Italian Immigrants and Sports, 1925-1941," *Journal of Sport History*, IX (Summer, 1982), 5-19.

38. Jordan, *A False Spring* (New York: Dodd-Mead, 1975) and *The Suitors of Spring* (New York: Warner, 1974); Ralbovsky, *Destiny's Darlings* (New

York: Hawthorn, 1974) and *Lords of the Locker Room* (New York: Wyden, 1974). Also see: Roger Kahn, *Good Enough to Dream* (New York: Doubleday, 1985), an account of his role as the president and part owner of the Utica Blue Sox of the New York-Pennsylvania League in 1983; and Frank Dolson, *Beating the Bushes: Life in the Minor Leagues* (South Bend, IN: Icarus Press, 1982).

39. Ralbovsky, *Lords of the Locker Room*, 47-48.

40. (Englewood Cliffs, NJ: Prentice Hall, 1970).

41. Paige and David Lipman, *Maybe I'll Pitch Forever* (New York: Doubleday, 1962); Holway, *Voices* (New York: Dodd-Mead, 1975). Also see: Henry Aaron as told to Furman Bisher, *Aaron, r.f.* (Cleveland: World: 1968); William Brashler, *Josh Gibson* (New York: Harper and Row, 1978) and "Looking for Josh Gibson," *Esquire*, LXXXIX (February, 1978), 104-108ff; Janet Bruce, *The Kansas City Monarchs: Champions of Black Baseball* (Lawrence: University of Kansas Presss, 1985); Roy Campanella, *It's Good to Be Alive* (Boston, Little, Brown, and Co., 1959); Bill Heward and Dimitri V. Gat, *Some Are Called Clowns: A Season with the Last of the Great Barnstorming Teams* (New York: Crowell, 1974); Jerry Malloy, "Black Bluejackets," *The National Pastime* (1985), 72-77, and "Out at Home," *The National Pastime* (1983), 14-28; Donn Rogosin, *Invisible Men: Life in Baseball's Negro Leagues* (New York: Atheneum, 1983); Theodore Rosengarten, "Reading the Hops: Recollections of Lorenzo 'Piper' Davis and the Negro Baseball League," *Southern Exposure* (1977), 62-79; and Art Rust, Jr., *"Get That Nigger Off the Field"* (New York: Delacorte, 1976).

42. Seymour, *Baseball*, 2 vols. (New York: Oxford University Press, 1960, 1971); Voigt, *American Baseball*, 3 vols. (Norman, OK: University of Oklahoma Press, 1965, 1970, 1982).

43. Allen, *100 Years of Baseball* (New York: Bartholomew, 1950); Wallop, *Baseball* (New York: Norton, 1969); and Honig, *Baseball America* (New York: Macmillan, 1985).

44. Wallop, *Yankees* (New York: Norton, 1954). Wallop's novel came to life on stage and screen as *Damn Yankees*, the latter starring Tab Hunter.

45. Kahn, *The Boys of Summer* (New York: Harper and Row, 1971).

46. Graham, *The New York Giants* (New York: Putnam's, 1952) and *The Brooklyn Dodgers* (New York: Putnam's, 1945); Allen, *The Cincinnati Reds* (New York: Putnam's, 1948); and Lieb, *The Boston Red Sox* (New York: Putnam's, 1947), *The St. Louis Cardinals* (New York: Putnam's, 1944), *The Baltimore Orioles: The History of the Colorful Team in Baltimore and St. Louis* (New York: Putnam's, 1946), *The Detroit Tigers* (New York: Putnam's, 1946), *The Pittsburgh Pirates* (New York: Putnam's, 1948) and with Stan Baumgartner, *The Philadelphia Phillies* (New York: Putnam's, 1946). Also of note: Robert Hood, *The Gashouse Gang* (New York: Morrow, 1976). Through his interviews with some of the surviving members of the 1934 St. Louis Cardinals team, Hood breathes a little fresh air into an otherwise stock history. The same can be said of Allen's later account for Putnam's, *The Giants and the Dodgers: The Fabulous Story of Baseball's Fiercest Feud* (New York: Putnam's, 1964).

47. Ritter, *Glory* (New York: MacMillan, 1966); Honig, *Baseball* (New York: Coward, McCann, Geoghegan, 1975).

48. As cited throughout this paper, such book and article titles include *Touching Base, Fear Strikes Out, Balls, Ball Four, Pine-tarred and Feathered, The Old Ball Game, Busting 'Em, The Imperfect Diamond, High Inside, Home Games, "Diamond in the Rough,"* and *"Out at Home."*

49. Angell, *Summer Game* (New York: Popular Library, 1972).

50. Boswell, *Why Time Begins* (New York: Penguin, 1985). In the same vein, see Boswell's earlier *How Life Imitates the World Series* (New York: Doubleday, 1983).

51. Hall, *Fathers Playing Catch* (New York: Dell, 1985).

52. Hall and Ellis, *Doc Ellis* (New York: Coward, McCann and Geoghehan, 1974).

53. Lardner, *You Know Me, Al* (New York: Scribner, 1914); Tunis, *Kid from Tomkinsville* (New York: Harcourt, Brace, 1940).

54. Mark Harris, *Bang the Drum Slowly* (New York: Bobbs-Merrill, 1956) and *The Southpaw* (1953) and *A Ticket for a Seamstitch* (1955); W.P. Kinsella, *Shoeless Joe* (New York: Houghton-Mifflin, 1982); Robert Coover, *The Universal Baseball Association, Inc., J. Henry Waugh, Prop.* (New York: Random House, 1968); and Bernard Malamud, *The Natural* (New York: Farrar, Straus and Giroux, 1952). For an analysis of some baseball novelists, see: Eric Solomon, "Jews, Baseball, and the American Novel," *Arete*, I, 2 (Spring, 1984), 44-66.

55. Carkeet, *Greatest Slump* (New York: Harper and Row, 1984); Greenberg, *Celebrant* (New York: Everest House, 1983); Roth, *Great American Novel* (New York: Farrar, Straus and Giroux, 1973); and Kennedy, *Billy Phelan* (New York: Penguin, 1983).

56. Kennedy, *Ironweed* (New York: Viking, 1983); Doctorow, *Ragtime* (New York: Random House, 1975); Kesey, *Cuckoo's Nest* (New York: New American Library, 1975); and Woidode, *Bedroom Wall* (New York: Farrar, Straus and Giroux, 1975).

57. Twain, *A Connecticut Yankee in King Arthur's Court* (1899); Faulkner, *Sanctuary* (1931); Fitzgerald, *The Great Gatsby* (1925); Lewis, *Babbitt* (1922); *Dos Passos*, 1919 (1932); Hemingway, *The Old Man and the Sea* (1952); and Salinger, *The Catcher in the Rye* (1951).

58. Meat Loaf, "Paradise," *Bat Out of Hell* album (Epic Records: CBS, 1977).

59. Fogarty, "Centerfield," *Centerfield* album (Warner Brothers Records: Warner Brothers, 1985).

60. Charles M. Schulz, *Big League Peanuts* (New York: Holt, Rinehart and Winston, 1985).